LOOK HOMEWARD

A Life of Thomas Wolfe

OTHER BOOKS BY DAVID HERBERT DONALD

LINCOLN'S HERNDON (*1948*)

DIVIDED WE FOUGHT
A Pictorial History of the Civil War, 1861–1865
with Hirst D. Milhollen, Milton Kaplan, and Hulen Stuart (*1952*)

(ed.) INSIDE LINCOLN'S CABINET
The Civil War Diaries of Salmon P. Chase (*1954*)

LINCOLN RECONSIDERED
Essays on the Civil War Era
(*1956; revised edition, 1961*)

(ed.) WHY THE NORTH WON THE CIVIL WAR (*1960*)

CHARLES SUMNER AND THE COMING OF THE CIVIL WAR (*1960*)

THE CIVIL WAR AND RECONSTRUCTION
with J. G. Randall
(*1961; revised edition, 1969*)

(ed.) DIARY OF CHARLES FRANCIS ADAMS
Volumes I and II
with Aïda DiPace Donald (*1964*)

THE POLITICS OF RECONSTRUCTION, 1863–1867 (*1965*)

THE NATION IN CRISIS, 1861–1877 (*1969*)

CHARLES SUMNER AND THE RIGHTS OF MAN (*1970*)

(ed.) GONE FOR A SOLDIER
The Civil War Memoirs of Private Alfred Bellard (*1975*)

THE GREAT REPUBLIC
A History of the American People
with Bernard Bailyn, Robert Dallek, David Brion Davis,
John L. Thomas, Robert H. Wiebe, and Gordon S. Wood
(*1977; revised editions, 1981, 1985*)

LIBERTY AND UNION (*1978*)

LOOK HOMEWARD

A Life of Thomas Wolfe

BY

DAVID HERBERT DONALD

LITTLE, BROWN AND COMPANY
Boston   Toronto

FIRST EDITION

ACKNOWLEDGMENTS OF PERMISSION TO REPRINT
COPYRIGHTED MATERIAL APPEAR ON PAGES 561—562.

Library of Congress Cataloging-in-Publication Data

Donald, David Herbert, 1920–
   Look homeward: a life of Thomas Wolfe
   Bibliography: p.
   Includes index.
   1. Wolfe, Thomas, 1900–1938—Biography. 2. Novelists,
American—20th century—Biography. I. Title.
PS3545.0337A674 1987   813´.52   86-10460
ISBN 0-316-18952-9

MV

Published simultaneously in Canada
by Little, Brown & Company (Canada) Limited

PRINTED IN THE UNITED STATES OF AMERICA

For
BRUCE

Contents

List of Illustrations

(following page 292)

Preface

I FIRST HEARD of Thomas Wolfe when I was nine years old. In the fall of 1929 I sat on the front steps of our house in Goodman, Mississippi, and eavesdropped while my mother and her friends talked about a scandalous new novel called *Look Homeward, Angel*. Later, when my mother was not looking, I sneaked off with her library copy and searched for the dirty words they said Wolfe had used. I couldn't find them, and I don't remember much from this juvenile reading of *Look Homeward, Angel* except the scene where W. O. Gant came home drunk, built up a roaring fire in the living room, and for forty minutes chanted:

> O-ho — Goddam,
> Goddam, Goddam,
> O-ho — Goddam,
> Goddam — Goddam.

It was the first time I had seen a curse word in print.

Later, as an adolescent, I really read *Look Homeward, Angel* and was certain that Thomas Wolfe had told my life story as well as that of his hero, Eugene Gant. Like so many other teenagers, I was convinced — without any just cause — that I too was misunderstood by my family and unappreciated in my community, and, like Eugene, I enjoyed writhing in romantic agony. Afterward, along with everybody that I knew, I was swept up in the turbulent rhetoric of *Of Time and the River* (1935). My friends and I were certain that we were unrecognized "artists," like Eugene Gant, and we believed that we also had Faustian appetites. *The Web and the Rock* (1939) was a little disappointing, but *You Can't Go Home Again* (1940) restored my faith in Wolfe. As a young man, packing to leave rural Mississippi forever to take up residence in the strange and terrifying North, I shivered appreciatively when I read: "We are so lost, so naked and so lonely in America. . . . Immense and cruel skies bend over us, and all of us are driven on forever and we have no home." But somehow, I gained reassurance from Wolfe's prediction: "I believe that we are lost here in America, but I believe we shall be found. . . . I think the true discovery of America is before us."

It would be pleasant to record that my youthful enthusiasm for Thomas Wolfe persisted, but it did not. Perhaps I was simply growing up. Or perhaps I was unconsciously influenced by the dominant critical view of the 1950s, which condemned Wolfe's gigantism, his rhetorical extravagance, and his lack of form. At any rate, as my research and writing increasingly focused on the Civil War and the Reconstruction era, I lost interest in his novels.

Then during the 1970s I rediscovered Wolfe. Quite by accident, my wife and I, after a vacation in the North Carolina mountains, found ourselves in Asheville, and we decided to visit the Wolfe house, "The Old Kentucky Home." Now a state historic site, carefully preserved and beautifully tended, Julia Wolfe's boarding-house is without doubt in better shape than at any time when Thomas Wolfe lived in it, but it is still what Wolfe's father called it, a "murderous and bloody Barn." Downstairs, the cluttered living room, with its uncomfortable upholstered furniture, a piano, a small collection of dog-eared books, and a large assemblage of bric-a-brac, pretends to a domesticity that is contradicted by the cramped pantry, with zinc-covered table, where the Wolfe children had to eat so that there would be more space in the dining room for the boarders. The upstairs floor is a rabbit warren of rooms, sparsely furnished with sagging beds, creaking chairs, and rickety tables. Electric light bulbs hang by naked cords from the ceilings. Even in the summer the house is drafty, and in the winter the wind rattles the ill-fitting windows. I began to wonder how growing up in such a bleak and culturally impoverished setting affected a writer.

At this time I was beginning a study of Southern society and culture after the Reconstruction era, in which I planned to discuss the development of Southern literature from Thomas Nelson Page to William Faulkner. After visiting the Old Kentucky Home I realized that it would have to include a section on Thomas Wolfe, and I reread his novels and stories.

To my surprise, the experience proved richly rewarding. I discovered that, even if Wolfe's fiction had no other merit, it ought to be read because it offers a remarkably full social history of the United States during the first four decades of the twentieth century. Wolfe's careful dissection of Asheville, as "Altamont" (or "Libya Hill" in the posthumous novels), is a masterful picture of small-town life in America. No other novelist has written so knowledgeably about American higher education — at the University of North Carolina, Harvard University, and New York University. Hating urban life, Wolfe was fascinated by New York City and in hundreds of pages he tried to capture it on paper. Only occasionally did he record the greatness and the excitement of the big city, but no one has better described the harsh impersonality of New York's "manswarm" or chronicled the city's "infinite repetitions of lust, cruelty, and sterility, of hatred, defeat, and dishonor, of gouging and killing."

I found that Wolfe's novels are also a barometer of American culture. Absorbed with the artist and his need for self-expression, *Look Homeward, Angel* accurately reflected the temper of the 1920s. *Of Time and the River,* published after the onset of the Great Depression, showed some awareness that the problems of society might be more important than the frustrations of the individual. But Wolfe's last novel, which described the consequences of the stock market crash, demonstrated that he was, as Alfred Kazin has said, "the most alert and brilliant novelist of depression America, and an extraordinarily imaginative analyst of . . . the social disorganization of the thirties."

But in the long run Wolfe's books must be judged as literature, not as history. They are remarkably uneven; Thomas Wolfe wrote more bad prose than any other major writer I can think of. But much of his work is extraordinarily brilliant and moving. Wolfe created dozens of unforgettable characters: W. O. Gant, the stonecutter; Eliza Gant, his property-loving wife; Helen, their daughter, high-strung and hysterical; Luke, their fast-talking, stammering son; Professor Hatcher, who taught the celebrated class in playwriting; Esther Jack, the perfection of womanhood, whose face was shaped like a violet; Lloyd McHarg, the alcoholic Nobel Prize–winning novelist; Foxhall Edwards, the long-suffering editor — to name only a few.

Though Wolfe's novels lack form, episodes in them are strong and crisply defined. From his years of training as a playwright Wolfe learned how to make individual scenes vibrant and memorable. In the manuscript of his first novel the encounter between W. O. Gant and "Queen" Elizabeth, madam of the town brothel, who is looking for a tombstone for one of her "girls," was so beautifully constructed that Maxwell E. Perkins, his editor at Scribners, pulled it out and made it Wolfe's first published short story. Wolfe was at his best in death scenes. His account of the final days of Benjamin Gant is deeply moving, but it is surpassed by the scene in *Of Time and the River* called "The Death of Stoneman Gant," based on what Wolfe was told about the last hours of his father.

But what is even more memorable about Wolfe's novels is the author's unique literary voice. There is hardly a page in any of his books that could have been written by anybody else. Some of Wolfe's best effects are, surprisingly enough, on a small scale: when W. O. Gant first met Eliza's family, her father began making heavy-handed puns, and in response "Gant grinned with a thin, false painting of mirth." Or take his Imagist portrait of Ben:

> My Brother Ben's face, thought Eugene,
> Is like a piece of slightly yellow ivory;
> His high white head is knotted fiercely
> By his old man's scowl;
> His mouth is like a knife,
> His smile the flicker of light across a blade.★

But it is in Wolfe's lyrical passages — those Whitman-like chants that Maxwell Perkins disparagingly called "dithyrambs" — that his prose is most distinctive. In these his style is opulent, and his language is rhythmical. Here, for example, is part of Wolfe's ode to October, the month of his birth:

★To stress the poetic quality of these passages I have presented them here in verse form. For numerous other examples, see John S. Barnes, ed., *A Stone, A Leaf, A Door: Poems by Thomas Wolfe* (New York: Charles Scribner's Sons, 1945).

October is the richest of the seasons:
The fields are cut, the granaries are full,
The bins are loaded to the brim with fatness,
And from the cider-press the rich brown oozings of
    the York Imperials run.
The Bee bores into the belly of the yellowed grape,
The fly gets old and fat and blue,
He buzzes loud, crawls slow, creeps heavily to death
    on sill and ceiling,
The sun goes down in blood and pollen
Across the bronzed and mown fields of old October.

There are dozens of these passages. Among my favorites are Wolfe's magnificent recreation of locomotives snaking their way north through the Southern mountains, his lament on the frigidity of New England ("Oh, bitterly, bitterly Boston, one time more"), and his evocation of the spine-tingling first sight of New York, "far-shining, glorious, time-enchanted." These are not the work of a cautious writer or of a conventional writer, and they have their faults. But they help to explain why so many of Wolfe's contemporaries thought him a genius. Rereading them makes it clear that Wolfe deserves to rank among the very great American authors.

Excited by Wolfe's books, I decided, seven years ago, to write his biography. In it, first of all, I have told the story of Wolfe's short and troubled life. With access to all of Wolfe's papers, I have been able to trace his career more fully than any previous biographer. Earlier writers, who had to consider the feelings of Wolfe's surviving brothers and sisters, were obliged to use circumlocutions when speaking of Wolfe household in Asheville, but since all close relatives are now dead, I can be candid about that desperately unhappy family. The passage of time has also made it possible for me to discuss freely his passionate affair with Aline Bernstein, to whom he wrote, "My life is a prison into which only one person has ever entered. That person is you." Their extraordinary love letters, which have not been available in full to previous Wolfe biographers, make it possible for me to trace this most important relationship in Wolfe's adult life, from his initial infatuation through their protracted, bitter quarrels to their final, angry break from each other.

In telling Wolfe's story I have so far as possible avoided intruding my own comments on the events of his life. I believe that present-day readers no more desire moral judgments or psychoanalytical diagnoses from an author of a biography than they want heavy-handed moralizing and editorial pronouncements from a novelist. I am not persuaded that anything would be gained if I interrupted my account of Wolfe's attitudes toward Jews to announce that such bigotry is intolerable and uncivilized — as of course it is. Nor am I convinced that my portrait of Julia Wolfe would be more credible if I characterized her as an anal-retentive type.

This does not mean, of course, that I have simply let the facts speak for themselves. The record of Wolfe's actions is so full that his biographer has constantly to make choices. Every quotation or incident included reflects my judgment of what is important and what is inconsequential in Wolfe's life. Throughout, I have interwoven interpretation with narrative. But I have tried not to stress an interpretive structure that would reduce Wolfe to a case study, whether psychological, literary, or sociological. My purpose has, instead, been to present him as a man, like all men full of contradictions and ambiguities.

Second, this book offers a group photograph — taken from Wolfe's perspective, to be sure — of what can properly be called the Great Generation in American literature. Because Sherwood Anderson, Theodore Dreiser, Sinclair Lewis, Ezra Pound, and Eugene O'Neill had already begun to liberate American literature from the restrictions of Victorian convention and propriety, Wolfe and his contemporaries were free to experiment with new forms, new language, new ideas. This first full generation of American modernists, all born between 1895 and 1905, included not merely F. Scott Fitzgerald and Ernest Hemingway, with whom Wolfe was most often linked, but Stephen Vincent Benét, Erskine Caldwell, Hart Crane, John Dos Passos, James T. Farrell, William Faulkner, John O'Hara, John Steinbeck, Allen Tate, Robert Penn Warren, Glenway Wescott, Thornton Wilder, and Edmund Wilson. Most of these men Wolfe knew personally. A few of them he liked very much, and a good many of them he cordially detested. His story is, then, part of the history of this astonishingly gifted group of writers, who were the founders of modern American literature.

But chiefly this book is a study of the creative process, the story of Thomas Wolfe's evolution as a writer. I began with the assumption — a widely shared view, I believe — that Thomas Wolfe was an artless writer who occasionally achieved some remarkable effects almost by chance. I thought of him as an author who poured out millions of words recounting his own experiences, words that had to be selected, shaped, and formed into something resembling novels by his literary agent and his editors.

As I worked through Wolfe's voluminous correspondence and the numerous drafts he kept of everything that he wrote, a very different picture emerged. Far from being a literary naif, Wolfe was a well-educated man, with thorough grounding in the classics and in English literature from the University of North Carolina and with advanced training in English history, the history of drama, and the work of the Romantic poets from Harvard University. Fitzgerald was correct in noting that Wolfe had "a deeper culture" than his contemporaries. He had, in fact, the best formal education of any American novelist of his day: Fitzgerald attended Princeton and Dos Passos went to Harvard, but Caldwell, Farrell, Faulkner, Hemingway, and O'Hara were not college graduates.

Everybody knows the stories about Wolfe's prodigious reading, but only a study of his letters and notebooks reveals how much his writing was influenced by it. Wolfe was one of the most "literary" of American authors — that is, his books were reflections not merely of what he had experienced but of what he had read. The hundreds of poetic fragments silently interwoven into the text of his novels demonstrate his familiarity with English lyrical verse, and the comic exaggeration of so many of his characterizations is a reminder that from childhood he knew his Dickens. At Harvard he encountered James Joyce's *Ulysses,* which did so much to shape the language and structure of *Look Homeward, Angel,* and later he discovered Proust.

I was even more surprised to find that Wolfe was an experimental writer. He reached maturity in a decade when authors were restless with old forms, when Pound and Eliot were revolutionizing English poetry, when Gertrude Stein and Joyce were introducing new forms of narrative, when O'Neill was creating an American drama. Cramped by the conventional form of the novel — indeed, he preferred to speak of his "books," not his "novels" — Wolfe, like Dos Passos and Faulkner, tried out new techniques of fiction. In most of his books he included prose-poems of lyrical rhapsody; in *Look Homeward, Angel* he frequently used interior monologues; *Of Time and the River* developed the Antaeus myth in modern setting; and some of the stories in *From Death to Morning* were exercises in nonsequential, asynchronous fiction. In the unpublished "Hound of Darkness" manuscript Wolfe used cinematic technique to present simultaneous happenings at a dozen widely scattered places in the United States on a single night, July 18, 1916.

Wolfe's manuscripts also show that, far from simply dashing off whatever first came to his mind, he was a self-conscious writer, who drew up detailed outlines of his books in advance, paid close attention to their structure, and gave much thought to the themes and symbols he intended to develop. (When it came to line-by-line revision of his writing, on the other hand, he was not careful. If a passage he wrote did not suit him, he rarely fiddled with reworking a sentence or a paragraph but crumpled up the page and started over again.)

It is reasonable to ask why this artistry has so rarely been perceived in Wolfe's published books. The answer is, in part, that Wolfe did not wish to come between his readers and the story he was telling. As a very young writer, attempting to write Expressionist dramas, he learned that avant-garde techniques might impress the sophisticated but that they confused the larger audience that he desperately wanted to reach. He sought to seem simple. (At the same time he resented becoming a prisoner of his own legend and complained when readers pictured him "as a great 'exuberant' six-foot-six clod-hopper straight out of nature who bites off half a plug of apple-tobacco, tilts the corn liquor jug and lets half of it gurgle down his throat, wipes off his mouth with the back of one hairy paw, . . . and then wads up three-hundred thousand words or so, hurls it at a blank page, puts covers on it and says 'Here's my book!' ")

But a larger part of the story emerges from a study of the publishing history of Wolfe's books. Not one of them was printed in anything like the form in which it was originally written. Wolfe had great difficulty in finding a public for his work. No producer was willing to present either of his plays, "Welcome To Our City" or "Mannerhouse." He was twenty-nine years old before anything that he wrote, except for college compositions, appeared in print. His first novel had been rejected by a series of publishers when Charles Scribner's Sons accepted it. By this point Wolfe himself was so uncertain of its merits that he agreed, though reluctantly, to the cuts, reorganization, and revision that Perkins required. The result was a book very different from the one that he had originally written.

When *Look Homeward, Angel* was published, its reception appeared to confirm Perkins's wisdom. From this time Wolfe accepted his editor's literary judgment as superior to his own, and he grew more and more dependent on him. An understanding of the relationship between Wolfe and Perkins is, therefore, essential to an evaluation of Wolfe's career after the publication of his first novel. It would be easy to describe their friendship, as Malcolm Cowley has done, as one between a talented but undisciplined author and a superbly gifted editor who dedicated his career to making his friend a success. Or just as readily one could write of Wolfe as a struggling genius whose work was turned into conventional fiction by an unimaginative editor. I have tried, instead, to tell a story without a hero and without a villain. Wolfe and Perkins needed each other, and they developed a symbiotic relationship that was in one sense enormously beneficial to both men but in another, hurtful and limiting.

I believe my account of the relationship between Wolfe and Perkins will help readers to understand not merely this special friendship, which in the end produced so much unhappiness, but the ambivalent relationship that necessarily exists between authors and their publishers. Thomas Wolfe's biography offers an inside view of the world of publishing, which is at once so frustrating to the literary artist and so essential to his survival.

I hope this biography will spur persons who are not familiar with Thomas Wolfe's work to read his novels. For those who already know and admire Wolfe, I have supplied a fuller account of what he was trying to do in his books. I doubt that anything I have said in this biography — or anything that anybody could say — will convince readers who dislike Thomas Wolfe that he was a great writer, but I like to think that it might persuade them to read his books afresh. For all three groups of readers I offer a portrait of a remarkable man, at once complex and simple, suspicious and withdrawn but open and affectionate, humorlessly self-absorbed but with a superb sense of humor, tragically limited and brilliantly gifted.

Lincoln, Massachusetts   David Herbert Donald

LOOK HOMEWARD

A Life of Thomas Wolfe

I

A Secret Life

"THIS IS A FIRST BOOK, and in it the author has written of experience . . . which was once part of the fabric of his life," Thomas Wolfe alerted readers of *Look Homeward, Angel*. "Now that it is to be published, he would insist that this book is a fiction, and that he meditated no man's portrait here." The disavowal was patently an afterthought, for Wolfe's novel was filled with readily identifiable portraits of people he had known in his native Asheville, North Carolina, and in Chapel Hill, where he attended college. Most easily recognized were Wolfe's caricatures of members of his own family. Anybody who lived in Asheville in 1929 knew that W. O. Gant was William Oliver Wolfe, Thomas Wolfe's father, and that Eliza Gant was Julia E. Wolfe, his mother. The Gant children corresponded in age and appearance to Wolfe's siblings, and in the case of Benjamin Harrison Gant and Grover Cleveland Gant the author used the actual names of his brothers. Eugene Gant, the protagonist of the novel, was unquestionably Thomas Wolfe himself.

Yet everyone well acquainted with the Wolfe family in Asheville must have recognized that parts of the story were fictional. The Edenic character of Eugene Gant's infancy in his father's house on Woodson Street was wholly unlike the turbulence of the Wolfe household at 92 Woodfin Street. In the novel the Gants' home was a place of rich abundance. Everything about it was oversized. The father, a lavish provider, brought home whole hogs to be made into sausage or cured into bacon or hams, wagonloads of beans and corn to be devoured or canned. There Eugene Gant's mother cooked enormous meals. For a midday dinner the Gants might have "a huge hot roast of beef, fat buttered lima-beans, tender corn smoking on the cob, thick red slabs of sliced tomatoes, rough savory spinach, hot yellow corn-bread, flaky biscuits, a deep-dish peach and apple cobbler spiced with cinnamon, tender cabbage, deep glass dishes piled with preserved fruits — cherries, pears, peaches." In the narrow front yard of the house, which rose sharply from the street, Eugene remembered that "the flowers grew in rioting glory . . . the velvet-leaved nasturtium slashed with a hundred tawny dyes, the rose, the snowball, the redcupped tulip, and the lily." In the long back yard, which stretched uphill for four hundred feet, W. O. Gant had planted peach, plum, cherry, and apple trees, and his grapevines covered their trellises and reached out to frame the second-story windows of the house. "Wherever his great hands touched the earth," the novelist said, "it grew fruitful for him."

In *Look Homeward, Angel* Eugene Gant's memories of his infancy were nearly all warm and ego-boosting. Eliza Gant, who was at the end of her child-bearing years when he was born, treasured this "last coinage of her flesh." His father, to be sure, had gone on a drunken spree before the baby came, but he came to dote on this son that he sired in his forty-ninth year. He worried when the baby, not yet a year old, seemed slow to talk, but his fears were relieved one day when he carried Eugene into the back yard, where the infant espied a cow grazing in a neighbor's yard. "Moo," uttered the prodigy. Immensely pleased, the father took him back into the house to display his linguistic talents to his mother, and all afternoon he told the story to guests and neighbors, getting the baby to repeat his utterance over and over.

From the large wicker basket that served as his playpen Eugene came to recognize his brothers and sisters. He saw little of his oldest brother, Steve, who was nearly twelve when Eugene was born, but he had very distinct memories of his sister Daisy, a year older than Steve, who sometimes gave the baby his bath, scrubbing until it seemed that his skin would come off. Helen, who was ten years old when Eugene was born, and Luke, who was six, became members of the baby's retinue of entertainers. In later years Eugene had only a slight memory of Grover, that child with "the warm brown face, the soft eyes," but he felt a special affinity for Ben, Grover's twin. As an infant, Eugene took it for granted that his brothers and sisters existed in order to play peekaboo with him, to make funny faces for his amusement, and to read children's picture books to him so frequently that he memorized the words and then took satisfaction in demonstrating that he too could "read."

I

If this was autobiography, it was, to say the least, highly selective. The household into which Thomas Clayton Wolfe was born on October 3, 1900, was stressful and overcrowded. There were only three proper bedrooms, and Julia and W. O. Wolfe each occupied one of them. The other children shared the remaining bedroom or were jammed into cubbyholes.

Thomas Wolfe's mother, like Eugene Gant's, was over forty years old when he was born, and she had already produced seven other children (one of whom died in infancy). Like Eliza Gant, she thought of this baby as her "unexpected treasure" — but not, perhaps, an altogether welcome treasure. She nursed Tom until he was more than three years old, long after he had begun to talk and walk, not so much in order to be warmly mothering as to prevent another pregnancy.* She installed the baby in her own bed — originally, no doubt, so that she could take care of his infant needs but also, in all probability, in the hope of deterring further sexual advances from her husband. Tom slept with his mother until he was eight years old. She was a desperately unhappy woman, trapped in a loveless marriage.

W. O. Wolfe, her husband, was indeed sometimes as proud of Tom as W. O. Gant was of Eugene. But, like Julia, he did not initially welcome this addition to his large and expensive family. Indeed, three days after Tom's birth he entered the room where Julia was nursing him, pulled out a knife, and threatened: "I'll kill you and the baby and myself . . . and end the whole thing right

---

*The belief that nursing women could not become pregnant was widespread, but this was a highly unreliable method of birth control. Indeed, Julia said that during the years after Tom's birth she had had two or three additional pregnancies, which terminated in miscarriages.

now." The episode was not unique, for W. O. Wolfe was a chronic alcoholic, whose drunken moods ranged from whining self-pity to outright violence. "A spree drinker," as Julia called him, he could do without liquor for several months and then, feeling a desperate thirst, he "would go through a brick wall" to get whiskey. He did not again threaten his son's life, but he made a regular practice of denouncing his wife as a whore and of cursing her family as "mountain grills."

Decades after her husband's death Julia continued to wonder what had caused her to marry a man who was in nearly every way her exact opposite. Daughter of Major Thomas Casey Westall, who had served in the North Carolina militia during the Civil War, she came from an old western North Carolina family that had lived in or near Buncombe County for generations. The Westalls were Scotch-Irish, solid and conventional, limited in outlook, Democratic in politics, Presbyterian in religion. Most of the men were small farmers, tanners, hatters, and carpenters. If there was anything that distinguished Julia's branch of the family, it was a belief in the supernatural, which she shared. She had a repertoire of stories about how both her father and her grandfather had predicted the exact day and hour of their deaths, how certain members of the Westall clan had been seen in two places at the same time, and how she herself had a vision predicting her sister's death and ascent into Heaven.

Born just before the Civil War, Julia grew up during the hard Reconstruction years. Her family was so poor that she had only a few scattered months of schooling as a girl and later managed to attend two female "colleges" — they were really high schools — for about a year and a half. But she was bright, independent, and self-confident, and she was convinced that, despite lack of preparation, she could do anything. For several years she passed herself off, with considerable success, as a schoolteacher. Saving what little she earned, she followed the advice of her father, who was then doing construction work in Asheville, and invested it in town lots. Then she became a book agent — that is, she went from door to door soliciting subscriptions for books about to be published and taking orders for those that were already available.

It was as a book agent that she first met William Oliver Wolfe. She knew something about him before she ever saw him, in the way that people do in a small town like Asheville, which had only five thousand inhabitants in 1880. He had moved there recently from Raleigh and had set up shop for the sale of tombstones and other monuments, while his wife Cynthia ran a not very successful millinery store. Some time after Cynthia's death in February 1884, Julia called at Wolfe's shop to solicit his subscription for the *Golden Treasury of Poetry and Prose,* edited by R. H. Stoddard and F. F. Browne. Conversation about this book led to a discussion of others, and that, in turn, resulted in an exchange of romantic novels, like Augusta Jane Evans's *St. Elmo,* which they were both reading. He invited her to the theater, and they spent many evenings together. Presently his notes to her took on a more urgent tone. *"Darling,"* he wrote, "dont you see I find it impossible to stay away from you."* By October they were engaged, and they were married in January 1885.

Perhaps she was attracted to him because he was six feet, four inches tall and handsome in an aquiline way, while she was short and homely. Perhaps it was that he was one of the few eligible bachelors in Asheville, while she was already twenty-four years old and had recently broken off the only real love affair of her life. Or perhaps it was that, as one of her Westall relatives cruelly remarked, she was deceived by W.O.'s "veneer of chivalry, a charm of manner manifesting itself in the exaggerated salaam and sweep of the wide-brimmed hat common to the Southern Colonel of the period."

From the outset it was not a romantic marriage. In asking Julia's hand, W.O. made his motives clear: he had built his stucco house on Woodfin Street for Cynthia, who had died, and now his mother-in-law, who had been keeping house for him, wanted to return to Raleigh. He needed someone to look after him and to cook for him. For her part, Julia announced that her heart had been broken in her earlier affair and that she could never love anyone else. She needed someone to provide for her. On that practical basis they agreed to marry — and both were disappointed. After the wedding Julia simply moved into Cynthia's house and used Cynthia's furniture. "Nothing was mine," she remembered bitterly, "a second handed house, and furniture — even to a second handed husband."

---

*The spelling is W. O. Wolfe's. Throughout this book I have preserved the spelling and punctuation of quoted material, except where the error might confuse readers.

"Mr. Wolfe's idea," said Julia decades later, "was to marry and learn to love afterwards." The plan did not work. The more she learned about her husband, the more outraged she became. She had, of course, known the basic facts of his life before the wedding. He had been born in Pennsylvania, near the hamlet of York Springs, not far from Gettysburg, in 1851. He came from an undistinguished German-English family of farmers, who spelled their name "Wolf"; always fond of a flourish, he had added the final "e." His family was poor, and he received almost no education. Left fatherless as a boy, he had been apprenticed to a Baltimore stonecutter and, after learning his trade, went South during the Reconstruction period. After doing stonework on the South Carolina capitol and the state penitentiary in North Carolina, he settled in Raleigh, where he opened his own business. There, as he had told Julia, he married Hattie Watson, but they were soon divorced.

What he did not tell her was that the dissolution of his first marriage came after a notorious divorce trial in which he charged his wife with frigidity and she claimed that he was impotent. The suits and countersuits had cost him his house, his business, and his reputation in Raleigh. Nor did he tell Julia the full story of his second marriage. He had had an affair with Cynthia Hill. When she became pregnant, he sent her away to have an abortion, but she had a miscarriage instead. After Raleigh people, already outraged by his divorce proceedings against Hattie, learned the facts, he was forced to marry Cynthia, who was eight years older than he was and tubercular to boot, and public opinion made it prudent for them to move. They chose Asheville, where his reputation was unknown and where, in any case, the mountain air might be good for Cynthia's lungs. And he did not let Julia know that he had had a sexual liaison with Cynthia's sister-in-law in the same house where his wife lay dying from tuberculosis.

Even more important, W.O. did not warn Julia that he was an alcoholic. Not until two months after the wedding did she discover that he periodically went on binges. As she sadly learned over the years, the pattern was always the same: after several months of total abstinence — during which he often spoke about the evils of alcohol and on one occasion even joined a temperance society — he would begin drinking steadily. After each of these binges, W.O. was remorseful and pledged never to touch liquor again. But of course he did, and his drinking became worse over the years. Several times Julia had him sent to Richmond or Greensboro, North Carolina, to take the Keeley Cure for alcoholics, but he always fell off the wagon again.

Julia could not control him. Brought up by her father, a teetotaler and a temperance lecturer, "to shun anybody who took a drink," on the grounds that "it was demoralizing, degrading," she did not know how to cope with W.O.'s sprees. Indeed, sometimes she had to flee to the neighbors for protection. Never knowing when her husband might come home drunk, and sickened by "the humiliation and disgrace of it all," Julia cut herself off from social contact with her family and friends. "The best years of my life," she told Tom later, "was robbed of happiness and home life — all social activities were given up — both for myself and children — all on account of [the] Liquor habit."

To add to these problems, W.O. and Julia were basically different in temperament. He lacked her interest in money and property. He made a good enough living from his tombstones, so that the Wolfe family was better off than nine out of ten families in Asheville. A skilled craftsman, he lettered inscriptions with precision, and he had a talent for carving little lambs, or hands folded in prayer, on his monuments. Occasionally he sold one of the seven-foot funerary angels, made of Carrara marble, which he accepted on consignment and displayed on the porch outside his shop. But what he made he spent freely, on himself and on his family. After his losses in Raleigh, he realized that whatever he accumulated might disappear overnight.

Vainly Julia tried to get him to save or to enter a more lucrative business. There was not enough money in death, she decided; people did not die fast enough. She was sure that there was a fortune to be made in real estate, but he vowed that he never wanted to own another piece of property. She saw that her brothers were making money in the lumber and construction business and urged her husband to team up with them. At one point she got him to enter into a partnership with her brother William Westall, who was becoming one of the wealthiest men in Asheville, but W.O., who detested all of her family, dissolved the business after only a year.

The antagonism between Julia and W.O., which existed from the beginning of their marriage, erupted into open warfare during

Tom's infancy. Up to that time she had restrained herself in order to protect the children, for she knew that her husband, for all his deficiencies, was a good provider. But during Tom's earliest years W.O. began to suffer from inflammatory rheumatism, which affected his hands and arms. As he entered his fifties it was not clear how much longer he could continue his trade and support his large family. Anxious, he began to drink more than ever, and in his cups he would tell Julia that they were all going to the poorhouse. He blubbered that she ought to help support the family and reminded her that one of her neighbors — who probably did not have seven children to care for — was taking in sewing. She responded by feeding some boarders at her already overcrowded table.

It was probably this experience that led her to undertake the experiment of running a boardinghouse at St. Louis during the World's Fair of 1904. Most of the children accompanied her, and Tom retained a clear mental picture of "The North Carolina," the house on Fairmount Avenue where his mother took in selected boarders. But his sharpest memory of St. Louis was of the night when his sister Mabel led him into a darkened room and showed him the wasted body of his brother Grover, stretched out on a "cooling board." Grover had contracted typhoid fever in St. Louis, and his death put an end to Julia's first attempt at independence.

She returned to Asheville disconsolate over the loss of Grover. "I could have given up any child I had," she said later, "and it could not have hurt any worse." For months afterwards she was so sorrowful that she could take little interest in her family or her home. When her husband tried to cheer her up by offering to have the house painted, she told him indifferently, "Do it any way you want to do it." Her apathy was so great that her minister urged her to stop brooding and to remember her Christian duty to her other children. At the root of her depression there was more than the death of a specially beloved child. This sorrow brought to the surface of her mind all the accumulated unhappiness of her marriage. She longed for escape.

In the summer of 1906 she hit on another way to save herself and her children. Learning that a rambling Victorian house at 48 Spruce Street, near the center of Asheville, was for sale, she made a down payment on it in August. The next month she reopened it as a boardinghouse, retaining its previous name, "The Old Kentucky Home." Initially W.O. favored her plan, because it promised to increase the family income, and he co-signed the mortgage. But after a few weeks she discovered that in order to make money from the boardinghouse, which held as many as nineteen guests, she had to live in it, and at this point her husband drew the line. He refused to move from his house on Woodfin Street. Feeling that she had no choice, Julia took Tom, her baby, with her to the Old Kentucky Home, while the older children remained with their father, a few blocks away.

II

In *Look Homeward, Angel* when Eliza Gant opened "Dixieland," her boardinghouse, it disrupted the Gant family. The dissolution of the Wolfe family had begun long before Julia moved to the Old Kentucky Home. Frank, the oldest son, was already away from home much of the time, working at transient jobs, forging checks occasionally against his father's account, and scrounging on his mother's generosity. Within two years, Effie, the older sister, married Fred Gambrell, moved with him to South Carolina, and began her life of quiet domesticity as the mother of many children. Mabel, who was sixteen, remained at the Woodfin Street house, cooking and cleaning for her father and becoming a kind of surrogate wife for him. Ben, Grover's twin, unwilling to ask for help from either his father or his mother, left school in the ninth grade and got a job in the circulation department of the *Asheville Citizen*. Fred, who was only twelve, oscillated between Woodfin and Spruce streets; he began to stutter, and he wet his bed at night.

For Tom, the move to Spruce Street marked a recognition that the turbulent disorganization of his family was not some transient phase but a permanent condition. To be sure, he still lived with his mother, and he slept in her bed. She always though of him as her baby, and she attended to his needs as if he were still an infant. She told him when to bathe, she picked up the clothing he strewed on the floor of his room and in the hallway and bathroom, and she tidied up his books and toys and papers. In less busy moments, she was affectionate and concerned, and perhaps too possessive.

But she was so involved in running her boardinghouse that she often simply ignored him. The Old Kentucky Home was not one of Asheville's better places to stay, for, as one of Julia's relatives said, it had a reputation for being "'an untidy, dirty, squalid, down at the heels, second class boarding house. Drab as to furniture, meager in food." But Julia was an excellent manager, and by giving it her undivided attention, she made it pay. So successful was she that she worked off her mortgage promptly and presently expanded the operation by adding six new rooms and a sleeping porch upstairs.

Constantly shifted from one room to another, obliged to eat his meals in a little pantry that Julia had scooped out in order to make more room for the boarders in the dining room, Tom was never sure whether his mother would caress him or neglect him. Growing up as an appendage to Julia, he did not develop a full sense of autonomy, the feeling that he was an independent person in his own right. For the rest of his life he felt obliged to attach himself to a stronger, older, wiser person, on whom he could lean, in order to feel complete.

From his father he also received mixed signals. Prematurely aged by a strenuous and dissolute life, W.O. often seemed more like a grandfather than a father to Tom. Most of the time he was affectionately indulgent. After school when Tom stopped by the monument shop he might be warmly welcomed, and W.O., who was not doing much in the way of business, would walk him over to the drugstore, where, "before the onyx splendor of the fountain, under the revolving wooden fans," he would treat him to "limeade so cold it made the head ache, or foaming ice-cream soda, which returned in sharp delicious belches down his tender nostrils." In the evenings W.O. sometimes took his youngest son to the outdoor movie at the Riverside Park, and for the rest of his life Tom remembered seeing *The Fall of Troy*, with the spectacular wooden horse and the boulders that the Trojans hurled at the attacking Greeks, so obviously made of cardboard that they floated through the air like feathers.

But at other times, particularly when W.O. was suffering from rheumatism or was beginning to drink again, he was not so agreeable. In this state he never scolded or abused Tom, but he berated the rest of the family and with querulous self-pity enumerated the sacrifices — mostly imaginary — he had made for them. With malicious satisfaction he complained to Tom that Julia's "mismanagment" was leading to "an entire failure of her boarding house," which he called "this murderous and bloody Barn," and he predicted that the ruin of the whole family would surely follow. His other standard lament was that he was getting too old to work and "if I have to depend on the weakling crowd of boys I am unfortunate enough to be the father of I will certainly go to the poorhouse."

Tom never knew which reception to expect, and the uncertainty increased his fear — so uniformly found among the children of alcoholics — of desertion. It also fueled his suspicion, which he retained until the end of his life, that those nearest to him were about to betray him.

At the house on Woodfin Street his welcome was also unpredictable. Much of the time Mabel was happy to see her youngest brother, who was at this time a handsome fellow. His face was framed by a mass of black curly hair, which Julia insisted that he wear long, in ringlets; his complexion was dark, but his coloring was pale; and his most striking features were his large, dark-brown eyes, which were not bright or sparkling but had a flat, observing quality, rather like the lenses of camera. As a youth he was not exceptionally tall, and only the astonishing size of his feet gave indication that he would one day exceed his father's height. Altogether, when he was dressed up in one of the fancy sailor suits that Julia made for him, he was a charming little boy, and Mabel liked to feed him, talk to him, and play with him.

Then, suddenly overcome by the anomaly of her situation as a surrogate wife and mother, Mabel would view Tom as a symbol of the forces that had disrupted the family and would turn on him. At these times she sneered at what she called his "queer, dopey, freaky little face"; she protruded her lower lip in a grotesque mockery of his own; she let her head "goggle and droop stupidly," as she claimed his did. She announced that he was a Westall, not a Wolfe. "Bastard," she shouted. "There's none of papa in you." Then, after she had reduced the child to tears and impotent fury, her mood would abruptly change, and she would begin praising Tom as "the pick of that family."

Buffeted back and forth, Wolfe grew up lonely and confused. In reponse to the contradictory signals given by his parents and his siblings, he developed a pattern of emotional ambivalence, which he retained for the rest of his life. In a conversation or a letter he would blurt out his candid feelings and then — especially when they were negative or hostile feelings — instantly attempt to retract them. Even in his adult years, except when he was under the influence of alcohol, he was rarely able to express his emotions straightforwardly, without feeling obliged to disavow what he had just said.

Members of his own family most often experienced these abrupt reversals of Tom's moods. For instance, he loved Fred — but when he was with his brother for any length of time, Tom's "pulse beat bitter dissonance to each pulse of his, his hair rose and bristled at his nearness, his flesh crawled, [he] could not endure him." He would launch out and attack Fred's meddlesome interference or his incompetence. Then, sometimes in midsentence, his emotional current would be reversed, and, "filled suddenly with all the warmth of [Fred's] goodness and devotion," he would retract all the harsh things he had just said. Later both Thomas Wolfe's editor and his lover became intimately acquainted with his pattern of instantaneously shifting emotions.

As a little boy Tom was not able to express his anxiety, but it manifested itself in the slight stammer that he developed after Julia moved to the Old Kentucky Home. He did not have a severe stutter, like his brother Fred's, but he often had difficulty articulating the initial words of his sentences, especially when he was talking to strangers or was excited. When he was in relaxed conversation or, in later years, when he was making a formal presentation in a debate or a lecture, the impediment disappeared. Those who knew Wolfe best were scarcely aware of it, but people introduced to him for the first time nearly always noticed it.

His unhappiness also caused him to have terrifying dreams and a fear of the night — "not ordinary fear," he explained, "but a kind of night sickness — a spiritual nausea," which "hung like a cloud over my life." Later he passionately voiced his feelings as a child: "My overloaded heart was bursting with its packed weight of loneliness and terror; I was strangling, without speech, without articulation, in my own secretions — groping like a blind seathing with no eyes and a thousand feelers toward light, toward life, toward beauty and order, out of that hell of chaos, greed, and cheap ugliness."

An uncomprehending casualty of the warfare between his parents, Wolfe grew up with no sure sense of his self or of its relationship to the outside world. In some ways he always remained

an infant — as an adult, a gigantic infant, to be sure — unwilling
to give up its mother's breast. He desired to devour everything in
sight, whether it was mountains of food or libraries of books. He
had grandiose fantasies of unlimited success, power, brilliance,
and endless love. In other ways he was always a small boy —
unable to drive a car or to use a typewriter, unwilling to bathe
regularly, uninterested in keeping his clothes clean.

Self-absorbed, he took a childish pleasure in the functioning of
his own body. Even as a man he felt great satisfaction when he had
a bowel movement, and he wrote about his joy "to feel the seductive thrill of its approach . . . , to restrain in gently, to submit
to its growing ecstasies, and finally to submit." His penis especially interested him. Years later he told Edward C. Aswell that as
a child, he had always found it "somehow pleasant in a deep and
subtle way, to touch and handle" his organ. When he was eight
years old he "loved to hold his penis whenever he was excited or
aroused by anything," and "he would not merely hold it through
his clothes or put his hands inside his pants as others did, but
would often take his penis out, no matter where he was, and hold
it fondly, but at the same time abstractedly, with his attention so
fixed on other things that he hardly knew he did it." He continued
to do this, he said, until older boys shamed him out of the practice.
Even as an adult he continued to play with his genitals. When he
was able to afford tailor-made suits, he ordered that the cloth be
doubled at the crotch, because his trousers always wore out at that
point.

Feeling unloved by both of his parents, Wolfe grew up with an
insatiable need for recognition and praise and with an extraordinary sensitivity to criticism of any kind. At the same time his sense
that his mother and his father had failed him produced in Wolfe,
as it does in other narcissistic personalities, an urgent "need to
reunite with a powerful and nourishing figure" who could take
their place. It was not by accident that Wolfe made a man's quest
for his father the central theme of so much of his writing.

III

But these developments were part of the secret life of Thomas
Wolfe. Members of his family, preoccupied with their own problems, were not aware that he had any particular cause for unhap-

piness. If other people had been asked, they would have said that he was reasonably well cared for. After all, his family lived in not one but two fairly satisfactory houses in the center of Asheville; he was always given plenty of food; his clothing was adequate, though he was growing so rapidly that nothing ever seemed quite to fit him. To most people he seemed an ordinary little boy, a little spoiled perhaps, but brighter than most.

In September 1906, when his playmate, Max Israel, started attending the local public school on Orange Street, Tom decided that he wanted to go too, even though he lacked a month of being six years old. Julia let him tag along with Max, thinking that the teacher would send him home. But, with that flexibility that is possible only in a small school system, she let him stay. "He seemed ready for school," she explained to Julia a few weeks later, "and was in fact making better progress than some in the room who were seven or eight years of age."

Like any other child, he had some initial difficulties in adjusting to school. He found it embarrassing to ask to be excused in order to go to the toilet. He squirmed and he suffered and, at least once, in the second grade, he wet his pants while he was standing before the class to read. The bigger boys bullied him and made fun of his shoulder-length curls, which Julia insisted that her baby must keep. Not until he was eight years old, when he contracted head lice and had to have his hair cut, did he begin to look like a regular boy.

But for the most part he loved the Orange Street School. He liked the songs they taught him, especially "The Jolly Miller's Song." With the other students he memorized poems, and he always remembered Robert Louis Stevenson's verses, "The Swing," and his line about trains: "the stations go whistling by." In the third grade he began to study American history. He knew all about the redcoats and the Liberty Boys of 1776 and was patriotically confident that "one American [was as] good as 3 Englishmen." When his class studied the Civil War he learned about "The Yankees" and "How we almost 'whupped' them."

But most of all he liked to read. After going through all the children's books at the school library, he started on his father's respectable collection of books. He spent hours looking at John Clark Ridpath's *Cyclopaedia of Universal History,* as much absorbed in the illustrations as the text, and he fancied himself living among the Egyptians or fighting with Charles the Hammer. Early he developed a taste for poetry, for he was used to hearing his father recite old-time favorites, like Gray's "Elegy Written in a Country Church-Yard," which he knew by heart. When W.O. lived in Baltimore, he had often gone to the theater, and he memorized and declaimed with great passion Hamlet's first soliloquy, Marc Antony's funeral oration, and the final scene between Desdemona and Othello before he strangles her. As soon as he could, Tom began reading these himself, especially in anthologies that his family owned, like *Wit and Humor of the Ages* and *The Golden Treasury of Poetry and Prose*. Years later his mother pointed out that "these books still have his dirty finger prints."

By the time Tom entered the second grade, W.O., always concerned for his son's education, bought a card for him at the public library, which he renewed every year. As soon as school was dismissed, Tom usually went to the library, which was then on the square near his father's shop, and buried himself in books until dinnertime. He went through many of the Horatio Alger books, the Oliver Optic series, Gene Stratton Porter's sentimental novels, and O. Henry's short stories. Grace Jones, the librarian, told Julia that "Tom had read more books than any boy in N.C. and he doesn't stick to children's books. He reads everything."

He was, however, considerably less advanced in writing and in spelling. In what may be the earliest example of his handwriting, he scrawled his name and address on the reverse side of Ben's neat 1906 exercise book — giving his address at 92 Woodfin Street much more frequently than 48 Spruce Street — and he tried his hand at drafting a letter:"Dear Sir I am glad to here from You. An I am glad to See you I gess I will clos my letter now. I have nothen more to say." By Christmas of that year his spelling had improved, or at least he was taking more pains, for his letter to Santa Claus contained few errors; it requested, among other things, a slate and chalk, a signet ring, a sweater, a "great big drawing tablet," "Some Pictur books," an air rifle, a sled, and a soldier suit. But he made many mistakes in his composition book for the third grade, and his teacher complained, as has everybody else who has ever read his manuscripts, "Your writing is very poor."

His education was not confined to the classroom, for, unlike most of his playmates, he had a good many opportunities to travel. Occasionally he went on trips with his father, but more frequently he accompanied his mother, who was beginning to suffer from rheumatism and liked to escape the Asheville winters, when there were very few boarders at the Old Kentucky Home anyway. In 1909 they went to New Orleans for Mardi Gras, and for the rest of his life he remembered visiting the French Quarter, and "the strangeness of hearing a foreign language in an American City." That fall they traveled to Hot Springs, Arkansas, where she hoped the waters would relieve her swollen joints, and the next year Julia, who was beginning to speculate in Florida real estate, took him to St. Petersburg, Tampa, and Jacksonville. During these trips she sometimes hired a tutor for him. Occasionally she entered him in the local schools if they were staying for any length of time, or she taught him herself. At first he loved these trips and the chance they gave him for having his mother all to himself. But as he grew older he was embarrassed by Julia's lifelong habits of frugality, such as tucking all the rolls and bread served at dinner in a restaurant into her capacious purse, to be consumed as breakfast the next morning, and they quarreled a great deal.

At about the same time that Tom started school he began going to Sunday school at the First Presbyterian Church, where all of the children were expected to remain for the regular church service afterward. The Scottish minister, Dr. R. F. Campbell, who presided over the church for a generation, preached straight Calvinistic doctrine — "nothing," as Mabel said, "but the Bible, and the Father, Son, and Holy Ghost." Tom completed at least the third grade of Sunday school, and apparently he liked the church well enough, for he retained memories of "the children singing 'Shall we gather at the River the Bew-tee-ful the Bew-tee-ful R-hi-ver,' " of "the dark walnut stained-glass light in the church," and of "the remote yet passionate austerity of the preachers voice, the lean horselike nobility of his face as he craned above his collar saying 'heinous.' "

As a child he had entirely conventional ideas about religion. A prayer that he wrote out when he was eight years old mostly repeated the familiar "Now I lay me down to sleep," but he added: "God, . . . Make Papa well." During these early years he gained, either in church or through his own reading, a considerable familiarity with the Bible. Nearly all his later writings contained biblical phrases, especially echoes of the Psalms.

Yet religious education had surprisingly little impact on Wolfe. There is nothing to suggest that he ever had a profound religious experience; he took no interest in doctrinal arguments; and, unlike many youths, he bore no burden of sin, confessed no sense of guilt. He never talked about religion with his parents, who were infrequent churchgoers. Presently he began to play hooky. There was no special rebelliousness in his action; he simply drifted away. Later, when he came back to Asheville during college vacations, he often made a point of visiting the First Presbyterian Church — usually after the service was over — to pay his repects to Dr. Campbell. But their relationship was only a social one, and when Campbell officiated at Wolfe's funeral he had to admit: "I wish I had something definite to say about his religious life."

Attending the Presbyterian church did help to make young Thomas Wolfe aware of social distinctions in his home town. Up till the age of six or eight, he was totally absorbed in the life of his tumultuous family, and the rest of Asheville served as a backdrop for that domestic drama. Then he found that his public school classmates attended several different churches. The children of "rather common" families, many of whom lived in the less prosperous east side of Asheville, were likely to be Baptists, while those from families that were "a little better, but still common," were often Methodists. The Episcopal church attracted those who "were more flashy and a lot of social swells." Though Tom was a little troubled that his own Sunday school class included so many "swank boys from the West side of town," he concluded that the Presbyterians "were the best there was. . . . They stood for order, quietness, . . . financial substance, and solid rectitude."

As he grew older he discovered other social divisions in the city. He knew very little about the blacks of Asheville until he was old enough to run errands for his mother. Julia usually had a black maid or cook at the Old Kentucky Home, but she got along badly with all her help. "She was not, never had been, used to service," Wolfe wrote later; she suspected them of stealing from her, she nagged them about their work, and she "never had their respect." When one of them quit without notice, she would send Tom down into the Negro section — "Niggertown," as he always referred to it in his fiction — to find a replacement. These expeditions gave Tom his first real contact with blacks, who comprised about one-fifth of the city's population, and he saw them under the worst possible circumstances. He never had a cherished black mammy, with whom he could associate ideas of comfort and

affection, and he had no acquaintance with any of the sturdy rural
black families of the region. Instead, as he recorded in *Look Homeward, Angel,* he entered a "city of rickets," where he was obliged
to poke "into their fetid shacks, past the slow stench of little rills
of mire and sewage, in fetid cellars, through all the rank labyrinth
of the hill-sprawled settlement." It was scarcely surprising that he
grew up with the conventional view of white Southerners of his
era that Negroes were a "black millstone" on the progress of the
South and that these lazy, inefficient, primitive people should be
transported back to the "jungles" of Africa.

Julia also forced him to explore the white sections of Asheville.
Believing that "a boy should be taught to be independent and
self-respecting," she insisted that he had to help his brother Fred,
that gregarious natural salesman, who was in charge of the door-
to-door sale of the *Saturday Evening Post* in the city. Tom hated the
work; he squirmed with embarrassment at Fred's pep talks to the
groups of boys who worked for him, he resented his brother's
bullying, and he suffered an agony of shame each time he had to
approach a prospective customer. Yet he was very good at the job.
In one typical week, when the *Saturday Evening Post* for August 28,
1909, reached Asheville, he sold one hundred fifty copies, while
the seventeen other boys who worked for Fred sold between one
and sixty-one copies each; Fred himself, the supersalesman, sold
two hundred five copies that week. To urge his helpers on, Fred
offered to give a prize to the boy who sold the largest number of
copies of the magazine. "I aint in it," Tom explained in a letter to
Effie, "if i was i would beet them all to pieces. So he don't want
me in it — the boys would not feel like working if I Beet them."

While selling his magazines in all sections of Asheville, Tom
came to sense that his family occupied an anomalous place in
society. It was easy to identify the groups that the Wolfes did not
belong to. Asheville was a remarkably cosmopolitan small city,
for the mountain air and the scenery of the Great Smokies attracted large numbers of summer residents from all over the country. They filled the great hostelries, like the Battery Park Hotel,
which was perched on a steep hill — now leveled — in the center
of the city, and spilled over into boardinghouses like the Old
Kentucky Home. Some of the wealthiest visitors were so enchanted with the area that they stayed. George Vanderbilt constructed his own French château, which he called Biltmore, on a

huge tract of land south of the city. On a slope to the north Dr. E. W. Grove, who made a fortune from his patent medicines, built his own fantastic castle, the Grove Park Inn. A very few of the best-educated Asheville families, like the Pearsons and the Sondleys, associated with these wealthy outsiders, but the Wolfes clearly were not in this class. When Tom was growing up he thought of a millionaire as "a fabulous creature like the hippogriff or the centaur."

Nor did the Wolfes and most other permanent Asheville residents mix socially with the sizable numbers of people who came to the city for reasons of health. Asheville's elevation and its pure mountain air were reputed to benefit those infected with tuberculosis. Local people profited from the expenditures of these invalids, but they also feared them, since there was no known cure for the disease. Tom encountered these "lungers" when Julia allowed him to sell the *Saturday Evening Post* in the sanatoriums and hospitals that ringed the city. But all residents of Asheville who could do so avoided them, and the better boardinghouses in Asheville — but not the Old Kentucky Home — specified in their advertisements "No Consumptives Taken" or "No Invalids."

Another segment of the population that Tom's family had nothing to do with was the Jews. Like most Southerners of the time, the Wolfes were anti-Semitic. Tom was brought up to think of Jews as "beaknosed Shylocks from Yankeedom," and he and his playmates took joy in terrorizing the Jewish boys of their age and in spying on their parents. Though there were only sixteen Jewish families in all of Buncombe County in 1906, they were so readily identifiable by their exotic names and their Sabbath observances that it was easy for Wolfe, both as a boy and a man, to believe that their numbers in the town were rapidly increasing "by that strange advertisement of the race which brings stealthily the swarm where honey is found."

But if it was clear which groups in Asheville the Wolfe family did not associate with, it was harder to identify their place in the large, native-born working- and middle-class population of the city. They were socially invisible. In later years a surprising number of people who grew up in Asheville, often in the same neighborhood as Tom, reported that they knew about the Wolfes but "didn't have anything to do with them." One of Wolfe's roommates in Chapel Hill, a native of Asheville who had not met Tom until he entered the University of North Carolina, tried to locate the family's position in society: "The Wolfes belonged to that large group of lesser lights who had never achieved more than a certain respectibility of name and neighborhood acceptance. The father, who earned a none too bountiful living, and that with his hands, had little claim to either social or civil distinction; and the Wolfe home, shabby and inadequate to the family's size and comfort, did not measure up to 'society' standards."

In consequence, Thomas Wolfe grew up in a kind of social no-man's-land. His family had neighbors but not friends. They had relatives in the city but rarely saw them. Julia's brothers, who became prosperous businessmen, had little to do with their sister and her numerous, rowdy offspring, whom they called "those wolves." W.O. reciprocated their dislike, and he taught his children that Westall was "a synonym for selfishness, coldness, and unpleasant eccentricity." W.O. had cronies among the local artisans, but these never felt socially comfortable with Julia. In short, as Tom wrote, the Wolfes "were a lovely family — everyone knew them — no one came to see them — they couldn't go with the swells — the common people were awed by them."

IV

The spring of 1912 brought a marked change in Tom's life. J. M. Roberts, the principal of the Orange Street School, decided to resign in order to open his own private academy, the North State Fitting School, which would prepare Asheville boys for college. Hoping to identify likely candidates for the new school, he read a story aloud to all the boys in the sixth grade and told them to reproduce it in their own words. Taking the papers home, he asked his wife Margaret to help him evaluate them. After reading one particularly ratty-looking paper, she asked, "Who is this boy Thomas Wolfe?" Her husband identified him and said that he had expected him to write a good paper. "Well," Mrs. Roberts said, handing the paper to him, "he is a genius."

But it took persuasion to get W.O. and Julia Wolfe to enroll Tom in the North State Fitting School, because there was a tuition fee of one hundred dollars a year. Julia was always reluctant to part with money except for her real estate speculations. W.O. blustered that he already supported the public schools with his taxes and that there was no reason to pay more for the boy's education. Tom's brothers and sisters, all of whom attended the public school system, were opposed, thinking that Tom, as the baby, had already received too much special treatment. But Tom was so eager to go that he kept begging his parents. Finally W.O., who almost doted on his youngest son and wanted him to become an educated man, gave in and agreed to pay the tuition from his earnings at the monument shop. "If the boy wants to go," he announced, "he can go."

Tom always remembered his first sight of Margaret Roberts. The North State Fitting School was about to open, and the Robertses were still cleaning up the big pre–Civil War house in south Asheville where the classes would be held. Mrs. Roberts had a broom in her hand. Thirty-four years old, of middling height but desperately thin, she had, he thought, "the most tranquil and the most passionate face he had ever seen." After Mr. Roberts introduced the awkward boy, she saw that his glance drifted to the bookcases in the room, and she asked what he had been reading. Since he had been hiding himself in the public library most afternoons, he had read a great many books — mostly books for boys and light fiction. Gently she called his attention to Charles Reade's historical novel *The Cloister and the Hearth,* and allowed him to borrow her copy. For a time he thought that it was the greatest novel ever written, as he thought that Margaret Roberts was the grandest person he had ever met.

This instant adoration of Mrs. Roberts saved him from what otherwise might have proved a disastrous first year at the North State Fitting School. By going to a private school he pretty much severed his friendship with the other boys of his neighborhood, like Max Israel and Charley Perkinson, who continued in the public school system. But he did not find it easy to make new friends. Many of his classmates at the Robertses' academy were wealthier and more sophisticated than he was, and these "swells," as he called them, looked down at the gawky, unpolished son of a drunken marble man and a stingy boardinghouse keeper. Like many other day-schools for boys, North State stressed sports, but Tom was totally unathletic and made no friends on the playing field. He disliked most of his classes, for he thought Mr. Roberts was a poor instructor in Latin, since he taught "by formula and by repetition," and developed a positive hatred for Hortense Pattison, who taught algebra, a subject he never could master.

But his classes with Mrs. Roberts were richly rewarding. Bearing in mind the admission requirements for the University of North Carolina, she guided her students through a survey of English and, to a lesser extent, American literature. She introduced him to Francis Palgrave's *Golden Treasury*, and he discovered the beauties of the lyric, though his taste still ran to poems like James Russell Lowell's "The Present Crisis" ("Once to every man and nation") that had a "swinging obvious gallop." Under her direction he began reading Shakespeare, Scott, Dickens, Thackeray, and Stevenson.

Indeed, he read so much that his other schoolwork suffered, even in classes that Mrs. Roberts taught. Often he made only a perfunctory effort. Required to prepare sentences that showed the differences between "annex," "unite," and "coalesce," he submitted: "They will coalesce." Mrs. Roberts warned that his work was unsatisfactory and threatened to tell his mother unless it improved. "You are a boy of great ability, but you must study too," she wrote on one of his papers. "You read a great deal and that is good, but too much reading is not to be desired any more than too little."

So poorly did Tom perform during his first year that Mrs. Roberts objected when Julia proposed to take him out of school for several days in March in order to attend the inauguration of Woodrow Wilson, the first Southern-born President elected since the Civil War. She said that he would fall behind, especially in algebra. But after he excitedly told her about all the benefits he was sure he would derive from the trip, ending up with, "But don't you understand — I'll hear the President and I'll see *the home of the United States!*" she had to capitulate. Tom and Julia visited the Capitol, the Library of Congress, and the Bureau of Engraving, they toured Mount Vernon, and they watched the inaugural parade. What they both remembered best was that outgoing President William Howard Taft had a complexion "as pink as a baby's."

Wolfe's later years at the North State Fitting School were more successful. He learned how to study, and his grades improved. His classmates began to accept him as one of the group — still not an athlete, but in his own way "an eccentric genius." In turn, he concluded that the other students were "all fine boys." In a required essay in his junior year, he announced that the school was superior to all others because of the "new and novel" — even at an early age Wolfe was given to redundancy — methods of instruction that sometimes permitted students to suggest their own assignments and because of "the fairness and the justice meeted out by the teachers." "There is not one thing about the school that I dislike," he concluded, "and I therefore spend an enjoyable time." No doubt there was a certain amount of toadying in the essay, but two decades later Wolfe declared that he had spent "the happiest and most valuable years of my life" at the Robertses' school.

What he did not say in his essay — but what was obvious to anyone who knew him — was that he enjoyed the school because of Mrs. Roberts. This superb teacher, frail, overworked, and high-strung as she was, reached out to all the boys in her classes, believing that "in each there was something worth loving, or some thing needing love." For a much smaller number she felt "a really personal love," and Tom was one of those. Something about him deeply appealed to her. Perhaps initially it was that he was so skinny and so disheveled that he obviously needed care, and she worried that he did not get enough sleep or enough to eat. Later it was his eagerness to read any book that she recommended and the enthusiasm he shared with her for nineteenth-century English romantic poetry. But mostly, after the first year, what struck her was the delight he took in writing. "I never corrected much except your mechanical mistakes," she reminded him later. "I was wise enough, though not naturally wise, to see that by nature you had the touch of the pen, and that you would soon be far beyond your teacher."

For his part, Wolfe always recognized his debt to Mrs. Roberts. Recommending her for a position in the Asheville public school system in 1921, he tried to explain what he owed to her, in terms that a school administrator would understand. She "succeeded in getting under my skull an appreciation of what is fine and beautiful in literature," he wrote. Beyond that, "she exercised an influence that is inestimable on almost every particular of my life and thought." But this public testimonial did not do justice to his feelings, and in a personal letter he reminded her that she had rescued him from his family's turmoil and distress. Addressing her as the "mother of my spirit who fed me with light," he asked:

"Do you think that I have forgotten? Do you think I ever will? You are entombed in my flesh, you are in the pulses of my blood, the thought of you makes great music in me."

The love that Wolfe bore for Mrs. Roberts was pure and ideal, and he never thought of associating it with sex. Indeed, he came to an awareness of sexual matters surprisingly late for a boy raised in a large family of brothers and sisters and brought up in a boardinghouse where a certain amount of promiscuity among the guests was tolerated. Since his parents always slept in separate rooms — and most of the time in separate houses — he was shocked to discover when he was eight years old that Effie and Fred Gambrell shared the same bed. Even as he approached puberty he had only a vague idea of female anatomy until he and some of his classmates learned the facts of life from a seventeen-year-old who, tucking his male organ between his legs and writhing his hips erotically, demonstrated what a woman looked like.

Then, when Wolfe was about thirteen, he accidentally discovered a new satisfaction in masturbation. Perhaps it was not entirely coincidental that he had his first orgasm when he and Julia, for unknown reasons, briefly came back to his father's house on Woodfin Street. After that he masturbated frequently. "It opens to you the kingdoms of the earth," he found. His favorite place for the activity was the back-porch toilet at Spruce Street, where in cool privacy he fantasized about voluptuous women, wearing silk stockings, who submitted to his will. Curiously enough for a boy brought up as a Presbyterian in a Southern community, he felt no guilt over the practice, flippantly remarking later: "Every man his own Harem . . . If a man can not be his own master, at least he can be his own mistress."

Overtly his sexual fantasies had nothing to do with Mrs. Roberts, who was so pure that Wolfe could not think of her ever having carnal relations with her husband, even though they had two children. Unable to express his feelings toward Mrs. Roberts, he turned them against her husband, whom he condemned as "a crude countryman, full of sound and fury." Enviously he observed that Mr. Roberts had "huge privates" and that while he was teaching he "caressed them with thick chalky fingers — Chalk from his tool to his throat." A decade after Wolfe graduated from the North State Fitting School and wrote the thinly disguised account of Mr. and Mrs. Roberts that appeared in *Look Homeward,*

Angel — where he called them Mr. and Mrs. Leonard — he decorated his pages with drawings of enlarged male genitalia.

V

During the four years that Wolfe spent at the Robertses' school he began the process, which he did not live to complete, of disengaging himself from his quarrelsome and manipulative family. Later he came to think of it as "the building of a Wall," behind which he could shelter "'a secret life." Yet he recognized that protecting his autonomy had its costs, and he asked himself: "May not every liberation from the crowd . . . every motion toward freedom be really an isolation behind a wall? For is not that thing which frees us also that thing which isolates and walls us in?"

He needed all the independence that he could muster, for during his high-school years his family was further disintegrating. His father worked hardly at all, now that his hands were crippled by rheumatism. He drank less after he discovered that alcohol aggravated his suffering from prostatitis. Much of the time he rocked on the porch of the Old Kentucky Home, ogling the female boarders and telling anybody who would listen about his early years in Pennsylvania, his encounter with Confederate cavalrymen on the road to Gettysburg — whose leader, if one could believe the old man, was General Fitzhugh Lee — and his apprentice days in Baltimore. When he lacked an audience, he sank into whining self-pity and took less and less interest in his family.

Julia, on the other hand, was flourishing. Her frugality made the Old Kentucky Home a paying proposition, but she was not satisfied. She spent more and more of her time on real estate speculation, convinced that it would make her as rich as her brothers, and she thought of herself as a hard-nosed investor. Years later Frank Wolfe retained a mental picture of "Julia E. in her be-littered sun parlor, with maps and plats of Castle Valley, Skunk Hollow, Porcupine Gap, and a few other too numerous places to mention twisting her mouth and telling a lot of buzzard-looking real estate men what a grand future these places had."

She had led such a disappointing life that she developed a carapace of insensitivity to others, even to her own children. Tom wrote later that she shared the monumental self-confidence of all the Westalls, who were "invincibly assured that the universe pro-

ceeded from them and responded to each heart beat of their lives,
[so that] the hostility of the world, the scorn of other men
would only harden them in their virtuous self-belief . . . of
their own infallibility." Julia was more than a little serious
when once she corrected Tom for saying that the two greatest
Americans had been born in February, George Washington and
Abraham Lincoln. There was, she reminded him, a third: his
mother.

The Wolfe children now went their separate ways. Effie rarely
appeared in Asheville. Frank drifted back when he was broke. All
the other children hated him, and none more than Tom. He loathed
Frank's rotten teeth and foul breath; he remembered that Frank
once struck him with a monkey wrench and then tried to mask his
fear of discovery as contrition; he was furious to discover Frank
and one of the female boarders in his father's bed.

Mabel, in a surprising display of independence, joined another
Asheville girl, Pearl Shope, to form a musical team, and for two
or three years they sang and played the piano at hotels, chatauquas,
and movie houses all over the South. In Tom's senior year of high
school she married Ralph Wheaton, a respectable, commonplace
young man, who was a salesman for the National Cash Register
Company. But even after they moved away from Asheville,
Mabel, who remained childless, was ready to rush back and care
for her father, who, she believed to the end of her life, "loved me
a little more than he did the others." Fred, the cheerful, stammering salesman, saved up enough money to enter Georgia Tech in
1912; he remained there for nearly three years, until he flunked
out.

That left Ben, the loneliest, the most isolated of the Wolfe children, for whom Tom since infancy had had a special affection.
Thin, with humped shoulders and a sunken chest, his sallow face
afflicted with boils, Ben looked like no one else in the family, and
he joined neither side in the perennial family war. With equal
skepticism he listened to his father's and his mother's complaints
against each other, saying to the invisible guardian angel that rested
on his shoulder, "Listen to that, won't you?" He did all that he
could to protect Tom. The two boys slept in the same room after
Tom left his mother's bed. From his modest salary at the *Asheville
Citizen* he gave his youngest brother pocket money and occasional
small gifts. A thoroughly conventional young man, Ben believed

in the importance of dressing neatly, and he tried to keep Tom clean and neat.

Ben fiercely resented Julia's reluctance to buy clothing for her youngest son — who, in fact, grew so fast that it was hard to keep him in garments that fit. Once when Ben discarded a pair of five-dollar shoes, she decided they were too good to be thrown away, and she gave them to Tom, saying, "It's a pity not to use them." Much too small, they hurt his feet and produced a "sky-scraper toe-nail," but she made him wear them. When Ben discovered what was happening, he wrestled the shoes off Tom and threw them away, and then he blasted Julia for her stinginess. In the privacy of their room he warned Tom not to be taken in by the protestations of his parents that there was not enough money for his care and education. The Wolfe family was now well off, he said, and if penuriousness had blighted the lives of the older children, it must not be allowed to ruin Tom's. "Get all you can from them," he advised.

Ben's emotional support, along with Mrs. Roberts's affection, helped make Tom's last two years at the North State Fitting School happy ones. Now recognized as one of the most gifted students and allowed, because he was Mrs. Roberts's favorite, greater freedom than most of the other boys, he pitched himself enthusiastically into extracurricular activities. After his voice changed, he became an effective member of the debating team. He and a classmate won their case against building up American naval strength to meet any threat that might emerge from the World War that had just broken out in Europe, and Tom received a gold medal for being the best speaker.

Less happy was his participation during his senior year in the city-wide festival honoring the three hundredth anniversary of William Shakespeare's death. Students were to represent characters from Shakespeare's plays in a pageant, the costumes for which were ordered from Philadelphia. Tom was Prince Hal in *Henry IV*. When the costumes arrived on the day of the performance, Prince Hal's leggings turned out to be at least four inches too short for the six-foot youth, whose stage debut converted historical drama into farce.

Not even this fiasco greatly upset Wolfe, because he was by this time involved in what proved to be a lifetime love affair with Shakespeare. The Independent Publishing Company offered a gold medal for the student who wrote the best essay on Shakespeare, and Tom immersed himself in the assignment. Tearing the picture of the poet from the paper, he tacked it above his study table at home, inscribing it with Ben Jonson's invocation: "My Shakespeare, rise!" For days his brothers and sisters made fun of him, requesting "My Shakespeare" to pass the sugar and so on. But his essay on "Shakespeare: The Man," which paid tribute to the writer as "an intellectual ocean toward which all rivers ran and from which all the realms of learning are now refreshed," won the prize, and the judges praised the paper's *"symmetry, . . .* the internal evidence it betrays of wide, sympathetic and appreciative reading, and *especially . . .* its unity as an *interpretation* and *appreciation* of the Genius and Spirit of 'Shakespeare the man.' "

At Mrs. Roberts's suggestion, he read his essay in the declamation contest, held during the graduation exercises at the school, and he won another gold medal, beating the other contestants, as he said, because their voices had not yet changed while his booming baritone could be heard throughout the hall.

After sweeping all the literary honors at graduation, Tom announced to his parents that he intended to go to college. His plan was a surprise even to the Robertses, who thought he was very young and believed that he could benefit by another year in preparatory school. It was even more startling to his family. Except for Fred, who had paid his own way, none of the other Wolfe children had received a higher education. Julia was unwilling to spend the money. Finally W.O. intervened, just as he had done when Tom asked to be sent to the North State Fitting School. Convinced by the boy's argument that, with a college education, he could become a congressman, a governor, or an ambassador, W.O. agreed to pay for Tom's college, Drawing the money from his own earnings, not from what Julia made at the Old Kentucky Home, W.O. told his youngest son he could go to the University of North Carolina.

But that was not what Tom wanted. He dreamed of attending Princeton. When Julia vetoed that as too expensive, he asked to be sent to the University of Virginia, which he was sure was "a dwelling place of culture, the last and greatest academy of the old aristocracy, an American Oxford." But W.O. insisted that the contacts he made at the state university would be useful for a career in North Carolina law and politics. "You belong to

North Carolina and you must go to Chapel Hill," he told the boy.

Throughout the summer of 1916, Tom and his father had, as Mabel reported, "a *fuss* daily over *where* to go to school." In late August Tom seemed to be winning, for W.O. asked Mabel to take the boy to Charlottesville. But Tom's letter asking information from the University of Virginia went unanswered, and he felt forced to decide for the University of North Carolina. After he committed himself he heard from the authorities in Charlottesville, but he recognized that it was too late to change. "Carolina is a good school," he concluded, "and perhaps everything is for the best."

II

The Magical Campus

L ONG AFTER WOLFE GRADUATED from college he described his years at the University of North Carolina as "close to magic," and to the end of his life he had a special feeling of warmth and affection for Chapel Hill. In his autobiographical jottings he referred to the university as "the magical campus."

But that was not the view of the sixteen-year-old freshman who enrolled in September 1916. The university, which had about a thousand students, seemed bewilderingly large. Along with other freshmen he was given an orientation tour of the campus. They were reminded that they were attending the oldest state university in the country, chartered in 1789, and were shown the Davie Poplar, where the founders of the university tethered their horses when they decided that the elevated wooded tract at Chapel Hill was the best location for the institution. The guides pointed out Old East, the oldest university building, begun in 1793, and called attention to the Old Well, still the central place for students to meet. Wolfe must have been impressed by the university library, with its seventy-five thousand volumes, though he later remarked on "the general discomfort and inaccessibility of books" in these quiet rooms.

As part of the orientation program, freshmen heard talks from students as well as teachers on "What Is a College For?" "Foundations of a Liberal Education," and similar grand subjects. Albert

Coates, an upperclassman already identified as a future leader of
the university, explained the honor system to the new students.
Marion Ross urged freshmen to join one of the two campus literary societies, the Philanthropic, which mostly attracted men
from the eastern part of the state, and the Dialectic, to which many
western North Carolinians belonged.

Unfortunately, all this good advice came too late to help Wolfe
in making his living arrangements. Since there were few dormitories, most students stayed in rooming houses, and he had been
led to choose one just to the west of the campus run by Mrs.
Mattie E. Hardee, who was originally from Asheville. Wolfe's
father, doubtful of his son's ability to handle money, insisted that
he pay for his room and board two months in advance. The food
at Mrs. Hardee's was exceptionally good, but the room was over-
priced. What was worse, her son, an upperclassman, adopted toward the freshman "the disgusting posture of master and slave."
When the two months were up, Wolfe moved out of Mrs. Hardee's
and began a singularly peripatetic way of life for the next four
years, moving frequently from rooming house to dormitory and
back, each time changing roommates.

Nor was the orientation program of much use to him in choosing courses, for the work of freshmen was largely prescribed. He
was required to register for algebra, which was followed in the
second semester by trigonometry. From the start he realized he
would have "to 'bone' on math," but he never got the hang of it.
By memorizing formulae he managed to earn a "C" in the fall
term, a "D" in the spring.

Freshman English was also required, and he had to study a fat
volume of *Essays for College Men,* written by such worthies as
Charles W. Eliot and Lord Bryce. Freshmen were expected to
worry out the meaning of sentences that, as Wolfe recalled later,
ran something like: "But, even more, we submit, and in a still
larger sense, may we not assume the growing importance of the
psychological and, as it were, the sociological factors in determin-
ing the moral and, so to speak, intellectual quotient of tomorrow's
citizenship?" Disliking his first English teacher, Wolfe got along
well with a second, James Holly Hanford, who required all his
students to write a theme on "Who I Am." The more sophisticated freshmen, recognizing that their biographies contained little
drama, made up stories about themselves, and they initially as-

sumed that Wolfe's unvarnished account of life at Spruce Street, with details about W.O.'s drunkenness and profanity, must be fictional too.

Well prepared after studying Latin for four years under Mr. Roberts, Wolfe enjoyed his course on Cicero and Livy, which also included toward the end some odes of Horace, and he worked hard at it, underlining his texts and writing in translations between the lines. Unused to students who were conscientious and interested, his teacher, George G. H. Henry, thought his translations were so fluent that he must be using a "pony." Unable to persuade Henry that he was doing his own work, Wolfe then bought the translation, which most of the other students were already using, recited in its jerky phrases, and brought his grade up from a "C" in the first semester to a "B" in the second.

Only from his course in Greek did he receive any intellectual stimulation. After two years of preparation in the language at the North State Fitting School, Wolfe was able to keep up with the assignments given by Professor W. S. ("Bully") Bernard, and he probably did better work than was indicated by the "C"given him both terms by that sharp-tongued campus eccentric. His copies of the *Iliad,* the *Odyssey,* and Xenophon's *Symposium* were heavily marked up and annotated. Bernard's occasional lectures on Greek history and culture excited him, and he followed the professor's advice to read Greek plays in Gilbert Murray's translation. After he left college Wolfe lost most of his mastery of the language, though he claimed a decade later that he could "still read my Homer after a fashion" and "could put up some sort of battle with Xenophon." More important, he continued to share Bernard's passion for Greek civilization. In all Wolfe's early fiction he referred to Greek myths, believing that they encapsulated fundamental human experiences. "There's not much cant and twaddle to the Greeks," he wrote a friend in 1927; "they are really the *living,* aren't they? The dead are all about us."

If Wolfe's academic record during his freshman year was unremarkable, his participation in extracurricular activities brought him an unwelcome distinction. This green, ungainly freshman, who was already six feet, three inches tall and weighed only 135 pounds, seemed created to become the butt of the pranks of upperclassmen. Of all the members of his class, he alone believed the story that freshmen had to pass an examination on the college catalogue, and he memorized its pages. He credited the report that freshmen had compulsory chapel on Saturday morning, and he attentively listened to a burlesque sermon by a sophomore. Along with other freshmen he joined the Dialectic Literary Society (which was always called "the Di") and attended the initiation ceremony in the comfortably furnished society rooms lined with portraits of such distinguished former members as Governor Zebulon B. Vance. Announcing that all the initiates must make speeches, the president called first on a sophomore, who pretended to be a freshman, in order to set the desired tone of rhetorical extravagance. He turned next to Wolfe, who took the whole occasion with the utmost seriousness, held forth for twenty-two minutes about his pleasure and pride in being among such distinguished company, and concluded with a high-flying peroration predicting that some day his own portrait would hang alongside Zeb Vance's.

"Degradation" was the word Wolfe used in his autobiographical jottings to summarize his situation. In part his unhappiness was like that of any other freshman thrust into new surroundings, with no friends and no guidance. But Wolfe was especially vulnerable because of his puppy-like eagerness to be agreeable, to do whatever was expected of him. Then, too, his appearance made him a marked man — not merely because he was so tall (and was very conspicuous in an age when the average height of American men was much less than it is today), but on account of his curious scissor-like walk and his head, which appeared too small for his elongated body. In addition, his clothing never fit, and his wrists and shanks generally protruded an inch or two beyond his suit. The problem was not that he lacked money. At a time when over half the students at the university worked to earn their way through college, W.O. uncomplainingly paid all of Tom's fees and expenses. But his clothing looked odd partly because he had never learned to take care of himself — Julia and Ben had always done that for him — and chiefly because he was growing at the rate of about two inches a year.

Contributing to his vulnerability was his sense that his family was socially inferior to those of his classmates. Certainly his essay on his father's drinking and cursing, which he read aloud, did not help the situation. Nor did Julia when she visited Chapel Hill in the spring and began passing out her cards advertising the Old

Kentucky Home. With her characteristic nod and wink she told Tom's acquaintances that if they drummed up a little business for her boardinghouse she could offer them special rates. "M-M-M-Mabel, Mabel, my God," Tom exploded to his sister, "she's ruining me over at Chapel Hill. I'll swear she's just r-r-r-ruining me with my friends."

The fact that he came from the western part of the state put him under an additional disadvantage. For generations the social leaders of the university had come from the wealthy plantation region of eastern North Carolina, and during the past few decades the sons of prosperous Piedmont businessmen and manufacturers had been accepted into this elite. From these groups came the members of the oldest and most prestigious fraternities on campus, like Delta Kappa Epsilon and Zeta Psi. Sitting on the porches of their fraternity houses, which looked like palaces to students obliged to live in the dormitories or in rooming houses, these self-styled aristocrats studiously ignored the non-Greek-letter men who passed by on the sidewalk. These fraternities scorned students like Wolfe, who seemed to be uncultured mountaineers.

Wolfe had difficulty in understanding this kind of discrimination. After all, he was not a country boy but a resident of Asheville, one of the larger towns in the state. Though Asheville was situated in the mountains, he knew very little about them. As his mother once observed, he thought of the rim of hills that surrounded the city primarily as a place for an occasional picnic. To be sure, he had numerous Westall, Penland, and Patton cousins who lived in the hills beyond Asheville, but he rarely encountered any of them for his father had taught him to scorn these "mountain grills." He did not understand why he was now cast in the role of a mountaineer, an outsider.

Feeling very lonely, he accepted all proffers of friendship that came his way. Soon he was drawn into the little circle of freshmen who gathered around John S. Terry, a junior six years older than Wolfe, who made himself a kind of mother-confessor for the greenest students at the university. Active in the Di, the YMCA, and in several campus literary groups, Terry carefully monitored the academic and social life of his protégés. He taught the ungainly ones how to dance, and in that innocent age when there were only a few women students, nobody thought it odd when this 270-pound upperclassman led one freshman after another onto the dance floor. At this time Terry's homosexual inclinations were hidden, perhaps even from himself, and he got his satisfaction from eliciting the confidential confessions of his freshmen about temptations of the flesh, real or imaginary, that they experienced. Initially Wolfe basked in the warmth of Terry's group, but he soon began to find it confining. Terry had fixed, conservative ideas about the university, about religion, about literature, and, in particular, about the importance of sexual purity, and with scornful laughter he drove out of his circle anyone who challenged his views.

It was almost by accident that Wolfe offered such a challenge. In early December when two older freshmen seemed to take a special interest in him, he responded quickly to their offer of friendship. They persuaded him to go with them to a brothel in nearby Durham, promising that the experience would make a man of him, and he went to bed with a whore named Mamie Smith. Shortly afterward he went back again on his own. When he returned to Asheville for the Christmas holidays, he slipped off from home to visit a prostitute in a cheap hotel. Before she would have sex with him, she examined him and announced that he had gonorrhea. Desperately frightened, he turned for advice to Ben, the only member of his family he trusted, and Ben made him see a doctor. To his surprise the physician was not shocked or disgusted; he treated the patient and, instead of giving a lecture, laughed and said: "We are all brothers and sisters below the waist, son. . . . Better luck next time!"

Tom was so miserable and ashamed that he decided not to go back to Chapel Hill after the holidays. But Julia firmly told him that he had to return; he had to stand straight like his father, throw his shoulders back, and be a man. On the train ride from Asheville he discovered that his sexual adventures had been whispered around town, and several of his classmates taunted him about his brothel visits. After the new semester began, Terry and his circle heard the story and, when Wolfe failed to prove that he was sufficiently repentant, he was dropped from the group. Now he felt more of an outcast than ever.

The episode apparently had no permanent consequences for Wolfe's health, and once he was cured of gonorrhea he began visiting the prostitutes in Durham and Raleigh again. He experienced no guilt over his behavior. After all, his father had for years been frequenting the whores on Eagle Terrace, and that was the way a man should behave. But years later Wolfe expressed sorrow over "the wrung loins of boyhood." "I weep for lost virginity," he wrote in his autobiographical jottings. "Is it not as painful in a boy as in a girl?" But however sad in retrospect, his initiation by prostitutes reinforced the division he had already begun to erect between love and sex. Not until many years later did he learn that sometimes the two can be one.

During the spring term of his freshmen year, Wolfe continued to be lonely and unhappy. His academic work was mediocre. He achieved some modest recognition at the Di Society for his public speaking and was eventually made a member of the freshman-sophomore debate team. The only thing that gave real interest to his college life was the fact that the United States was getting close to entering the World War that had been raging in Europe since 1914. Like most of his classmates, Wolfe was fervently pro-Ally, and he believed every atrocity story that circulated about the barbarities of the Huns. Longing to take part in the war, he watched enviously as one hundred students and ten faculty members went away to military camp in January and four hundred more reported for voluntary military training in February, after the United States broke off diplomatic relations with Germany. When war was declared in April, many additional Carolina students rushed to enlist, but Wolfe, who was only seventeen, was too young. He had to be content with taking part in the voluntary training program on campus, where students drilled without guns or uniforms. But this was only play-soldiering, and Wolfe found it as disappointing as his other experiences at the university. At the end of the term he left Chapel Hill determined to transfer to Princeton in the fall.

I

During the summer of 1917 Wolfe lived at the Old Kentucky Home and worked in Ralph Wheaton's office of the National Cash Register Company. The job, as his father reported to Ben, "dont amount to much. He only gets $5.00 a week but [it] keeps him from loafing the streets." Evenings he spent in the company of his mother's boarders for, as W.O. discovered in July, he had "become suddenly *girl struck* with two or three affairs lately." "He had better cut it out," his father told Ben, "for the present at least."

The most attractive visitor at the Old Kentucky Home was Clara Paul, who was five years older than Tom. She had come from the hot eastern part of the state to spend a few weeks in Asheville before her planned wedding in the fall. Not pretty, but fresh and innocent, she promptly won Tom's heart. He fancied that he was "honestly — desperately in love" with her, and years later he told Mrs. Roberts, "I've never quite got over it." Aware of his interest, Clara wrote her sister that "a nice young boy here, the son of my landlady, has a crush on me." "He hopes to become a writer," she added. "He has right much talent, I think. The most trivial thing he says sounds like poetry." Though she was flattered by his attentions, she told him right away that she was engaged and "could never return his feeling." Years later, in *Look Homeward, Angel,* Wolfe described the brief, passionate affair of his hero, Eugene Gant, with "Laura James," but in actuality he and Clara Paul never got beyond holding hands in the moonlight. Even if they had wanted to do so, they were inhibited by the constant presence of her younger brother, who served as her chaperon. Tom accepted the situation very well, and indeed he even found some advantages in it. He did not usually allow himself to think of nice girls in sexual terms — that was restricted to prostitutes — but the fact that Clara was unavailable permitted him to moon about her and to observe "how her firm little breasts seem to spring forward, filled with life."

No inhibitions restricted his relations with other women at the boardinghouse who were known to be of dubious virtue. Frequently during this summer he crept up the quiet dark steps to have sex with Miss "Smith" — as she called herself — a semiprofessional prostitute on vacation. She "would not perform," he remembered, "without some little gift — so long as she was sure I attached some value to it." Since he had no money, he paid her with the medals he had won in high school. He continued his nocturnal visits until Julia ejected the woman from the house. The summer experiences with Clara Paul and Miss Smith reinforced his division of women into angels and whores.

Dreading to go back to Chapel Hill, he explored the possibility of transferring to Princeton, and he went so far as to solicit a letter of recommendation from Hanford, his English teacher. But his father would not hear of the plan. Now very ill with cancer of the prostate, W.O. was shortly to begin a series of visits to the Johns

Hopkins Hospital for surgery and radium treatment. He had little time or sympathy for his son's discontents with the University of North Carolina, and in September shipped him back to Chapel Hill.

Once there, Wolfe resolved to make the best of his situation, and he discovered that the lot of a sophomore was a great deal pleasanter than that of a freshman. His classmates were now accustomed to his odd figure and his disheveled clothing. They were no longer surprised by his initial stammer, especially when he was not sure of his audience, or his habit of blurting out half a dozen words rapidly, pausing to swallow "with his Adam's-apple dancing up and down like an elevator on the loose," and then producing another verbal ejaculation.

Then, too, he was maturing, and he began to lose the callowness that had marked his freshman year. "I suppose I'm a greater surprise to myself than to anyone under the sun," he wrote to his mother about this transformation. "I am changing so rapidly that I find myself an evergrowing source of interest."

One reason for the improvement was the fact that he was leading a more orderly existence than at perhaps any other time in his life. The University of North Carolina was now a military camp, preparing the students for participation in the war. The student body was divided into four companies, which spent hours each week in close-order drill and bayonet practice. In addition, all male students were required to attend five hours of military lectures every week. Wolfe was an enthusiastic member of Company C, and, despite his aversion to keeping regular hours, he went on daily marches with his company in the early morning and in the late afternoon. He reported to his mother that these military activities took up fifteen hours each week, and of course he had in addition to carry his usual load of classes.

In his sophomore year his courses were generally more interesting. He suffered through the required course in general descriptive chemistry, taught by the distinguished scientist and former president of the university, Francis P. Venable, and was bored by "the lectures of an irritable and aging professor," whose classroom demonstrations never came off, and his hours in the laboratory proved that "he had no talent for experiment — his fingers were all thumbs." But he continued to enjoy his Latin course, where he read Plautus, Terence, Horace, and Tacitus. With Professor

Bernard he studied Plato's *Crito* and *Apology* in the original Greek, and he went on to read other dialogues in translation. He developed a lifelong interest in the personality of Socrates, and he was fascinated by the Platonic notion that the human soul yearned for its prenatal ideal state. This concept was later central to *Look Homeward, Angel*.

He also began studying English literature with Professor Edwin A. Greenlaw, with whom he took courses nearly every term of his remaining years at Chapel Hill. Wolfe found in Greenlaw a new kind of teacher. Rigorously trained under Professor George Lyman Kittredge in the graduate school of Harvard University, he had come to the University of North Carolina after a brief stint at the University of Chicago. His appointment was part of a systematic effort to upgrade the quality of scholarship at North Carolina, an attempt to transform what had hitherto been a low keyed parochial college into a modern research university. Formidably learned, Greenlaw had a lofty scorn for those who merely dabbled in literature or who taught an "appreciation" of letters. He required students to analyze texts, to ascertain precisely what an author had said and what he meant. In his world of scholarship there was no room for flights of imagination. But Greenlaw was not a narrow textual critic. In his courses he stressed the relationship between literature and the society that produced it; the series of high-school anthologies that he later edited was called *Literature and Life*.

At first Wolfe found Greenlaw's approach difficult. He was used to writing enthusiastic effusions about the books he read, and his work lacked the focus and precision that Greenlaw demanded. Early in the semester he prepared a theme on "The Third Type of Shakespearean Humour as exemplified by Jack Falstaff," which concluded: "I can imagine this inscription on his [Falstaff's] tomb. 'Here lies Jack Falstaff — (and lies and lies and lies.)'" Greenlaw welcomed his student's enthusiasm but criticized "the quite obvious superficiality of your analysis. You have not penetrated the subject — merely glossed it." The paper received a grade of "B-minus." But Wolfe sensed that Greenlaw's criticisms were not those of a pedant but of a man with a mind "devouringly hungry but formalized," and he worked hard to meet his professor's expectations. In Greenlaw's course he received his first "A" at the university.

But not all of his sophomore year was devoted to his studies or to military drill. He enthusiastically went out for extracurricular activities, for, he wrote his mother, "it will never do to make the text book your god." His classmates welcomed his participation, because the war was draining off so many of the older students who usually ran the campus organizations, directed the literary societies, and edited the school paper and the college magazine. Wolfe discovered that the war had created opportunities for him. Partly for this reason he did not think of the World War as a blighting experience, and, unlike so many other American writers who were just a few years older, he never did consider himself a member of a Lost Generation. "What we felt was not disillusionment or bitterness," he wrote later; "we felt exultancy and joy. For us there was the sense of something magnificent and wonderful impending in the air. . . . We felt . . . that the war was glorious and magnificent, and that it offered us a thousand chances for glory, adventure, and joy."

With so few able-bodied men around, he could try out for any activity without fear of failure or ridicule. He even trained — briefly — for the track team. His most sustained efforts were in the Di Society, where he vigorously participated in debating. Though Wolfe later made fun of the "clap-trap tradition" of oratory in the South — "the right hand by Calhoun, the proud stamping foot by Henry Clay, the rolling eye by Daniel Webster" — he recognized that, next to athletics (which were discontinued during the war), public speaking was the most prestigious extracurricular activity at the university, and he enthusiastically participated in debates about government control of the railroads, the unionization of labor, minimum wage laws, and old-age pensions.

He discovered, however, that he was in more demand as a writer than as a speaker. He had made his peace with John Terry, who was now an assistant editor of the *University of North Carolina Magazine* and asked him to write for it. The November 1917 issue carried Wolfe's first published writing, a poem called "A Field in Flanders," about the "war-ripped field," where

> *. . . within a smoking, bloody Hell,*
> *Ten million risk their lives for Freedom's sake.*

It was followed in the next issue by his ode, "To France," which
began:

> O *France, you truly are sublime,*
> *The thought of you shall make men thrill*
> *Throughout all ages and all time.*

The March 1918 *Magazine* was full of Wolfe's patriotic rhetoric.
His short story, "A Cullenden of Virginia," told of the recreant
son of an old family who recovered his courage on the field of
battle and vindicated his tarnished honor in a charge over the top,
in which he was killed. More fervid was his poem "The Challenge," written in the meter of James Russell Lowell's "The
Present Crisis," which he had memorized in high school. It addressed the German Kaiser:

> *You, proud ruler, made the challenge, we have*
> *answered all in all,*
> *Aye, we answered with all gladness, for we heard a*
> *great creed's call.*

"In the name of embattled democracy," Wolfe recalled many years
later, "I let the Kaiser have the works."

Though there was nothing in these early publications to suggest
that Wolfe was anything more than a very patriotic young man,
they created a ripple of interest across the state. In the university
newspaper, the *Tar Heel,* Professor R. H. Thornton, who taught
journalism at Chapel Hill, singled out "The Challenge" for praise,
declaring that "the poem has many excellent lines and the dignity
of true poetry." In April the *Asheville Citizen* reprinted the poem,
noting that "it is full of fire, and its r[h]ythm is well sustained."
When Mr. Roberts saw the poem, "he threw up his hands and
cheered." "Then," W. O. Wolfe reported to Tom, he "called his
whole school together and read it aloud to the entire school." The
Presbyterian minister, Mr. Campbell, and other "men and woman
. . . who are among our best citizens and capable of judging" also
praised it. Later, after the poem was published in the *Winston-
Salem Journal* and in a Florida newspaper, W.O. wrote that it has
"been coppied with your name as author more or less all over the
country." "Don't let it turn your head or make you vain," he
warned his son, but he added, "I suppose *I* am *the one* it has turned
fool."

With better grades, participation in debating, and publications, Wolfe's standing in the university markedly improved by the middle of his sophomore year. The older social fraternities still ignored him, but he was now approached by the members of Pi Kappa Phi, which his classmate Clement Eaton characterized as a "bobtailed fraternity which had recently been formed by a group of frustrated boys who had not been asked to join one of the well-established and somewhat snobbish fraternities." In contrast to the older Greek-letter societies, which recruited chiefly from the social elite of the state and from the athletic teams, Pi Kappa Phis made a deliberate, and largely successful, effort to initiate men who were likely to become campus leaders. Extraordinarily pleased by this recognition, Tom assured his father that joining the fraternity "is the greatest thing I ever did and will mean much."

Feeling accepted gave Wolfe greater social poise than he had exhibited as a freshman, when he always seemed about to commit some grievous faux pas. For instance, he coped very well when one of his roommates, George Lay, invited him to spend the Thanksgiving weekend with his family in Raleigh. Lay's father was rector of St. Mary's College for girls, and he had four daughters of his own. The Lay family took meals in the college dining hall, and of course all two hundred girls stared at their visitor. Very self-conscious, Wolfe wrote that, "shot with four hundred arrows," he tried to "slide and sidle to his place" at the table, but in fact, according to Elizabeth Lay, who was also a student at the university, "he didn't seem bothered by it at all. He took everything in his stride." All the Lays liked him, and one of the younger daughters developed a schoolgirl crush on the visitor, particularly admiring "the way his hair curls up in front." He so enjoyed the visit that he returned in January and perhaps on other weekends as well before his roommate joined the army. Back in Asheville, his family was impressed by the company he was keeping. "How many girls did you flirt [with], or make love to," asked Julia, while W.O. expressed satisfaction that his son could "mingel with refined and cultured people" like the Lays.

By spring Wolfe felt self-confident enough to attend the Easter dance at the university, one of the principal social events of the year. Characteristically he made up his mind at the last minute, so that there was great difficulty in finding him a dress suit and dancing shoes. "You should have let us know about it 2 weeks ago," W.O. scolded, "that we might have had more time. You being so tall with . . . abnormal arms and legs it is next to impossible to get anything [to] wear near fit you without having it made to order." In the end he was able to borrow an evening suit from Ralph Wheaton. Though the sleeves and trousers were a little too short, he looked respectable enough, and, having no date of his own, he moved among the couples on the dance floor, tapping the shoulder of a friend to cut in on his partner.

Now much in demand, he felt "the flowering of the joining spirit" that spring. He seemed to belong to every organization on campus. He was initiated into Sigma Upsilon, a literary fraternity, and into a student club called Amphoterothen, which encouraged extempore speaking. Appointed one of the three associate editors of the *Yackety Yack,* the college annual, he was also named assistant editor of the *Tar Heel.* In May he was elected permanent class poet. "I . . . feel very proud that you have won such renown on the Hill," W.O. wrote him, and he boasted to Ben that Tom was "having untold college honors heaped on him," since "he has been elected and initiated into every society belonging to the university." A little fearful lest too much success turn Tom's head, he added, "All this is well enough if he behaves himself accordingly."

II

Wolfe's parents expected him to return to Asheville again at the end of his sophomore year, and W.O. told him of a job he could get at Azalea, five miles east of Asheville, where some other college boys were earning good wages. But Tom was restive and wanted to demonstrate his independence from his family.

His reluctance to stay at home stemmed partly from the fact that he was dissatisfied with the way his college expenses were being handled. For every expenditure — even for a dollar-and-a-half Greek textbook and one dollar for pressing his suit — he had to ask his father for money. W.O. generally gave him what he asked for, even though he frequently complained that times were hard and that he was too ill to earn very much, and sometimes he included an additional five dollars for spending money. Consequently Tom was never in need, but on the other hand he never had much money in his pocket. Early in his sophomore year he told his mother that he was "going to try to borrow or steal a bank account in order to spare myself the embarrassment of writing home." But his parents refused his request, and W.O. continued to dole out money in small quantities for specific expenses.

Through some college friends he learned of what appeared to be a solution to this problem. There were "fair promises of wealth in Norfolk," for rumor had it that even unskilled laborers could earn good wages in the wartime military installations near that city. The fact that Clara Paul, now married, lived in nearby Portsmouth made Norfolk seem an even more attractive place to work that summer. Both Julia and W.O. objected to his plan, thinking that Tom was too young to leave home, but they finally acquiesced and gave him train fare for the trip. He first found a job as a time-checker at Langley Field, where he rode around on a horse to tally up the hours put in by the work gangs. Once or twice on weekends he went to Portsmouth, but, as he proudly wrote to his mother, "I have not as yet seen fit to look up Clara Paul." Eaten up by mosquitoes and bedbugs, he quit the job after a month and spent nearly all that he had earned in a "week of riotous living" in Norfolk.

At that point a friend convinced him that they could make good money if they passed themselves off as carpenters, and they pooled what little money they had to buy carpenter's tools. They got jobs but were fired the first day for incompetence. By selling the tools they managed to scrape together just enough money to rent a room, but they had literally almost nothing to eat until Fred, who was in the navy and stationed at Norfolk, rescued them and filled them up at a navy mess.

After that Tom found work loading grain and ammunition at a Newport News pier. It was hard labor, but by the end of the summer he was in good physical condition. Of course, not all of his time was spent working. He learned to shoot craps, and on one occasion won seven dollars. With Fred he went to see Dinwiddie Martin, a blind friend of the Wolfe family, who was then in Norfolk; he became the prototype of the sinister and corrupt Rumford Bland in *You Can't Go Home Again*. And there were regular visits to the brothels, where sailors and civilians lined up for sex. Wolfe's favorite whore was Lillian Walker, and he remembered one hot night when "I screwed her — rolypoly and moist as she was, with the wind of the electric fan (to which paper streamers of red white and blue had been attached) beating upon our naked and animate bottoms."

In September, feeling very proud that he had proved his independence, he headed for home. Ben, who had been working for a newspaper in Winston-Salem, had also come back to Asheville, and Tom found him in a bitter, despondent mood. He had tried to enlist, but the doctors had rejected him for military service because of "weak lungs" — which almost certainly meant an arrested case of tuberculosis. "Good God," he exclaimed bitterly, "I wonder what I'm living for." He blamed his parents for his condition — W.O. because he had failed to provide for his family, Julia because she had accepted all boarders, however diseased, at the Old Kentucky Home so long as they paid her. Once again he advised Tom: "Get all you can from them."

Tom returned to the university in late September, but the term had hardly begun before he was summoned back to Asheville. Ben had succumbed to the dread Spanish influenza epidemic that was sweeping the country, and because his lungs were already so weak it turned into pneumonia. Reaching the Old Kentucky Home in early morning, Tom found his brother in a desperate condition, fighting for every breath. When Ben saw him, he gripped his wrists and gasped, "Why have you come home? Why have you come home?" The family gathered around the sickbed. Mabel helped nurse Ben until she collapsed from exhaustion. Fred, now a civilian, returned from Ohio, where he was working. W.O., too feeble to climb the stairs, had to be hoisted up to the second floor of the Old Kentucky Home. But Ben, fiercely resenting his mother's stinginess, refused to allow Julia in the room. Observing "the running down of the machine," the family doctor predicted the end: Ben was "drowning . . . in his own secretions."

Ben's death on October 19, at the age of twenty-six, broke Thomas Wolfe's closest tie within his family. Since childhood the two boys had had a special relationship, which had been strengthened during the past few years by their resentment of what they believed was the hypocrisy and parsimony of their parents. From the other members of the family he increasingly distanced himself after he enrolled in the university. He had as little as possible to do with Frank. Effie, Mabel, and Fred were all busy leading their own lives. Julia was so preoccupied with her boardinghouse and her real estate speculations that Tom was out of touch with her; he wrote her so infrequently during his college years that she felt obliged "to remind you, you still have a mother." Years later she confessed, "It seems like I didn't know him after [he went to Chapel Hill], didn't understand him any more." Tom did write to his father, reporting his successes at the university and frequently requesting money, but W.O. was now terminally ill; his life, as one of the doctors at Baltimore told Mabel, was like a gate that was hanging from one rusty hinge.

Tom had difficulty in accepting his brother's death as a fact. Death had heretofore seemed to him "something which happened to old people and strangers," but now he had to acknowledge "that this bright and particular flesh should be mortified, made one compressed with the earth he trod uniquely." At first when he returned to college, "Ben's death stayed remote — appeared to fade," but then, just when it seemed forgotten, the memory "returned from time to time to absorb and damn the moment." Tom never exorcised Ben's ghost. Years later, even while he was writing on some very different subject, he would break off to jot down another sketch of Ben, "sitting with his long legs crooked beneath him, on one of the high revolving stools of the all-night lunch, holding a cup of coffee in one hand and a cigarette in the other," or Ben as he reported the plays in a World Series baseball game from the wire in the office of the *Ashveville Citizen,* dressed "in his shirtsleeves, and he has neat armbands to hold them up, a pair of earphones is clamped to his head, a cigarette dangles from his lips, . . . he is irritable and scowling . . . ; Ben's stomach is all sunken in and his trousers hang on his hip bones, he has a belt with a silver buckle and his initials on it." So real were these images, he wrote, that Ben "seems to me a manifestation of permanence; an object of fixed reality in my life, on which I may place my hands at any moment . . . and he is gone." Shortly after *Look Homeward, Angel* appeared in 1929, Tom told a cousin that he "wrote the book for Ben." He dedicated his second book, *From Death to Morning,* to Ben's memory and "to the proud and bitter briefness of his days, the brave and tender scorn of his short life."

III

Attempting to reknit the fabric of his life after Ben's death, Tom threw himself into the round of college activities. The university had now been converted into a unit of the Student Army Training Corps. The dormitories were barracks, and Swain Hall, the student commons, was a mess hall. Tom applied for admission to the SATC but was again rejected on account of age. In consequence, he, a handful of other noncombatants, and the two dozen or so women who attended the university dominated the usual college activities.

Beginning the year as an assistant editor of the *Tar Heel,* Wolfe was elevated to managing editor when his predecessor took a job running the alumni magazine. Then when the editor-in-chief left for training in the marines, he took over his duties too, without an additional title. In the spring he was chosen editor-in-chief for 1919–1920, his senior year.

The campus newspaper took up a great deal of his time during his last two years at Chapel Hill. As students went off to war or, a little later, were struck down in the epidemic of Spanish influenza that swept the university, he often had to work with only one or two assistants. Occasionally he had to write much of the copy himself, and on Thursday night he usually stayed up until past midnight drafting stories. Early the next morning he would go over to Durham, where the paper was printed at Seeman's printing shop. There he sometimes found that he had too much copy and, to the dismay of the paper's business manager, would throw out advertisements to make room for stories. Or he might discover that more copy was needed, and he would urgently summon his colleagues to rush over from Chapel Hill with more news or features.

Already he clearly thought of himself as a writer, and so did his colleagues. The owner of the printing shop in Durham, Ernest Seeman, often took Wolfe and his friends to lunch on Fridays, because he enjoyed hearing these young people talk. Once, he remembered, one of the other students asked, "Say, Tom, when you get to be a famous writer are you going to use your middle initial or just sign 'Tom Wolfe'?" "Hell, no," Wolfe replied; "how would it look if Shakespeare had signed his stuff 'William J. Shakespeare'?"

Now recognized as a big man on campus, Wolfe was not yet sure how he wanted to present himself to his classmates. Some of his closest friends knew him as a very busy, reasonably hardworking student, who prepared for his courses, especially those in literature and philosophy, and spent a good number of hours in the library, and his fraternity brothers fondly remembered "the gentler and quieter affection and good feeling that Tom so often displayed." But this was not the picture of himself that he preferred. Instead, much of the time he tried to capitalize on the role in which he had been unwillingly cast when he first entered the university, that of the untutored man of the mountains. One of his classmates remembered that he still burned from the snubs of the self-styled aristocrats on campus, and, in order to ridicule their pretensions, he "tousled his hair, rolled up his trousers legs to midway his ankles, disarranged his neck-tie and, staring up at the sky, walked nonchalantly down the gravel walk-way along fraternity row while members sat on their porches staring up at the sky."

But he liked best the part of the eccentric young writer of genius. The stories of his sloppiness in dress, of his failure to change shirts until his roommates complained, and his carelessness about bathing and combing his hair were known all over the campus. There was an element of truth in them all, for Wolfe never did care much about how he looked, and during his junior and senior years he was so active, so busy, and so happy in what he was doing that he simply could not take time to have his suits pressed or his shirts sent to the laundry. He did wear his hair unusually long, for he developed a patch of eczema on his neck and wanted to conceal it. And since he kept late and irregular hours, he often stumbled into an early-morning class after the bell had rung, occasionally bringing his breakfast with him in a paper bag.

But there was also something a bit theatrical about his behavior. Doubtless he was in a hurry when he had to prepare an essay for Clarence Hibbard's course in journalism, and he may not have had any paper handy; but it made a better story when he appeared in class with his theme written on the backs of advertising bills that he picked up along Franklin Street. His teachers came to expect this kind of self-dramatizing conduct, and because he was an exceptionally gifted student they often played along with him. One of the most frequently repeated anecdotes about Wolfe at the University of North Carolina had to do with an essay he presented orally in one of Professor Greenlaw's classes. Wolfe arrived late, as usual, and Greenlaw called on him first: "Brother Wolfe, we welcome you. Will you read us the burning words you have written?" Standing up in his overcoat, for the room was chilly, Wolfe began reading from a sheet of paper he held in his hand. Then, attempting to give the impression that he had had a sudden inspiration in the middle of the night and lacked proper writing paper, he broke off in midsentence and fished out another sheet from his pocket and read from it, and after that produced an envelope with a continuation. At one point he dug out a matchbook, from which he read a sentence. At the end, reaching deep into his pockets, he found a roll of toilet paper, on which he had written the conclusion of his theme. By this time, of course, the class was convulsed with laughter over Wolfe's carefully calculated performance, but Greenlaw got the last laugh by commenting that the quality of his essay was worthy of the paper it had been written on.

Stories like this gave Wolfe a reputation during his junior and senior years as a campus wit, and he thoroughly enjoyed the role. After the war ended in November 1918, the tone of high seriousness disappeared from his writing, and his contributions to the *Tar Heel* strove to be humorous. He started, for instance, a series called "Fables of Sultan Peikh A Bou," one of which featured a druggist called Dr. C. Astor Oile. His conversation was now marked by "a pyrotechnical exuberance" of jokes and stories, and, as one classmate remembered, "if you ever saw a little knot on the campus and went up there and heard a bunch of boys laughing, . . . Tom would be in the middle telling some big lie or laughing." He developed a range of humorous anecdotes, though he was especially fond of telling about the advertisement allegedly used for a patent medicine called "Tan-Bark" in which a lady reported: "Before taking 'Tan-Bark' I could not sleep with my husband, but since taking one bottle I can now sleep with any man."

By the fall of 1919, when students who had served in the army began straggling back into the classroom, those who had begun their studies in the same year as Wolfe were astonished to find that he had become "king of the campus." His standing as what his classmate Paul Green called "the boss man around here" had been confirmed the previous spring when he, along with only six other students, was elected to Golden Fleece, an honors society vaguely modeled after Skull and Bones at Yale. It was, as W.O. proudly recorded, "the highest honor [that] can be bestowed on a college man" at the University of North Carolina.

IV

During his junior and senior years Wolfe also excelled in his class work, for his courses were challenging and he was studying with the best professors at the university. He continued to work with Greenlaw, who during his junior year focused his course in English composition on the issues that would face the peace conference at the end of the war. Assigning groups of students to represent the different nations at the peace conference, he had them debate questions concerning disarmament, the remilitarization of Germany, reparations, freedom of the seas, and the creation of a League of Nations. Wolfe was one of the most active participants in what he called "Greenlaw's great experiment," and he not merely took part in the debates but saw that the course received enthusiastic publicity in the *Tar Heel*. At the end of the quarter the class drew up a collaborative report, which was published as a pamphlet, *The Peace Treaty Including the Constitution of the League of States, Adopted by the English 21 Conference of the University of North Carolina*. It was impressive enough to receive commendation from the *New York Times*.

Pleased with this effort, Greenlaw followed it in the spring quarter with another experiment. This time the class dealt with the problems of the American city, and groups of students were assigned to represent the businessmen, the laborers, the politicians, and the reformers. Because the Armistice was followed by a sharp increase in the number of strikes in the United States, the class focused on the reactions of these groups to hypothetical labor stoppages in certain key industries. In order to set the tone, Greenlaw read John Galsworthy's play *Strife* aloud to the class. As the project got under way, it was transformed into the writing of a collaborative novel that dealt with the conflict between capital and labor. As spring came and graduation ceremonies approached, most students were slow to draft their assigned sections, but Wolfe worked hard on his two chapters, which dealt with the breaking of the strike. Greenlaw said that he "had achieved 'style' — what most men don't get till forty." Vastly pleased, he recorded that Greenlaw was "one of the great creative forces in my life."

Wolfe's interest in the problems of labor spilled over into an ethics course that he was taking from Professor Horace Williams, who became — along with Margaret Roberts and Edwin Greenlaw — one of his "three great teachers." This eccentric professor, who had been at the university since 1891, represented a type of teacher often in evidence in Southern colleges of the period, the resident iconoclast. Essentially self-taught, though he had received an undergraduate education at the University of North Carolina and a smattering of graduate training at Yale and at Harvard, Williams thought of himself as a questioner and a seeker, a North Carolina Diogenes. He seemed subversive because he dared to announce that he was a Republican in an overwhelmingly Democratic state, a religious liberal in a society that was determinedly fundamentalist. Hostile to the increasing emphasis at the university on science, which he considered a modern form of vulgar superstition, he was equally opposed to the recent stress on "scientific" scholarship in the humanities. When Greenlaw insisted that every statement about literature must be documented, Williams scornfully asked where the footnotes were in St. Paul's Epistle to the Galatians.

Williams's purpose was to teach his students how to think (and he was willing to attempt to teach his colleagues too). For this reason he required no reading in his courses, though he usually assigned a textbook, like Charles C. Everett's *Science of Thought* (1869), and occasionally referred to it in a casual way; he wanted his students to find their own solutions, not to follow authority. "We read nothing," Wolfe remembered. "We began to feel [a] certain contempt for people who did read." Williams made his classes question their most basic values by having them discuss homely, concrete problems. For instance, what should a man who was engaged to marry one woman do when he discovered that he was in love with another? He used examples that he knew his students would understand. One day he informed his class that he had bought a mule for one hundred fifty dollars — and he did have a farm outside Chapel Hill — which had now paid for itself three times over. He had recently been offered three hundred dollars for that mule. Was he ethically and morally entitled to make a profit by selling the animal? What were the nature and the source of that profit? With grave, meditative faces his pupils, many just off the farm and familiar with mules, pondered his problem. They would offer answers, and Williams, quick and sharp in repartee, fenced with them.

This "magnificent twister" delighted Wolfe. He recognized that Williams was "an old but crafty boxer, baiting you on, turning the laugh on you, laughing finally at you with his dry husky laugh," but, proud of his debater's skills, he enjoyed sparring with the professor. He also discovered that Williams encouraged intelligent dissent. For instance, the professor praised Clement Eaton, one of his students and later a distinguished historian, who refused the government bonus of sixty dollars when he was mustered out of the SATC at the end of the war, declaring that since he had been a student for the entire time of his service he did not deserve the money. Enthusiastically Williams announced that Eaton's action "raised the moral level of the campus two and one quarter inches." Daringly Wolfe disagreed, suggesting that Eaton turned down the bonus simply because he did not need the money.

Williams encouraged intellectual independence, because he did not want his students to become carbon copies of himself. He particularly welcomed dissent from Wolfe, whom he identified as one of the future leaders of the state. Wolfe became one of "his boys" — one of the little group encouraged to visit Williams's house in the evening to continue philosophical discussions, permitted an independence and even an impertinence in classroom discussion denied to others. After an initial trial quarter, Wolfe's papers always received the highest grade, regardless of the quality of the work. What the professor was looking for in a student was not industry or care; as he told Wolfe later, he sought out those who had "that capacity of intelligence to take fire and *blaze* through its own heat." That capacity he believed he had discovered in Wolfe, and he later spoke of him as "one of the six remarkable students in my thirty years" at the University of North Carolina.

In addition to stimulating students, Williams also tried to indoctrinate them with his own idiosyncratic philosophical system, which was vaguely Hegelian. To many of his disciples it seemed powerful and original as he developed it in the classroom; only later, when he published his lectures under the title *The Evolution of Logic* (1925), and an autobiography that was intended to rival that of Henry Adams, *The Education of Horace Williams* (1936), did they discover that it was a rickety makeshift structure. Hating the notion that there were antagonistic forces in the universe, he tried to use the Hegelian dialectic "process of unifying oppositions" to show that "every object is made up of exact opposites." Life, then, was a process of synthesizing the apparently irreconcilable.

Williams's "dialectic" had a special appeal for Wolfe, since all his life he had been pulled between the antagonistic personalities of his father and his mother. Williams's "Hegelian Monism" offered him a comforting unity, for it did "away to a considerable extent with the Yea-and-Nay answer to all things." "If it doesn't account for the combined," Wolfe concluded, "it accepts it and pretends to understand it."

Wolfe applied Williams's philosophy in his composition on "Mass Movements in Labor," which he then expanded into a fuller paper on "The Crisis in Industry." The essay originated in Greenlaw's course, where the students were trying to write about industrial strife, but the treatment clearly reflected Williams's ideas. Both essays were, for an eighteen-year-old, grammatical and carefully written. But, in line with Williams's aversion to facts, neither reflected any reading or research; it is not clear that Wolfe had any specific knowledge of the major strikes, including a bitter work stoppage in the steel industry, then taking place. His analysis was entirely abstract. Controversies over hours, wages, and fringe benefits, he announced, were not fundamental; "these petty, paltry bickerings" concealed labor's real demand for "its right to self-direction," which capital denied. The solution was a proper illustration of Horace Williams's principal of Hegelian synthesis: the two antagonistic forces must be brought together in "a system of democratic co-operation in industry with equal rights and responsibilities for labor and capital." How this solution was to be achieved and how it would work were not discussed. Much impressed, Williams awarded the 1919 Worth Prize, for "the best thesis submitted in the courses in Philosophy," to Wolfe's *The Crisis in Industry*. Printed in a fourteen-page booklet by the University of North Carolina, it was Wolfe's first work to be issued as a separate publication.

For several years after graduating from the University of North Carolina Wolfe kept up a correspondence with Williams, for whom he felt "the most exquisitely tempered bond of sympathy," and he frequently thought back to his "amazing lectures," the "expres-

sions of a subtle and many-prismed personality." Though in his
final years he came to see that Williams's philosophy was "at best
a tortuous and patched-up scheme," he never completely shook
off its influence. To Horace Williams's teaching can be attributed
in considerable measure Wolfe's lifelong lack of interest in books
on social and economic theory, his tendency to avoid serious discussions by scoring debating points over his opponent, and his
unwillingness to accept advice or criticism.

V

The lessons that Wolfe learned from Professor Frederick H. Koch
during his junior and senior years at the University of North
Carolina had more immediate consequences for his literary career.
Koch came to the university in 1918 after a notably successful
career at the University of North Dakota, where, in the most
unlikely surroundings, he had initiated a drama program in which
students both wrote and produced their own plays. Greenlaw and
others at Chapel Hill hoped that he would be equally successful in
North Carolina.

Though Koch had considerable knowledge of the history of
drama and of the techniques of stagecraft, these were not his chief
interests. His ambition was to promote the writing and production of what he called "folk plays." Apparently he fixed on this
goal during his brief period of study with George P. Baker, professor of dramatic literature at Harvard, who taught that every
nation has its own form of theater. From this Koch deduced that
every society should have its own drama and, indeed, that almost
anybody, with a little encouragement, could write plays.

Exactly what a folk play was Koch never made explicit. Years
later, when thoroughly disillusioned with the theater, Wolfe concluded that Koch himself "did not know very clearly" what he
meant; he allowed his students to gather that a folk play was "a
communal emanation . . . of thousands of people, mysteriously
transferred to paper by a single elect spokesman." That was not
quite fair, for Koch's intent was relatively simple. He did not want
his students to compose imitations of Sheridan or Ibsen or Synge;
instead, he asked each of them to write plays that came "from the
soil" and depicted people and places within the writer's own experience.

When Koch arrived in Chapel Hill, there was no auditorium on the campus where a play could be presented. The university was an armed camp, and most students were too busy trying to be soldiers even to think of writing plays. Only nine students enrolled in his first class — eight women and Thomas Wolfe. Seeing that the professor was taken aback, Wolfe spoke up: "I don't want you to think that this Ladies Aid Society represents Carolina. We have a lot of he-men seriously interested in writing here, but they're all disguised in uniforms now. I tried to get myself into one myself but they didn't have one long enough for me!"

Resolutely Koch pushed ahead with his plan to introduce the drama to Chapel Hill; he was, as Wolfe unkindly labeled him, "the Little Man with the Urge." In North Dakota he had learned that self-promotion leads to success, and he tried the same tactics in North Carolina. Everybody at the university quickly learned to recognize this bustling little man, nattily dressed in the Norfolk jacket and the Windsor tie that he affected, carrying his pipe and walking with his dog. He made himself constantly available. Though he was middle-aged, there was something incurably boyish about him. "Koch is still twelve years old," one of his students rather unfairly commented. He liked to fraternize with the students and even went so far as to subject himself to hazing when he was initiated into Omega Delta, a student society that supported the drama. Wolfe, a member who took these affairs very seriously, gave him "a healthy swat or two on his pants-tight backside" that brought him up erect, "with his professional dignity as well as his anatomy ruffled and stinging." Koch insisted that everyone call him "Proff" (with two f's, please). And everywhere he went he promoted the drama, and himself. Stopping students and colleagues on the campus pathways, he would reach into an inner pocket, produce a newspaper clipping, and ask, "Have you seen this one? Look, here, what this newspaper says about me."

As an instructor Koch was permissive. He simply wanted to encourage his students to write plays. "I can't tell you how to write a play," Koch confessed. "There's only one real way. Go ahead and write it. . . . And starting is the hardest part of the game. I can only advise you now to draw up a synopsis of your plot and your story and wade right in. Go on through to the end without stopping, if possible."

Members of Koch's class were tremendously excited by the

notion that any one of them could simply sit down and dash off a play, and they all began to work in earnest. The professor gave almost no direction. He did tell them that, once they had produced drafts, they should then "go back, condense, expand, and revise as much as is necessary," but how much was necessary he failed to say. He had learned very early, he used to say, that most writers needed encouragement, not criticism. The only suggestions for improvement they received came from other classmates to whom they read their work aloud, and these comments were usually no more sophisticated than "That's great stuff" or "Rotten."

Unlike the women in the group, Wolfe had trouble finding a subject for his play. He had probably enrolled in the course because of his great admiration for George Bernard Shaw and, improbably enough, he attempted "a satiric comedy" that would be illuminated by Shavian repartee. It was, he wrote later, "a dismal failure." Hoping to rescue his sole male student, Koch pulled out of his folder labeled Play Ideas a twelve-year-old clipping with a Chicago date-line, which he had saved from the *Grand Forks Herald*. It told the story of two gangsters, one of whom had been killed in a shoot-out. The other was captured while attempting to place flowers on the grave of his dead friend. This little story, Koch thought, might provide Wolfe a plot for his play. As for its setting, Wolfe ought to remember that they were writing folk dramas, about people and scenes with which they were familiar, and Koch suggested that it might take place in the western North Carolina mountains, which Wolfe presumably knew so well.

Wolfe knew as much about Chicago gangsters as he did about Carolina mountaineers, but he welcomed Koch's suggestion because he was never very good at inventing plots. Besides, he had learned to play the role of mountain man very successfully at Chapel Hill, where nobody else knew any more about Appalachia than he did. He began transposing the Chicago residents in the clipping into "a set of mountain characters, the principal being Buck Gavin, an outlaw." Soon he convinced himself that he was writing "about people I have known and concerning whom I feel qualified to write." The result was his first play, "The Return of Buck Gavin."

In January 1919 Koch called a meeting of the Carolina Playmakers — as he called his group — to hear a reading of Wolfe's play, along with two other folk plays and a college play, and the next month it went into production. At the tryouts no one volunteered to play Buck Gavin, and Koch told Wolfe: "I guess you'll have to do it yourself, Tom. You may not know it, but you really wrote that part for yourself!" "But I can't act, 'Proff,' " Wolfe replied, "I've never acted." "You're a born actor," Koch told him, "and you *are* Buck Gavin."

When "The Return of Buck Gavin" was presented, along with two other one-act plays, on March 15 and 16 in the Chapel Hill high-school auditorium, Wolfe made a striking impression in the title role. "Tom looked just like a 'mountain outlaw,' " Professor Archibald Henderson remembered, and "his formidable stride, his deliberate movements, [and] his look of suspicion and distrust" made him seem "a natural for the role." Even the usually boisterous undergraduates in the audience were impressed, for the *Tar Heel* noted, "There was no trace of the tendency often seen in college audience of laughing at the serious moments."

"The Return of Buck Gavin" was a creditable initial effort for an eighteen-year-old. Wolfe took great pains to describe the interior of the cabin home of his mountain outlaw in a remote cove of the western North Carolina mountains, and he tried to make his characters authentic by writing dialogue like "I calc'late I knowed why" and "This is sartin' the best way out an' I'm not worr'in'." It was also unintentionally very funny. He included a parody of this play in his draft of his first novel and called it "The Return of Jed Sevier," but it was not included in *Look Homeward, Angel,* perhaps because it was hard to tell the spoof from the original.

Though Wolfe later belittled his play as something that he "wrote . . . on a rainy night, . . . in three hours," he was very proud of it at the time, and he was elated when it was singled out for comment in an article on the Carolina Playmakers in the national magazine *Review of Reviews*. The success of "The Return of Buck Gavin" impelled him to produce other hastily written one-act plays in the same general style. One, called "The Convict's Theory," had to do with two brothers in the North Carolina mountains who were bootleggers. One of them had killed another man, blamed his brother, who was imprisoned, and then married his brother's girlfriend. Released from prison, the convict returned to kill his brother but stopped when he learned that his fiancée was now his brother's wife. Obviously a hastily composed first draft, the play was full of "folk talk" like: "That's nothin' t' y' —

so keep yer trap closed." It contained almost no action. Another, which obviously derived from his course with Greenlaw and his essay *The Crisis in Industry,* was called "The Strikers." It showed little comprehension of either management or labor, and again it contained no action. The first six pages of the forty-eight-page manuscript were devoted to setting the scene and contained not one word of dialogue. Somewhat more promising was a play about a feud between mountain families called "The Mountains," which Wolfe began at Chapel Hill but finished in Cambridge.

The only other play by Wolfe actually produced while he was at the University of North Carolina was "The Third Night," which played for two nights in December 1919 on the improvised stage of the high-school auditorium. Set again "in a deserted mountain section of North Carolina, some miles west of Asheville," it depicted the psychological disintegration of Captain Richard Harkins, "a degenerate Southern gentleman" — Wolfe played the role himself — who killed the father of his fiancée and was appropriately haunted by a spectral appearance of the man he murdered. This little play marked a slight advance over its predecessors. Wolfe used the effective, if trite, theatrical device of having the face of the murdered man appear at the window in a vivid flash of lightning, and he also tried to experiment with somewhat more complex characterization by making one of the captain's henchmen a mulatto, who had absorbed "many of the superstitions of the black race." Still, it was a very talky play, with little action, and most of the dialogue was in what the author thought was mountaineer dialect. And Wolfe continued to have difficulty in devising plots; "The Third Night" was freely adapted from Lord Dunsany's "A Night at the Inn."

VI

During the spring of his senior year at Chapel Hill Wolfe was too busy being a public figure to spend much time writing plays. He was in charge of the *Tar Heel* and set its editorial tone by pledging "to give the student body the best service possible" and the news "as soon as possible and put in the best form." As an important figure on the campus, he got to meet the governor of the state and the candidates for public office who spoke at the university. He did not hesitate to remind them that they should take a high tone in their remarks, for they were "speaking to a fair-minded, impartial group of men, who have small respect for petty appeals of a partisan nature."

Always ready for fun and frolic, Wolfe was much in demand as a speaker at smokers and initiations, and he shared "the huge pretense of idiot geniality" that prevailed at the university. Usually his remarks consisted of "the good natured, but somewhat ill-considered, slap stick which finds favor on a campus," but occasionally he went too far, as when he introduced the distinguished and very self-important mathematician and writer, Professor Archibald Henderson, to the senior smoker as "a man, who, among the literati, is known as one of the world's greatest mathematicians, and among the mathematicians is known as one of the world's greatest literary figures."

In April he agreed to serve as special editor for an issue of the *Tar Baby,* the campus humor magazine, that parodied the *Raleigh News and Observer,* the most influential paper in the state. According to campus legend, Wolfe wrote most of the forty-page issue himself. Much of it consisted of the adolescent humor expected of undergraduates, and stories bore headlines like "Purlington Pearls are Phearlessly Pilfered." But a tongue-in-cheek editorial that accurately imitated the cautiously balanced stand of the *News and Observer* on all issues gave a hint of Wolfe's future as a satirist. And a front-page story on the wedding of "O. I. Saye" to a Hillsboro girl and the advertisement of "The Witless McBoob Co." for "Ladies Thingermabobs" gave an intimation of the kind of wordplay that Wolfe used so effectively in *Look Homeward, Angel.*

Both of Wolfe's parents came to the commencement exercises in June. W.O. was too feeble to attend all the ceremonies, but he did go to the baccalaureate sermon and he heard Tom, as the class poet, read his verses, "1920 Says a Few Words to Carolina." Julia went to everything, including the senior ball, and she beamed as her son, along with 164 others, stepped up to receive his diploma. Undoubtedly both parents read the brief biography of Tom in the college annual, *Yackety Yack.* After listing his many honors, the sketch, written by his fraternity brother Nat Mobley, concluded: "He can do more between 8:25 and 8:30 than the rest of us can do all day, and it is no wonder that he is classed as a genius."

After his parents left, Wolfe stayed on in Chapel Hill for a few days, packing his belongings and making some farewell visits. "I hate to leave this place," he wrote a friend; "there's an atmosphere here that's fine and good." Undoubtedly he spent much of the time thinking about his future. His father, now very much out of touch with the world, was under the impression that, having finished college, his son was now ready to enter politics, but this was not a career that had any interest for him. Nor did law, which attracted so many of his classmates, even though he knew that W.O. preferred this profession. An academic career must have seemed a possibility. In a dramatic fragment about Horace Williams written some years later, the philosopher told him, "You'd make a great teacher." But Wolfe had perhaps been too close to some of his professors at Chapel Hill and knew too much about the "bitterness of faculty life." He also read a warning in Greenlaw's career, for that formidably learned man seemed "with deliberate fatalism to have trapped himself among petty things" and was wasting himself compiling anthologies. Wolfe turned down the suggestion of an academic career on the ground that he did not have the scholarly temperament, "the ability to be painstaking and thorough within limits, within narrow limits." "I can't limit myself that way," he concluded.

That left him with the vague idea that he should become a writer, though he did not articulate this ambition even to himself. Like his family, he was used to thinking of a writer as "a very remote kind of person, a romantic figure like Lord Byron, or Longfellow . . . a very strange, mysterious kind of person, who lived a very strange, mysterious and glittering sort of life, and who came from some strange and mysterious and glittering sort of world, very far away from any life or any world that *we* had ever known." Unable to confess such an outlandish aspiration, he convinced himself that he wanted to become a journalist — an ambition that his family could understand.

Then he further persuaded himself that he needed to study at Harvard University — even though Harvard had no school of journalism. "I want this year's graduate work at Harvard in preference to year at the Columbia Journalism School, or some other," he stated in his application, "because I feel that such work as I may get at Harvard will be of more real value than the somewhat technical training of journalism schools." Actually, he chose

Harvard because all three of his major professors — Greenlaw, Williams, and Koch — had studied there. Williams told him that Cambridge was "the place to study," because there "the inspiration is constant and consuming." "Far more books come out of Harvard than any other place," he added.

Once Wolfe had convinced himself that he should go to Harvard, he still had to persuade his family. Julia was silent. W.O. was now too sick to discuss the subject, but with the obstinacy of the very ill he refused to give Tom more money. "No, I'm finished with you now," he told his son. "If you don't take up law, . . . take up something else or go to work." The other children were also opposed to the plan. Effie and Frank lived too far away to have much influence on the decision, but Mabel and Fred felt that enough money had already been spent on Tom's education. In addition, both thought that Tom had not borne his share of the burden of taking care of their father. During the summer he and Fred had an angry quarrel over this question, and Tom bluntly told his brother: "I don't want you or any one else to tell me what my duty is to Papa. . . . If you value the friendship of the only decent brother you have, . . . you will maintain, as I have maintained, the proper relations between us."

All summer Wolfe was uncertain what to do. He got some support for his plan to study journalism from Heywood Parker, a prominent Asheville lawyer, who advised, "There's more future to that than there is in the law." But at about the same time the head of the Bingham School, a military academy in Asheville, offered him a job teaching English. Wolfe hated the idea, sure that within ten or fifteen years he would become "a sour, dyspeptic, small-town pedant." He was, however, willing to consider the job if there was a reasonable likelihood that his father would die within a year. He wanted to be near W.O. during his last days — and he also believed that at his father's death he would inherit enough money to be able to quit the Bingham job and pay his way at Harvard. But the family doctor refused to make any predictions. "I can't tell you anything about how long your papa's going to live," he said; "he may outlast you or me."

Desperate, Tom told his family, "I'm going to Harvard if I have to borrow the money." Julia, who had taken little part in these discussions so long as there was a chance that W.O. would finance his youngest son's graduate education as he had paid for his years at Chapel Hill, now had to make a decision. Torn between her real love for Tom and her extreme reluctance to part with money, she allowed affection to triumph over avarice. "You go on up there," she told him. "I'll pay for it."

III

By God, I Have Genius

WOLFE INTERRUPTED the long train ride north to get his first glimpse of New York City. In that "ecstatic Northern city," he accidentally encountered Albert Coates and T. Skinner Kittrell, both recent graduates of the University of North Carolina, who were attending the Harvard Law School. Along with William T. Polk, who had also been at Chapel Hill and was studying law, they had rented the top floor of a house at 48 Buckingham Street in Cambridge, near the Harvard Observatory, and they suggested that Wolfe join them. Eagerly he accepted, for he was going to arrive at Harvard only two days before classes began and knew that a room would be hard to find.

Wolfe needed all the support that his friends could give him, for he found Cambridge a strange and hostile place. With six thousand students, not counting those in university extension programs, Harvard was much larger than the University of North Carolina. At Harvard, he learned, "no one knows you and you don't care." There were "all kinds of queer freaks in the student body," he discovered. Some of the undergraduates "go to classes dressed in golf tweed and stockings, use the broad ā, and so on," and a few drove up to their classes in their Packard or Stutz roadsters. But he preferred "these foolish and boisterous" undergraduates to the graduate students, who were "the intellectual peasantry — dull, cold, suspicious of any idea they had not been told to approve."

Only after Wolfe reached Cambridge did he seriously think about what he was going to do at Harvard. Though he was enrolled in the Graduate School of Arts and Science, he certainly did not want to become what he called "a Ph.D. man." The only possibility that appealed to him was one that Koch had suggested: that of studying to become a playwright with Professor George Pierce Baker.

Baker had taught courses in drama at Harvard since 1905, but it was not until 1912 that he became head of a kind of independent subdivision of the department of English that offered instruction in the writing, staging, and production of plays. He concentrated his energies on the few graduate students (along with an occasional special student) who were permitted to enroll in his English 47, The Technique of the Drama. Rarely did he accept more than ten or twelve students a year, and for this reason those admitted were often referred to as "Baker's Dozen." Students who were successful in this course were allowed to enroll for a second year in the more advanced English 47a, which had the same title. Members of these two courses, together with some graduates of the program who lived in the Boston area, a handful of stagestruck Harvard and Radcliffe undergraduates, and a few other faculty members interested in the theater, formed the 47 Workshop, which staged performances of the best plays produced in Baker's courses.

When Wolfe attempted to register for English 47, he learned that the course was full. Those admitted had applied much earlier and had submitted two original plays as evidence that they were qualified. Not knowing what else to do, Wolfe went over to the Bakers' house on Brattle Street in order to plead for special permission to enroll. Mrs. Baker, who answered the door, never forgot her first impression of the ungainly, powerful young man, whose "wrists showed beyond his sleeves and his ankles beyond the trousers," and she always remembered "his grave face, alert and yet sad, above the great body, that of a mountaineer out of place in Brattle Street." When Baker learned that Wolfe had worked under his former student Koch at the University of North Carolina, he agreed to admit him to the program. "When you come into my course it is with the intention of eventually being a playwright," he told Wolfe; "if you have the ability I'll make one out of you."

I

Wolfe expected much from Professor Baker, and he was not disappointed. Respected as an authority on John Lyly and other minor Elizabethans, he was esteemed as a teacher at Harvard, but his real life was in the world of the theater. He knew everybody — writers, actors, producers, directors, financial backers, and critics. He corresponded with Arthur Wing Pinero, Henry Arthur Jones, Gordon Craig, Harley Granville-Barker, and other giants of the theater world. He conversed on equal terms with Lady Gregory about the work of the Abbey Theater in Dublin and with David Belasco about the hits on Broadway. He was author of the recently published *Dramatic Technique,* which has remained a sensible, standard guide. Baker was, in fact, a central figure in the revival of the American theater that had begun before the First World War. As American audiences grew bored with the well-made plays of Victorien Sardou, the younger Alexandre Dumas, and their imitators, theatergoers wanted dramas like those of Henrik Ibsen and George Bernard Shaw, which tackled serious psychological and social problems. Directors on Broadway as well as the leaders of the Theatre Guild, which produced less conventional plays, were looking for new dramatic talent. All turned to Baker's group as a source for stage managers, scenic designers, directors, and innovative writers. Baker could open for his students the doors to success and fortune.

He did not make their way easy, for he spared neither his students nor himself. Students in English 47 had three principal writing assignments. For the first he handed each student a different short story, to be converted into a play; his purpose was to show how different the art of fiction was from that of the drama. In the second assignment, each student had to write an original one-act play, which was read aloud to the entire group for criticism. After revision, the most promising of these efforts were given a Workshop production, usually on two consecutive nights, in the Agassiz Theatre in the Radcliffe yard. Finally, each student was expected to write a full-length original play, of three or more acts.

Wolfe found the work very hard, for he had never hitherto had to apply himself and was inclined to believe that he could rely on inspiration. Consequently, his performance on the initial assignment was, as he admitted, "rotten"; his script followed the story Baker had given him too closely, so that most of the action took place offstage. On a second try he was more successful, for he broke loose from the story, and Baker, who always tried to encourage new students, said that he had "struck a keynote greater than that the short story author thought of."

He learned enough from that first failure to take the writing of his one-act play very seriously. At the University of North Carolina he had sometimes dashed off a play in an afternoon, but at Harvard he took great pains with his work. "I'm really working, Proff," he wrote Koch. "I'm reading voraciously in the drama, stocking up with materials the same as a carpenter carries a mouthful of nails: I am studying plays, past and present, and the technique of these plays, emphasis, suspense, clearness, plot, proportion and all the rest."

For his theme he went back to a play about a feud between mountain families that he had started at Chapel Hill, and he told Baker that he was going to write "a North Carolina play," rather than one of the "blasé, high society dramas (à la Oscar Wilde)" such as his classmates were attempting. Baker, who had already typecast Wolfe as a mountain man, urged him to go ahead with a subject that he presumably knew so well. Pleased, Wolfe was convinced that he had "struck gold, pure gold."

Throughout the fall Wolfe worked on his play, which he called "The Mountains." It told the story of the Weavers and the Gudgers, who are engaged in a feud. The senior Dr. Weaver has no heart for continuing it but family pressure has forced him to do so. His son, Richard, fresh out of medical school, has vowed to have no part in the feud. But in the end both are swept into fighting the Gudgers. Hoping to make this play something more than the story of a quarrel between two mountain families, Wolfe sought to raise deeper issues, such as the professional and moral responsibility of the older Dr. Weaver to treat an ailing Gudger child.

From his reading in "the best of the modern dramatists, Shaw, Pinero, Barrie, and others," he had learned that stage directions ought not merely to describe appearances "but to discern through them the character and temperament of the person described."

Consequently he included elaborate physical and psychological sketches of his characters. Young Richard Weaver was presented in terms drawn straight from Horace Williams's philosophy: Richard "can visualize only two forces in life; — a Spirit that seeks truth and one that denies it. Life to him means a conflict between these two. . . . Richard knows of only one way to absorb his negations; that is to forget them and conquer them, — or be conquered." Wolfe also supplied minutely detailed descriptions of the set, down to "a very knowing looking iron sparrow" on the mantel, which invited "the touch on his back that will make him dive like a shot into the [match] box and bring up a match impaled on his long beak."

The purpose of the play was to reveal a kind of geographical determinism that shaped society in the Appalachian mountains. It was not personal weakness nor even family tradition that swept the reluctant Weavers into combat with the Gudgers; instead, it was the mountains themselves, which hemmed in their lives and shaped their fate. If there was a villain in the story, it was one particular mountain, called Old Bald Pate, the outline of which, as seen from the Weavers' window, resembled "strikingly the profile of an old, hook-nosed, sardonically grinning man." Convinced that most people derived what little they knew about the Appalachian region from *The Little Shepherd of Kingdom Come,* by John Fox, Jr., and other saccharine novels, which depicted mountain life as "a romantic affair, with beautiful golden-haired girls, and dashing outlaws," Wolfe hoped to show instead that it was "a terrible sordid story."

Recognizing that his play was "'faulty in places at present," Wolfe was nevertheless convinced that he had written "an honest, true, and in places, powerful piece of work." He eagerly awaited Baker's public reading of his effort on January 25. Confident of its success, he told his mother that it would be given a full-scale production at the Agassiz Theatre in March and that it might also be performed on the tour that the Workshop players were planning for Buffalo, Cleveland, and New York. Much pleased, Julia hoped that his play would mark "a beginning for a *great big name* also a promise of financial *substance.*"

II

But the reaction of the Workshop members to the reading of "The Mountains" was decidedly negative. Many of the auditors expressed impatience with the Weavers; since both were doctors and educated men, they should simply have stopped the senseless feud with the Gudgers. Others asked why Wolfe blamed the moral failures of his characters on the mountains and accused him of "dragging in symbolism by the horns." Most found the play too long, confused in emphasis, and depressing.

Wolfe was devastated by their response. Later he said that his critics "took an idea that was fundamentally good and destroyed my enthusiasm in it; they destroyed the budding germ of a play that might have grown from that idea; they destroyed my play." They also destroyed any chance that "The Mountains" might be performed at the Agassiz Theatre that spring, and they eliminated any possibility that it might be part of the repertory of the Workshop players when they made their tour.

The hostility with which his play was received confirmed Wolfe's dislike of his colleagues in the 47 Workshop. Initially he had tried to make friends with them, for he was impressed by their experience and sophistication. But he soon came to realize that their world-weary air of condescension meant that they truly liked nothing that they read or saw. When he asked one of his classmates, "Have you ever read Galsworthy's 'Strife'?" — which at Chapel Hill had been the latest thing in drama — he was told, in an accent of resigned regret: "I'm sorry. I can't read him. I simply can't read him. Sorry —." His Workshop peers were equally sorry about Shaw, who was "amusing" but not a real dramatist since he never learned to write a play; about Barrie, who was "insufferable on account of his sentimentality"; and even about Eugene O'Neill, whose "dialogue was clumsy, and his characters stock types." Presently Wolfe referred to his classmates as his " 'ass'-ociates in English 47."

They, in turn, reciprocated his dislike. Some of them resented the fact that he had gained admittance to the playwriting program so easily, when they had had to work hard to secure Baker's permission. He was so much younger than most of his classmates that he could not mix with them easily, and when he did try to join in their conversations he seemed callow. The untidiness of his appearance, which was most marked during his Harvard years, added to his social undesirability. His classmates noted that his clothes were never pressed, that his linen was not changed regularly, and that he bathed infrequently. Many in Baker's group had little to do with Wolfe. A few deliberately snubbed him. Years later one of Baker's assistants, Ward Morehouse, said frankly: "Oh yes, I knew Wolfe, but I never liked him. I was introduced to him a couple of times, but whenever I saw him in the [Harvard] yard, I cut him."

Rebuffed and bewildered, Wolfe felt a sense of "bitter rebellion from the group," and after the initial class meetings he sat through most of the meetings of English 47 in silence, his eyes darting suspiciously at his classmates. Only infrequently did he attend the performances put on by the 47 Workshop. To this period, when he closed himself off from his classmates, he later traced "the ineradicable stain of Solitude upon my spirit."

Perhaps his social isolation might have been less had Professor Baker been giving his full attention to his classes, but in 1920–1921 he was rushing to complete and produce a gigantic pageant celebrating the three hundredth anniversary of the landing of the *Mayflower* at Plymouth. Busy and distracted, he was much of the time absent from Cambridge. He left the day-to-day management of his courses to his assistant, Kenneth Raisbeck, who early in the semester did try to make Wolfe feel at home by inviting him to dinner. But Wolfe did not understand what Raisbeck's role was; he was put off by the extraordinarily affected accent of this young man from Moline, Illinois, and by the luxurious furnishings of his little apartment on Massachusetts Avenue. During Wolfe's first year at Harvard their acquaintance remained a casual one.

III

Fortunately for Wolfe, not all his work during his first year at Harvard was connected with the 47 Workshop. In addition to a dull course on American literature, taught by Chester Greenough, whom Wolfe described as "a professor with a starched prim face," he was enrolled in John Livingston Lowes's course on the English Romantic poets. Lowes was different from any other teacher Wolfe had ever encountered. He was as enthusiastic about the Romantic poets as Mrs. Roberts was, and he was even better informed about them than Professor Greenlaw was about his special interest, Edmund Spenser, but he went beyond appreciation and information to ask why these poets wrote as they did and what were the sources of their poetic ideas. Lowes's lectures drew on his exhaustive study of Samuel Taylor Coleridge, which he published in 1927 as *The Road to Xanadu,* and they were designed to show how the "incongruous, chaotic, and variegated jumble" of Coleridge's reading was transformed in the poet's "deep well of unconscious cerebration" — a phrase he borrowed from Henry James — and became "a structure of exquisitely balanced and coördinated unity — a work of pure imaginative vision."

Lowes's approach so impressed Wolfe that, despite his aversion to research, he tried to explore the sources of some of Coleridge's ideas himself, with enough success that he received credit in a footnote to *The Road to Xanadu* — where his name was misspelled "Wolf." But he wanted to reverse the development that Lowes traced. If it was possible to find the origin of images and ideas in a great poem like "The Rime of the Ancient Mariner" in the vast, disorderly reading that Coleridge had done, was it not equally likely that enormous and diverse reading could lead to the production of a great work of literature? Excitedly Wolfe wrote to Professor Greenlaw that Lowes's lectures, which showed "conclusively how retentive of all it reads is the mind and how, at almost any moment that mass of material may be fused and resurrected into new and magic forms," were leading him to devour books wholesale. During his last two years at Chapel Hill he had not read very much, but now he buried himself as much as possible in Widener Library, and he was delighted to report that "the ghosts of old, supposedly forgotten books are continually walking forth now, almost as distinct in their detail as when I read them."

His special haunt was the Farnsworth Room, a reading room for English literature, which had comfortable lighting and luxurious leather couches, on which he could sprawl as he devoured one book after another. He read promiscuously, without plan or pattern. In a representative day he completed H. G. Wells's novel *The Undying Fire,* Swift's *Tale of a Tub,* two essays of Ralph Waldo Emerson, and Leslie Stephen's biography of Alexander Pope. Often he wandered through the stacks of Widener Library, "like some damned soul, never at rest — ever leaping ahead from the pages I read to thoughts of those I want to read." In his fiction he described his counterpart, Eugene Gant, as reading with a watch in his hand, timing his "laying waste of the shelves." With practice Wolfe's speed of reading improved, so that by 1923 he boasted: "The Widener Library has crumpled under my savage attack. Ten, twelve, fifteen books a day are nothing."

As Wolfe ransacked the library, he thought of himself as another Coleridge. He was, he said, "not afraid to read in his experience, in his life, a possible portent of my own. Certainly there was a bond in our common thirst for information." Learning from Lowes that Coleridge had "made use of a thousand elements of apparently unrelated experience," he hoped to make his own life "a vast tapering funnel into which everything must be poured."

Lowes was impressed by his strange young student who took his theory of literary criticism so seriously. He liked Wolfe's long research paper on the supernatural in the philosophy and poetry of Coleridge and told Wolfe that "not one man in a 1000 could write a report like that." Calling Wolfe into his office, he suggested that he work toward a Ph.D. degree and become a college teacher, remarking that "the teaching profession was all too shy of men who could do that kind of writing." Wolfe was, of course, gratified, for, as he told Mr. and Mrs. Roberts, the kind of encouragement that Lowes offered was "something as astonishing for a Harvard prof as giving a woman a seat in a N. Y. st[reet] car would be to a New Yorker." But he wanted to be a writer, not a professor.

IV

Lowes failed to realize that it was loneliness, rather than love of scholarship, that caused Wolfe to spend so much time in the library. He felt desperately isolated in Cambridge. He did have an uncle in the vicinity, his mother's brother, Henry A. Westall, who lived in nearby Medford and worked in Boston. Expressing a hope that "the frigid social atmosphere [of Cambridge] has not congealed your warm Southern blood," Mrs. Laura Westall frequently invited him to dinner. He enjoyed these occasions, for both his aunt and his uncle were eccentrics. Henry Westall, after receiving a law degree in the South, gave up the legal profession to study theology at the Harvard Divinity School, where he met Ralph Waldo Emerson, James Russell Lowell, and Henry

Wadsworth Longfellow. As a minister he shifted from the Episcopal to the Presbyterian to the Unitarian church — only in the
end to abandon the pulpit because he discovered that he was an
agnostic. His marriage was an unhappy one. When his wife was in
the kitchen, he would whisper to Wolfe that she was insane. In
turn, when he left the room, Laura Westall told her nephew "what
a fearful handicap it is to be born a Westall," and "what an unbalanced, lopsided clan we are in general," warning that he must
watch himself "to keep the family traits from cropping out."
Wolfe thought them "a great pair" and was sure that his visits to
Medford were providing him "materials for a great play."

Yet most of the time he was alone. Except for meals at the
college commons in Memorial Hall, he did not see much of the
three other boys from North Carolina with whom he lived. They
liked him; they enjoyed hearing him mimic Professor Baker and
the people in the 47 Workshop; and they had a good time when
they all went into Boston to buy bootleg whiskey in the basement
of the Parker House or to eat a huge steak dinner at the Durgin-
Park restaurant. But the law students were working very hard,
and they could not spend too much time listening to Wolfe's
endless anecdotes.

The Boston climate added to his unhappiness. Shortly after his
arrival in Cambridge he came down with a wretched cold, which
lingered on, and then he developed "a rattling, tearing, sort of
cough, full of phlegm." His lung was sore, and least once he
coughed up blood. Probably he already had a tubercular lesion.
Throughout his years at Harvard Wolfe's letters contained frequent complaints of coughs and colds, as well as general lamen-
tations about the miserable New England weather.

Most of the time he felt out of touch with his family. His dying
father managed to send a line or two to his youngest son, but, as
W.O. admitted: "I write so few letters these times that I have
forgotten how." "You can see by his few lines to you," Julia
explained, "that he can't be interested even in you," and she speculated that W.O. had taken so many medications "that his mind or
thinking faculties are inactive — in a dormant state." He heard
more frequently from his mother, who urged him to take care of
himself, to buy "heavy weight union-suits for winter," and to
"have a nice suit of clothes made."

But letters from Julia often brought more grief than pleasure, for she scolded him repeatedly on his management of the money she sent him. In general she continued to treat him in financial matters like a little boy, sending him only small sums at a time and paying his college bills only at the last possible moment. In turn, he demonstrated that he fully deserved her distrust about his handling of money. He kept very poor records of his expenses, and when he did send his mother an itemized account, the figures he listed did not match the total. He so frequently overdrew the checking account that she set up for him at the Wachovia Bank & Trust Company in Asheville that bank officials requested that it be closed out — or that Wolfe's overdrafts be charged automatically to his mother's account.

What was worse, he spent money lavishly. During only the first six months of his first year at Harvard, his expenditures totaled $1,256.45 — at a time when Harvard tuition was only $255 a year and when the university catalogue estimated that student expenses for a full year should run between $545 and $805.

Wolfe could not explain to his mother what became of the money that poured so freely through his hands. Not much of it went for lodgings; during his three years at Harvard he always lived in a furnished room, not an apartment. He spent a good deal on food. "I am afflicted with a big appetite," he reminded his mother. Meals at the Harvard cafeterias did not satisfy his hunger, and he often ate out in restaurants in Cambridge and in Boston. And a considerable amount went for liquor, for he had begun his lifelong pattern of drinking heavily when he was unhappy or unsuccessful.

Because of Julia's strong objections, he had never tried alcohol until the Christmas after Ben's death. Then, while the other members of the family went shopping, he liberally sampled a selection of liquors that Fred had brought his father, just before the Volstead Act went into effect. When the family returned, Tom was in bed, fully clad and completely looped. "Fred," he smiled up at his brother grandly, "that's good liquor!" After that he drank with his friends in Chapel Hill but rarely to excess. But in Cambridge it seemed that everybody drank, some because they believed that in America true artists had to be alcoholic, some because it was sophisticated to know about bootleggers and nightclubs that admitted only customers who knew the passwords.

At Harvard Wolfe rarely drank by himself, for "the idea of

solitary drinking of stealthy alley potations from a flask, filled him with sodden horror." But he rarely declined when others suggested a drink. The first powerful draught of bootleg liquor seemed to give him a fierce strength, a "growing clarity and sheathing of thought and language." Feeling "exultancy, the desire to release an animal cry, exuberant power, benevolent destructiveness to all the world," he poured down drink after drink. Under the influence of alcohol he felt "unreasonable suspicion, choking anger, . . . fury, grief, shame, impotent rage." Though he sometimes experienced a thick numbness of his tongue muscles and once or twice became insensible, he usually did not realize that he was drunk, and, like his father, he often managed to maintain an appearance of sobriety even when he was hopelessly intoxicated. Then, after the initial ecstasy wore off, he lapsed into profound depression, and "weariness, horror, boredom . . . engulfed him like a heavy noxious effluvia."

V

Alienated from the Workshop group and deeply hurt by their criticism of "The Mountains," Wolfe could not bring himself to write the three-act play that Professor Baker required of students in English 47. He started a drama that would celebrate the ideology of the New South. Remembering a bit of North Carolina history that his father had once told him, he thought of telling the story of Colonel Tasher Weldon, "a typical Southern aristocrat," who has lost everything in the Civil War except his vast holdings of mountain timberland. His younger son, Eugene — Wolfe's first use of the name that thereafter he gave to heroes fashioned in his own image — urges the colonel to forget about the glorious antebellum days and to work the land himself. But Weldon refuses, "tragically failing to realize that new times have come," and he finally is forced to sell his land to a lumber company for a pittance. As his stately mansion is razed to make way for progress, Eugene and his fiancée, "glorious forerunners of the New South," make a fresh beginning in a life of love and hard work.

But he never completed this play, partly because he was paralyzed by criticism, and partly because the idea behind it came to seem increasingly naive. He had come to Harvard to study the modern drama but, much against his will, he found himself also forced to study the modern mind. At Chapel Hill he had learned to think in simple black-and-white clichés: democracy, education, science, and progress were good; aristocracy, ignorance, religious fundamentalism, and nostalgia for the past were bad. But in Cambridge he encountered complex modernist ideas and sensibilities, and he had difficulty in dealing with them.

Some of the intellectual trends then fashionable at Harvard he rejected completely. He refused to join his Workshop associates in the faddish admiration for "Cocteau, Gide, Morand and Proust, American jazz and the negro spiritual." He had nothing to do, then or later, with the belief that writers of the 1920s were members of a Lost Generation, whose careers had been blighted by the Great War.

Nor was he receptive to the neohumanist ideas then in vogue at Harvard, where Irving Babbitt, along with his disciple Paul Elmer More, repudiated romanticism and naturalism and defended an ideal of moderation and balance. In his final year at Harvard he did audit Babbitt's lectures, but he mostly remembered the professor's skill in avoiding clear-cut statements, as he praised imagination but urged that it be kept in check and implied but never quite said that the world was going to seed because of Jean-Jacques Rousseau.

He was even less receptive to the Cambridge enthusiasm for T. S. Eliot as poet-philosopher of classicism, restraint, and despair. Willing to concede that Eliot was the living "critic with the greatest subtlety," he disliked his "modest omniscience." "Whoever is impressed with the 'classicism' of T. S. Eliot," he observed, "should buy immediately a copy of that other fine modern expression of the classical spirit, The Thundering Herd, by Zane Grey." Years later he satirized the Wastelanders, as he called Eliot's admirers, by writing of a man who "thought of nightingales in Newark, and muttered of his ruins; he knew six words of Greek and spoke of Clytemnestra. He muttered bitterly, was elegant and lost, and yet he did not die: he watched the windows, wore his rubbers when it rained, wept when his wife betrayed him, and went abroad to live."

But to some new ideas he was more receptive. At Kenneth Raisbeck's apartment he first saw a copy of James Joyce's *Ulysses,* which still had to be smuggled into the United States because it was considered pornography. Leafing through it randomly, he was at first "greatly amused" and thought the novel "misbegotten in some way." He read some passages aloud to Raisbeck, and soon they both broke into "whoops of joy, and yells of happy but derisive laughter." Recovering himself first, Raisbeck, who was far more sophisticated than Wolfe, pointed out that if *Ulysses* was funny, parts of it were also *"quite* astonishing," and he added, in his mannered way, "I *mean,* the whole thing's there. It really is you know." Wolfe was slower to appreciate *Ulysses,* but in time he came to recognize that Joyce had written a "great book which was to leave its mark upon the life of a generation and in some measure, alter the vision and shape the consciousness of everyone who read it."

Two new American novels had a more immediate impact on his thinking. When he read Sinclair Lewis's *Main Street,* which was published in 1920, it alerted him to the endless opportunities that life in a small town offered to a satirist. "I have read your books since I was twenty," he told Lewis later; "I think you are a man of genius with the most enormous talent for writing." Even more to his liking was Sherwood Anderson's *Winesburg, Ohio,* published in 1919. Anderson's impressionistic portrayal of small-town residents as grotesques, who lived in an atmosphere of highly charged but complex sexuality, had a lasting influence on Wolfe. "It seems to me ever since I first began to read your books when I was a kid of twenty," he wrote Anderson in 1935, "that you got down below the surface of our lives and got at some of the terror and mystery and ugliness and beauty in America better than anyone else."

He was also much impressed by H. L. Mencken, whose name he seems never to have encountered at the University of North Carolina. But at Harvard everybody read Mencken's *American Mercury* and chuckled over the irreverencies of his *Prejudices,* which ridiculed American piety and American politics. Workshop members especially liked Mencken, because he seemed to support their view that the American artist — a word they usually pronounced "ottist" — was "crucified by life, misunderstood and scorned of men, pilloried and driven out by the narrow bigotry and mean provincialism of the town or village." Wolfe found it easy to appreciate this kind of talk, for he too enjoyed Mencken's attacks on the provincialism of American culture. "Middle class morality, middle-class religion, middle-class politics, middle-class intelligence," he echoed, were "small, mean, and cowardly."

Yet he also had reservations about "the self-observing vigor" with which Mencken attacked idols. In particular he had difficulty accepting Mencken's strictures on the South, as in his celebrated denigration of Southern culture as "the Sahara of the Bozart." His problem was not so much with Mencken's ideas as with the way his Northern classmates used Mencken's invective and denunciation to ridicule the social and political backwardness of the South and to condemn Southern whites for their uncivilized treatment of the Negroes.

These were not issues that Wolfe had thought much about before coming to Cambridge. Until he came to Harvard he never considered himself a Southerner — any more than he had thought of himself as a man from the mountains until he was so labeled at Chapel Hill. After all, Asheville, a city with few links to the antebellum slavery era, was not especially Southern. But in Cambridge his accent and his origins immediately marked him as a Southerner. Like many another Southern student in the North, he discovered that there were some advantages to his newly found regional identity. "Your Southerner in northern states," he remarked, "soon learns what is expected of him, and is not unlikely to surrender and become professional. His words crawl and drip with syrupy reluctance from his mouth, the most commonplace facts of his existence become rosy in this romantic glow, and, if he is not careful, he is apt to be found referring to his own father as 'the Colonel.' "

But being a Southerner in the North also had its price. He had to listen to supercilious remarks about the South's ignorance and poverty, to attacks on its demagogues and its lynch law, and to ridicule of its religious fundamentalism and its hostility to the teaching of evolution. On most of these subjects, he fancied that he, a graduate of the University of North Carolina, the center of progressive thinking in the South, was remarkably liberated, since he belonged "to a new generation of Southerners who refuse to share in the beautiful but destructive conspiracy of silence of their fathers" about the problems of the region. But he was astonished to find that his Harvard associates thought him hopelessly backward on the central problem of the South: race relations.

Throughout his life Wolfe had difficulty dealing with issues of race. Like most white Southerners of his generation, he believed that blacks were "members of a savage and inferior race," just out of the jungle, who were incapable of any true civilization. From this stereotype he could easily have moved toward a conventional Southern defense of segregation and repression of the blacks, or he could have accepted the opinion of his Harvard acquaintances that blacks deserved education and equality. But, with characteristic ambivalence, he wavered between these two positions and came up with a third. The racial problems of the South, he speculated, stemmed from neither the whites, who were in control, nor the blacks, who were oppressed, but from "the discontented mulattos who feel, with justice, that they are neither fish nor flesh." Promiscuous interracial sex, he concluded, had produced so many "yellow skins" that in the South "something very much like a yellow plague [is] walking our streets."

Impressed with his own insight, he drafted scenes for several never-completed plays about the role of the tragic mulatto. Most dealt, fairly sympathetically, with a Southern farmer who hid the fact that he had one-eighth — or sometimes one-thirty-second — black blood, passed the color line, and married a white woman before he was exposed. In "The House at Belmont" Eugene, Wolfe's alter ego, informed his brother, who was having an affair with a light-skinned mulatto, "that the misdeeds of such white men constitute a crime against society which will one day be reaped in shame and dishonor to the race."

VI

Attempting to deal with so many new ideas all at once, Wolfe made little progress on his proposed play about the New South during his second semester at Harvard. Indeed, the quality of all his work declined. Feeling that he had performed "superhuman" labor during his first term, he cut back to only two courses. He intended to spend any spare time learning French, so that he could pass the proficiency examination required for the M.A. degree. He did take the French examination in the spring, but he failed it; consequently "the accursed French requirement" still had to be worked off.

Wolfe ended the academic year in a state of uncertainty. His family wanted him to come home, but he felt he that he had now outgrown Asheville, where the average young woman had "the brain capacity of a fourteen year old child" and "the damn-fool boys" thought of nothing but dancing and idle chatter. Besides, he feared that if he left Cambridge he might never be allowed to return. He knew that he could expect nothing from his father, who grew weaker each day. As Julia wrote, W.O. "does not take any interest in anything[,] even admits he . . . does not think or care for the family anymore." Both Fred and Mabel were opposed to spending any more on their brother's education. And his mother had an infinite capacity to procrastinate when it came to releasing money.

So he remained in Cambridge, finally persuading his mother to pay the tuition for summer school so that he could take the one additional course needed to fulfill the requirements for the master's degree. Perhaps his threat to work his way to Europe on a transatlantic steamer convinced her, for she would rather pay for his staying at Harvard than allow him "to mix with so many rough low bred people and perhaps diseased people." He took only one course, that of Professor Charles H. McIlwain on English history, and he found it stimulating. McIlwain "with his sane, clear judgments" was "magnificent, a real scholar," and Wolfe was "delighted, thrilled, charmed" to discover that the required books by Freeman, Stubbs, and Maitland were *"literature, something modern history too often is not although it is scientif-ically more correct."*

He also found time to relax. He explored Boston and was fascinated by its diversity and ethnic complexity. At this time he began his lifelong habit of eavesdropping on conversations on the streets and in restaurants, afterward jotting down a phonetic rendering that he hoped would permit him to recreate distinctive speech patterns in the dialogue of his plays. He frequented the second-hand bookstores in Cambridge and Boston and picked up at bargain prices some of the best books in his library. When friends and acquaintances visited, he showed them the sights, taking them to Widener Library, then out to Lexington and Concord, and back to the narrow streets of Boston.

Most of the summer he was in high spirits, chiefly because Professor Baker had invited him to return to the 47 Workshop for a second year. This was not a privilege extended to all first-year students. Of the eleven students Baker admitted to his course in playwriting for 1920–1921 only six passed what Wolfe called "the real test of success and future promise" by being allowed to enroll for another year.

Baker encouraged Wolfe to continue because he genuinely liked this voluble young giant from the Appalachians. A rather stiff New Englander, Baker was charmed by Wolfe's Southern accent and his Southern manners. At a time when many students were cultivating an air of sophisticated world-weariness, Wolfe's hearty enthusiasm and his total lack of pretentiousness were refreshing. Baker could not help admiring Wolfe's endless energy and his voracious appetite for knowledge. Baker was touched by his enchantment with drama, for he shared Wolfe's belief that the theater was "a species of fairyland" and his conviction that a great play should be "something bigger and finer than drab, sordid, commonplace, everyday life." Aware that Wolfe had difficulty expressing his ideas in dramatic form, the professor nevertheless found his work promising. Always generous in praising the work of his students, he was enthusiastic about "The Mountains"; he told Wolfe that he was proud of the play and announced to the class that "it had done in one act what he had seen three act plays fail to do." Even though not entirely convinced of Wolfe's future as a dramatist, Baker recognized Wolfe as "a genius somewhat out of control" and urged him to continue in the Workshop.

Encouraged by Baker's approbation, Wolfe did a little work during the summer on his proposed play celebrating the New South, but he did not get far with it. "Somehow or other," he explained to Baker, "my thoughts keep going back to my one act play 'The Mountains' and I feel in my heart I shall yet make a long play out of it." More and more he discussed this play with friends. As he talked, one of them remembered, "those mountains of his became fantastic. They were there all about us, almost palpable . . . , they shone in the sun and were as white as the light or their shadows became symbols of frightening disaster."

But as the summer session came to an end, Wolfe grew worried. He had heard almost nothing from home all summer, and he did not know whether his mother would finance a second year at Harvard. "Perhaps you have time to spare me a thought occasionally," he nudged her. "Believe me, I am deeply sensible of my obligation to your generosity in money matters but even so I do not think I should be passed over completely in your correspondence." As he continued to hear nothing from her, he became more agitated. "Can I . . . believe my own Mother has forgotten me! What have I done to deserve this treatment at your hands?"

On September 19, with classes beginning just three days later, he still had no word from home. Protesting that he was "no gold-digger, no parasite," he demanded to know just where he stood. "If the time has come for me to go out on my own, so be it," he announced, "but please try not to treat me with indifference . . . that has characterized your correspondence, or lack of it, for the last year."

Feeling desperate, he momentarily reverted to the religious beliefs that he had discarded at the end of his childhood, and he began to repent his sins and to pray for divine intervention. "I, Thomas Wolfe," he wrote, "do look back with a bitter and intense sorrow at my manner of living these past four years, for . . . I have been loose, weak, and totally lax in a moral way. I call to God to give me strength to utterly forget the sorrow and misery of that period. . . . To-night I make unto me a convenant and I call infinite and allmighty God to witness that I hereby abjure the mental and carnal fleshpots . . . which have well-nigh destroyed me. . . . Help me to keep clean, O God, help me to be a man."

His unstated prayer, for a second year at Harvard, was answered. Though Julia had been silent she was not cruel. She had been preoccupied all summer with taking care of her husband, whose health was deteriorating rapidly, and in September he had to be rushed back to the Johns Hopkins Hospital for further treatment. She summoned Tom to meet her in Baltimore, and for two weeks they looked after the old man, now very frail and infinitely weary. Toward the end of their stay she promised to finance another year of graduate work.

VII

Elated, Wolfe headed back from Boston, stopping off in New York to see *Liliom, The First Year, Daddy's Gone a-Hunting,* and *The Return of Peter Grimm.* He returned to Cambridge in time for the full-dress production of "The Mountains," which the Workshop players presented at the Agassiz Theatre on October 21 and 22. Though he had made some revisions since the public reading of the play in January, it remained what John Mason Brown, the future critic who played the part of the older Dr. Weaver, called "a mountain play to end all mountain plays." The theme was still the fatal grip that the mountains held on their inhabitants, and Brown only slightly exaggerated when he recalled that the hero "walked to a window and shook his fists vehemently at an inoffensive peak painted on the backdrop, crying, 'Goddamn you, Baldpate (for that was the mountain's name), yuh hemmin' me in!' " It was not, in fact, a very good play, though it was much more competently crafted than anything Wolfe had previously written, and it was hardly more flawed than Arthur Ketchum's "The Other One" or William F. Manley's "The Crowsnest," which appeared on the same bill.

After watching the first performance, Wolfe noted that the acting was "discouraging." It improved a little on the second night, but even he recognized that "The Mountains" needed to be condensed. Still he was not prepared for the unsigned criticisms that were required of those who attended Workshop performances, for they indicated that his play had been "a complete and dismal failure." The audience found the play depressing and thought Wolfe's characters psychologically unbelievable. Furious, he addressed to Professor Baker an angry reply to the criticism — which he may never have sent. "I sweated decent honest blood on what I thought was a decent, honest play," he stormed. "I at least deserved a decent, honest criticism," adding, in a rare understatement: "I'm no pachyderm." He concluded belligerently: "I thank God that the far-reaching wisdom of the founders [of the 47 Workshop] saw fit to remove the names from the criticisms, for if I knew who wrote [them], I would no longer be responsible for my actions."

Crushed by the reception of his play, Wolfe thought that Baker, who had showed *"generous* enthusiasm" before the play was staged, now treated him with coldness and neglect. Taking Baker's failure to praise as censure, Wolfe asked Ketchum, one of the older students in the 47 Workshop, for his candid opinion of his future. To his "almost inconceivable anguish and despair," Ketchum predicted that he would never become a playwright and suggested that he ought to find a college teaching position.

Dejected, Wolfe holed up in his room at 67 Hammond Street and spent most of his time alone, reading and brooding. His course work during this second year of graduate school was light, since he had enough credits for the master's degree and had no desire for a doctorate. He studied seventeenth-century drama with Professor A. N. Murray, and his final term paper deserved both the "A" grade it received and the professor's comment, which applied to Wolfe's writing at any point in his life: "You show genuine understanding. . . . In writing you are inclined to repeat yourself and the essay would profit by a reordering." This year he was less interested in Professor Lowes's course, on the literature of the Renaissance, and his papers were less professional. Lowes's comment on one of them was both perceptive and balanced: "This paper shows both insight and a gift for expression. The last, in particular, needs (as Coleridge says) to be 'curbed and ruddered.' The study sprawls a little — yet you can be terse and telling, as you show again and again."

Most of Wolfe's time was supposed to be devoted to English 47a, Baker's advanced course on playwriting, but he did not have a particularly productive year. Early in the first term he gave Baker a synopsis and the draft of a first act of what he called a "problem play." "I am on so unsure a footing, so troubled with doubt and misgiving," he wrote, "that I feel the necessity of waiting your opinion before going on." The problem he wanted to deal with was spiritual, not social, for the play addressed Horace Williams's old question of where, in a world of change and contradiction, some "fixed, immutable, unchanging principle" could be found. Most of the play apparently was to be a long, philosophical dialogue between an elderly professor, clearly modeled after Williams, and a much younger man named Ramsay, who bore some resemblance to Coleridge and more to Wolfe. "There is," he alerted Baker, "much that is personal in this statement." There was also much that was high-flown and so abstract that no audience would sit through it. Baker apparently discouraged the project.

Characteristically, though, Wolfe was not willing to give up either this proposed problem play or "The Mountains." Instead he doggedly went about expanding the latter into a three-act play, inappropriately cramming into one of the acts most of the highfalutin dialogue he had written for Ramsay and the professor in the other play. By February he had completed a prologue and the first two acts. The next month Baker read to the class the opening scene, which explained the origin of the Weaver-Gudger feud, and "pronounced it the best prolog ever written here."

But the three-act version of "The Mountains" simply did not work. Though the prologue was indeed good, the play as a whole was too long and too talky. When Wolfe submitted a final version in the spring, Baker flipped throught the typescript rather hastily, apparently seeing in its pages little that was new and less that was interesting. In several places he made marginal notes: "talk rather thin," and "too much mere talk." Beside one of Wolfe's long stage directions, which described not merely the appearance but the mind of a character, he asked prophetically: "Aren't you anticipating your text and writing as a novelist?" The play was never produced, and Wolfe received only the grade of "B" in English 47a — the lowest on any course during his three years in graduate school.

He was aware that his work had declined in quality. In March he notified Baker that he expected to withdraw from his course, and from the university, at the end of the term. He did not have the money for another year at Harvard. In addition, he wrote: "The conviction has grown on me that I shall never express myself dramatically. I am therefore ending the agony by the shortest way; I would not be a foolish drifter promising myself big things."

About the same time he registered with the Harvard University Appointments Office for teaching positions in English composition and literature at Northern or Midwestern colleges and preparatory schools. Hoping to find a post in a large city where there was an active theater, he applied for openings at New York University and at Northwestern University, and the department of English at Northwestern showed an active interest in his candidacy.

It must have seemed especially unfair to Wolfe that as he was preparing to leave Cambridge and the playwriting group the 47 Workshop made fun of his plays. In the spring they put on, as they did each year, "The 47 Varieties," skits that parodied the plays that they had produced during the year. One was called "The Maountains," which had a chorus that pretty well expressed, and at the same time ridiculed, the idea behind Wolfe's play:

> O the Maountains, the Maountains,
> They styarve a man, they styarve a man.
> They grin, like sin,
> They pin you in,
> Till you go out and kyarve a man.

It was all intended as good, clean fun, but Wolfe was hurt. "Easy for second rate people to burlesque bad writing," he observed later. "They understand it, and they gain a reputation for cleverness by it."

VIII

In June Wolfe was still in Cambridge, waiting for the commencement exercises, at which he would receive his master's degree, when he received a telegram announcing that his father was sinking rapidly and was not expected to live. He took the first train home, but before he could reach Asheville his father died, at the age of seventy-one. Of course he was saddened by the news, for W.O. had always been affectionate and generous toward his youngest son. At the time of his death W.O.'s wallet still contained a tattered newspaper clipping of Tom's wartime poem, "The Challenge," of which the old man had been so proud. "Before he grew so diseased and still had interest in earthly things," Julia reminded Tom, "he had his whole soul wrap[p]ed up in you and what he thought you would one day be."

Yet the death of an aged parent who had been mortally ill for many years came as neither a surprise nor a devastating loss. As Tom wrote Professor Baker: "His ending, following a last critical illness of only two days was an infinite relief from the long, protracted period we have lived in terror of." Years later, in *Of Time and the River,* Wolfe indicated that the death of his father, "who had become a ghost and shadow of his father to him," was not entirely unwelcome. As Eugene Gant, Wolfe's fictional counterpart, heard the sad news, "all he felt was the tongueless swelling of wild joy. It was the wild and secret joy that has no tongue, the impossible hope that has no explanation." If those words meant anything — and in Wolfe's case it is not always possible to know, since once his rhetoric was in full bay the meaning of his language was secondary to the rhythm — it was that his father's death was a welcome reprieve, for the legacy he expected to inherit would enable him to return to Harvard for another year and to continue his training as a playwright.

Perhaps it was Wolfe's unwillingness to admit, even to himself, that he stood to profit from his father's death that caused him at just this time to begin speaking of W.O. in a remarkably laudatory fashion. Shortly after his father's funeral he wrote Baker praising W.O.'s fondness for Shakespeare, Scott, and Dickens and his "inexhaustible memory for poetry," and he announced that W.O. had been "really one of the most vigorous and distinguished personalities that I have ever known." Later, his eulogies of his father became even less restrained. "He is the most unique human being I have ever known," he concluded; "I am convinced there is nobody in America to-day anywhere like him." He urged Julia: "Mama, in the name of God, Guard papa's letters to me with your life. Get them all together and watch them like a hawk. . . . There has never been anybody like papa." What made this urgent request so surprising was the fact that W.O.'s letters — and there are only a few of them — were brief and unrevealing, and they were written with the stilted formality of a self-educated man.

Besides convincing himself that his father had been a great man, Wolfe began to romanticize the earliest years of his own life, giving to them an Edenic quality and blotting out the tumult and the family tension. He remembered himself as "the baby in the basket [who] became conscious of the warm sunlight on the porch, and saw his sister go up the hill to the girl's school on the corner (the first thing I remember)." And slowly, as things took shape in the world of infant darkness and the big terrifying faces became familiar he recognized his father by his bristly mustache. He was on his way to inventing the scenes of infantile paradise with which he began *Look Homeward, Angel.*

Wolfe spent the summer in Asheville helping his mother adjust to widowhood and waiting for his father's estate to be settled. For the most part it was a pleasant time. He saw a good deal of his cousin Marie Westall, who was about his age. W.O.'s death had brought Julia and her brother T. C. Westall together, and Tom enjoyed browsing in his uncle's excellent library and talking about books with Marie. Once he read aloud to her from Tennyson's "Maud," with, as she recalled, a marked but charming lisp. He passed many hours with Mrs. Roberts, telling her about his work and reading scenes from his plays. As always, she was wholly supportive. "Boy, nothing can stop you!" she told him. "It's in you, writing is — it's the marrow of your bones!"

But he also found that much in Asheville had changed. Some people that he knew had moved away, others seemed to have forgotten him, and children had grown up during his absence. A new spirit of optimism and boosterism was abroad in the city. The

population of Asheville reached fifty thousand in 1920, and the
city fathers promised that it would be one hundred thousand by
1930. In an unprecedented real estate boom, three times as many
building permits were issued in 1922 as in 1920, and the assessed
valuation of property in the city skyrocketed by 250 percent during the same period. The Jackson building, Asheville's first "sky-
scraper," now loomed where W. O. Wolfe's monument shop had
once stood. The old Battery Park Hotel, built on the highest
elevation within the city, had been purchased by Dr. E. W. Grove,
who demolished it and brought in steam shovels to level the hill
on which it had stood. In its place he erected an ugly and archi-
tecturally conventional hotel. Since mountains hemmed in
Asheville on all sides, land for development was in short supply.
Some promoters expected the city to expand to the east, once a
tunnel could be bored through Beaucatcher Mountain, but it was
not opened until 1928. Others tried to buy out and raze the cluster
of Negro shanties, which were not far from the Old Kentucky
Home, so that white middle-class houses could replace them. The
Asheville Chamber of Commerce saw in all these changes the
march of progress, but Wolfe thought that behind the boom there
was only "greed, greed, greed — deliberate, crafty, motivated."

It seemed to him that as the city grew in numbers and wealth it
became more, and not less, provincial. Members of the revived
Ku Klux Klan, which was rabidly antiforeigner, anti-Negro, and
anti-Semitic, openly paraded through the streets of Asheville and
hobnobbed with the local police. Opposed to the teachings of
evolution in the public schools, Fundamentalists were mounting a
campaign against science that would come to national attention a
few years later in the trial of John Scopes in neighboring Tennessee. These developments reinforced Wolfe's concern over "the
spiritual and intellectual meagreness" of "a community swarming
with the activity of growth and speculation." In the lives of
Asheville residents he noted the absence "of the simplest spiritual
necessities, — good books, good plays, good pictures, and good
music." After dating students at Radcliffe and Wellesley, he was
particularly offended by the vacuity of Asheville girls, many of
whom "were naturally endowed with charm, grace, and sweetness; some were voluptuously beautiful," but they were nearly all
"blighted by an inbred conviction that charm and stupidity went
hand in hand."

Though the boom times that Wolfe witnessed in Asheville were new, the attitudes that he deplored were not. It is not clear that the city in the 1920s was any more or less a cultural backwater than it had been when he was growing up. It was Wolfe, not Asheville, that had changed. He now looked at his home town through lenses provided by H. L. Mencken and Sinclair Lewis, and he made tacit comparisons between Asheville and Boston and New York.

At the end of the summer Wolfe received an unwelcome surprise. W.O.'s children assumed that he left a sizable estate, derived chiefly from the sale of the old house on Woodfin Street and his business lot on Pack Square, and they all knew that his will provided a bequest of five thousand dollars for each of his surviving children. Tom had been counting on this money for a long time. He had proposed borrowing against his share of the estate both when he first went to Harvard in 1920 and again when he wanted a second year of graduate study. Now he learned from W.O.'s executors, Fred and Ralph Wheaton, Mabel's husband, that the expenses of the old man's prolonged illness had eaten up nearly all of his estate; only eleven thousand dollars was left. In an effort to make a reasonably fair settlement, the executors proposed to give Mabel, who had spent so many years caring for her father, the promised five thousand dollars, and Frank and Effie, both of whom had borrowed heavily from W.O., were to receive lesser amounts. Fred offered to forgo his share, and he asked Tom, in view of the money that had already been spent on his education, to do the same.

Tom had no choice but to agree. Disappointed, he prepared to give up the idea of a third year at Harvard and was ready to accept the offer of an instructorship at Northwestern University. At this point Julia intervened. She did not believe that the settlement of W.O.'s estate was fair to Tom, in whose future as a writer she firmly believed, and she offered to finance a third year at Harvard. He turned down the Northwestern job. "My finances are now in such a condition as will permit me to return for another year to Harvard," he reported happily. "Professor Baker has been so unfailingly kind and encouraging that I believe this extra year which is now made possible will be of the utmost importance to me."

IX

Wolfe returned to Cambridge with a new sense of vigor and excitement. Finding a comfortable room, with a fireplace and a southern exposure, at 61 Trowbridge Street, he settled in quickly to work. As one of the very few students permitted to work with Professor Baker for a third year of graduate study, he felt for the first time very much at home at Harvard. Except for Professor Langfield's course on aesthetics, in which he received his first, and generally unfavorable, introduction to the ideas of Sigmund Freud, he concentrated all of his efforts during 1922–1923 on playwriting. "I lived," he remembered, "in a radiance — drunken with joy and with power."

He had little to do with most of the others in the Workshop program, considering them "poor damned, dull, sodden, pallid misbegotten misfits." But he was now secure enough that he spoke up in class, attacking the work of his colleagues more severely than any critics had treated his own Workshop plays. He was especially critical of Philip Barry, partly out of envy that his play, *You and I,* was about to be produced on Broadway, and possibly out of resentment because Barry had outlined a play about mountain bootleggers that could only have been intended as a burlesque of Wolfe's "The Mountains." Sometimes Wolfe went along with his classmates to the afternoon teas given by Miss Carrie Norcross and Miss Leonora Loveman in their huge old house on Garden Street; later, in *Of Time and the River,* he lampooned these two worthy ladies, who were both cultivated and generous, as the vacuous and eccentric Miss Potter and Miss Flitcroft.

When he did converse with his colleagues, he "talked essays, dramas, and narratives," as Philip Barber remembered; "he no more expected to hear from his audience than an actor on stage would expect comment from beyond the footlights." Once he was launched, "words seemed to be coming into his mouth in great groups, to be spit forth one at a time." On these occasions "his eyes, usually wary and distant, became more prominent; his chest expanded, his voice took on volume and power; and he held himself taller and straighter. His head thrust forward, fiercely nodded for emphasis. Even his shirt seemed to become excited,

the drooping points of his collar turning up and out, his tie slip-
ping to the side."

During this third year at Harvard, Wolfe began to make a few
friends in the playwriting group. He thought well of Frederic
("Fritz") Day, though he grumbled that it was easy enough for
Day to write plays since he had an annuity of fifteen thousand
dollars a year; and he genuinely liked Henry Fisk Carlton, later a
distinguished writer of radio scripts, though he thought his plays
were flat and unexciting.

But he saw more of Kenneth Raisbeck than of anyone else. It
was an attraction of opposites. Even in appearance they were in
total contrast. Raisbeck's coloring was ruddy and he had apple-red
cheeks; Wolfe was exceptionally pale and his face, atop his gigantic
body, seemed remote. Raisbeck had good critical mind but little
creativity, and he admired the surging vitality of Wolfe's imagination. Wolfe envied Raisbeck's sensitivity and sophistication.
Raisbeck was mannered and affected; Wolfe was spontaneous and
thoughtless. But in many ways the two young men complemented
each other. They enjoyed going together to the theater and afterwards, over dinner, dissecting the plays they saw, Raisbeck with
a scalpel, Wolfe with a meat-axe. They delighted in discovering
new hole-in-the-wall restaurants in the North End of Boston,
where Raisbeck could pretend to speak French or Italian. They
drank a great deal of homemade wine and bathtub gin and staggered back to Cambridge together. Many of the Workshop group
knew that Raisbeck was homosexual and that he and one or two
of the other members took dangerous risks in picking up sailors on
Scollay Square, but he kept this part of his life separate from his
friendship with Wolfe. There was nothing sexual in their relationship; they were, they thought, linked in the love of Art and the
Theater.

As Wolfe got back to work, the effects of the broad reading he
had done during the two previous years began to show up in his
writing. He dropped forever his play about the deterministic force
of the mountains, and he abandoned the notion of writing a play
about Horace Williams's Hegelian philosophy. Instead he experimented with a variety of new ideas and proposed to Professor
Baker plays of remarkably dissimilar kinds. One was "The People," a futuristic drama, which echoed the antidemocratic views
he had picked up from Mencken. It was set in the Republic of

Moronia, where the sentimental and foolish people have deposed their wise king. When threatened by the neighboring Neskians, they turn back to the king for leadership, and he "smilingly, contemptuously, and silently" takes charge and wins a victory. Deposed again for showing his contempt for the populace, he is chased up a hill and forced to jump from a cliff to his death. As his body bounces on the rocks below, the people chant in unison, "Bump, bump, bump." Another, a kind of science-fiction play called "The Interstellar Interlude," consisted of conversations between "a dapper dark complected gentleman with sly saturnine features" and Henry Adams; the devil argues that hell is a much more satisfactory permanent place of abode than heaven. Still another featured the statue of the Egyptian king Mycerinus, which Wolfe admired in the Museum of Fine Arts in Boston. It comes to life and, among other things, explains the origins of the pyramids.

In addition to dashing off these trifles Wolfe began to make dramatic use of what he had observed on his recent visit to Asheville. Reaching toward a deeper emotional level, he drafted scenes about a family — variously called Bateson, Groody, Watt, and Breen — remarkably like his own. Since he was still trying to come to terms with his feelings about his father's death, it was not surprising that the central figure in all these drafts was a replica of W. O. Wolfe: "Merciful God!" he repeatedly exclaims, as Wolfe's father had done; in the morning he builds roaring fires; he gets uproariously drunk; and he frequents the house of prostitution run by "Queen" Elizabeth. In these fragments Wolfe's prose for the first time became more than workmanlike, and he was able to recapture the exact tone of voice and pattern of speech of characters whom he knew so well. After starting a fire, William Breen, contractor and dealer in monuments, arouses the rest of his family upstairs by hammering on the ceiling with a heavy pole and roaring: "Fred! Ben! Tom! Get up! Get up! Merciful God, what will you ever amount to. . . . Look at your old grey-haired Father — up at six o'clock, building the Fires. When I was your age I was up at four o'clock every morning."

Professor Baker was rather overwhelmed by this burst of creativity, especially from a student who had done very little writing during the previous year. As Wolfe kept bringing in scenario after scenario of new plays, all incomplete, he finally announced: "Mr.

Wolfe, you have written us six one-acters, and I don't want you coming in here again without the second act to one of them."

Baker's remark was intended to be encouraging, not critical, for he had come to have a high opinion of Wolfe. Both the Bakers had liked Wolfe from the first time that they met him; this gangling specimen from the South cleaned up and dressed neatly when he came to see them, and he was always on his best behavior at their house. Neither ever doubted his great ability, though they sometimes wondered about his lack of control. Baker had worried about Wolfe's social isolation in the Workshop group, and he was no doubt touched when Wolfe, in announcing that he would not return for a third year, had expressed his gratitude for Baker's "kindness and encouragement" and "for the inestimable benefits I know I have derived from your course." A reserved New Englander, Baker found it hard to voice his feelings, but when Wolfe returned to Asheville at his father's death he wrote him warmly supportive letters. Wolfe responded by pledging that "as time goes on . . . toward you and the Workshop I get loyaller and loyaller." By August Baker began a letter "Dear Tom," asking, "Mayn't I use that form? We are getting to be friends, I think."

During the school year Baker made it clear that he considered Wolfe one of his most promising students. Long locked in battle with Harvard president A. Lawrence Lowell and the more conservative members of the faculty, who opposed teaching the performing arts at the university, he longed to demonstrate the merits of his playwriting program by producing another successful dramatist. It had been a good many years since Edward Sheldon and Eugene O'Neill had emerged from Baker's Workshop. For a time Baker had great hopes for Raisbeck, but he failed to live up to his initial promise, and Philip Barry seemed unable to decide whether he wanted to be a playwright or an advertising man. Of Baker's current crop of students Wolfe was clearly the ablest. Baker singled him out by taking him to performances of *Aida, Madama Butterfly,* and *The Beggar's Opera,* and Wolfe was invited to join the Bakers for Thanksgiving dinner.

Along with encouragement, Baker tried to give Wolfe advice. On one occasion, after supper in the Parker House Grill, he told him that he had been unnecessarily depressed over the Workshop comments on "The Mountains" and that he needed "a certain toughening." The ability to take criticism, he observed, marked the difference between a great artist and a second-rate one. How Wolfe responded to this counsel is hard to determine. Baker kept no record of these conversations, but Wolfe had now begun his lifelong practice of blowing off steam by drafting letters that would say what he had forgotten to say, or was unable to say, in a discussion. Once he had written these, he rarely mailed them but instead put them in his files. His papers contain numerous angry, accusatory letters to Baker. After their talk in the Parker House Grill, for example, he exploded: "I do not need your Workshop people to help me in the construction of my plays. . . . Your Workshop audience is half-educated . . . and half-baked." In another draft he announced: "Being a great artist depends no more on such callousness [to criticism] than does [a playwright's] ability to swallow castor-oil. . . . It has nothing to do with it. You, or no man else, can make me a great artist, or a second-rate artist. . . . That is a matter which was settled in my mother's womb." Apparently he sent neither version. Drafts of them are in his files, but neither letter appears in Baker's papers. In all probability Baker believed that Wolfe was taking his advice to heart.

With Baker's encouragement and advice, Wolfe settled down to writing a long play. He had a special incentive because Richard Herndon, a New York producer, had established an annual prize for the best play written in the 47 Workshop. It carried a cash award of five hundred dollars and a contract for a New York production within six months. Wolfe's rival, Philip Barry, had won the competition the previous year for his comedy *You and I,* and Wolfe estimated that his royalties amounted to seven hundred dollars a week, for a play that might run for thirty weeks. Enviously he noted that Barry "stands to make a tidy little fortune." He hoped to do the same.

He called his play "Niggertown." "I trust that there will be found nothing to provoke mirth in the title," he wrote in a prefatory statement. "Within the limits of that crude word are bound up too much human misery to cause any amusement to thoughtful people. . . . It is a word that should not be printed: it should be stained on the page with sweat and blood." The play drew upon what he had seen and heard during his summer in Asheville, which he called "Altamont." By November he had a first act ready, which Baker read to the class and pronounced "first rate dramatic stuff." As his manuscript piled up, so did his typing bills. Attempting to help him, Elizabeth Munroe, Baker's secretary, gave him a used Corona typewriter. "I'm going to do my typing from now on and try to save on typing," he promised his mother. "I'll have to learn sometime and its better now." But Wolfe's manual dexterity was poor, and he never did master the machine. Throughout the fall term he continued to give his typist his handwritten, often almost illegible script, and by January 16 he had a draft of the entire play, in ten scenes, which he read to the class.

"I have spared neither myself nor that of which I wrote," he told his mother. As a result, his play was in every sense superior to anything that he had previously written. The plot of "Niggertown" was carefully worked out. In Altamont the intelligent, aggressive mulatto physician, Dr. Johnson, owns a beautiful antebellum mansion in the middle of the city. Will Rutledge, an aging white aristocrat, desires to purchase it because it was formerly his family home. The local real estate promoters also want Johnson to sell, because his house, along with the Negro shanties that surround it, stands in the way of a lucrative white housing development. Tempted to sell, Johnson discovers Rutledge's spoiled son attempting to seduce his daughter, attacks him, and repudiates the deal with Rutledge. Johnson rouses the Negroes to resist eviction, and the National Guard is called in to quell the minor race riot that ensues. In the resulting confusion Johnson is shot by a National Guardsman and his mansion, fired by the evicted tenants of Niggertown, burns to ashes.

Remembering Baker's argument, in *Dramatic Technique,* that conflict was central to effective drama, Wolfe built into his play a series of antagonisms: between Johnson and Rutledge; between Rutledge and his idle, playboy son; between Johnson and his daughter, who is all too willing to be seduced by a white man; between mulattoes and blacks; between Sykes, the black from Boston who represents the Society for the Promotion of Brotherly Love, Racial Equality, and Humanitarian Principles Between the Colored and White People (Wolfe's translation of the National Association for the Advancement of Colored People), and the lazy, promiscuous blacks of Altamont, who are mostly interested in a minstrel show.

Much of the dialogue was authentic, if exaggerated. Wolfe was at once recording and parodying the promotional talk he had heard in Asheville the previous summer when he made Joseph Bailey, the secretary of the Altamont Board of Trade, praise the amenities of the city: "We have eight schools, one of which cost over a half a million dollars, six banks, nine big hotels, over two hundred inns and boarding houses, and twenty-three churches, one of which cost half a million." Many of the "flat" characters — who were intentionally one-dimensional and made only brief appearances — were particularly effective. Some of them, like the Reverend Mr. Smallwood, "a big, red-faced, well-fed man, in the mid-forties," who is "the idol of his flock" and whose "pronunciation of the word 'Brother' warms the cockles of the heart," and old "Looky Thar" Sorrel, the Civil War veteran who points all too graphically to the bullet wound in the roof of his mouth "big enough to stick yore fist through," would reappear in Wolfe's novels.

Wolfe was learning to define character by action as well as by speech. One of the most effective scenes was largely in mime as Governor-elect Preston Carr, a reactionary politician who won office by campaigning against evolution and by indulging in bloviation of the sort favored by Warren G. Harding, reveals to the audience his true, empty self. Alone in his hotel room as he prepares for bed, he removes his toupee, his gleaming false teeth, the false soles of his elevator shoes, the shoulder padding, and the back brace that gave him an erect stance, and the abdominal supporter that prevented "an immediate fleshy landslide to his middle regions."

Greatly impressed by Wolfe's reading of "Niggertown," Baker immediately began planning a spring production. Concerned with the difficulties of staging a play with thirty-four named characters, in addition to extras in the crowd scenes, he asked him to estimate the minimal number of actors that would be required if some played double roles. Though Baker's reaction was very encouraging, it was clear that he did not fully understand what Wolfe was trying to do in this play. He urged him to revise in order to make each scene and incident deal with what he took as the main theme, the problem of the Negro in Southern society.

That was not what Wolfe had had in mind. "A play about the negro, a play in which each scene bore directly upon the negro, a play in which the negro was kept ever before you," he told Baker, "might be a better play: it would not be the play I started to write." "The play is not about any problem — least of all about the negro problem," he assured his cousin, Elaine Westall Gould. Rather it was "concerned with giving a picture about a certain section of life, a certain civilization, a certain society. I am content with nothing but the whole picture. I am concerned with nothing else."

He explained to Baker that the play required a large cast because it was intended to present, not the usual conflict among individual characters, but a cross-section of an entire society. "I have written this play with thirty-odd *named* characters," he said, "because it required it, not because I didn't know how to save paint." "Some day," he boasted, "I'm going to write a play with fifty, eighty, a hundred people — a whole town, a whole race, a whole epoch." To make this purpose clear he changed the name from "Niggertown" to the ironic "Welcome To Our City."

Believing that he had made his point, Wolfe floated through the spring in a euphoric state. He was supposed to meet a rigid schedule in revising his script and to give a perfect copy to Baker's secretary, for distribution to the actors. But, confident that he had "expressed dramatically the modern South," he saw little need for revision and none for cutting, and he failed to meet every deadline. "If you find me a raving maniac upon your return," Miss Munroe wrote Baker, who was out of town for a few days, "please remember it was in a good cause! Absolutely nothing makes an impression upon him, threats, tears or rage, or smiles of kindness." He was certain that his play was going to be a hit, and that Richard Herndon, the New York producer who funded the Belmont Theater prize, would like it. Cynically he asked: "If the New York Jews don't fall for this what in God's name do they want?"

Rehearsals, which began on April 23, proceeded smoothly enough at first. Baker, as was his custom, met with the cast, the stage manager, Philip Barber, and the author in the basement room of Massachusetts Hall, which the university reluctantly permitted the Workshop to use, and led the actors through the script. Wolfe lounged almost horizontally near Barber's chair, occasionally bolting upright, twisting sideways, or throwing himself forward, with his chin on his fists and his elbows resting on his knees. He knew every line of the play by heart and, to Baker's annoyance, would break into quick laughter when an actor delivered a speech he considered humorous.

But by the second week it became clear that "Welcome To Our City" was much too long and that it contained too many discursive subplots. For many years Baker had made it a practice never to tamper with a script without the consent of the author, and he tried to follow this rule when dealing with Wolfe. Stopping the actors, he suggested to him that one of the passages that burlesqued small-town manners should be cut. Wolfe countered with reasons why the lines should be retained. Baker listened politely but then turned back to the actors and read them the cuts. As he did so, Barber remembered, Wolfe started "weaving back and forth in his chair like a polar bear suffering from the heat," and finally he "sprang to his feet with a tortured yell, and rushed out into the night." Ignoring his behavior, Baker said to the cast, "Let's keep it that way for the time being," and the rehearsal proceeded. Some minutes later Wolfe casually returned to the room, as though he had gone out for a cigarette. But day after day this pattern of cutting, followed by anguished protests, continued.

Baker's nerves began to wear thin. He invented ways to get Wolfe out of the rehearsal room. He asked Mrs. Marjorie Fairbanks, who attended the Workshop productions, to think up an excuse for taking Wolfe off for a talk or a drink. This "crazy, wild, six-foot-seven southern boy," he told her, had written a brilliant play but was causing havoc at the rehearsals. "If you could just let him talk to you some of the time," he begged, "so the cast could recover and do a little play-acting." Another time, feeling harassed because Wolfe lay in wait for him after every class, full of new reasons why every cut in his play had to be restored, Baker expressed the hope that somebody would tie a rock around his neck and drop him off a bridge over the Charles River. "Tell me if he gurgles much," he requested.

Wolfe was even more upset. After a day's rehearsal he tried to calm himself by taking a walk along the Charles, often accompanied by Albert Coates. He could not endure the anguish that Baker was causing him. "When they tell me to cut a paragraph or a page or a scene from that play," he told Coates, "they are telling me to cut off a finger or a hand or an arm." He was, he said later, "desperate, frantic, half-mad over the whole business," adding, "My heart was a poisoned sponge within me."

When the time came to shift from the rehearsal room in Massachusetts Hall to the Agassiz Theatre on the Radcliffe campus, where the play was to be performed, it became evident that Wolfe, who had never taken any interest in scenic design, lighting, or directing plays, had totally failed to take into consideration the physical limitations of that auditorium. Nor had Baker or any of the experienced Workshop members given him warning. The Agassiz Theatre was designed to serve as a concert hall; the seating spread in a full 180-degree semicircle around the stage, so that an area of only about three feet square could be seen by the entire audience. The stage had no proper entrances; on both sides it opened out in hallways, and the one rear exit led into the Radcliffe library, through which actors had to run if they were required to make their next entrance from either wing. There were no dressing rooms, and when actors were not on stage they had to congregate in the hallways. Access to the stage was so limited that all the participants in one scene had to make their exits before anyone in the next scene could get onstage. The Agassiz Theatre offered no storage space for sets or properties. Though John McAndrew had designed an imaginative unit set that could serve for the whole play, it had to be adapted for each scene, by strategically placing furniture and properties. Wolfe's play called for seven such changes of scene, each of which required at least five minutes, during which the audience had to sit, with the house lights off, staring at a lowered curtain. Because of these physical limitations, the play necessarily moved at a slow and halting pace, and it was impossible for dramatic tension to build from one scene to the next.

By the day of the first performance of "Welcome To Our City" on May 11, even Wolfe had to recognize that his play could not be successful. In a note he recorded "for my personal satisfaction, my belief that the play which I have written has no better show than that of the snowball in the infernal regions." He could only hope that some miracle would make the production people and the cast present "a performance superlatively better than any they have previously given."

In fact, "Welcome To Our City" was not a failure. There were full houses for the performances on both May 11 and May 12, and nobody walked out, even though it was after midnight when the final curtain fell. Only two of the critiques that those who attended Workshop performances were required to submit have been preserved, and both were highly favorable. One suggested that some drawn-out scenes should be cut but concluded that Wolfe's play was "quite the most interesting piece of work that I have seen at the Workshop." Another member of the audience, who had expected a comedy of manners, was surprised and pleased that Wolfe had done something quite different: "That idea of making the life of a city the plot of a play seems to me not only intensely interesting, but almost limitless in its possibilities." "It is great," a Radcliffe student, who was from North Carolina, wrote Wolfe after the first performance. "I've rarely had a play grip me so completely." Another praised the author's originality, "deep insight into . . . human relations," and "unusual power in characterization."

Yet "Welcome To Our City" was clearly not the hit that Wolfe had hoped for. Its length and its discursiveness, which might have been minimized in a fast-paced Broadway production, were exaggerated by the inadequacy of the Agassiz Theatre for staging such a play. Some in the audience were unsure just what Wolfe was trying to say. Others failed to see what the racial conflicts in Altamont had to do with his central theme of civic corruption and greed. As his cousin told him, the society he portrayed was "not the South, any more than it is the West or the East. [It was] Main Street, if you like." Nobody commented on Wolfe's belief that the plight of the tragic mulatto — in this case, Dr. Johnson and his daughter — was at the root of the South's racial problems, but some must have been troubled that not a single character changed or developed during the course of the long play.

Wolfe was evidently downcast by the reception of "Welcome To Our City." During the months before it was put on stage he had talked of his expectation that Herndon would be impressed by his play and of his hope that it would win the Belmont Theatre prize, but now he failed even to submit it to the committee of judges, which consisted of Baker, Herndon, and Robert C. Benchley. He had told his mother in great detail about the writing of the play, but now he did not describe the performance for her. Sensitive both to what her son said and to what he did not say, she tried to cheer him up: "Don't get discouraged. All will happen for the best yet — just keep up your spirits and see if I am not right." When Mabel tried to encourage her brother by speaking of his genius, he replied that that word made him "feel like a swindler and a cheat." "I believe I have some *talent,*" he assured her, promising: "If I ever do anything worthy [of] the name of Genius, I will not be too modest to admit it."

Yet he did not feel defeated. He could, with good reason, blame the amateur cast and the imperfect staging for any coolness that the audience showed. In addition, Professor Baker kept him from falling into depression by inviting him to spend the week after the performances at his New Hampshire farm. Repeatedly he reassured Wolfe that "Welcome To Our City" had real merit. It was, he said, better than Elmer Rice's *The Adding Machine,* which the Theatre Guild had recently produced, and he believed that it ought to have a greater popular success. Confident that Wolfe was "a coming man" in the world of the theater, he took the script to New York himself, in order to make sure that the Theatre Guild gave it a careful reading.

"He is a wonderful friend," Wolfe wrote his mother, "and he believes in me." Throughout his life Wolfe looked for the approval of some older, wiser person — Mrs. Roberts, Greenlaw, Williams, and now Baker — who could give him guidance and confidence. With that approval he felt he could not be stopped. "I know this now," he told his mother, "I am inevitable, I sincerely believe. The only thing that can stop me now is insanity, disease, or death. . . . And I intend to wreak out my soul on paper and express it all." "No one in this country is writing plays like mine," he boasted. "I don't know yet what I am capable of doing, but, by God, I have genius . . . and I shall yet force the inescapable fact down the throats of the rats and vermin who wait the proof."

IV

I Shall Conquer the World

WOLFE DRIFTED through the summer of 1923 with no clear plans for his future. Most of the time he stayed in Cambridge, where he desultorily flirted with three different girls, but he also visited classmates in New York. From time to time he tried to revise "Welcome To Our City," which the Theatre Guild, at Professor Baker's suggestion, had asked to see. He knew that it had to be shortened in order to have any chance of acceptance, but when he tried to cut and condense, he ran into the problem that plagued him for the rest of his life. Every time he began a revision his incredibly tenacious memory recalled every word that he had included in all the previous drafts, and he could not bear to dispense with any of them.

Looking for help, he visited Henry Carlton, one of the few Workshop members whom he trusted, at his summer place in New Hampshire. Carefully Carlton went over his script, pointed out that there were too many subplots, and indicated how two or three of the least developed stories could easily be dropped. Wolfe seemed to accept this advice and, late at night after the Carltons had gone to bed, worked away on his manuscript. The next morning Carlton discovered that he had not deleted any of the underdeveloped material but instead had added new sequences to flesh it out. By the end of the summer "Welcome To Our City" was longer and less dramatically effective than the play that had been produced at the Agassiz Theatre. When Professor Baker saw this revised script, he shook his head sadly and told Wolfe, "Your gift is not selection, but profusion."

Wolfe's revision of "Welcome To Our City" was perfunctory because his heart was in a new play. He dug out of his files the unfinished script about the decline of an aristocratic Southern family unable to face defeat in the Civil War and the emancipation of the slaves. When he began it early in 1921, he had planned to celebrate the triumph of progress and hard work in the New South. Now, much under the influence of H. L. Mencken, he intended to extol the regime of slavery and aristocracy in the Old South in order to attack the "middle class mentality, the handshaking, flag-waving, back-slapping politics" that replaced it.

After experimenting with titles like "The Wasters," "The Prelude," and "The House," he decided to call his drama "The Heirs." In one version he again argued his notion that miscegenation was at the root of the problems of the South. Making the last survivor of a once powerful Southern planter family an idiotic "quadroon negro, product of the union of the eldest son and a mulatto," he hinted at a theme that William Faulkner later developed in *Absalom, Absalom*. But in a more fully worked out draft he concentrated on Colonel Ramsay, who returned from the war a broken and ruined man, and his children. While Ralph, the older son, spent what money the family had on the races and in the stews of New Orleans, his younger son, Eugene, after one abortive attempt to go to work, lay around the decaying mansion aimlessly spouting philosophical abstractions that sounded suspiciously like those of Horace Williams.

As he wrote Wolfe worried that the last of the money his mother had given him was trickling away. Vaguely he hoped that somebody would continue to support him while he was establishing himself as a playwright. Like other members of the 47 Workshop, he knew that in the past Professor Baker had helped one or two of his most promising students, sometimes making them part-time assistants, sometimes giving them money from his own pocket. "I do not say that I would have accepted such aid," Wolfe stated in a letter to Baker that he never completed or mailed; "but I would have felt considerably better about the whole thing."

A more likely source of funds was his mother. To nudge her in the right direction, he again talked of working his way to Europe on an ocean liner and speculated that he could live in Germany on only $7.50 a week. To his surprise Julia responded not with money but with a promise to accompany him. "If you go," she wrote, "I certainly will be with you even if I am an old woman I can get around alright. Aint so green either when the test comes."

Since that was not at all what Wolfe had had in mind, he tried another tack in September, asking Professor Baker to give his mother an evaluation of his prospects as a playwright. His pretext was that Julia was "subjected to unpleasant criticism from people who look on my career here as a failure, and on the money which has been spent as wasted." Thus instructed, Baker wrote Julia a long, and perhaps not entirely candid, letter declaring that Tom was pursuing "the career for which he is especially equipped" and predicting that he would certainly "make a reputation for himself with the next ten years of real significance." "I feel that you should be very proud of what he had already done," Baker continued, "and that he should be given entire freedom now to make a career for himself in the art in which he has already shown unusual ability."

It was, as Wolfe said, "a corking letter" — but it left him no further possible reason for staying on in Cambridge. In the middle of September he shipped off the revised and retyped version of "Welcome To Our City" to the Theatre Guild and then headed for home. "Everything I have is staked on this play," he wrote his mother. "I dare not think of failure."

I

As always, Julia was glad to see him, but she was unimpressed by Baker's suggestion that she ought to continue financing her son. For some time she had thought that he was working too hard and that it would be best for him to stay in Asheville where he could "get out next to nature and be a child again." "Go slow," was her recommendation; "you have plenty of time to make a name and money too."

He lingered uncomfortably at home for about a month. Acquaintances embarrassed him by asking about his prospects, and after a time he could not stand any more of "the silly little questions of 'What're you doing now?' — And the silly little 'oh' and the silly little silence that follows when you say you are writing."

Only the expectation that he would soon hear from the Theatre Guild made his stay tolerable.

But toward the end of October he learned that the Guild would not take his play. "In a great frenzy and despair of soul" because of the rejection, he decided to leave Asheville, where he felt everybody knew about his defeat, and visit his sister, Effie Gambrell, in South Carolina. Some college-age acquaintances, on their way to a football game in Columbia, gave him a lift in their Packard convertible. They were already in an exalted state, and Wolfe soon caught up with their drinking. By the time their car reached the outskirts of Greenville, where he was supposed to meet Fred, they were all very drunk, whooping and yelling like Comanche Indians. The police stopped them and put them all in jail to cool off.

At this point Fred, who himself had been drinking, arrived in town, learned that his brother was in jail, and bailed him and his friends out. After they were released, Tom told him that the police had thrown him into a cell with a Negro. The black man may have been a figment of his imagination or, conceivably, a janitor sweeping out the police station. At any rate, both Wolfe brothers were infuriated at this apparent breach of the rigid code of racial segregation. Protesting angrily, they got into a fight with the police, who rearrested Tom and threw Fred in jail too, on the charges of drunkenness, resisting arrest, and assaulting officers. Finally, one of Fred's friends in Greenville posted bail for them, and the police told them to "get into that god-damned car" and get out of town.

"In great distress of mind and spirit because of my arrest and the failure of my hopes to be a playwriter," Tom stayed for a few days with Effie and her family. Then he returned to Asheville, where he felt that everybody considered him a drunken failure. Feeling "disgraced and unable to stay there any longer," he took a short-term job raising money for the University of North Carolina alumni fund in New York.

He lived in an apartment at 439 West 123rd Street with four other Carolina graduates, sharing a bed with Lacy Meredith, who was often pushed out by "his hairy, gorilla-like frame." During the day he and the other fund-raisers tried to pick the pockets of well-established Carolina alumni in New York, like Junius Parker, chief counsel for the American Tobacco Company. In the evenings Wolfe raged against the Theatre Guild for failing to take his play, and once in his anger actually rammed his hamlike fists through a door of the apartment.

In December, when the Theatre Guild returned the script of "Welcome To Our City," Wolfe learned some of the reasons why his play had been declined. Aside from the fact that it was much too long and too loosely constructed, it did not meet the needs of the Guild. Just reaching financial stability after a very shaky start in 1919, the group could not afford to put on an expensive, experimental drama by an American. Since it rejected the "star" system, which led to long, profitable runs in the commercial theater, the Guild tried to choose for its major production each year the work of an established playwright, like St. John Ervine, John Masefield, or George Bernard Shaw. When forced to go farther afield, the directors tended to select plays by European dramatists who had a cult following, like Leo Tolstoi, August Strindberg, Ferenc Molnár, and Leonid Andreyev. Up to this point the Guild's modest efforts to cultivate native American dramatists had proved both costly and critically unsuccessful. Professor Baker had been only half joking when he told Wolfe that if he could give his name "a German or a Russian ending the Guild would take the play in a minute."

Added to these obstacles was the fact that all decisions of the Theatre Guild had to receive the unanimous support of the six directors of the organization. The vote on Wolfe's play is unknown, but Theresa Helburn, the powerful executive director of the Theatre Guild, had been in the audience when "Welcome To Our City" was presented in Cambridge and she must have reported that its staging in the Agassiz Theatre was dramatically ineffective.

Yet there was considerable support for Wolfe's play in the Theatre Guild. In returning the script, Courtenay Lemon, one of the play readers for the Guild, told Wolfe — if Wolfe's recollection of the conversation can be trusted — that he was "the best man the Workshop had yet turned out and the coming man in the theatre." Obviously touched by the young author's shabby, bedraggled appearance, Lemon hesitantly slipped him ten dollars. "I was pretty dirty, and ragged, for a fact," Wolfe admitted, but he still had a little money of his own and refused the handout.

Lawrence Langner, a patent lawyer who was one of the founders of the Theatre Guild, was even more positive about "Welcome To

Our City." He told Wolfe that the only problem was that he "had a play and a half at present," while the Guild needed "a shorter, simpler play." Urging the author to "go off somewhere — to the woods or the country and work a week on the play — cutting it down thirty minutes, and from ten scenes to eight, and 'tightening' it up, . . . making the main thread of the story, the plot, more plain in every scene," he promised that he would resubmit the revised version to the Theatre Guild.

As soon as his job for the University of North Carolina ran out, Wolfe went back to Cambridge to consult with Professor Baker about Langner's proposed revision. Baker was cordial, but he made it clear that he believed that Wolfe had wasted the past five months. If he had not been so stubborn about shortening the play, he said, it would have been accepted. But he was wary about the alterations that Langner suggested, fearing that they might "change the essential structure" of the play. Calling Wolfe's attention to Oliver M. Sayler's new book, *Our American Theatre,* which called "Welcome To Our City" as "radical in form and treatment as any play the contemporary stage has yet acquired," Baker predicted that the play would ultimately be a success. He strongly opposed Wolfe's plan to take a teaching job, arguing that it would give him no time to write and would perhaps impair his talent. As to how Wolfe was to make a living until that time he was vague, saying "Of course you must be prepared to make sacrifices. . . . You must be prepared to live close." It would, he suggested, "be a good thing for you if you took a year abroad now." When Wolfe said he had no more money, Baker seemed to think that only "pig-headedness" kept him from asking Julia to continue to support him.

Wolfe reported this conversation to his mother, unquestionably hoping that she would agree with Baker. But she was in Miami when his letter arrived, and then it took her several days to decide to part with more money. Eventually she promised: "I'll pay your way till you get these plays finished, and before [the] Theatre Guild — but you must settle down in some quiet place, and do like Prof. Baker said, get to work."

Before her letter reached Cambridge, Wolfe, bitter that both Baker and his mother had apparently turned against him, began looking for a teaching job. Learning from a classmate that the Washington Square College of New York University needed an additional instructor for the term that began in February, he applied on January 1 and had the Harvard Appointments Office send his dossier. Writing to Professor Homer A. Watt, the departmental chairman, Wolfe warned: "I have had no experience as a teacher. It is only fair to tell you that my interests are centered in the drama, and that someday I hope to write successfully for the theatre and to do nothing but that." Stating that he was now twenty-three years old, Wolfe added: "I do not know what impression of maturity my appearance may convey but it is hardly in excess of my age. In addition, my height is four or five inches over six feet, producing an effect on a stranger that is sometimes startling." If, despite these limitations and problems, New York University offered him employment, he promised "to give the most faithful and efficient service of which I am capable."

II

Impressed by Wolfe's credentials, which included strong recommendations from Professors Lowes and Baker, and charmed by the ingenuous candor of his letter, Watt offered him appointment as instructor in English, at a salary of eighteen hundred dollars a year, and Wolfe promptly accepted. Badly dressed in his new but ill-fitting suit and overcoat, which together cost him only $69.50, he showed up in New York during the first week in February, rented a room at the inexpensive residential Hotel Albert, on University Place between 10th and 11th streets, just a few blocks north of the university, and met his first classes on February 6.

The Washington Square College, located in the heart of downtown Manhattan, was different from any university campus with which Wolfe was familiar. In the 1880s New York University had largely been removed to the University Heights campus in the Bronx, where officials hoped to create a rival to Princeton. Most of the original gray-stone building on Washington Square, the original home of the university, was rented out to the American Book Company, but the small New York University schools of law, business, and pedagogy continued to occupy the top floors. Shortly before the First World War it became clear that if these schools were to prosper they had to offer some general college courses as well as professional training. At about the same time, the children of the Lower East Side, densely populated by Italians and East European Jews who moved there during the 1880s, were reaching college age, and they looked for education at a nearby institution. Faculty members from University Heights began to offer occasional courses at the Washington Square campus, and in 1918 the university created the Washington Square College, with a full-time faculty. It grew very rapidly, from 541 students in the first year to 2820 in 1924, when Wolfe began teaching.

A busy, efficient educational factory, the Washington Square College was, as Wolfe said, "a great, unvarnished, horrible, impressive machine which doesn't try to conceal its grinding." With almost no campus amenities — no gymnasium, no dormitories, no student center, few cafeterias — it was simply a place where students who could afford the tuition took courses, often while they were holding down full- or part-time jobs, and eventually received degrees. The permanent faculty was small, and most teachers were instructors or assistant professors who were just beginning their careers. In appointing them, the university was not strict about demanding higher degrees and paid little attention to scholarly publications. The Washington Square College was looking for strong, vigorous young instructors who were prepared to work hard, teaching section after section of basic college courses to a large student body that was, on the whole, poorly prepared.

The department of English consisted of Professor Watt and eight instructors and assistant professors, who worked under his supervision. Though Watt had received his doctorate from the University of Wisconsin for research on an obscure topic in medieval literature, he was no scholar, and he used to say that he did not take "the average administrator's attitude" toward his department. Happy enough to have on his teaching roster excellent young critics, like William Y. Tindall and William Charvat, he was proud that his department also included poets like Léonie Adams and novelists like Frederic Prokosch and Vardis Fisher. "I believe that there is room in a department, especially in New York City, not only for excellent teachers and good scholars, but for men who have a creative impulse," he told Wolfe. "Indeed, I have a feeling that the department can absorb with profit a reasonable number of temperamental gentlemen like yourself who have color and imagination to inspire students as well as to teach them."

Though Watt was "something of a tyrant" in the way he ran his department, he was unfailingly generous to Wolfe. Initially he was much taken by Wolfe's commitment to creative writing and by his obvious lack of academic ambition. When Wolfe proved faithful in meeting his classes, serious about instructing his students, and obliging in his willingness to perform departmental chores, the chairman rated him "a highly successful instructor." Later Watt, a very proper elder in the Presbyterian church, took vicarious satisfaction in Wolfe's bohemian style of life, and he enjoyed hearing about his more raffish experiences. In 1925, when Wolfe wrote him about his adventures in Paris with several women, Watt replied: "Your ability to land on your feet in spite of whatever misfortune you may encounter makes me think that you are more like a Thomas cat than a Thomas Wolfe."

A favorite of the chairman, Wolfe was offered reappointment at the end of his first term of teaching. When he declined, in order to go abroad and write, he was given to understand that there would always be an opening for him at New York University. During the next five years, the Washington Square College became his base of operations; in addition to his initial year of teaching, during the spring and summer of 1924, he taught there during 1925–1926 and 1927–1928, as well as during the fall term of 1929. Because he was granted a flexibility not offered to most of the other instructors, some of his colleagues spoke of him as "the departmental 'wild oat,' " to whom "any laxity or extravagance would be permitted." But they were careful not to say this in Watt's hearing.

Basically Wolfe's job was to teach elementary composition. During his first year he had two sections of English 1-2 in the general college course, which met on Tuesday, Thursday, and Saturday at 9 and 11 A.M., and one for pre-professional students, mostly older people who worked during the day, which met at 4 P.M. twice a week. In later years he also taught a more advanced course called "Ideas and Forms in English Literature." When he began at New York University, he thought that the teaching load of eight hours a week was light, and somebody told him that he could easily complete his work, "in and out of class, with three hours a day."

But, like every other beginning instructor, he discovered that teaching was a full-time job. He did not have to spend a great deal of time in preparing for his classes. The same texts were used in all sections of freshman composition at New York University — manuals of grammar and usage by Woolley, Gross, or Thomas, Manchester, and Scott, and a standard anthology like *The New World: College Readings in English,* edited by Harold Bruce and Guy Montgomery. Wolfe heavily marked up his own copies of these texts, in order to locate passages more easily, but his marginal comments reveal little more than the fact that he was a hardworking instructor, intent on teaching essential rules of grammar to his students.

He had one hundred and four students in his sections — considerably more than the ninety he had been promised — and each of them submitted a theme every week, all of which had to be read, criticized, graded, and returned usually before the end of the following week. Almost from the beginning Wolfe recognized that this part of his job was "drudgery," and he frequently complained in his letters of "the interminable work of correcting papers: — like the brook, *that* goes on forever." Even though many of the themes were mediocre and perfunctory, he took his job of criticizing them very seriously. What he called his Presbyterian conscience obliged him to write comments — often extended comments — on the back of each paper. In 1928, looking back over his years of teaching, he reported to Professor Watt with pride: "I think I have never put a grade on a student's paper without trying to add a few lines of sensible and honest criticism."

Quickly he gained a reputation as a stiff grader. During his first semester he failed about ten of the students, and as many more dropped out of his sections. But he did not lower his standards. In one large section of twenty-seven students, each of whom submitted nine or ten weekly themes, not one paper received an "A" grade and only eighteen out of about two hundred and fifty were graded "B."

Despite his severity, most students liked him and thought that he was a good teacher. Few accounts have been preserved of Wolfe's classroom performance during his first year, when he was struggling just to keep up with his students, but probably it was not much different from his somewhat more polished teaching in later years. Nearly all his students vividly recalled the extraordinary impression Wolfe made at the first meeting of a class because of his size. Years afterward some still believed that he was six feet seven inches tall and weighed over two hundred pounds. (He was, in fact, six feet, four and one-half inches tall at this time and weighed 182 pounds.) Most also remembered his deep, throaty voice, with its residual Southern accent. He began talking in a slow, sputtering way, but once he was launched he became fluent. As he paced back and forth in front of the class, he seemed "drunk with words and thoughts and electric with living."

Not at his best in explaining rules of grammar, Wolfe took every opportunity to introduce literature even in his composition courses. Because he wanted students both to feel and to understand literature, he often had them read selections aloud. But when, as so often happened, they failed to read poetry with expression, he himself would take over, holding the text in front of him but rarely referring to it, since he knew all the poems by heart. At these times he seemed enraptured, as were most of the students, who felt that there should be a big sign across the front of the room announcing: "Genius at Work."

Of course, not all students liked Wolfe or approved of his method of teaching. One young woman thought his extended comments on her themes were "not only very destructive, but . . . cold, hard, and defiant." Another was so upset by his rigorous grading that she cornered him in the public room of the Hotel Albert, complaining loudly and breaking down in copious tears. Others recognized that fundamentally Wolfe "hated to teach" and thought that he seemed "as if he was always in a hurry to 'get it over with.'"

Wolfe found the students at Washington Square College unlike any that he had known at the University of North Carolina or at Harvard. Most were second-generation immigrants; many were Jews. Years later, in *Of Time and the River,* he described Eugene Gant's sense of drowning in "the brawling and ugly corridors of the university," which were flooded with the "swarming, shrieking, shouting tides of dark amber Jewish flesh," only to be swept "into the comparative sanctuary of the class room with its smaller horde of thirty or forty Jews and Jewesses."

Much of the time he found it exhilarating to be plunged into this unfamiliar ethnic world. "I am making a contact which shall prove itself to be of the greatest value to me," he explained to Frederic Day, one of the few Workshop members with whom he kept in touch. "I came without racial sentimentality — indeed with a strong racial prejudice concerning the Jew, which I still retain," he admitted, but he added: "I shall learn — I am learning — a great deal."

But, with that ambivalence that was so much a part of his nature, there were many other days when he doubted that there was anything to be gained by familiarity with these exotic young people from the East Side. At times he almost hated his Jewish students — though he was careful not to make anti-Semitic remarks or jokes in his classes. The young women, most of whom were only two or three years younger than their teacher, seemed especially threatening, for he thought they were sexually precocious and emotionally uninhibited. Doubtless Wolfe sometimes mistook looks of boredom for sultry invitations, but he was no doubt correct in reporting that many of "the girls — some of them are very pretty, you know — have a 'crush' on me." He was careful to "maintain the proper distance" between himself and his female students.

The young men were harder to deal with. By and large they liked him, and they made their admiration clear by drinking countless cups of coffee with him between classes, by inviting him to their fraternity houses, and by urging their friends to choose Wolfe's sections. But Wolfe's students, like most of the others at New York University, were immensely articulate and assertive, and they liked to make each session of a class an intellectual wrestling match. Though they had enormous respect for education, they showed little deference to rank or title, and they grilled instructors with endless questions: "Why didn't [he] give them better topics for their themes? Why didn't they use another volume of essays instead of the one they had, which was no good? Why, in the list of poems, plays, biographies and novels which [he] had assigned, and which were no good, had he omitted the names of Jewish writers such as [Ludwig] Lewisohn and Sholem Asch? Why did he not give each student private 'conferences' more frequently . . . ? Why did they not write more expository, fewer descriptive themes; more argument, less narration?"

Unaccustomed to this sort of cross-examination and worn out by the effort of teaching, which left him "as limp (and as wet) as a rag," Wolfe developed a strong dislike to one of the most persistent of his tormentors, Abe Smith, a member of his eleven o'clock class. One day, after Abe followed him from the classroom, badgering him with questions and complaints, Wolfe exploded in exasperation and ordered the boy to transfer to another section. Stunned, Abe begged not to be ejected, growing misty-eyed as he told Wolfe that he and the other students thought his was the best class they were taking.

Immensely pleased, Wolfe relented, and the homely student insisted that his teacher must come to dinner with his family. In the dark East Side apartment, where Abe lived with his widowed mother, his two brothers, and the illegitimate child of his sister, Wolfe got his first introduction to Jewish-American culture. He learned that Abe's father and mother were Polish Jews, whose name had been changed to Smith "on the impulsion of brutal authority and idiot chance" by an ignorant immigration inspector. Abe's mother, "an old woman with a friendly, sharp face, and a single wistful tooth," saw that Wolfe needed looking after, and she sewed up the rips in his trousers and stuffed him with rich Jewish food.

Abe became Wolfe's most devoted follower. When Wolfe set out on his first voyage to Europe in the fall of 1924, only Abe, along with one other student, was allowed to see him off. They remained friends long after Abe graduated and began to prosper in his own business. He volunteered to type Wolfe's first novel, which became *Look Homeward, Angel,* and he also typed much of *Of Time and the River.* "I have always trusted and liked you since that first year at N.Y.U.," Wolfe wrote him in 1931. "I shall always remember your big nose and ugly face as you ran down the pier alon[g]side the ship as I left. . . . You are one of the few people among the 1800 million people on this earth that I hold in my heart's core."

But Wolfe's very thinly veiled portrait of Abe Smith as "Abe Jones" in *Of Time and the River* indicated how ambivalent his feelings were toward his Jewish students at New York University, even toward those who had befriended him. In that novel Abe Jones had an "enormous putty-colored nose that bulged, flared and sprouted with the disproportionate extravagance of a carica-ture or a dill-pickle over his pale, slightly freckled and rather meagre face; he had a wide, thin, somewhat cruel-looking mouth, dull weak eyes that stared, blinked, and grew misty with a murky, somewhat slimily ropy feeling behind his spectacles, a low, dull, and slanting forehead, almost reptilian in its ugliness, . . . un-pleasantly greasy curls and coils of dark, short, screwy hair."

Pitilessly Wolfe ridiculed Abe Jones's love for books and music, his fierce ambition to become a great scientist or writer, his unrealistic aversion "from the prospect of joining the hordes of beak-nosed shysters." It was not by accident that Wolfe withheld these sections of *Of Time and the River* when he asked Abe Smith to type his manuscript for him.

III

Much of the time Wolfe thought New York City was the most exciting place in the world. For him, as for his fictional heroes, it was the "shining city," the center of life and excitement. It offered him endless possibilities; it trembled with "the mighty pulsations of a unity of hope and joy, a music of triumph and enchantment that suddenly wove all life into the fabric of its exultant harmonies." Now in the theater capital of the country, he could see all the plays that people in the 47 Workshop used to talk about. Along with other teachers from Washington Square College he attended a preview of Eugene O'Neill's *Desire Under the Elms*. He was invited to the party celebrating the award of the Pulitzer Prize in drama to *Hell-Bent fer Heaven,* by a fellow North Carolinian, Hatcher Hughes. "The world is mine," he crowed to Mrs. Roberts, "and I, at present, own a very small but gratifying portion of it — Room 2220, at the Hotel Albert."

But, in a characteristic reversal of moods, he readily switched to the opposite view that the city was "a never-ending pageant of glitter, show, false-front, and vulgar wealth." Then he described the "hard-mouthed, hard-eyed and strident-tongued" crowds that "streamed past upon the streets forever, like a single animal, with the sinuous and baleful convolutions of an enormous reptile," and in his novels wrote of the menace in "the million faces — the faces dark, dingy, driven, harried, and corrupt . . . of the beak-nosed Jews, the brutal heavy [faces] of the Irish cops, . . . filled with the stupid, swift, and choleric menaces of privilege and power."

His unhappiness was linked to his lack of money. From the start he had to depend on his mother to supplement his salary. Since his initial New York University check was not due until March 1, she had to lend him enough to pay for his room and board during his first month in the city. After that he still found that he could not live on the one hundred fifty dollars he received each month, and repeatedly he asked Julia for more. "I have made it a point of honor to live, *so far as possible,* within my income," he explained to her, but on his salary he could not afford to fill his "ravening gut," which "grinds, grinds, grinds all the time." "Money, money!" he exclaimed. "Good God! What couldn't I do with it."

In addition, he was lonely in New York. Of course he was constantly meeting students and fellow residents in the Hotel Albert, but he had few friends. He did not see much of his colleagues at New York University, because many of them commuted from New Jersey or Long Island and were in the city only briefly. Since Washington Square College had no faculty club or faculty lounge, teachers mostly encountered each other in the large faculty room, where, in the absence of private offices, they were assigned desks. Unlike some other members of the English department, Wolfe never felt comfortable in this setting, where there was no privacy, and he spent as little time as possible at his desk.

But, contrary to the envenomed account he gave in *Of Time and the River,* most of his colleagues liked and respected him. He did not fit in well with the self-consciously artistic group that talked of Freud and Dada, and a few instructors who were seriously interested in Marxism thought him naive. But with fellow teachers who seemed to be outsiders like himself he was outgoing and considerate. During his second year of teaching, for example, he initiated an acquaintance with Henry T. Volkening, who had just joined the English department, when he learned that Volkening, too, loved literature but disliked literary criticism. Long after Volkening left the university and established his own literary agency, Wolfe kept up a low-keyed friendship with him and his wife, Natalie. Wolfe virtually adopted Younghill Kang, the Korean-born writer who came t Washington Square College in 1929. "In my first year at NYU," Kang wrote, "nobody really cared for me except Tom." Wolfe also took a special interest in Vardis Fisher, whom he recognized as a writer as ambitious as himself. After Wolfe became a celebrity, he tried to promote Fisher's *In Tragic Life,* declaring that it contained "some of the most powerful and magnificent writing that has been done in America in many years."

Wolfe felt even closer to James Buell Munn, whose desk was for a time next to his in the big faculty room, and the two men talked endlessly "about life, and art, and teaching, and writing." Munn fascinated him because he did not fit into any of the usual categories of New York University instructors. Though he had graduated *summa cum laude* from Harvard and had a Ph.D. in comparative literature, he had no driving scholarly interests and never published anything much except an anthology that he and Professor Watt edited. He was an effective administrator, serving as departmental chairman when Watt went on leave, but he had no drive for power. Not for some time did Wolfe discover that Munn's true interest was in philanthropy. A member of a wealthy New York family, which had long had connections with New York University, he secretly helped underwrite the university library. Each year he also made it a practice, without any publicity whatever, to select a few of the most gifted Washington Square College undergraduates for what one of his colleagues amusingly called "gentrification": Munn paid the tuition of these exceptionally talented children of the East Side — Abe Smith was one of them — helped them purchase suitable clothing, offered tickets to the Metropolitan Opera and the New York Philharmonic, and afforded access to his father's large private library.

Wolfe came to regard Munn, who was only ten years older than himself, with the reverence that he felt toward Edwin Greenlaw, Horace Williams, and George P. Baker, men who might play the paternal role in his life as W. O. Wolfe had never adequately done. He asked Munn for advice about his writing and even dedicated one of his plays to him. Calling Munn "one of the *high men,*" able to maintain his integrity and tranquillity "in a world of jangling exacerbation, swarming irritability, noise and distressed motion," Wolfe attributed his friend's strength to the fact that he was a true Christian. "I am not a Christian," he confessed to Munn. "My life is stained . . . and I have not always escaped the dirt. If I ever come to any kind of altar, and kneel down, . . . there will be some spots on me. If such a time and place should come, I should hope that one or two such as you might be there." For his part, Munn thought that Wolfe was "very kind, very simple, absolutely loyal, and of the finest integrity."

IV

"God didn't intend me to be a teacher," Wolfe wrote William Polk before his first semester was over. "I don't regret the experience,

but this year ends my Pedagogic career. I may, conceivably, tap
on the sidewalk with a cane next season, having bought a pair of
smoked glasses. I may shout 'Times, Woild, Joinal' — in a rau-
cous bellow. But — I shall not teach."

From the beginning of his appointment he had planned to go to
Europe in the fall. By September, when the spring and summer
terms were finished, he would have no more teaching duties, but
his salary from New York University, which paid instructors in
twelve monthly installments, would continue to come in until
February. He was convinced that this money would pay for his
passage to Europe and allow him to live there inexpensively for at
least four months.

Behind this plan was the recognition, arrived at almost immediately after he began work, that he could get little writing done
while he was teaching. After meeting his classes and grading his
papers, his creative energies were exhausted. "You can't serve two
masters," he discovered; "I have elected to serve one, and I must
see it through."

He was too exhausted to spend much time revising "Welcome
To Our City," and, despite the encouragement he had received
from Lemon and Langner, he did not resubmit it to the Theatre
Guild. Nevertheless, the Guild continued to take an interest in his
work, and Theresa Helburn asked Professor Baker whether he
was making the promised changes in his play. Such inquiries infuriated Wolfe, who now fancied himself — without any evidence
at all — as cast out from the Workshop group and rejected by
Baker because of his decision to teach. "Why do they pry around
so?" he responded angrily. "It goads me to fury. They could have
talked to me if they had had any genuine interest. And now, damn
them, they'll come to me — or not at all."

To spite the Theatre Guild, he submitted "Welcome To Our
City" to the Provincetown Players, a more experimental group
which produced plays in a small theater on MacDougall Street.
During the four months that they kept his script, Wolfe visited
their cramped offices frequently. "Each time," he reported, "an
evil-looking hag with red hair has gone into a little room, shuffled
some papers, and returned with the information that the playreader
had the play, that 'you shall certainly hear next week.' " Finally he
pushed his way past the receptionist into the back office, where he
spotted his manuscript buried under a layer of dust; it had never

been read. Reclaiming the play, he took satisfaction in writing a long, vitriolic letter, which offered "renewed assurances of my warm personal detestation" and ended with *"Go to Hell."*

He did not know where to turn next, but the manager of his hotel suggested that he give it to Anne MacDonald, who read plays for the Neighborhood Playhouse. This he did — but almost immediately he began bombarding her with letters, "full of proud and vaunting speech," insisting on a prompt decision. The Playhouse did not reject "Welcome To Our City," but it did not accept it either. One of the directors called the play "unusually fine" and said that it promised well for the future of the American drama, but he went to explain that no decision could be made until Alice Lewisohn, another director who made heavy financial contributions to the Playhouse, returned from Europe. "What she intends to do I don't know," Wolfe wrote his mother. "I'm sick of praise; I want money."

By now Wolfe no longer cared much about "Welcome To Our City," for his heart was in his new play, "The Heirs," which he was struggling to complete. "The new play is an epic," he boasted to Mrs. Roberts. "I believe in it with all my heart. Dear God! If I but had the time to write." While he taught through the oppressively hot summer term, he felt a desperate need to get back to the play. "I have become like some mad beast who sees through famished eyes a pool of forest water," he told his mother; "I have only one thought in mind, to get away — anywhere, anywhere out of this world about me — and finish my beautiful play."

In August he was able briefly to escape the heat of the city. Unexpectedly he had heard from Olin Dows, who as an undergraduate at Harvard had greatly admired Wolfe's plays when they were presented by the 47 Workshop. After studying at the Yale School of Fine Arts, Dows was looking for a place to live in Manhattan and asked Wolfe to help him get a room at the Hotel Albert. Because Dows was so shy and unpretentious, with a modest opinion of his talents as a painter, Wolfe did not know that he came from an enormously wealthy family that lived on a great estate at Rhinebeck, overlooking the Hudson River, near the Astors, the Delanos, and the Franklin D. Roosevelts. When the heat became intolerable in Manhattan, Dows invited Wolfe to visit Rhinebeck. There he discovered that the Dows estate ran to two thousand acres and that the family seemed "wealthier than the

Asheville Vanderbilts." The Dows family, for all its wealth, was not ostentatious or pretentious, and they were willing enough to accept Olin's "curious young friend." Wolfe was urged to come back whenever he could, and they offered him the gatehouse, where he could keep his own hours and write without being disturbed.

Over the next five years Rhinebeck became a place where Wolfe could escape the pressures of the city, and he maintained a steady affection for the Dows family. Dows's young sister he thought "one of the most beautiful and wonderful people I've ever known," and Dows was one of "the most unselfish and un-worldly men I have known."

A weekend on the Hudson offered respite, but Wolfe was looking for escape. As soon as he met his last class, on September 5, he began preparing to go abroad. Knowing that he had not been able to live on his salary in New York, his mother worried that he was venturing off to strange countries with so little cash and no possibility of securing work there if he ran out. "But I must go, mama," he assured her; "my life has turned to dust and ashes in my mouth, and I find myself unable to do [here] the only thing I care for — the only thing I ever shall." She insisted that he must come back to Asheville before going abroad, and during the month that he was at home she looked more closely into his finances. Not persuaded by his assurance that he could live on one hundred dollars a month in Europe or by his confidence that he could sell enough stories during the next year to support himself, Julia reluctantly gave her approval to the trip and let Tom understand that after going as far as he could on his own money he could call on her for further help.

Returning to New York, Wolfe sailed on the Cunard liner *Lancastria* on October 24. With his mother's warnings in mind, he pledged, "I shall economize, work, learn, and someday I'll ride to glory." "I shall conquer the world on this journey," he promised.

V

"To-day, for the first time in my life, I am beginning a more or less methodical record of the events which impinge on my own experience," Wolfe's journal of his first voyage to Europe began. He continued it for only two days. The trip was without incident, but because the whole experience was so new to him, he was convinced that it was an "amazing voyage," and he began to draft semifictional sketches about the ninety-six passengers, who included "knaves, fools, aristocrats, tradesmen, fat Americans . . . [and] English traders." What to do with his stories was by no means clear, since his writing was "a conglomerate of so many things — drama, comment, incident, opinion." Wolfe himself realized that much of what he had dashed off was "recorded hastily, . . . sometimes clumsily."

Arriving in England with no letters of introduction and no particular plans, Wolfe wandered about London for three weeks, walking "the queer, blind, narrow, incredible, crooked streets." Then he drifted off briefly to Bath and to Bristol. Early in December he moved on to Paris, where he felt afflicted by "a terrible and devastating impotence" since he could speak only a few words of French and had great difficulty in reading even the newspapers.

By his third day in Paris he located a room on the top floor of a pension on rue de la Université, in the Latin Quarter, where the concierge, who had been wounded in the war, groaned at the thought of carrying his three suitcases up five flights of stairs. Trying to be agreeable, Wolfe took two of the bags up himself and left the third for the next day. But that night, while the concierge's back was turned, someone slipped in and stole Wolfe's third suitcase, which contained the manuscript of "The Heirs."

Wolfe went "almost crazy" over the loss of his play. As he wrote his mother, "Nothing has hit me as hard as this since papa's death." But the language barrier kept him from adequately expressing his outrage until he ran into George Stevens, a Harvard undergraduate who had been involved in the 47 Workshop productions. With Stevens as interpreter, Wolfe filed a complaint with the local magistrate, who found that the pension had been negligent and fined the owner and his wife five hundred francs — about twenty-five dollars. Once Wolfe had the money in hand, he instructed Stevens to "tell the man that he was a dirty scoundrel, and the woman that she was dishonest."

Promptly moving to a small hotel in the nearby rue des Beaux-Arts — the Hôtel d'Alsace, where Oscar Wilde had died — Wolfe sequestered himself for the rest of December in order to rewrite his play. Initially he felt the loss of his manuscript as a crushing blow. Gradually, however, he came to think of the theft as a disguised blessing, since it forced him completely to rewrite a play over which he had struggled so many years.

The revised version dealt with the same theme as the earlier drafts, the rise and fall of a powerful Southern family, and the central character remained Eugene, the younger son of a wealthy, aristocratic planter. But in all other ways the new draft was strikingly different from its predecessors — so different, indeed, that Wolfe gave it a new name, "Mannerhouse."

Years later Wolfe remarked that "Mannerhouse" had been "written in a somewhat mixed mood of romantic sentiment, Byronic irony, and sardonic realism." The theme of the decline and ultimate extinction of a proud old family was "probably influenced a good deal by *The Cherry Orchard* of Chekhov"; Eugene "was a rather Byronic character, a fellow who concealed his dark and tender poetry under the mask of a sardonic humor"; his love scenes with the heroine were "undoubtedly influenced a great deal by the Hamlet and Ophelia situation"; and his ironic gallantry owed much to Rostand's *Cyrano de Bergerac.*

So far as it went, Wolfe's recollection of the influences on "Mannerhouse" was correct, but he failed to mention that it was even more strongly affected by the techniques of Expressionist drama, which attempted to represent on the stage what was happening in the minds of the characters, rather than what was happening to them. Wolfe had begun to read the plays of Expressionist writers like Gerhart Hauptmann and L. N. Andreyev while he was at Harvard, and he had at least some knowledge of the work of August Strindberg. But in the 47 Workshop Professor Baker had insisted on straightforward presentation of scenes, with dialogue that captured the distinctive regional and social origins of the characters, and Wolfe's interest in Expressionism had been curbed. But the experimental plays that Wolfe saw during his year in New York reinforced his belief that Expressionism was a liberating force in the theater. Now that he was no longer under Baker's influence, he introduced soliloquies and asides in "Mannerhouse" and gave his characters lines, often both lyrical and enigmatic, that were less like the steps of a logical argument than the unanticipated but meaningful juxtapositions of a dream. "Mannerhouse" was also, like most Expressionist dramas, awash in symbols, the most effective of which represented the decay, both physical and moral, working at the foundations, which would ultimately cause the collapse of the great Southern mansion: "the sound of a single large drop of water, which somewhere forms, swells, develops, and falls at length with an unvarying punctual monotony."

Consequently, "Mannerhouse" was decidedly different from all of Wolfe's other plays. Bearing "no relation to problem, none to history," it was no longer concerned with praising the New South or justifying the Old South; it dealt with psychological, rather than social, reality. Despite the author's pose of ironical detachment, "Mannerhouse" was the first of Wolfe's truly autobiographical writings. The play was, he admitted, "the mould for an expression of my secret life, of my own dark faith, chiefly through the young man Eugene."

VI

After completing "Mannerhouse" at the end of December, Wolfe felt free to explore Paris. Like so many other American artists of his generation, he had the notion that "one could work far better in Paris than anywhere on earth; that it was a place where the very air was impregnated with the energies of art; where the artist was bound to find a more fortunate and happy life than he could possibly find in America." But he had no clear objective, and, indeed, at this time it was not certain what his "work" was. With no acquaintances in the city, he simply wandered about, on the vague theory that he was observing and collecting material that he would be able to use at some point in his writing. Lonely in a foreign land, he was much of the time oppressed by "the sick anguish of homelessness, insecurity, and homesickness."

On New Year's Eve he was rescued by Kenneth Raisbeck, his friend from the 47 Workshop. Raisbeck spotted Wolfe at the entrance of the Louvre, drunk and loudly quarreling with the guards, who kept telling him — in French, which he did not understand — that the museum was about to close. Raisbeck intervened and took Wolfe away, and they began a round of cafés, bistros, and restaurants that lasted all night. Delighted to have somebody to talk to after weeks of being alone, Wolfe told all about his teaching at New York University and the loss of his manuscript. In turn he learned that Raisbeck had been without employment since Professor Baker left Harvard to head the Yale Repertory Theatre and that he had come abroad, where living expenses were lower, to write another play. He was now staying at a friend's studio on rue Edgar Quinet, and in the early morning hours he suggested that Wolfe sleep there, since he was obviously too drunk to return to his hotel.

Before noon the sound of women's voices awakened him. The owner of the studio was Mrs. Marjorie Fairbanks, whom Wolfe had met casually in Cambridge but did not immediately recognize, and she came in with her Boston friend, Helen Beal Harding. Very confused about relationships, Wolfe took some time to figure out that Raisbeck, Fairbanks, and Harding had been spending most of their time together in Paris. He kept thinking that Mrs. Fairbanks, a stout, managerial person who looked older than the others, must be a cousin or aunt of Raisbeck. He had even more difficulty in placing Miss Harding. Only slowly did he learn that she and Marjorie had grown up together; both came from proper Boston families listed in the Social Register. But there was a streak of rebelliousness in both women. During the World War, Marjorie had gone to France as a volunteer ambulance driver, and Helen, after a disastrous coming-out party to which almost nobody came because of a mix-up in the invitations, went to Presbyterian Hospital in New York to train as a nurse.

Both were obviously very fond of Raisbeck, and they welcomed Wolfe, as Raisbeck's friend, to their little circle. For the next few weeks the four were inseparable. They lunched or dined together nearly every day, and most evenings they went to cabarets and nightclubs. Raisbeck knew all the out-of-the-way places in Paris; Marjorie with her idiomatic French commanded prompt service; and Helen, who had more money than the others — though she was reluctant to spend it and kept close accounts — usually paid the bills. In their company Wolfe found that the unfamiliar French world "became in a moment wonderful and good" and "the whole earth seemed to come to life at once."

In *Of Time and the River,* hardly making an attempt to disguise the autobiographical nature of his story, Wolfe wrote of these weeks in Paris at great length and with much passion, but in fact they were largely uneventful. Apart from an ill-conceived day trip to see the Rheims cathedral, the four stayed in or near Paris, mostly at the usual spots. What fascinated Wolfe were the complex relationships among his friends, which he slowly began to discover. In time he realized that Marjorie Fairbanks, far from being a relative of Raisbeck, wanted to become his lover and hoped to marry him. She had left behind in Boston her husband and her son — but not her dog! — in order to be with him. Raisbeck responded to her advances by cruising the bars of Paris and picking up a young Frenchman named Albert, and he insisted that the others must accept his homosexual friend.

In this erotically charged atmosphere, Wolfe's own interests centered on Helen. Four years older than he was, tall and statuesque, she had a beautiful figure and lustrous black hair, which she parted in the center. Her face usually looked downcast and somewhat sullen, but she was radiant when she smiled. Unhappy that the others seemed to cast her in the role of dog-sitter and chaperone for Marjorie, she seemed genuinely fond of Wolfe, and Raisbeck and Marjorie encouraged a romance between them.

The situation was novel to Wolfe. For years he had found outlet for his sexual drives in "the coarse and honest appeasements of the brothel, and the lusty commerce of the whores"; he did not think of women of his own social class in sexual terms. Indeed, he writhed with "a terrible internal shame" at the very thought that people he knew and admired, like Professor and Mrs. Baker, or Mr. and Mrs. Roberts, had ever slept together. The same "unutterable shame" had overcome him when he once saw his parents, long locked in the mortal warfare of marriage, embrace after the death of his brother Ben. But now, for the first time, his Paris companions made him realize "sharply how delightful and seductive the companionship of a woman might be — a companionship that quickened the mind and senses . . . [and] was subtly and rarely sensuous and seductive."

So stimulated, Wolfe fancied that he was "hopelessly, madly, desperately in love" with Helen, and one evening in late January, when the friends were spending the night at St.-Germain-en-Laye, he put his arms around her, kissed her, caressed her breast, and even thrust his hand under her skirt. She did not resist, but at first she made no response at all. Then, bursting into tears, she confessed that she was in love with Raisbeck, who had no sexual interest in her or any other woman and tolerated her because of her money. As for Wolfe, she explained that her feelings were expressed in the words of a popular song: "I can't get the one I want, those I get I don't want."

For his part, Wolfe found that physical contact with Helen

brought on "a terrible horror of the flesh." When he touched her, all the forbidden images of sex flashed through his mind — between the Bakers, the Robertses, and, most of all, his parents. In his fictional recreation of this scene, in *Of Time and the River*, Wolfe described how Eugene Gant's desire faded, overcome by "senseless feelings of guilt and shame and profanation. . . . He had been with so many whores, and casual loose promiscuous women, that he would have thought it easy to make love to this big, clumsy, sullen-looking girl, but now all he could do was to hug her to him in an awkward grip, to mutter foolishly to her, and to kiss her warm sullen silk-downed face again and again." Frustrated by his impotence, Eugene tried to flog desire into life by identifying the girl with the whores he had known. "Oh, you big, dumb, beautiful Boston bitch," he cursed, "you sweet, dumb, lovely trollop." But it was no use, and they separated in anger.

VII

After that, Wolfe began to pull away from the group. Helen, embarrassed, had little to say to him. He quarreled angrily with Marjorie about money. His relations with Raisbeck deteriorated. Complaining of his friend's "ungenerousness and pettiness," Wolfe was also troubled by Raisbeck's increasingly overt homosexual activities and felt outraged that this man who was not at all interested in women was able to monopolize the attention of two such attractive females.*

At the end of January when the others rented a car and drove to the south of France, Wolfe remained behind in Paris. He spent much of the time writing long letters to Helen, most of which he never mailed. In some of them he tried to minimize the importance of "our little comic opera." In others he ridiculed her "large grim body" and her "elephantine resolve, to do life thoroughly, taking an occasional note." When she replied, he claimed that her

*In *Of Time and the River* Eugene Gant, in his final encounter with Francis Starwick, called him "you dirty little fairy," and the two men fought. The episode is possible but unlikely; even Wolfe's rhetoric in this passage is false — as it generally was when he tried to invent scenes and characters. Shortly after their quarrel Raisbeck wrote to ask if a renewal of their friendship was possible. "It is not only possible, I believe, but desirable," Wolfe replied, stipulating that he was speaking only of "friendship between us,— not communal friendship" with the "two ladies in Paris."

letter, written no doubt on "the impulse of a petulant and brutal vanity," exhibited "a petulance of spirit, a failure to understand and accept, and a corresponding desire to wound." Years later, looking back over the drafts of his letters to Helen, he felt "almost choked with shame."

Even if Wolfe had wanted to accompany the others on their trip, he did not have enough money. By the time they left he had used up the funds he came over with, ninety dollars that he had borrowed from Helen, and most of the one hundred twenty-five dollars he had cabled his mother to send him; he had only eight hundred francs (about forty dollars) left. To make his situation worse, Fred wrote that he ought to come home. He had already had three months of vacation, his brother wrote; if he was serious about getting his plays produced, surely he ought to be in New York.

Greatly offended at this reasonable advice from his "own blood brother, whose terrible selfish soul went wrapped in flattery for years," Tom pleaded with his mother for five hundred dollars more, so that he could spend the next five or six months in the south of France and in Italy. *"Please, if you are able, stand by me a little longer."*

When another check from Julia arrived, he left Paris and went to the château country, wandering about "alone, almost without plan" — indeed, as he admitted, "in an insane fashion." At Orléans he was taken under the wing of a half-crazed countess, who told interminable stories of touring the United States in behalf of the Allied war effort and astonished Wolfe by drinking horse blood for her anemia. Later he visited "the magnificent chateau of a real marquise" at Tours. There he finally decided that it was time to settle down and write, for his mind was swarming with "various projects, cloudy, vague, and grandiose in their conception, of plays, books, stories, essays."

First he worked over the notes he had made during his ocean voyage, turning them into a series of sketches that he called "Passage to England." Attempting to characterize his fellow-travelers, he began inventing scenes in which they appeared and conversations that they might have had. For the first time he encountered a problem that plagued him for the rest of his life: the possibility that his semifictional writing could be an invasion of privacy or even an outright libel. Clumsily, he sought to avoid the issue by attaching a prologue with "a rather fantastic plot-work." In it he claimed that his sketches represented a dream or a delusion, since the narrator had missed the sailing of his ship and had remained in New York. Consequently "Passage to England" had the subtitle, "Log of a Voyage That Was Never Made."

After that, he turned to sketches about his adventures in England and in France. With the overoptimism that always characterized his estimates, he calculated that he wrote "40,000 or 50,000 words — a short novel." Some of these short pieces were clearly autobiographical, like his account of the very tall young man aboard the ship, "a man for whom most of the contrivances of the earth are just uncomfortably a little too small; the beds a trifle too short, the tables a bit too low, and food and the drink a mite too scanty."

In many of these sketches, the work of a very homesick young man, Wolfe let his mind drift back to his childhood and to people he had known in Asheville: "a Swiss jeweller who did his work for years in a tombstone shop [which belonged to W. O. Wolfe] and read the World's Almanac; a negro woman named Molly Earle who was a cook through the week, and who delivered two hour sermons in the public square, on Sunday afternoons, . . . in a voice which rose to a steady scream . . . ; an undertaker who wept with joy when he revealed the body of my brother [Ben], declaring, with the pride of an artist, that 'it was the finest job he had ever done.' "

"Tired of writing for the four winds" and feeling a desperate need for an audience, Wolfe hoped that George McCoy, his college friend who was now editor of the *Asheville Citizen,* would publish "Passage to England." But he realized that some Asheville residents might recognize themselves in his pages and that others might be offended by the negative tone of his remarks about his home town. Announcing that it would have been "too petty, too dishonest," to worry about these matters while writing and claiming that his criticisms were presented in sadness of spirit, he asked Mrs. Roberts to censor the whole manuscript before it was published. "Boy, nothing can stop you," she replied enthusiastically. "You have done *something* both from standpoint of subject-matter and style that I haven't seen done anywhere." But she went on to say that she did not think the *Asheville Citizen* could publish it. "You say . . . it is all done in sadness of heart," she continued, "but . . . your big foot, however much of sadness may be controlling your leg muscles, comes down with squashing force upon the godlets of our daily lives and Sabbath meditations." In the end, only a small, innocuous segment of his manuscript, called "London Tower," appeared in the Asheville paper.

Failure to publish "Passage to England" and Wolfe's other 1925 sketches resulted in no great loss to American literature, for most of the pieces were poorly conceived and imperfectly executed. They did, however, show that Wolfe was thinking seriously about the best way to present his ideas and that he was consciously striving to attain a distinctive literary voice. "Manifestly," he noted, "the whole course and purport of my intent is to fashion in English prose a personal and distinctive style." Of the many models he could follow he was especially fond of Thomas De Quincey, whose ornate style combined humor with splendid imagery; he had two copies of *Confessions of an English Opium-Eater* in his own library. De Quincey's balanced sentences and rich, heavy vocabulary were especially appealing to Wolfe, who, from the days when his father had declaimed poetry, was as conscious of the sound as of the meaning of words.

Wolfe's "Passage to England" and his other 1925 sketches showed that he was approaching — though he certainly had not yet achieved — the sonorous, allusive style that would make *Look Homeward, Angel* and *Of Time and the River* so distinctive. For instance, the concluding segment of "Passage to England," though far from skillful, revealed that Wolfe was beginning to use the overheated adjectives, the balanced antitheses, the rhythmical prose of the novels:

> The terrific compression of life upon that ship was sickening. Nowhere in the world, perhaps, can the scheme of things be so terribly and honestly presented. Here, the terrible fabric, the tragic interweft of human existence, is most closely woven; here it is quite possible to show what the conservative will deny to the larger scheme — that no pebble falls into the ocean but leaves its ripple at the earth's farthest shore; that no soft fat man from Cleveland [one of the passengers] may have his bath of salt twice daily, but by the tortured labor of a lean hard man from the seven ends of the earth; that no lady lies in silks but the tragic balance must be held where another lies in rags.

Running out of money, Wolfe went back to Paris to pick up another check his mother had sent him. Awaiting him there also was a letter from Professor Watt, who offered him another appointment, this time at a salary of two thousand dollars, in the department of English at Washington Square College. "I should like to have you working with us on the regular staff here," Watt assured him. "Please do come back, Wolfe. . . . We miss your diminutive form in the faculty room."

Pleased by this evidence of Watt's confidence, Wolfe nevertheless delayed accepting the appointment in the vague hope that somehow there was a way to escape "the deep damnation of Freshman composition." While waiting for the miracle, he headed for the south of France, where he stayed for a few days at St. Raphael with friends from the University of North Carolina. Then he pushed on to Genoa, Milan, and Venice. By midsummer he was back in Paris, where he decided, since no angel had stepped forward to befriend him, that he had to accept the New York University appointment. Hoping to see just as much as he could before returning to America, he went again to London and briefly visited the Lake Country, where the great Romantic poets had done their finest work. By August his time and his money ran out, and he booked third-class passage to New York on the *Olympic*.

VIII

On the last night of the voyage, as the great liner rocked in the waters outside New York harbor, an acquaintance persuaded Wolfe to join him in sneaking across the barriers to visit some friends he had made among the cabin-class passengers. Ordering a drink in the verandah-like café that afforded a clear view of the wake of the ship, they were joined first by Mina Kirstein (later Mrs. Curtiss), a handsome, extraordinarily tall young woman, who taught English at Smith College. In her fruity voice, she announced that her friend would join them in a minute. Soon a small, vivacious woman appeared and was introduced as Aline Bernstein. In the initial pleasantries Wolfe got an impression of Mrs. Bernstein as "a matronly figure of middle age, a creature with a warm and jolly little face, a wholesome and indomitable energy for every day, a shrewd, able and immensely talented creature of action, able to hold her own in a man's world."

It was the last time he ever had such an objective view of her, for Aline immediately captivated him. She was bright, she was sophisticated, and she was amusing. She was also stunningly attractive. "I was in the real flower of my physical self," she said later; "I was beautiful. Please do not take it ill that I say this, it is not a boast, only a corroborative detail." Her pansy-shaped face and her remarkably fresh, ruddy complexion were enchanting. Wolfe came to think that she was "the most beautiful woman that ever lived"; in his fiction he described her counterpart, Esther Jack, as a "creature of incomparable loveliness to whom all other women in the world must be compared."

As the evening wore on, Wolfe learned something of the history of this extraordinary woman. Before meeting her he had been told that she was connected with the theater, but he did not know that her father, Joseph Frankau, was a prominent actor or that her childhood had been spent in a theatrical boardinghouse on West 44th Street, in the heart of the theater district. He also learned that she was an important figure on the Neighborhood Playhouse and that she designed sets and costumes for many of their productions. Not until the night was nearly over did she tell him that she had carried a copy of "Welcome To Our City" on her trip to Europe, in an effort — vain, as it proved — to convince Alice Lewisohn that the Neighborhood Playhouse ought to produce it.

By that time they had both been drinking too much, and Wolfe's deep ambivalences toward the theater began to emerge. It was at once the door to fame and success and, because it had so consistently rejected his plays, a source of corruption and evil. In Aline Bernstein the good and the evil of the theater world seemed to be joined. Arguing, they stumbled down to her cabin, ostensibly to find some brandy, since all the bars on the ship were now closed. Before long, as the *Olympic* lay anchored off Staten Island, he took her in his arms, she muttered something about having a compassionate nature that "did not want to see him suffer," and they made love.

They did not see each other the next day when they disembarked, and Wolfe promptly took a train to Asheville. He found the real estate boom was at its peak. Talking about Bigger and Greater Asheville, everybody seemed to be getting rich, and Julia and Fred, who had invested money in property in Asheville and in

Florida, were "all hypnotized" by the prospect of seeing their land skyrocket in value. Obsessed by success, acquaintances in Asheville were willing to extend their "generous falsehoods, which are so full of hope and good will for all things," to Wolfe, and they spoke of him as holding the "chair of English" at New York University. Much of the time he was simply amused, but one night he came down to the office of the *Asheville Citizen,* where J. M. Roberts, Jr., the son of his former teachers, now worked, and read selections from "Passage to England" that satirized the community. When they emerged just before dawn into the town square, Wolfe turned to young Roberts with a sudden realization: "If it's published, I'll never be able to come home again."

After a few weeks at home, he had to return to New York and to his teaching duties. Settling in again at the Hotel Albert, he taught three classes in freshman English and an introductory course in literature for schoolteachers. Once again he was caught up in his job. "My work thus far has given me no time for writing, or for anything else," he wrote his mother in October. "At the present . . . it seems that I shall have little time for writing this year." He did not like teaching, but he worked very hard at his job. So effective was he in the classroom that Professor Watt recommended him as a suitable instructor for the advanced course on modern drama.

Busy as he was, Wolfe had time to think about his brief encounter with Aline Bernstein, and he was disappointed that she made no attempt to get in touch with him. After brooding for several days he composed a letter — "one of those pompous, foolish, vainglorious letters that young men write," he later called it — expressing a desire to see her again but defensively announcing that he would not be disappointed if she did not wish to do so. Wolfe's letter has been lost, but in *The Web and the Rock* his hero, George Webber, wrote a similar missive to Esther Jack, announcing: "In a life which for the most part has been lived alone, I have learned to expect or ask for nothing. . . . Whatever else the world may say of me, I have never truckled to the mob, nor for a moment bent the pregnant hinges of the knee . . . to flatter the vanity of the individual." After carrying the letter around in his pocket for days, unable to decide whether to mail it, Wolfe finally thrust it into a mailbox — and was instantly consumed with regret that he had done so.

The next morning Aline called him at the hotel and asked him to be her guest at the Neighborhood Playhouse production of the *Grand Street Follies,* for which she had designed the sets and costumes. Meeting her in her own environment for the first time, Wolfe was impressed by the deference that the others in the theater showed her. During an intermission she took him backstage, where Wolfe, who thought that he knew everything about playwriting but was totally ignorant about design, lighting, and sets, marveled that she was able so quickly to bring order out of the chaos of ropes and flats and stage properties. After the show was over, he went with her to her little workroom, where she showed him her "swift, sketchy, and yet beautiful costume drawings." Wolfe, who sought throughout his life to capture fullness and completeness, was amazed that Aline was able to suggest an entire character by "the jaunty sketching of a jacket, an elbowed sleeve, or perhaps just the line and pleating of the skirt." Deeply impressed, he raised no objection when they parted almost formally at the end of the evening, shaking hands.

At their next meeting, on October 3, Wolfe's twenty-fifth birthday, Aline got to know more about him. Indeed, that day was a kind of preview of their turbulent relationship over many years. He was late for their noon appointment on the steps of the New York Public Library, as he was always to be late for all of their meetings. He took her to an Italian speakeasy on West 46th Street where he knew the proprietor. In Wolfe's fictional re-creation of this meeting, in *The Web and the Rock,* George Webber, warmed by the good food and the bootleg drink, poured out to Esther Jack the story of his life, telling her "every secret hope, every insatiate desire, every cherished and unspoken aspiration, every unuttered feeling, thought, or conviction." By the end of the afternoon he was very drunk, but she managed to get him into a taxi. In the middle of rush-hour traffic on Broadway, it dawned on him that she was going to leave him at his hotel, and he furiously charged her with deserting and betraying him. Shouting to the driver to stop, he lurched out of the cab, ignored Esther's entreaties to come back, slammed the door in her face, and disappeared in the crowd.

Ashamed of his behavior, Wolfe was sure that he would never see this adorable, fascinating woman again, but the next morning she telephoned him. That evening she became his mistress. At first they met two or three times a week, then every day. Often he came by after the curtain fell at the Neighborhood Playhouse and they went out for a late supper, frequently at a Childs restaurant on Madison Avenue. They could not go to his cramped room in the Hotel Albert, where the permanent residents kept a close eye on his comings and goings, and she did not think it proper to make love to him in her brownstone on West 77th Street, where her husband, children, and sister lived. All in all, the first few months of their affair were uncomfortable.

In December Aline began looking for a place of their own. She had a perfect excuse for wanting a studio, because skyscrapers were being built around her house on the West Side that shut out the light so necessary for her work as an artist and draftsman. Before Christmas she found the ideal place: the loft of an old brick house at 13 East 8th Street.

It did not initially look promising. The building had been badly neglected. The bottom floor was occupied by a dingy tailor shop, and the two main floors, which had obviously been used as work-rooms, were empty and dilapidated, with rubbish covering the floor and coils of electrical wiring hanging from the ceiling. But at the top there was an enormous studio or loft that ran the entire length of the house. When Aline located it, it was filthy. But huge skylights radiantly illuminated it, and it was so big that even a man of Wolfe's height could march back and forth in it — taking care, however, to duck a little at the front and rear, where the roof sloped. The studio had electricity, running water but no bath or shower, and heat until about five o'clock, when the furnace was shut off.

Aline had the place cleaned up, and in January they moved in. For the sake of propriety and cleanliness Wolfe continued to keep a room at the Hotel Albert, but increasingly he spent most of his time in the studio. He claimed a couch at one end of the room, which became almost immediately surrounded by books, manu-scripts, student papers, dirty coffee cups, cigarette ashes, and piles of his unwashed clothing. Aline set up her drafting desk at the other end, always neatly arranged and spotless, and she came to the studio most afternoons, returning at night to her house. The rent was only thirty-five dollars a month, and Wolfe insisted on paying half of it.

Sharing the studio was a signal that their affair was serious. It had begun casually enough, and their initial encounter could have been just another shipboard romance. After all, Aline was nearly eighteen years his senior. She was comfortably married to a stockbroker, Theodore Bernstein, who was wealthy and devoted if not passionate, and she had two teenage children, Teddy and Edla. She had already established herself as one of the leading scenic designers in the United States. Wolfe, on the other hand, was young and poor, a dramatist whose plays nobody would produce, a writer whom nobody wanted to publish.

When they first began seeing each other in New York, Wolfe's initial feeling was one of surprise at his good fortune, accompanied by a sense of pride. "I was a young fellow who had got an elegant and fashionable woman for a mistress," he said later, "and I was pleased about it." With satisfaction he told his mother that "a very beautiful and wealthy lady, who . . . designs scenery and costumes for the best theaters," had taken an interest in him and was helping him financially. Julia's pious hope that his "financial friend" did have "that beautiful character you speak of" did not upset him very much.

Presently Wolfe discovered, "without knowing how, when, or why," that he was desperately in love with Aline. She proved to be everything that he had ever wanted in a woman. She was a great listener. For years he had needed someone to listen to his endless anecdotes, his re-creation of everything that he had thought and done during the previous twenty-four hours, and his stories, almost as detailed as those of his mother, about his relatives and acquaintances in Asheville, and Aline was always interested, sympathetic, and ready to be amused. But she also was a great talker. Remembering the advice of her beautiful but promiscuous aunt Nana that "you could say the most remarkable things, side by side in a recumbent position, things you could never dream of saying standing up or facing each other in chairs," she lay on the bed beside Wolfe and told him about her life: about her grandfather Frankau, a German Jew who had settled in Hartford, Connecticut; about her father, who had known all the great actors in the American theater; about her aunt's boardinghouse in the theatrical district; and about the early death of her parents, which left her and her sister, Ethel, at the mercy of penurious relatives.

Aline cooked as well as she talked. She took an artist's pride in creating a beef ragout, in sauce of Rembrandt brown, with little onions, carrots, and tomatoes. She specially prided herself on her salads, which she designed with an eye to color, "running the whole gamut of greens, from the green-yellow-white of endive, through the lettuces, to the sharp dark tone of water cress, with plenty of chopped hard-boiled egg in the dressing." Wolfe had never tasted such wonderful food. "There is," he concluded, "no spectacle on earth more appealing than that of a beautiful woman in the act of cooking dinner for someone she loves."

Aline was also a superb lover. She taught him that sex could be something more than a physical release or a commodity to be sold and bought. With her he was for the first time able to overcome his numbing inhibitions, which had stricken him when he touched Helen Harding. For Aline enjoyed sex. In a fragmentary passage Wolfe recaptured one intimate moment, when "with proud crowing love" he asked fondly, "Can you feel that?" and she responded, panting, "God, can I feel it! That pole, that tree."

No doubt it was easier for Wolfe to have sex with Aline than it had been with other women, because she was a Jew, one whom he thought of as belonging to a different and often sinister race, but a race noted for its sensuality and opulence. An added attraction, surprisingly enough, was her age, for Aline, though she appeared ever young, was old enough to be his mother, able to shower on him the maternal affection that Julia had never been able to express. In Wolfe's draft of *The Web and the Rock,* he described the lovemaking of George Webber and Esther Jack, which could only have been based on his experience with Aline. Holding Esther's breasts, George asked her, "Am I your child?" "Yes," she answered breathlessly, "yes." "Are these my breasts?" "Yes," she replied, "yes." "Have you any milk there for me?" When she said that she had none, he snorted, "Hah, . . . if you really loved me, you would have milk for me."

At the same time Aline appealed to him because she was so small — eighteen inches shorter than he was — so diminutive, with her tiny feet and hands. Because she was slowly growing deaf, she often cupped one of her delicate hands behind her ear, and the gesture aroused in Wolfe an overmastering wave of tenderness. At such times he wanted "to rush over to her and bite her, to kiss her a million times, to hug her hard and breathless till she cried out, to fondle, caress, and love her as one might some dearly beloved child." "She had been his mistress and his mother," he concluded, "and now she had become his child."

Of course Wolfe's view of Aline — like any lover's image of his beloved — was at best a partial one, for there was much about her that he did not know and could not understand. He was never able to puzzle out what she meant when she said, that first night on shipboard, "I want to die — I hope that I die in a year or two. . . . It seems that I've come to the end of everything. . . . There's nothing more that I can do." It took years for him to understand that, along with generosity and openness, Aline had what Mina Curtiss called "the eat-your-cake-and-have-it-too side of her character." If she was passionately in love with Wolfe, she also deeply loved her stolid, dependable husband and was fiercely devoted to her children. And, though she enjoyed her hours in the studio, she had no intention of choosing it in preference to her beautiful house, her well-trained servants, and her elegant parties where she welcomed luminaries like Eugene O'Neill, Alexander Woollcott, Thomas Beer, and Carl Van Vechten.

But Wolfe knew little of this during the initial months of their affair, and what he did know did not trouble him. Life with Aline afforded him, as he said, "the happiest hours I had ever known." They could hardly bear to be separated from each other, and when they were apart their letters expressed their love. "That way I care for you is like a cube root," Aline wrote him. "It just multiplies in every direction." "My dear," he responded, "believe me — the thought that I am loved by such a person as you are gives me the most enormous pleasure of my life."

Basking in the assurance of Aline's love, Wolfe began to take a dim view of his family. When he went home at Christmas, he found Asheville a scene of "death, doom, desolation, sickness, disease, and despair." "My family," he reported to Aline, "is showing its customary and magnificent Russian genius for futility and tragedy." Over the next few months he grew increasingly bitter because he was obliged to support himself by teaching while his mother now owned Florida real estate apparently worth a fortune. Ignoring the fact that Julia had financed his three years at Harvard and had paid for most of his year abroad, he complained that his family had always mistreated him. He was, he told Mrs. Roberts, the son who had "called for wine, and was given the sponge, and whose bread as a child was soaked in his grief."

Wolfe's affair with Aline did little to promote his career as a dramatist. Initially he thought that her numerous connections in the theater would help him, and indeed there was a flurry of interest in his plays shortly after he returned from Europe. In October Kenneth McGowan, of the Provincetown Theater, asked to see both "Welcome To Our City" and "Mannerhouse." Courtenay Lemon of the Theatre Guild scolded Wolfe: "Why haven't you been in to see me, and brought your new play, faithless one?" In January he submitted "Mannerhouse" to the Neighborhood Playhouse, informing Miss Lewisohn, who was a close friend of Aline's, that it had "the focal power of one idea, developed with enormous concentration." "Read it carefully, Miss Lewisohn," he enjoined. "Certainly men must have felt like this, but I have never seen it expressed."

Nothing came from any of these submissions. All the producers agreed with what Aline privately thought: that Wolfe's "plays were poor, they have no quality at all as plays, they have not a thing to do with the theatre." People who knew Wolfe also concurred in her judgment that he was temperamentally "unfitted for an association with theatrical people." "No one who has not been in the theatre knows . . . the constant working together and the constant criticism that is necessary to make a theatrical production," she explained. "He simply could not take criticism from any one."

In time Wolfe himself came to accept that verdict. Enviously he watched as plays by Philip Barry and Henry Carlton, classmates in the 47 Workshop, were produced on Broadway, and he grew so depressed when Paul Green, who had been a classmate at the University of North Carolina, won a Pulitzer Prize for *In Abraham's Bosom* that he went on a three-day drunk. Contrasting his failure with their successes, he concluded that his aspiration to become a playwright "was not only wrong — it was so fantastically wrong as anything could be." "Whatever other talents I have for playwriting — and I think I had some," he observed, "the specific requirements of the theatre for condensation, limited characterization, and selected focus were really not specially for me."

Even before Wolfe's plays went on their final round of rejection, he had begun to turn to prose narrative as a way to achieve "a more full, expansive, and abundant expression of the great theatre of life than the stage itself could physically compass." His "Passage to England" and his other 1925 sketches had been tentative efforts in that direction. During the winter of 1925–1926 he wrote a good many more random, disconnected pieces that he did not show to anyone but Aline, and as they talked together about their lives, he began to jot down recollections of his childhood and of Asheville.

As summer approached, Aline found that she needed to go back to Europe for the Neighborhood Playhouse and, seeing that teaching exhausted Wolfe, asked him to come too. Though she had to return to America in the fall, she offered to finance him for six months abroad, so that he could have the time to work without interruption on a book about his childhood.

V

I Must Spin Out My Entrails

"I AM WRITING A BOOK — a novel — trying, you see, to find a breach in the wall somewhere," Wolfe began a letter to a friend in the summer of 1926. Then, wryly remembering his failures as a playwright and a journalist, he added: "Epic Poetry and the essay still remain." For the next two years Wolfe's novel, which was eventually published in 1929 as *Look Homeward, Angel*, absorbed most of his time and all of his creative energy.

He began the novel during the happiest months of his life. In June he and Aline, discreetly sailing on separate ships, left New York, and they met by prearrangement in Paris. For the first time Wolfe had his mistress to himself for more than a day. Now she did not have to leave him to rejoin her family, or to meet with the directors of the Neighborhood Playhouse, or to oversee the sets for a new production. In Paris she was all his, and his passion for her, his delight in her body, almost frightened her. After a week they moved on to Chartres, where they continued lovemaking as well as sightseeing. Aline remembered the time as "Heaven."

Before they left for England Wolfe bought a notebook, like the ones French children used for schoolwork, and began jotting down what he called the "outline" of the book he planned to write. It was not truly an outline but a series of elliptically expressed thoughts and abbreviated references to material he expected to include. The first page that has been preserved began:

Over the fence, near Britt's is a cow. I immitate its sound. "Moo"
First articulate speech. Father delighted, tells story over and over
getting me to repeat the sound all afternoon for guests and neighbors. The smell, the sound, the day I remember accurately; it was
Sunday (the hot smell of dock weed in the rank rich South)
    Spring 1902 — They kept me in a great wicker laundry basket —
I remember climbing to the edge and seeing vast squares of carpet
below me. . . .

In England Wolfe kept adding to his outline, first during their
week in London, where Aline briefly introduced him to James
Joyce, and then in Bath. After visiting the cathedrals in Lincoln
and York, they turned west toward the Lake Country, where so
much of the great English Romantic poetry had been written.
Along the way, at Ilkley, Aline made a most practical contribution
to Wolfe's career as a writer: she bought him three sturdy ledgers,
bound in red cloth. Years later he naively called this purchase "one
of the most important events in my life as a writer." Writing in
these big ledgers "gave me joy and hope," he observed with a note
of wonderment; "I could no longer lose the pages, because they
were bound together."
    They spent two weeks at Ambleside, on Lake Windermere,
where Aline had rented a cottage. To avoid shocking the very
respectable housekeeper, they had separate but adjoining bedrooms. Anyway, Wolfe was in the habit of staying up most of the
night writing, while Aline was an early riser. In the morning,
while he slept late, she worked on her stage designs and did
watercolors. They took long walks in the afternoons and after
dinner they often went to the local pub, where Wolfe, towering
above the locals, tried his hand at darts. Always he was writing
and writing, adding thousands of words to his outline and gaining
more and more confidence as he worked. One afternoon he told
his mistress that people would remember her long after she was
dead because she would be "entombed in his writing."
    They were interrupted only once, when Theresa Helburn and
her husband drove up unexpectedly in a long blue Rolls-Royce to
see how Aline was getting along. Knowing that Wolfe bitterly
resented successful theater people, Aline feared their visit would
trigger one of his tirades or send him into deep, drunken depression. But he was in a good mood. Much impressed by the expensive car, he volunteered to ride in the front with the chauffeur, so

that he could stretch his long legs, and the other three poured into the back seat. Together they drove through the Lake District, stopping for tea at Dove Cottage, where Wordsworth had lived. They so enjoyed the crumpets and the cake and the conversation that they left without ever entering the cottage. For Aline it was a blissfully happy day, and Wolfe seemed to enjoy it too. But that evening, after Miss Helburn and her husband left, she found Wolfe lying across his bed, sobbing, "You love these people more than you love me."

Wolfe's unhappiness was transient, but it suggested the mounting tensions as the time drew near for Aline's return to America, to her family, and to her stage designing. Desperate at the thought of losing her forever, Wolfe urged her to divorce her husband and marry him. Perhaps his proposal was a serious one: he had met the one great love of his life and he wanted to keep her. But he also knew that he could freely make the offer because it was certain to be rejected. Aline would never publicly humiliate her husband, and she was deeply loyal to her children. Besides, Wolfe could not support himself, much less a wife, and Aline's earnings from the theater, which were enough to subsidize a struggling young writer, would not house, feed, and clothe them both.

Aline's rejection of Wolfe's proposal subtly changed the quality of their relationship. In the future he did not have to think of himself as an aspiring but unpublished young writer dependent upon the encouragement and money provided by a benevolent patroness. Instead, he could picture himself as the young genius who had offered his self-sacrificing love to a woman who, as he wrote later, "is securely married, has grown children, and enjoys a position of great wealth and security which she has absolutely no intention of deserting for this great love."

Their last days together in Great Britain were unhappy, and they quarreled frequently. After a trip to Glasgow, they returned to London, so that Aline could make final arrangements for sailing. When her train left for Southampton, she looked back and saw him on the station platform, looking pale, miserable, and deserted.

I

After Aline left, Wolfe searched for comfortable, inexpensive quarters in London where he could write. On Wellington Square,

in the Chelsea district, not far from where Thomas Carlyle and
Henry James had lived, he found an adequate apartment, consisting of a bedroom and a large sitting room, equipped with a deep
padded chair for reading, a table for writing and eating, book-
shelves already stocked with books, and a cupboard for tea things.

Promptly he fell into a regular routine. At 8:30 every morning
the proprietor, a former butler, came in with a cup of tea and a
newspaper. Later his "huge, fat, one-eyed wife" served a substantial breakfast. Then, while the rooms were aired, Wolfe walked
along the Thames, enjoying the view that Whistler had so often
painted. When he came back he worked till noon, and then he
went to the American Express office for his mail and had lunch
in Piccadilly or Soho. During the afternoons he took "enormous promenades through the East End of London," and once he
walked all the way to Hampstead Heath. Returning to his digs
to bathe and dress, he went out to dinner, afterwards often
walking several more miles. When he got home he wrote until
about midnight.

Leading such a quiet life, he made rapid progress on his outline,
and soon he had a second notebook filled with jottings. As he
wrote, his entries became fuller and he included, along with notes
of names, places, and key words that reminded him of episodes in
his life, more and more general reflections:

> The place of the artist: no one owes him anything for writing —
> He may regret the stupidity or ignorance that keeps his work un-
> known, but he must accept it as one of the possible conditions
> under which he must work — No one asked him to write — let
> him expect nothing. . . .

By early September he had finishing his outline, and he claimed,
with characteristic exaggeration, that it was "the length almost of
a novel." It covered the events of his life from his birth through his
years in Cambridge.

Now he had to transform these stream-of-consciousness jottings into a novel. It was not a task for which he was prepared. For
all his wide reading, he had given little attention to the craft of
fiction; indeed, he was acquainted with surprisingly few modern
novels. He had read a good deal of H. G. Wells, something of
Arnold Bennett and Joseph Conrad, and one novel of John
Galsworthy. He did not know the novels of E. M. Forster or

Virginia Woolf. D. H. Lawrence, the author whose career was in some ways closest to Wolfe's own, was still only a name to him. While he and Raisbeck had sniggered in Cambridge over *Ulysses*, he was not yet much influenced by Joyce.

With the American novel he was even less familiar. By his own account he had read nothing of Herman Melville; there is nothing to suggest that he had studied William Dean Howells or Mark Twain; and he confessed that he never could finish a novel of Henry James. Theodore Dreiser he respected as a "gigantically thorough realist," and he pigeonholed Willa Cather as a "woman writer." He was not yet acquainted with the work of contemporaries like F. Scott Fitzgerald, Ernest Hemingway, John Dos Passos, and William Faulkner. He had read Sinclair Lewis's satirical accounts of middle-class Americans, and he admired Sherwood Anderson's poetical prose.

Because he had read so little modern fiction, Wolfe was unaware of the controversy that was raging among critics and authors over the nature and technique of the novel. Much influenced by Percy Lubbock's *The Craft of Fiction* (1921), which codified the shrewd insights Henry James had offered, writers began to turn away from the sprawling, discursive, and often moralistic fiction of the nineteenth century in favor of objective, realistic, carefully planned novels. James and Flaubert, not Dickens or Trollope, became the models for aspiring novelists. But when Wolfe began to write fiction, he did not even know that this debate was going on. Less than any other of his generation was he affected by the anxiety of influence — the writer's need to deal, whether through imitation, rejection, or modification, with the patterns and themes of his predecessors. Instead, Wolfe simply planned to write as he pleased. So far as he had any models for his book they were the eighteenth-century novels that he loved, like Henry Fielding's *Tom Jones* and Laurence Sterne's *Tristram Shandy*. He favored the leisurely, ruminative style of Robert Burton's *The Anatomy of Melancholy*, one of his favorite books, and the fevered rhetoric of Thomas De Quincey's *Confessions of an English Opium-Eater*.

At the outset he had no clear idea of the form of his novel. For a time he toyed with imitating Thackeray's *Vanity Fair*, in which the narrator takes puppets out of a box and makes them characters. Wolfe thought of making Aline, as "Mrs. Glickstein," the "puppet woman" in his "fictional biography." After he abandoned that idea and returned to the more conventional technique of having an omniscient narrator recount the story, he planned a novel in six parts, or books. Soon he realized that was too long, and he telescoped his six books into five, and then into four. Even so he predicted that his novel would be "Dickensian or Meredithian in length."

Whatever the structure, he wanted his novel to "swarm with life, be peopled by a city." Free from the constraints against which he had struggled as a playwright, he would write about things that could not effectively be presented on a stage: "Sounds (a train far off in Southern Hills, a horse at night on a deserted street; particularly cobbles); Odors; Tastes (Food; drink); Sights (Places, Pictures); Touch; Books and Music and Women (Smell — Of Horses and of Leather on a Summers day, and of Melons, bedded in straw in a farmer's wagon — particularly watermelons)." His book would present "a huge rich pageant," and now that he was no longer limited by the proprieties of the theater, it would be "in places terrible, brutal, Rabelaisian, bawdy."

From the beginning he knew that his novel would be autobiographical. His book, he announced early, would be "immensely flavored with me," it would be "about me" — but his personal experiences would be "transmuted and recreated in writing." It was not just "romantic Egotism," which he freely admitted, that caused Wolfe to write about himself. While he was trying to become a playwright he found that he had little talent for devising plots or inventing characters, but he could very effectively recreate people he had known and events that had touched his own life — as he had done in the incomplete Groody or Broody plays about his family. He was not alone in turning to autobiographical fiction. A number of his contemporaries — notably D. H. Lawrence and Ernest Hemingway — did so too. At a time when basic beliefs in Western society seemed to be disintegrating, creative spirits like these felt forced back upon their individual experiences — especially those of childhood — in the hope of discovering some new and sustaining myth.

The first writing Wolfe did after completing his outline was not promising. He started with recollections of his years in Cambridge and Boston. Ultimately he filled five ledgers with sketches as disjointed and as abstract as his "Passage to England" pieces had been. Alongside a straightforward description of the Farnsworth

Room in Widener Library he wrote a reverie on the state of his teeth, a fantasy on his imaginary career as a prizefighter, and a comparison of Jesus and Socrates. Later he noted on the cover of one of these ledgers that he could use little of the contents in a book because there was too much "moralizing." Only a small part of this material found a place in his first novel, but some passages, greatly reworked, appeared in his second, *Of Time and the River.*

Not until the end of October, when he turned to the first section of his novel, did he begin to write organized, consecutive chapters. No longer was he simply filling blank pages with words; he was excavating his own past. When writing of his infancy and childhood he discovered a theme, or pattern, in his life. His story would be "the story of a powerful creative element trying to worm its way toward an essential isolation; a creative solitude." This secret life had to protect itself first from the "savage glare of an unbalanced, nervous brawling family," later from school, society, and "all the barbarous invasions of the world." At this time he thought of calling his novel "The Building of a Wall." The wall, Wolfe understood, was an ambivalent symbol: it kept out hostile forces, but it could also become a prison. "May not every motion toward freedom be really an isolation behind a wall?" he asked.

To illustrate this dual process he planned to tell the story of a character who closely resembled himself, to whom he gave the name "Eugene," meaning "well born" or "of noble race" — the same name he had bestowed on the Coleridge-Wolfe figure in his unfinished play about Professor Weldon and on the ironically romantic hero of "Mannerhouse." He let his father, mother, sisters, and brothers keep their own Christian names. The family name he changed to "Gant," perhaps because it conveyed an impression of lean strength. His mother's family name was altered from Westall to "Pentland" — an obvious variant of Penland, the family name of his maternal grandmother.

His novel was intended to expose Asheville — which he continued to call "Altamont," as he had done in "Welcome To Our City" — in much the same way that Sinclair Lewis in *Main Street* had caricatured Sauk Centre, Minnesota, as Gopher Prairie. He wanted to exhibit the spiritual impoverishment, the cultural barrenness, and the social snobbery of the American small town. At the same time he would attack the boom-town mentality of the 1920s by showing the gullibility of the Asheville "Boobs" — a term of H. L. Mencken's that he liked. Asheville residents, like his mother and Fred and Mabel, were so easily deceived that "the near-swindlers and the near-thieves who stay within the letter of the law" could persuade them to invest in schemes "for manufacturing gasoline from Florida grapefruit" or for "importing Bulgarian wool grown on cactus bushes."

While paying off old scores against Asheville, Wolfe also intended to get even with members of his own family. As he thought back to his childhood, he told his mother, it seemed "a dream full of pain, ugliness, misunderstanding, and terror." At first he found that it hurt to write of his mother and father, of his quarrelsome brothers and sisters, of the emotional deprivation and anguish of spirit that he had felt as a child. As he wrote, "the great fish, those scaled with evil, horrible incandescence, hoary with elvish light, have swum upwards." But in the process he drained some of the bitterness that had been building up in him for years. Even as he filled his pages with much that was sordid and unhappy, and sometimes with "monstrous evil," he felt that he had "somehow recovered innocency." "I am beginning to have the decent heart of a child," he wrote Aline. "I have written it almost with a child's heart."

In a sense writing about his infancy and childhood served Wolfe as a kind of self-administered psychoanalysis. Though he never studied psychoanalytic theory systematically, he had become acquainted with Freud's ideas at Harvard and he had heard much about analysis from colleagues at New York University. Aline taught him more. Before she met Wolfe she had begun therapy with Dr. Beatrice Hinkle, a disciple and translator of Jung. When Wolfe entered her life, he insisted that she must tell him every detail of each visit she made to Dr. Hinkle, and he became so interested that he once expressed a wish to undergo analysis himself. There is no reliable evidence that he ever did so,* but almost

---

*There is an unconfirmed report that Wolfe in 1928 sought treatment from Sigmund Freud in Vienna. Unable to pay Freud's fees, he was referred to his pupil, Dr. Helene Deutsch, but he could not afford her charges either. She in turn is supposed to have referred Wolfe to Heinz Hartmann, who was then beginning psychoanalytical practice in Vienna (Paul Roazen, *Helena Deutsch: A Psychoanalyist's Life* [Garden City, N.Y.: Anchor Press/Doubleday, 1985], p.27). This story was recounted by Dr. Deutsch many years after

certainly he did read Dr. Hinkle's *The Re-creating of the Individual* (1923), which was a nontechnical introduction to Jungian psychology.

Even a smattering of psychoanalytical theory helped Wolfe better to understand his family and, to a much smaller extent, himself. He began to see why, when his mother put an end to sexual relations with her husband, W. O. turned to his daughter Mabel for affection, lavishing praise on her, allowing no one else to control him in his drunken bouts, and taking her with him when he went to Hot Springs for treatment of his rheumatism.

Such understanding begat compassion if not forgiveness, and Wolfe concluded: "The sad family of this world is damned all together, and joined, from its birth in an unspoken and grievous kinship: in the incestuous loves of sons and mothers; in Lesbic hungers and parricidal hatreds; in the terrible shames of sons and fathers, and the uneasy shifting of their eyes; in the insatiable sexuality of infancy, in our wild hunger for ourself, the dear love of our excrement, the great obsession of Narcissus, and in the strange first love of every boy, which is for a man."

As Wolfe developed a more compassionate view of his family, he changed the direction of his novel. No longer was he going to write of a young artist who had to protect himself behind a wall. Instead, his theme would be "that all men are alone and strangers, and never come to know one another." From London, as he worked on his book, he wrote to his mother in fuller understanding: "I know that none of us is to be blamed very much for anything. Strangers we are born alone into a strange world — we live in it . . . , alone and strange, and we die without ever knowing anyone. It is therefore beyond the power of any one of us to condemn, judge, or understand. I'm simply sorry for every one."

This unavoidable human loneliness he expressed in terms of the doctrine of preexistence — the belief that the soul left the blissful, unchanging sphere of immortality to enter a human body at the time of birth. Brought up in a superstitious family, by a mother who claimed to have visions and to be able to predict the future, Wolfe did not find this notion implausible. As Aline said: "Tom believed that people knew more than they knew — that is, what

---

Wolfe's death. No surviving letters or manuscripts indicate that Wolfe had any contact or communication with Freud, Deutsch, or Hartmann.

their ancestors had known." He had first formally encountered the idea of preexistence while reading Plato at Chapel Hill, and he had studied it more closely in Professor Lowes's Harvard course on the Romantic poets. Doubtless the idea was now fresh in his mind because of his recent happy stay at Ambleside, in Wordsworth's country. He also connected it, in some loose way, with what he knew of Jungian psychology.

He found the idea of preexistence a valuable literary device to underscore the unavoidable loneliness of all humans. His hero Eugene was unique in his solitude — and he was also Everyman. Like all mortals, he had come into the world trailing clouds of glory; his birth had been but a sleep and a forgetting of his pre-existent state; and during his earliest years he, like all other infants, had fading intimations of "the great forgotten language, the lost lane-end into heaven."

In a change of plan he decided to call his novel "O Lost." Dropping the wall as a symbol, he substituted images derived from Wordsworth's *The Prelude*: "a stone, a leaf, an unfound door." Once again these recurrent symbols were ambivalent. If the "door" was in one sense the sought-after passage for return to the lost state of preexistent bliss, in another it was an opening into the common world of humanity. "I have not felt the world's imprisonment," he wrote in one fragmentary passage; "I have wanted a key that would let me enter, not a key to set me loose."

II

Wolfe remained in London for a month after Aline's departure, breaking only for an overnight trip to Brighton. Days passed and he spoke to no one but servants, bus drivers, and the mail clerks at the American Express office, whom he hated. Without Aline he felt alone and lost. He had "a strange sense of unreality" about his life. Falling asleep after long hours of writing, he often had bad dreams. When he woke, he sometimes felt he was a "phantom in a world of people: or the only person in a world of phantoms."

By the middle of September he thought that he was going stale and went to Belgium for ten days. On this trip he began the practice, which he followed for the rest of his life, of carrying a small pocket notebook for recording random ideas, overheard conversations, names and addresses, and lists of paintings that impressed him at museums. One day he went to the Waterloo battlefield in a tourist bus, with James Joyce and his family as fellow passengers. Too shy to reintroduce himself, Wolfe observed Joyce closely: "His face was highly colored, slightly concave — his mouth thin, not delicate, but extraordinarily humorous. He had a large powerful straight nose — redder than his face, somewhat pitted with scars and boils." "The idea of Joyce and me being at Waterloo at the same time and aboard a sightseeing bus," he wrote Aline, "struck me as insanely funny: I sat on the back seat making idiot noises in my throat, and crooning all the way back through the forest."

On a short visit to Antwerp he enjoyed the "great vulgar Flemish paintings" that filled the museums. "From my father, I came by Dutch blood," he explained to Aline, "and the love of opulence has always been in me." Rubens's "broad, deep bellied goddesses" aroused him erotically. "I see myself sunk . . . between the mighty legs of Demeter, the earth Goddess, being wasted and filled eternally." The paintings evoked a fantasy that would frequently appear in his writings: "Upon a field in Thrace Queen Helen lay, her amber belly spotted by the sun."

Wolfe returned to London in time to celebrate his birthday alone. At a Spanish restaurant off Regent Street, which he and Aline had frequented, he ordered a bottle of sherry with his dinner and filled a second glass for the empty chair opposite him. When the waiter asked if he was expecting someone, Wolfe replied: "Yes — a ghost." The waiter was so frightened that he did not come near him for the rest of the evening.

Obliged to give up his comfortable lodgings in Chelsea, Wolfe took an unsatisfactory room near the British Museum and, after a quarrel with his landlady, moved on to Oxford, where he hoped he would be less distracted. There he found quarters in an isolated house he called Hilltop Farm, which was a twenty-minute walk from the center of town. His life began "running with horrible precision." He wrote during the morning and had lunch in his room; in the afternoon he walked into Oxford, where he browsed through the bookstores; then he returned to Hilltop Farm, worked, and ended the day with a late visit to the local pub. From time to time he went to Merton College to visit William J. Cocke, a Rhodes scholar who was also from Asheville, and Cocke's friends marveled at Wolfe's enormous bulk and his unkempt appearance.

Cocke wrote his parents that Wolfe was "simple as a child, and as gullible, but very good hearted," and he concluded that he was "quite a genius." What Wolfe's Oxford acquaintances remembered longest, however, was his attempt, when a little drunk, to ride a bicycle — something he had never done before. He became a momentary celebrity when somehow he managed to ride it backward down the High Street — but he fell off and pulled a tendon in his leg.

During these months in England he rarely heard from his family or most of his friends in America. Occasionally his mother wrote him her customary reports of disease, death, and disaster, but her letters seemed to come from another world. Wolfe could only urge her to "be content on what you have, feed and house yourself properly," and he begged her to stop thinking about money, which, in the Wolfe family, had always been "a breeder of suspicion, of jealousy, of falsehood among brother and sister."

Aline was his only remaining link with the real world. She wrote frequently, and he replied in letter after letter. Because it took so long for mail to cross the Atlantic by steamer, their correspondence was constantly out of synchronization. If they tried to straighten things out by cabling, further confusion often resulted. When Tom cabled "Continent," did he mean that he was leaving England for the Continent or that he was — as he had promised — not seeing other women?

Aline wrote short letters, and because they were well organized, with a beginning, a middle, and an end, Wolfe thought they could not be sincere. He would start a letter, write three or four pages, lay it aside, and then add more to it from day to day, until it grew to the size of a small book. Aline worried because she received letters so irregularly, and often she had trouble deciphering his handwriting. All in all, their correspondence was something like a duet between a tuba and a piccolo.

Both needed desperately to communicate with each other, but the range of their letters was limited. Wolfe wanted most of all to talk about his book, but since Aline had not read any of it he could only give an accounting of his progress, with exaggerated estimates of the number of words he had written and unduly optimistic predictions about completing his novel. For the rest, he wrote mostly about his growing dislike of England and the English. As winter came on he found the weather "heavy, foggy, physically depressing." He had expected to discover among the students at Oxford "the flaming faces of future Shelleys and Coleridges." Instead, he found them much like American undergraduates, except that they wore a "sort of uniform — light baggy flannel trousers of grey, a black coat, a striped shirt and collar." "I fear," he told Aline, "that their ideas upon examination would also wear a uniform of baggy grey flannels." The townspeople were equally uninteresting. Even the "nice women have long teeth, or false teeth, red leathery cheeks." "I wonder," he speculated, "how they engender fire for begetting children."

In England during the long strike of coal miners that precipitated a brief general strike in 1926, Wolfe was appalled by the antilabor hysteria in British newspapers, which tried to link the strikers with Bolshevism. For the first time he realized that "desperate and panicky wealth tied to government" was so "evil and rotten a thing," and he began to believe that "this ugly, ancient palsied thing that lies and cants . . . and uses all the words [such] as liberty, patriotism, God and King" ought to be wiped out.

Aline's subject matter in her letters was even more restricted. She knew Wolfe did not want to hear about her family; consequently her husband, referred to as "Mr. Bernstein," appeared only once in their correspondence. Since Wolfe was sensitive about the fact that she was paying for his stay abroad, she had to be careful in referring to his finances or even in urging him to buy new clothes. She liked to talk about her work and her friends in the theater, but these letters reminded Wolfe of his failure as a playwright. One of them made him so sick that he had to rush out of the American Express office to vomit in the street. "Never speak to me in a letter again of a play," he enjoined, "unless to tell me that you did well in your own work."

With so many constraints, it was no wonder that their correspondence soon assumed a stylized form. "I love you completely" was his main theme — but he was certain that she was being unfaithful to him. She protested that she was so much in love that she still bled from where she had torn herself apart from him — but she felt sure he could never return to her because "You are a young man, I am a middle aged woman." His letters tended to become rhetorical tirades, of which W. O. Wolfe would have been proud. He accused Aline of "giving 3,297.726 violent hours to meetings, drawings, hammerings [in connection with her stage designs], beddings, fuckings, eatings, lyings" and only 2.374905 minutes to "the high passionate and eternal things of life." Hers were theatrical fantasies, in which she wished she could distill herself into an "elixir of Aline" so as to be near him, or they were dramatic gestures, as when she pricked her finger with a needle so that she could mark the page with a drop of her blood. Both of them, as Wolfe shrewdly observed, tended to "fall into a *manner* when we write — a manner of passionate declarations, a framework on the surface of the great wall of our hearts."

Mannered or not, Wolfe thought that his letters to Aline contained "some of the most extraordinary things that have ever been written." To some extent they served him as literary exercises; he deliberately used them to warm up for writing his novel. He was consciously rhetorical. He claimed that one letter, which exhibited wild oscillations of mood, was constructed "like a symphony which begins with bestial snarling notes, and ends in mighty soaring triumph." Sometimes he was detached enough to comment on his own style. After ending an attack on Aline with: "I will say prayers to your God to water with his tears the shrivelled seed that is your soul," he added immediately: "Yes, in spite of the s's, I'll do it."

Wolfe hoped that by anticipating the worst in his letters he might forestall defeat. Hardly had Aline left England before he began to write that his whole life had been "an unlovely failure," that he could "never create anything worthwhile." Impatiently he brushed aside her prediction that his novel would succeed and that his plays could be revised and produced. He was not the Masked Marvel, he told her; she must not think of him as a steadfast star but as "a wandering flame in hell." "I have felt the agony of defeat more than most people," he assured her. "It has been hard for me ever to see myself playing second fiddle. But in my lucid moments, which are growing surprisingly numerous, I see now that I have always been beaten, that I have never won anything."

He managed to combine this tone of patient pessimism with the growing sense of excitement he felt about his novel. It was "evolving into one of the most extraordinary things ever done." "Something takes possession of me when I write," he explained; there was a kind of "unnatural drunken ecstasy" about the process of writing a book. But, he quickly added, "no one will care to publish it, few to read it." "I am deliberately writing the book for two or three people," he told her, "first, and chiefest, for you." It was for her that he continued the "holy labor" of writing. Even as he predicted failure he kept to his task of adding pages to the manuscript. "I must," he said, "spin out my entrails again."

The same kind of preventive magic was behind his repeated accusations that Aline was having affairs with other men. He thought he might avert disaster by predicting it. Even before they left for Europe he had begun making "occasional taunts of infidelity." When Aline angrily protested that he lacked faith in her, he explained in language that the Hamlet-like hero of "Mannerhouse" might have used: by charging her with infidelity he would be "prepared for anything — either to be exalted by love, or to be sanctified by treachery: it is necessary to get nourishment from honey and bile." The fears that he had infrequently voiced when they were both in the United States he now trumpeted across the ocean. Hardly had Aline left England before he charged that she was already having so many affairs with other young men that he was now "antlered like a mountain goat." The more often she assured him that she was leading a quiet life, the more convinced he was that she was lying. Undoubtedly, he speculated, while he slept "in ominous midnight," she was being driven by "the hungry flesh of forty" to lift "her skirts, behind the door, with sow grunts, and belly burlesque."

Now that the Atlantic separated them, a new element entered into his letters. For the first time he began calling Aline "My Jew." Initially he was trying to be affectionate, if derisory, and to some extent she encouraged him. Sometimes she signed her letters "St. Rebecca," and she wished there was a Jewish nunnery she could enter, so as to prove to him her fidelity. "We would wear dark brown velvet habits, with gold and ivory rosaries," she told him, "and sleep on the best mattresses. But nuns, nevertheless." Once in describing a Theatre Guild first night, attended by "all the Jews in the world," she told Wolfe: "You could have made a lovely pogrom, you could have cut all their throats and seen all the dollars trickle out." But as the months of separation lengthened, his anti-Semitism became more open and more offensive. By December, writing while in his cups, he concluded that Aline was only "a titillative New York Jew with a constantly dilating and palpitative vagina."

The virulence of his attacks on Aline was related to her obsession with the differences in their ages, which she prophesied would
lead him to discard her. Repeatedly he tried to reassure her. "I was
born, my dear, with an autumnal heart. With me since I was
twenty ripeness has been almost all." In his youth, to be sure,
"blind and dizzy in all romantic legendry," he imagined that he
would be a handsome young minister, a captain of the Yale football team, or a "vanquisher of Dago armies" (fantasies that he was
incorporating into his novel), who would marry a millionaire's
daughter younger than himself. But since he met Aline he had
dreamed only of "Helen and Demeter moving their rich bodies in
the ripening fields." "You," he wrote her, "are timeless like Helen,
like deep-breasted Demeter, like Holveig."

When Aline answered that she wished she were the golden young
woman he had dreamed about, he exploded: "You fool, do you
ever pay attention to what I say, when I wreak myself out for you,
however clumsily, or have you grown into one vast writhing
belly, one crying wail, . . . understanding or caring nothing?"

He had promised her to remain chaste while they were separated, and during this longest period of continence since adolescence he began to have strongly sexual dreams and fantasies. He
had an improbable nightmare about D. H. Lawrence, who was
having sex with "an old woman with a lewd whore's face." He
imagined the sexual release he would experience when he joined
Aline again. Then, he wrote her, "you must let me bite your jolly
red face, breathe your pitted arm-stench, enjoy your gluttonous
and well-oiled womb. Also I shall make clotted marks of blue
upon your firm round arms, and clutch between my hands the
heavy melons of your plumskinned little-girl's butt. I shall sit in a
chair, or on the edge of a bed, with you standing between my legs
and I shall breathe your seminal odors; yes I shall catch your heavy
sagging tit between my teeth and draw desperately for rich
milk. . . . I shall tear small rich mouths in your flesh and drink
your blood slowly like wine."

After several months of chastity his fantasies became even more
aggressive. Somewhat incoherently he wrote Aline that he would
like "to feel a strong young woman's legs widened across a horses
back to thrust my knees horsily between her strong legs and to
drink the good smell of horse and woman, and to smell her strong
good-smelling Horsecock." Alternatively, "I should like to be the

Leusian Bull of Europa with my long Bull tongue I would lick her tits and with long Bull-Lunges from its aureole of shaggy hair thrust bellywards the raw gleaming Bullprick stre[t]ching and filling her throatwards."

Behind his lust and anger lay panic. His stay abroad was coming to an end, but his book was far from finished. Although he had done a great deal of work and had written, according to his estimate, one hundred thousand words, he had completed only the chapters on Eugene's life up to the age of twelve. He worried that Aline would scold him for having wasted his opportunity, and he feared that when he came back to America he would have to take a job that would interfere with his writing.

III

By mid-November Wolfe found that his writing sounded as tired as he was, and he decided to spend his final month on the Continent. He passed a few days in Paris, "the city of superficial observation," where he went to the usual tourist resorts and used up a good deal of Aline's "spendable lendable unendable commendable money." Then he visited "that grotesque gabled city," Strasbourg. Crossing the Rhine for his first visit to Germany, which he thought of as the homeland of his father's family, he grew almost wild with excitement and exultancy, rushing from one side of the railway compartment to the other to look out at the river. Obsessed by the notion that somebody or something was trying to thwart or check his return to the land of his fathers, he cried aloud: "I have fooled you, you swine."

Even before he left England he was sure that Germany was "a land where this strange life shall find a home." There, he believed, "below old dreaming towers a river runs; upon the rocks the loreli comb their hair; the winds about the castle crags at night are full of demon voices; and the gabled houses of the toyland towns are full of rich and gluttonous warmth." He found the land as enchanting as he had anticipated. Everything was wonderful — the "ugly powerful language," which he could not read easily or speak, though he convinced himself that he had "a strange power of instinctive assimilation and understanding"; the "large solid-looking museums" of Munich; and especially the Hofbrauhaus, that "enormous sea-slop of beer, power, Teutonic masculine energy and vitality," where he, along with twelve hundred Germans, drank beer.

But he could stay only for a few days. It was time to return to the United States, and now he was ready to go. "Head and heart tired" of crowded Europe, he thought longingly of "the vast uninhabitation of America and the wind moaning pines." He would always be, he assured Aline, "as American as Kansas." After six months abroad "I should like to see people I have known again; breathe the air of my own soil; return return."

But returning meant renewing his affair with Aline, and he did not know how they would live. During his months abroad he besought her "to arrange some method of life and work for us," asking: "Don't you think its only fair? Or, is having me back again, owning me, all that matters?" More than once he reminded her — however inaccurately — that in their relationship "You have given up nothing; you have had me in secret," while "I have torn my accursed heart away from its moorings, I have ladled it up to you with smoking blood; I have unspun my entrails, counted my slow pulses, distilled my brain for you."

Now that he was coming home he hoped, rather ponderously, that she would make "some attempt . . . to lift and enhance the quality of our relation." He begged her to understand that she might "wreak out a grievous wrong on much the highest spirit you have ever known simply by celling it in the dungeons of clandestine adultery." "Whatever door you and I may enter," he wrote her from Stuttgart, in a letter that he did not mail, "let us write up upon it before we close it: 'Unashamed.' Except your love, I ask you no more than that, but be advised that I will take nothing less, as you shall find."

Aboard the *Majestic*, sailing from Cherbourg to reach New York just after Christmas, he brooded over the future. As he neared America he jotted in his pocket notebook: "What rut of life with the Jew now? Is this a new beginning or a final ending?"

IV

Aline was at the dock. Her pansy-shaped face was more beautiful than ever and, since she had lost eight pounds, she looked exceptionally trim. As she spotted Wolfe among the passengers, she began to wave and to jump up and down, until it seemed that she was dancing.

During his absence she had thought a good deal about his teaching and the demands that it made on his time and his creative energies. Almost as soon as Wolfe returned, Professor Watt invited him back to New York University as an instructor, but Aline begged him not to accept. Insisting that he must keep on writing, she again offered to pay his expenses from the money she earned as a scenic designer. He hesitated but finally agreed to her plan. "No employment at university," he noted of this winter in an autobiographical sketch; "lived on money my mistress gave me."

She also found him a place to work. While he was abroad she had looked for an apartment, but the rooms were too small, the rents were too high, or the leases were too long. Finally she turned back to the loft at 13 East 8th Street, which they had shared before they went to Europe. But this time their arrangement was more open. Wolfe no longer made a pretense of keeping a hotel room, and he slept as well as worked in the loft. Aline kept her desk at one end of the huge room, and he sprawled over the rest. She paid all of the rent — thirty-five dollars a month — and gave him enough money for food and expenses.

She also tried to respond to his demand that their relationship be made, in some sense, public. On December 31, 1926, just after Tom got back from Europe, they went to the Fine Arts Ball, which was held only three blocks from their loft. After dancing awhile, they joined Aline's friends in the box reserved for the Neighborhood Playhouse. These were people that Wolfe despised, and he particularly disliked Albert Carroll, a female impersonator often featured in Playhouse productions. Already withdrawn and sullen, Wolfe took offense when a young man entered the box and embraced Aline rather intimately. "I'm sorry," he interrupted, "but you mustn't put your hands on her." When the man challenged his right to intervene, Wolfe lunged out and threw him back into a chair. A fistfight seemed imminent, but friends kept the two apart until Aline could drag Wolfe downstairs on the pretense that she wanted to dance again. Finally she managed to get him out of the building. As they walked back to 8th Street, she wept, telling Tom that his attack had been unwarranted, that the young man was "just a kid." He admitted that he had acted badly — but he was not repentant. He could not bear seeing other men pawing Aline. Crying, she left him, saying: "We must never go out among people again."

After that disastrous experiment in openness, Wolfe began to lead an almost solitary life, spending nearly all of his time in the loft and seeing no one but Aline. He usually began writing in the late afternoon, just as the workers in the pressing shop below were leaving, and after five or six o'clock he was the only occupant of the building. The heat was turned off at night, and he often had to wrap himself in blankets to keep warm while he wrote, hour after hour, in his big ledgers. "I am no better than an idiot usually by midnight," he wrote Mabel, "because I drink some dozen or eighteen cups of coffee during the day of my own brewing. It gets me simply crazy with nerves, but it keeps me alive and cursing." By four o'clock in the morning he fell exhausted into the bed, sleeping till noon, when Aline came in bringing food, news, gossip, and love.

Wolfe remained sensitive about his living arrangements and his financial dependence on Aline. He was afraid, he wrote Olin Dows, with whom he had lost touch while abroad, that there were rumors that he was living a bohemian life in Greenwich Village, committing "the worst excesses of Nero, Caligula, or the most evil devotee of Gomorrhaean lechery." Instead, he assured his straitlaced friend, "you will find me respectable, hard-working, poverty-stricken, dirty — and I'm afraid, somewhat dull." When his mother congratulated him on having rich friends who supported him, he replied that apart from the rent for the studio he accepted from Aline only "enough to feed me." Tartly he added: "I think I am more to be congratulated on being unwilling to use them or gouge them, because they have cared enough for me to help me."

"Get the book done," he had enjoined himself just before landing in New York. The solitude of the loft and his long working hours allowed him to make good progress. Now, much more consciously than ever before, he began thinking about the kind of novel he was trying to write. He started to read a great deal of fiction, mostly in the library of the Harvard Club, where he went to get his mail and to take infrequent showers, since the loft had no bath. More and more he began to pattern his book on Joyce's *Ulysses*. Perhaps his two chance encounters with Joyce had renewed his interest in that novel. Possibly he read some of the critics who were beginning to praise the high poetry of *Ulysses* and to understand its carefully wrought structure. More likely he gained a better understanding of Joyce's work from his occasional conversations with a "few friends from the old sunken world," who visited him in his garret. Mostly these were former colleagues from nearby New York University, such as Boris Gamzue, who was a night worker like Wolfe and who would from time to time persuade him to go out after midnight to a nearby Village restaurant for a bite to eat and a hot rum poncino. Wolfe also saw a good deal of William Y. Tindall, who was on his way to becoming one of the most perceptive of the early academic critics of Joyce.

Wolfe missed his own copy of *Ulysses* — still a banned and rare book — for he had stored it, along with his other books, at his Uncle Henry Westall's house in Medford. Repeated entreaties failed to persuade the old man to send the books to New York, for Westall, now married to a second wife much younger than himself, was vacationing in Florida and starting a new family. In March Wolfe went up to Boston and with the assistance of his cousins engaged in "forcible entry and a bit of high grade burglary" to recover his books.

That night, over wine at a North End Italian restaurant he had so often frequented with Raisbeck, he jotted in his notebook phrases from the "Bronze by gold" section of his copy of *Ulysses*: "gouty fingers nakkering, jogjaunty-warmseated, ardentbold — grampus." It was Joyce's verbal experimentation that most excited him. "I am weary of the . . . old language," he wrote. "We must mine deeper — find language again in its primitive sinews. . . . Joyce gets it at times in Ulysses — it is quite simple but terrific."

Wolfe's own novel was, as he later candidly admitted, his " 'Ulysses' book." "Like Mr. Joyce," he explained, "I wrote about things that I had known, the immediate life and experience that had been familiar to me in my childhood." From Joyce he learned the technique of the interior monologue, a method he most successfully used to recreate his father's unuttered thoughts, linked only by free association. Walking home from a movie with Eugene, Gant's attention is momentarily caught by a shop window where "new sewing-machines glinted in dim light." The sight causes him to make a mental leap: "The Singer building. Tallest in the world. The stitching hum of Julia's machine. Needle through your finger before you know it." And he winced. Passing a drugstore, he mused silently: "Drink Coca Cola. They say he stole the formula from old mountain woman. $50,000,000 now. Rats in the vats. Dope [i.e., Coca-Cola] at Wood's [pharmacy] better. Too weak here."

Wolfe also adapted from Joyce the practice of punctuating his narrative with familiar tag lines of poetry, which often served as an ironical commentary on the scenes he was describing. On his way home from school, Eugene passes the office of Dr. H. M. Smathers, the dentist, who asks his patient tenderly, "Do you feel that?" and receives the reply "Wrogd gho ghurk!" "Spit!" orders the dentist, and Wolfe inserted a line, without attribution, from *Paradise Lost*: "With thee conversing, I forget all time." Farther on, Eugene sees the simpering mannikin in the window of Bain's millinery store, advertising "Hats for Milady," and Wolfe interjects, without identification, a phrase from William Cowper: "O that those lips had language." On the street he encounters Mr. Buse, the oriental rug merchant, whose broad dark face is wreathed in Persian smiles. Wolfe comments, from Shelley's "Ozymandias": "I met a traveller from an antique land." In one of his ledgers Wolfe wrote out a long list of such poetic fragments, mostly from Shakespeare, Milton, and the English Romantic poets, and he systematically worked them into his narrative.

Most of all he was impressed by the "Wandering Rocks" section of *Ulysses*, in which Joyce, in a sequence of eighteen seemingly disjoined scenes, walked his readers through the labyrinth of Dublin streets between 3:00 and 4:00 P.M. on June 16, 1904, observing dozens of characters crossing and recrossing each other's paths. As originally written, a very large portion of the second book of Wolfe's novel consisted of similar sweeps of telescoped time. One of these sequences (which became Chapter XIV of *Look Homeward, Angel*) gives an interlocking picture of seemingly unrelated incidents in Altamont between 3:25 A.M., when Ben leaves for work on the newspaper, and a little after six, when Eugene awakes to Gant's imperative summons from downstairs. During these hours Ben arrives at the newspaper office; the circulation manager scolds a newsboy for failing to collect his bills; Ben and Harry Tugman, the press operator, walk over to the Uneeda restaurant; Berenice Redmond, a prostitute, goes to bed, with the request that she not be disturbed until one o'clock; Ben and Tugman meet the drunken Dr. McGuire, who must perform an operation within forty-five minutes; the pretentious Dr. Jefferson Spaugh and the undertaker, "Horse" Hines, enter the restaurant and engage in heavy-handed banter with the others; Gant gets up and starts the fire at Dixieland; Judge Webster Taylor, specialist in demonology, arises, as does Julia Gant; Moses Andrews, a Negro aged twenty-six, is discovered behind a billboard with his throat cut and his pockets picked; eight Negro laborers walk by, carrying lunch pails; Paperboy No. 3, having finished his route, returns for sex with the Negro woman, May Corpening; Ben and Tugman go back to the newspaper office; and Gant routs Eugene out of bed.

Wolfe linked these disparate, fragmentary events not merely through chronology but by relating them to the gradual emergence of light, beginning with a night "brightly pricked with cool and tender stars" when Ben goes to work, proceeding through "the lilac darkness," on to the "nacreous pearl light" of early dawn, to the "soft and otherwordly light" of morning, which was "like the light that fills the sea-floors of Catalina where the great fish swim." Uniting them also are the sounds of a train, first far distant in the mountains, then climbing the last ridge into Altamont, next whistling "with even, mournful respirations" as it approaches the town, and arriving at the station just as the episode concludes.

But if Wolfe borrowed techniques from Joyce, *Ulysses* did not have much influence on the structure of his novel. In part this was because the first book, dealing with Eugene's infancy and early years, had been written before he studied Joyce seriously. In part, too, it was because as yet no critical consensus about the form of *Ulysses* had emerged. Not until the publication of Gilbert Stuart's book on *Ulysses* in 1930 did American readers begin to discover behind the rather humdrum wanderings of Leopold Bloom a masterpiece of allegory, tightly constructed. While Wolfe was writing his first novel he certainly did not view *Ulysses* in this light. Had he done so, he probably would have rejected Joyce entirely and concluded, as he did years later, that *Ulysses* suffered from "the sterile perfection of its planned design."

V

When Wolfe's writing was going well, his relations with Aline were close and loving. So long as he was able to convince himself that his novel would be completed in the spring and in the hands of a publisher by summer, they were happy together. Their daily meetings were times for lovemaking, good food, and laughter. He jotted in his notebook some of the silly wordplay they indulged in:

> *The floors have no doors; the floors have cuspidors.*
> *The ceiling has no feeling.*
> *The chairs have no stairs, hairs.*
> *The bottle has no throttle.*
> *The walls have no balls.*

In March Aline made another attempt to introduce him to the New York world of writers, poets, and actors in which she moved. At her urging he went to a party given by Philip Moeller, one of her lifelong friends who was associated with the Theatre Guild, in his Greenwich Village studio. Wolfe enjoyed meeting Carl Van Vechten, a novelist then in vogue because of his discovery of decadence and negritude. (Van Vechten became Van Vleek in Wolfe's later novels.) But to the poet Elinor Wylie, the guest of honor, he took an instant dislike. Perhaps she seemed threatening because she was so strikingly beautiful. Perhaps he was upset because there were not enough chairs and she told him to sit on the floor while she read her poems aloud. Affronted, and probably a little drunk, he slouched in the doorway until he could bear it no longer and then launched a vituperative attack on Wylie, William Rose Benét, her husband, and the assembled crowd of poseurs and literary dilettantes. "I hated them so," he wrote Mabel, "that I managed to insult them all before the evening was over." Aline did not urge him to go out again.

As his unfinished novel — like that of George Webber in *The Web and the Rock* — "spread and flowered like a cancerous growth until it now had engulfed him," he grew increasingly weary and irritable, and Aline was often insensitive to his moods. One of their first serious quarrels came when, elated after the dress rehearsal of a new play for which she had designed the sets and costumes, she walked over to the loft to share her joy with him. Finding him "lying on the bed with his arms dragging on the floor, and the coffee cups all over the room, and the cigarette stumps," she did not pause to recognize that he was tired and drained but began talking of "the beautiful things I had made, and how I had been praised, and how I needed to be loved, more and more." Even more dangerous, she asked if he had been working too. His "eyebrows made a straight line of anger across his face, his mouth tightened and his lower lip thrust out, little beads of spit gathered in the corners and edged his lips," and he began abusing her. Since she lived in the theater, he announced, she must be foul, for the theater was a foul place. He accused her of unspeakable deeds behind doors, momentary obscenities, little satisfactions of the lowest order. She replied in kind. They raged at each other in hatred and anger until it seemed that they could never be lovers again. Reconciliation came soon, but things were never quite the same again. They had learned how to hurt each other.

In May they had one of their bitterest quarrels. After attending a meeting of actors and directors of the Neighborhood Playhouse, which was about to be closed, they got into a long discussion of "Our Relation." She blurted out that Alice Lewisohn had said that she did not produce "Mannerhouse" because she found Tom "the most arrogant young man she had ever known." Still angry over the rejection of his play, furious that Aline had failed for more than a year to tell him of Miss Lewisohn's statement, and suspicious that there were other such secrets that she was withholding, he charged that she "essentially" hated him. She counterattacked that he wanted to leave her. He replied by asking "casually" whether Aline's daughter was a whore. "I said [it] because I wanted to hurt her," he recorded in his pocket notebook. "Don't you *ever* say that again," she exploded, declaring that he had "the dirtiest lowest mind she had ever known." Having discovered his lover's most vulnerable spot, Wolfe would in the future make accusations about her daughter — accusations that had no factual basis — again and again when he wanted most to wound Aline.

Both lovers derived a certain satisfaction from these quarrels, and even more from the passionate peacemaking that followed them, but these episodes were costly to both. For the first time their affair began to affect the Bernstein family, from whom she had kept the relationship discreetly screened. But now Wolfe, in drunken fits of suspicion, started calling her home after midnight, in the hope of discovering that she was out with another man, and he sometimes left messages with her troubled husband. Wolfe, too, suffered. He began to have "damnable nightmares" about Aline's having sexual intercourse with a man who ran a carnival show on a riverboat. In the dream, after discovering them together, Wolfe destroyed his novel, "tearing it to pieces and feeding it to the fire."

As summer began and the loft on 8th Street grew unbearably hot, both Tom and Aline were relieved when Olin Dows invited him to Rhinebeck. A little nervous about living among "the swells," Wolfe did not stay in the main house but took up lodgings in the gatekeeper's cottage, "a little bit of heaven with a little river, a wooded glade, and the sound of water falling over the dam all through the night." Below him was "the mighty Hudson — the noblest river I know of." Mostly he kept to himself, doing his own cooking or eating food sent down from the main house, but sometimes he joined the family and their other guests for dinner. On July 4 he went with the Dows family to the Astor mansion, to see the annual fireworks display. Storing up his impressions of these River People for a later book (they were to appear at length in *Of Time and the River*), Wolfe felt conspicuous and out of place in this elegant world of wealth. He believed that he was thought of as "Olin's wild Bohemian friend," but everybody treated him with great courtesy. He was obliged to admit that he found the River People "lovely" — though he concluded that if he lived long among them he would think them dull.

Wolfe took his ledgers to Rhinebeck with him and continued to write steadily there. He had now completed the first two books of his novel and was well into the third, which dealt with Eugene's college years. While he was visiting Dows he wrote in one ledger a marginal exhortation to himself: "Get up to Ben's death before going to New York." Whether he did so is unclear; he was always overoptimistic about his schedule. He also decided that, if his novel was ever to be finished and have any chance of publication, he would have to limit himself to these three books, concluding his story shortly after Eugene's graduation from college.

In the third book on which he was now working, Wolfe's writing lacked the control exhibited in his Joycean second book. Though it contained some excellent passages, it was far less carefully crafted and less original; indeed, it was similar to several other autobiographical American first novels of the 1920s. His loss of mastery in this third book was mostly the result of fatigue; he had been writing, almost without interruption, for nearly twelve months. In addition, with Eugene Gant removed from his family in Altamont, Wolfe was dealing with a social setting, in the university and at Chapel Hill, that was less compact and less clearly defined. Recognizing that this third book was weak, he decided to introduce some fictional love scenes — episodes that were notably absent from his autobiographical outline. Forgetting that he had never known love, though he had experienced sex, before he met Aline, he was at his worst in inventing a pallid affair for Eugene with Laura James, the beautiful boarder at Dixieland, and an improbable adventure with a sensuous Italian woman aboard a ship at Newport News. Reviewing these chapters, and also his plays, years afterwards, Wolfe himself wondered: "Why am I always ashamed and afraid to write a love scene?"

VI

While Wolfe was away, Aline went to the 8th Street loft and found it a terrible mess. He had left food out, and there were flies by the hundreds. His belongings were scattered all over the place. In the rubbish on the floor she discovered two ardent love letters she had written him, unopened. She also found an uncashed check from Henry Westall — at a time when she was still paying all of Wolfe's bills. "Please come down," she wrote urgently. "I want terribly to talk to you." Then, in very faint ink, she added a hesitant postscript: "Would you like to go to Europe with me — Vienna, Prague, Budapest."

Wolfe accepted the offer, though he had vowed not to leave New York until the book was finished. "Very tired — both in body and brain," he felt he needed a change and respite from the heat, from which he suffered greatly. He rationalized his decision by saying that he had always planned to go to Europe again when the book was completed and that it would be better to do so now, so that he would be in New York during the fall "to try to launch the thing and some of my plays."

Still being discreet, they took passage for Europe on two separate ships, and Aline's left first. While waiting for his own liner, Wolfe saw a good deal of a North Carolina friend, Donald MacRae, now a physician at the Manhattan Maternity Hospital. Always collecting new experiences, he went with Dr. MacRae into the delivery room of the hospital. Dressed in the longest white gown the nurses could find, he watched as the doctors explained every step in delivering the baby of a big, husky Irish woman, who was already in labor. To the amusement of the young physicians, Wolfe screwed his face into a knot and clenched his teeth in sympathetic suffering every time the woman screamed with pain. Since she had difficulty in giving birth and seemed to fight against the doctors' efforts, the chief obstetrician kept coaxing her: "Come on, momma! Do your stuff now! Give us some help, momma! Push! Push!" Finally he had to administer ether and to deliver the baby by forceps. Wolfe watched closely as "the little skull began to come, and then the little body." When the doctor held the baby up by his heels and spanked him, he gave a good loud yell, and Wolfe, tremendously excited, gave one of his own: "Come on baby! Come on!"

The doctors thought it was funny that Wolfe became so emotional about what was to them an everyday occurrence, but he found the birth was "one of the most terrible and beautiful things I have ever seen." "This thing has made a great music in me," he wrote Mabel, and as usual he connected what he had seen with his own experiences: "Something gathers in my throat and my eyes are wet when I think of all the pain and wonder that little life must come to know; and I hope to God that those feet will never walk as lonely a road as mine have walked, and I hope its heart will never beat as mine has at times under a smothering weight of weariness, grief, and horror; nor its brain be damned and haunted by the thousand furies and nightmare shapes that walk through mine."

Days later he was still musing over what he had witnessed. He began to weave the experience into the lyrical proem of his novel: "Naked and alone we came into exile. In her dark womb we did not know our mother's face; from the prison of her flesh have we come into the unspeakable and incommunicable prison of this earth."

On July 12 he sailed for Europe on the *George Washington*, for a two-month vacation with Aline. He continued to write in his ledgers while she bought new clothes in Paris and took a close look at a play in which the Actors-Managers group (the successors of the Neighborhood Playhouse) was interested. But this time their stay abroad was not a happy one; they could not recapture the golden days at Ambleside. They did a great deal of sightseeing and assiduously went to museums, but now there was no magic in them. Wolfe concluded that the Louvre was "the greatest junk heap in the world." In Prague he got into a quarrel with a waiter who, he thought, was trying to cheat them. This time Munich, which Aline loved, disgusted him because of the "foul people" with "Hun-heads and triple necks." Aline was upset at Strasbourg when soldiers at the railroad station laughed to see a couple so disparate in age and height. In Vienna they had a terrible fight in a restaurant, and Aline left, walking weeping through the streets, with Wolfe following in great embarrassment.

They were both relieved to part in Paris. By prearrangement Aline went home first, and Wolfe, to preserve the appearance of propriety, remained alone for several days. After she left, he got a copy of *Sourire* to read the "Whore House Items," went to an all-night pharmacy and bought a prophylactic kit, and just before dawn had sex with a prostitute. Noting carefully that one hour after intercourse his heart was beating eighty-one times a minute, he recorded in his notebook: "in over two years first time I've betrayed her."

VII

Arriving in New York on September 18, Wolfe almost immediately resumed teaching duties at New York University, where the ever-encouraging Professor Watt had renewed his appointment, at a salary of $2200, and had arranged for him to have nearly all of his classes between 6:30 and 9:00 P.M., from Monday through Thursday, so that he could have uninterrupted days and long weekends for writing. Wolfe promised himself that he would give only minimal time to his teaching, but once classes were under way he once again found that he was absorbed in his duties.

Now that Wolfe had some income, he and Aline could afford more comfortable quarters, and presently they found an apartment at 263 West 11th Street, only a few minutes' walk from the university. It was, he wrote his mother, "a magnificent place in an old New York house owned by a wealthy old bachelor." It had two enormous rooms and a bath, and rented for only $135 a month. Aline, who paid half the rent, used the front room for her designing, and her section of the apartment was always orderly, with fresh paper on the drawing board and her inks, her pens and pencils, her compasses and triangles arranged neatly.

Wolfe occupied the back room overlooking a little garden bricked in by a wall. His room was always a chaos of great ledgers, scattered manuscripts, piles of student examinations, open books tossed facedown on the floor, coffee cups, cigarette butts, and sweat-stained shirts piled in a corner. A New York University colleague called it "a stinking lair."

In this chaos he continued stubbornly and steadily to write. He hoped to get back to Asheville for Christmas but found that he could not afford the time. "At present I am taking every spare minute for my book," he wrote his mother. "I *must* finish it by the first of the year and give it to a publisher for reading." While he was completing the final chapters, he asked his friend and former student, Abe Smith, to type what he had already written. Smith agreed but had difficulty in deciphering his handwriting. In the end Wolfe dictated most of the novel to him at the typewriter, making minor changes and improvements as he read the manuscript aloud.

Desperately tired as he taught, wrote, dictated, and revised all at the same time, Wolfe vented his frustration on Aline. Now that he was earning a living and was no longer fully dependent on her, she seemed less available and less nurturing than in the past. She was deeply involved in getting the Civic Repertory theater under way, a "people's theater" that would combine fine drama with popular prices, but Wolfe suspected that she was beginning a new affair with a younger and more successful man. He started to roam the streets of New York at night and often, fortified with raw gin, he worked himself into a fury. Then, after midnight, he would call Aline, accusing her of having been out on some "bawdy mission." Even her husband was obliged to notice what was going on. Long afterwards Wolfe tried to explain his conduct to Aline: "I was obsessed by the work I was doing, driven on desperately to finish it, . . . the horrible pain lengthening out day by day, and no escape."

Aline was equally suspicious of him. When she cleaned their apartment, the discovery of a dusting of woman's powder or of a hairpin convinced her that he was sleeping with "silly cheap little tarts." Sometimes she was right. But she could be embarrassingly wrong. Once Wolfe gave an informal little dinner party for three of his New York University colleagues, one of whom was a woman. Watching from the street, Aline saw the woman's silhouette on the blind of the apartment and stormed in to make a scene. The three young professors of English were startled at the incursion of this "violent middle-aged woman," but Wolfe quieted her and took her out of the apartment. When he returned he explained that she was his mistress, who "had come up to catch him in the act."

Despite all interruptions he continued to write, and by the end of December he was completing "the big scene" for the conclusion of his book, Eugene's encounter with the ghost of his brother in the Altamont public square, when Ben counseled: "*You* are your world." In his final ledger Wolfe then drafted a long introduction, which he hoped would give his novel a "downward movement, back through time." He traced the early history of the Gant (Wolfe) and Pentland (Westall) families. Then he arranged to have young W. O. Gant and Bacchus Pentland — "Stinking Jesus," the prophet of Armageddon, and the brother of Gant's future wife — meet on the road that led to the battle of Gettysburg. The object of this "constant excavation into the buried life of a group of people" was to show that the turbulence and divisiveness of Eugene Gant's own family were not just accidental but were virtually foreordained.

By this point his relations with Aline had so deteriorated that time past and time future became confused in his mind. A passage on how W. O. Gant was publicly derided because of the infidelities of his first wife became an account of Wolfe's own situation as he viewed it:

> The world laughs. — But the world is a boy of twenty-four, who sought, [was] stricken and possessed by a woman of forty, . . . who resists, mocks, curses, laughs, weeps, is shaken by her tears, believes in her protests, is remorseful because of his disbelief, and then who burns out his light in madness when her brief fidelity grows jaded; and she returns to the stealthy tournament of her lovers.

It was well that by this point the writing of the novel was almost finished. Though utterly exhausted, suffering from toothache and from eye strain, he was able proudly to report on March 31, 1928:

"I finished the book on which I have been working for the last twenty months a few days ago, and I sent a copy to a publisher for reading." To Dean James Munn of New York University, who had repeatedly befriended him during his years as a teacher, he gave a copy of the typescript, with a note explaining its crudities and imperfections: "My energy is completely exhausted — I felt as if I should drop dead when I came to the last comma."

VI

Like Some Blind Thing
Upon the Floor of the Sea

MY GREATEST DEFICIENCY is a total lack of salesmanship,"
Wolfe wrote Mabel while he was still working on his
novel. He recalled that in trying to place his plays he
had sent the scripts to only two or three producers and, when they
did not respond promptly, had peremptorily demanded that they
be returned. "I have never known where to go, where to turn, or
what to do," he explained, but he predicted: "This time, certain
friends will probably attend to that part of it for me."

Aline was his most certain friend, and in March 1928, after Abe
Smith had completed the final typing of "O Lost," Wolfe turned
his manuscript over to her, prefacing it with a long "Note for the
Publisher's Reader," which managed to be both apologetic and
defiant. Surely Aline, with her charm, her tact, and her countless
acquaintances in the world of art and letters, could find him a
publisher.

She tried hard. First she turned to the young firm of Boni &
Liveright, partly because she knew Liveright as a theatrical producer, partly because the two eccentric partners had a reputation
for publishing new or unconventional talents like Dorothy Parker,
Stark Young, Theodore Dreiser, and Ernest Hemingway. For
weeks Wolfe waited in hope, uncertainty, and despair. On April
30 T. R. Smith, a director of the firm, on whose advice Liveright
heavily relied, rejected the manuscript with what Wolfe thought

were "a few contemptuous words." In the past year Boni &
Liveright had published four similar autobiographical novels by
young men and all had failed. They had no choice but to decline
this one. The manuscript, Smith wrote, was "so long — so terribly long." But even if rigorous editing controlled the length,
"the whole thing" seemed wrong. The bored, indifferent tone of
Smith's letter made it inevitable that Wolfe would later write a
burlesque of his firm, calling it "Rawng & Wright."

Next, Aline turned to her friend Ernest Boyd. The pontifical
Irish-American critic was not much interested in fiction and referred her to his wife, Madeleine, who was just starting her own
literary agency. Uncertain about the competence of this Frenchwoman, whom Boyd had met while teaching at Trinity College,
Dublin, Aline hesitated but was finally reassured when she learned
H. L. Mencken thought well of her. The Bernsteins' chauffeur
delivered Wolfe's manuscript, and by the time he reached the
Boyds' sixth-floor walkup on 19th Street he was panting from its
weight.

Deterred by the size of the parcel, Mrs. Boyd left it unopened
for two weeks, but when her husband went on a lecture tour she
forced herself to begin reading it. Intending to spend only a couple
of hours on it before going out to a cocktail party, she grew
absorbed. Disconnecting the phone, she forgot about going out,
forgot about eating, and hardly moved from her reading chair
until her legs went to sleep and she looked up to find that it was
three in the morning. Thrilled, she began to run up and down the
hall of the apartment, shouting at the top of her voice: "A genius!
I have discovered a genius!"

When Wolfe and Mrs. Boyd met on May 22, they took an
instant dislike to each other. Unpersuaded by the Gallic extravagance of her enthusiasm, he was offended by her talk of royalties
and the agent's percentage. He also furiously resented her remark
that he suffered from "literary diarrhea." For her part Mrs. Boyd
found Wolfe distrustful and suspicious, and she was offended by
his boasting about "all the women who were trying to jump into
bed with him." Firmly she explained that he badly needed a bath,
that she did not admire his looks, and that in no circumstances
would she go to bed with him. He concluded that she was "a fat
Frenchwoman, hardboiled and out for the guilders." Nevertheless
they agreed to work together, for he knew no one else in the

publishing world who took an interest in his book, and she needed to make a success out of this, the second manuscript that had come to her as a literary agent.

Having an agent, Wolfe discovered, did not mean having a publisher. Enthusiastic about the manuscript, Mrs. Boyd tried unsuccessfully to place it. First she sent it to Pascal Covici, whose Chicago firm was publishing daring novels by Ben Hecht. Covici took about a month to read "O Lost" and liked it, but before agreeing to publish it he moved to New York to start the new firm of Covici-Friede, in which the chief manuscript reader was his partner's wife, Mrs. Donald S. Friede. Mrs. Friede's verdict on Wolfe's novel was altogether negative: "A semi-autobiographical novel of over 250,000 words . . . fearfully diffuse . . . marred by stylistic clichés, outlandish adjectives and similes, etc." Admitting that the manuscript "holds one's interest by its vitality," she judged: "Probably Mr. Wolfe could write if he dumped this overboard and began again." The firm informed Mrs. Boyd that it would be interested in Wolfe's next book, if it was of reasonable length.

Next she tried Longmans, Green and Company. Wolfe's huge package was added to the stack of unsolicited manuscripts, which young William M. Sloane and another college boy were supposed to screen. Because of its size they allowed it to collect dust as long as possible and then jockeyed with each other over who should have the burden of skimming this interminable novel. Finally they shared the reading of about 50,000 words, found the book "terrible," and sent the manuscript back — "presumably," as Sloane remembered, "in a truck."

Meanwhile Aline continued her own efforts to find Wolfe a publisher. After some persuasion her friend Melville Cane, a poet and a lawyer who was also a director of the new publishing firm of Harcourt, Brace and Company, agreed to talk with him about his novel. Wolfe brought the manuscript to Cane's office in two small suitcases, and the lawyer unhappily agreed at least to sample the work. When he did, he was impressed by "the driving, passionate force behind the writing," which he found "eminently civilized, with a personal style." Nevertheless he concluded that "what the manuscript lacked basically was a shape," that "what was important lost its full effect because of intrusions of the commonplace," and, finally, that its "elephan-

tine length" made it unpublishable. Attempting to be kind, he told
Wolfe that he had "a fine, moving, and distinguished piece of
writing," but suggested that next time he ought to write a
novel only as long as Sinclair Lewis's recently published *Elmer
Gantry*.

I

The reasons for these repeated rejections were understandable.
Wolfe's manuscript was indeed formidably long — 1,113 typed
pages, containing approximately 330,000 words. This was more
than three times the length of the average American novel of the
1920s. Also, Wolfe's story was unusually complex, for about 380
named characters, along with dozens of unnamed minor figures,
appeared in it. He had fulfilled his 1923 prediction to Professor
Baker: "Some day I'm going to write a play [though it turned out
to be a novel] with fifty, eighty, a hundred people — a whole
town."

Wolfe's language offered problems. At times his vocabulary
was difficult and inaccessible. On the very first page he used
"alexin" — a word (referring to a substance that destroys bacteria)
so technical that it did not find a place in the *Oxford English Dic-
tionary*. Other examples were "adyts" (shrines or sanctuaries),
rarely used since its introduction in 1594, and "esemplastic," which
Coleridge had coined to suggest "unifying." Elsewhere, however,
his vocabulary was coarse and explicit. Crudely joking doctors in
the all-night restaurant in Altamont asked a newcomer who had
prepared a paper on carcinoma of the liver why he didn't write one
on "halitosis of the bunghole." Eugene Gant's brother, the
supersalesman of the *Saturday Evening Post*, responded to a question about how he was getting along: "Couldn't be better, General — slick as a puppy's peter!"

Readers were also bewildered by the great variety of styles that
Wolfe employed. By far the largest part of his long novel consisted
of hundreds of straightforwardly presented scenes, in which only
a few characters, recreated through a combination of dialogue and
description, interacted. But interspersed among these dramatic
vignettes were cadenced passages in which he reconstructed the
inner life of his characters. Thus to convey a sense of W. O. Gant's
prodigality and profuseness, Wolfe wrote:

His life was like that river [the Mississippi], rich with its own deposited and onward-borne agglutinations, fecund with its sedimental accretions, filled exhaustlessly by life in order to be more richly itself, and this life, with the great purpose of a river, he emptied now into the harbor of his house, the sufficient haven of himself, for whom the gnarled vines wove round him thrice, the earth burgeoned with abundant fruit and blossom, the fire burnt madly.

So much even the average reader could readily follow, but along with dialogue, description, narration, and generalization there were lyrical passages, usually in a loose iambic pentameter rhythm, in which the author soared above the characters and events he was portraying. For instance, after Eugene's brief tryst with Laura James on the slopes above Altamont, Wolfe broke forth in a dithyramb:

Come up into the hills, O my young love. Return! O lost, and by the wind grieved, ghost, come back again, as first I knew you in the timeless valley, where we shall feel ourselves anew, bedded on magic in the month of June. . . . Where [is] the music of your flesh, the rhyme of your teeth, the dainty languor of your legs, your small firm arms, your slender fingers, . . . and the little cherry-teats of your white breasts? . . . Quick are the mouths of earth and quick the teeth that fed upon this loveliness. You who were made for music, will hear music no more: in your dark house the winds are silent. . . . Come up into the hills, O my young love: return. O lost, and by the wind grieved, ghost, come back again.

Despite the abundance of incident in Wolfe's novel, readers who screened unsolicited manuscripts for publishers — especially those pressed for time — found difficulty in discovering in it anything resembling the structure of a conventional novel. Anticipating their puzzlement, Wolfe in his prefatory note explained: "The book may be lacking in plot but it is not lacking in plan." Indeed, he noted — perhaps to convince himself — "The plan is rigid and densely woven." It consisted of two essentially opposed movements: a downward movement that described "the cyclic curve of a family's life — genesis, union, decay, and dissolution," and an outward movement, tracing "the effort of a child, a boy, and a youth for release, freedom, and loneliness in new lands." But later in the same introductory note Wolfe in effect conceded that his manuscript did not fall into any conventional category of fiction: "I have never called this book a novel. . . . It is a book made out of my life, and it represents my vision of life to my twentieth year."

A reader of the manuscript could be forgiven if he was unable to figure out just what that vision was. By the author's own admission this was an autobiographical work, a novel of development, a story of how a young artist found himself in spite of all the obstacles his family and his society put in his way. Yet it was very different from other semiautobiographical novels of the period, like Floyd Dell's *Moon-Calf* (1920), F. Scott Fitzgerald's *This Side of Paradise* (1920), or Glenway Wescott's *The Apple of the Eye* (1924). Wolfe's hero did not even make an appearance in the first fifty pages of his manuscript, which dealt with the early history of the Gants and the Pentlands. More important, Eugene Gant, while indisputably the central figure in the story, was the least fully realized character. Later Wolfe himself saw that "perhaps the chief fault, the unconvincing element of his first book," was the presentation of Eugene as an "ironic and romantic kind of fellow — a sort of genius of the village, who, like Shelley, Keats, or Byron . . . would that he were a hart and could flee away into the wilde wood, or could tread with goat huffs the antic hay or prance around with Bacchus and his pards."

Equally puzzling was the social setting of Wolfe's book. This clearly was a novel about a part of the South, written by a Southerner — but it was not like any of the Southern novels that readers in the 1920s were used to. At this time, as Wolfe later observed, "the better known gentlemen and lady writers of the South were writing polished bits of whimsey about some dear and mythical Land of Far Cockaigne [like James Branch Cabell], or ironic little comedies about the gentle relics of the Old Tradition of the South [like Ellen Glasgow], or fanciful bits about negro fish mongers along the battery in Charleston [like DuBose Heyward], or, when passion was in the air, about the romantic adulteries of dusky brethren and sistern on a plantation in South Carolina [like Julia Peterkin]." Wolfe himself had experimented with all these conventional modes of writing about the South — indeed, "O Lost" included an unacknowledged parody, in the scene describing Eugene's visit to Charleston, of Miss Glasgow's novel *The Deliverance* — but had found them all wanting. Wolfe's South was a land of fraud and violence. The better sort of people in his Altamont were pretentious, hypocritical, avaricious shysters; the main avocations of the rest seemed to be fornication, adultery, whoremongering, incest, and miscegenation. In 1928, before William Faulkner's major novels had appeared and when Erskine Caldwell and Richard Wright were still unpublished, it was little wonder that manuscript readers were appalled by this picture of the South. As Wolfe commented some years later, "O Lost" took "the lid off some things that had never been shown without the lid before."

But if Wolfe's novel did not fit any of the accepted categories of Southern fiction, it was not clear that it was quite like any other writing either. In exposing the meanness and narrowness of small-town life in the United States it bore some resemblance to Sinclair Lewis's *Main Street* and *Babbitt* — but, as Wolfe observed, there was an undercurrent of evil in it that made "*Babbitt* an innocent little child's book to be read at the Christmas school entertainment along *The Christmas Carol* and *Excelsior*." It was somewhat like Sherwood Anderson's best work in its revelation of the strangeness and isolation of lives in the United States, but, unlike Anderson, Wolfe refused to write about Americans "as if we are a lot of simple and superstitious peasants" or "to make a virtue of being ignorant and crude and simple."

In short, Wolfe's manuscript had such difficulty finding a publisher because it was startlingly idiosyncratic. It had connections with the work of Joyce (who was, however, still virtually unknown in American publishing circles), to the Psalmist, to Coleridge, Shelley, and Keats — but it did not belong to any recognizable American literary tradition. Wolfe himself was acutely aware of the problems that the strangeness of his writing caused. Beginning a new book even before "O Lost" found a home, he invented a conversation between his novelist-hero — as always, himself under another name — and an interested publisher. "The trouble with your work at present — and I do not mean it is a fault in your work, but something your readers will have to get used to," the businessman said, "is that it is hard to find a tag to fit it."

II

Wolfe understood why publishers declined his manuscript, and he tried to joke about his "Monster," his "Leviathan." Nevertheless, he was bitterly hurt, and each rejection cast him into deeper despair. He calculated that he had had "five years of being kicked in the face," and this latest failure was more than he could bear.

His strong body, punished by overwork and failure to exercise, by gargantuan eating and intemperate drinking, began to give him trouble. He suffered from headaches. Always fearful of doctors, he reluctantly had his eyes examined, and when the ophthalmologist put silver nitrate in his eyes — which Wolfe knew was used to prevent venereal infection in newborn babies — he feared the worst. An abscessed tooth, which required painful, expensive, and in the long run unsuccessful dental surgery, continued to plague him. When a friend from his Harvard days encountered Wolfe again in 1928, he found him "an entirely different person, slovenly, glowering, and looking like some one pursued."

Wolfe's teaching suffered. While he was writing his book, even though he had been under terrible strain, he continued to take care with his classes, and a number of students recalled their excitement when he read portions of his manuscript to them and asked for their comments. But once the book was finished, he declined Professor Watt's offer of an appointment for the next year, on the ground that he must make a break now or never. "One of the chief reasons for my leaving now is not that I dislike teaching, and find it dull," he explained somewhat disingenuously, "but that I may like it too well." After taking that decisive step, he found it increasingly difficult to remain interested in his teaching, and many times he had to prime himself with liquor before he felt able to meet the students. Once during the late spring, when he was trying to teach them to avoid clichés and to use fresh, appropriate language, he turned to the window that opened on Washington Square, where the trees were in full leaf, and asked them to describe the beautiful evening. "*One* good word, please," he begged. An eager young woman in a tight black dress, twisting her favorite curl around her finger and setting her lips in a languorous smile, offered with slow, easy assurance: "Balmy." Wolfe looked down at the floor, stared wildly out of the window, and suddenly exploded: "Aw Shit!"

Now that he had decided against teaching again, he had to plan how to earn a living. He talked grandly about the money he could earn by helping his Harvard Workshop colleague, Henry Fisk Carlton, write radio scripts and movie scenarios, but nothing came of these plans. Aline thought that he might prepare advertising copy for the J. Walter Thompson Company, and she persuaded Mrs. Helen Resor, the wife of the president of the firm, to read portions of "O Lost." Impressed and no doubt confident that an author so profuse in adjectives could write lyrical tributes to Fleischmann's yeast and Simmons' Beautyrest mattresses, Mrs. Resor offered him a job — but on the condition that he pledge to stay with the firm for at least three years, because of the time it would take to train him. Attracted by the money and the security but fearful of making such a long-term commitment, Wolfe stalled and resorted to the bottle. It was probably about this time that he told William Y. Tindall the story, doubtless exaggerated, of waking up in the gutter on West 42nd Street and staring up at the Salvation Army lassies who were using him as an object lesson on the evils of drink.

More than ever before he vented his unhappiness and his anger on Aline. They quarreled frequently, and reconciliations became more and more difficult. By now he had lost "all physical love, desire, passion" for her, but his declining sexual interest was accompanied by mounting jealousy. "He could hardly bear to have me talk to another man," Aline recalled. "Dreadful black clouds of fantasy" colored his view of her, and every time they met he accused her of whorish promiscuity. He thought that her unfaithfulness was demonstrated by her inability — or was it unwillingness? — to find a publisher for his book. Angrily he berated her because she was "of no use" to him.

By May it was clear that they could not continue together. Wolfe announced that they ought to separate and not see each other, at least for the summer. He could not write if he was constantly upset by emotional scenes, and he needed time and distance to think objectively about their future relationship. By this time she was ready to agree. "I really think that it is necessary for us to be away from each other now," she told him, and in early June she made plans to sail for Europe with Theresa Helburn. Fearing that he might be recaptured in the net from which he thought he had escaped, Wolfe refused to come to the Bernsteins' house to say good-bye or to see Aline off at the dock. Finally he agreed to see her just one more time if she met him on the corner of Seventh Avenue and 40th Street, where he felt all the passing people would protect him from another scene. As they parted, he kept telling her that she must make no demands on him, no attempt to see him.

A few days later he made a brief visit to Asheville, his first in two years. Suffering from the collapse of the real estate boom, his family seemed glad enough to see him but not much interested in his problems. Mrs. Roberts, however, noticed how much he had changed and, misreading the consequences of suffering, overwork, and intemperance, wrote that she had "never seen any face so added to by spiritual beauty as yours has been in the past two years."

III

At the end of June Wolfe himself went abroad. He explained to his puzzled mother, who had had to pay half his train fare to Asheville, that he had saved up a little money from teaching and that he could live more cheaply in Europe than in New York. In fact he worried about running out of funds during his travels until Olin Dows offered to advance him five hundred dollars or more whenever he needed it. That sum, Dows said, minimizing his generosity, was less than what he often paid for a single painting.

Wolfe told himself that he needed to go abroad to acquire a fuller knowledge of several European cities, which he planned to make the setting for a new novel. He wanted to be near Aline, who was spending most of the summer at a water cure at Carlsbad — but not so near that they could actually meet and have to make painful decisions about the future. But most of all he felt that travel was "a spiritual necessity to him; in some measure it fulfilled a deep hunger in him for knowledge and change, and it awoke him from the lethargy into which he fell when he had been for too long in one place."

Landing at Boulogne on July 9, he passed the next two months in aimless wandering — to Amiens, Paris, Brussels, Antwerp, Cologne, Bonn, Wiesbaden, Frankfurt. In order to avoid thinking about his problems he became an assiduous sightseer, filling his pocket notebooks with page after page of lists — of books he examined in bookstores, of museums he visited, of paintings and statues that attracted his attention. He had little interest in happenings in the larger world, though he did celebrate the Democratic nomination of Al Smith for President, chiefly because Smith was opposed to Prohibition. In Brussels he was thrilled to see a mass parade representing the Socialist parties of Europe, and as he watched the battalions of laborers and peasants march by for two hours under the brilliant red banners, he felt that "at last the poor, the weak, the entire under half of the earth had been drawn together in a powerful disciplined organization," and he predicted that this was the beginning of "a new Crusade, richer and vaster than any of the old ones."

But he was really interested only in himself. Frustration and failure caused him, at least briefly, to rethink his goals and his tactics. "For the past six or eight years," he recognized, "I have exhausted myself in an effort to know and do everything." He had wanted to read all the books in the stalls along the Seine, to eat all the preserved fruits and candies and pâtés in the confectioners' stores along the rue St.-Honoré, to visit all the places that he had never seen. Because his appetite could never be sated, he had worked himself into "a frenzy of despair and hopelessness." "Now," he announced, "I am willing to put up boundaries somewhere." "I am getting a new sense of control," he assured himself in Paris. "I must begin to put up my fences now."

His restraint was short-lived. By the time he reached Cologne, his old passion to read and see everything flared up again. Once more he began visiting bookshops, attempting to look at every volume, buying large numbers of books that, with his halting German, he could barely decipher. He had a fantasy of finding in a bookstore one volume that would summarize all the other books that had ever been written. Once again he felt compelled to inspect every museum in every city he visited, attempting to examine every room. The canvasses of Pieter Brueghel were his favorites because they contained dozens of figures and actions, each with its own story, so that by seeing one painting he could simultaneously see many.

He knew that he was gorging like an anaconda, but he did not know how to stop. "The desire for it *All* comes from an evil gluttony in me — a weakness — a lack of belief," he recognized. When he attended a German production of *Faust*, he saw that it was a "statement of my *own* trouble." "Faust's own problem touches me more than Hamlet's," he wrote; "his problem is mine, it is the problem of modern life. He wants to know everything, to be a god — and he is caught in the terrible net of human incapacity."

The tension between knowledge of what he should do and recognition of what he would do affected the writing of his second novel, which he had begun before leaving the United States. Responding to criticisms that "O Lost" was too long and too difficult, he decided to make "The River People" short and snappy. Jokingly he wrote to Dean Munn that after a careful examination of 4,362 modern novels he had concluded that his new book should contain exactly 79,427 words. It was going to have everything that a successful story needed: "rich people, swank, a poor but beautiful girl, romance, adventure, Vienna, New York, a big country house, and so on." One of his principal characters he called Joel Pierce, who was modeled closely after Olin Dows. Dows was amused and interested when Wolfe told him he would figure in the novel "as he ought to be — always grand, noble, and romantic." He patterned the heroine, Lili Weinberg, after Greta Hilb, an Austrian whom he had met on shipboard during his last voyage back to America and with whom he had flirted so clumsily and outrageously that her husband referred to him as "Elephant Baby." The link between these two characters from such different backgrounds would be another of Wolfe's autobiographical figures, whom he thought of naming Eugene — like the heroes of "Mannerhouse" and "O Lost" — but whom he finally called Oliver, after his father.

The plot of "The River People" was straightforward. Oliver Weston, an unsuccessful playwright, had had his portrait painted by Joel Pierce while at Harvard and had been nursed back to health in Paris by "Li" Weinberg. In New York he brought together these two people whom he so admired, and they fell in love. They could not marry until Li could get a divorce from her Austrian husband and Joel could overcome the opposition of his cousin John. After a winter together in Vienna, where Oliver found them an apartment, Li secured her divorce, and they returned to America to plan a wedding at the Pierce estate on the Hudson River. But, for unexplained reasons, John killed Li, and Joel was left only with his portrait of her, his one truly successful painting.

Throughout the summer Wolfe wrote sections of "The River People," convinced that it had the ingredients "for a good and moving book — also, perhaps, stuff for a bad and trashy, but possibly successful book." He was never sure which book he was writing, and the project failed to hold his interest. Lili Weinberg was never a realized character, though Wolfe enjoined himself to emphasize her "lightness and gayety and sensual quality over everything else — the great profundity and sorrow beneath." Joel Pierce, with his spartan regimen of diet and exercise and his modest but realistic assessment of his limits as a painter, was more credible — but only as a foil for the oversized, unkempt Oliver Weston, who had Faustian longings to "visit every state in the union and every town with a population of more than five thousand" and to discover "in the orange groves of Southern California, on the ranches of Wyoming, and in the James River Valley of Virginia" beautiful women who were "like great ripe peaches" and who were also excellent cooks.

As the summer wore on, Wolfe wrote less about Joel and Li and more about Oliver, who, he explained rather unnecessarily, was "a figure of myself." After he visited the house in Bonn where Beethoven had been born, his story took a new direction. Perhaps a picture of the composer, "striding across an uneven field, with a great wrack of stormy clouds behind him, and the wind blowing in his fiery wild hair, and a tempest of music gathering in his terrible strong face," reminded him that many of his friends thought that he looked like Beethoven. Certainly the sight of the huge brass earhorns that Beethoven "used to catch a little of the magic he created" made him think about "this *extra* grand thing about deaf people who are grand anyway to begin with, and who have the beautiful and noble souls of artists," like Beethoven, Helen Keller — and Aline Bernstein. For a day he walked around with his ears stuffed with cotton, so that he, too, could be attuned to the "deep and glorious music in the hearts of all of us which very few of us ever come to hear in all the savage jargon of this world." Shortly afterward he drafted a chapter for "The River People" in which Oliver Weston lost his hearing.

Even with the focus back on himself, Wolfe could not sustain interest in this second novel. He tried to force himself. In his notebook he commanded: "Go upstairs and write, write, write!!!!" But the words did not come. If "I can break this lethargy, which has kept me from doing much writing — if I can write 50,000 words, 2,500 a day — for . . . three weeks . . . ," he kept promising himself; but he could not and he did not. By the end of September he concluded: "I have almost lost the power of writing."

IV

His paralysis stemmed in part from his record of rejection as a writer. Learning that thirty-six thousand new books were published in Germany each year and calculating that there must be at least one hundred thousand published in the rest of Europe and in the United States, he reflected sadly: "I have never had talent enough to get a single thing printed. . . . I have never succeeded in interesting anybody enough in anything I ever wrote to run it through one of the printing presses which are belching millions of tons of print into the world every month." "This terrible vomit of print that covers the earth" killed his desire to be an author. "I can not lift my head above the waves of futility and dulness," he explained. "I have no hope, no confidence, no belief in my ability to rise above the level of even the worst of it."

But he also owed his writing block to his anguish and uncertainty over his relationship with Aline. No sooner had she left for Europe than he began to feel the "unspeakable burden of pain and shame" because of the way he had behaved toward her. All during the summer he agonized over his past conduct. While he was wandering through Cologne, the memory of his obsessive suspiciousness and his cruelty toward his mistress swept over him and, as he wrote her, "I almost go blind with the pain of it. . . . I have caught at my throat with my hand, twisted with a cry in the streets, covered my face and eyes until all the people have stopped to look at me."

In letter after letter he tried to analyze what had gone wrong and to explain the present state of his feelings. These were the most beautiful and touching love letters that he ever wrote. Entirely absent from them were the anti-Semitic flings that had blotted his earlier letters. Except in one letter, which he probably did not mail, he no longer accused her of being unfaithful. Instead, he gave constant assurances of his devotion: "I can not deny, Aline, that I love you more than any one in the world." "My total feeling . . . is one of infinite love. You are beautiful and you are good — no one will ever take the place in my life that you have taken." "I love you with a single and absolute love that rises above and dominates every other thing in my life."

It is easy to understand why Aline, when she received such letters, wondered why they were separated. "I believe you love me much more being so far apart," she wrote after she returned to New York. When Wolfe called her the bright star in his life, she replied a little tartly: "It seems as though your desire is for me to burn on for you, your star, but to burn on at a distance." Nevertheless she kept assuring him: "My heart will be always yours, and my soul and my truest devotion."

Repeatedly, if confusedly, he tried to explain, both to Aline and himself, why, since his love for her was so great, he had behaved so badly. The pressures of completing his novel and the disappointments of repeated rejection by publishers had contributed to his actions but did not account for them. "I can not explain things in any reasonable way," he told her. "Love made me mad, and brought me down to the level of the beasts." "I know . . . how I have wasted everything most precious — paramountly yourself — and made a wreck of everything I wanted to make beautiful," he admitted. "I do not know the reason for it. . . . My brain . . . is like something that hunts round and round inside an iron cylinder trying to find some way out when there is none." He did not know how to unroot from his soul "the snake headed furies that drive us on to despair and madness."

By blaming his actions on madness, Wolfe meant that he was unwilling and unable to explore why he had behaved as he did. Part of his reluctance stemmed from fear that he might do or say something that would further wound Aline. "*I love you,*" he assured her, "and I no longer want to say anything to trouble you." Nothing should blur his message: "I know to the bottom of the cup how badly I have acted, and my heart is simply dead with such despair that I can hardly lift my tongue to speak."

No doubt Aline was right when she concluded, years later, that the basic problem was that Wolfe "was terrifically jealous, in every way, sexually jealous, and jealous of his work." When they were both in New York, it was sexual jealousy that had tormented him. "I could not endure her loving anyone else or having physical relations with any one else," he said, "and my madness and jeal-

ousy ate at me like a poison, like a horrible sterility and barrenness." But after they separated he recognized that he had no
grounds for thinking that Aline was sleeping with anybody else.
He correctly suspected, however, that his demands on her time
and emotions had become too taxing. When she returned from
Europe in August, she began giving more attention to other young
artists and writers, like Russel Wright and Irene Sharaff. Her interest in these new protégés helped account for the somewhat
brisk tone of her brief responses to Wolfe's long, tortured letters.

But other kinds of jealousy continued to torment him. He was
envious that Aline had her devoted family and a wide circle of
loyal friends while he had only her — and not even all of her. He
claimed that the differences in their letters showed the differences
in their situations. "I bring all sorts of things into my letters," he
explained, "because I used always to dream of a life with you in
which all this would figure. . . . I used to feel that love was part
of my life — or that my life and all the million things that went
boiling through my brain was part of love. I have never been able
to cut them apart as you have your life, your many activities, your
relations with other people, and your feeling for me. And," he
concluded, "I think a great deal of our trouble has come from
that."

He was less open in admitting that he was also jealous of Aline's
work. While he was struggling vainly to get anything into print,
she had risen to become one of the principal stage designers in
America. Trying not to offend her, he no longer berated her for
flaunting her triumphs in his face, but there was an unmistakable
note of envy in some of his letters. After explaining that he did not
know where he was going or what he would do, he added: "I
suppose you are looking forward to your return to New York
where you will have several shows to do. You are fortunate in
having work which gratifies you so completely and in which you
are so successful."

Convinced that the theater was full of falseness and chicanery
and most actors were lechers or perverts, he pictured Aline surrounded by theatrical people with "little furtive eyes all wet with
lust," by "brutes heavy of jowl and gut, and ropy with their
sperm." "You are the most precious thing in my life," he assured
her, "but you are imprisoned in a jungle of thorns, and I can not
come near you without bleeding."

Later he hinted at another reason for his conduct toward Aline by blaming his "feeling of inferiority, induced by some terrible shame, distrust, and humiliation of the past." She got at part of the truth when she said that the trouble stemmed from "the irrevocable difference in our ages." The age gap was truly unbridgeable because the more Wolfe needed her love, comfort, and nurture, the more she seemed in his mind to be playing the role in his life that his mother had never adequately played. He best expressed his deepest feelings in a semifictional account, intended for *The Web and the Rock*, in which the hero shouts at his much older mistress: "I've destroyed my youth and thrown my life away over a woman old enough to be my mother! . . . I've polluted my blood with a foul incestuous shame that all the rivers of the world could never wash away."

Since incest-guilt was at the root of his quarrels with Aline, it was hard to know what, if any, future they could share. Tacitly acknowledging that the affair had ended, his letters during the summer and fall of 1928 had an elegaic tone. Much of the time he seemed to be laying a wreath on the tomb of a dead love. "No matter what I have thought or believed," he assured her, "the feeling has become very clear in my mind that it has been a very grand thing to have known you. . . . I do not know what it may mean for my life to have known you. . . . The whole engine of my life mounted to its greatest drive and expenditure when we were together, but whether on this account it will hereafter be a better engine I can not say."

Observing that he wrote of their love in the past tense, Aline sensed that he was saying he had left her forever. Her certainty grew when there was a chance for them to meet in Berlin after she finished her cure at Carlsbad. Though Wolfe was only a hundred and fifty miles away, in Cologne, he refused to join her, explaining: "To see you for three days in a new and strange place before you sailed would be too bad and too unsatisfactory. Its effect on me would be explosive." No more satisfactory was his failure to answer her repeated question whether he ever intended to come back to her. Always evading a direct reply, he assured her of his undying love and expressed the hope that some day they would meet in "loving friendship." Furious, she responded: "I will never be satisfied with this loving friendship you talk so much about. The phrase stings me to helpless anger. I am your true love until

I die, how dare you write to me to make 'other arrangements for my happiness.' "

In part, Wolfe's evasive talk about a future Platonic relationship reflected his constitutional reluctance to make hard choices. "It is part of my temper," he knew, "to postpone pain and a final decision as long as possible." But even more it indicated his deep uncertainty, not merely about Aline but about himself and his future. He did not know where he was going. "I am at times," he explained, "like some blind thing upon the floor of the sea feeling its way along."

During much of his stay abroad he seemed to be groping toward self-destruction. Isolated, lonely, and depressed, he began taking symbolic leave of the world. When Aline returned to New York, he sent her directions that read very much like a last will and testament: "I give you all my books and manuscripts, or such of them as you will have, and anything else you may find at Eleventh Street." Whatever she did not want, she should give to the Soldiers and Sailors Home. She could keep or destroy his books and papers "or give them to the junkman or some charity," but she must not show them to her friends and acquaintances. Finally he enjoined: "Do not let anyone use the cot on which I slept for any purpose, either sitting or lying down, as long as it stays in the room where I slept and where my books are. . . . This is all that I ask, but I pray that any one who violates my wish on this matter may be cursed with a most bitter and bloody grief."

There is nothing to indicate that Wolfe contemplated suicide, but his actions during the summer and fall of 1928 showed an unprecedented willingness to take risks and a disregard for his life. As Aline pointed out, he spent most of the months aimlessly banging about Europe, drinking, brawling, and consorting with unsavory companions. In August, for instance, when he arrived in Antwerp without announcement or reservations, he could not find a room in the city, and after midnight he went out to the little town of Malines, where he finally found a place to sleep above "a dirty little drink shop." Throwing himself on the bed, he tried to rest, but through the thin partition he heard "three villains" whispering about the rich "Englishman" next door. A little after three in the morning they quietly tried his door, but he let out a blood-curdling yell and threw his size-thirteen shoe at the entrance. When the would-be robbers retreated, he began to sing and to talk loudly to himself, hitting the wall with his big walking stick and from time to time bursting into sudden fits of insane laughter. Not until dawn, when the streets began to fill with people, did he dare to doze off.

A little later, in Germany, he tried to disguise his identity by growing a mustache. "It covers my lip," he discovered, "and gives me quite a piratical look." When he registered at his hotel in Frankfurt under his proper name and nationality, the clerks believed that he was someone else traveling incognito. They insisted on answering all his questions in French, and he heard the head porter tell the desk clerk, with a knowing smile, that their guest's "English was good, but spoken with a pronounced accent."

But not until he reached Munich in September did his indifference — indeed, his aversion — to living become fully evident. Arriving shortly before his birthday, he was there for the Oktoberfest, the fall celebration of the doubly strong October beer. Day after day he went out to the Theresienwiese to attend the festival. The sight and sound and smell of the thousands of Germans who gathered to consume great slabs of beef and to drink liter after liter of the potent beer both attracted and repelled him. He had what he called a "crowd neurosis," for he had been "afraid of people in groups and crowds since his childhood." In the throngs at the Oktoberfest "a fear greater than any he had ever known rose up and inundated his heart. He was terribly and desperately afraid." But, with characteristic ambivalence, he also found the crowds in these "immense and appalling" beer halls irresistibly fascinating, for it was here that he thought he could find "the heart of Germany, not the heart of its poets and scholars, but its real heart." Watching the Germans eat and drink themselves "into a state of bestial stupefaction" and then, linking arms, stand and sing their drinking songs, he thought he was witnessing "in this great smoky hell of beer" what must be "the magic, the essence of the race."

On September 30, accompanying some acquaintances to the Theresienwiese, he decided to stay on after they had had their fill. That evening he went from one of the great beer halls to another, and by the time the fair began to close at 10:30 he had drunk seven or eight liters of dark beer — almost a quart of alcohol. Heading for a side exit from the tent, he ran into a group of Germans who were singing a final song before leaving, and they stopped him in a friendly enough fashion. One grasped him by the arm and, when

Wolfe backed away, held on. Always panicked when another man touched him, now desperately so because he was drunk, he pushed the German away and knocked him over a table. Then he ran out of the tent.

But the exit he chose led only to an enclosed space at the side of the tent, and the Germans whom he had insulted came after him, one brandishing a folding chair from the beer hall. Cornered, Wolfe turned on his assailants, and they fought in a "horrible slippery mudhole." The details of the struggle were never clear in his mind. He was not sure whether there were two or three assailants, but, pummeling each other, all slipped and fell into the mud. "At that time I was too wild, too insane, to be afraid," he wrote, "but I seemed to be drowning in mud." Blinded by blood from wounds on his head, he got back on his feet, lashed out at one of the Germans and, when he fell, leaped on him. He and his attacker tried to choke each other, and Wolfe held on, determined "to kill this thing or be killed." Then a woman, who belonged to the party of Germans, jumped on his back, beat him over the head, and gouged his face and eyes with her nails, crying, "Leave my man alone!"

By the time the police arrived, some of the Germans had run away. They picked up Wolfe, who drunkenly insisted on reclaiming his battered old hat from the mud, and took him first to the police doctors. After dressing his head wounds, they discovered that his nose was broken and told him that he must see a surgeon the next day. After interrogation they let him return to his pension, where other American tourists suggested the name of an American physician, Dr. Eugene F. DuBois of Cornell, who was an advanced resident in the famous clinic of Dr. Friedrich von Müller in Munich.

The next day Dr. DuBois, who looked "professorily American . . . with winking eyeglasses, and a dry prim careful voice," saw that Wolfe was admitted to the clinic and that he received the personal attention of Dr. Lexer, the chief of surgery. After examining and probing in his thorough Germanic manner, Dr. Lexer announced that Wolfe's broken nose would mend itself and, as Dr. DuBois reported later, he "did a rather poor job of cleaning up the scalp and suturing some but not all of the cuts." Dr. Lexer's failure to notice one gash on the back of the head, hidden by heavy, matted hair, earned him Wolfe's undying enmity. When Wolfe complained, the doctor had his whole head shaved so that no other injuries could be overlooked. Bruised and aching, entirely bald, with a broken nose stuffed with blood-soaked cotton wadding, Wolfe passed his twenty-eighth birthday in the hospital.

V

Wolfe recognized that the Oktoberfest was a turning point in his life. For months he had been "insane with the brooding inversions of my own temper, disappointed, and sick at heart because of the failure of acceptance of my book, lost to everyone who cared for me — not even leaving an address — sick with a thousand diseases of the spirit." For months he had been telling Aline Bernstein that he deserved punishment for his abominable behavior toward her. Now that he had received it, his burden of shame was lightened. The beating he received at Munich marked an end of the downward, self-destructive path he had been following. It is understandable that, for the rest of his life, he planned to write a book he would call "The October Fair."

The transformation in Wolfe was not, of course, instantaneous. When he was released from the hospital on October 4, he tried to resume his usual strenuous round of sightseeing, determinedly working his way through room after room of the huge Deutsches Museum, visiting parts of Munich he had not previously seen, and attending the theater. An old Englishwoman, Mrs. Louise Parks-Richards, who had taken an interest in him before his accident, tried to involve him in a book she was writing on the Passion Play, and, though his nose was still badly swollen and he had to wear a loose skullcap to cover his "bald scarred dome," he went with her to Oberammergau, where they met the men who played Pilate and the Christus in the play. But Wolfe could not keep up the pace. He was depressed, very tired, and "weak as a cat." Easily upset, he grew very anxious when a police detective questioned him again, and he was half-convinced when Mrs. Parks-Richards told him she had heard him described on a radio broadcast as "an American criminal."*

*Apparently testing his ability to create entirely fictional situations, Wolfe wrote Mrs. Bernstein on October 10, 1928, of the death of old Mrs. Parks-Richards, while she was listening to radio reports on the Graf Zeppelin's trip to America. Mrs. Bernstein easily detected that the story was made-up. John S. Terry believed another of Wolfe's inven-

With a sense of making his escape he fled to Austria, spending first a few days in Salzburg and then settling in Vienna. Though he still suffered from a heavy cold, he was now in better spirits and believed "that life is going to be different and more beautiful." Indeed, the next eight weeks, mostly spent in Vienna but with a week in Budapest and a one-day excursion to the Hungarian village of Mezökövesd, a tourist attraction because of its needlework, were among the happiest of his life. He loved Vienna, and he poked into every street and every museum, still ostensibly collecting background information for the Viennese chapters of "The River People," for he had vowed to make his "picture of life there as seductive and appealing as possible." All in all, he recorded in his notebook, "I am steadier in spirit since coming to Vienna than for months."

News from America helped lift his spirits. Rebuffed by so many publishers, Madeleine Boyd had shrewdly maneuvered the senior editor at Charles Scribner's Sons, Maxwell Evarts Perkins, into asking for Wolfe's manuscript. On October 15 she learned that Scribners was interested in the novel, and she immediately wrote Wolfe. Aline, with whom she shared the good news, also wrote and cabled him. Because both used his Munich address, the news did not reach him in Vienna until the end of the month.

Outwardly he refused to get excited. After all, Mrs. Boyd did not write that Scribners had accepted his novel; she merely said that Perkins — whose name meant so little to Wolfe that he could not keep it in mind and referred to him as "Mr. Peters" — was "very much interested, would like to see you to talk things over." Wolfe had had similar responses from other publishers, and he tried to avoid experiencing again the agony of rejection. He saw no reason for changing his travel plans, and he wrote Aline: "In my present state Scribners does not make even a dull echo in me — I have seen so much in print that I feel it is criminal to add to it."

But he was not so blasé as he tried to sound. When he heard from Perkins himself, he answered promptly, and in a most ingratiating way. "Your words of praise have filled me with hope, and are worth more than their weight in diamonds to me," he

---

tions — referred to briefly in his pocket notebook as "How I Murdered The Old Woman in The Antiquariat."

responded. He had no way of knowing it, but his plea for "the direct criticism and advice of an older and more critical person" was the best possible approach to Perkins.

Scribners' interest encouraged him to get back to work on "The River People." He did not add much to his improbable love story of Joel and Li, but he drafted chapters on "Oliver's" fight at the Munich Oktoberfest and on his hospital experiences with an uncaring German doctor and a friendly American physician. Then his tale took still another direction, and he wrote an amusing chapter on the decision of Hoyt and Hoyt, "which did a thriving business in the works of Victorian novelists, memoirs of Woodrow Wilson written by ex-cabinet ministers, and in the confessions of aged and respectable actresses and politicians," to publish Oliver Weston's "unprinted and unprintable Leviathan." As if to ward off another defeat, he concocted a summary of the unfavorable reviews of Oliver's novel, which sold only 237 copies.

Wolfe's spirits had begun to revive even before he heard from Scribners, and after the purgative fight in Munich his letters to Aline took on a new tone. No longer was he willing to accept her rebuke that he had wasted his time and his energies. He rejected as "twaddle" her charge that he ought to work harder. When she wrote that she still had faith in his great talent, he responded: "OW! Did someone put you up to using 'still,' or did some flash of devilish cleverness show it to you? You could not have found a little word that could sting better." Did she mean "*Still* (in spite of —); *still* (no matter what other people say); still (although you are thus far a total failure); still (because it makes me feel so noble and grand to keep on saying I believe in you when no one else does)"?

For the first time in months he was able to think clearly about his future as a writer. "I'm glad I'm alive," he assured Aline after his wounds began to heal. "I've meant to lead a good life, and I've led a bad and wasteful one. But out of all this waste and sin I believe in spite of all logic, that some beauty will come." "Ramping and chafing to get to work again," he began once more to believe that he had something to say that would be new and important. "However many millions [of] things and books and people there may be in the world, no one has exactly the same picture of life as I have," he was confident; "no one can make the same kind of picture as I can — whether it be bad or good."

He recognized that it was time to return to America. He had

been alone so long in foreign lands that he sometimes felt "like a man who is out in mid ocean in a rowboat," and he needed to be back among people he could talk to. When he came home he knew he could encounter "horrible fatal things" that would sicken him: "the bigotry, the hypocrisy, the intolerance, the ku kluxers, the politicians." But he was determined to think only of "the glorious elements of America, the great towers, the wealth, the hope, the opportunity, the possibility of everything happening."

"I am going home," he wrote Aline from Budapest; "I am going to try to get hold of something, and to do something with my life." What that would be he did not know. He would, of course, go at once to see the people at Charles Scribner's Sons, and he would again get in touch with Mrs. Resor about a job with J. Walter Thompson. Maybe Olin Dows would help him find work. "I have no sense of what is going to happen to me in the future," he declared. "At any rate I lived in a garret once and was not unhappy there; I am willing to work; and I have not yet lost all hope entirely." Finally, he turned to the subject that concerned Aline most: "I do not know what your relation to me will be now, but I have always loved you, and it seems to be the one fixed thing in my life." At the end of a quick guidebook tour of Italy he sailed on December 21 from Naples, on board the *Vulcania*, bound for New York.

He arrived in New York on the last day of 1928, with only twenty-seven cents in his pocket — all that remained of the three hundred fifty dollars Aline had cabled him in Vienna for his return passage. At the Harvard Club he found a message from Charles Scribner's Sons, asking him to call at his first opportunity.

VII

A Miracle of Good Luck

ON JANUARY 2, 1929, Wolfe made his first visit to the offices
of Charles Scribner's Sons, at 597 Fifth Avenue. If he
expected to find a sumptuously furnished executive suite,
he was disappointed. The editorial department, which was above
the Scribner Book Store on the ground floor of the building, was
a nest of small offices, simply equipped with somewhat battered
but functional wooden desks and chairs and, here and there, with
filing cabinets. A receptionist directed him down to the corridor to
the office of Maxwell E. Perkins.

Looking up from the desk where he was working, Perkins got
his first glimpse of Wolfe, framed in the doorway of the office.
Apart from Wolfe's height of nearly six feet, six inches, what
struck Perkins first was the fact that his visitor had a dispropor-
tionately small head, surrounded by an aureole of unruly hair,
which had not yet grown to manageable length since his hospital
experience in Munich. Something about Wolfe's figure, or the
brightness of his countenance, made Perkins think at once of
Shelley.

Charles Scribner II, the head of the firm, was in Perkins's office.
Obviously he had heard about Wolfe's manuscript and was curious to see this latest discovery of his senior editor. He withdrew
after a brief conversation, and Wolfe was left alone with the man
with whom he would work closely for the next eight years.

At this time Wolfe knew almost nothing about Perkins. He saw
before him a man sixteen years his senior, of moderate height and
with striking, regular features, a trifle delicate to be considered
handsome, and with graying, receding hair, combed neatly back
from his forehead. Like Aline Bernstein, Perkins was slightly deaf,
but he had no difficulty in hearing Wolfe's deep, resonant voice.
Possibly Wolfe already knew that Perkins was a Harvard graduate,
who initially hoped to become a writer himself but instead had
worked as a newspaper reporter in New York before joining the
advertising department and later the editorial staff of Charles
Scribner's Sons. A novice in the world of publishing, he had no
idea that Perkins had for several years quietly been building up the
Scribners fiction list, which already included Henry James and
Edith Wharton, by publishing the works of a younger generation
of American novelists. F. Scott Fitzgerald was Perkins's discovery
and, with Fitzgerald's help, he also added Ernest Hemingway to
the Scribners list.

Wolfe did immediately recognize, however, that he was dealing
with an intelligent, gentle man, genuinely interested in him and
his work. After a few general questions, Perkins spoke of the scene
in "O Lost" that showed W. O. Gant, the stonecutter, selling a
marble angel to the madam of Altamont's leading brothel, to be
placed, with an appropriately saccharine inscription, at the grave
of one of her "girls." "I know you can't print that!" Wolfe interrupted; "I'll take it out at once, Mr. Perkins." But Perkins assured
him that the chapter formed a superb short story; that, indeed,
only the week before he had read it to Hemingway, who agreed
with his opinion; and that he asked about it simply to ascertain
whether Wolfe would write a brief new introduction so that it
could be published in *Scribner's Magazine*. Wolfe's spirits plum-
meted, for he feared that this one story was all that Perkins wanted
from his huge manuscript.

Then Perkins went on to talk about the book as a whole, referring to careful notes he had made on each chapter. He was more
familiar with the manuscript than the author himself, for Wolfe
had not looked at it for more than six months. Wildly excited by
Perkins's interest, Wolfe burst out with promises to cut this and
that — only to have the editor respond each time: "No, no — you
must let that stay word for word — that scene's simply magnificent." Perkins was not much troubled by episodes that Wolfe

feared were "too coarse, vulgar, profane, or obscene," though he warned that a few words might have to be changed. What did worry him was the fact that the manuscript was "somewhat incoherent and very long." Recognizing that Wolfe's book followed no orthodox form, Perkins suggested that it would gain unity if "the strange wild people" in the story were always presented "as seen through the eyes of a strange wild boy" — the hero, Eugene Gant.

Feeling that for the first time in his life he was getting criticism that could help him, Wolfe was ready to agree to anything immediately. But Perkins urged him to take two or three days to think over the proposed revisions, promising that, if necessary, Scribners might offer him a small advance to live on while he was making the changes. As Wolfe left he was introduced to John Hall Wheelock, the editor who was Perkins's closest associate at Scribners, a sensitive, soft-spoken poet, who said that "O Lost" was one of the most interesting manuscripts he had read in years. Wolfe departed euphoric.

Perkins was also pleased. Despite his promise to Mrs. Boyd, he had not initially read every word of Wolfe's manuscript. Fascinated by military history, he had been caught up in Wolfe's opening pages that described the encounter between young W. O. Gant and the Confederate soldiers — including Bacchus Pentland, his future brother-in-law — on the road to Gettysburg, but after that his attention waned. He passed "O Lost" on to Charles Dunn, who had for many years been reading unsolicited manuscripts for Scribners. Excited by Wolfe's scene in the Uneeda Lunch No. 3, where Ben Gant and the townsmen engaged in ribald early-morning conversation, Dunn urged Wheelock to read the manuscript. About the same time Wallace Meyer, who had recently rejoined the Scribners firm, got interested in it. Both asked Perkins to take another look at the book, and Wheelock provided a detailed analysis and criticism. Perkins did so, though he still harbored doubts about the book and more about its author, of whose harum-scarum escapades in Europe he had learned from Mrs. Boyd.

His interview with Wolfe calmed his fears. Like his distinguished predecessor as senior editor at Scribners, William Crary Brownell, Perkins thought it was more important to judge a man than a manuscript. He liked what he saw in Wolfe. Moreover, he learned enough in that conversation to be able to persuade Charles Scribner and other editors at the firm that Wolfe was an author willing and eager to take suggestions and criticisms, so that his gargantuan manuscript could be reduced to a reasonable length.

A week later Wolfe returned to Scribners with a plan for revision. He agreed to cut out the opening fifty-one pages, which traced the early history of the Gant and Pentland families, to shorten the third book of the novel, which dealt with young Gant's college years, in order "to keep Eugene's relations with his family uppermost," and also to eliminate "all unnecessary coarseness in language." If Scribners offered "some definite assurance of their willingness to publish the book," he promised to deliver one hundred pages of revised manuscript each week. Pleased, Perkins told him that the firm had "practically made up" its mind to publish his novel and smilingly agreed that he might tell his good news to "a dear friend" — Aline Bernstein. As Wolfe pranced out of the office, Wheelock said, "I hope you have a good place to work in — you have a big job ahead."

Wolfe left Scribners "drunk with glory." First he told Aline. Then he informed Mrs. Boyd, whom he now formally named his representative in a statement as naive as it was all-inclusive: "I, Thomas Wolfe, hereby authorize Mrs. Madeleine Boyd to be my literary agent." Two days later he received an official letter of acceptance from Scribners, together with a contract, which gave the author a royalty of ten percent on the retail price of the first two thousand copies of his book that were sold, escalating to fifteen percent on all additional copies. Scribners also offered five hundred dollars as an advance against these royalties. Even after Mrs. Boyd's fee of ten percent was deducted, this seemed an enormous amount to him. For the next several days, as he wrote Mrs. Roberts, he "felt like that man in one of [Stephen] Leacock's novels who 'sprang upon his horse and rode madly off in all directions.' " He would sit for hours at the Harvard Club, staring at his contract and the letter, and then rush out and walk eighty blocks up Fifth Avenue, unaware even of where he was heading. He carried the contract and the letter around in his pocket, and from time to time he would pull them out to "gaze tenderly at them, and kiss them passionately."

But after a day or two he realized that he had work to do and that he must get settled. As always, he turned to Aline for help, and together they found a two-room apartment at the rear of the second floor at 27 West 15th Street. Here he was alone most of the time, but Aline set up her drafting table near the back window, which had the best light. Wolfe also recognized that he could not live indefinitely on the advance he had received from Scribners, and once more he turned back to New York University for employment. Professor Watt had no openings in the English department for the semester that was about to begin, but the university was able to offer him one course in freshman English composition at the College of Fine Arts, which met in a loft off Fifth Avenue in the Thirties, and Dean Munn, probably from his own pocket, paid him three hundred dollars to help grade papers from his course on "Literature and the Bible."

I

"I am at work on the revision," Wolfe wrote Mabel toward the end of January, "still happy, but more settled." Promptly he completed his first assignment, which was to prepare a brief new opening for "An Angel on the Porch" scene, so that it could stand as a short story. When *Scribner's Magazine* paid him one hundred fifty dollars for it, he was delighted, for that was twice as much as he had expected. At Mrs. Boyd's urging he tried to detach other sections of his novel for publication as short stories, but she had no luck in placing them.

When it came to shortening his huge manuscript, he was not so successful. Condensation was "a stiff perplexing job," he found; reducing his manuscript was like putting a corset on an elephant. "I stare for hours at the manuscript before cutting out a few sentences," he wrote Mrs. Boyd; "sometimes I want to rip in blindly and slash, but unless I know *where* the result would be disastrous." With only a little exaggeration he claimed that in the two months after Scribners accepted his book he "had cut out twenty or thirty thousand words, and added fifty thousand more." When he returned the first half of his revised manuscript to Scribners, Perkins found that it was only eight pages shorter than the original version.

At this point the editor began to take a more active role. On March 28 he called Wolfe into his office, reviewed the manuscript with him, and began to indicate specific cuts that ought to be made. From this date Wolfe's pocket notebooks were filled with lists of passages to be excised or sharply condensed.

In later years Perkins, mindful of the rumor that Wolfe was a kind of automatic word-producing machine, whose product had somehow to be packaged into novels by an editorial assembly-line at Scribners, minimized the extent and nature of the changes that he had insisted on. Indeed, he claimed that, apart from recommending the deletion of the "very long narrative" of W. O. Gant's early life, his assistance had been "in re-arranging, not in cutting." In particular he pointed to Wolfe's "wonderful account of Gant's return from his wanderings and his journey through the town in a trolley car in early morning." In the original typescript this passage immediately preceded the scene in the Uneeda Lunch greasy-spoon. Perkins thought that both episodes gave "an astonishing sense of the character of the town" but, juxtaposed, they weakened each other. Consequently he recommended shifting Gant's return to an earlier chapter. But in general he insisted that neither the editing nor the cutting of "O Lost" was "so very extensive."

Wheelock's recollection was more accurate: "I'm aware of no book that had ever been edited so extensively up to that point." In all, more than 90,000 words were eliminated from Wolfe's manuscript. This was far less than the 150,000 or 200,000 that he later remembered; nevertheless, it did represent a reduction of between one-third and one-fourth. Taken together, the discarded material was longer than the average novel of the decade.

Some of the changes Perkins urged were obviously necessary. For instance, two long passages that summarized Eugene Gant's — and Thomas Wolfe's — voyages and experiences after he graduated from college were clearly out of place in a book that ended with Eugene's twentieth year. These, in fact, were a kind of synopsis of Wolfe's second novel, *Of Time and the River*. Equally inappropriate were occasional paragraphs where Wolfe thrust his head from behind the curtains to speak directly to his audience:

> Meanwhile, Julia had begun to dream of Dixieland. Oh, but we could tell you more if we would. But not yet, not yet. The Time is not ripe. But it will come! Suspense! Suspense! Suspense!

Perkins insisted that a few indelicate passages be dropped — for instance, a nasty sentence or two about Eugene's childhood friend

who had sex with his pet hens. Out, too, came some bibliograph-
ical buffoonery, as when Wolfe referred to an edition of "the
writings of Jamlichus, Porphyry, Michael Psellus, and Proclus,
with annotations, a glossary and an introductory monograph by
Thomas Clayton Wolfe, Ph. D. (L. L. D. Oxon; Camb; Harv;
Sweet Briar; Bryn Mawr; Zurich; Centre College; Valparaiso; and
Allegheny College) and Stoke Poges Professor of North American Folk Lore at the University of Chickamauga."

But most of the changes reflected Perkins's belief that the novel
suffered from a "lack of form" and that the only way to give unity
to the book was by eliminating everything not directly related to
"Eugene's life up to the time when he was about to set off into the
world." The book should be restricted to events "all virtually
within the experience and memory of this boy Eugene." That rule
required discarding long sections on the Pentland family. Out,
too, came a description of the Altamont annual firemen's tourna-
ment. Out came an account of the Altamont amusement park.
Out came a parody of T. S. Eliot's "Sweeney Among the Nightingales." Out came a passage on sexual relations between white
paperboys and a middle-aged Negro woman. Out came most of
the story of Judge Webster Sondley, who begat mulatto children
and studied demonology. Out came the early life of John Dorsey
Leonard, the headmaster of Leonard's Fitting School, which was
in fact necessary for an understanding of Leonard's limited ability
as a scholar and of his unfailing support for his frail, tubercular
wife. Out, too, came sections that illustrated the social stratifica-
tion of the students in Leonard's school and that precisely located
Eugene and the whole Gant family in the Altamont social structure.

These and numerous other similar cuts significantly changed
Wolfe's novel. He had intended its three books as "a series of
widening concentric circles." The first gave a picture of the Gant-
Pentland family; the second portrayed Altamont; the third gave a
view of the state of Old Catawba and of the South as a whole.
What connected these was "the cyclic curve of a family's life."
Wolfe only imperfectly executed his plan, for both the introductory section and the final book showed a notable loss of control,
but his purpose was clearly there. Perkins, who had only the
faintest understanding of Wolfe's plan, thought much of his
manuscript was simply irrelevant. He was not an advocate of

perfectly planned fiction, for his favorite author was Tolstoi, but he did think that a novel ought to have a straightforward story line. In Wolfe's manuscript he found it in the development of Eugene Gant from infancy to manhood. By removing all passages that did not tell Eugene's own story, he helped transform Wolfe's book from a portrait of a society to an account of the life of one young man.

As always, tampering with his work hurt Wolfe. He felt that the publisher took pleasure in hacking off large chunks of his manuscript, and he grumbled in his pocket notebook about "the Passion For Condensation," observing: "It may be a very bad passion. Probably what we need is a passion for expansion. What most of us mean when we say we have a passion for condensation is simply that we haven't very much to write about." After one particularly painful session with Perkins, Wolfe bounded up the stairs to Mrs. Boyd's apartment shouting, to the consternation of the ladies in the hair salon on the lower floor, "Those sons of bitches, they are taking the balls off me!"

But in Perkins's office, where he went two or three times every week during April and May to receive new lists of passages that must be compressed or deleted and to submit his revisions for the editor's inspection, he offered no objections to the truncation and transformation of his book. His deferential acceptance of criticism — so unlike his truculent resistance in earlier years — in part reflected Mrs. Boyd's advice to accept Perkins's suggestions, for, she reminded him, the editor was "the sole and only excuse . . . for Scott Fitzgerald having been successful as he is."

But Wolfe deferred mostly because of his growing respect for Charles Scribner's Sons and his deepening affection for Perkins. From the beginning he was convinced that Perkins, Wheelock, and the others at Scribners were helping "in every way with criticism, editing, and a vast amount of patient, careful work." In the long hours he spent in Perkins's office, over the drinks they often had afterwards at the Chatham Walk, and during the long strolls they sometimes took in the evenings, Wolfe came to think of Perkins as not merely a superb editor but as a superior human being. The two grew to be friends as well as co-workers. For Perkins, the father of five daughters, Wolfe became in a sense the son he never had — a son the more dear because he exhibited the extravagant impulses, the excessive appetites, the torrential loquacity in which Perkins would never allow himself to indulge. And for Wolfe, Perkins's modesty, patience, common sense, and generosity made the editor seem almost like a father — like the wise, all-seeing father he tried to believe that W. O. Wolfe had been. "Young men sometimes believe in the existence of heroic figures, stronger and wiser than themselves, to whom they can turn for an answer to all their vexation and grief," he wrote Perkins at Christmas. "You are for me such a figure: you are one of the rocks to which my life is anchored."

Accepting the cuts and the structural alterations that Perkins recommended, Wolfe made no objection when Scribners requested a different title for the book. "O Lost" — that reminder of the haunting refrain, "O lost, and by the wind grieved, ghost, come back again," which linked the segments of the unabridged manuscript — was less important in the shortened version. Anyway, the Scribners sales force thought it lacked appeal. Always happy when he was drawing up lists of titles, Wolfe proposed "The Exile's Story," "The Childhood of Mr. Faust," "The Lost Language," "They Are Strange and They Are Lost," and dozens of others before he settled on *Look Homeward, Angel*, from a line in Milton's "Lycidas": "Look homeward, angel, now, and melt in ruth."

More troubling was Perkins's recommendation that at several places he ought to vary the descriptions of some of the characters. He could not do it, he told the editor; he had described the people exactly as they were. For the first time it dawned on Perkins, with horror, that the book was "often almost literally autobiographical — that these people in it were his people." Appalled, Perkins insisted that at least the names of living persons should be altered. Consequently, in "Eugene's" family, the father remained "W. O." and the two dead brothers, "Grover" and "Benjamin," but the mother became "Eliza," the two sisters "Daisy" and "Helen," and the two brothers, "Steve" and "Luke." The names of the Wolfes' neighbors, such as Colvin and Parkinson, were altered to "Duncan" and "Tarkinton." The names of streets and buildings in Asheville ("Altamont") underwent transparent alterations: Grove Street became Vine Street; the Orange Street School became the Plum Street School; and the Oaks Hotel became the Ivy Hotel.

It was much harder to know what to do about scenes — especially disreputable ones — in which readily identifiable characters participated. For one thing, work at Scribners on the manuscript had already gone too far to permit what would have amounted to a rewriting of the book. For another, Wolfe insisted that the characters in his novel were not literally true to life. When Perkins warned that he ran the risk of libel suits, he argued, on the one hand, "that all serious creative work must be at bottom autobiographical" and, on the other, "that these people are *great* people and that they should be told about." To mollify the publisher Wolfe agreed to preface his novel with a note to the reader asserting "that this book is a fiction" — but claiming that all "fiction is fact selected and understood." "Dr. Johnson remarked that a man would turn over half a library to make a single book," he observed; "in the same way, a novelist may turn over half the people in a town to make a single figure in his novel."

II

The months while Wolfe was revising *Look Homeward, Angel* and seeing the book through the press were among the happiest of his life. After returning from Europe he had resumed his relationship with Aline Bernstein, but with less ardor and less suspicion on both sides. She was much occupied with designing and constructing a new house in Armonk, New York. High-rise buildings now surrounded the Bernsteins' brownstone on West 77th Street, and the whole family wanted to escape to the suburbs. Supervising every detail of the new residence, Aline went out to Armonk frequently, and sometimes Wolfe accompanied her.

Mostly, though, he was busy with his own work. Because his mind and heart were elsewhere, he found his teaching duties onerous, but he continued to write long comments on the papers he graded. His relations with his colleagues were prickly. He thought that they resented his success in placing his novel with a major publisher and claimed that many of them "turned slightly green, yellow, and purple from stored-up poison and malice." When he speculated publicly on the royalties that his book might earn, one fellow teacher remarked snidely that "any book which wins popular acclaim is cheap." Some colleagues who did not envy Wolfe thought he was old-fashioned and out-of-date. Like so many other academics in the United States at the time, members of the New

York University English department were becoming increasingly left-wing in politics, and they scorned Wolfe's ignorance of Marxist dialectics and his indifference to social problems. They called his concern for literary values escapism, and one remarked that for Wolfe to write about his childhood experiences was like a "dog returning to his vomit."

Spending as little time as possible at the university, Wolfe worked long hours in his apartment, where James Lewis Mandel, one of his students, retyped the revised portions of the manuscript of *Look Homeward, Angel.* As always, Wolfe's rooms were disorderly. His bed was never made, the floor was littered, and his large round table was covered with "papers, ledgers, books, unwashed dishes, ashes, cigarette butts, pencils and glasses." In person he was equally untidy, for his trousers were always unpressed, his shirt was soiled, his hair unkempt, and his fingernails grimy.

Even while he was revising *Look Homeward, Angel,* he was thinking about his next book. Now that it was established that he was a novelist, not a playwright, he began to devour an extraordinary amount of fiction, drawing some from the Bernsteins' very good collection of books but more from the library of the Harvard Club. For the first time he began systematically reading American novels. He had little success with Henry James, who, he thought, had "too much fluency" and was inferior to Thomas Hardy; but he carefully studied Melville, Stephen Crane, Fitzgerald, Hemingway, and Gertrude Stein. At the same time he began reading contemporary British novelists, such as Aldous Huxley and D. H. Lawrence. To Virginia Woolf he took a strong dislike, noting that her "real name was Virginia Stephen. She has no right to call herself Virginia Woolf. The . . . only real branch of the family left was in North Carolina, of which Thomas Wolfe is the illustrious representative."

Searching for models, Wolfe had no clear idea what his next book would be about. He did know that he was bored with "The River People" and was not going to develop that story further. Aside from that, he simply wanted to write about America and Americans, to experiment with a new form suitable for American rather than European subjects, and to use the American vernacular. He filled his little notebook with fragments of conversation overheard in bars and restaurants and on the streets:

Will you send me a ticket?
Sent you a *tick* et.
And I did.
What about your girl friend?
I suppose you found you better go.
I don't know how it's going to turn
    out — that's one of the reasons.
That's *absolutely* true.

From the start he planned to include in his next novel passages of cadenced prose — and more of them than he had used in *Look Homeward, Angel*. He began developing one lyrical passage that, much reworked, became the proem to *Of Time and the River*: "Of wandering forever and the earth again. From these dark tide winds and waters of our sleep on which a few stars sparely look, call up the strange dark fish, the swart eternal whisperings." He also started working out a theme that would suggest the repression of New Englanders: "O bitterly bitterly Boston one time more."

He was not fixed on making the new book a continuation of the story of Eugene Gant. Of course he expected that it would incorporate and reflect his own experiences, but he thought that the hero of the new book ought to be "a physical picture of my soul — a mixture of the ape and the angel" — in contrast to Eugene Gant, whose body was physically identical to Wolfe's. He thought of making this new protagonist a man of "about middling height, but the stoop of his heavy shoulders and the great length of his arms which dangled grotesquely and apishly almost to his knees made him appear at first sight a good deal shorter." Because of his "curious loping prowl that suggested the motion of a gorilla," schoolmates gave him the name "Jocko." Already Wolfe had in mind a clear picture of George Webber, the hero of *The Web and the Rock* and *You Can't Go Home Again*.

The structure and content of the new book remained vague in his mind. He discarded most of what he had written for "The River People," retaining only some autobiographical sections. He thought of weaving these into a novel called "The Fast Express," which would include stories about his hero's years in Boston and Cambridge, about the death of his father, and about the fast express train that brought the young man home. But, with his usual aversion to leaving out of his fiction any part of his experiences, he also wanted to include an account of his tumultuous love affair with Aline Bernstein. In order to fill in Aline's part of the story, he encouraged her to reminisce about her childhood, about her actor father, about her aunt Nana, about New York at the turn of the century. Some of the stories she wrote out for him, but most she told him, like a modern Scheherazade. Her recollections were so full and so fascinating that at one point he thought of making a separate novel out of them, called "The Good Child's River," and he assigned to her the theme: "Long, long into the night I lay thinking of how to tell my story." Then, growing even more comprehensive and ambitious, he planned to combine all these segments into a long novel, to be called "The October Fair," which would culminate in his fight at Munich.

How to combine such enormously diverse materials into a single book puzzled Wolfe, and he considered several strategies. Increasingly dependent on Perkins for advice, he asked the editor for suggestions. One night, after a long session in the Scribners office, the two men took a walk through Central Park. Idly Perkins remarked that a grand story could be written about a boy who for some reason had never seen his father but set out to find him. Excitedly Wolfe responded, "I think I could do something with that." Not long afterwards he recorded the theme for his new book in his notebook: "In Search of My Father."

At the moment, though, he could only talk about a second novel because he was still making final revisions in the first. He spent most of the summer reading proofs of *Look Homeward, Angel*. As usual he suffered from the sweltering heat of New York City, where he claimed he could smell all seven million inhabitants, and he was delighted to get away to Boothbay, Maine, where he and Aline had rented a cabin for two weeks. Relaxing on the shore, fishing from an old, rotting pier, enjoying Aline's superb cooking, he was more hopeful and expansive than he had been for years. To Wheelock, who was handling the proofs of *Look Homeward, Angel* at Scribners, he wrote: "I feel packed to the lips with rich ore. . . . I want to tear myself open and show my friends all that I think I have. I am so anxious to lay all my wares out on the table . . . , to say: 'You have not seen one tenth or one twentieth of what is in me. Just wait.'" This was, as he knew, "the most colossal egotism," but he explained that "there are moments when . . . I feel that no one else has a quarter of my

power and richness . . . that, one way or another, I am a fine
young fellow and a great man." About this time he drew up a list
of the greatest English and American authors of the nineteenth
century and put beside it a short roster of twentieth-century
American novelists. It contained only two names: Wolfe and
Hemingway.

Receipt of galley proofs dampened his fine exuberance. As he
read the galleys — the long sheets on which the initial printing
was done and corrections made, which were afterwards divided so
that about three printed pages came from each galley — he found,
as all authors do, that his words looked different in print than in
typescript. Away from the daily influence of Perkins, he began to
worry about cuts that he had agreed to and started inserting new
material until Wheelock warned him that the printer was "a little
bit upset" by these changes, which cost a great deal and might
delay publication. Even so he kept making further additions, which
he considered "necessary because of certain omissions and gaps
which . . . either the printer had caused, or Mr. Perkins and I had
failed to consider when we made the cuts."

Toward the end of July, when Aline returned to her family, he
went on a brief tour of Montreal and Quebec, neither of which he
found interesting. In August he came back to New York in time
to look over the page proofs of his book, to hear the rumor —
unfounded, as it proved — that either the Book-of-the-Month
Club or the Literary Guild would adopt his novel, and to see his
first story published in the August issue of *Scribner's Magazine*,
accompanied by a photograph of the author and a romantic write-
up of his life. "I was more madly in love with myself than ever
when I read it," he wrote a friend, and he was equally in love with
his publishers. "Scribners have been magnificent — their best
people have worked like dogs on the thing — they believe in me
and the book," he declared. "To have found a firm and association
with men like this is a miracle of good luck."

III

During the final months before the book appeared, Wolfe's chief
worry was how it would be received in Asheville. Alerted by
Perkins's concern over its autobiographical nature, he began to
prepare for attack — and for counterattack. He drafted letters to

the editors of the Asheville newspapers, ostensibly answering their invitations — which, of course, he had not received, since his book was not yet published — to respond to criticisms of his novel. In some drafts he took a humble tone, asserting that "no praise and commendation could be of higher value to me than that of my own people" and declining to reply to critics because a novelist's book should speak for him. In other versions he went on the offensive, denying that he had attacked his town, his state, and the South and claiming that there was beauty as well as bitterness, ugliness, and pain in his novel. But if, after reading the book, "the indignant Methodist ladies and gentlemen suspect me of fleshly carnalities, let them suspect no more," he concluded defiantly. "I am enthusiastically guilty. I have eaten and drunk with sensual ecstasy in ten countries. I have performed the male function with the assistance of several attractive females, a few of whom were devout members of the Methodist church."

The only such letter that he mailed, though, was to Mrs. Roberts, whom he assured: "My book is a work of fiction, and . . . no person, act, or event has been deliberately and consciously described." His statement was, to say the least, disingenuous. It would be hard to find a character, a building, a street, or a scene in *Look Homeward, Angel* for which there was not a real-life prototype. Relying on his formidable and accurate memory, he had recreated the whole fabric of life in Asheville — especially its seamy side.

One reason he so strongly insisted, both before the book was published and afterwards, that everything in *Look Homeward, Angel* was fiction was to deflect criticism by his townsmen and his family. Another was his belief that it would detract from his stature as an artist if readers felt that he did not so much create as report on his characters. Furthermore, he knew that he had largely invented the conversations and thoughts attributed to the real-life people portrayed in his book. For instance, in "The Angel on the Porch" scene, W. O. Gant was a very slightly disguised version of his father, who did indeed exhibit a simpering marble angel on the porch of his shop on Pack Square, and "Queen Elizabeth" was a pretty accurate version of Asheville's prosperous madam, whose establishment on Eagle Terrace Wolfe's father had frequented in his more virile days. But the conversation between the two was made up. So was Elizabeth's decision to buy, and Gant's reluctant decision to sell, the angel to mark the grave of one of her "girls." Indeed, Wolfe's inventiveness later led to no little scandal as stone angels from W. O. Wolfe's shop began to be identified in and around Asheville, and speculation did not cease until it was shown that the marble figure described in *Look Homeward, Angel* marked the grave in Hendersonville, North Carolina, of an unquestionably respectable wife of a Methodist minister.

Still, he was worried enough about the autobiographical nature of his book to go back to Asheville before it was published, in the hope of softening the impact on his family. As usual, a visit home brought him both happiness and frustration. Now nearly seventy, Julia had only roomers, not boarders, at the Old Kentucky Home, and she had more time for her youngest son. She worried that he was not getting enough good food up North and promised to fatten him up. "I've got a good ear of corn on that stalk for your dinner next week," she said, pointing to her garden. She launched on the interminable seas of her memory, recounting bits of family history, reciting the tale of her recent losses in real estate speculation as the land booms in Miami and Asheville collapsed. More freely than ever before she talked about the birth of her children and told him, apparently for the first time, of the self-induced miscarriage she had had in Florida, when the fetus "was just like your papa if he'd been all stewed down to that shape." Remembering her long, turbulent years with W. O., she concluded: "I had less married life than any woman I know."

Wolfe also spent a good deal of time with his sister Mabel, who now lived in an expensive house on Kimberly Avenue, looking across the golf course to the Grove Park Inn. She gave a party in his honor and invited the best that Asheville could muster in the way of writers and educators. But Wolfe got an inkling that Ralph Wheaton's future with the National Cash Register Company was uncertain, and he was sensitive to the constant, nagging friction between his sister and her demanding mother-in-law.

With Fred he visited Effie's family in Anderson, South Carolina, "that hot dismal town — ever the same — the pretty drawling girls with bribing words of rape, red clay, cotton, bigotry and murder." On the way back to Asheville they got into a pointless argument over whether a waiter in a restaurant had insulted them. Tom exploded in anger at his brother, Fred broke into tears, and

Tom began to cry too. He loved his family, he blubbered, but he "couldn't get along with them."

After a week in Asheville Wolfe reported to Perkins: "We get one another crazy . . . I'm about ready for a padded cell." He realized that he had been away so many years that he was no longer really part of his family, or of Asheville, and, brooding over "the sadness, the sadness, the sadness and the loneliness of my life," he asked: "To *what* did I belong, to *what* do I belong — *who* wants me?"

As he prepared to leave, he tried clumsily to tell his family about his book and to alert them that they were characters — and certainly not wholly admirable characters — in it. "My family knows what it's all about," he reported to Perkins, "and I think is pleased about it — and also a little apprehensive." In fact, they had only the vaguest notion of what his book was about. Mabel, with whom he talked most extensively, thought it was probably "one of those boring philosophies or criticisms" but feared that it might be "a book on the Negro situation." Anyway, she was sure that no more than ten people in Asheville would read it. She was, then, both confused and a little frightened when her brother told her as he was waiting for his train back to New York: "Now when I come next time, Mabel, I'll probably be wearing a beard or whiskers. I'll have to come incognito. . . . I have written a few things about people here in Asheville that I'm afraid some of them aren't going to like."

IV

Back in New York, Wolfe began teaching again at New York University. He had been reluctant to accept the appointment as instructor in English at a salary of twenty-four hundred dollars a year, but his friends at Scribners reminded him that, however successful his novel might be, he would not receive any royalties until April 1930. Once again, he conducted courses in composition and literature, but his nerves were ragged as he waited for publication date, October 18.

He received his first copy of his first published book on his twenty-ninth birthday. It was an occasion of supreme excitement. Lovingly he held it in his powerful hands, turning it over, ruffling the pages, leafing back through it again. It was a sturdy, compact volume of 626 pages which sold for $2.50. Bound in dark-blue cloth, it had a dust jacket that he found "very attractive — bright colors, jagged lines, very modern design." Everything about the book pleased him. He was especially happy over the dedication page, where he acknowledged his indebtedness to Aline Bernstein with a simple "To A.B.," followed by lines from John Donne's "A Valediction: Of My Name, in the Window," which began:

> Then, as all my soules bee,
> Emparadis'd in you, (in whom alone
> I understand, and grow and see). . . .

The first of his author's copies of *Look Homeward, Angel* went to Aline, with the inscription: "At a time when my life seemed desolate, and when I had little faith in myself I met her. She brought me friendship, material and spiritual relief, and love such as I had never had before." The next copy went to his mother with the less intimate message: "I present this copy of my first book, with love and with hope for her happiness and long life," and he then mailed one to Mrs. Roberts, more warmly inscribed "To the Mother of my spirit." When Mrs. Boyd returned from Europe, he sent a copy to her also, as one of "the two friends who have done most for this book." But the rest of the inscription, which noted that Mrs. Boyd had placed his manuscript with Scribners, was equivocal: "What skill, what art, what effort it took to do this, I do not know but whatever it was, she did it, and all my thanks and gratefulness go to her for it."

On publication day the Scribner Book Store devoted one of its Fifth Avenue windows to a display of *Look Homeward, Angel*. Wolfe could hardly tear himself away from it. He walked back and forth in front of it so frequently and ogled the display so intently as to alarm passersby and to alert the policeman on the beat. He stopped in other bookstores to ask whether people were buying his novel. Taking a seat on a bus, he was thrilled to discover that the girl next to him held a copy of his book in her hand, but he was too shy to speak to her.

Eagerly awaiting the reviews, he was stunned by the first reactions, which were from North Carolina. To be sure, in the *Asheville Citizen* his college friend George McCoy and his fiancée praised the book as "a genius's combination of reality, which will not shrink from even the most sordid details of everyday life, and of a child-like expression of the most delightful fantasy." But the *Asheville Times* was bluntly critical of this story told "with a frankness and detail rarely ever seen in print." Most of the characters in *Look Homeward, Angel* were real people, the review continued, and they could readily be identified by any resident of Asheville. Wolfe had presented them all in the most unpleasant light possible. "If there attaches to them any scandal which has enjoyed only a subterranean circulation, it is dragged forth into the light. If they have any weaknesses which more tolerant friends are considerate enough to overlook, these defects are faithfully described." In the *Raleigh News and Observer*, Jonathan Daniels, another of Wolfe's University of North Carolina classmates, was even more severe; his review was headed: "Former Asheville Writer Turns In Fury Upon N.C. and the South." Admitting the "splendid vividness" of Wolfe's writing, Daniels protested that the book was full of "lurid details of blood and sex and cruelty" and suggested that it was written to pay off old scores. "In 'Look Homeward, Angel,' " Daniels announced, "North Carolina, and the South are spat upon."

The book caused a sensation in Asheville, Within ten days Asheville bookstores had sold more than one hundred copies and were begging Scribners to send more. Purchasers passed the book from hand to hand, noting the more shocking passages about the Gant family and trying to identify other characters. Rental libraries received dozens of calls for the book a day but were unable to supply the demand.

Just how angry townspeople were is hard to determine, for only a few criticisms of the novel were put in writing. One Asheville woman, who had published some poetry, thought Wolfe's book vulgar and blasphemous and questioned the legality of sending such an obscene book through the mails. A former resident protested to Scribners, "in the name of decent womanhood and citizenship," against "the cruel exaggerations" in the novel. But most hostile comments were oral. At a bank directors' meeting one man said: "The boy should be spanked for his impertinence," and at club meetings women expressed themselves as being "too shocked for words." Jack Westall, Tom's cousin, remembered later that he overheard some muttered threats against the author and that from time to time a man would say: "I talked to so-and-so and he doesn't give a damn how big the whipper-snapper is —

if he comes back to this town they'd tear him to pieces." Oliver Wolfe, another cousin, reported that "at church, on the streets, at club and social gatherings, everywhere it is the principal topic discussed." Supposedly the book was denounced from at least one Asheville pulpit.

Though readers resented Wolfe's sordid picture of life in Asheville and his exposure of his family, friends, and acquaintances, most attacks on *Look Homeward, Angel* were ostensibly made on the ground that it was full of foul and indecent language. So strong was the view that it was a dirty book that Leon McNeirney, the owner of the Arcade Book Store in Asheville, felt obliged to make a public explanation that he was selling *Look Homeward, Angel* as literature, not smut. Miss Nan Erwin, the town librarian and a proper Victorian, borrowed a copy of *Look Homeward, Angel*, was shocked by the dirty words, and refused to order a copy for the library. When readers asked for the book, they were told, without explanation: "I'm sorry, we do not have it." Years later another Asheville resident cheered her decision to ban "the obscene vaporings" and "the bare bestial foulness" of *Look Homeward, Angel* and begged: "Do not let any influence persuade you to let his buckets of night soil sit on your shelves."

How much of this hubbub reached Wolfe's ears in New York is unclear. Later he claimed that his mail was loaded with letters "full of vilification and abuse." One, he said, began simply and directly: "Sir: You are a son-of-a-bitch. . . ." He said that another threatened to kill him if he came home. "One venerable lady" he had known most of his life — probably Mabel's mother-in-law — declared that she would not intervene if a lynch mob dragged his "big overgroan karkus" across the public square. Though Wolfe throughout his life preserved every scrap of his correspondence, no such letters appear in his files.

If Wolfe exaggerated the abuse he received from the general Asheville population, he understated the criticism that his book drew from his closest friends. As early as August, when *Scribner's Magazine* carried his story, "The Angel on the Porch," Mrs. Roberts expressed a fear that his account of his father and the town prostitute might distress his family. When her copy of *Look Homeward, Angel* arrived, she was recovering from a long and desperate illness. Eagerly she unwrapped the parcel, and by chance turned to Wolfe's chapters on the Leonards and the Altamont Fitting

School — a very thinly disguised account of the Robertses and their academy. His fictional portrayal of Mrs. Roberts was admiring and poetic, but she thought he had depicted her husband as "only a snob, a pedant, a dullard, and . . . a man who was brutal to a frail wife." This uncalled-for attack, by a man who had been her favorite student and who had very recently visited her house and talked to both her and her husband with warm friendship, so upset Mrs. Roberts that she was again confined to her bed. She managed to write Wolfe a short letter that ended: "You have crucified your family and devastated mine." She did not write or see him for the next seven years.

As her letter suggested, the harshest effect of *Look Homeward, Angel* was on Wolfe's own family, for he had portrayed his father as lecherously alcoholic, his mother as penurious and parsimonious, Frank as a debauched drug addict, Mabel as a hysterical, unhappy near-alcoholic, and Fred as a semiliterate buffoon.

When Julia read the book, she was hurt and shocked. She wrote her son that his account of W. O. Wolfe was "too personal," arguing that if her husband "was here to fight for the living it would be all right. But the dead have no come-back." She found that people on the streets in Asheville now looked at her strangely, and some of her friends tried to telephone their condolences to her for having such an ingrate for a son. But indomitable as always, she cut off her callers brusquely, and she refused to give any public evidence of her pain. When someone dared to call her "Eliza," she laughed and said that she did not care what Tom wrote about her, that he could call her Caroline Peavine — the name of a disreputable old mountain woman who used to beg on the streets of Asheville — so long as he made a success of his writing. In later years, when questioned about Wolfe's characterization of his family, she used to snap back: "He's the only Asheville author who ever sold 100,000 copies!"

Among Wolfe's brothers and sisters, only Effie, who was briefly characterized in the book and came off without much damage, took no offense; she considered the novel a work of literature, and she was proud of it and of her brother. Frank was very angry. "I blew up when his book first came out," he recalled a few years later; "on the impulse of the moment, I could have committed murder." Fred did not read the book through, but he was upset when he dipped into it here and there and when other people told him about its contents. When he finally brought himself to write to Tom, he said that, in sampling the book, he "got a Hell of a lot of Jars, but along with the Jars also found a hundred dam[n] good laughs."

The publication of *Look Homeward, Angel* hurt Mabel most. In an attempt to gain a social standing in Asheville that her parents had never attained, she was now very active in civic associations and women's clubs. As soon as the first copies reached Asheville, she began receiving calls, at all hours, from well-meaning friends in these organizations, who assured her "that nobody would believe a word of it, that we were never that sort of family, that they had known us all their lives and knew that we were decent people, and *what did that boy mean anyway in writing such a terrible book about his flesh and blood?*" Mabel asked herself the same question, but in writing to her brother she tried to put the best face on the situation: "You know how Papa always wanted us to succeed, and how he always said, 'Don't be a nonentity.' . . . Well, we Wolfes aren't nonentities now." She urged Tom to keep working on his next book and concluded: "We're getting along fine. Mama is all right and none of us are going to die from it."

The news from Asheville greatly upset Wolfe. Years later he realized that "he had foreseen some forms of local glory in his own home town and now that it had all turned out so differently . . . his wounded pride as well as his bewildered doubt were taking refuge in a sense of martyrdom." But at the time he lashed out at the "unfair and unintelligent" comments of his townsmen. To Vardis Fisher, a fellow instructor at New York University and another aspiring novelist, he read the adverse criticisms, "weeping, cursing, hating." "They all hate me," he told Fisher. "They're so damned little that they smell little!" In talking with Henry Volkening, another colleague, he indulged in a fantasy of retribution. The time would come, he predicted, when the same people who now criticized him would be "building monuments to me, comparing me with O. Henry (hah!), naming their children after me, and nigger children too (hah!), and stuffing me with food, just so they can get a good look at me, and tell me of my great contribution to the great literature of the South (hah!)." Then, coming down to reality with sudden sadness, he added: "But I do wish that they would try to understand, and that they would let me alone."

Repeatedly in the months after *Look Homeward, Angel* was published he tried, without much coherence or success, to explain and defend what he had written. He could not bring himself to admit that, when he wrote the book, the prospects for publication were so remote that he had not felt under any constraints, whether of propriety or legality, in revealing and exaggerating the most disreputable secrets about Asheville that he knew. Nor was he able to say that writing his novel had been a way of purging himself of his bitterness toward members of his own family and of repaying old social snubs, and that, once the book was finished, most of his hostility and aggressiveness toward Asheville had disappeared. But he did admit that the interest the public took in his book was a great surprise, for he had thought that maybe two dozen people in Asheville would read it, not "every realtor, attorney, druggist, or grocer."

Over and over again he begged members of his family and Mrs. Roberts to remember that he was an artist, not a sensation-seeking hack writer, and that the artist was the captive of his own creative process. Without much logic he reminded friends that his book had been begun "in a little room in London" and completed "in a New York sweat shop garret"; consequently it was "neither about North Carolina nor the South, nor any specific group of people. . . . It is about all the people I have known anywhere." His intent, he insisted, had not been to expose the peccadilloes of Asheville but to develop his constant theme, which ran from the first to the last page of his book: "that men are strangers, that they are lonely and forsaken, that they are in exile on this earth, that they are born, live, and die alone."

To appease his family he wrote that Perkins and all his New York friends thought that the Gants, as portrayed in *Look Homeward, Angel*, were "grand people," "remarkable people." He tried to reassure his mother by reporting that everybody thought of Eliza, her counterpart in the novel, as "a very strong, resourceful, and courageous woman, who showed great character and determination in her struggle against the odds of life." "No matter what Asheville thinks now," he predicted, "they will understand in time that I tried to write a moving, honest book about great people."

V

He also told his family about the favorable reviews that his book was receiving almost everywhere except in North Carolina. To be sure, in the first New York review Harry Hansen mixed praise for Wolfe's "rich emotion" and his "understanding sympathy" with criticism that he imitated Thackeray's manner and "George Meredith's musing over destiny, fate, love, ah me! ah me!" and concluded with the disquieting observation that only Wolfe's "second novel will tell us whether he has staying power as a novelist, whether he will be more than a one-book man." But most of the other reviews were wholly positive. Though the *New York Times Book Review* relegated *Look Homeward, Angel* to page seven and assigned it to the relatively unknown Margaret Wallace, her review was full of praise for this novel "of great drive and vigor, of profound originality, of rich and variant color." Even more enthusiastic about Wolfe's "mammoth appreciation of experience and of living," Margery Latimer in *New York Herald-Tribune Books* concluded: "If I could create now one magic word that would make everyone want to read the book I would write it down and be utterly satisfied."

Reviews in magazines were mostly appreciative too. Wolfe writhed in agony because several critics complained that the book was too long and lacked form. "He would show them too that he could compress, maybe like Dostoevsky," he promised Volkening; he would prove that he could write to conform to "any damned acceptable pattern they wanted." But even he was obliged to recognize that *Look Homeward, Angel* received "the best reviews . . . a first book has had in several years." In the *New Republic* Geoffrey T. Hellman reported that this "extraordinarily fine novel" combined "literary ability, taste, and a scholarly background." Basil Davenport in *The Saturday Review of Literature* announced that Wolfe had the "robust sensitiveness" of Rabelais but that *Look Homeward, Angel* had "a violent emotional intensity" lacking in *Gargantua*. In *Scribner's Magazine* the young poet Robert Raynolds placed Wolfe in the same category as Melville and Whitman. Carl Van Doren discovered "a kind of magnificence" in *Look Homeward, Angel*, and his review in *Wings*, the house organ of the Literary Guild, answered Hansen's: "Mr. Wolfe with his first novel has made himself a novelist who must be taken into account, whether he ever writes another novel or not."

Wolfe was especially pleased that, except in North Carolina, Southern reviews were generally positive. Though Donald Davidson, one of the leaders of the Agrarian movement, which extolled the values of stability and continuity in Southern life, complained that *Look Homeward, Angel* had "a sickness in its marrow," because Wolfe thought he could separate his artistic goals from his social values, he was obliged to call the book a "superb performance," "brilliant," "powerful," and "magnificent." Stringfellow Barr, the editor of the *Virginia Quarterly Review*, hailed Wolfe as "the first novelist of the new dispensation in the Southern States." Particularly gratifying was a review signed "Zoilus" in the *Richmond Times-Dispatch*, which praised "the richness of the material, the tumultuous glow of the prose, the newness of the epithets, the down-right healthiness of the tale" and claimed that *Look Homeward, Angel* was not a local or sectional book but one of universal meaning. Delighted to find such a review — "the most understanding one I have yet read" — in a leading Southern paper, Wolfe asked that a copy be sent to the *Asheville Citizen*, where it might counteract adverse reactions in his home town.

Most of the letters Wolfe and Scribners received about *Look Homeward, Angel* were warmly encouraging. Thomas Beer, the author of *The Mauve Decade*, said that Wolfe was the best young writer who had emerged since Glenway Wescott — and left Wolfe wondering "why Wescott I don't know." Professor Irwin Edman of Columbia University wrote that Wolfe was "a first-rate prose writer, . . . an understanding novelist, and . . . a philosopher in fiction." Witter Bynner, the poet, told Wolfe: "It isn't fair to respect and admire a book as much as I do *Look Homeward, Angel* without saying so . . . to the author. Faults, yes, but good ones. Great stuff!" A fellow North Carolinian and one of the ablest novelists on the Scribners list, James Boyd, told Perkins that *Look Homeward, Angel* struck him as being less a work of fiction than "a great inchoate bellow of the human soul," but he expressed "an uneasy feeling that the little fellows had better move over for this bird. . . . And on personal grounds there's no writer I'd rather move over or down for myself."

Even more gratifying was the mail Wolfe received from young, would-be writers. His first fan letter was from Mark Schorer, then an undergraduate at Harvard but later to become a professor at the University of California and the biographer of Sinclair Lewis, who wrote breathlessly: "I have just finished your book, and, oh, it's tremendous. It is simply a marvellous thing." Kimball Flaccus, an aspiring poet at Dartmouth, confessed that *Look Homeward, Angel* had opened his eyes "to all the joy, the sadness, the tenderness, the tragic terror of life." Completing his own first novel, August Derleth wrote from Sauk City, Wisconsin, that he had read *Look Homeward, Angel* through three times, and he exclaimed: "How sure your strokes are — how real your emotions. You have recaptured for me my own youth."

But sales were not so encouraging as the reviews and the letters. With an advance sale of 1,600 copies and four additional printings in the first six months after publication, *Look Homeward, Angel* fared well for a first novel. It was a success compared to William Faulkner's *The Sound and the Fury*, which was published during the same season and with which Wolfe's novel was often reviewed, usually to the disadvantage of Faulkner's book; the initial printing of 1,789 copies of *The Sound and the Fury* was enough to satisfy all demands for that book for more than a year. But compared to Hemingway's *A Farewell to Arms*, which Scribners published earlier in the fall of 1929 and which promptly sold 20,000 copies, Wolfe's novel did only moderately well, and he was greatly disappointed.

Entirely absorbed in his own affairs, he did not understand that his book had appeared at the worst possible time. Within a week of its publication the stock market collapsed and within a month thirty billion dollars in the market value of listed stocks had been wiped out; the United States fell into the deepest depression of its history. But, accustomed to living on a very small income, Wolfe hardly noticed what was happening to the country's economy. Consequently he was both puzzled and hurt when not even his students at New York University took up his offer to autograph copies of the book. They had to measure the pleasure of owning his novel against the need to buy lunches and textbooks.

Sensing his disappointment, his more sympathetic colleagues at the university rallied to help promote the book. Professor Watt arranged for him to lecture before the Women's Club of Glen Ridge, New Jersey, on November 1, when he illustrated the modern novel by reading liberally from *A Farewell to Arms* and told the ladies: "Beautiful and Pretty Literature cannot be governed or judged by the standards and capacities of 16-year-old boys and girls." What most of the audience remembered about the lecture, however, was the fact that Wolfe borrowed a watch from a member of the audience, placed it on the speaker's lectern, said in his booming voice, "When I first begin to talk I'm very nervous, but after I get started I'm quite all right" — and in a nervous gesture swept the watch off onto the floor. He later repeated the same talk at New York University to a group of evening college students. More effective promotion came from his colleague Tindall, who lectured on *Look Homeward, Angel* in his classes on the modern novel at the Washington Square campus. In this first serious literary criticism of Wolfe's novel, Tindall granted that the book was relatively formless but compared Wolfe favorably to such contemporaries as Cabell, Conrad Aiken, Wescott, and Thornton Wilder and linked him with the Elizabethan dramatists, Rabelais, Melville, and Whitman. Wolfe was "the novelist of the future," Tindall concluded, because "it is Wolfe rather than Hemingway who expresses [the] spirit of the young nation."

VI

The publication of *Look Homeward, Angel* made Wolfe a literary celebrity, and at first he basked in his fame. His mailbox was filled with fan letters, and his phone rang constantly. During the winter of 1929–1930 it seemed that everybody in New York — at least everybody who counted in New York — wanted to see and hear Thomas Wolfe.

He had dinner invitations almost every night. Sometimes the occasions were informal and pleasant, as when Dorothy Kuhns, who had known Wolfe in the 47 Workshop at Harvard, invited him to join her and her husband, the novelist DuBose Heyward, for a family dinner with a few friends. Mrs. Heyward herself probably got no dinner that evening, for Wolfe, who ate only one real meal a day and was ravenous by evening, cleared plate after plate as she brought in fresh helpings from the kitchen, all the time talking, volubly and passionately, about his work, his experiences, and his plans. Toward the end he halfheartedly apologized: "I eat too much, I write too much, and I talk too much." Other dinners he found crashing bores. At the request of the Scribners publicity department he agreed to attend one on Park Avenue, where he found himself along with other literary lions at the head table, which was on a platform, while several hundred matrons were at tables on the floor below. With comic indignation he pictured himself as "sitting like Jesus Christ on a dais, surrounded by his disciples."

At this time in his life Wolfe was especially attractive to women. Lean and romantically handsome in a very masculine way, he also looked so much like a little boy who needed a mother to take care of him. More than one socialite offered to take on the task. He told Tindall that he was pursued by enamored debutantes, crying "Fuck me, fuck me." From his tenacious memory he later produced a long list of "Free Pieces of Cunt" he had during these months, noting: "I fucked these women for nothing — save the best price of all."

Now that Wolfe was so much in demand, his relations with the Bernsteins became easier. No longer was he Aline's poor hanger-on; he was a celebrity, whom any hostess would welcome. While their house in Armonk was being completed, the Bernsteins moved into a huge apartment in the Marguery, at 270 Park Avenue, which Aline furnished with understated elegance. Wolfe was nearly always invited to their parties, and for the first time he came really to know some of Aline's closest friends who were not in the theater.

He particularly liked Thomas Beer (who was portrayed as Stephen Hook in Wolfe's later fiction), for he recognized that this shy, mannered writer was so fundamentally insecure that he disguised his uncertainties in a pose of aloofness and a habit of avoiding direct eye contact — just as Wolfe hid his own in excessive volubility. Though Wolfe had been acquainted with Mina Kirstein Curtiss, who was probably Aline's closest woman friend, since 1924, he had not hitherto liked her; she was a professor of English at Smith College, and intellectual women always put Wolfe off. But in the winter of 1929–1930, with his ego boosted by success, he found Mina, who was still grief-stricken after her husband's death, both more vulnerable and more appealing. She, in turn, grew fond of him, partly because she discovered that he "could have the greatest sensitivity and sweetness when he forgot himself," partly because, since she was five feet, ten and one-half inches tall, Wolfe was "one of the few men who ever made me feel diminutive and feminine." (Later Wolfe would caricature her as

the "sensual-looking Jewess," Lily Mandell.) Much more mixed
was his reaction to another of Aline's intimates, Emily Davies
Thayer. Growing up near the Biltmore estate outside of Asheville,
Wolfe could not help being impressed by the fact that Emily's first
husband had been William H. Vanderbilt, and he was attracted by
this astonishingly beautiful, seductive blonde; on the other hand
he found her insolent, sexually aggressive, and fundamentally
trivial. (Wolfe would pillory her as Amy Carleton in *You Can't Go
Home Again*.)

The most memorable party at the Bernsteins' that Wolfe attended was on January 3, 1930, when Aline decided to offer her
guests a special entertainment. Charmed by the work of the young
sculptor Alexander Calder, and particularly by the miniature circus figures he had constructed, mostly out of wire, she invited him
to put on a performance at her apartment. "It's often a circus there
anyway," she told him. "I'll invite all my friends."

After dinner "Sandy" Calder arrived, carrying two heavy black
salesman's cases and wearing hockey-player's shin guards — because, he explained, he had to be on his knees so much during a
performance — and, as Aline's guests watched in speechless astonishment, proceeded to transform her drawing room. To give
authenticity to his circus ring, Calder pushed her delicate eighteenth-century chairs into a corner and scattered sawdust over her
new, light-colored rug. Mr. Bernstein's first editions were yanked
from the shelves so that Calder could post circus banners and
pennants. Casually the sculptor informed his hostess that he had
invited some guests of his own, who would serve as audience for
the show. Then the doorbell rang, and Calder's friends, including
the Japanese sculptor Noguchi, trooped in. Mistaking Mina
Curtiss, who was wearing a simple black dress with a white collar,
for the maid, they unceremoniously handed her their coats and
hats and, without greeting the Bernsteins, took possession of the
drawing room. For over an hour Calder, on his knees, arranged
his miniature figures of dancers, horses, elephants, and trapeze
artists.

Finally satisfied, he produced from one of his black bags a small,
tinny phonograph, which played only one record, Sousa's "The
Stars and Stripes Forever," and ordered Edla, the Bernsteins'
daughter, to keep winding it in order to provide circus music. He
directed one of his friends to distribute packets of unshelled pea-

nuts to the guests, so as to create the proper circus atmosphere. Then he introduced his circus characters and began seemingly interminable, and usually unsuccessful, efforts to have his wire acrobats link hands in midair. Boring as this was, it was not so appalling as his demonstration of the sword-swallowing act, in which, with obvious difficulty, he rammed a hatpin through a little stuffed male figure.

Bored and offended, most of the Bernsteins' guests retreated to Aline's bedroom, from which Theo Bernstein emerged periodically to check on the damage being done to his apartment. But Wolfe and Mina Curtiss stood side by side against the wall for a long time, in horrified fascination with what was going on. Feeling a need to escape and seeing on Wolfe's face an expression "suggesting that he might lean over at any moment and crush all those lively little insects with his two great hands," she suggested going into the kitchen for something to eat. Inspecting the refrigerator, he grabbed a big stalk of celery and began taking bites out of it. "It isn't washed," she kept telling him. "You're eating dirt." "And a fine, healthy thing to be doing after what is going on in there," he retorted.*

Finally, after midnight, the circus was over, Calder's uninvited guests departed, leaving behind them a wake of peanut shells and paper bags, and Calder busied himself with packing his wire figures. Suddenly there was a distinct and unmistakable smell of smoke: the apartment building was on fire and everybody had to get out. Hastily the Bernsteins, Wolfe, and Mina Curtiss prepared to leave, urging Calder to hurry up with his packing. But when they reached the stairs Aline remembered that the cook was still in her room. Going back, they found that, terrified, she had locked herself in, and no urging could persuade her to come out. Finally Wolfe threw his weight against the door — once, twice, and again a third time — until the lock broke, and he rushed in and carried the woman out in his powerful arms. Through the early-morning hours the residents of the Marguery, their servants, and the employees of the apartment building shivered in democratic equality in the courtyard while firemen extinguished the flames

---

*Calder did not know that Wolfe was in his audience: "He did not have the good sense to present himself and I only heard from him much later — some nasty words on my performance, included in a long-winded book."

that had begun in the basement and sent clouds of deadly smoke up the elevator shafts.

Years later, in "The Party at Jack's," Wolfe treated this whole episode as a parable of the decadence of upper-class American society and of the subterranean rumblings that brought about its collapse during the Great Depression. In that fictional account he omitted all mention of the heroic role he himself had played in saving the cook's life. At the time, though, the fire seemed less a symbol of social breakdown than a hint of Judgment Day: "Huge churnings filled the sky, aerial ruin. Cloven in upper air, the million-windowed towers split, fell with slow thunderings. Exultant, he watched until (No, surely not . . .   O of course not . . . By God, there it goes . . . Goodbye, New York.)"

VII

In fact Wolfe by this time was about ready to say goodbye to New York. Being a literary celebrity, he painfully discovered, had its drawbacks. "Because of telephone calls, invitations to speak, dine, or visit, . . . interviews and excitement," he found it hard to do any sustained writing, though he continued to make notes on his experiences and observations. One scene that he could not forget was that of a dead man in the B.M.T. subway at Times Square, "a shabby fellow of 48–55 . . . slumped in one of the subway benches — a small puddle of urine stained the concrete at his feet," but he was unable to develop this image into a story because of the interruptions and demands on his time. (Later the subway scene would be an episode in his "Death, the Proud Brother.")

Because he was a published author, people believed that he now had money, and he did not know how to say no to the salesmen and panhandlers who kept bothering him. In fact, as he was painfully aware, he was not due any money from the sale of *Look Homeward, Angel* until April and during most of the winter had to live on his meager New York University salary. Anticipating the day when he would receive a large check, he began bitterly to resent the fact that Mrs. Boyd, as his agent, would receive ten percent of it. Soon he began calling her "this damned fat woman who wants to drink my heart's blood." What angered him even more was Mrs. Boyd's insistence that, as his designated literary agent, she was entitled to ten percent of the earnings on Wolfe's next book, too. Once again he turned to Melville Cane for advice, seeking the "legal terminology to tell her to go to hell."

As he grew jaded, Wolfe discovered that the literary world in New York was as full of poseurs and frauds as the theater set. Sometimes he found the pretentiousness unbearable. Wheelock took him to a party given by Marjorie Allen Seiffert, a poet published by Scribners, where the guests included William Rose Benét, the novelist Floyd Dell, and the poet Genevieve Taggard, all of whom extravagantly praised the poetry of Edna St. Vincent Millay. Wolfe said something derogatory, and Benét — who may have remembered an earlier party when Wolfe insulted his wife, Elinor Wylie — replied sharply. Grandly and irrelevantly Wolfe responded, "Go back and read Homer." "Don't tell me to read Homer — I read Homer before you were born," Benét snorted, so offended that he put on his hat and coat and left the party, slamming the door. Afterward Wolfe characteristically was remorseful for having driven Benét away — but he did not change his opinion that the New York literary circle consisted mostly of sycophants and backscratchers.

Equally troubling was his discovery that those who made much of him were less interested in the real Thomas Wolfe than in the legendary figure that they imagined him to be — a real-life Eugene Gant, with insatiable appetites and unappeasable sexual desires, of Faustian yearnings to read everything, see everything, do everything, from whose pen poured out millions of words. There was a great deal of truth behind this legend, which Wolfe himself had done more than anybody else to create, but that did not make the role easier for him to play. Nobody, it seemed to him, understood that most of the time he was a quiet, sensitive, hardworking fellow; that, among American novelists of his generation, he had the best and longest formal education; that he had an exceptional mastery of American, English, French, and German literature; and that he had experimented with adventuresome new techniques in writing his fiction. Instead, as he complained later to F. Scott Fitzgerald, everybody insisted on picturing him "as a great 'exuberant' six-foot-six clod-hopper straight out of nature who bites off half a plug of apple tobacco, tilts the corn liquor jug and lets half of it gurgle down his throat, wipes off his mouth with the back of one hairy paw, jumps three feet in the air and clacks his heels together four times before he hits the floor again and yells out 'Whoopee, boys, I'm a rootin tootin, shootin son of a gun from Buncombe County — out of my way now, here I come!' — and then wads up three-hundred thousand words or so, hurls it at a blank page, puts covers on it and says 'Here's my book!' "

Clearly it was time for a change, and by spring Wolfe felt financially able to make a break from New York. While his book was not a bestseller, nearly ten thousand copies were purchased, and his royalties were substantial. In April Scribners sent him a check for over three thousand dollars — more than he had hitherto earned in any year of his life.

There was a chance that his second book might be even more successful, and several other publishers expressed a discreet interest in luring him away from Scribners. Sometimes he misinterpreted their advances. The beautiful and brittle Blanche Knopf, who was responsible for the fiction list of the aggressive firm that her husband headed, invited him to a dinner party for what Wolfe called "the literati, actorati, and plain rotty-rotty." Speculating all evening whether Mrs. Knopf's "cunt was moist firm and deep and if she was a great fucker" and planning "as usual with all pretty women to ram *it* lusciously and tenderly home in her," he was astonished when Mrs. Knopf made it clear that her interest in him was literary and financial, not sexual. The upshot, Wolfe recorded plaintively in his diary: "I am bade goodbye at the doorway, I do *not* fuck Mrs. K, and I am used again, worn, pawed and revolved about."

In order to forestall such approaches by other publishers, Perkins as early as December 1929 urged Wolfe to apply to the John Simon Guggenheim Memorial Foundation for a fellowship. Perkins himself supported Wolfe's application by describing "a young man of extraordinary promise"; James Boyd asserted that he had "the temperament from which great novelists are made"; Dean Munn said that he had "the spark of authentic genius"; Robert Norwood, rector of St. Bartholomew's Church in New York, volunteered that he was "an indubitable genius"; and Professor Watt called him "the type of real genius which the Guggenheim Foundation was established to help develop."

Realizing that the Guggenheim awards would not be announced until March, Perkins also persuaded Scribners, a firm notably conservative about showering money on authors, to offer Wolfe forty-five hundred dollars as an advance against royalties on his next book, to be paid in monthly installments of two hundred fifty dollars, beginning in February 1930. About the same time A. S. Frère-Reeves, a principal editor at William Heinemann Ltd., agreed to publish a slightly expurgated English edition of *Look Homeward, Angel*, and gave the author an advance of one hundred pounds.

Guaranteed a substantial income for the next eighteen months, Wolfe finally was able to submit a definitive resignation from New York University, effective at the end of term, in January 1930. For all his complaints about the drudgery of teaching, he left with some regret, and he took great pains to see that the man who took over his classes, the insufferably superior Russell Krauss, would "protect his abandoned flock." He insisted that the reluctant Krauss must sit in on his final three or four classes.

A final tie was harder to cut: that with Aline. After the publication of *Look Homeward, Angel* they both recognized that their affair was coming to an end, but neither knew how to break it off. He hated to make hard decisions; always ambivalent, except when under the influence of alcohol, he was unable to tell Aline that he wanted out without immediately retracting his wish. Believing that she was invincible, that there was nothing that she could not do, Aline would not let him go, because that would mean accepting defeat. Though she was now nearly fifty, she could not concede that she was too old for her lover.

For months, then, they fenced and feinted, and Wolfe's diary was filled with accounts of a "terrible scene" or "a sobbing hell" with Aline. Sinking under "the old sensation of being caught, caught, caught," he tried to lash himself into action by inventing quarrels with her husband. In his fantasies he would imagine saying to Mr. Bernstein: "What kind of man are you? Why don't you kill me? That's right, Goddam it, kill me, shoot me through the head, spatter my brains out on the pavement, hire thugs and gunmen, have me tied up naked to a post and spit on me, vomit over me, urinate on me, and debagg me, castrate me with a rabbi's circumcision knife, and feed my genitals to ladies' lapdogs."

When these tactics failed to give him courage to break with Aline, he began once more to vent his anger at all Jews, especially those, like the Bernsteins, who lived in New York. Obliged to admit that emotionally and psychologically the most interesting people he had ever met were Jews, he was sure that "intellectually they are sawdust and ashes." More important, he was certain that they were sexually promiscuous. On seeing a young Jewish woman in a restaurant with Noguchi, he scribbled obscenely in his little notebook: "Do you like to fuck Japs? Why not tell the truth? Jew women will fuck anything if it is in the mode."

He tried to get other people to advise him to end the affair with Aline. Several times he attempted to interest Perkins in his problem, without ever mentioning Aline's name, but that reticient New Englander refused to get involved. Importuned, he finally agreed that, if things were as Wolfe reported them and if the disparity in ages was so great, the relationship obviously had to end. Comforted, Wolfe relayed this judgment to Aline, who was not convinced of anything except that Perkins was now her enemy. The only unequivocal support he received was from Madeleine Boyd, who asked ironically: "Do you think you are the only person in the world who has ever had an affair like this?" When Wolfe expressed fear that Aline would have a breakdown or commit suicide if he left her, Mrs. Boyd responded: "The Jews love to dramatize their emotions." "Besides," she added, "she's at that time of life when women get hysterical." When she saw that her reference to menopause startled Wolfe, she continued: "Aha! You didn't know about that! I can see there are still some things that you must learn."

In the end Wolfe's actions declared what he could not bring himself to say. When he applied for a Guggenheim Fellowship, he knew that one of the conditions of the award was that he must work abroad, but he did not tell Aline of his application. Then one day after he received notice of the award, while walking with her along 14th Street, he broke away to enter a travel agency. When he emerged with steamship schedules, she said bitterly: "Well, that's your way of informing me, is it? . . . If you go away and leave me this time, it will be for good. . . . I know you'll never come back to me."

Wolfe remained determined to break away. "I find myself at the same depth of fruitless and sterile exhaustion as I had reached two years ago. I am unable to create, unable to concentrate, and I am filled with fever, with bitter and restless anger against the world; and I am beginning to feel this against Aline," he recorded in his diary. "This must be the end!" He enjoined himself to hold firm against her entreaties: "Now, keep hold: strike hard — keep your breath cool and calm, and endure. Do all that can be done with calmness and with decency. . . . Leave without fear or shame — Do not bluff — endure."

Sad and desperate, Aline finally acquiesced, in the hope that after another journey abroad he would again return to her. He gave her some encouragement by having Melville Cane draft a will for him, entrusting his books and his manuscripts, in the event of his death, to Aline and dividing his royalties equally between his mother and his mistress.

Aline bought him new underwear, socks, and neckties, helped him pack, and on May 9 accompanied him to the dock in Hoboken, where the S.S. *Volendam* was preparing to sail. They drank champagne, and before she left she hung around his neck one of her most treasured possessions, a medal that the artist Marsden Hartley had made for her.

As the ship sailed, Wolfe calculated that he had "$14,000, no ties, and the ability to travel where I choose." A few days earlier he had set himself an agenda:

> What I shall Do:
>   I shall get on a great ship.
>   I shall eat fine food and drink red
>   rich wines and splendid beers and
>   liquors.
>   I shall try to fuck beautiful women.

Now he had taken the first step.

VIII

Penance More

FROM THE BEGINNING Wolfe's Guggenheim year abroad was plagued by troubles. Hardly had he landed in France when he learned that *Look Homeward, Angel* failed to win the Pulitzer Prize in fiction. One Pulitzer juror, Robert Morss Lovett, did not care for the book, but a second, Albert Bigelow Paine, thought it "the work of a genius, slightly demented, as a genius is likely to be." The chairman, Professor Joseph B. Fletcher of Columbia University, disliked Wolfe's novel, arguing that the author was more than " 'slightly demented,' " and pushed through a recommendation of his own first choice, Oliver La Farge's *Laughing Boy*. Newspapers mentioned that *Look Homeward, Angel* was the runner-up for the fiction award, and the people at Scribners, though naturally disappointed, told Wolfe that it was "certainly a great honor to be second in such a selection."

Wolfe kept his own feeling about the Pulitzer award to himself, but afterwards he wrote a story about a millionaire who turned away from a promising novelist with "a look of sorrow and commiseration" because he was only the runner-up for the prize. Later Wolfe told friends that he did "not believe in the prize for the purpose for which it is given" and declared "it might be a very bad thing" for him to win it. Accordingly, when his second novel was published in 1935, he insisted that it be withdrawn from the competition. The implacable Professor Fletcher, still chairman of the fiction committee in 1935, grimly responded that it was not necessary to withdraw *Of Time and the River,* since Wolfe was not "in serious danger" of winning the prize.

Even more unsettling was the bill Wolfe received, shortly after he arrived in France, from two New York dentists who had completed some complicated extractions and bridgework for him just before he left the United States. Aline Bernstein had recommended these doctors, warning that their work was expensive. But he was stunned when he received their bill for five hundred and twenty-five dollars — more than twice what he was expecting and more than one-fifth of his Guggenheim stipend for twelve months. He told them that he could not afford to pay it. Unmoved, the doctors turned their bill over to a collection agency, which threatened legal action.

Feeling desperate, Wolfe appealed to Perkins and the others at Scribners for help. He was sure that the bill was excessive and that the dentists were big-city crooks, out to ruin an innocent country boy. Anyway, the dental surgery had not been necessary. Angrily he began drafting letters — which he did not send — to the doctors: "You have destroyed my teeth and my health. You will get no money out of me, but if possible I shall force you to pay for the damage you have done me." Worried that they might attach the royalties Scribners owed him, he formally signed over to Perkins "all money that is due to me, or will be due to me." Ultimately the bill was settled for a fraction of the original charges, but Wolfe spent much of his Guggenheim year in frantic, angry correspondence about this problem.

He was the more upset by this controversy because the dentists tried to involve Aline in it. When they complained to her and asked for Wolfe's address abroad, she sent the bill along to him, adding, "I cannot pay it as I am literally penniless." That was just one of the letters with which she bombarded him from the day he sailed. Often she began on a cheerful note but nearly every letter mentioned her husband's losses in the stock market crash and reported on her recurrent illness. Always there was the refrain of endless love: "I love you with every fibre of my being, and I hate myself with the same intensity. I want to do away with so weak and miserable a soul. . . . I love you." Most of her letters ended in the chiding tone that all-knowing mothers use toward fractious children: "Tom if you'll only work and not drink all over Europe

there will be at least some justification for your desertion of me."
"If you take yourself away from me, you must work well to make
up for it. . . . Will you keep a schedule of 5 hours a day?"

All this drove Wolfe frantic. Aline's letters reminded him how
much he had hurt her by leaving — even though he felt that the
break was necessary for his self-preservation. Her suggestion that,
though "penniless," she might be forced to pay his dentists' bills
infuriated him to the point of drafting a letter — which he never
sent — to Theodore Bernstein: "Your wife is not responsible for
any bill of mine or for any other action of mine. I am indebted to
her in no way, and there is no reason why she should write me,
cable me, or attempt to molest and injure me in any way." To
keep from being in constant emotional turmoil he refused to answer Aline's letters and did not respond to her cables.

But if Wolfe thought that by breaking with his past he could
begin a new and happier life in Paris, he was disappointed. He
genuinely disliked the French, who were so different that they
were like "creatures from another planet." By now he knew Paris
so well that the usual tourist attractions had no interest for him,
but he could not settle down to work in this noisy, distracting city
full of "the little nervous taxis with their honking New Year's
horns . . . the big green buses with people hanging over the back,
and all the people swarming along the street, talking with their
hands, sitting in front of cafes talking a blue streak, usually about
nothing."

He had no circle of friends in Paris. The world of the French
intellectuals was closed to him, as it was to nearly all foreigners.
Through A. S. Frère-Reeves, of W. H. Heinemann, which was
about to publish *Look Homeward, Angel* in Great Britain, he did
have an introduction to the small circle of English men of letters
who lived in or were visiting Paris. Reeves saw that his American
author met Michael Arlen, the stylish society novelist, Derek
Patmore, the critic, and Richard Aldington, whose *Death of a Hero*
castigated the British for sending their sons to slaughter in the
World War. But Wolfe felt an outsider in this group, who seemed
"so strange and foreign" that he did not keep up his acquaintance.

He almost certainly could have gained access to the adoring
circle that surrounded James Joyce in Paris, for Mrs. Jean Gorman,
the wife of Joyce's authorized biographer, took a special interest in
this new American novelist. But Wolfe's feelings toward Joyce

were now mixed. As critics began to discover the profound sym-bolism and the careful architecture of *Ulysses,* Wolfe, who had enjoyed the frankness, the humor, and the verbal pyrotechnics of the novel, grew disenchanted with it. Joyce's "Work in Progress" (which later became *Finnegans Wake*) caused him to believe that Joyce mistook "the nauseous rumblings of his gut for the trumpet of doom." Anyway, Wolfe suspected that Mrs. Gorman's interest in his work, his plans, and his friends was excessive, and he vowed to have nothing to do with this "prize bitch" and "these scandal-mongering apes and baboons" who were her friends.

Consequently the only people in Paris that he saw much of were American literary and artistic expatriates. Some he found pleasant and inoffensive: Terence Holliday, owner of the Holliday Book Shop in New York; George Seldes, the journalist; Lewis Galantière, who wrote occasionally for *Hound and Horn* and the *New Republic.* But most of the expatriates seemed shallow, and some of them had been in Aline Bernstein's circle in New York. He had left New York to escape these same people.

The most attractive as well as the most repellent of these New York acquaintances was Emily Davies Thayer. When she learned that he was in Paris, Emily pursued him with notes scrawled in her childish hand: "Dear Tom: Where are you? I want to see you. . . . Love, Emily." Lonely in Paris, Wolfe "got a warm and happy feeling" when he first heard from her, and for a week or so he saw her frequently.

Then things changed. He suspected that Emily was reporting his whereabouts and activities to Aline. He was disgusted by her systematic and rather dogged exploration of the life of degeneracy and refused to join her in smoking a pipe of opium. He detested her gigolo, a young Frenchman named Raymonde, who, Wolfe said, looked "like a bad edition of the late Rudolph Valentino." What really hurt, though, was Emily's remark over lunch one day that Raymonde was also a genius, and she told Wolfe that he and her lover "had much in common" and "were both to be broth-ers." Wolfe became violently sick and rushed from the restaurant to vomit. A few days later he thought Emily publicly insulted him when she paraded him, along with Raymonde, "as someone who was madly in love with her."

Finding it impossible to escape her attentions, Wolfe fled to Rouen at the beginning of June. When he returned to Paris, he moved to a different hotel, where he thought he could avoid her and could settle down to work.

I

Even with all these interruptions Wolfe managed to do a great deal of writing. He had come to Europe desperately tired and emotionally drained. On shipboard he vainly tried to resume his practice of writing for long, consecutive hours during the night, but the words would not come and his mind went blank. Then on his first night after landing at Boulogne he discovered a way to stimulate his creativity. After attempting to write for an hour or so in his hotel room, he decided to give it up and go to bed. He undressed slowly and, since the night was warm, he did not put on his pajamas but walked naked over to the window and looked out over the town sleeping in the moonlight. As he stood there, all at once his weariness dropped away, and he was eager to write again. Curious about the change, he tried to reconstruct what had happened and remembered that, unconsciously, he had reverted to a habit of his childhood. While standing nude at the window, he had been gently fondling his testicles and penis with one hand. His sensations were not specifically sexual; his "penis remained limp and unaroused" as his hand explored "the male configurations — the long and dangling shaft, the soft, smooth head with its flaring rim and its tiny mouth, and the rough seed bag hanging free with the weight of the two solid nuts, which lay warm and heavy in the palm as he cupped his hand beneath them." But touching his private parts gave him such a "good male feeling" that his energy returned. Switching on the light, he sat down naked at the table, picked up where he had left off, and "the words flowed in full spate again" until dawn, and "with amazing speed, ease, and sureness he filled page after triumphant page."

It was to this never-failing source of creative energy that Wolfe regularly resorted. When fondling his genitals during his solitary late-night writing sessions, he "found that the sensuous elements in every domain of life became more immediate, real, and beautiful to him, and easier to capture in words." This dreamy masturbatory state did not lead to the construction of plots or the writing of dialogues; instead it put him in the mood to produce some of his most beautiful semipoetic chants and rhythmical pas-

sages. From these nocturnal sessions came the earliest version of
his paean to autumn:

> October is the richest of the seasons; there is the harvest in, the
> granaries are full. October is the richest of the seasons: all of the
> blood and meat of living is plumped full. . . .

He also began experimenting with phrases that would become
his ode to spring, his affirmation of life over death, which became
the proem to *Of Time and the River:*

> Immortal love, alone and aching in the wilderness we cried to you.
> You were not absent from our loneliness. . . .
> For lovely April, cruel and flowerful, will tease
>   us with sharp joy, with wordless unfulfilled desire.
> Spring has no language but a cry.

Not all that Wolfe wrote during these months abroad was lyrical, but nearly everything he composed was brief and disconnected, for he was experimenting with new forms of fiction. He
was never much interested in the development of character; the
people in his books and stories rarely experience growth or change.
He had no interest in plot. But he felt "haunted by the Idea . . . of
Time and Change" and wanted to share that mystery with his
readers. Like William Faulkner, in *The Sound and the Fury* and,
later, in *The Wild Palms,* and like John Dos Passos, especially in
Manhattan Transfer, he took liberties with the conventions of time
and place. Not even attempting to write a well-constructed novel,
he wanted his "book" — the term he always preferred to
"novel" — to present, as in a frieze or panorama, a sequence of
apparently unrelated scenes: "a woman talking of the river, the
ever-moving river, coming through the levee at night, and of the
crippled girl clinging to the limb of the oak"; the "hoboes waiting
quietly at evening by the water tower for the coming of the fast
express"; the "rich American girl moving on from husband to
husband, from drink to dope to opium" (obviously Emily Thayer);
"the engineer at the throttle of the fast train"; the "school teacher
from Ohio taking University Art Pilgrimage No. 36, writing back
home"; and so on.

What would unite these seemingly unrelated episodes was the
fact that they all impinged on the life of his hero, David ("Monkey") Hawke. In order to avoid the charge of autobiography,

which had so plagued him after the publication of *Look Homeward, Angel,* Wolfe followed his plan to make David Hawke as different as possible in appearance from himself: he was "about five feet nine, with the long arms and the prowl of an ape." But, he explained to Perkins, "I have made him out of the *inside* of me, of what I have always believed the inside was like."

But David Hawke was intended to be something more than a thin disguise for Thomas Wolfe: he was to be the representative American whose life history would be that of all Americans. Wolfe planned to have his adventures follow the pattern of the ancient Greek myth of Antaeus, the Libyan giant, who was searching for the father he had never seen, Poseidon. His quest brought him into conflict with many enemies, but he overcame them all since each time he fell to the earth, which was his mother, his strength was redoubled. Only when Antaeus encountered Hercules, who lifted him into the air so that he could not touch earth, was he subdued. Wolfe believed that the Antaeus myth expressed "the two things that haunt and hurt" Americans: "the eternal wandering, moving, questing, loneliness, homesickness, and the desire of the soul for a home, peace, fixity, repose." In his own life Wolfe had been torn "between a hunger for isolation, for getting away, for seeking new lands — and a desire for home, for permanence, for a piece of this earth fenced in and lived on and private to oneself, and for a person or persons to love and possess." He sought, then, to write a book that was both personal and universal. The first line would be: "Of wandering forever and the earth again."

His new book would be gigantic in scale because it would take hundreds of thousands of words fully to reveal "the richness, fabulousness, exultancy and wonderful life of America." Wolfe was now engaged in a prolonged love affair with his native land. While at Harvard he had joined H. L. Mencken in jeering at the American "booboisie" and he had rejoiced when Sinclair Lewis exposed the spiritual emptiness of Main Street Americans. "Welcome To Our City" had attacked provincial America, and *Look Homeward, Angel* was begun in the same spirit. But even while that novel was going through the press, Wolfe's views had begun to change and he deleted some blatantly antidemocratic passages and a reference to America as "the great mongrel nation."

Now that he was abroad, his affection for his native land became a passion. He had barely landed in France before he began

writing of his "most unspeakable desire, longing, and love for my
own country." The longer he remained in Europe the deeper his
homesickness became. "America may be all the terrible things
these English and French people tell me it is," he conceded, "but
. . . it is the only place in the universe to which I feel even partially
a kinship — its sights and sounds and smells are part of my blood
and brain." About this time he bought a copy of Joyce's *A Portrait
of the Artist as Young Man,* which he apparently read for the first
time, and he underscored the next to the last sentence from Stephen
Dedalus's diary: "I go to . . . forge in the smithy of my soul the
uncreated conscience of my race." Like Dedalus he intended to
become a "voice for the experience of a race," the bard of America.

Wolfe knew that he was breaking with the literary fashion of the
1920s, which satirized and denigrated the United States. He anticipated attacks from "the wastelanders, the lost generationeers,
the bitter-bitters, the futility people, and all other cheap literary
fakes." These young Americans of modest talents had made
Gertrude Stein's pronouncement about a "lost generation" their
excuse for loitering in the cafés of Paris and failing to write anything of consequence, all the while blaming their impotence on the
thinness of the American culture from which they sprang. "There
is not any 'lost generation,' " Wolfe insisted; "every generation is
lost" and "one generation is very much like another."

Shortly after he returned to Paris Wolfe had an encounter with
F. Scott Fitzgerald that strengthened his hostility toward expatriate American writers. They met at the urging of Maxwell Perkins,
who wanted Scribners authors to know each other, and they tried
to be amiable. Each sent back to Perkins an admiring report of the
other. Fitzgerald, Wolfe wrote, "was very friendly and generous,
and I liked him, and think he has a great deal of talent, and I hope
he gets that book done soon." Fitzgerald told Perkins that he had
"a great find" in Wolfe, for "what he'll do is incalculable." He
compared Wolfe to Ernest Hemingway, the third of Perkins's
special authors, concluding that "he has a deeper culture than
Ernest and more vitality" but noting that Wolfe was "slightly less
of a poet" and lacked Hemingway's "quality of a stick hardened in
the fire." A little later Fitzgerald told Perkins that he had discovered a "family resemblance between we three" — Hemingway,
Wolfe, and himself — since all three were attempting "to recap-

ture the exact feel of a moment in time and space, exemplified by people rather than by things . . . an attempt at a mature memory of a deep experience."

Despite these agreeable reports to Scribners, the two men did not really get along well, for they were different in almost every way. Fitzgerald's compact figure, his chiseled features, and his meticulous dress were as different from Wolfe's gigantic size and disheveled appearance as his concern for form and plot were from Wolfe's rhythmic prose and extravagant rhetoric. Even at their first meeting they disagreed over the writer's proper relationship to his country. Wolfe insisted that Americans were "a homesick people, and belonged to the earth and land we came from as much or more as any country" he knew, but Fitzgerald, who had spent many years abroad, objected that "we were not, that we were not a country, that he had no feeling for the land he came from." On one occasion they had a good many drinks together at the Ritz Bar, where Fitzgerald, a fixture at that establishment, was surrounded by "Princeton boys, all nineteen years old, all drunk, and all half-raw." Wolfe listened as Fitzgerald engaged in "a spirited conversation . . . about why Joe Zinzendorff did not get taken into the Triple-Gazzaza Club," and one Princetonian told him: "Joe's a good boy, Scotty, but you know he's a fellow that ain't got much background." "I thought it was time for Wolfe to depart," Wolfe recorded, "and I did."

II

The encounter with Fitzgerald made Wolfe painfully aware that he did not belong in Paris. In early July he fled to Montreux, where he found a good room in a quiet hotel overlooking Lake Geneva and planned to settle down for an uninterrupted period of writing. But he had hardly arrived before he again ran into Fitzgerald, whose wife was in a nearby sanatorium and who was very lonesome. Fitzgerald took him off to a casino and a nightclub and seemed determined to tempt him to drink too much. "It would be very easy for me to start swilling liquor at present," Wolfe reported to Perkins, "but I am *not* going to do it. I am here to get work done, and in the next three months, I am going to see whether I am a bum or a man." Though Wolfe privately thought Fitzgerald was "a drunken and malicious fellow," the two men continued to see a good deal of each other. One evening as they were walking together in Montreux, Wolfe found that he could reach up and touch the electrical wires above the street and, delighted as a child at his discovery, began to pull on them "with the casualness of a conductor ringing up fares," while he produced a blackout in the city.

In moving to Switzerland Wolfe had taken great care to conceal his whereabouts, but shortly after he encountered Fitzgerald there it seemed that everybody knew his address. He suspected that Fitzgerald, whom he thought a social climber, had endeavored to ingratiate himself with the wealthy Emily Davies Thayer by passing along the information and that Emily had forwarded it to Aline Bernstein. Whether his suspicions were correct or not, he soon began to receive a flood of letters and cables from Aline, all ending with the lament that she had been driven "nearly crazy" because he had been "so wantonly cruel" in deserting her. She warned that if he did not reply to her letters, she would borrow money and sail to Europe to find him. One cable read simply: "Help me Tom — Aline."

Desperate at this reopening of a wound that he had hoped was healing, Wolfe felt he had to reply in order to forestall Aline's trip. The drafts of his message indicated his hopelessly mixed feelings. Some included phrases like "I love you dearly," but an entry in his pocket notebook read: "This woman . . . wrecked me, maddened me, and betrayed my love constantly, but she will not leave me alone now. I hope the whore dies immediately and horribly, I would rejoice at news of this vile woman's death." The cable he finally sent was curt and unrevealing: "Let's help each other Be fair Remember I'm alone."

Upset by Aline's threats, Wolfe took out his rage on the hotelkeeper at Montreux, who he claimed had overcharged him. Breaking his promise to Perkins, he "went on a spree, broke windows, plumbing fixtures, etc. in the town, and came back to the hotel at 2 A.M., pounded on the door of the manager and on the doors of two English spinsters, rushed howling with laughter up and down the halls, cursing and singing." The next day he moved to Geneva.

There he found no peace either, for he began to receive British reviews of *Look Homeward, Angel,* which Heinemann published on July 14, 1930. Aware that he was abnormally sensitive to criticism,

Wolfe had urged Frère-Reeves not to send him any reviews, but the initial notices were so favorable that the editor could not restrain himself. The *Times* of London announced that Wolfe had "a talent of such torrential energy as has not been seen in English literature for a long time." Derek Patmore said Wolfe's language had "the rich magnificence of the Elizabethans," and Richard Aldington called *Look Homeward, Angel* "the one good book which has come from 'Ulysses,' because Mr. Wolfe is the first writer . . . to learn what Mr. Joyce has to teach without imitating him." The prestigious *Times Literary Supplement* acknowledged that the book was long and diffuse but praised Wolfe's "great talent, so hard, so sensual, so unsentimental, . . . so proudly rising to the heights," and promised anxiously to observe his future, "for if Mr. Wolfe can be wasted, there is no hope for today."

But Frère-Reeves also sent a second batch of British reviews, which were markedly unfavorable. Admitting that *Look Homeward, Angel* was "in a way impressive," the *Spectator* lamented: "What a pity he has been so long (and lofty) winded, and so painfully literary." "I cannot form the remotest conception of what 'Look Homeward, Angel' is about, though I have been humbly gnawing at it for weeks, and have read many passages many times," grumbled Gerald Gould in the *Observer*. In the *London Evening News* Frank Swinnerton wrote a patronizing put-down deploring Wolfe's "over-excited verbosity" and protesting that the book became "intolerable" when Wolfe engaged in "ecstatic apostrophe" and suddenly began "crying 'O this' and 'O that,' as if he were parodying the Greek Anthology."

Wolfe was crushed. For a man who grew up believing that he had "at least as much English blood in my veins as the royal family," who was trained to know and love English — much more than American — literature, rejection by British reviewers was devastating. Recalling the "hate and rancor" his book had stirred up in Asheville, the "venom and malice among literary tricksters in New York," and now the "mockery and abuse over here," he decided: "Life is not worth the pounding I have taken both from public and private sources these last two years." He demanded of Perkins an accounting of any royalties due to him and informed Scribners: "I have stopped writing and do not want ever to write again."

Deeply depressed, he left Switzerland, taking his first airplane ride, to Lyon. Though in the past he had always been terrified of heights, he felt "no trace whatever of this dizziness and fear" in a plane. On the contrary he thought air travel was "a glorious experience," partly because "it's so nice to think what you could do to a lot of people (each of us has his little list) with a few carefully chosen explosives." From Lyon he moved on to Marseilles and then to Arles, and the travel, the sun, and most of all the excellent food restored his spirits. By September 13 he was sufficiently recovered to wire Perkins: "Working again. Excuse letter."

III

Wolfe went to Germany because he felt more at home there than in any place except the United States, and he decided to visit Freiburg because it was in the Black Forest. "The inside of me was like a Black Forest," he explained, "and I think the name kept having its unconscious effect on me." Initially he enjoyed his stay, but his tranquillity was disturbed by the strident campaigning for approaching national elections. In the hope of strengthening his centrist government against the Communists on the left and the growing Nazi party on the right, Chancellor Heinrich Brüning had dissolved the Reichstag and called for new elections on September 14. The newspapers were filled with exhortations from nineteen rival political parties, each of which claimed to have a way out of the Depression that would put the millions of unemployed Germans back to work. "I have never seen such excitement in my life," Wolfe reported as the ordinarily quiet city was disrupted by riots on election day. He was not troubled by the enormous increase in the Nazi vote, which swelled Adolf Hitler's delegation in the next Reichstag from 12 to 107 deputies; he thought "the German fascisti" were simply "young fellows . . . hot under the collar about the international situation," and he shared their bitterness toward the French "swine" who were occupying the Rhineland. Still, he felt vaguely ill at ease, torn between his admiration for "the simple common people" who were "clean, kind, friendly and as *honest* as they make them" and his aversion for their leaders with their "fat corrupt faces."

Returning briefly to Paris, he picked up a waiting batch of letters from Aline, which brought on "a kind of terrible fear . . . of some further grief, failure, humiliation, and torture." Then in early October he moved to London and settled into a flat at 15 Ebury Street, which Frère-Reeves had found for him. It was a quiet place, above the offices of a Russian physician, who Wolfe suspected was an abortionist. Wolfe's needs were attended to by the elderly charwoman, Mrs. Lavis, who was, he said, "a perfect priceless damned Kohinoor" diamond. Mrs. Lavis, with her unshakable loyalty to the British royal family, made her appearance in Wolfe's fiction as Daisy Purvis in *You Can't Go Home Again*.

Here, for the first time in his Guggenheim year, Wolfe settled down to a regular schedule. During the previous six months he had been constantly adding material to the great ledgers that he carried everywhere he traveled, but these entries were very different from the sustained, consecutive narrative of his first book. For example, one ledger included, with no attempt at continuity or connection, a proposed dedication of his new book to Perkins (composing such dedications was always a favorite activity with Wolfe, for it gave him an excuse for not actually writing his novel); a rhapsody on October; a description of the passengers on the ship where he and Aline had first met; reminiscences of Aline's childhood; a characterization of "Mona" (who was Mina Curtiss); a rhapsody beginning, "But in the night time, in the dark, Lee came on across Virginia"; an account of "an interesting and magnificent old man dying of cancer"; and a dozen or more proposed outlines for his new book. "I am all broken up in fragments myself at present," he observed before he left France, "and all that I can write is fragments."

The more disorganized Wolfe's materials became, the more earnestly he insisted to his friends at Scribners that his new book had "a beautiful plan and a poetic logic." Doubtless Perkins and Wheelock realized that he was really trying to convince himself, for they offered only the most general comments whenever he sent in a long prospectus for the new novel. "Every time you write about the book," Perkins assured him, "I get as excited as I did when I began 'The Angel.'"

With no help from New York, Wolfe spent the winter in London attempting to bring order to his material. It fell, he recognized, into three large categories. A good many long fragments, to which he sometimes gave the general title "Faust and Helen" but more often called "The October Fair," formed a fictional account of his affair with Aline Bernstein. Another group of manuscripts, which he named "The Good Child's River," was based on the recollections that Aline kept sending him; it reconstructed her life in the years before he met her. To a third category of material Wolfe gave an eighteenth-century title: "The Strange Life and Adventures of Mr. David 'Monkey' Hawke, a gentleman of good family, of his early youth, of his wanderings in America and Europe, and of his remarkable search to find his father, and how he found him." All three of these stories were incomplete; they were only in a very loose sense interrelated; and each of them, if finished, would run far longer than the average novel. Wolfe clearly recognized his problem: "I have started three books and have written twenty or thirty thousand words on each — I *must* finish one. Which?"

But he was unable to choose among them. He needed to write the love story in order to understand the most turbulent emotional involvement of his life. Aline's history was important if only because it would demonstrate that he could write something other than autobiography — about people he did not know, and about a time before he had even been born. And he was deeply attached to the story of "Monkey" Hawke, because Perkins had suggested that he write a book about a man's search for his father. Perkins was dismayed to discover that Wolfe was taking a casual remark so seriously, but Wolfe insisted that the theme was "immensely and profoundly true," since "all of us are wandering and groping through life for an image outside ourselves, for a superior and external wisdom we can appeal [to] and trust." In addition there was a very practical advantage to following the theme that Perkins suggested, because it permitted the author to bring the story to an end at any point by having the son find his father. Wolfe was aware that, not merely in writing but in living, he had trouble in coming to a conclusion.

During the winter months in London, then, he continued to work on all three story lines simultaneously, turning from one to another as he became bored or tired. Completely alone in the house on Ebury Street at night, he read during the early evening, ate the meal that the doting Mrs. Lavis had left for him or cooked up something for himself, and about midnight settled down to work, priming himself with awesome quantities of tea and coffee. Often he wrote until daybreak, when the light struck the yellow walls and the smoky brick of the street, the milk wagon came by, the housemaids went out to scrub the stoops, and the shops opened. Only then did he have a drink and go to bed, where Mrs. Lavis would find him later and bring him toast and tea and gossip.

IV

Though Wolfe thought he "lived about as solitary a life as a modern man can have," he was not a hermit during his months in London. Frère-Reeves introduced him to "some celebrated people," as Wolfe proudly informed his mother. He was made to feel at home in several solid, middle-class families, such as that of Donald Carswell, a "literary architect," at Hampstead Heath. Afterwards Wolfe caricatured his hosts as gray-looking people, wearing gray-looking glasses, drinking weak tea and eating cold Sunday lamb. He also came to know some of the visitors to the Russian doctor. Perhaps through these acquaintances he was introduced to Ivy Litvinoff, the stylish, English-born wife of the Soviet commissar for foreign affairs. At first he enjoyed sleeping with her, but she turned him off by her insistence that she "be beaten with straps (. . . 'O *whip,* O whip,' she said) across her bottom."

On his long afternoon walks Wolfe for the first time became aware how serious the economic depression was. Owning no securities or investments, he had not been affected by the stock market crash in the fall of 1929, and, living on his Guggenheim stipend, which had more and more purchasing power as prices everywhere dropped, he had taken little notice of unemployment or destitution on the Continent. But now, everywhere around him in the gray, cold streets of London, he saw "thousands of poor wretches who have no shelter for their heads and no money for a meal." Unemployment in England, he concluded, was permanent: "There are too many people for so small a country, and there is not enough work to go round. The people have endured hardship poverty and insufficient food for so long *that* has affected their spirit."

His hope that things were better in "a great rich country" like the United States was shattered by the news he received from home. Julia Wolfe had lost most of her paper fortune when the Asheville real estate boom collapsed in 1926, but now the failure of the Asheville banks cost her the rest. Ralph Wheaton lost his job, and he and Mabel were obliged to give up the fashionable house they were buying on Kimberley Avenue. Fred was about to lose property in Miami Beach that was nearly paid for. When Wolfe heard the bad news, he responded immediately with an offer of help. He mistakenly thought that sizable royalties had accumulated from the English edition of *Look Homeward, Angel,* and he knew that he could draw more against the advance that Scribners had offered him. "If you or Mabel or Mama are in need of a little money to tide you over at present," he informed Fred, "I am sure that I could come through with a thousand dollars, perhaps more." Grimly he warned, though, that he would not send money to further the family delusion that fortunes could be made through speculation in property: "If I had ten million dollars, they could have half of it to grow cocoanut trees at the North Pole, but not one God-damn cent for real estate."

When Fred asked for a loan of five hundred dollars, Wolfe urgently requested Perkins to send this sum to his brother. "Mr. Perkins," he begged, "I know it's a bad year for everyone, but *if I've got it there* at Scribners, or even if I haven't got it, for God's sake get that money for the boy, and I will work my fingers to the bone." Perkins obliged promptly.

But Wolfe found it difficult to work his fingers to the bone when he was distracted, and interruptions to his work became more and more frequent. In December Sinclair Lewis, who had just received the Nobel Prize in literature, arrived in London and asked Wolfe to call on him. It was not an invitation Wolfe could decline, for Lewis had been unstinting in his praise of *Look Homeward, Angel*. In October, quite without warning or introduction, he wrote Wolfe that the novel had "authentic greatness" and exclaimed: "I wish there hadn't been quite so many brisk blurbwriters these past twenty years, using up every once respectable phrase of literary criticism, so that I might have some fresh phrase with which to express my profound delight." Shortly afterwards, when the Nobel Prize was announced, Lewis gave an interview in New York in which he praised several young American writers but singled out Wolfe, who, he said, "may have a chance to be the greatest American writer" — indeed, Lewis added, "I don't see why he should not be one of the greatest world writers." Then at Stockholm, in accepting his prize, Lewis assailed the "Victorian and Howellsian timidity and gentility in American fiction" and pointed to younger writers, such as Ernest Hemingway, William Faulkner, and John Dos Passos, who were creating an authentic American literature. He gave special praise to Wolfe, "a child of, I believe, thirty or younger, whose one and only novel, *Look Homeward, Angel,* is worthy to be compared with the best in our literary production, a Gargantuan creature with great gusto of life."

Wolfe received Lewis's commendations with mixed feelings. On the one hand, as he wrote Lewis, he was "honored and deeply grateful" for such praise. On the other hand, he was at just this time moving away from Lewis's harshly satirical view of American life. Besides, Lewis's predictions were a bit daunting. "The Great American Writer business is pretty tough stuff for a man who is on his second book," he complained, explaining that it would start critics gunning for him before he could finish his new novel. "I hope he's write [sic] but I hope they give the young fellow a few more years to blaze out in all this glory."

Nevertheless, when Lewis called, Wolfe had to respond. On their first encounter both men were astonished by what they saw. Wolfe found Lewis "the most fantastically ugly man" he had ever met — tall, emaciated, with "bony, freckled, red-haired, knuckly hands," a face "so scaled carbuncled, scabbed, broken out in lumps and patches, that it suggested the corrugations of a washing board," and eyes that seemed to have been "permanently poached." Lewis, for his part, gazed up at Wolfe in amazement, exclaiming: "God a-Mighty, you're a big son-of-a-bitch, Tom!"

The two men took an instant liking for each other, and Wolfe abandoned his writing schedule for as long as Lewis remained in England. Lewis insisted that Wolfe accompany him on an unannounced visit to Frère-Reeves in Surrey. Wolfe's slightly fictionalized account of their trip, during which the driver repeatedly got lost and Lewis lapsed into a comatose alcoholic state, later became the "Lloyd McHarg" episode in *You Can't Go Home Again.* Omitted from this published account were Wolfe's more graphic details about Lewis's drunken stupor; put to bed, he roused himself to thrust a long, bony finger down his throat so as to induce an incredible fountain of vomiting, which Wolfe had to catch in the chamber pots and other receptacles Frère-Reeves had prudently provided.

Years later, when the "Lloyd McHarg" story appeared in print, Lewis was hurt by Wolfe's description of his ugliness, and he objected that the account was both inaccurate and exaggerated. Still, he admitted, "Wolfe had a perfect eye. He made each paling in a fence stand out, made each one distinctive." But some time later when asked whether he was a friend of Wolfe's, Lewis replied: "No. . . . You couldn't be a friend of Tom's, any more than you could be a friend of a hurricane."

Already thrown off his schedule by Lewis's visit, Wolfe was even further distracted during his stay in London by Aline Bernstein. He had thought their affair was finally ended. For a time it seemed that Aline did too, as she lapsed into silence. But during the fall she began writing him more and more desperate letters: "You would put upon my love the ugliness of your desertion and infidelity, but that does not change my undying fire." "What life if Tom is false and bad to me." Then began the cables: "Life impossible no word from you are you willing to accept consequences desperate."

Wolfe stuck to his resolve not to reply, but he took these messages seriously. So convincing were Aline's suicide threats that he began buying all the New York newspapers he could lay hands on, searching through their "horrible mortuary columns" under the letter "B" for the "dreadful news" of Aline's death. But he was almost equally troubled when he found nothing, for he "imagined she had died or killed herself, and that her embittered and griefstricken friends and family were saying nothing to me."

Then he chanced upon reviews of Vicki Baum's play, *Grand Hotel,* which praised the stunning sets designed by Aline Bernstein. Chance acquaintances from New York mentioned that they had recently seen Aline, that she was "very radiant and happy," and that she had scored another triumph with her designs for Philip Barry's *Tomorrow and Tomorrow.* About this time Aline's sister, Ethel Frankau, who was on a buying trip to London for Bergdorf-Goodman, came to see Wolfe. When he told her of the frantic messages Aline had been sending him, she replied that her sister "had never been happier or calmer or more joyful and successful than this Fall." Wolfe asked why Aline kept sending "these cables threatening death, misery, and destruction," and Ethel replied that her sister was an "emotional woman," who might "think she meant these things" for five minutes or so. She advised him not to take these communications "too seriously."

When Ethel left, Wolfe rushed to the lavatory and vomited for two hours. Aline's conduct, he believed, was "one of the vilest and basest things I have ever heard." Reviewing her actions, he concluded: "That a person that I have loved so dearly, and who has professed her love, faithfulness and faith for me so often, could deliberately and trivially do this ruinous and damnable thing to a young man without influence or money who is leading a desperately lonely life abroad, trying to get on with his work . . . seems . . . to be a vile, cruel, and cowardly act."

Tormented by Aline, frustrated by the approaching end of his Guggenheim year with no second book near completion, Wolfe early in 1931 decided to ask for help, and he turned to Maxwell Perkins, who was, he thought, "the real head of Scribners." Perkins was not merely "the best publisher and the best man . . . on the face of the earth," he explained to Fred. "This man has been more than a friend, he has been a father to me, and strictly between ourselves, I think of him as a father and care for him as such." Up to this point Wolfe had maintained "a partial reserve in speaking" to Perkins about his own affairs, though he had "hinted at things, and got at them indirectly." But now the time had come when "I must now tell you certain things — much more plainly than I have ever been able to tell them to you in person, but if I cannot tell them to you, who in God's name am I to talk to?" In a five-thousand-word letter he poured out to Perkins the whole tortured history of his affair with Aline and asked for help: "I am in *terrible trouble,* and I need a friend."

Perkins's initial reaction to Wolfe's unsought confidences was cautious. With his formal, conservative upbringing, he found the whole Wolfe-Bernstein affair messy and unpleasant. Since he had never experienced anything like this himself, he lacked confidence in his ability to give Wolfe good advice. Still, he was certain that Wolfe had been right in leaving Aline. "I can only feel angry with *her,*" Perkins responded to Wolfe's outpouring, adding: "There is an egotism in woman beyond any known in man, and they infuriate me. . . . Did any one of them ever admit she was in the wrong about anything?"

But the more Perkins reflected on Wolfe's problem, the more deeply involved he became. Up to this time he had thought of

Wolfe as one of several remarkably gifted young writers in whom he took a fatherly interest, a likable, loquacious young Southerner who was always good company for a drink or a walk. But now Wolfe's call for help touched some deep emotions in Perkins. Obviously his author desperately needed, and eagerly sought, organization and guidance, and that was what Perkins felt best equipped to offer. A great admirer of Napoleon, whose profile he used to sketch during boring conferences, Perkins thought he had a talent for strategy and tactics but knew he would never be a leader of men himself. Early in his marriage he had told his wife that his ambition was to be "a little dwarf on the shoulder of a great general advising him what to do and what not to do, without anyone's noticing."

V

But Perkins's generalship was not yet needed. After pouring out his troubles to his editor, Wolfe felt enormously relieved and was able to get on with his work. Though he was "damned tired," he kept on writing even during a brief, unhappy vacation in Paris at the end of December. Daily for the next two months he kept adding to his manuscript. "I am," he assured Henry Volkening, "rapidly becoming a great authority on the subject of *Work* because I, my boy, have done some — 'and penance more will do.' " That phrase from "The Ancient Mariner," he suggested, would make a good title for almost any book, "for that, I think is what it takes to write one." At the end of February, after a brief visit to Amsterdam, he sailed for home, bringing with him, as he reported to the Guggenheim Foundation, "six enormous book-keeping ledgers with about 200,000 words of manuscript and a great many notes." Admitting that "a great deal remains to be done," he was confident that his book was "so firmly on the rails now that nothing can stop it." Before sailing he cabled Perkins: "Need no help now. Can help myself most. Work six months alone."

In planning his return to the United States, Wolfe was determined not merely to avoid Aline but all the other "little sneering Futility People" he had known in New York. For a time he thought of finding a place to live and work in New England, perhaps near Sinclair Lewis in Vermont or near Perkins in Connecticut. But more and more he began to turn to "the quaint old town of Brooklyn," which would be inexpensive, relatively isolated, yet within easy reach of the Scribners office in Manhattan. There also he could be near several old, undemanding friends, particularly John S. Terry, his rotund classmate from North Carolina, who now taught in the English department at New York University.

With the help of friends he found an inexpensive apartment at 40 Verandah Terrace, a short, unpretentious street on the edge of the Syrian section, not far from the Brooklyn Bridge. Initially it seemed highly satisfactory. It cost only sixty-five dollars a month, including gas and electricity. He had two rooms, one on the main floor, where he slept, and the other, immediately below, on the ground floor, where he worked. Before the house was divided, this had been the kitchen, and it still contained a stove, on which his landlady, Marjorie Dorman, from time to made him coffee and breakfast. A window grated with iron bars admitted light to this room from the street, and in the rear it looked out on a small, patiently cultivated garden. He liked Miss Dorman, a warm-hearted, heavy-drinking woman, big, plain, and rather statuesque, who had formerly been a reporter for the *Brooklyn Eagle,* and he was fascinated by her eccentric family. With only a little exaggeration he portrayed her father in his story "No Door" as "an inventor who does not invent," who perfected "a corkscrew with the cork attached that would not cork; an unlockable lock; and an unbreakable looking-glass that wouldn't look."

Wolfe sought in Brooklyn a life of privacy and anonymity. About once a week he walked over the Brooklyn Bridge to Manhattan and visited Perkins, Wheelock, and others at Scribners, and occasionally he stopped in at the Harvard Club to read in the library. But he almost never went to the theater, which had such painful memories for him, and rarely visited museums or attended concerts, for his interest in art and music died with his love for Aline. He no longer attempted to keep up with the latest books and magazines but read and reread a handful of volumes that he kept within easy reach on the top shelf of his bookcase: Shakespeare's plays, Coleridge's poems, Donne's poems, *The Anatomy of Melancholy, Ulysses,* and *War and Peace,* which he began because it was Perkins's favorite novel but which he now considered one of the few books "the world could not do without." After reviewers of *Look Homeward, Angel* compared him to

Whitman and Melville, he began seriously to read *Leaves of Grass* and *Moby Dick*. More and more he turned back to parts of the Bible — chiefly the Book of Job, Ecclesiastes, the Song of Solomon, and the Revelation of St. John the Divine.

He tried to keep to a fixed schedule. He began working on his book about midnight and, because no chairs or tables were ever quite comfortable for a man of his height, he usually stood while he wrote, using the top of the refrigerator as his desk. About four or five in the morning, exhausted, he tumbled into bed and slept till around eleven, when, assisted by many cups of coffee, he got back to work. Often in the early afternoon Abe Smith, his former student at New York University, now a young, married business-man, came by to type his interminable manuscript. Abe — or one of the several other young people who succeeded him — stayed until about six, when Wolfe, very reluctantly, let him escape. Then Wolfe went out to eat, usually at an inexpensive restaurant that served large helpings of food, for this was his one substantial meal of the day. Afterwards he walked, both to clear his head and to absorb new impressions later to be worked into his writing. He went everywhere, even into the most dangerous sections of Brooklyn, like the docks at Red Hook, and everywhere he talked to people — policemen, cab drivers, prostitutes, bartenders, shop-keepers. No one ever molested him, perhaps because of his size. Years later customers at a nearby Syrian store in Brooklyn re-membered him simply as a very big man, who wore a dark over-coat and no hat. "He looked like a walking coffin," said one.

It was a lonely life, but initially it was a rewarding one for a writer. "Brooklyn is a fine town — a nice, big country town, a long way from New York," he assured Henry Allen Moe, the secretary of the Guggenheim Foundation. "You couldn't find a better place to work."

When Wolfe wanted company, he could reach out easily to old and new friends in Brooklyn, knowing that they would not annoy him with highbrow literary talk. Terry, who lived nearby and was a bachelor — Wolfe did not know of his homoerotic attachment to his "chauffeur" — was always available for endless hours of talk about the South. He often ate or drank with Marjorie Dorman. She introduced him to the beautiful, garrulous Harriet Hoppe, another former *Brooklyn Eagle* employee, who promptly fell in love with him. He got to know the family of Dr. Arthur Jacobson, a Danish-born expert on tuberculosis. A great cook, Mrs. Jacobson at least tolerated Wolfe's visits at mealtimes; the older daughter, whom he dated occasionally, did not like him, and the younger thought him a hulking presence; but the authoritarian Dr. Jacobson took a great interest in this young writer. Privately, he speculated that Wolfe's intense creativity was like the hectic energy exhibited by many of his tubercular patients.

Wolfe also got in touch with some of his friends from earlier years. William Y. Tindall, his former colleague at New York University, occasionally visited him on Verandah Terrace. After dinner and much talk, Wolfe would walk his guest back across Brooklyn Bridge in the dark, chanting a passage from his manuscript on Pale Pity and Lean Death, "two horsemen, riding, riding, riding in the night."

Wolfe also made a point of seeing the young Korean Younghill Kang, with whom he had also taught at New York University. Learning that Kang had written a novel, he introduced him to Perkins, and when Scribners issued *The Grass Roof,* Wolfe wrote the only book review he ever published. His appraisal seemed to apply more to Thomas Wolfe than to Younghill Kang: "He has made a record of man's wandering and exile upon the earth, and into it he has wrought his vision of joy and pain and hunger."

Reviving an even earlier friendship, he went to see Henry Carlton, whom he had first met in the 47 Workshop, in Croton-on-Hudson, and there he met a remarkable young woman, to whom he was immediately attracted. Claire Turner Zyve had been brought up on a ranch in Wyoming, had gone to college in Colorado and California, and had earned her doctorate at Teachers College, Columbia University. Now separated from her husband, she was head of a new, experimental school in Scarsdale. Noting that Claire had "lots of sense and character" and was "very good looking to boot," Wolfe was much impressed that she earned five thousand dollars a year.

For her part, Claire was "entranced and intrigued by this man" even at their first meeting, and she began seeing a good deal of him during the spring of 1931. Sometimes she visited him on Verandah Terrace, where she noted with amusement his habit of dumping all his clothing onto the floor of his closet, so that when he dressed to go out, he had to root around in the pile to find a shirt, socks, or a tie, never pausing to consider whether what he was wearing matched. Once he took her to the loft on 8th Street in Manhattan, where he had written so much of *Look Homeward, Angel.* More often they met at her apartment on Mitchell Place, below 49th Street in Manhattan, which, as he remembered it, had a view of the East River.

Inevitably there were turbulent episodes in their friendship. A word or a glance could send Wolfe, always suspicious that somebody was laughing at him, into a tantrum. Sometimes he felt that he was being persecuted, perhaps by the people at Scribners, even by Perkins himself. Sometimes he suspected that Claire was trying to use him to meet influential people. Her casually expressed interest in the Town Hall Club festered in his memory, and years later it reappeared, in *You Can't Go Home Again,* when the "beautiful and brave young woman, country-bred," whispered to his hero at a most passionate moment: "I want you to use your influence to get me into the Cosmopolitan Club."

But these tempests usually ended as abruptly as they began. Mostly it was a joyful time for them both. Claire remembered when "I went to buy bread and you said 'hurry back' and I hurried glad with the thought of you waiting." Tom found her "so clean, sweet, and desirable" that she made him loathe the Southern girls he had known, who were "foul, dull, stupid, nasty — with a litter of gummed combs and hair upon the dresser, and a rancid swimming chamber-pot below the bed." When he left her apartment in the morning, he told her, he had "a feeling of the most enormous exultancy and joy to think that there were young women like you in the world."

VI

But Wolfe had hardly begun creating a new life for himself before it started to fall apart. In March Aline Bernstein, from a chance newspaper item, learned that he had returned to the United States. She had been ill for several months, suffering severe pain from an infected sinus and occasionally having attacks of vertigo. Now she collapsed and from her hospital bed wrote him — in care of Charles Scribner's Sons, since she did not know where he was living — begging to see him again. "Apparently to love you as I do is insanity," she admitted — but she could not help herself. At the same time, knowing that he was now writing the story of their passionate love affair, she insisted: "There is one favor I am asking, will you let me see your book before it is published. I believe you owe me that."

When Wolfe learned that Aline was seriously ill, his rage against her abruptly subsided. Explaining in great detail why her letters and cables had driven him into a frenzy, he pledged: "Aline, I love you more dearly than anyone or anything in the world, I will love you all my life, and it will never change. . . . If your present trouble and illness is in any way due to me, I want to tell you I would rather shed my own blood than cause you any pain." Remembering the past, he insisted that there should be no more "tricks and concealments" between them, and he urged her to tell her family and friends that they loved each other — "but that we are not physical lovers." He promised that he would "never write a word that may concern you, without your seeing it, and your decision in it will be in all ways final." In order to protect his privacy, he did not give Aline his address but communicated with her through Abe Smith.

"Your letter, and Abe, literally saved my life," Aline responded, and very soon she was on her feet again. Declaring that she could not help loving him all her life, she agreed to accept his insistence that there should be no more sex between them. Pitifully she begged him to "spare a couple of hours for your friend," and she promised to be quiet and loving if he would see her.

Reluctantly Wolfe agreed, and she began to visit him at Verandah Terrace once a week, usually on Thursdays. Coming in from Armonk, she used to talk with him, reminisce about her father and her girlhood, and cook for him. And, inevitably, they became more intimate, as she delicately reminded him by references to the brown silk handkerchief she left in his pajama pocket and "the indisposition in your tender place," which needed treatment with zinc ointment. More blunt, Wolfe recorded that they had sex six times during the summer.

As Wolfe had feared, renewing his relationship with Aline brought to an end his efforts to lead a new and different life. He continued to see Claire Zyve, but during the summer their affair cooled. She sensed in him a lack of "understanding and compassionate consideration." "He didn't really care about and care for other human beings in the way that most of us as human beings do," she came to recognize. Even when he was making love, he seemed "a kind of analyst and a scientist probing into what the human being was. . . . It was just as though the woman were under a microscope and being looked at by him and dissected by him . . . a dissection of that species which is called woman." She wanted from him "a different kind of friendship."

He misunderstood Claire's wishes. He thought she was trying to convert a happy relationship between two free spirits into a marriage — though, in fact, she was not even divorced and had no desire to marry him. He suspected that she was using her sexual favors "as a sort of bribe," and that infuriated him. He sent her one long, confused letter trying to explain his feelings and drafted another, more explicit one in his pocket notebook. He was incapable of giving her "the utmost and final love of my heart and spirit," because that he had already given to Aline. But even if he were free to love her fully, things would never work out. "I am ugly, cruel, and mad in a way you know nothing about: if anyone loves me I torture them, curse and revile them, and try to drive them away." This was the way he had treated Aline, "the only person who ever loved me with all her heart." "If I loved you, and you loved me," he assured Claire, "I would treat you the same way." By fall they had begun to drift apart.

During the summer his love affair with Brooklyn also began to fade. As the July sun beat down, he came to see the city not as a pleasant overgrown country village but as "a vast sprawl upon the face of the earth, which no man alive or dead has yet seen in its foul, dismal entirety." The "huge gigantic Stink" of Brooklyn overwhelmed him: it was "cunningly contrived, compacted, and composed of eighty-seven separate several putrefactions," including melted glue, burned rubber, "deceased, decaying cats, . . . rotten cabbage, prehistoric eggs, and old tomatoes." At the same time his quarters on Verandah Terrace became less comfortable. His downstairs room, so cold and clammy during the winter, was now a hotbox, and he tried to keep cool by having no curtains or shades on the two windows. He did not know that his apartment was becoming a local sightseers' attraction, as passersby on the opposite side of the little street paused to stare and giggle at the half-clad giant who stood inside, leaning over his old Frigidaire, interminably writing, writing, writing. He was, however, disturbed to discover that his landlady had fallen in love with him and — though she was about fifty years old — was telling her friends that he would be the "father of her children." She also began drinking too much and, as Wolfe wrote his mother, "Whether you get cleaning, or heating, or lighting depends on whether she has a dollar, or spends it on gin."

Much more distressing was the fact that his writing was not going well. When Aline reentered his life, he dropped work on the adventures of young David Hawke and on the love story of David and Esther and gave almost all of his time to "The Good Child's River." For this account of Aline's childhood he relied not merely on her recollections; he spent much time in the public library searching through issues of the *New York Times* for the 1880s and jotting down long lists of news stories and theatrical events that would give authenticity to his novel. Though he wrote much, he finished only one section of Aline's story, an account of her father's purchase of one of the first automobiles in New York City. An attempt to recreate the past both authentically and objectively, "In the Park" was also an experiment in language, for he sought to merge meanings and sounds. In Central Park, where the automobile broke down, the passengers heard "the sharp, fast skaps of sound," the first morning calls of birds, like "smooth drops and nuggets of bright gold," and then "with chittering bicker and fast-fluttering skirrs of sound the palmy, honied bird-cries came . . . the rapid kweet-kweet-kweet-kweet-kweet of homely birds, and then their pwee-pwee-pwee: others had thin metallic tongues, a sharp cricketing stitch, and high shrew's caws, with eery rasp, with harsh, far calls." He submitted "In the Park" to *Scribner's Magazine*. When the editor rejected it, he seemed to be giving a verdict on what had happened to Wolfe's career since Aline Bernstein came back into his life.

As if to underscore the point, Perkins at the end of August told Wolfe that he should have the manuscript of his new book finished by the end of the next month. Brought up short, Wolfe was obliged to assess what he had written and where he stood. "There is no remote or possible chance that I will have a completed manuscript of anything that resembles a book this September," he informed Perkins, "and whether I have anything I would be willing to show anyone next September, or any succeeding one for the next 150 years, is at present of the extremest and most painful doubt to me." Two years ago he had been confident of producing "at least a half dozen long books."

Now, worn out by too much publicity, too much gossip, and his never-ending struggle with "a middle-aged Jewish woman old enough to be my mother," he was not sure he could complete even one. "I am not in *despair* over the book I have worked on," he told Perkins. "I am in *doubt* about it — and I am not sure about anything."

By the fall of 1931 Wolfe was at one of the lowest points of his life. As he celebrated his thirty-first birthday alone in the cheap Blue Ribbon restaurant, he summarized his situation in his pocket notebook: "I have done little — finished and published one book — know not where I am on the other."

His money was running out. Since his return from Europe he had been living on the small accumulated royalties earned by *Look Homeward, Angel*, but during the past six months fewer than two hundred fifty copies of the regular edition had been sold and he received very little from the inexpensive Modern Library edition. He had no bank account and no savings.

Just when he most needed money, he discovered that Madeleine Boyd was cheating him. From the very beginning he resented the commission that she took, as his agent, from his royalties. Now he learned that back in February Verlag Rowohlt agreed to translate and publish his novel in German and had sent Mrs. Boyd a contract and an advance against royalties of two hundred fifty dollars. She cashed the check but did not show the contract to Wolfe, obviously because she knew he would ask for his ninety percent of the advance. When Wolfe and Perkins confronted Mrs. Boyd in the Scribners offices, she broke into "gushets of tears," which, Wolfe noted callously, "spurted from her eyes . . . with the easy fluency of a pissing cow." At this point Perkins, who could stand almost anything except the sight of a woman crying, urged Wolfe not to be harsh on her. She was, after all, a woman and, by nature, incapable of understanding such matters as money and contracts. When she promised to pay Wolfe the money she had embezzled, Perkins persuaded him not to prosecute her and not even to dimiss her outright as his agent.

The amount of money involved in this unpleasant episode was not large — but neither were Wolfe's needs. He estimated that he could live quite comfortably on two hundred dollars a month. This modest budget did not, of course, include provision for the emergency assistance that his family, from time to time, called upon him to give. Julia's assets were almost completely wiped out, but, dauntless, she lived on in the Old Kentucky Home, took in an occasional roomer, and never accepted any of Tom's repeated offers of help. Fred had touched Tom for a loan while he was still in Europe, and Mabel got one hundred fifty dollars from him to help get her set up in the Gramercy Apartments in Washington, where she rented rooms to federal employees. When Tom learned that the mortgage on Effie's house in Anderson, South Carolina, was about to be foreclosed, he rushed three hundred dollars to her, but she realized that she could hold off the bank for only a year at most and returned the money to him with gratitude. From Frank, on the other hand, Tom received neither thanks nor a refund, for his oldest brother promptly went on a spree with the "loan" he received from Tom.

The troubles that Wolfe's family were experiencing helped him understand that the Depression was a "horrible human calamity." On his nocturnal rambling in Brooklyn and Manhattan he came upon the derelicts of economic disaster — "a man whose life had subsided into a mass of shapeless and filthy rags, devoured by vermin," and "wretches huddled together for a little warmth in freezing cold squatting in doorless closets upon the foul seat of a public latrine." But it was less the material than the spiritual bankruptcy of his countrymen that appalled him. "We seem to be lost," he observed. "The faces of the people in the subway are sometimes horrible in their lack of sensitivity and intelligence — they ruminate mechanically at wads of gum, the skins are horrible blends of the sallow, the pustulate, the greasy: and the smell that comes from them is acrid, foul and weary."

Wolfe felt that the United States was "at the end of . . . an 'era' — that the old system is shot to hell, and we will have to get busy and find a newer and better one." The basic problem was the result of overproduction and underconsumption: "we are glutted, literally starving in the midst of plenty, unable to market at a profit what we produce." Predicting that economic conditions would worsen, he warned his mother: "It may be that the whole Capitalistic system is finished — if so I think we should welcome some other one that is not so stupid and wasteful."

VII

By December 1931 Wolfe recognized that he would have to change from the pattern of life into which he had sunk. Down to his last few dollars, he needed to make some money. His new novel was nowhere near completion — indeed, it was not clear that it could ever be completed. Rejection of "In the Park" showed him that there was no market for his fictional treatment of Aline Bernstein's girlhood, to which he had devoted most of his time for the past six months.

He dug into his pile of accumulated manuscripts in the hope of retrieving something that could be made into a salable short story and came up with a sketch of his uncle, Henry Westall. Originally intended for *Look Homeward, Angel,* it had already been revised once or twice since 1928. At the moment it was part of the unfinished saga of David Hawke, and the uncle was called "Bascom Hawke." Wolfe worked for nearly a month shaping this segment of his novel into a story, and he left it on Perkins's desk, hoping it would be suitable for *Scribner's Magazine.* "I've simply tried to give you a man," he explained. "As for plot, there's not any, but there's this idea which I believe is pretty plain — I've always wanted to say something about *old men* and *young men,* and that's what I've tried to do here."

"A Portrait of Bascom Hawke" was indeed a study in youth and age. Old Bascom is one of Wolfe's best extended caricatures, a tall, bony creature with his amazingly flexible features and his scornful, snuffling laughter: "phuh-phuh-phuh-phuh." A seeker, who had come out of the South after the Civil War to work his way through Harvard Divinity School, he had tried to find God in many churches only to end as an agnostic, and he now was living the burned-out end of his life as a title-conveyancer in a Boston suburb. In contrast, David Hawke, his young nephew, who is much less fully portrayed, is just coming into his full manhood and has a Faustian appetite for experience and knowledge. David seeks to learn from the wisdom and experience of his uncle, but Bascom says sadly, "Sometimes everything seems so long ago." As the old man sinks into silence, the young man goes "out into the streets where the singing and lyrical air, the man-swarm passing in its million-footed weft, the glorious women and the girls compacted in the single music of belly and breasts and thighs, the sea, the earth, the proud, potent, clamorous city, all of the voices of time fused to a unity that was like a song, a token and a cry."

Perkins enthusiastically recommended "A Portrait of Bascom

Hawke" to Alfred Dashiell, the editor of *Scribner's Magazine,* who also liked it. Perhaps they enjoyed the story as a portrait of an aging eccentric, even though Bascom was a two-dimensional character and Wolfe's dialogue, as John O'Hara remarked, was "incredibly bad." But they may also have understood that Wolfe was less interested in telling a good story than in making an aesthetic assertion. For several years he had been troubled by the influence of T. S. Eliot and other nay-sayers on literature. To their images of the waste land of barren earth, dry bones, dust and ashes, he countered in the rhetorical questions that concluded his story:

> The dry bones, the bitter dust? The living wilderness, the silent waste? The barren land?
> Have no lips trembled in the wilderness? No eyes sought seaward from the rock's sharp edge for men returning home? Has no pulse beat more hot with love or hate upon the river's edge? Or where the old wheel and the rusted stock lie stogged in desert sand: by the horsehead a woman's skull. No love? . . .
> Was no love crying in the wilderness?

A celebration of youth and joy and life, "A Portrait of Bascom Hawke" was Wolfe's first published statement as self-appointed bard of America, prose poet of affirmation. With this story he helped American literature make the transition from the disillusionment of the 1920s to the affirmations of the 1930s.

Fully aware of the significance of his story, he was delighted when *Scribner's Magazine* accepted it for publication in the April 1932 issue. The appearance of the short story — it was really a novella of about thirty thousand words — would, at least temporarily, put an end to the literary gossip that he was a one-book author who had written himself out in *Look Homeward, Angel.* Though he professed to be indifferent to such criticism, he was acutely aware that he had published no fiction for more than two years and much of the time felt surrounded by a "circle of leering eyes which draws in about the poor wretch who is trying to write his second book."

On a more practical level, the five hundred dollars that *Scribner's Magazine* paid him meant that he could meet his bills, including his rent on his new apartment at 111 Columbia Heights in

Brooklyn, to which he had moved on the first of November, after Marjorie Dorman's household had become too disorganized for comfort. He now had an entire floor of a brownstone in one of the best parts of Brooklyn — across the street from the building from which crippled Washington Augustus Roebling had supervised the construction of the Brooklyn Bridge and in which the poet Hart Crane had lived. With two big, sunny, high-ceilinged rooms, a kitchen, and a full bathroom, he could for the first time in his life spread out his belongings comfortably, and since he could rent another bedroom upstairs he could now put up overnight guests.

Urgently he begged his mother to come up and visit him in January. Though he genuinely enjoyed seeing her, he had a special reason for wanting her at this time: he needed help in making a final break from Aline Bernstein. In a literary sense he had already made the break by turning from Aline's recollections and "The Good Child's River" back to his own and his family's experiences. But he knew from years of experience that, alone, he did not have the courage to bring to a final end his relationship with Aline, a relationship that was, he was convinced, sapping his creative energies and blighting his life.

He planned a confrontation between his mother and his mistress. He knew that Julia strongly condemned Aline's behavior and hoped that "the *Jew* woman" would leave her son alone: "If she don't his future is lost — so far as literary work goes — It is a sad state — but all *sex* and nothing different." "Nothing good can come of such an alliance," she warned Tom, "and if she is a friend, she will let you alone to do your work."

Wolfe knew, then, that his mother would express her opinion forcefully if she met Aline. To guarantee that she would do so, he did something he had not done for more than two years: he begged Aline to lend him five hundred dollars and personally to bring the money over to his apartment. Then, to make sure that there was no confusion about which woman was allegedly corrupting Julia's son, he curtly rejected Claire Zyve's offer to help entertain his mother during her visit.

On the morning after Julia arrived in New York, Aline came to Brooklyn with the cash. Julia was trying to serve her son breakfast, but he was in a more excited state than usual, for he had just learned about Madeleine Boyd's embezzlement of his German royalties. He vowed that he would have his agent put in jail. Quietly Aline said: "Well, I'll look into it; I'll find her and see what she can do about it."

Unreasonably, Wolfe then turned on her. "You're the cause of it," he insisted. "In the first place you gave her this manuscript ["O Lost"], to sell, and you're the cause of my getting mixed up with that kind of a woman." "You're two of a kind," he said accusingly, "you just walk the streets together."

Julia tried to calm her son down. So did Aline, who kept saying that she would do anything for him. "You know how much I love you," she insisted. "You know I love you, Tom."

"Well," said Julia, turning on the visitor, "it's all right if you love him as a — ah — friend, a dear friend, — or do you love him as a mother?"

"No, . . . you don't understand — you don't understand."

"Well, I think I do understand," replied Julia. "Any other kind of love I consider an illicit love. A woman with a family," she said reproachfully. "I understand — you have some grown up children that are almost as old as Tom."

"But you don't understand," Aline helplessly repeated.

"My mother's not an ignoramus," Tom interjected; "she knows what she's talking about." Then he turned sharply on Aline: "Get away, let me alone."

She refused to go until he gave her a kiss. While she was insisting, Julia manuevered her to the door, pushed her through, then shut and locked it behind her. After a few minutes Aline began ringing the door bell, but Julia announced: "The doors are locked and I have the key. That woman's not coming back."

Aline went away, but the next day she wrote Tom a bitter letter, regretting that "the horrid cruel phrases of your mother and yourself" had made her lose control. What right, she asked somewhat illogically, did Julia have to call her love licentious — she who had forced him as a boy to wear tight shoes in order to keep from spending pennies on new ones, she who had walked out on her husband so as to make money by running a boardinghouse? People like Julia could only understand money, she claimed. In order to show her own contempt for wealth, she announced that on her way back to Manhattan she had thrown off Brooklyn Bridge one of the hundred-dollar bills she had brought him. On each of the next four days, she promised, she would throw another hundred-dollar bill off the bridge, "just to show God I don't come from Asheville."

Julia was present when Aline's letter came. "Call her up right now," she insisted. Tom should tell her to leave the hundred-dollar bills on the bridge and throw a nickel over. Then, being a Jew, she would jump into the river for the coin. "I've never known one yet that if you drop a nickel but what they'd jump over and scramble for it." Tom joined his mother in cackling at her crude anti-Semitic witticism, and at Aline's final defeat.

Aline too realized that she had reached the end. She wrote Wolfe again, insisting that neither he nor his mother understood her. "I am not the evil person you both believe me to be," she protested. "I have literally given you my soul, and if I am not to be utterly destroyed I must take it back." It was time, she concluded, that "we see each other no more." Two years passed before they met again.

Feeling a little ashamed at this cheap victory over his lover — "There's lots of good things about the woman, yes," he muttered after she left — Wolfe was exultant at last to have his freedom, and he thoroughly enjoyed the rest of his mother's visit. They spent endless hours reminiscing about W. O. Wolfe, about Tom's brothers and sisters, about the Westall and Penland families, and about Asheville.

When Julia left to visit her brother, Henry Westall, Wolfe decided to write a story based on her recollections. It is told almost entirely in the words of an elderly woman, whom Wolfe called Delia Hawke, who is visiting her son in New York City, where the horns of the boats on the river occasionally distract her. Elaborately she interweaves an account of her long, tempestuous marriage to Will Hawke and a tale about an escaped convict who came to her house in the night, begging for shoes so that he could make his way over the mountains. What connects the two stories is the character of Delia — a thinly disguised Julia Wolfe, who was, as her son now had good reason to know, "the most completely fearless and independent person I have ever known." The story grew into a short novel — again running to about thirty thousand words — and Wolfe realized he might find difficulty in placing it. He also recognized that parts of it were probably too explicit for a family magazine.

But, excited by his story, which he called "The Web of Earth," exultant over his liberation from Aline, he dashed over to Manhattan to see Perkins. He needed reassurance from his editor, because this short novel was different from anything that he had previously published: the author's voice hardly appeared, and the whole story was told in the woman's own language as "her octopal memory weaves back and forth across the whole fabric of her life until everything has gone into it." He also wanted to consult Perkins about entering "The Web of Earth" in the short novel contest that *Scribner's Magazine* had been conducting annually since 1930.

The two men talked until the Scribners offices closed and then walked down to Grand Central Station, where they waited in a bar for Perkins's train to New Canaan, Connecticut. When the train was announced, they unsteadily headed for it, and Wolfe got on board to finish talking about his manuscript. As the train started, he leapt up, jumped onto the platform from the moving car, and fell on the concrete pavement. As he lay there, stunned and looking, as Perkins said, "a bit like a dead whale washed up on a Cape Cod beach," somebody pulled the emergency cord on the train, passengers got out to look at him, and railroad doctors rushed to the scene.

When Wolfe opened his eyes and saw the "crowd of staring, greedily curious and insatiate people pushing and thrusting all around him," his first emotion was that of shame — shame that he had injured himself "neither through unavoidable accident, nor in some way that might have served a useful or a generous purpose for another person, that I had broken [my arm] uselessly, horribly, stupidly, wastefully, and for no reason at all." The accident epitomized the whole story of his life of "ruinous defeat — my inability to complete or put an ending to my work, my failure to make any productive use of such talents as I had." Emancipation from Aline, it was clear, had not brought him freedom from his fears and anxieties.

VIII

The accident made it impossible to finish "The Web of Earth" before the deadline for the short novel competition. Though he did not break his left arm, as he at first feared, he had badly bruised it and had severed a vein. Dr. Jacobson ordered him to rest for several days. Anyway, he did not feel well enough to write, though he persuaded Harriet Hoppe to come in and help with his correspondence. Then Julia came back from Boston and mothered him through a miserable cold that he had picked up.

By the end of February he completed the story. Perkins read it, pronounced it "grand," and declared that it was the most perfectly constructed work that Wolfe had ever written. *Scribner's Magazine* happily accepted it for publication but it was too late to win a prize.

Before Wolfe had time to lapse into despondency again, Perkins brought him exciting news. Without telling Wolfe, he had already entered "A Portrait of Bascom Hawke" in the short novel competition. The jury, consisting of Edmund Wilson, Burton Rascoe, and William Soskin, declared a tie between Wolfe's story and John Herrmann's "The Big Short Trip," a novella about a traveling salesman, heavy with social significance and written in pseudo-Hemingway style. The decision gave Wolfe half of the five-thousand-dollar prize. Winning this award, he said, was "like picking gold up in the street."

The Scribners prize, announced in April 1932, gave an enormous boost to Wolfe's morale. Not only did it provide him enough money to live on for twelve months; it also gave him confidence in his work. Freed from further interruptions by Aline, he now turned back to his novel and reviewed what he had been writing for the past two or three years. It was "not a volume but a library." He had been possessed by "some fantastic hope" that he "would be able to write one gigantic and monstrous tome which would say everything that could be said about everyone and everything." Now it was clear that his pile of manuscripts contained the material for many books — sometimes he spoke of eight, sometimes ten — and the sensible way to proceed was to write one book at a time.

That revelation lifted him from "the very bottom of a deep black pit of depression and despair," and soon he was writing again "with a great rush." The segment of his long work that he planned to complete first, and to publish as a separate book, was called "K-19," the number of the Pullman car that regularly shuttled between Asheville and New York City. After an opening incantation beginning ". . . of wandering forever and the earth again" (which he later used in *Of Time and the River*), the book

recounted the interrelated life stories of passengers traveling from
New York to North Carolina, who were "now imprisoned in a
projectile of roaring steel hurtling across the continent under the
immense and lonely skies that bend above America." The structure of the novel was left deliberately loose; there was no plot.
Sometimes Wolfe thought of writing about ten passengers in detail; at other times he expected to deal with thirty-eight.

During the spring of 1932 he worked on "K-19" with fierce
energy and growing excitement, writing three, four, and sometimes five thousand words a day. He made such progress that he
convinced himself that he could complete the manuscript by midsummer. Perkins shared his enthusiasm and announced that
Scribners would publish Wolfe's 200,000-word novel in the fall.
The publisher prepared dummy books, including the cover, the
title page, and the first ten pages of the first chapter, for salesmen
to show to bookstores.

The contents of "K-19" are only partially known, because much
of Wolfe's manuscript for this novel was cannibalized for use in his
later books. One of the main stories was to be that of an evil,
blind, syphilitic Asheville lawyer, who appeared in Wolfe's later
fiction as Rumford Bland. Another concerned Monty Bellamy,
modeled after Lacy Meredith, a friend from North Carolina with
whom Wolfe had briefly shared a room. The longest separate
surviving section, "The Man on the Wheel," told the story of
Robert Weaver, the fictional version of Henry David (Harry)
Stevens, whom Wolfe had known in Asheville, Chapel Hill,
Cambridge, and New York. It was a story of desperation and
madness, which stemmed partly from some genetic fault and partly
from the frenzied spirit of the 1920s, when "the tempo of our
unrest increased with the tempo of the inept and savage life that
roared about us — a glare of days, a bedlam of machinery, a
phantasmagoria of movement, sound and violence." In the story
of Robert Weaver could be read "the whole grieved chronicle of
wandering and unrest, which was . . . everywhere around us, in
the very air we breathed, the earth we walked on, the city that
rumbled with a strange and secret rumor like a gigantic and distant
dynamo, even in the most silent hour of night, and the wheel, the
wheel, the wheel, the eternal wheel that was our only home!"

In July Perkins read the segments of "K-19" that Wolfe had
completed and advised him not to publish it. Since Perkins ex-

plained his reservations about the manuscript orally, rather than in writing, his reasons for rejecting it can only be guessed. It was evident that Wolfe had written very rapidly, and often carelessly. Obsessed by a compulsion to "say the final and ultimate word about everyone and everything," he cluttered his pages with long, irrelevant passages having nothing to do with his main story line. Perhaps Perkins was troubled that "K-19" duplicated so many scenes and conversations already presented in *Look Homeward, Angel*. It was also reasonable for him to wonder whether Wolfe was any more able to complete this book than any of the others that he had projected. Since "The Man on the Wheel" alone ran to about ninety-thousand words and since there were to be at least nine other major characters on the train ride, it was clear that the final manuscript would be gargantuan.

Just how sensitive a reader Perkins was is uncertain, but he could well have noticed the dissonance between the lives Wolfe described in "K-19" and the narrator's voice that framed and linked their stories. For instance, Robert Weaver was a vapid, volatile man, bent on self-destruction; but Wolfe chose to conclude his story with the narrator's affirmation of life. Choosing rhythms that T. S. Eliot had employed in "Ash-Wednesday," he threw out a deliberate challenge to those he contemptuously called "The Wastelanders":

> Because I shall not go into the dark again; nor suffer madness, nor admit despair; because I shall not go. Because I shall build walls about me now, and find a place, and see a few things clearly, letting millions pass. . . .
> All things belonging to the earth will never change — the leaf, the blade, the flower. . . .
> Under the pavement trembling like a pulse, under the buildings trembling like a cry, under the waste of time, the hoof of the beast again above the broken bones of cities, there will be something growing like a flower, forever bursting from the earth again, forever deathless, faithful, coming into life again like April.

Whatever his reasons, Perkins turned the book down and told Wolfe it simply was not good enough to follow *Look Homeward, Angel*. No doubt that verdict reflected his Napoleonic ambitions for his author and himself, but it also showed the editor's awarencss that Wolfe was so sensitive to criticism that he might not survive damaging attacks on his second novel.

Without protest Wolfe accepted Perkins's judgment on the book. Naturally he was disappointed, for he had spent much time and energy on this aborted project, but he consoled himself with the belief that he would "eventually use almost all" of this manuscript in future books. Indeed, even the story of Robert Weaver, though in greatly condensed form, found a place in *Of Time and the River*. Wolfe had grown accustomed to deferring to Perkins's judgment in literary matters, because he was, after all, "the greatest editor in the country."

IX

A Miserable, Monstrous
Mis-begotten Life

THOUGH WOLFE ACCEPTED SCRIBNERS' DECISION not to publish "K-19," it left him in doubt about his future as a
writer. He knew that he still had abundant creative energy. "The well certainly has not gone dry," he told a correspondent; "in fact, I seem to have tapped a whole subterranean river and
the water is spouting up in columns and geysers more than it ever
did." But when asked whether he would ever produce another
book equal to *Look Homeward, Angel*, he responded frankly: "I
will be damned if I know myself."

What he did know now was that writing a second book could
not be rushed. He felt that Scribners had pushed him too hard to
complete the novel Perkins had rejected. "I have just begun to
discover," he announced, "that publishing is a business and that
publishers have dates and deadlines like other business men, but,
although this is the way to *publish,* it is not the way to write." His
second book, he declared firmly, "will be published when I am
done writing it and when I think it is fit to be published."

That was brave talk, but he had to make a living until he was
ready to publish. For a time he toyed with the idea of going to
Hollywood and writing movie scenarios. Knowing that other serious writers like Faulkner and Fitzgerald were earning what
seemed to be princely salaries at the studios, Wolfe confessed that
"my mouth waters and my tongue lolls out of my mouth in my

greedy lust" to do likewise. But when a friend offered to give him railroad fare and to put him up for a few weeks in Los Angeles, he backed away. "I may do better in the long run if I stumble and sweat in my own way and try to do some work which I may be capable of rather than work for which I have no capacity whatever," he explained.

So when a scout for one of the studios, Mrs. Ad Schulberg, the mother of the novelist Budd Schulberg, approached Wolfe, he could not take her seriously. The tale of his lunch with this "very elegant, highly perfumed and fancy talking Hollywood lady" became one of his anecdotes that improved with each retelling. He claimed that she convinced him that if he would only sign a Hollywood contract he could "then start raking the thousand dollar bills into an open valise." Then it turned out that all Mrs. Schulberg could offer was a promise to "do something wonderful and mysterious and immensely prosperous" for him if he came out to California. When he asked who was going to pay his fare, she suggested that he could hitchhike.

Wolfe realized that his only source of immediate income was from the sale of short stories excavated from his pile of manuscripts. During the last six months of 1932 he shaped three fragments into relatively self-contained units, and Alfred Dashiell, the editor of *Scribner's Magazine,* accepted them all. The first of these, "The Train and the City," published in May 1933, consisted of two almost unrelated segments: a rhapsody on the coming of spring in the city, and an account of a race between two trains pounding their way across New Jersey. The rhetoric was luxuriant, and Wolfe's favorite overheated adjectives abounded: "wonderful," "terrific," "tremendous," "immense." Marjorie Kinnan Rawlings, the author of the recently published bestseller *South Moon Under,* remarked that Wolfe pounded the drums so lavishly as to give "the effect of an awfully enthusiastic German band," and she rather longed "to empty pitchers of water from the third story, to shut up the tumult."

"Death the Proud Brother," which appeared in the June issue of *Scribner's Magazine,* was more ambitious and more controlled. It was an account of four deaths that Wolfe's narrator — presumably David Hawke, though his name was not given — witnessed in New York. At least one of the episodes, that of the nameless man who died quietly in the subway, was drawn from Wolfe's own experience; Thomas Beer told him of another, the death of a riveter who fell from the iron beams of the building under construction for Bergdorf-Goodman (which Wolfe called "Stein and Rosen"). All that linked the four sections was the fact that each described the death of an anonymous man in the big city. The story ended with a chant praising the "immortal fellowship, proud Death, stern Loneliness, and Sleep."

More complex in structure and more successful in effect was Wolfe's third long story, "No Door," which was published the next month. It consisted of episodes evoking the varieties of loneliness. Initially he intended to include many such segments, but he finally reduced the number to four. When these proved too long for a single issue of *Scribner's Magazine,* he removed a long part of one for subsequent separate publication as "The House of the Far and Lost." On first reading, nothing appeared to connect these fragments except the first-person voice of the narrator — again, presumably David Hawke. The story moved, without connection or transition, from South Brooklyn in October 1931 to what was obviously Asheville in October 1923 to Oxford in 1926 to Lower Manhattan in April 1928.

But in a complex way "No Door" did have unity. All four accounts of loneliness were filtered through Wolfe's own experience. He told Mabel that she should read the story if she was "interested in knowing anything about my own life for the last ten or fifteen years." More important, the sections were linked by a leitmotif of repeated words and phrases. In this time of his unhappiness and apparent failure, Wolfe once again returned to the image of the door that he had employed in *Look Homeward, Angel;* but in this story it was not a door to be discovered and opened but one that was so firmly closed that the narrator had "no wall at which to hurl my strength, no door to enter by, and no purpose for the furious unemployment of my soul."

In addition, the four accounts of different kinds of solitude, frustration, and isolation were held together by the lyrical passages with which Wolfe began and ended the story. The opening was a prose-poem he had been working on for at least two years, essentially the proem that he had planned for the ill-fated "K-19":

> . . . of wandering forever and the earth again . . . .
> Where shall the weary rest?

When shall the lonely of heart come home?
What doors are open for the wanderer . . . ?

The questions were answered in the concluding dithyramb, a variant of the chant with which Wolfe had inappropriately planned to end "K-19":

Lean down your ear upon the earth, and remember there are
    things that last forever. . . .
Under the pavements trembling like a pulse,
Under the buildings trembling like a cry,
Under the waste of time, . . .
There will be something growing like a flower,
Forever bursting from the earth, forever deathless, faithful,
Coming into life again like April.

Readers of *Scribner's Magazine* were doubtless puzzled by these three remarkable pieces, in which Wolfe experimented with a new form of fiction. Nonlinear and nonchronological, they owed much to Joyce, but their abrupt cuts, flashbacks, and montages reflected even more the influence of the cinema. Demonstrating his verbal virtuosity, his skill in rendering the New York–New Jersey vernacular, and his lyricism in the cadence of the Old Testament poetry that he so loved, these stories clearly appealed to a special audience, willing to make the considerable effort that Wolfe's prose demanded. They were "stories" that told no story; what had driven the narrator to the point of madness and fury was never made clear; and both "Death the Proud Brother" and "No Door" contained unexplained references to "the woman" and "Esther" (as Wolfe had decided to call Aline Bernstein's fictional counterpart). It is easy to understand why a friend told Wolfe that he was bankrupting *Scribner's Magazine*: "A few more pieces [like these three stories] . . . and that magazine will be on the rocks. . . . I can't believe any American magazine can publish literature and survive."

Nor could Wolfe survive on the sale of short stories. He received two hundred or two hundred and fifty dollars for each of them — about what it cost him to live for a month. His expenses were now a little lower since he moved in August 1932 to 101 Columbia Heights, where he found a smaller apartment that cost fifteen dollars a month less. But he still had to buy food and pay his typist. When *Scribner's Magazine* accepted one of the stories he "had just $7.00 left in all the world." And, of course, he could not count on producing or selling a new short story every month.

If he had another book it might bring in a substantial income and also revive the sales of *Look Homeward, Angel*. From time to time Wolfe and his friends at Scribners tried to devise ways for him to publish a second book without actually having to write it. There was talk of collecting his stories, for "A Portrait of Bascom Hawke," "The Web of Earth," and the three latest pieces would have made a sizable volume. Afterwards Perkins regretted that this was not done, but at the time both he and Wolfe believed all these segments would be worked into his big, still unfinished novel. After "No Door" appeared in *Scribner's Magazine* there was a plan to expand and publish it as a small book, in a limited edition. Though Wolfe never systematically reworked "No Door," he continued for nearly a year to say that this little book was going to be published, but Scribners never pursued the project seriously. Consequently, at the end of the grim Depression winter of 1932–1933, he had no second book. What was worse, there was no immediate prospect of his completing a second book.

"It was a black time," Wolfe recalled later. "I was a creature stumbling with fatigue, almost bereft of hope, almost ready to admit defeat, to admit that I was done for as a writer, and could not possibly complete the work I had set out to do."

I

Perkins observed Wolfe's struggles with sympathy but, initially, without much comprehension. He was, after all, a busy man, the senior editor in a major publishing house, who had to look after many authors — all of whom, it seemed, had problems. He had to persuade Scott Fitzgerald to finish *Tender Is the Night,* to watch over Ernest Hemingway as he was writing *Green Hills of Africa,* to encourage Marjorie Rawlings as she began a second book, and to oversee the final revision of Douglas Southall Freeman's *R. E. Lee.* He was used to having Wolfe drop in his office about once a week, to talk excitedly about whatever was on his mind at the moment and to report enthusiastically that his manuscript had now grown to 200,000 — or maybe 400,000 or 600,000 — words, but he had actually read only small portions of what Wolfe had written. So far as he could tell, everything should be going well with Wolfe's second novel. He said later that he simply did not know "why Tom did not finish his book" or "fully understand what was holding him back all this time."

By early 1933, however, it was clear that Wolfe needed guidance and encouragement, and changes in the firm of Charles Scribner's Sons made it possible for Perkins to give both. The death of Arthur H. Scribner in 1932 led to the elevation of Charles Scribner III to the presidency of the company, and at the same time Perkins became both editor-in-chief and vice-president. If these new positions burdened him with managerial responsibilities, they also gave him a freer hand in shaping editorial policy. Now he was authorized to offer authors advances — though advances from Scribners were never on a grand scale — when he thought the risk worth taking.

Always confident that Wolfe was basically a good risk, Perkins tried to find out what was holding up his second book. His usual approach to such a problem was to get one of his authors who had solved his difficulties to advise another who was in trouble. So in January 1933 he arranged for Wolfe to have lunch with Hemingway, who had just come up to New York from Arkansas, at his favorite restaurant, Cherio's on 53rd Street. The two writers had never met, but each professed admiration for the work of the other. Praising the "superb concision" of A Farewell to Arms, Wolfe envied Hemingway's ability to say one thing and suggest ten more: "his words not only pull their own weight in a sentence, they also pull a very rich weight of profound and moving association and inference." Always jealous of other writers, Hemingway tended to sneer at Wolfe as Perkins's "World Genius," whose failure to produce a second book probably derived from insufficient "bed sports." Still, he claimed he was "simply wild" about Wolfe's writing and expressed a desire to meet him.

At the luncheon Perkins was almost entirely silent. "I hoped," he explained later, "Hem would be able to influence Tom to overcome his faults in writing, even though they were the defects of his qualities, such as his tendency to repetition and excessive expression." Wolfe, too, listened attentively as Hemingway held forth on writing. He urged Wolfe to follow his practice and "break off work when you 'are going good' — Then you can rest easily and on the next day easily resume." The only time he got a rise out of Wolfe was when they discussed critics. Hemingway remarked scornfully, "Why, you don't read reviews, do you!" "You just bet I do!" Wolfe replied. "And if I knew Miss Suzy Stross was writing a piece about me in the Skunkstown, Ohio, Busy Bee I'd stay up all night to get the first copy off the press." But mostly the conversation was low-keyed and reassuring. Hemingway, Perkins remarked, "*can* be blunt, but he can also be more gentle in speech than anyone I know. He wanted to help Tom, and everything went well, except I think Tom wasn't in the least affected."

After the lunch Wolfe, who thought only unproductive writers were envious of other authors, remained confident that Hemingway would write "a grand book about American life." Hemingway was less generous. He told Perkins that Wolfe obviously had great talent, a delicate, fine spirit — and limited intelligence. In *Green Hills of Africa* he called Wolfe "sad, really, like [the boxer, Primo] Carnera," and speculated that sending him to Siberia or to Dry Tortugas "would make a writer of him, give him the necessary shock to cut the overflow of words and give him a sense of proportion." Many years later Hemingway called Wolfe "a glandular giant with the brains and the guts of three mice," "the over-bloated Lil Abner of literature."

Failing to get much assistance from Hemingway, Perkins saw that he himself had to help Wolfe get under way with a second novel. Since he suffered from allergies and sinus problems, which increased his deafness, Perkins now went several times a year to the Johns Hopkins Hospital for treatment, and in January he persuaded Wolfe to accompany him, promising that afterward they would go on to Washington and visit Mabel. During their several quiet days together, the two men talked at length. Perkins confessed, Wolfe said, that he "had been almost desperate about me, trying to figure what was wrong and how to get me out of it." This admission led Wolfe to drop all pretense and to say that, though he had written many thousands of pages, he was not certain how, if at all, they could be made into a book.

During their long conversations Perkins persuaded Wolfe to forget about experimenting with new forms of fiction. Wolfe abandoned his plan to begin his book with a portrait of America made up of numerous vignettes linked only through theme or leitmotifs. He discarded his original opening for the book, about which he had talked and written so frequently since 1930; his twenty-one-page wonderfully polyphonic rhapsody, "Antaeus, or A Memory of Earth," was never published. Instead, he agreed to write a straightforward chronological narrative.

Rejected, too, was Wolfe's plan to make his novel a commentary on the nature and meaning of time. For many years he had felt "haunted by a sense of time and a memory of things past." From reading Proust he knew how a great artist could use a trivial episode in the present to evoke the memory of an intricate sequence of past happenings, and he understood, with T. S. Eliot, how time present and time future are both contained in time past. He hoped to discover a way to combine, in a single narrative, three kinds of time: the "element of actual present time, . . . which carried the narrative forward"; the "element of past time," which revealed how each moment of a man's life was conditioned "by all that he had seen and felt and done and experienced"; and the force of "time immutable," that "time of rivers, mountains, oceans and the earth, . . . a kind of eternal . . . time against which would be projected the transience of man's life, the bitter briefness of his day." He went so far as to take elaborate notes on the articles in the *Encyclopaedia Britannica* dealing with time and time measurement. Increasingly he had come to feel that the element of time was so important in his study that he should change the title from "October Fair," which really referred only to the culminating scene in the Munich beer hall, to "Time and the River." But in these long conversations with Perkins he decided to relegate his whole concern for the complexities of time to a secondary place — though, characteristically, he clung to his new title, even when it no longer had much to do with the philosophical thrust of his book.

From these discussions with Perkins came the decision to give up the idea of making the new book the story of David (or, as Wolfe sometimes called him, John) Hawke, that apelike, athletic figure who physically was everything that Wolfe was not but who from the start had been psychologically identical with the author. Wolfe turned back to his original fictional alter ego, Eugene Gant. The decision probably did not take much persuasion on Perkins's part. Wolfe knew that he wrote best about his own and his family's experiences. When he had tried to write objectively about other people, he had nearly always failed: "The River People" was so unsatisfactory that he abandoned it; his attempt to recreate the early life of Aline Bernstein in "The Good Child's River" aroused no enthusiasm in his publisher; in "K-19" the only passages that had real life were those that contained Wolfe's own observations and feelings. He had already come to the conclusion that "nowhere can you escape autobiography whenever you come to anything that has any real or lasting value in letters." By replacing David Hawke with Eugene Gant, *redux,* he was simply recognizing what had become obvious to everyone: that he was, in fact, an autobiographical novelist.

With the new book defined as a sequel to *Look Homeward, Angel,* Wolfe and Perkins decided that it ought to begin where the earlier book left off. Most of what Wolfe had written about the early years of David "Monkey" Hawke had to be scrapped, for the childhood and adolescence of Eugene Gant had been abundantly recorded already. Scrapped also was Wolfe's plan to make a man's search for his father the central theme of his second book. There was no question that Eugene Gant — unlike David Hawke — knew perfectly well who his father was. If he ever forgot, he had only to read the very complete account of W. O. Gant's life in *Look Homeward, Angel.* In an effort to save some of the passages he had already written, Wolfe came up with a different formulation: the new book should convey the "feeling . . . that when a man's father dies the man must then discover a new earth for himself and make a life for himself other than the life his father gave to him or die himself."

Perkins and Wolfe also agreed that "Time and the River" should, like Wolfe's first book, be written in the third person — that is, it would be told by an omniscient narrator. Up to this point, what Wolfe had written for the new book was mostly in the first person: David Hawke had told the story of Bascom Hawke and was the unidentified narrator of Wolfe's other stories. Now all this had to be changed, and "I" had to become "he." The shift had unfortunate consequences. In *Look Homeward, Angel* it was perfectly natural for a narrator to tell the adventures of young Eugene Gant, occasionally commenting, with affectionate humor, on the emotional excesses of the hero. But in the voluminous drafts of Wolfe's second novel there was no such separation between narrator and hero. Even the most luxuriant of Wolfe's dithyrambs — for instance, his ode to October, his chant on the three horsemen, Loneliness, Death, and Sleep, or his rebuke to the frigidity of New England, "O bitterly bitterly Boston one time more" — were composed as the utterances or thoughts of David Hawke, a young man in his early twenties. When the hero was changed from "I" to "he," these lyrical passages became detached. They seemed no longer the musings of a sensitive young man but the considered thoughts of Thomas Wolfe, who was now in his thirties, no longer a romantic figure but now, as he sadly admitted, "a great lumbering fellow about six feet five who weighs 235 pounds," with a bald spot in his hair.

Neither Perkins nor Wolfe ever really understood how this shift from the first- to the third-person narrator affected *Of Time and the River.* Perkins did recognize that the change created a problem with Wolfe's lyrical passages and chants — passages that he never liked much anyway. "They did not belong in a novel in the conventional view," he remarked. "They were not in any sense narrative, they broke up the story." Yet he felt that many of them were "too lovely or too magnificent to dispense with" and favored including some — perhaps setting them apart, in italics, from the narrative. Wolfe simply thought that changing the narrative "to a third person point of view" would give the book "a much greater sense of unity than now seems possible."

II

Though these changes required a drastic modification of Wolfe's plans for a second novel and obliged him to discard hundreds of pages that he had already written, he readily accepted them all. Shortly after his trip to Baltimore and Washington he reported that Perkins's advice had given him "suddenly . . . a way of getting started" on the new book — on which he had been working for the past three and one-half years. He was so encouraged by "the plan we have agreed on" that he felt a great surge of creative power.

Once he and Perkins returned to New York, Wolfe gave his editor about four hundred typed pages that he thought were in final shape, and he began working hard to fill in the gaps in the story. By March he claimed that he had written an additional 100,000 words, and by the middle of April 150,000 more words. (As always, Wolfe's estimates of his productivity were greatly exaggerated.) To this latest batch of material he attached a long note, outlining the entire book and indicating what had already been written and what remained to be done. From the manuscript and the outline he hoped that Perkins would be able "to judge if the project is feasible or just a mad delusion on my part." "Now finally it is up to you to tell me whether . . . what I am trying to do . . . is worth doing and if I shall go ahead," he wrote his editor. "For God's Sake do it without delay and with merciful even if brutal honesty."

Wolfe was still planning "one of the longest books ever written," composed of four parts. Hoping to make use of Greek myths to give universality to his story, as Joyce had done, he continued to call the first book "Antaeus: Earth Again"; in it his hero, who was comparable to the Libyan giant Antaeus, contended with "the million-visaged shape of time and memory." "Proteus: The City," the second book, would reveal "all the thousand protean shapes of life in the city," to which Eugene Gant moved. "Faust and Helen" began with Eugene's meeting with Esther Jacobs on board a ship returning from Europe and recounted their passionate love affair. The final book, "The October Fair," set altogether in Europe, would deal with "the Faustian hunger to drink and eat the earth"; it culminated in the fight at the Munich beer festival.

The prospect of tackling so vast and so incomplete a manuscript would have daunted any editor but Perkins, but he readily accepted the challenge. With a typescript of about 450,000 words and an outline of the whole work on hand, he felt that "the book is really almost in existence now." On May 2 Perkins offered Wolfe a contract for "Time and the River," with an advance of two thousand dollars and a royalty of ten percent of the retail price on the first two thousand copies sold and fifteen percent thereafter. Apparently Wolfe objected to the royalty rate, for the next day a new contract was drawn up giving the author fifteen percent on all copies sold. Noting that "it is desirable that said work should be published in the Fall of 1933," both contracts required Wolfe to deliver his completed manuscript "not later than August 1st 1933."

Wolfe and Perkins must have known that this was an unrealistic schedule, because shortly afterwards the contract was again revised and the delivery date for the manuscript was changed to February 1, 1934. At the same time someone remembered that Wolfe, back in 1930, had already drawn a little more than a thousand dollars in advances against this same book, and the contract was further changed to make only an additional one thousand dollars available to the author.

None of these contracts was especially generous, even by the standards of the time. Scribners was reluctant to advance large sums to Wolfe because Perkins and his associates did not think he was capable of managing his finances. The firm took over the responsibility for filing and paying Wolfe's income tax, informing the Collector of Internal Revenue that he was "not so constituted that he is able to look after matters of this kind — which is often the case with writers." Since Wolfe had no bank account and Perkins did not succeed in explaining to him how to open and manage one, Scribners was afraid that he would lose or squander any large advance. Rather than sending him a check, therefore, they set up a royalty account at Scribners, from which he could draw small amounts of cash, ranging from five to one hundred dollars, as he needed money. The system caused a certain amount of irritation, and Robert Cross, the head of the accounting department at Scribners, complained that Wolfe was making the firm offer the services of a bank and objected to Wolfe's frequent withdrawals. Six months after signing the contract, Wolfe had already overdrawn his advance.

At the time the contract was drawn up, Perkins was optimistic about the early completion of "Time and the River." He knew, of course, that there would be "unlimited work and struggle before it is fully accomplished," since there was much to be argued about and "much revision and all that." But he thought that even the imperfect manuscript on his desk contained "half a dozen chapters in it that are beyond anything even in 'The Angel'; and it may be a distinctly finer book than that." Writing to Charles Scribner III, who was traveling in Europe, he proposed "a sort of plan" to go off with Wolfe in June or July "to the country and spend a couple of weeks, and get the book into shape." He canceled plans for his own summer vacation so that he could work on Wolfe's manuscript and, partly in order to be more available to his author, moved from New Canaan to Manhattan, where his family settled in at Turtle Bay, on the East River, within easy walking distance of the Scribners office and just across the river from Wolfe's apartment.

Wolfe too was confident — unreasonably so — that he would have a finished manuscript in Perkins's hands, if not by August 1,

1933, then certainly by February 1934. A review of the outline that he gave Perkins ought to have warned him that the task before him was huge. By his own reckoning, not one of the four books of "Time and the River" was anything like complete. The first had "the final three or four scenes lacking to make it a complete draft." Though Wolfe claimed he had a draft of most of the second book, "Proteus: The City," he was able to give Perkins only the first section; a year later his account of "Professor Butcher" (as he then called George P. Baker, who was in the published book to become "Professor Hatcher") and the members of the 47 Workshop was still incomplete. If "Faust and Helen" was "mainly written either in full or in scenes and sections," the final book, "October Fair," was still "unwritten save for notes and rough drafts." But, bolstered by Perkins's faith in him, he believed he could do the impossible.

As a result, the spring and summer of 1933 were some of the most productive, as well as some of the most tormented, months in Wolfe's life. He forced himself to put in eight hours a day. Though he still occasionally used the top of his refrigerator as a desk, so that he could write while standing up, he mostly worked these days at his sturdy but battered oak table, and, to make his big shoulders more comfortable, he removed the upper crosspiece of the chair in which he sat. Using soft lead pencils, which he cut into fourths because the stubby segments better fit his massive fist, he filled page after page of cheap yellow typing paper, interrupting his writing to pace back and forth through his apartment or to enjoy a cigarette at the window. He did not compose his book consecutively, starting with the opening pages and pushing systematically to the end; instead, he turned to whatever part of the story interested him at the moment and worked on it until he grew bored, and then he shifted to another segment. He wrote quickly, almost never pausing to revise. Though he would occasionally strike through words or phrases and substitute others, he would usually just crumple up a page that was not going well and start again on a fresh one. About forty words in his scrawling, almost indecipherable handwriting filled a page, and as he finished each sheet he would push it impatiently from the table and start another. His flustered typist would rescue the pages from the floor, attempt to arrange them in order, and try to puzzle out his handwriting.

When his writing was going well, Wolfe was in a buoyant

mood. In August when he turned to a segment that ultimately became a large part of the first book of *Of Time and the River,* describing "a train smashing northwards across the State of Virginia at night with three drunken youths, as drunk with the exultant . . . fury of going to the city for the first time . . . as with the corn liquor they keep passing from hand to hand," he was sure he was doing "a very exciting piece of writing . . . so good I almost cry about it." When it went badly, he complained of "the accursed and interminable labor of his miserable, monstrous misbegotten life" and pitied himself as "God's great galley slave of words."

Whether his writing went well or badly, he was so keyed up by the end of the day's work that he could not relax or sleep. Often he went on long nocturnal rambles through Brooklyn and Manhattan. Sometime not even these were enough to make him sleepy, and he began drinking heavily. "I like to drink and I had been familiar with the use of alcohol since my twenties," he recorded in an autobiographical note, "but now, for the first time in my life, I began to use it consciously, and almost deliberately, as an anodyne."

The pattern of Wolfe's drinking was always the same. Beginning, either alone or with friends, in a bar or restaurant, he first felt the expansive influence of alcohol. As Charles Norman, the poet, who saw something of Wolfe during these days, observed, "whisky seemed to lubricate his mind, and he talked without stopping until the early hours . . . quickly characterizing people by his trick of repeating some person's peculiarity as he went along." But as he drank more and more, his face would become white and tense, and his suspicions and fears would begin to surface. He imagined that he was surrounded by enemies. Once, in a bar on Seventh Avenue, a stranger struck up a conversation with him and, trying to make a point, slapped him on the back. Wolfe, who was always revolted by physical contact with another male, told him to keep his hands off and, when he refused, pushed him out into the street. A Scotch and soda and three beers later, he continued to brood over the incident and concluded that the stranger was a homosexual, probably "someone employed by Mrs. Bernstein, her husband, her daughter[,] son or a sister or . . . the Theatre Guilders, the Thomas Beer and Knopf crowds, or the nameless and lamentable nighttime filth of B'dway."

Maudlin self-pity often followed these belligerent episodes.

Once at 3 A.M., he was found stretched out on the floor and drunk in the men's room at the Plaza Hotel. The attendant, who did not want to call the police, begged him to leave, but he cried and said he would not go until Mrs. Bernstein came to get him. So early in the morning Aline — who had not talked to Wolfe for two years — was routed out of bed in the nearby Gotham Hotel. She found Wolfe babbling incoherently but, with the help of the attendant, she managed to fold him into a taxi and sent him back to Brooklyn.

After exhaustion or alcohol finally drove Wolfe to bed in the early morning hours, he slept badly, tormented by anxiety dreams. In one recurrent dream he was back at New York University, "rushing through those swarming corridors, hurrying frantically from one classroom to another, trying desperately to find the classes I had . . . forgotten." Then, in the department of English, he came upon a "mounting pile of unmarked student themes — those accursed themes that grew in number week by week — that piled up in mountainous and hopeless accumulations."

Some of his nightmares were sexual. He woke in anguish from a dream in which he was dying, "mad, barren, sterile, drugged by a whore and castrated by her masters, forced to swallow my own genitals." Or he dreamed that he "lay quilted in abominable filth and nastiness with women who had loved him as a child . . . ; he held clasped in his arms, pressed to his lips . . . women . . . whose bodies were ugly, sallow, withered or wasted by an old disease."

Tormented and exhausted, Wolfe could not keep his pledge to Perkins to stay at his desk until his book was finished, and from time to time he felt compelled to get away, if only for a day or two. In March he met Julia in Washington to see the inaugural parade of President Franklin D. Roosevelt. Occasionally he visited his brother Fred, who was now trying to sell farm machinery in Harrisburg, Pennsylvania, and they drove out to York Springs to see relatives of their father and to admire the bountiful fields and the great stone barns that W. O. Wolfe had so often talked about.

Even when Wolfe stayed in New York he tried now and then to break away from his work, but many of his associates found him hard to put up with these days, especially when he was drinking. Often he "snarled at the whole world" and vented his "horrible, ugly and furious temper" both on very old friends, like Henry Carlton, with whom he quarreled bitterly and without apparent cause, and on newer acquaintances, like Alfred Dashiell, at whom he lashed out when he felt "beset with demons, nightmares, delusions and bewilderments."

The only people he could get along with were those who demanded nothing from him and gave him unqualified admiration. John Terry, fat, wheezing, unflappable, was always available for endless conversation. Kyle Crichton, who worked at Scribners, enjoyed going with him to the Yankee Stadium or the Polo Grounds, especially on weekdays when crowds were thin and the two men could take their pick of seats and hang their long legs over the seats in front of them. Then, munching a hotdog and drinking Nedick's orange juice, Wolfe would launch into a monologue and reveal "inside information about conditions on the Chicago White Sox, state his position on a possible change of managers at the St. Louis Browns, and end with a full report of what was happening in Cleveland." Crichton thought he was "a perfect compendium of baseball lore" until he discovered that before going to the game Wolfe had bought early editions of the afternoon papers and "with that frightening memory of his" had absorbed all the sports news and gossip in them.

Wolfe also saw a good deal of Robert Raynolds, the young Western novelist who had so enthusiastically reviewed *Look Homeward, Angel*. Though he avoided most other writers, whom he thought pretentious and competitive, he found Raynolds so low-keyed and so admiring as to pose no threat. Perhaps Wolfe also took comfort in the fact that Raynolds, who was very thin, was almost as tall as he was. He even managed to laugh when, as he and Raynolds got on an elevator, the Negro operator remarked: "The Lord, He didn't economize on length when he made up you two gentlemen. . . . A thin one, like the gee-raffe, and a thick one, like the elyphunt; sure the works of the Lord are wonderful!" In September, exhausted by overwork and what he thought was ptomaine poisoning, he fled to Raynolds's house in Vermont to rest and recover. When he felt better he decided, with his usual compulsiveness, to look at every mountain peak in the state, and while Raynolds drove Wolfe admired the sturdy, neat Vermont houses along the roads and spoke longingly of finding himself a small place where he could finish his book. "And I need a nice little wife, too," he told his new friend at one stop. "Well, she's going to be a good cook, and she's going to raise vegetables and chickens and hams and bacons." When Raynolds added, "And little Wolfes," he danced in the road with happiness.

Wolfe got the same sort of comfort from Clayton Hoagland, who worked for the *New York Sun,* and his beautiful wife, Kathleen, both of whom he met through some North Carolina acquaintances. In August he began going over to visit them in Rutherford, New Jersey, enjoying the ride across the Hudson and the short train trip. He basked in their wholehearted, undemanding admiration, he delighted in Kitty's rich Irish accent, and he stuffed himself with their excellent food. Kitty's mother, Mrs. Dooher, took a fancy to him and catered to his fondness for an improbable delicacy, cold fish sandwiches. When Wolfe joined them as they gathered around the piano and sang old songs like "Jeannie with the Light Brown Hair," he felt like a member of the family. Before he left he would always ask Mrs. Dooher to tell his fortune, but while she dealt the cards he would wring his hands with nervousness and start to prowl up and down the room. "If you see death there," he begged her, "don't tell me. Don't tell me."

But after relaxation there was always work, and it seemed never to end. He had now accumulated such a formidable pile of manuscripts that he bought a wooden crate, four feet long and two or three feet high, to store them in, and he kept this box in the middle of his room. But however much he added to the pile, there was always more to come. Sometimes, he wrote Mabel, he felt "like the old horse running forever around the circle of a treadmill or like that mule they tell about who ran himself to death trying to catch up with a bundle of hay that someone had tied a foot in front of his nose."

III

By the end of the summer of 1933 Wolfe was broke again. He had used up the advance Scribners gave him on "Time and the River." *Look Homeward, Angel* had earned only about one hundred twenty dollars in royalties for the year. Rowohlt Verlag published a superb translation of his novel, *Schau Heimwärts, Engel!* but under Hitler's currency restrictions Wolfe would have to spend any royalties it earned in Germany itself. The sale of occasional stories to *Scribner's Magazine* was, as he said, "the only source of income I have at the present time."

Recognizing that he needed to economize, he moved once more, to nearby 5 Montague Terrace in Brooklyn, where he rented an apartment on the fourth floor of a five-story brownstone house for only forty-five dollars a month. He wrote his mother that he had found "a very nice roomy kind of place," but in fact his apartment consisted of a fair-sized living room, a small bedroom with bath, and a kitchen that one of his typists called "the miserable make-shift kind that New Yorkers tolerate." In the living room he had a Victorian sofa, which had lost its stuffing, a lounge chair, the springs of which had fallen out onto the floor, his console radio, and his work table, covered with papers, used ashtrays, and dirty coffee cups. There was one bookcase, full of volumes piled helter-skelter: *Anna Karenina, Ulysses,* books in the "Jalna" series by Mazo de la Roche, W. Somerset Maugham's *Cakes and Ale,* copies of *Look Homeward, Angel,* and paperback books Wolfe had brought back from Europe. Other books spilled out onto the fireplace mantel, the table, and the floor. His crate of manuscripts occupied much of the space, and piles of other papers were stacked against the walls. Even more cheerless and dismal was his bedroom, containing "a rusty iron bed with a thin mattress, a battered bureau and piles of books in every unoccupied space, clothes thrown carelessly all around." With "no evidence of music, no pictures on the wall," it was, as one of his typists claimed, "a very temporary-looking habitation."

Because he needed money so badly, even for this dismal apartment, he began to think about selling his stories to periodicals that had larger circulations and paid larger fees than *Scribner's Magazine.* In the spring he was almost ready to sign up with the well-known literary agency, Curtis Brown, Ltd., but he never actually did so. He did, however, write to the editors of *Harper's Magazine, The Forum, American Mercury,* and *The Atlantic Monthly,* asking whether they were interested in publishing his stories, which ran from ten to thirty thousand words in length. Several of the editors replied that such pieces were too long for short stories, though some suggested that they could possibly be published as novelettes or serials.

In the end it was Perkins who found Wolfe an agent for his short stories: Elizabeth Nowell. Four years younger than Wolfe, Nowell after graduation from Bryn Mawr had applied for a job in the editorial department of Scribners, only to have Perkins inform her that women were not allowed there because they were "too distracting." She then went to work in the Scribner Book Store downstairs, where she and Perkins became well enough acquainted that he made no objection when she was brought back upstairs as an assistant in the art department. In the fall of 1933 she left Scribners to join the literary agency headed by Maxim Lieber, and she was looking for new clients.

Perkins thought she would be just right for Wolfe. She was bright, articulate, and experienced, and Wolfe already knew her well enough so that he would not instantly distrust her. Perkins was sure that she would not get sexually involved with Wolfe. This was a matter of some importance, for Wolfe thought any woman who did not want to go to bed with him must have something wrong with her. "Tom was always horny as hell," Miss Nowell noted years later, "and you had to keep him at arm's length." She made it clear from the beginning that theirs would be a business relationship, and she addressed him as "Mr. Wolfe" or, much later, simply "Wolfe." In turn, he always referred to her as "Miss Nowell" or "Nowell" — never as "Liddy," her nickname. He found that having a business relationship with a woman was not so much difficult as puzzling, but he played by her rules of the game. "So help me, Nowell," he told her once, "I've never made a pass at any girl. I've never had to — They always do it first."

With Perkins's blessing, Miss Nowell introduced Wolfe to her boss, Lieber, an ambitious, enterprising literary agent who represented such novelists of social protest as Alvah Bessie. At dinner Wolfe began pumping Lieber to discover how well, relative to other publishers, Charles Scribner's Sons treated its authors. With Lieber's encouragement, his questions brought to surface all his real and fancied grievances about Scribners. He complained that "Perkins wouldn't let him have his own money in a bank account: that he had to come and beg it from [Robert] Cross to pay his secretary and Cross would always say 'What, Mr. Wolfe, you here again!' " He and the agent seemed to be getting along famously until Lieber made a derogatory remark about Sinclair Lewis. With a characteristic reversal of emotion, Wolfe instantly became very angry and said something about "these people who are so little that they smell little, criticizing a great man like that!" With difficulty they calmed him down, but after that it was clear that Wolfe was Miss Nowell's, not Lieber's, client.

Shortly afterward Wolfe gave Miss Nowell several manuscripts to read — all parts of his long novel — which he hoped could be made into salable short stories. One he called "Boom Town," an account of "John Hawke's" return to Asheville in 1925, when the "delirium of intoxication" over real estate speculation was driving residents to "ruin and death." It was one of Wolfe's weaker stories, full of all sorts of extraneous material, such as the removal of the casket of the first wife of John's father from one cemetery to another and the excited, eccentric behavior of John's stuttering brother, "Lee." In addition, it contained some of Wolfe's worst rhetorical excesses: the American earth that kept "stroking" past the night train was not merely "the old earth, the everlasting earth, the huge illimitable and unbounded earth," but it was the earth "so rude, sweet, wild, harsh, strange, magical and instantly familiar, and from which there was no word, no language and no door."

Nevertheless Miss Nowell was excited by it, and she and Wolfe spent several evenings together shaping the manuscript into a story of reasonable length. Sometimes Lieber joined them. As Miss Nowell read the story aloud, suggesting that this or that passage could be cut, Wolfe paced angrily up and down the office, blustering and cursing violently. When he finally agreed to a deletion, Lieber would ask him to write a few words to make a smooth transition, and he would dash off a paragraph instead of a sentence. Knowing that he could not place the story if it ran to more than fifteen thousand words, Lieber proposed to reduce the length by eliminating "Lee's" frequent "wh-wh-whats" and "wh-wh-wheres." At this point Wolfe "turned livid with fury, ranted, stormed, and literally foamed"; he could not and would not change his character's speech "because he did stammer. I ought to know because he was my brother."

After months of working on this manuscript — and after quietly, on her own, eliminating the stammer — Miss Nowell succeeded in placing "Boom Town" in *American Mercury*. When her ten-percent agent's fee was deducted, Wolfe cleared one hundred eighty dollars — less than what *Scribner's Magazine* had been paying him for his stories. While he welcomed this "addition to my lean and hungry pocket book," he concluded that his stories could not be made acceptable to general magazines without "changing the entire structure" and — in a reference to his brother's stuttering — without altering the "quality of a fundamental character," and he asked Miss Nowell to return his other manuscripts. He was, however, not so much disappointed with her as with himself, for having attempted "to do something I do not understand." When Harry Hansen selected "Boom Town" for inclusion in *The O. Henry Memorial Award: Prize Stories of 1934,* Wolfe's respect for Miss Nowell's editorial talents increased, and in 1935, when she left Lieber to set up her own literary agency, he was one of her first clients.

IV

At Scribners, meanwhile, optimism over early publication of Wolfe's second novel had changed into doubt whether it would ever be ready for publication. By the end of July Wheelock informed a newspaper reporter "that the publication of Thomas Wolfe's new novel has been postponed and it is not possible at this time to set a definite date."

During all these months of struggle Perkins watched Wolfe's exertions with anxiety and with sympathy. Wolfe's difficulties in finishing his book continued to puzzle him. As he explained to Frère-Reeves, who was eager to publish the new novel in Great Britain: "The trouble with Tom is not that he does not work, for he does, like a dog. It is that everything grows and grows under his hands, and he cannot seem to control that. He takes up an episode which is to be part of the book, and a small part, and by the time he is through with it it is big enough to make a volume by itself."

By the fall of 1933 Perkins began to fear, as Wolfe himself did, that this promising novelist was approaching "the final doom of an utter, inevitable, and abysmal failure." Observing that Wolfe was "tortured by anxiety" and was "in a state of growing desperation," Perkins told his colleagues at Scribners: "He *can't* go on like that! If he does, something terrible is bound to happen!" He feared that if the book was not finished soon Wolfe "would meet with some personal disaster, possibly even insanity." Shaking his head with concern, Perkins told his colleagues: "I think I'll *have* to take the book away from him!"

That was exactly what Perkins did, on December 13. Calling Wolfe to his house, he quietly informed him that the book was

Julia E. Wolfe and W. O. Wolfe, Thomas Wolfe's Parents

"He was never . . . able to see them touch each other with affection, without the same inchoate and choking humiliation: they were so used to the curse, the clamor, and the roughness, that any variation into tenderness came as a cruel affectation."

— *Look Homeward, Angel*

Tom Wolfe, at about three years old

When Tom was three "they bought him alphabet books, and animal pictures, with rhymed fables below." His father "read them to him indefatigably: in six weeks he knew them all by memory. Through the late winter and spring he performed numberless times for the neighbors: holding the book in his hands he pretended to read what he knew by heart."

— *Look Homeward, Angel*

The Wolfe family at the Woodfin Street house
(Thomas Wolfe is in the left foreground.)

W. O. Wolfe's "strange house grew to the rich modelling of his fantasy. . . . He built his house close to the quiet hilly street; . . . he laid the short walk to the high veranda steps with great square sheets of colored marble; he put a fence of spiked iron between his house and the world."

— *Look Homeward, Angel*

W. O. Wolfe's monument shop on Pack Square

"It was a two-story shack of brick, with wide wooden steps, leading down to the square from a marble porch. Upon this porch, flanking the wooden doors, he placed some marbles; by the door, he put the heavy simpering figure of an angel."

— *Look Homeward, Angel*

Tom Wolfe, at about five years old

"He was not quite six when, of his own insistence, he went to school. . . . His only close companion, . . . a year his senior, was going, and there was in his heart a constricting terror that he would be left alone again."
— *Look Homeward, Angel*

"The Old Kentucky Home" on Spruce Street

Julia Wolfe's boardinghouse "was situated five minutes from the public square, on a pleasant sloping middle-class street of small homes and boarding-houses. . . . A big cheaply constructed frame house of eighteen or twenty drafty high-ceilinged rooms: it had a rambling, unplanned, gabular appearance."

— *Look Homeward, Angel*

Thomas Wolfe, at about seven years old

His mother "had allowed his hair to grow long; she wound it around her finger every morning into fat Fauntleroy curls: the agony and humiliation it caused him was horrible."

— *Look Homeward, Angel*

Mabel Wolfe (Wheaton)

"She was . . . almost six feet high: a tall thin girl, with large hands and feet, big-boned, generous features, behind which the hysteria of constant excitement lurked."

— *Look Homeward, Angel*

Fred Wolfe

"He came with wide grin, exuberant vitality, wagging and witty tongue, hurling all his bursting energy into an insane extraversion."

— *Look Homeward, Angel*

Ben Wolfe

"Pigeon-toed, well creased, brushed, white-collared," Benjamin Harrison Wolfe "loped through the streets, or prowled softly and restlessly about the house. . . . He was a stranger."
— *Look Homeward, Angel*

Thomas Wolfe (at about nine years old) and his mother

"Stricken by severe attacks of rheumatism, [Julia] . . . began to make extensive, although economical, voyages into Florida and Arkansas in search of health and, rather vaguely, in search of wealth. . . . She turned always into the South, the South that burned like Dark Helen in [Tom's] blood, and she always took him with her. They still slept together."

— *Look Homeward, Angel*

Thomas Wolfe at North State Fitting School

"Stuck on a thin undeveloped neck beneath a big wide-browed head covered thickly by curling hair . . . , was a face so small, and so delicately sculptured, that it seemed not to belong to its body. . . . The mouth was full, sensual, extraordinarily mobile, the lower lip deeply scooped and pouting. His rapt dreaming intensity set the face usually in an expression of almost sullen contemplation."

— *Look Homeward, Angel*

Mrs. Margaret Roberts

She had "the most tranquil and the most passionate face he had ever seen. . . .
Her hair was coarse and dull-brown, fairly abundant, tinged lightly with
gray. . . . Everything about her was very clean, like a scrubbed kitchen
board. . . . She made a high music in him. His heart lifted."

— *Look Homeward, Angel*

Thomas Wolfe, freshman at Chapel Hill

He "was not quite sixteen years old when he was sent away to the university. He was, at the time, over six feet and three inches tall, and weighed perhaps 130 pounds."

— *Look Homeward, Angel*

*Thomas Wolfe in the Carolina Playmakers' Production
of his play "The Return of Buck Gavin"*

"I'm not ashamed of the play," Wolfe wrote in 1924, "but I wrote it on a rainy night, when I was seventeen, in three hours. Something tells me I should hate to see my name attached [to it] now."

— *The Letters of Thomas Wolfe*

Thomas Wolfe as a college senior

He "was a great man on the campus of the
little university. He plunged exultantly into
the life of the place. . . . He joined
everything he had not joined. He made
funny speeches in chapel, at smokers, at
meetings of all sorts. He edited the paper, he
wrote poems and stories—he flung outward
without pause or thought."
— *Look Homeward, Angel*

Programs for Wolfe's plays at the 47 Workshop, Harvard

Disappointed by the reception of "The Mountains" and "Welcome To Our City," Wolfe wrote Professor Baker: "By God — no one knows me — no one knows my capacity. Those who liked my play looked on it as a fortuitous accident. . . . But already I have a bigger play under construction . . . bigger, truer, nobler." It turned out to be not a play but a novel, *Look Homeward, Angel.*
— *The Letters of Thomas Wolfe*

Thomas Wolfe and Kenneth Raisbeck

Wolfe's closest friend in the 47 Workshop, Raisbeck failed to live up to his early promise as a playwright. "He had no poetry in him, but he was one of those who write poetry," Wolfe concluded, "no sinew of creation, but he was one of those who go piously through the ritual of creating."

— Wolfe's Pocket Notebooks

PHOTOGRAPH BY DORIS ULMANN, COURTESY OF MRS. PAMELA RANKIN-SMITH

Wolfe just before publication of Look Homeward, Angel
(The photograph is inscribed to Abe Smith,
Wolfe's loyal former student and typist.)

"He had the head of an angel."
— Aline Bernstein

Mrs. Aline Bernstein

"A very beautiful and wealthy lady, who . . . designs scenery and costumes for the best theaters in New York, . . . has seen me daily and entertained me extensively."

— *The Letters of Thomas Wolfe to His Mother*

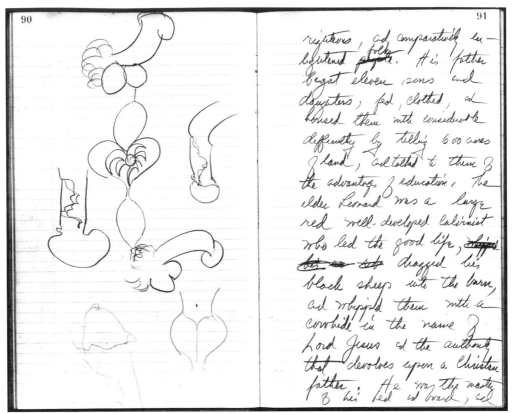

A page from Wolfe's "O Lost" ledger,
describing Mr. Leonard (J. M. Roberts)

Wolfe drafted his first novel in large bound ledgers, the blank pages of which he often filled with crude sketches. The graffiti accompanying this account of John Dorsey Leonard (his fictional portrait of J. M. Roberts) suggest how jealous he was of the husband of his idolized teacher, Mrs. Roberts.

Sketch of Thomas Wolfe by Olin Dows, 1923

"A young fellow I knew at Harvard — by name Olin Dows — wrote from Cambridge and asked me if I could get a room for him here in the hotel near me," Wolfe told his mother in the summer of 1924. "I knew the boy slightly — he's just twenty — and he saw my play at Harvard, and was enthusiastic, and painted me — he's studying art."

— *The Letters of Thomas Wolfe to His Mother*

Maxwell Evarts Perkins

"Young men sometimes believe in the existence of heroic figures, stronger and wiser than themselves, to whom they can turn for an answer to all their vexation and grief. . . . You are for me such a figure: you are one of the rocks to which my life is anchored."

— *The Letters of Thomas Wolfe*

Elizabeth Nowell, Wolfe's literary agent

"This girl," Wolfe wrote a friend, is "far and away the best agent I ever knew, absolutely honest and reliable, is not out to make money for herself — believe it or not, this is true — and is genuinely interested in your work."

— *Between Love and Loyalty*

A page from Wolfe's manuscript that became Of Time and the River

Wolfe drafted most of his second novel in pencil on loose sheets of paper. Much of it — like this passage — was originally written in the first person but was changed to the less effective third person before it was published. This paragraph appears on page 622 in *Of Time and the River.*

Aline Bernstein's favorite photograph of Wolfe

"How can I thank you for Tom's picture!" Aline Bernstein wrote Van Vechten shortly after Wolfe's death. "It is superb, the finest photograph of any body I have ever seen. It has all of his piercing quality, I have been looking at it a long time, and felt as though I was looking into his own face."

Carl Van Vechten's Portrait of Wolfe

According to one of Van Vechten's correspondents, Wolfe "said that his own photographs were customarily bad. Then he mentioned . . . almost parenthetically . . . that the only ones he had really liked had been some which you had taken of him."

Wolfe and the manuscript of Of Time and the River

Wherever Wolfe lived in New York, the most important feature in his living room was a huge wooden crate, in which he stored his manuscript. "There is an immense amount of it, millions of words," he wrote Fred, "and although it might not be of any use to anyone else, it is, so far as I am concerned, the most valuable thing I have got."

— *The Letters of Thomas Wolfe*

Wolfe at 5 Montague Terrace, Brooklyn

Wolfe's living room, Robert Disraeli recorded, was large, with two windows facing the harbor. "It was a bare room containing much used furniture: old chairs, two tables, two well-stuffed bookcases, a couch, a radio, a worn carpet, a refrigerator and a miscellany of dishes." Wolfe usually removed the upper crosspiece in the backs of chairs he sat in while writing, so as to give more room for his enormous shoulders.

Wolfe demonstrates his height

At his apartment on Montague Terrace Wolfe received the photographer Robert Disraeli with suspicion, claiming that too many of his visitors emphasized his height. "What did they do to make you uncomfortable?" Disraeli asked. Wolfe illustrated. "You see," he said, "they think it funny that I can touch the ceiling light without even stretching." Disraeli raised his camera and made a shot of that. "Even though he protested," the photographer recalled, "I suspect he rather liked the idea that he could show the world how tall he was."

Reprinted from

The Saturday Review

of LITERATURE

NEW YORK REVIEWERS PICKET PUBLISHERS OF THOMAS WOLFE'S 500,000 WORD NOVEL, "OF TIME AND THE RIVER."

SATURDAY REVIEW OF LITERATURE, MARCH 9, 1938

A cartoonist imagines reviewer reaction to Of Time and the River

Scribner's Book Store on Fifth Avenue, New York, devoted an entire window to Wolfe's *Of Time and the River*. On one side it featured the front-page review in the *New York Times,* on the other the front-page review in the *New York Herald-Tribune*. Above a great stack of copies of the novel was displayed a greatly enlarged copy of this cartoon from the *Saturday Review of Literature*.

Wolfe in Berlin, 1935

"I must leave here in a few days although every one is urging me to stay," Wolfe wrote Perkins from Berlin in May 1935. "I have never known such friendship, warmth, good will and affection as these people have shown me."
— *The Letters of Thomas Wolfe*

Wolfe and Mrs. Thomas Hornsby Ferril, Central City, Colorado, 1935

After lecturing at the University of Colorado Writers' Conference in Boulder, Wolfe went on an automobile trip with the poet Thomas Hornsby Ferril and his wife. At Central City they inspected the reconstructed mining town where the gold rush of 1859 had begun. (As the poster behind them indicates, Central City was planning a gala for 1936.) Then they pushed on to Shaffers Crossing, where bandits used to lie in wait for the gold trains.

Julia and Tom in Asheville, 1937

Returning to Asheville for the first time since 1929, Wolfe told newspapermen, "It's grand to be back." Still worried by the furor that *Look Homeward, Angel* had caused in his home town, he announced, "If anything I have ever written had displeased anyone in Asheville I hope that I shall be able to write another book which will please them."

Mrs. Julia E. Wolfe, 1937

Seventy-seven years old, Julia Wolfe was as tough and indomitable as ever. She had stood by her son stanchly when Asheville was outraged by *Look Homeward, Angel,* and, now that he was widely praised, she was equally ready to claim credit for his success. "She does literally believe that he was a great writer because of pre-natal influence," Maxwell Perkins wrote, "that it was due to the fact that she read many books during the months before his birth."

Edward C. Aswell

"He is a young man, just my own age, married and with a child just a year old.
I think he is a very fine fellow."

— *The Letters of Thomas Wolfe to His Mother*

Wolfe on his final western journey, at Zion National Park, Utah, 1938

Nearing the end of his 4500-mile automobile trip of eleven national parks, Wolfe wrote: "It has been furious, hectic, crowded and wildly comical, but I've seen a whole lot of the country and a lot of people and things. Furthermore I've got it all down — in a huge notebook — the whole thing smacked down with the blinding speed and variety of the trip."

— *The Letters of Thomas Wolfe*

finished. Stupefied, Wolfe replied that it was not finished, that it could never be completed, that he was not equal to finishing it. But Perkins firmly repeated that the book was complete, whether he knew it or not, and told Wolfe to go back to his apartment, arrange his manuscript in order, and turn it over to the publisher.

Wolfe did as he was told. He had always distrusted his own critical judgment about his writing, and now he was so weary, distraught, so dispirited that he was unable even to argue about it. During the past twelve months, as he broke off relations with most of his older friends and university colleagues, he had become increasingly dependent on Perkins, to whom he now looked for guidance on matters personal, social, and financial as well as literary. As the editor later said, "He had become absurdly dependent, though I never wanted to make him so." "There is just one person in the world today," Wolfe wrote, "who believes I will ever come to anything, that person is Maxwell Perkins, but that man's belief means more to me than anything on earth, and the knowledge that I have it far outweighs the disbelief of everyone else."

Following his editor's orders, Wolfe dug into his wooden crate, excavated a pile of manuscript that ran to about half a million words, and on December 14, "in a state of great trepidation and great hope also," laid it on Perkins's desk. During the next two weeks, while Perkins was reading this, he pulled out another segment of half a million words, which constituted the last half of his novel, and gave that to his editor too. Along with the manuscript, he presented Perkins with a twenty-page typed outline of the whole book.

"I must shamefacedly confess," he wrote Perkins after he turned over his manuscript, "that I need your help now more than I ever did. You have often said that if I ever gave you something that you could get your hands on and weigh in its entirety from beginning to end, you could pitch in and help me to get out of the woods. Well, now here is your chance."

"Immediately after lunch," Perkins replied, "I am going to begin on the ms., and expect greatly to enjoy it, for I have always enjoyed reading what you have done, and working in connection with it. It is a thing that does not happen to publishers often."

V

Shortly after New Year's Day, 1934, Perkins and Wolfe began systematically working on the manuscript of "Time and the River." (The title was changed to *Of Time and the River* sometime between March and September.) During the first two weeks they agreed on a major change in the structure and length of the novel. The manuscript that Wolfe gave Perkins was a fictional account of his own life from 1920, when he left Asheville for Harvard, to 1928, when, after prolonged quarrels with Aline Bernstein, he fled to Germany and was injured there in the Oktoberfest. After quickly going through the typescript — which formed a pile two feet high — Perkins concluded that Wolfe had written not one but two books, describing "two complete and separate cycles." The first was an account of "the period of unrest, wandering, search, and hunger in a man's youth"; the second, a story of "the period of greater certitude, of intenser concentration, and [it] was dominated by a unity of a single passion" — namely, Eugene Gant's love for Esther Jacobs. The two, Perkins argued, ought to be separated, and he proposed that they concentrate on the first "cycle" and make it Wolfe's long-awaited second novel.

Perkins explained and defended the division with several arguments. First of all, he said the complete manuscript was formidably long — much too long for publication in one volume. There was no question about that, though Wolfe might reasonably have asked whether it was necessary to publish a single book. Perkins himself did not always think so, for at least at one point he thought of "publishing the manuscript in separate volumes perhaps two hundred thousand words each, regardless of whether any volume reached a definite conclusion, . . . until the whole work should be complete." There was powerful support in his own firm for publication of Wolfe's novel in two volumes. If he needed precedents for successful multivolumed novels, he might have turned to Thomas Mann's *Joseph in Egypt* trilogy or to Romain Rolland's five-volume *Jean-Christophe*. Or, to stick closer to home, he could have thought of Freeman's four-volume biography, *R. E. Lee,* which Scribners was about to publish, to universal acclaim and with considerable financial success.

More often Perkins claimed that Wolfe's manuscript had to be broken into two books because the account of Eugene's affair with

Esther was of inferior literary quality. Indeed, to the end of his life Perkins maintained that Wolfe's relationship to Aline Bernstein was "always too fresh to be written of objectively." In all probability Perkins, a veteran publisher, had another, unstated reason for pressing Wolfe to discard the last half of his novel. All publishers live in fear of devastating libel judgments, and the danger with so clearly an autobiographical writer as Wolfe was real. There had been murmurs about legal action from Asheville after *Look Homeward, Angel* held up too clear a mirror to life. Later, according to the popular columnist Walter Winchell, Wolfe's brother Frank, so meanly portrayed as Steve Gant in that novel, contemplated bringing suit, and Uncle Henry Westall talked of going to court after "A Portrait of Bascom Hawke" was published. Recently Wolfe had heard from Mrs. Clarence Osborne of South Carolina, whose life had been made miserable because she appeared in Wolfe's first novel as "Mrs. Selborne," a woman of easy virtue. It might be possible for Charles Scribner's Sons to ignore such obscure people in remote places, but the firm could not overlook the grave possibility that Aline Bernstein, or some member of her family, might well sue for libel if Wolfe's account of their love affair was published. Perkins knew that Aline had demanded, and received, Wolfe's ironclad promise not to publish anything about her or her family without her prior approval, and he must have been certain that such approval would not be forthcoming for the manuscript now before him. Indeed, Aline had been greatly "hurt and excited" by the publication of an almost incidental passage in "No Door" that referred to her as "Esther."

If Perkins had any doubts on this subject, they were resolved when Aline in the fall of 1933 published *Three Blue Suits,* short stories about men she had known. One of them, "Eugene," was her version of her affair with Wolfe. It was autobiography very thinly disguised as fiction; Eugene Lyons resembled Wolfe in every particular, and even his first name was borrowed from Wolfe's Eugene Gant. Wolfe, who had described so many readily identifiable characters in his own fiction, was outraged by Aline's "uncharitable and unjust" story, which he thought was sure to "get pawed over and whispered about by wretched, verminous little people who want to poke around, pick out identities and gloat over . . . scandalous morsels." If Wolfe could get so excited over a little book, published inconspicuously by the newly formed

Equinox Cooperative Press, Perkins had every reason to think that Aline Bernstein might explode if Charles Scribner's Sons published a major book, half of which was devoted to her love life. In short, Perkins's reasons for wishing to divide Wolfe's manuscript were probably more legal than literary.

Without questioning, Wolfe accepted the partition of his book. If he had regrets, Perkins consoled him by promising to include a "Publisher's Note" at the beginning of the new book. It announced that *Of Time and the River* was a sequel to *Look Homeward, Angel* and the predecessor to four additional books about the Gants and the Pentlands. One of these, "The October Fair (1925–1928)," was supposed to contain the discarded second half of his long manuscript, and it, Scribners announced, had "now been written."

The decision to cut off the last half of "Time and the River" resulted in the publication of the least considered and most hastily written part of Wolfe's manuscript. Wolfe's later claim that he wrote *Of Time and the River* "in less than a year before its publication" and only after having completed "the two books which are to follow this one" was an exaggeration; for many years he had been writing drafts of the stories included in his second novel, and he certainly did not complete two additional books first. Yet in his extreme way he was making almost the same point as Perkins, who said that the writing of *Of Time and the River* "started almost backwards." In general, during the final months of preparing his manuscript for the printer, Wolfe worked back from the now discarded "Faust and Helen" section of his story to an earlier period, before Eugene Gant met Esther Jacobs. Since so much of *Of Time and the River* was written in "frenzied haste," Wolfe himself felt that it lacked "the power and richness that long and painstaking effort will sometimes give to a piece of writing."

Another consequence of the partition of Wolfe's manuscript was that *Of Time and the River,* the published first half, was deprived of anything like a conclusion. That book did not end; it simply stopped. After tiresomely chronicling Eugene Gant's racketing about France, the author unceremoniously put him aboard a ship for home, where, on the next to the last page of a 912-page book, he saw Esther Jacobs and "from that moment his spirit was impaled upon the knife of love." So unceremonious was the conclusion that the printer, who had patiently set type for the whole

enormous book, asked plaintively on the last sheet of the typescript: "Is more to follow?"

More important, this division of Wolfe's manuscript left *Of
Time and the River* without any true organizing principle or theme.
Wolfe had intended his full-length manuscript to present "a coherent legend of the savage hunger and unrest that drives men
back and forth upon this earth and the great antagonists of fixity
[and] everlasting change, of wandering and returning, that make
war in our souls." He wanted his final section "to conclude the
fury of movement, unrest and wandering that drives men across
the earth." After the bloody fight at the Oktoberfest, which was
the climax of his aimless, pointless, confused wandering, Eugene,
lying in the hospital bed at Munich, was to begin "weaving his life
back now out of the fury which for ten years has devoured it
and finally exploded it, into silence, peace, repose." Now this
resolution of the tension between "wandering forever and the
earth again" was removed, and Eugene was left as a sensitive
young man who was involved in a series of largely unrelated
adventures.

VI

Once Perkins had persuaded Wolfe to agree to this basic change,
further revision came much easier. With only 344,000 words left
in the book, editor and author could settle down to steady work
on the manuscript. At about eight o'clock every night, including
Sundays and holidays, they met in the editor's boxlike office at 246
East 49th Street. Though Wolfe was once or twice very late in
arriving, he ordinarily was, for him, unusually punctual. Then,
for two or three hours, Perkins read, marking each passage that
required revision or deletion — lines, paragraphs, pages, and even
sections — with four precise brackets. He discussed each proposed
change with Wolfe and, if the author agreed with his suggestion,
he then drew a vertical line through the passage or, occasionally,
marked it with a large "X." If the revision was a small one, Wolfe
would take out one of his stubby, soft-lead pencils and, using the
corner of Perkins's desk, write in changes or sentences while the
editor proceeded with his reading. Larger changes and missing
passages Wolfe worked on during the day in his apartment. About
ten-thirty or eleven o'clock they stopped working and went over

to the Chatham Walk, a bar that Wolfe particularly liked because there he could feel the vibrations from the great trains far beneath the sidewalk, as they came into or left the city. Before midnight the two men strolled over to Perkins's house on Turtle Bay, and after that Wolfe walked across the bridge to Brooklyn.

The first weeks of their nightly work sessions were low-keyed and businesslike. Both men thought that the manuscript required "the most radical cutting," and Wolfe knew he had to let Perkins show him what to delete. It still hurt to have pieces of his manuscript cut out, but in Perkins's presence he tried to remain calm. For instance, the editor found the 100,000-word introduction to the novel, a scene in which young Eugene Gant departed from Altamont on an overnight train that took him to Baltimore, so long that it destroyed any sense of suspense. He proposed omitting two-thirds of the description of the passengers at the Altamont station and making smaller cuts in the rest of the section, and Wolfe agreed. But when he got back to Brooklyn, he called up Terry at 2 A.M. and for two hours talked in an agonized voice about what had happened. "John," he insisted, "I've written all that one could write, or need ever write, about a train; and it's one of the best things I've ever written. But, by God, they tell me I've got to cut it. I just don't see how I can do it. This ought to stand as a final piece of writing about a train." But when he saw Perkins the next day he did not reopen the question, and they went on to the next section.

For nearly two months their collaboration went so smoothly that both men were optimistic. In early February, recognizing that he still had "a tremendous lot . . . of cutting, revising, rewriting, and even getting new pieces typed out of my notes," Wolfe announced, "I am really out of the woods at last." "I think there's no doubt that we will get through this time," he told Fred, "and have a very big book — how big I don't care to think — when we get through." Perkins, too, was confident. Though he knew the manuscript required several more months of work before it could go to the printer, he told Fred on March 6: "I don't see what can prevent us from publishing this fall now."

But by March both men were becoming irritable. Wolfe forced himself to write eight hours each day before he came to Perkins's office, and he was so tired that he told some friends: "I would like to sleep for about two months solid and get fed meanwhile by some pleasant and nourishing injection that wouldn't disturb my slumber in the slightest!" Perkins, too, was worn out, for he met with Wolfe after putting in his full day of work at Charles Scribner's Sons, and he had had no vacation for two years.

Problems and disagreements rose in part because of the nature of the "Time and the River" manuscript. Working on this new book was nothing like their earlier collaboration on "O Lost," for there was a single, handwritten version of that book, mostly written consecutively in numbered ledgers, and a typescript that was largely a transcription of the ledgers. But for *Of Time and the River* there never was a basic, continuous manuscript draft, and the typescript Wolfe put before Perkins was, as Wolfe said later, "really not a book so much as it was the skeleton of a book." It consisted of transcriptions of passages omitted from *Look Homeward, Angel,* drafts written during his Guggenheim year abroad, fragments from the abandoned "K-19" and "The River People" books, and segments composed in great haste during Wolfe's creative flurry in early 1933. Parts were beautifully typed; parts were smudged carbon copies; many sections contained numerous corrections and revisions in Wolfe's handwriting; long segments consisted of galley proofs or printed copies of stories Wolfe had published in *Scribner's Magazine.*

Editing this incredibly messy manuscript was the more difficult because, now that the second half of the book had been discarded, there were now no reasonable ground rules for deciding what ought to be included and what should be dropped. The principle that Perkins tried to work on was that this book, like *Look Homeward, Angel,* "got its unity and its form through the senses of Eugene"; consequently, everything "outside his perception and knowledge at the time" ought to be excluded. That rule eliminated a good many, but not all, of the more obvious digressions. For instance, in order to illustrate the tensions in the Gant family while Eugene was waiting to learn whether a New York producer had accepted his play, Wolfe composed an account that ran to 240 typed pages — about eighty thousand words, or the size of an average novel — that, covering a period of only about five minutes, recaptured every move, gesture, and word uttered in a long, and largely pointless, conversation designed to get Eliza Gant from the kitchen of her house into a car waiting in front, so that she, Luke, and Eugene could take a short ride. Whatever else could be said about this section, it dealt with Eugene's own experiences, and Wolfe wanted to keep it in because of "the nature of the talk, the living vitality and character of the language, the utter naturalness, the floodtide river of it all." But, of course it was too long and had to be cut, and the tired and irritable men quarreled over how much had to come out.

Almost every change now caused a controversy. On one occasion, after Perkins suggested a big deletion and Wolfe rejected it indignantly, the two men sat silent in the office for at least fifteen minutes. Perkins went on reading, and Wolfe tossed his head about, swayed in his chair, and let his eyes rove over the office. In the corner, under Perkins's winter hat and overcoat, hung the skin of a huge rattlesnake, with seven rattles, that Marjorie Rawlings had sent him. "Aha," exclaimed Wolfe, pointing to the corner, "the portrait of an editor." That evening, at least, they broke up in laughter and adjourned to the Chatham Walk.

The arguments between the author and the editor became such a matter of common knowledge that John Chamberlain wrote in the *New York Times* of "Mr. Perkins wrestling with Thomas Wolfe for three days, catch-as-catch-can, over the attempted excision of a phrase." By the end of March, after many struggles over the manuscript, Wolfe agreed that the only way to proceed was for Perkins to go through it all, marking it up with his blue pencil, postponing explanations and arguments until later.

As if to demonstrate that he could inflict as much pain on his editor as Perkins caused him through his cutting, Wolfe during these weeks came up with stories and rumors about other publishers and his manuscript. He told Perkins that somebody at the Viking Press had read a carbon copy of "Time and the River" and had declared that it certainly must not be published in its present form. He claimed to have an offer from *American Mercury* to serialize his enormously long novel, devoting all the space in three consecutive issues to it; the offer would, of course, require that Scribners delay publication of the book. And he took pleasure in informing Perkins that "Cap" Pierce, an editor at Harcourt, Brace & Company, had approached him with an advance of ten thousand dollars; Wolfe said that he had virtuously rejected the offer because Pierce made derogatory remarks about Perkins. Pierce may have actually made some informal approach to Wolfe, though Alfred Harcourt, the head of his firm, did not authorize him to do so; but Wolfe could not have taken his manuscript to another publisher had he wished, for he had a contract with Charles Scribner's Sons and had accepted an advance against royalties for this same book. But the story was good enough to cause Perkins worry, and that probably was why Wolfe told it.

Throughout April, as Perkins continued "struggling along with the book . . . cutting it hard now, and reducing it greatly," Wolfe, who was both angry and bored, started taking little vacations. He spent a good deal of time with the Hoaglands in New Jersey. He planned another trip to Vermont, to see the Raynoldses, and he did visit a new friend, Catherine Brett, who taught in a school for the handicapped and retarded at Dingman's Ferry, Pennsylvania. "Tom has been ranging around the country again," Perkins reported, "and is in an unmanageable state, but I think he will soon calm down, and I hope we can get things into definite shape."

Toward the end of May Perkins succeeded in getting Wolfe back in harness. When he returned from Dingman's Ferry, he felt so refreshed that he "got off a terrific burst of work" and wrote another seventy-five thousand words or so needed to fill gaps in his story. The most important part of this new material was his story of the death of W. O. Gant. In his original manuscript Wolfe had planned simply to mention Gant's death, since it occurred while Eugene was in Cambridge, but Perkins persuaded him that he needed at least a short account of it. The next night Wolfe came in with a five-thousand-word passage about Gant's attending physician, Dr. McGuire, his unfaithful wife, and his loyal nurse. "This is good, Tom," Perkins told him, "but what has it to do with the book? You are telling the story of Eugene, of what *he* saw and experienced. We can't waste time with all this that is outside it." The next night Wolfe turned up with an equally long passage about the anxiety and desperation Eugene's sister, Helen, felt as her father's death approached. "How in God's name will you get this book done this way, Tom?" Perkins exploded. "You have wasted two days already, and instead of reducing the length and doing what is essential, you are increasing it and adding what doesn't belong here." Wolfe was penitent — but he kept bringing in more and more copy until he finally had what, when transcribed, became a 153-page account of "The Death of Stoneman Gant." Instead of seeing that this, "one of the most wonderful episodes Wolfe ever wrote," was really a separate, beautifully constructed short novel, Perkins gave up on his exclusionary principle and included most of the new manuscript in *Of Time and the River*. "What [Wolfe] was doing," he explained later, "was too good to let any rule of form impede him."

By this time Perkins felt that if only he could keep Wolfe working and cooperating for another six weeks, the first third of the book would be ready to send to the printer. But Wolfe began exhibiting "an overwhelming reluctance to let it go." "There are so many things I want to go back over and fill in and revise," he explained, "and all my beautiful notes I long to chink in somehow." Perkins feared that they "might have to go through the whole struggle again." One hot evening in June they reached absolute deadlock. Perkins announced that another large cut had to be made — probably in the very long account of Eugene's visit to the wealthy Pierce family on the Hudson — and Wolfe could not bring himself to agree. "Literally," Perkins recalled, "we sat here for an hour thereafter without saying a word, while Tom glowered and pondered and fidgeted in his chair. Then he said, 'Well, then will you take the responsibility?' And I said, 'I have simply got to take the responsibility. And what's more,' I said, 'I will be blamed, either way.' "

Shortly afterward, seeking moral support, Perkins persuaded Scott Fitzgerald to join him and Wolfe for lunch. When the subject turned inevitably to the progress they were making on Wolfe's manuscript, Perkins said, "You tell Tom to cut something and a great hand comes over and slowly crosses out a word, but you tell him to improve it, to add to it, and the words just flow." Fitzgerald observed, "You never cut anything out of a book that you regret later." But Wolfe wondered whether this was true, and Fitzgerald proved no more persuasive than Hemingway had been.

Beginning to feel desperate, Perkins on July 10 sent the first batch of Wolfe's huge typescript to the printer. He knew very well that the final sections of the book had still to be revised, but he felt that the only way to keep Wolfe from tampering with what had already been done was to take it out of his hands. He also hoped that his action would spur Wolfe on to finishing his work. So uncertain was he at this point about the outcome that, for perhaps the only time in his life, he became impatient with his dear friend Elizabeth Lemmon, for inviting Wolfe to take a brief vacation at

Welbourne, her beautiful house in Middlebury, Virginia. Completing work on the book, he warned her, was "a desperate matter" for Wolfe; nothing should interrupt him, because "he must finish it."

In August the first galley proofs began to come in. Seeing his book in print made Wolfe despondent. He sat for hours in the Scribners library, revising the first forty galleys (which corresponded to the first 133 pages of the published book). Taking great pains with minor revisions, Wolfe also attempted to put back in some of the material that earlier in the year he had allowed Perkins to cut out, and he added new passages to suggest that Eugene Gant's experiences had a universal, rather than a purely personal, significance. Told that he could not make substantive changes, he lost interest, did not read the rest of the proofs, and failed to return them. Indeed, the next spring, when he was packing for another trip abroad, they were still strewn over his apartment, still unread. Wheelock struggled valiantly to correct them, but inevitably hundreds of typographical and grammatical mistakes appeared in the printed volume.

VII

As the book was in the final stage before publication, Perkins had one last struggle with Wolfe, who began to worry that it did not have sufficient social content or demonstrate sufficient social awareness. At this time he was seeing a good deal of certain left-wing writers and critics, particularly V. F. Calverton, to whose *Modern Monthly* he gave several short stories that Elizabeth Nowell thought he could well have published elsewhere for money. There is nothing to suggest that Wolfe read or understood Marx — or, for that matter, any other economic or social theorist — but, according to Joyce Maupin, a member of Calverton's circle, he "considered himself a socialist." Part of his interest in radical movements and ideas stemmed from calculation: he had a sense that there was a cabal of left-wing critics who were likely to "pan his book" for failing to show sympathy for the working classes. At the same time, he genuinely did have a sympathy for the victims of the Great Depression, and he insisted that he was the son of a workingman. For both reasons he wanted to make his book resonate with sympathy for working people — a term by which he mostly meant members of the petty bourgeoisie, for he knew very little about factory workers.

Perkins strongly objected. He was politically much more conservative than Wolfe, and they got into excited arguments about socialism and Communism. Wolfe was not altogether serious, but he liked to tease Perkins and, as he said, after a second round of drinks sometimes engaged in talk so radical as to "make Trotsky look like a republican." Perkins, incorrectly, believed that he "wanted . . . to be a Communist" and was trying to make his book follow the party line. "Old Tom," he reported to Hemingway in disgust, "has been trying to change his book into a kind of Marxian argument (having written most of it some years before he ever heard of Marx)." A novelist's social and economic beliefs, he argued, would come out in his writing, even though they were not made explicit. As he told Hemingway: "What convictions you hold on economic subjects will be in whatever you write, if they are really deep."

To convince Wolfe how inappropriate it would be to make his novel a working-class apologia, Perkins drafted a proposed publicity release to be issued by Charles Scribner's Sons:

> Thomas Wolfe, . . . whose new novel 'Of Time and the River' . . . is in process, has joined the Communist party. He took this step after long and serious thought and study. He is one of the very few who call themselves Communists who have actually been taken into the party itself into which admission is very difficult. His proletarian sympathies, though never directly expressed, are implicit in his new novel, as in some degree they were in his famous Look Homeward Angel.

This, in all apparent seriousness, he submitted to Wolfe for his approval. Of course it was a kind of double joke, for Wolfe most certainly had not joined the Communist party — and there is no evidence that the party ever tried to recruit a man so temperamental, individualistic, and unsystematic in his thinking — and Perkins knew better than anybody else that Wolfe never gave long, serious study to Communist or any other economic theories.★

★In response to my request, made under the Freedom of Information Act, the Federal Bureau of Investigation informed me that it never opened a file on Thomas Wolfe. It did so for many prominent writers and intellectuals suspected of having Communist sympa-

Once again Wolfe had to capitulate, and most of the passages that offended Perkins were removed. Helen, Eugene Gant's sister, was allowed to leave the group of businessmen who came to the house during her father's final illness and to join the workingmen who also came to pay their condolences, and she felt "an indefinable but powerful sense of comfort and physical well-being" when she was with them. But she was not permitted the realization that Wolfe's manuscript gave her: "that she herself was really one of these people — 'working people' such as these." Nor was the narrator's explanation of her choice of associates retained: "The true fellowship of working people is not one of mind and spirit but of blood, unless one comes from people who have worked with their [hands] their lives are jaded, feverish, impotent and sterile, their only dignity a feeble mocking of their own futility, a stale irony of hugging desolation to the bone and while enjoying lavish incomes."

By this point the book was nearly finished and Perkins had taken such full control that he came to regard Wolfe's presence as something of a nuisance. He was on the whole relieved when his weary author took the train to Chicago to see the World's Fair in September. When Miss Lemmon repeated her invitation to visit Welbourne, Perkins was this time glad to see Wolfe go. While Wolfe was in Chicago, Perkins, without consulting him, returned the first galleys to the printer, after which significant changes in the early part of the book were impossible.

It was probably while Wolfe was absent that a major change was made in the middle section of his book. He had planned, after bringing Eugene Gant to Boston, to present without interruption his story "A Portrait of Bascom Hawke" — with Uncle Bascom Hawke changed to Uncle Emerson Pentland, and John (or David) Hawke to Eugene Gant. Not until after this long episode did Wolfe introduce Professor Hatcher's celebrated playwriting class. In accordance with this original plan, the printer set up the first 153 galleys of *Of Time and the River*. Reading the galleys in Wolfe's absence, Perkins and Wheelock came to realize that the Bascom Hawke–Emerson Pentland story was really a digression, since the eccentric uncle and his idiosyncratic family played no significant

---

thies. For American writers and the Communist party, see Daniel Aaron, *Writers on the Left: Episodes in American Literary Communism* (New York: Harcourt, Brace & World, Inc., 1961).

role in the life of the hero, Eugene Gant. To prevent readers from losing the main thread of the novel, they decided to cut the Bascom Hawke story into sections, splicing between them segments of Wolfe's manuscript that dealt with Professor Hatcher and the playwriting group. Consequently the printer had to reset nearly the entire first quarter of the book in new galleys. The costs, which were formidable, were not reported to Wolfe until after the book was published.

As Perkins grew bolder in his editing of Wolfe, he also became worried about what he was doing. Sometimes he wondered whether he had taken the manuscript away from Wolfe too soon. To Elizabeth Nowell he speculated that "maybe if Tom was allowed to go ahead and make a book as long as he wanted, it would shape up into a perfect whole." Shortly before *Of Time and the River* was published, Perkins confessed to Miss Lemmon: "I've taken awful risks about that book, but I had to do it. It had to be done, and because of the peculiar circumstances of the case I almost know that no one else could have done it as well and finished it." But he anticipated that he would be "damned for it some day."

VIII

The prolonged struggle over *Of Time and the River* left Wolfe emotionally confused. Perhaps his strongest feeling, as the whole process of revising and editing drew to a close, was one of "tremendous relief." After so many years of struggle, after so many false starts, after so much blundering and misdirected activity, he was finally going to have a second book. Now he could thumb his nose at those who doubted him. In his euphoric mood he liked to think that what critics "mean or think doesn't get under my skin quite as deep as it did a few years ago." He ignored Mark Van Doren's uncharacteristically acerbic comment in the *Nation* that "Thomas Wolfe's one novel to date, 'Look Homeward, Angel,' needs to be followed by others before anybody can know whether Mr. Wolfe is an artist in anything beyond autobiography."

For the first time in years, Wolfe could begin to think about the future. Of one thing he was certain: he was tired and drained and needed a rest. He also wanted to be out of the country, away from all the excitement and publicity, at the time *Of Time and the River* was published. Finally, he was "fed up with Brooklyn." "I . . .

have lived here long enough and finished a big job here," he decided, "and now it's time to go." When he came back from Europe, he planned to find a place to live in Manhattan.

In planning ahead, he was even willing to think about using new techniques for writing his future books. For the first time he tried dictating his work to his typist. It was not an altogether satisfactory venture and on the whole he thought that pushing a pencil might be better for writers, because that "never allows us to forget the grim nature of our occupation." In a more daring innovation he asked a new friend, Belinda Jelliffe, the wife of the prominent psychiatrist, Dr. Smith Ely Jelliffe, to help him select a typewriter. "Silly to have to pay to have my stuff typed," he told her — much as he had told his mother when he was at Harvard. "I'm going to do it myself." With her assistance he bought a portable and began pecking away at it in a kind of free fugue: "i have lived in brooklyn and i have lived i n boston . . . and they had angreat statehouse with a gilded dome . . . i dont think it up it just comes so while isearch out onthe key i have been in many places i h ave eaten a great many magnificent meals i . . . have fucked a graet many women from a great many states. . . . " The experiment did not last long, and Mrs. Jelliffe believed that only the fact that Wolfe had paid fifty dollars for the machine kept him from pounding it into a twisted bunch of metal.

But, along with relief, Wolfe felt regret as the date for the publication of *Of Time and the River* approached. Though every word of that book was his, he knew that it bore astonishingly little resemblance to the book that he had planned. He could not repress his unhappiness that Perkins had insisted on taking the manuscript from him in December 1933, for he believed that another six months would have allowed him to finish it properly. He continued to lament "the tremendous chunks and pieces we have had to cut out" of the manuscript, and he was bitter toward the publishing industry for allowing financial considerations to determine the proper length of a novel. In his almost daily arguments with Perkins he voiced his belief that the editor "deformed" his work. "Max, Max," he reproached his editor, "we should have waited six months longer — the book, like Caesar, was from its mother's womb untimely ripped — like King Richard, brought into the world 'scarce half made up.' "

As usual, Wolfe tried to persuade himself that "Max Perkins's

judgment is likely to be so much better than mine, particularly
since I have worked and lived and thought about this thing so long
that I no longer have any detachment concerning it." He never
questioned the purity of Perkins's motives or his "unfailing faith,
the unshaken belief and friendship." "No success that this book
could possibly have," he wrote to a friend, even while he and
Perkins were quarreling nightly, "could ever begin to repay that
man for the prodigies of patience, labor, editing and care he has
lavished on it." He wanted to make that sentiment public — and
perhaps to convince himself of its truth — by dedicating *Of Time
and the River* to Perkins, and he drafted at least eight versions of a
dedication praising that "gentle, brave and dauntless friend," that
"great editor, an unshaken and enduring friend, and a grave and
honest man." The most personal variant ended: "In all my life,
until I met you, I never had a friend."

Always averse to personal publicity, Perkins had a special reason for not wanting *Of Time and the River* to be dedicated to him.
During their prolonged work together on the manuscript, Wolfe
had made it clear that the editing had caused the author to lose
faith in his book, and he now told Wolfe: "You must not act
inconsistently with that fact." At the same time Perkins could not
refrain adding, in a sentence in which the reservations were at least
as significant as the affirmations: "Working on your writings,
however it has turned out, for good or bad, has been the greatest
pleasure, for all its pain, and the most interesting episode of my
editorial life." When Wolfe took this as a signal to go ahead,
Wheelock insisted that he prune his praise and keep to "a level of
propriety that would not embarrass Max altogether." Perkins accepted a somewhat toned down dedication as "a most generous
and noble utterance."

Still not satisfied that he had done justice to the editor, Wolfe
proposed to add a preface to *Of Time and the River,* explaining how
his book had evolved "through infinite processes of error and
bewilderment" and showing how, during the whole time, his
editor had been "a kind of editorial Moby Dick, hanging on grimly
to the fin of a plunging whale." At first Perkins looked kindly on
this preface, but when it developed into a candid confession he
became alarmed. Gently failing to remind Wolfe that Moby
Dick was a whale, not a whaler, he raised "a literary objection" to
the preface and argued that it made "the book seem personal and

autobiographical" — the very charge that for years Wolfe had been attempting to refute. To Wolfe's English publisher Perkins explained that the proposed preface would have been "harmful" — meaning, without doubt, that Wolfe was confessing to so much editorial assistance that the integrity of his work could be questioned. After argument Wolfe dropped the preface, but he thought that some day he might be able to make a magazine article out of it.

During the first weeks of January 1935, while *Of Time and the River* was being printed and bound, Wolfe was at loose ends. "Everything so far as I am concerned is finished for the book," he reported to his mother. "They won't let me do anything more to it and . . . I can't make any more changes even if I wanted to." The one thing he could do was to help the Scribners promotion department to get some pre-publication publicity for his forthcoming book. Usually very reluctant to give interviews, he finally consented, in part because the chosen reporter from the *New York Herald-Tribune,* Sanderson Vanderbilt, bore the name of the first family of Asheville, which did not associate with the Wolfes. Wolfe thought the situation had the elements of comedy.

It did. When Vanderbilt arrived at Wolfe's apartment on Montague Terrace, the author was out for lunch, but he left a note telling the reporter to make himself at home. He not merely came in and looked around; he practically made an inventory, meticulously noting that Wolfe's icebox, "evidently not used," stood in his bathroom; that his lamp lacked both shade and bulbs; that his telephone "proved simply an ornament," since service had been disconnected when Wolfe did not pay his $17.18 bill; and that the old green alarm clock next to Wolfe's bed worked only when flat on its face. With equal precision Vanderbilt recorded that Wolfe, when he dashed in an hour late, had been "sufficiently fortified" at lunch. In his elevated state Wolfe announced that he was going to trace the development of America in a series of six novels, which would be written in a distinctive way because "We've got a new language here — we can't talk like Matthew Arnold or James Russell Lowell; he's an American, of course, but he's trying to talk like an Englishman." To complete all these novels, "I've got to write 5,000,000 words," he told Vanderbilt, adding: "you fix it up if it sounds like boasting, because, damn it, I need some money and I want to sell this book." "Sunday," Wolfe exclaimed suddenly, peering out of his window into the dusk, "Wouldn't you know it's Sunday just to look out at that queer light." Lighting another cigarette, he ran his fingers through his thinning black hair. "I'm a nut," he cried.

Publication of the interview was embarrassing, not merely because it made Wolfe look silly but because it identified his Brooklyn address, and he began to have many uninvited visitors. "I'm one of their favorite haunts around here," he told Mrs. Jelliffe when she came to see him. The unwanted attention goaded him into making his long-planned move. Mrs. Jelliffe promised to store his few usable pieces of furniture and persuaded him to throw away his broken chairs and worn-out clothing. She also helped him pack his books and papers in large wooden crates, while he resisted discarding any scrap, protesting: "Dont throw that away. That may be a part of a valuable manuscript." The boxes were to be stored at the Scribners office while he was abroad. Temporarily he moved to a Manhattan hotel.

It required the help of all Wolfe's friends to get him aboard the *Ile de France* on March 2 in time to sail. As he got ready to leave his hotel, he remembered that he had a batch of laundry left in Brooklyn, which he must have before leaving, and from a public telephone booth in the lobby engaged in a long, loud conversation with the laundryman, beginning with a quite humble plea for delivery of the parcel and proceeding to a precise and eloquent cursing of the man, his ancestors, and his descendants. Then, feeling cheerful because he had done his duty, he checked out of the hotel, telling the woman at the desk as he signed the papers: "Better keep that, my girl; it will be valuable." With his bags, books, newspaper, notebooks, typewriter, overcoat, and an extra pair of shoes dangling from his arms by their laces tied together, he took a taxi with Mrs. Jelliffe to Scribners, where he said he must see Perkins once more. She offered to keep the taxi waiting, but he insisted that all the packages and luggage must be unloaded, carried into the building, and then taken upstairs to Perkins's office. After the two men talked for half an hour, the whole process had to be repeated in reverse. Mrs. Jelliffe was worried that he would miss the boat, but on the way to the dock he spotted a fruit stand and insisted on stopping and buying a huge, bulging brown bag of apples and oranges. At the ship Miss Nowell joined them, as did Mr. and Mrs. Raynolds. Later Terry puffed in, bringing the missing package of laundry, which proved to contain a few shirts, which Wolfe seized, and some worn pillow cases, torn sheets, three socks of varying colors, and old towels, which he thrust into Mrs. Jelliffe's arms with the plea: "You *will* take care of this for me, won't you?" While Wolfe was saying goodbye to his friends, the purser, who had noticed his height, quietly removed the short, standard bunk from his cabin and installed a special long bed. "It is incredible that they have done this for me!" Wolfe burst out. "Oh, I am so grateful and happy!"

X

The Famous American Novelist

WOLFE REACHED PARIS on March 8, 1935, the day that *Of Time and the River* was published in New York. He got little rest during the rough voyage for, as he wrote Belinda Jelliffe, he felt "still tormented, still driven on by drink, goaded by useless requests, beset by wild and foolish apprehensions" over how his new novel would be received. The night before he landed he sat up late, "drinking . . . saying spells, prayers etc for fate of book," but he had little belief in either Providence or luck and concluded: "Now over, done for, I feel a ruined man."

Paris was no place for a ruined man "to get rest or sleep or any peace or quiet." During his first three days in the French capital he went around in a daze, eating a great deal, drinking in many bars, and frequenting whorehouses, retaining no clear memory of where he had been or what he had been doing. Early one morning in his hotel bed he "had the horrible experience of seeming to disintegrate into at least six people. . . . Suddenly it seemed these other shapes of myself were moving *out* of me — all around me — one of them touched me by the arm — another was talking in my ear — others [were] walking around the room — and suddenly I would come to with a terrific jerk and all of them would rush back into me again." "I really was horribly afraid I was going mad," he told Perkins later; "it was as if I were on the back of some immense rackety engine which was running wild and over which I had no more control than a fly."

Not until March 11 could he muster courage to face his "grand test" of picking up his mail at the American Express office, which would tell him how *Of Time and the River* had been received. There he found a cablegram from Perkins: "Magnificent reviews, somewhat critical in ways expected, full of greatest praise." Convinced that the phrase "somewhat critical" meant that his editor was withholding bad news, Wolfe responded by cable: "I can face blunt fact better than damnable incertitude. . . . Give me the straight plain truth."

Believing that his book was a failure, Wolfe continued rambling around Paris, observing the whores, the pimps, the taxi drivers, and the waiters, stumbling from one bistro to another, and getting into a pointless fistfight at Harry's New York bar. Fortunately he had a letter of introduction to Mrs. Adelaide Massey, an American expatriate studying at the British Institute in Paris, and she took the bedraggled author in, treated his black eye and bruises, dosed him with castor oil, and made him get some rest. At her suggestion he called on Sylvia Beach, the publisher of James Joyce and the owner of Shakespeare and Company, the celebrated English bookstore in Paris. Though Wolfe had fortified himself for the occasion with six or seven drinks, Miss Beach thought he was reasonably sober as he discussed the influence Joyce had had on his writing and how he now "was trying to get out from under it." She concluded that Wolfe was "indubitably a young man of genius" but that he might be "perhaps very unsatisfactory as a social being." Wolfe remembered her mostly because of her "vivid concentration of white front teeth."

Finally, on March 14, Wolfe received what even he had to admit was an unequivocal cablegram from Perkins: "Grand excited reception in reviews, talked of everywhere as truly great book, all comparisons with greatest writers, enjoy yourself with light heart."

Enormously relieved by "the grand wonderful beautiful news," Wolfe spent another ten days observing "the changeless change of Paris and the French." He understood very little of what he saw and failed to recognize that the French were still floundering in the trough of the Great Depression and that the French government was dangerously threatened by scandals at home and by fascist dictatorships abroad. In fact, his only real interest was in the French cuisine, and his pocket notebooks recorded the "wonderful dinners" he ordered, with the courses carefully noted: poached turbot, chicken with yellow thick sauce and rice, apple tart with cream.

Discovering that his money was melting fast, he decided to go to England, where Frère-Reeves found him a service flat at 26 Hanover Square, equipped with a valet who, Wolfe said, was like Ruggles of Red Gap (he had just seen Charles Laughton in the movie of that name) and a pretty maid who served him ham and eggs, grilled sausages, kippers, toast and marmalade, and a big pot of tea for breakfast. For once, he was almost content. "I'm beginning to eat and sleep regularly for the first time in months or years," he reported.

Contrary to Perkins's advice, Wolfe began to buy American newspapers and magazines, to see how his book was faring. At first he looked only for advertisements of *Of Time and the River* and checked its standing in the bestseller lists. Because sales were slow in Atlanta and New Orleans, he complained, "My own South has apparently left me flat," but he was delighted to find that his novel was first or second (after Edna Ferber's *Come and Get It*) in the reports from New York, Philadelphia, Washington, and San Francisco. Encouraged, he then began looking up reviews, fearing that extracts Perkins kept sending him were "too *hand-picked.*"

Much of what he read was heartwarming. On March 10 *Of Time and the River* received front-page coverage in both the *New York Times Book Review* and *New York Herald-Tribune Books,* and on the previous day the *Saturday Review of Literature* carried an extended review by its editor, Henry Seidel Canby. Nearly every other important newspaper and literary magazine in the United States followed suit. Influenced, no doubt, by the unprecedented ten-thousand-dollar advertising budget that Scribners announced for the book, editors made sure that *Of Time and the River* received serious attention from major critics.

Most reviewers were impressed by the size and range of the book. No doubt many shared Herschell Brickell's feeling that a 912-page novel was "rather baffling to the assayer who has to work against time as do those of us who write about books every day," and a contemporary cartoon showed book reviewers on strike, carrying placards with messages like: "Thomas Wolfe Ignores 8 Hr. Day Makes Reviewers Work 24 Hrs." But, at a time when some critics were announcing the death of the novel, the publication of this huge volume, with its publisher's note that this was the second in a planned series of six novels, was welcome news that fiction, at least in America, was very much alive. Proudly Canby asserted that Wolfe had "more material, more vitality, more originality, more gusto than any two contemporary British novelists put together."

The power, the beauty, and the life of *Of Time and the River* were evident to most reviewers. Peter Munro Jack found it "a triumphant demonstration that Thomas Wolfe has the stamina to produce a magnificent epic of American life." Brickell announced that there was "a chance at least that Mr. Wolfe's big book will be the Great American novel." And Mary Colum called *Of Time and the River* "one of the best books ever produced in America, one of the three or four most original books produced in the last decade or so."

Nearly all reviewers compared Wolfe to the greatest of writers. Some measured him against Dickens and Walter Scott, others against Joyce and Proust. Burton Rascoe thought *Of Time and the River* ranked along with the works of Rabelais, Sterne, and Fielding. V. F. Calverton put him in a class with Melville, Poe, and Whitman. Some announced that Wolfe surpassed his predecessors. At last, rejoiced John Chamberlain, America had a novelist who has "escaped the blight of the Nineteen Twenties," with its "fetish of perfection and . . . horror of repetition," and he predicted that Wolfe "may supply the motive power to change our literature."

But, along with praise, most reviews expressed reservations about Wolfe's style. Even before *Of Time and the River* was officially published, Isabel M. Paterson, in *New York Herald-Tribune Books,* complained that all the "principal characters are highly exaggerated," and proposed, as "an interesting experiment," to "take one of his chapters and eliminate all the superlatives, the adjectives indicating altitude, volume, and violence . . . and see what would remain." Finding Wolfe's style "wondrous, Elizabethan" at its best but "hyperthyroid and afflicted with elephantiasis" at its worst, Clifton Fadiman in the *New Yorker* asked "whether he is a master of language or language a master of him." In the *New Republic* Malcolm Cowley reported that one-third of the novel was "extraordinarily strong and living" but that at least an equal portion was "Brobdingnagianly bad," "possibly worse than anything that any other reputable American novelist has permitted himself to publish."

The absence of any conventional form in *Of Time and the River* also troubled critics. Even Canby's warmly appreciative review pronounced the novel "an artistic failure," since it lacked both plot and structure. Many complained that, except for the Gants and Pentlands who had already made their appearance in *Look Homeward, Angel,* Wolfe's characters were undeveloped caricatures, and nearly all agreed that Eugene Gant was neither a strong nor a credible figure. "I believe in Thomas Wolfe," Fadiman announced; "but I do not believe in Eugene Gant." Cowley added that Eugene — or perhaps Wolfe — was "a God-intoxicated ninny."

A more fundamental criticism was that neither Eugene Gant nor his creator had anything of consequence to say. *Of Time and the River,* Fadiman concluded, "is defiantly, frenziedly anti–intellectual" and "what ideas it has are confused and sparse." "Eugene's intellectual processes are inchoate," Chamberlain agreed, adding: "Eugene's inability to think about America (as distinct from his capacious ability to feel its vastness, the terror of its distances) communicates itself to the author, [who] . . . is forever spilling over into prose poems about a continent." To Robert Cantwell these prose-poems seemed "confessions of imaginative bankruptcy," and Wolfe's "ostentatious Americanism" failed to conceal the fact that he really knew surprisingly little about his country, except for "that stretch lying between Asheville, North Carolina, and Boston, beside the railroad tracks."

But, after such strictures, nearly every reviewer concluded with an affirmation that Thomas Wolfe was a major novelist and that *Of Time and the River* was an important book. Most expressed the hope that in future books Wolfe could correct his errors and, along with his hero, become less adolescent and more mature. "If he does he will not be merely an important figure in American literary history," Chamberlain predicted; "he will be America's greatest novelist."

Always painfully sensitive to criticism, Wolfe winced at every negative judgment he read. Cowley's generally adverse review, in particular, made him "tremble with despair and hopelessness and a feeling of 'die, dog, die.' " It seemed that reviewers were saying that he could be a good writer if he "would only correct 3,264 fundamental faults, which are absolutely, profoundly and utterly incurable and uncorrectable." He shot off a long, self-pitying letter to Perkins railing against his critics: "In Christ's name, Max, what is wrong with us in America? . . . Is . . . there in us a sterile, perverse, and accursed love and lust for death that wishes to destroy the very people . . . who have something to give that may be of value and honor to our life? . . . I have given my life to try to be an artist, an honor to my country, to create beauty, and to win fame and glory, and . . . what has it got me? At the age of thirty-four I am weary, tired, dispirited, and worn out. . . . In Christ's name what do these people want?"

Yet this time the criticism did not send Wolfe into a tailspin of despair, as the much less damaging reviews of *Look Homeward, Angel* had done. He was now a little less thin-skinned. In addition, he had had some warning of what to expect, for Perkins had predicted that critics would object to "too many adjectives, and much repetition of a sort, and too much loud pedalling." More important, Wolfe recognized that much of the criticism, though painful, was justified. Better than anybody else he knew how imperfect *Of Time and the River* was. It had been "written too fast, with frenzied maddened haste, under a terrible sense of pressure." The published book was indeed episodic and incoherent, and he knew that it was flyspecked with "countless errors in wording and proof-reading," caused partly by his failure systematically to change the narrative from first- to third-person and chiefly by the inability of his typists to decipher his handwriting. He sent to Scribners long lists of mistakes to be corrected in subsequent printings: "light hundred miles" to be changed to "eight hundred miles," "the chains of the continent" to "the drains of the continent," and so forth and so on. Freely he admitted that he was responsible for these blunders, since he had failed to read his proofs. But, he told Perkins, "I was not ready to read proof. I was not through *writing*."

The encouraging sales figures for *Of Time and the River* also made it a bit easier for Wolfe to endure the admonitions of his critics. His friends at Scribners kept him up to date on the reception of the book. "Personally," Wheelock reported, "I do not recall any book during my quarter of a century with the House [of Scribners] which has been greeted with such overwhelming admiration, enthusiasm and excitement." On a more practical note Perkins wrote on April 20 that *Of Time and the River* had already sold twenty thousand copies. Since Wolfe's royalties amounted to about nine thousand dollars, the editor assured him, "you ought to have the security you want for at least two years." In addition, the success of the big book helped Elizabeth Nowell place four more of Wolfe's short stories, excavated from his stockpile of manuscripts. In June and July, in addition to pieces published in such low-paying periodicals as *Modern Monthly* and the *Virginia Quarterly Review,* Wolfe had stories appearing in *Harper's Bazaar, Esquire,* and *Cosmopolitan,* and the *New Yorker* carried his most famous story, "Only the Dead Know Brooklyn."

Besides, Wolfe had other things to think about in London than the criticism of his book in the United States. The Heinemann people, who were arranging to publish *Of Time and the River* in England in August, did their best to keep him busy and happy. Frère-Reeves and his wife introduced him to the finest restaurants in the city, and day after day his notebooks logged the meals he ate: "roast beef, Yorkshire, braised onion, mashed potato, rhubarb tart, cream, whiskey and soda, 1/2 pint old ale, brandy, coffee," and so on. Mrs. Reeves took him to the best tailor in London, who served by appointment to the Prince of Wales, and he ordered two regular suits, evening clothes, and shirts, all measured to his enormous size, and also bought himself a new overcoat and hat. He was, he promised, going to be "the damndest fop and tripple-gazzaza dude that American literature has ever known."

In this expansive mood Wolfe thought of making a little book out of his travel notes abroad. Ignoring the fact that, as some of his English friends tried to tell him, he really knew nothing of social, economic, or political conditions in either France or England, he proposed to tell "what it is like being back in Europe for an American after the last four years in America." Now planning to go to Germany, since Hitler's currency regulations required that royalties earned by *Schau Heimwärts, Engel!* be spent in that country, he talked of also visiting Russia, perhaps in time to witness the May Day parade. He wrote Perkins that his travel journal — "very much pruned and condensed, of course" — might be published as "The Busman's Holiday."

But then he began drinking too much, quarreled with Frère-Reeves and his wife, and announced that he would not see them again. Later he realized that he had behaved "like a callow, oversensitive, damned fool who had acted badly," but, too proud to apologize, he was left pretty much alone. He went by himself to the National Gallery, where he and Aline Bernstein had spent so much time. "First time I have looked at pictures in years," he noted in his diary, reporting that now the Old Masters mostly aroused in him a state of profound apathy. Lonely, he got in touch with a few of his acquaintances from earlier visits to London and went back to look at the places where he had formerly lived. Remembering that Wallace Meyer, of Scribners, had predicted that by the time Wolfe was forty he would "like a camel . . . begin to live off [his] hump," he wondered: "Is that happening to me now? Am no longer so ravenously hungry for new sights, new experience as I was ten years ago?"

Partly to force himself to have new experiences, he decided to go to Cambridge, where the "carved lovely stone" of King's Chapel and Clare College and the "backs," the gardens now in full bloom, let him understand why poetry had always flourished here, where "beauty joins with beauty." Then he spent about a week poking about the county of Norfolk, collecting verbal portraits of village types. Later he liked to describe a shy, gentle young naturalist, "with receding chin, brown silky moustache, and protruding stick-out teeth," who defined the limits of his competence: "I'm very sure of myself with the grahses but I'm still a trifle shy with the sedges." Most of the Englishmen he met he liked, but he was troubled that so many had the "look of malnutrition — and not a malnutrition of their life, but of the last hundreds of years."

After a while his aimless rambling and casual conversations with strangers in hotels and trains began to pall. "I came away 'abroad' to be alone," he noted, "but what I am really tired of, what I am sick to death of, what I am exhausted and sickened and fed up to the roots of my soul with — is being *alone*." On April 29 he crossed the North Sea to spend a few days in that "little backyard of a country," the Netherlands, and then he was off to Berlin.

I

During the next six weeks Wolfe was almost never alone. To his astonishment he found that he was a celebrity in Germany. Rowohlt Verlag, his publisher, which had issued the translation of *Look Homeward, Angel* in 1933, had prepared for his arrival with a strenuous publicity campaign. Advertisements gave extensive quotations from the highly favorable reviews. Hermann Hesse called Wolfe's "magnificent novel" the "most powerful piece of

fiction from present-day America that I know of." "Here is greatness," Ulrich Sonnemann announced in the *Berliner Tageblatt. Look
Homeward, Angel* was "simply amazing," and "nothing less than
phenomenal," wrote Hermann Linden in the *Frankfurter
Nachrichten,* and he compared it to "a fiery comet streaming
through the darkness of thousands of lesser and dimmer novels."
"Wolfe did not write this book, he sang it; it often becomes hymn
or song," reporter Kurt Münzer in the *Vienna Neue Freie Presse,*
who declared it "an incomparable book!" Everybody knew about
this new American novelist, and the German literary world was
eager to greet him.

So was the small American colony in Berlin, where the United
States ambassador, William E. Dodd, tried to represent the democratic ideals of his country to a government that had repudiated
those ideals. On learning that Wolfe was coming to Germany,
Martha Dodd, the ambassador's daughter, who had been assistant
literary editor of the *Chicago Tribune,* wrote warmly welcoming
him, and on the day after his arrival she invited him to tea at the
embassy.

Though Wolfe's room at the Hotel am Zoo was only a few
blocks from the United States embassy on the Tiergarten, he characteristically arrived late at the party. "The animated conversation," another guest recalled years afterwards, "was suddenly
interrupted by the appearance of a gigantic, embarrassed man who
was introduced as the expected writer. I shall never forget the
scene: the dark, imposing head towering above all the guests, the
almost coquettishly deferential modesty of the giant who was
soon the center of the party, and who was blushingly putting
himself out to say something friendly all the time and to brush
aside any compliments."

After this introduction to Berlin society, Wolfe was promptly
swept up in a "wild, fantastic, incredible whirl of parties, teas,
dinner, all night drinking bouts, newspaper interviews, radio proposals, photographers, etc." "I don't know what my status quo
may be back home," he wrote three weeks later, "but in Berlin I
have been the white haired boy." Major newspapers carried pictures of him and stories about him. When there was no news,
reporters invented some. One paper announced that "the famous
American novelist Thomas Wolfe" was entertaining a party of
beautiful motion-picture actresses aboard his magnificent sailing

yacht, which he supposedly maintained at a fashionable lake resort a few miles from Berlin.

In part Wolfe's success in Berlin was due to the orchestrated publicity campaign of his publisher. Ernst Rowohlt, a giant-sized man with light blue eyes and hair the color of straw, knew how to catch the public's eye. The publisher of distinguished German and foreign authors, he carefully cultivated a reputation for eccentricity. People who knew little about his books were familiar with stories of his extraordinary capacity for drink and of his practice, on occasion, of biting large pieces of glass out of tumblers and chewing them. He professed to publish books without regard to the politics of the authors — but he was careful not to go so far that the Nazi government would crack down on him. In short, he knew how to make an author famous — especially an author whose second novel he was having translated and planned to publish the next year.

Wolfe was happy to go along with Rowohlt's plans. He even wrote for one of the Berlin papers an account of his first meeting with the publisher, which lightly spoofed the reputation both men had for high living. Rowohlt, he said, invited him to a quiet family dinner, so that he could get away from the "hectic breathless life" of parties and nightclubs. "A restful evening together," he promised; "there won't be any drinks, no alcohol whatever." Then he modified that rule, to allow a little "light, ordinary Rhine wine," because "it is the very thing for my kidneys." But he vowed to send Wolfe off to bed early. And everything, Wolfe wrote, went as Rowohlt had planned. They did have an excellent, quiet dinner. They drank very simple wine — "a glass now and then, for the benefit of our kidneys." To be accurate, they drank fourteen bottles, "tasting like heaven," to which, around 4 A.M., they added three or four more of Munich ale. And, as he had promised, Rowohlt did get Wolfe back to his hotel "early" — at 5 A.M.

The circumstances were right for making Wolfe a literary lion. Since Hitler came to power in 1933 many of the leading German authors had gone into exile; many more had lapsed into silence, terrified by the anti-Semitic purges carried out by Hitler's thugs, intimidated by the constant espionage of the secret police, and gagged by strict censorship of the press. The arrival of a distinguished American novelist in Berlin gave a moment of hope to

German men of letters who knew — as Wolfe did not — that his most favorable German reviews had come from writers hostile to the Nazi regime, while the most critical comments were by Hitler's literary lackeys. By celebrating Wolfe's visit writers could indirectly express their opposition to the Nazi government. Novelists and poets who had secluded themselves during the past two years began to meet and talk with Wolfe at the Romanische Café, on Budapester Strasse, which had long been a gathering place for literary Berliners but had since 1933 been almost deserted.

But Wolfe's triumphant reception in Berlin was primarily due to Wolfe himself. No amount of public relations or literary protest could have succeeded had Wolfe not been personally attractive and appealing to the Germans. They liked everything about him. They enjoyed seeing this American giant striding along the Kurfürstendamm, Berlin's equivalent of New York's Fifth Avenue, or poking into the fine shops of the Tauentzienstrasse, usually accompanied by Heinz Ledig, Rowohlt's son, who was so much shorter than Wolfe that he seemed always rushing to catch up with his friend. They liked to watch him having chicken soup at the Café of Anne Menz on the Augsberger Strasse at three in the morning, or devouring nougat cakes at the Café Bristol. They relished reports of how Wolfe, after an all-night session in the Kurfürstendamm cafés, drove with his friends out to the Grunewaldsee and had breakfast at the Schloss Marquardt, where he pulled a colored cloth off a table, wrapped it around himself, Indian-fashion, and announced, "I'm Sitting Bull!" They admired his democratic fraternization with all sorts of Germans, from notables to shopkeepers, waitresses, cab drivers, trolleymen, and doormen. And most of all they relished his undisguised love of Germany, with "its noble Gothic beauty and its lyrical loveliness," and of the German people, who were, he said, "the cleanest, the kindest, the warmest-hearted, and the most honorable people I have met in Europe."

In fact, for a few weeks in Berlin Wolfe was more completely happy than at any other time in his life: he was famous and admired; he had plenty of money — which had to be spent, since he could not take his royalties out of the country; he had wonderful food, endlessly available; he was deluged by invitations and opportunities. His female admirers filled his hotel room with flowers, with suggestive cards attached. Never before had he been able to indulge his sexual appetites so freely. When, on occasion, volunteers ran out or his tastes were jaded, he visited the sophisticated Berlin brothels. More explicitly than ever before he was able to connect his craving for sex and his craving for food. Seeing a handsome waitress at Anne Menz's restaurant, he rubbed his knife and fork together like a butcher's knife and steel, remarking, "She's a fine piece, I'll cut a slice of her." In intercourse he actually bit one of his partners on her calf, leaving tooth marks that slowly faded to green and blue bruises.

While thoroughly enjoying his promiscuity, Wolfe at the same time rather fancied that he was in love with Martha Dodd, whom he first thought of as "a little middle western flirt — with little shining stick out teeth, and a little 'sure that will be swell' sort of voice," but who, on closer acquaintance, proved to have "quite the loveliest most incredibly luminous eyes" he ever saw. On her part, she was fascinated by this American giant: "his stride, his size, his endless talk, his wild gestures and imprecations."

Wolfe was exceptionally happy during a trip to Weimar, on which Martha and a friend accompanied him. Visiting Goethe's house, he studied carefully the saddle-chair in which the great German author wrote, and he was not a little pleased to discover that he was taller than Goethe, whose Faustian longings he shared. As they left the study a storm was rising, and, standing under the magnificent trees whipped by the wind, Wolfe began talking, as Martha recalled, "like one possessed in a luminous, uniquely phrased, wild and ennobled flow of language," so torrential that the only phrase that remained in her memory was "the demented music of the trees." After visiting the crypt where Schiller and Goethe were buried side by side in Weimar, Wolfe wrote Perkins that this "wonderful and lovely old town . . . seems to me . . . to hold . . . much of the spirit of the great Germany and the great and noble spirit of freedom, reverence and the high things of the spirit which all of us have loved."

That use of the perfect tense perhaps suggested that Wolfe, for all his naiveté and political ignorance, was beginning to sense that all was not right in Hitler's Germany. He came to that conclusion with great reluctance, for he loved Germany as he could love no other foreign country, and he loved it with the same lack of critical perspective that always affected his judgments on his own country. Americans better informed than he knew well before 1935 that Nazi Germany was a totalitarian society, which ruthlessly curbed freedom of speech, freedom of expression, and, indeed, freedom of thought; they watched with growing horror as the Nazis drove Jews and members of other "inferior races" from the government, the universities, and industry and subjected them to humiliation, degradation, and violence; and they observed apprehensively Germany's systematic rearmament in preparation for another world war. But Wolfe was unwilling to believe that anything untoward was occurring. Anti-Semitic himself, he thought the Nazis were simply exhibiting what he considered normal hostility toward the Jews. And since Hitler had not yet remilitarized the Ruhr, he was able to assert that German rearmament was defensive. He believed that Hitler was accomplishing much that was positive. In 1929, during the last years of the Weimar government, he had witnessed the poverty, the unemployment, and the fierce political battles that had racked Germany, and he could not help being impressed by the new sense of order and the feeling of "wonderful hope which flourishes and inspires millions of people who are . . . certainly not evil, but the most child-like, kindly and susceptible people in the world."

Not much impressed by Wolfe, Ambassador Dodd made no effort to promote his political education, but Martha Dodd and her brother, Bill, tried to convince him of the fundamental viciousness of the Nazi regime, and some of his German acquaintances also warned him of the deadly dangers of Hitlerism. At first he refused to believe what they said. Ultimately he was forced to admit that the stories about the Nazis that they told him were "damnable" — always introduced by the proviso "if they are true." To Perkins, who did not share his enthusiasm for Germans, he mentioned some "disturbing things" he had learned and promised a report of them when he got back to the United States. "I like this country and the people here," he wrote his brother Fred, "even if I cannot subscribe to everything that they do." But he did not like to have his illusions about Germany shattered, and he especially objected to being instructed by Martha, because she was a woman. Her opinions had to be discounted, he concluded, because she was "leaning toward the Communist side."

He also quarreled with Martha because she objected to his excessive drinking. Once she and Donald Klopfer, the co-founder of Random House, who was also visiting Berlin, found Wolfe dead drunk in the gutter and had to haul his huge carcass into the American embassy, where they revived him. Another night when Wolfe and Ledig, both obviously inebriated, barged into the embassy, she berated him for wasting his talents and held out her copy of *Of Time and the River* to remind him of his duty as a writer. Furious, Wolfe lunged out at her, snatched the book from her hands, "ripped it out of its cover, tore its thousand pages with his bear's paws, and threw the little bits like a shower of confetti out of the window into the steel-blue morning of the Tiergarten." Angrily Martha protested, "How can a writer do a thing like that!" He autographed another copy of the novel, which he inscribed coldly, "To Martha Eccles Dodd yrs V'ry Tr'ly, Thomas Clayton Wolfe." Five minutes later, sobering a bit and momentarily repentant, he reinscribed the same copy, "To Martha from Tom with love and friendship."

By the end of May, Wolfe's visit to Germany began to go downhill. His arguments with Martha became more frequent. He received the disquieting news that Madeleine Boyd was suing him for her commission on the royalties from *Of Time and the River*. The deep chest cold he had picked up early in his visit hung on, and he felt tired and dispirited. To make everything worse, he noticed "disquieting penile symptoms" and concluded that he had contracted gonorrhea. Panicking, he simultaneously feared that he had infected the three respectable women with whom he was sleeping and accused them of giving him the disease. Experiencing "one God damned horrible week of doubt and worry," he canceled his planned visit to the Soviet Union and went instead to Denmark.

In Copenhagen he put himself under the care of a physician. Thoroughly frightened, he brooded about illness and death and began experimenting with what would become one of his most memorable lyrical passages:

> Something has spoken to me in the night, and told me to lift up my heart again and have no fear, and told me I shall live and work and draw my breath in quietness again and told me I shall die, I know not where.

Then his Danish doctor told him that he did not have gonorrhea but only a mild venereal infection, which could soon be cleared up. Enormously relieved, Wolfe was soon back in regular form, sleeping with a Danish woman he picked up. But the memory of the scare remained with him and a reporter for the *Copenhagen Daily News* noted his "sad eyes" and thought him "a big sad boy, quite unspoiled by the sudden world success which has fallen upon him with his last book."

By now Wolfe recognized that it was time for him to return to the United States. "I have stayed over here too damned long," he wrote Terry, "and now I am aching to get home." On June 30 he boarded the *Bremen* for the voyage back.

II

Until the *Bremen* reached New York on July 4, Wolfe was still not sure that *Of Time and the River* was a success, for he distrusted the encouraging letters Perkins had sent him. But a welcoming cable from John Hall Wheelock that reached him on shipboard reassured him: "Dear Tom you return a conqueror." Even more convincing were the reporters who came aboard as soon as the *Bremen* docked, assigned to interview him as a celebrity.

Tanned and healthy, dressed in one of his beautifully tailored English suits, with his shirt, ties, socks, and shoes, for once, all in coordinated shades of tan and brown, Wolfe mugged happily for the photographers and talked freely with the reporters. He spoke at length about his published books and about the influence of James Joyce, which he said he had now outgrown, and he made predictions about the future of American literature. He was ingratiatingly modest about his own achievements: "I know I write too much of everything . . . I am going to learn, though. I'll work hard and I know I can do it." To his chagrin, however, most reporters were only interested in his comments on the snobbishness of the British and his anecdote about how he had tried to get his London valet to talk to him, on a man-to-man basis, by plying him with drinks, only to have the man inform him, with an absolutely deadpan expression: "Begging your pardon, sir, but here in England we're all a bit of a snob." They also reported Wolfe as saying that he was glad to be home because he had only five dollars in his pocket.

When he finally disembarked, after all the other passengers had come ashore, he found Maxwell Perkins on the dock, sitting rather forlornly on one of his suitcases. "Why, Max," he exclaimed, "you look so sad. What's the matter?" In fact, Perkins had been brooding over the difficulties he had been having with Aline Bernstein while Wolfe was abroad. The publication of *Of Time and the River,* in the final pages of which Aline appeared, very thinly disguised as "Esther," roused her fear that Wolfe would next publish an account of their love affair. This, she wrote Perkins firmly, was "not a matter for public consumption." She did not care what Wolfe wrote about her, she said, but she would not permit revelations that would distress her family, and particularly her recently widowed daughter. "I will not have them traduced," she told the editor bluntly, "no matter what means I take to prevent it." To emphasize her objections, she visited Perkins in the Scribners offices. He refused to promise that the love story would be suppressed. When Perkins let it slip out that he had once urged Wolfe to end their relationship, she became hysterical, and her screams could be heard all over the editorial floor. Finally she recovered, and, as she was leaving, Perkins offered her his hand, but she refused to accept it, saying: "I consider you my enemy." In subsequent conversations Perkins, who was hard of hearing, thought he heard her mention a gun but was uncertain whether she intended to aim it at him, Wolfe, or herself. While waiting on the dock, Perkins was wondering how to break all this to Wolfe and how to explain that "The October Fair" could not be published.

Before Perkins could tell his news, Wolfe swept him into a taxi and, after depositing his luggage at the Hotel Lexington, took him on a tour of his favorite spots in the city. One was the loft at 13 East 8th Street, where he had written so much of *Look Homeward, Angel.* After repeated knocking at the door of the building roused no response, Perkins discovered a fire-escape ladder that went right up to the top floor, and they climbed in, feeling adventurous and also a little guilty at being housebreakers. Perkins, who apparently had never seen the loft before, concluded that it was the best apartment Wolfe ever had, and Wolfe scribbled on the wall outside the door: "Thomas Wolfe lived here." Then, after drinks at the Hotel Lafayette, they crossed over into Brooklyn and from the rooftop of the Prince George Hotel looked out over the East River at the skyline of Manhattan softly radiant in the setting sun.

They had dinner on a converted coal barge that floated in the East River off 52nd Street, and Wolfe asked Mrs. Jelliffe to join them there. While they were waiting for her, Perkins related the problems he was having with Aline Bernstein, but, to his surprise, Wolfe was not at all troubled. Perhaps he knew that, if he really tried, he could always win Aline over. Perhaps he was simply so excited by coming back to New York that nothing could depress him. Dismissing the whole subject, Wolfe announced, "Well then, now we can have a good time." Not even a visit from Scott Fitzgerald, who was drinking with a rather disreputable-looking blonde, ruffled Wolfe's good humor.

After a long dinner with Perkins and Mrs. Jelliffe, Wolfe announced, "I want to go up in high buildings. All the way home I've been looking forward to going up in the highest building." They went to Radio City, where they persuaded a guard to let them go up to the highest level. Wolfe, as Mrs. Jelliffe recalled, "strode around, gazing in all directions over the city below, like a mythical country, pale in the gathering dusk, lights coming on all over town." He refused to have supper at the restaurant at the top of Radio City, saying that it was too expensive and "Rockefeller had enough money." So they went over to the rooftop restaurant at the St. Moritz, where they could look down on the city while they ate. Afterward, when Mrs. Jelliffe went on her way, Perkins and Wolfe strolled along the East Side, with their coats off because of the summer heat, and they wandered, always talking, from one bar to another. They were still together when the sun came up.

All in all, July 4, 1935, was the happiest day of Wolfe's life. It marked, he recorded in his pocket notebook, his "Return to Glory." He had money, he had friends, he had fame. It seemed to him that the Independence Day fireworks bursting over New York City signified "Fame Exploding in the City." He always remembered that day when he and Perkins stood together at the top of the tall buildings "and all the strangeness and the glory and the power of life and of the city were below."

When Charles Scribner's Sons reopened after the holiday, Wolfe came in to claim his mail and messages that had accumulated during his trip abroad. Hundreds of letters awaited him, mostly filled with praise for *Of Time and the River*. "One of the really great books of our age," one correspondent called it; "a superb thing," wrote another; "nothing short of a masterpiece," announced a third. A reader wrote that she was "reading it on buses and riding, lost and blinded, far beyond my stop, reading it at lunch counters and not knowing what food was traveling automatically into my mouth, reading it after breakfast when I should be washing dishes and before dinner when I should be cooking, reading it on the subway, at the circus." Another correspondent, infected by Wolfe's style, proclaimed: "Out of yourself, you have created a living breathing force, the earthly vitality of which flows from you, the creator, to the being of its beholders, in a slow but ample stream; awakening, stimulating and yet quieting all the longings and frustrated hopes of all mankind." To be sure, an occasional correspondent like the Episcopal bishop of Albany denounced *Of Time and the River* as "both lewd and blasphemous" but could not detail his complaints because the language would be too embarrassing to dictate to his secretary. But, on the other hand, there was the woman from White Plains who asked: "Is it too abrupt, too startling to tell you that I want you for my husband?"

Though Wolfe rented a room at the Lexington Hotel, he spent most of his first three weeks after he returned from Europe in the Scribners offices, where he hired a typist to help him answer his correspondence. Often he was so delighted by his fan mail that he burst out of the small room assigned to him in order to share his letters with the editors. He was especially proud of a note from Sherwood Anderson, one of the few modern American writers whom Wolfe truly admired. *Of Time and the River,* Anderson wrote, showed him "very simply and directly that I'm no novelist. Some things I can write but you — you are a real novelist." Often Wolfe stayed in the office late at night, reading his mail. Once he apparently forgot to go back to his hotel at all and slept on the table in the board of directors' room.

Wolfe did not have much time to bask in his fame, for he had to turn immediately to the suit that Madeleine Boyd had brought against him while he was in Germany. Now separated from her husband and almost destitute, Mrs. Boyd was desperately searching for a source of income, and her lawyer believed he had found it in the all-inclusive appointment that Wolfe gave her in 1929 as his literary agent. She argued that this agreement entitled her to an agent's commission of ten percent not merely on the royalties earned by *Look Homeward, Angel* but on royalties from *Of Time and the River* and "all other books [by Wolfe] that may be published by Charles Scribner's Sons." The lawyer claimed that Wolfe owed Mrs. Boyd at least ten thousand dollars in unpaid commissions.

Angrily, Wolfe exploded against such injustice: "If *America* has really at last become a place . . . where the *thief,* the *criminal,* the *shyster* can batten on *blackmail, lies,* and *filth,* and *steal* the earnings and the life of the *good* and *decent man* and *artist* . . . , then by God, I no longer want to be an American. I will renounce . . . a place that has become so *damnably rotten* and *accursed* — by God, I will [go] to Germany and become a citizen, because *by comparison* it is a haven of freedom, honor, honesty, and salvation. . . ."

He put the blame for Mrs. Boyd's suit not on the hasty, comprehensive authorization that he had given her when he was still an unpublished author with little prospect of earning anything from his books, but on the failure formally to cancel that agreement in January 1932, when he and Perkins had confronted her with evidence that she had missappropriated his German royalties. At that time Wolfe had yielded to Perkins's advice that she deserved a reprimand, rather than a dismissal. Now, bitterly, he reminded the editor that "we" — which really meant Perkins — had been "foolish, benevolent, soft-hearted, weak," because they did not *"make the thief sign the confession of her theft* when she was weeping, sobbing, crying in abject fear at the discovery and possible consequences of her crime."

On his return to New York, Wolfe learned that Scribners had retained Cornelius Mitchell, of Mitchell and Van Winkle, on Madison Avenue, to represent him in the Boyd suit. Mitchell did not think Mrs. Boyd had a strong case and was confident that it would never go to trial. Still, he wanted to have as much evidence as possible in the event that Mrs. Boyd's lawyer proposed a settlement, and repeatedly he required Wolfe to search through his great boxes of papers and manuscripts for correspondence proving that Mrs. Boyd had failed to turn over foreign royalties on *Look Homeward, Angel* promptly. Whatever Wolfe dug out for Mitchell, it was never quite enough, and the lawyer's repeated demands kept Wolfe in a state of frazzled irritability.

While attempting to deal with this new problem, Wolfe had also to cope with an old one: Aline Bernstein. Wolfe knew that Aline was indirectly involved in the Madeleine Boyd case. Though she and Mrs. Boyd were no longer close friends, she felt that Wolfe had an obligation to the agent who had done so much to bring about the publication of his first novel and thought that he ought to pay Mrs. Boyd off. There was a possibility that she might testify in court in Mrs. Boyd's behalf. Wolfe also knew from Perkins how passionately Aline objected to his fictionalized account of their love story in "The October Fair." But shortly after his return from Europe he discovered that her opposition was not so unyielding as she had led Perkins to believe. "I will have nothing to do with the law in connection with you or your publishers," she wrote Wolfe, but she insisted that the price for her acquiescence was "a personal and human agreement with you." Wolfe was willing to have such a reconciliation if it did not mean renewing their affair. Misinterpreting Aline's intentions entirely, he began to think that he might buy his way out of his emotional obligation to her by repaying the money that Aline over the years had given him.

With so much at stake, there was bound to be a dramatic scene when he and Aline met again. About a week after he returned to New York, while he and Perkins were having their usual evening drinks at the Chatham Walk, Wolfe noticed a woman on the other side of the room who was wearing the kind of flowered print dress that Aline always preferred, but he could not identify her since a large hat shaded her face. Perkins, who had a better view, recognized Aline and told Wolfe, who promptly went over to greet her. Both were so obviously overcome by emotion that Perkins took them off to the privacy of the Scribners offices. Leaving Aline sitting in the anteroom, Wolfe pulled Perkins into the editor's office to discuss his plan to repay his debt to her. When they emerged, they found Aline holding a bottle of pills in her hand. Assuming that she was about to poison herself, Wolfe knocked the bottle from her hands, and she fainted, as the pills rolled out on the floor. Quickly they summoned a doctor, who had an office on the ground floor of the Scribners building, to revive her and to ascertain whether she had swallowed a lethal dose. After picking up the scattered pills and telephoning the pharmacy that had filled the prescription, the doctor determined that no medication was missing, and Aline, reviving, declared that she had simply felt faint and had reached into her bag for a handkerchief. The whole scene ended in bathos.

Wolfe offered to see Aline home, but she wanted to be alone and insisted on taking a cab to Armonk. In his anxiety he followed her.

She was barely inside her bedroom when Wolfe's giant figure appeared, pressed against the Dutch door that opened directly on the garden. When she let him in, he berated her as "a lecherous old woman" but confessed that he could not get her out of his soul. They sat up all night talking, and Wolfe confided that "he could not have any relations with any woman but me, and that I was so bad that he could not stand it." Wolfe was, she concluded, "Crazy!"

Perhaps he was — or perhaps he was simply exhibiting a dramatic flair that had been notably lacking in his plays. Certainly he was upset by her apparent attempt to commit suicide, but he was certainly lying when he told Aline that she had caused him to lose his potency; a score of female conquests in Europe and America could testify to the contrary. But convinced that Aline was "inwardly praying for nothing better than to be a leading character in a book of mine," he thought this confession was the surest way to remove her objections to the publication of "The October Fair." His calculation proved exactly right. After he left, Aline wrote a friend about their meeting and concluded: "His next book I'm sure will all be my stuff, and I may as well give it to him."

III

While Wolfe was abroad he had been invited to participate in the sixth annual Writers' Conference, to be held in Boulder, Colorado, during the last ten days of July and the first week of August. The program, which had already been printed, listed Robert Frost and Robert Penn Warren as lecturers and Whit Burnett and Martha Foley, the co-editors of *Story* magazine, as leaders of discussion groups. Bernard DeVoto was named as the "visiting novelist." But when DeVoto was obliged to withdraw, the program director, Edward Davison, an English poet then teaching at the University of Colorado, asked Wolfe to replace him, offering two hundred fifty dollars, plus expenses, for a ten-day visit. Wolfe's main obligation would be to deliver one evening lecture on the novel, but he would also participate in one or two roundtable conferences, attend a few sessions of Warren's course on the novel, and consult individually with a few student-writers. Davison added that, en route to Boulder, Wolfe could pick up an additional seventy-five dollars by giving an informal talk at Colorado State Teachers College in Greeley.

When Perkins cabled the invitation to Berlin, Wolfe accepted promptly. The Writers' Conference at Boulder was one of the most prestigious of the summer workshops, and an invitation to teach in it was a recognition that Wolfe had truly arrived as a novelist. The fee Wolfe was offered was a considerable one. But most attractive of all was the opportunity to visit the American West. For all Wolfe's rhapsodies about the greatness and diversity of America, he had never been west of St. Louis. His trip to the Chicago World's Fair, in the fall of 1934, had made him aware both of the vast size of the United States and of how little he had yet seen, and he then wrote to his mother: "America is a huge tremendous country and someday I hope to see it all. . . . Someday I am going to see the Far West, too and hope to explore the country thoroughly before I'm done." Now he had his chance.

But first he had a lecture to prepare. He jotted down possible topics: "Some problems of a writer," and "The Artist in America." He thought of calling his talk "What is a novel?" but found the question easier to ask than to answer, since "You can not fix the form of a novel as the form of a sonnet is fixed — a novel is *War and Peace* and *Moby Dick* and *David Copperfield* and *The Pickwick Papers* — But it is also *Pride and Prejudice, The Red Badge of Courage, Ulysses,* and *The Nigger of the Narcissus.*" He considered speaking about the special problems of Southern writers, who had a heritage "twisted, dark, and full of pain," which derived partly from "the evil of man's slavery," partly from "the huge ruin of our defeat," but chiefly from "the weather of our lives, the forms that shaped us and the food that fed, from the unknown terrors of the skies that bent above us, the pineland barrens and the haunting sorrow, from the whole shape and substance of the dark, mysterious and unknown South."

Alfred Dashiell, the editor of *Scribner's Magazine,* who was on the advisory council of the Writers' Conference, helped steer Wolfe away from these abstractions and urged him to adopt "a plain, straightforward way of talking." For Wolfe that meant lecturing about the subject he knew best — himself. "How would it do," he asked Professor Davison, "if, so to speak, I 'shot the works'? That is, if I just got right down into the sawdust and told the people out there the plain, straight story of what happened in the writing of this last book." "I believe it really might be interesting and perhaps of some value to the people at the conference," he added.

When Davison gave his approval, Wolfe began to rummage through his boxes of manuscripts, pulling out what he had previously written on his experiences as a writer. He resurrected a long preface that he had drafted, but not used, for the Modern Library Giant edition of *Look Homeward, Angel,* in which he described Asheville reactions to his first book. He also dug out the even longer introduction he had prepared for *Of Time and the River,* which Perkins had not allowed him to use because it revealed too much about Wolfe's dependence on his editor. Blending these together, he wrote out a lecture, to which he gave the working title "The Making of a Book." By the middle of July he was able to assure the officials at Colorado State Teachers College that, although he had "almost no experience as a public lecturer," he would "have something to say to you that will be of some interest and value."

Because he was so busy answering his mail, attending to Mrs. Boyd's suit, and polishing his lecture, Wolfe did not leave New York until July 27. After stopping in Greeley, he arrived in Boulder on the last day of the month, after the Writers' Conference had been in session for nine days. He tried to slip quietly into the class that Davison was teaching on poetry, but the eyes of the students swiveled from the dapper, mannered English poet to this "big, tall barrel of a man in a dark suit, looking too warm for that hot afternoon." They had no trouble identifying Wolfe, since "he looked exactly like his pictures, not quite so handsome as the handsomest ones, a stubborn, high-strung face, with eyes as bright and curious as a child's. His hair curled out back of his ears, giving him a faintly cherubic aspect." At the end of his lecture Davison introduced Wolfe to the audience, and he beamed a silent greeting to the students.

From that moment Wolfe seemed omnipresent to Boulder. Feeling "instantly at home" in Colorado, where the immensity of American space and the brilliance of the sky lightened his spirits, he was determined to enjoy every minute of his stay. The day after he arrived was Colorado Day, when people from Boulder and the surrounding countryside gathered for speeches, food, and free wrestling matches. Wolfe was in the middle of the crowd, for once unconscious that his immense height was attracting attention or that people were thinking, "Look! There goes Thomas Wolfe!" He was intent on those wrestling matches.

He fraternized easily with the students in the program, who were charmed by his lack of reserve and pretension. Finding his British suits too heavy for the Colorado summer, he bought a pair of white flannel trousers, and, one student remembered, "wore them to a party and went around telling everybody who would listen that he was thirty-five years old and this was his first pair of white pants." He went with students for a barbecue on the top of Flagstaff Mountain and pretended, as he snapped out for the meat, to be the big bad Wolfe devouring the three little pigs, and he was delighted when the students gathered around him and sang, "Who's Afraid of the Big Bad Wolf?"

Toward his teaching colleagues and members of the university he was equally amiable. As usual, he accepted too many invitations, stayed so long at one party that he was always late for the next, and kept his hosts up late into the night talking about his past and his future writing and elaborating an idea that increasingly fascinated him of doing a book about "America at Night." Shrewdly he remained aloof from the controversy that raged between the local teachers in the conference, like Blanche Young McNeal and Mignon Baker, who emphasized practical instruction in how to write and sell short stories, and the visitors, like Burnett and Foley, who joined Davison in stressing creativity and experimentation in form. Adroitly he avoided all personal confrontations. At one dinner party, when asked about reviews of *Of Time and the River,* he replied that he had been pleased by favorable ones but had also learned much from the more critical ones. There was one review, Wolfe said, that had taught him more than any other, and "the author is at this table." He turned to Warren, who had just published a sharply critical appraisal in the *American Review,* chiding Wolfe for confusing the sentiments of his narrator with those of Eugene Gant and concluding that Wolfe would do well "to recollect that Shakespeare merely wrote *Hamlet;* he was *not* Hamlet." Years later Warren remembered, "It was a remarkably generous thing to say and do."

Wolfe did his share of the formal instruction at the Writers' Conference. He took part, with Warren, in one roundtable discussion of approaches to fiction and he talked in Davison's course on the appreciation of poetry. He gave encouragement and attention to several aspiring novelists, whom Davison referred to him, and encouraged three of these young writers to send their manuscripts to Perkins. His enthusiasm for a young social historian, Dixon Wecter, led to the publication of *The Hero in America* by Scribners in 1941.

But all this was preliminary to Wolfe's lecture on the evening of August 6, which was the culmination of his visit and, indeed, of the conference. As the time grew closer, he grew increasingly worried that his very personal talk would be out of character with the earlier formal lectures on such topics as "What Is a Short Story?" and "The Recent Southern Novel." When he lumbered up on the stage that evening, he was very nervous and had obviously forgotten all he had learned about public speaking as a student at Chapel Hill and as a teacher at New York University. Clutching the podium, he "swayed like a captive elephant" and for some time seemed unable to get beyond "Ladies and gentlemen." Later he confessed, "It took me the first fifteen minutes to quit stuttering, hemming and hawing, and fiddling around for an opening." But once he was under way, talking about his own experience as a writer, his words came easily. Asked to give an hour lecture, he was so carried away by his own story that he went on for ninety minutes before he glanced at his watch. Horrified, he apologized to the audience, which had been spellbound, and asked, "Shall I go on?" They cheered and cried "Yes, yes, yes!" He continued for nearly another hour, and no one showed any signs of weariness. "If I do say so as shouldn't," he wrote later, "I did the job up pretty brown . . . . they were hanging on by the eyelids when I finished."

After thunderous applause, Davison rose to end the session by announcing that "here at last was a genuine expression of the New American Art," and he predicted that Wolfe's lecture "would go far to making the University of Colorado one of the great literary centers of the country."

When the conference ended on August 9, Wolfe should have headed back to New York. Mrs. Boyd's suit was pressing, his lawyer needed further documents from his files, and Perkins was trying to get a collection of his short stories ready for fall publication. But, euphoric because his lecture had gone so well, Wolfe wanted to stay and enjoy his fame. "For the first time in my life," he told a reporter, "I've gotten some celebrity and a bit of money. It would be silly to say I don't enjoy it." He was also so thrilled by "the beauty, power and magnificence of this country" that he resolved to see more of the West before returning to New York.

From Boulder he went on to Denver, where he spent some time with Thomas Hornsby Ferril, the gifted Western poet, for whom he had developed a great liking. Then the Ferrils drove Wolfe through the Rocky Mountain National Park and, after spending a day at their cabin in Grousemont, he went on to Colorado Springs, where he met a former colleague from his New York University days, Desmond Powell, about whom Wolfe wrote several unpublished sketches, calling him "The Diabetic." With this old friend Wolfe was expansive and unreserved. They discussed why the best novels deal with adolescents, not with older people. Arguing — as he always did — that all good fiction is basically autobiographical and that time has to pass before a writer can see his own experiences clearly and completely, Wolfe suggested that it was the middle-aged who wrote most successfully about youth. "Why aren't there any novels about old men?" he asked rhetorically. "I'll tell you why: it's because nobody ever gets old enough to write them!" They talked much about the American landscape. "You can live with mountains," Wolfe told Powell; "mountains never make you doubt yourself." The sickly Powell admired Wolfe's gusto for living and noted with real pleasure that at breakfast, "while lesser men sat around and ate crunchies and tweeties and other monkey food," Wolfe devoured a large steak, topped not just with butter and salt and pepper but with tomato ketchup and Worcestershire sauce.

After Colorado, Wolfe moved on to New Mexico, for he had been invited to visit Mabel Dodge Luhan, once the lover of the revolutionary John Reed and the patroness of D. H. Lawrence, at Taos. His feelings about Mrs. Luhan were mixed. He recognized that she was a literary figure of some importance, whose salons had once been the center of the avant-garde in New York City, and he was gratified that she praised *Of Time and the River* for recreating "the tempo, color, feeling, taste, smell and sound of this continent." On the other hand, he was always rather afraid of strong-minded, literary women, and somehow he pictured Mrs. Luhan as "a big fat spider ready to pounce on any celebrity" who stumbled into her web.

As a result, his visit to Taos was a comic misadventure. Meeting two attractive young women in Santa Fe, he gratefully accepted their offer to drive him to Taos. Along the way they stopped repeatedly to admire the scenery and to toast in raw gin the glories of the West. Invited to dinner, Wolfe and his two uninvited companions did not reach Mrs. Luhan's house until 9:30. She had already gone to bed, leaving her female companion to receive her guest. Quite drunk, Wolfe came in, settled himself in one upholstered chair, and put his feet up on another. Protesting that "Mabel" — as he insisted on calling a woman he had never met — did not know how to treat guests, he announced that he was used to having women stay up all night for him. When Mrs. Luhan's companion reproved him, he owlishly told her that she was drunk and would feel differently in the morning. At this point this strong-minded lady told the two young women, who were friends of hers, that they had better leave, and she prepared to put Wolfe to bed. Before they got into their car, Wolfe stumbled out after them, shouting curses on Mabel Dodge Luhan, and all three of them left. Shortly afterwards he reported, imprecisely but with satisfaction, to Perkins, who shared his dislike of strong-minded women: "I had a fight with Mabel Luhan the moment I walked into her house." There is nothing to indicate that he was even slightly abashed when he received Mrs. Luhan's note, written the following day, regretting any unpleasantness or misunderstanding, because, she said, "This is your first trip west and it should be a wonderful experience for you and not have any stings in it."

Boarding the Southern Pacific Railroad, Wolfe next headed for California. On the train young Dr. Henry A. Murray, then director of the psychological clinic at Harvard, spotted him because he so completely resembled Eugene Gant and introduced himself as a great admirer of Wolfe's novels. Charmed by this intelligent psychiatrist, Wolfe began pouring out the story of his success at Boulder and gave an almost verbatim repetition of his lecture. He was so eager to tell about his adventures that he "was sort of sputtering, and saliva was coming out of his mouth as well as the words." After they talked for an hour, dinner was announced, and Murray had an opportunity to watch as Wolfe had two full orders of the steak dinner, shoveling the food into his mouth. "He was devouring and embracing the dinner," Murray recalled, "and really taking it into his arms and pushing it into his face." Shrewdly the doctor noticed that Wolfe "ate somewhat the way he talked, except that things were going the other way."

Once Wolfe reached Los Angeles, he wanted, like every other tourist, to see Hollywood, and he got in touch with two former classmates who were working for the Metro-Goldwyn-Mayer Studios. They introduced him to Sam Marx, Irving Thalberg's story editor, who had read Wolfe's novels and stories and was delighted to give him a personally conducted tour. Happily Wolfe inspected the sets where *Mutiny on the Bounty* and the Tarzan movies were filmed, and he was fascinated by the contrast between "the false and unreal world" of the actors and "the technical, building, working world" of the set designers, stagehands, and producers. He was pleased to meet Clark Gable and Frank Morgan, but he especially asked to see Jean Harlow, the blonde bombshell, then at the height of her fame. She had never heard of Wolfe but after coaching by Marx, who realized that this beautiful but vacuous woman's "knowledge of literary greats might leave something to be desired," she was suitably impressed by the interest of a world-famous novelist, and soon they were as "convivial as life-long friends."

Marx tried to persuade Wolfe to become a writer for M-G-M. No formal offer was made, but he was authorized to talk of a salary around fifty thousand dollars a year — more than Wolfe had earned from all his writing. Interested, Wolfe explained that he had no experience in writing screenplays, but Marx said that he would be assigned a collaborator, someone that he approved, who would teach him. Wolfe thought about the proposition overnight. He was not snobbish about movies, and he had no qualms that he would be prostituting his talent by "allowing anything I'd written to be bought in Hollywood, made into a moving picture by Hollywood." But he knew that he could not function as part of a closely knit team of writers, adapters, directors, and producers, and gently he declined Marx's proposal, saying that "he had a lot of writing to do and didn't want the job."

From Los Angeles Wolfe went to Palo Alto, to visit Dr. Russel V. Lee, with whom he had become friends on the *Bremen* returning from Europe. He much impressed the Lees' cook, "because he was able to [eat] 12 eggs, 1 1/2 qts. of milk, and a loaf of bread for breakfast and later in the day consumed a whole leg of lamb for dinner." Dr. Lee took Wolfe to see the giant redwood trees in the Sequoia National Park. Finding them "the most satisfactory thing he had ever seen in nature," he stood in rapt admiration for an hour and, for once in his life, was utterly silent.

Then came a few days in San Francisco, where he met up again with Robert Penn Warren. They wandered about the streets at night, and Wolfe was especially delighted by the sights and smells of Chinatown. Both were nonstop talkers, and they "wrangled back and forth" about the South and about literature, finding themselves, as Warren remembered, in "not unfriendly disagreement." Pressed by Perkins to return to work, Wolfe headed East by way of Reno, where he inspected the gambling palaces and sporting houses, and Salt Lake City, where he paused just long enough to get a permit to purchase liquor in Utah.

On his way back he stopped, as he had planned to do from the beginning of his trip, at St. Louis, to visit the house where the Wolfe family had lived in 1904 during the St. Louis Exposition and where Grover Wolfe had died. A St. Louis reporter who interviewed him was overwhelmed by the size of this "astonishingly big fellow," noting: "To talk with him while he stands beside one is decidedly uncomfortable, he dwarfs his companion so completely." The newspaperman found that Wolfe was eager to talk about everything: about the room where his brother had died (the details of which he stored in his memory, to be reproduced with absolute fidelity in his story "The Lost Boy"); about his writing and his plans; about his love for America. "He seems uncomfortable if he is not talking when in the presence of others," the reporter noted. "Words stream from him as though he were impatient of having to use them to transmit his thought. He stutters a bit in the urgency to say a lot quickly. . . . He never speaks in a didactic manner. He makes no pretensions to great wisdom. He is simply without inhibitions."

IV

Before Wolfe left on his Western trip he promised to return with renewed strength and energy, "ready to work this coming year as I have never worked before." But after he got back to New York in September he discovered that it was not easy to get back to his writing, and he was distracted by small but pressing problems. "My life is nothing without work, and yet I do everything in the world to avoid it — that is, before I get started."

First he had to find a place to live. He had had his fill of Brooklyn and was determined to find an apartment in Manhattan with a view of the river. Accompanied by Mrs. Jelliffe, he tramped up and down the East Side looking at apartments, but everything they saw was too expensive. "Only the rich can see the river, I see!" he grumbled, protruding his lower lip in a habitual gesture. "Well, I'm poor and I damned well will see the river!" Finally they located a place at 865 First Avenue — across from where the United Nations Building now stands. It cost eighty dollars a month, which he thought outrageously expensive, but it had a large bedroom, a living room, a kitchen, and a bathroom, and, best of all, from its windows he could watch the barges on the East River and could hear the hoarse warning signals of the tugs.

Then it had to be furnished. Mrs. Jelliffe and his other women friends vied in fitting out the new apartment. She brought out the broken-down furniture from his Brooklyn apartment, which she had stored for him. Aline Bernstein bought for him a specially made seven-foot bed, so that for the first time in his life he had a mattress long enough that he could stretch out fully. Mrs. Jelliffe noted that Aline had ordered it not merely long but wide, "perhaps with an eye to her own comfort." Mrs. Jelliffe urged him to buy venetian blinds for his windows, but Aline advised drapes made from material she had picked out, since "venetian blinds, under the most skillful pulling . . . always get out of order, and you know how ept your hands are at managing material things." Another female admirer sent him extra-large sheets, "of very fine linen, made in a French convent," and a huge handmade counterpane, which she was sure was "destined for nothing else but to be crumpled and twisted on Thomas Wolfe's seven-foot bed."

All this admiring attention Wolfe accepted complacently. He was surprised, though, when Mrs. Jelliffe told him that he had to pay her $8.74 for some ten-cent-store knives and forks she had bought for his apartment. "That's what you think!" he laughed. "Try and get it!" After Wolfe repeatedly refused to pay, Mrs. Jelliffe sent the bill to Charles Scribner's Sons, which issued her a check drawn against Wolfe's royalty account. Furious that a woman could get the best of him, Wolfe fumed: "You're like all the others: out to get all you can from a man, give nothing in return."

But even with all this assistance Wolfe's apartment remained sparsely furnished. It contained, as he said, "about three sticks of dilapidated furniture," and, like every other place that he lived, it looked like a place where he camped out, rather than resided.

Then there was the continuing distraction of Mrs. Boyd's suit, as lawyers on both sides endlessly demanded further statements and amplifications, copies of correspondence, and reports on royalty earnings. Wolfe thought the whole affair "outrageous," since in his view there was no ground for the suit at all: this "unscrupulous and dishonest person decided to sue me, make all the trouble she could for me, and worry, threaten, and torment me into making a settlement." His lawyers thought he would probably win if the case went to trial, but they warned that juries were unpredictable, especially where a woman plaintiff was involved. The suit dragged on until May 1936, when Mrs. Boyd's attorney reduced her claim from $10,000 to $1,876 and Wolfe's lawyers advised an out-of-court settlement. After consulting with Perkins, Wolfe himself came up with a final offer of $500, accompanied by an agreement that Mrs. Boyd was to continue receiving her commission on sales of *Look Homeward, Angel* but not on his other books if she pledged not to "make any utterances derogatory to the character or reputation" of the author. At a final meeting of the parties to the suit Mrs. Boyd's lawyer made a special plea for an additonal $150, on the grounds that she was nearly destitute. Perkins told Wolfe that "he ought to do the generous thing," and he did.

After the case was settled, Wolfe realized how much it had cost him not just in money but in "time and worry and trouble when I should be at work." He reported to his mother that he had, for the first time, discovered gray hairs in his head. And he considered Perkins responsible for the whole affair — not merely for the additional payment to Mrs. Boyd at the end but for his failure to insist that Wolfe dismiss her as his agent back in 1932.

During all these distractions Wolfe was trying to revise a collection of his short stories, for which he had signed a contract with Charles Scribner's Sons before he left for Europe. While he was abroad Perkins had begun arranging and editing the stories, and he hoped for fall publication in order to capitalize on the success of *Of Time and the River*. He had a dummy volume, bearing simply the title "Stories," made up to show the Scribners sales and advertising force the size and appearance of the new book. But Wolfe, enjoying his triumph in Berlin, gave him no help and instead warned: "Please don't go too far with the stories before I get there. There are things I can do that will make them much better, and if you will only wait on me I will do them and we will have a fine book of stories and unlike any I know of." Though Wolfe told Martha Dodd after he returned to New York that the stories were "ready," he did no work on the new book before leaving for his Western journey.

Pressed to meet a fall publishing date, Perkins had some of the stories set up in proof and urged Wolfe to come back to give them a final reading. Instead, Wolfe wrote him a stiff warning, which showed how deeply he still resented the fact that *Of Time and the River* had been sent to the printer before he thought it was ready: "You must not put the manuscript of a book of stories in final form until after my return to New York. If that means the . . . stories will have to be deferred till next spring, then they will have to be deferred, but I will not consent this time to allow the book to be taken away from me and printed and published until I myself have had time . . . to talk to you about certain revisions, changes, excisions, or additions that ought to be made." Perhaps deliberately missing the point, Perkins replied that he could not understand why Wolfe thought so badly of his stories and, understanding how to flatter him, argued: "They show how objective you can be, and how varied you can be. . . . [This book of stories] would be an answer to what you have had in adverse criticism."

But Wolfe was not to be bought off by compliments. Convinced that "there is as good writing as I've done in some of the stories," he wanted to be sure that they were presented so as to give the best effect. He now had a title, *From Death to Morning,* which he believed should dictate the arrangement of the stories and give them "a kind of unity and . . . cumulative effect," progressing from "Death the Proud Brother," written in a minor key, to the life-affirming "The Web of Earth." He also began wondering whether the book should consist only of stories that he had already published. "There is so much more that I want . . . to do, include, write," he told Perkins. "There are at least half a dozen big stories I should have written and that should be included, and all sorts of minor things."

Very anxious, Perkins corrected the galley proofs of the stories and asked for revised proofs, but he could not proceed further until Wolfe got back to New York. Wolfe's idea of adding other stories, as yet unwritten, was sure to throw the book off schedule completely and to jeopardize the prospect of simultaneous publication in Great Britain by Heinemann. "I shall fight hard against this," Perkins wrote Frère-Reeves. But, he observed, Wolfe "seems to feel a certain shame at the idea of turning out a book of reasonable dimensions."

But for once Perkins's misgivings proved unwarranted. Wolfe returned from the West in high spirits, eager to move on to new projects. He sat down at once to read and correct the proofs, and he did some revision. Rereading the stories gave him an occasion to think seriously about the character of his writing. Along with much praise, the reviews of *Of Time and the River* had so regularly objected to his rhetorical profusion and his stylistic extravagance — to what Marjorie Kinnan Rawlings called his "chestbeating" — that he was forced to reconsider his literary strategy. "The criticisms he received," Perkins noted, "have evidently at last impressed him with the truth of what we have been telling him, and often with very great violence, for years." In his lecture at Boulder he admitted that his writing had "a quality of intemperate excess, uncontrolled inclusiveness, an almost insane hunger to devour the entire body of human experience, to attempt to include more, pile in more, experience more than the measure of one life can hold or than the limits of a single work of art can well define."

Now, going over the texts of stories written several years earlier, he readily identified the passages to which his critics most objected, and he was genuinely uncertain whether to let them stand. Humbly he asked John Hall Wheelock, whose judgment for language he trusted, about deleting his final lyrical apostrophe to Loneliness, Death, and Sleep from "Death the Proud Brother." "This is the kind of thing that some of the critics have gone gunning after me for," he reminded Wheelock, "but it is also the kind of thing that many people have liked in my writing, and that some say they hope I never lose." "It's a pretty serious matter to me," he added, "because if it really is better that I cut out this *kind* of writing entirely, . . . I must seriously change my whole methods and style everywhere."

Perhaps Wheelock convinced him of the merits of this particular passage, or perhaps he suggested that he ought not tamper with a story already published, and the apostrophe remained in *From Death to Morning*. But the question Wolfe raised was not a casual one. In his subsequent writing he rarely included what Perkins termed "dithyrambs." Partly the result of criticism, his change in style was also a consequence of growing older; he found the poetic mood — often the product of what he called his "squeal" of rhapsodic joy — harder to sustain. Partly, too, the shift occurred because Wolfe, after his return to New York, dictated much of his fiction to a secretary, rather than writing it out in longhand, and he found it harder to create a cloud of language when a young woman was waiting to type out every word he uttered. As a result, in most of his writing after 1936 Wolfe used shorter, more direct sentences, made fewer literary and mythological references, and increasingly relied on satire as his principal literary device. *From Death to Morning*, then, was the last book he wrote in his "opulent manner."

XI

Almost Every Kind of Worry

WOLFE HAD A HARD TIME settling on a new book. When he left for Europe, he assumed that his next novel would be "The October Fair." This was the second half of his gigantic "Time and the River" manuscript, which dealt with the adventures of Eugene Gant between 1925 and 1928 — from Thomas Wolfe's first encounter with Aline Bernstein to the Munich beer hall fight. While he was in Europe he did not do much serious work on it, but he jotted down lists of characters, including some new figures who would have to be worked into the story. He predicted that "The October Fair" was going to be "far and away the best book I have written." Now that he had broken through the psychological barrier of publishing a second novel, he was sure that he could make rapid progress on a third one. "I'm going to hit this next book like a locomotive," he promised, "and I know I can ten times surpass all that I have done before."

At the same time, though, his mind was turning to another volume in the Gant cycle, "The Hills Beyond Pentland," which would deal with the ancestors and relatives of Eugene Gant from 1838 to 1926. For this book, he told Martha Dodd, he was "saving the best of everything I have in me." Since it would overlap both *Look Homeward, Angel* and *Of Time and the River,* it would give him an opportunity to work in a good many segments deleted from the manuscripts of those two novels. It was to consist of a fugue of memories, starting with Eugene Gant's scattered and feverish recollections of childhood as he lay on his hospital bed in Munich. Clearly much influenced by Marcel Proust's *Remembrance of Things Past,* Wolfe wanted to construct an elaborate counterpoint, with Eugene weaving together past and present in a triumph over time. In one version (later rather inappropriately used to preface *The Web and the Rock*), his narrator explained Wolfe's purpose: "Could I make tongue to say more than tongue could utter! . . . Could I weave into immortal denseness some small brede of words, pluck out of sunken depths the roots of living, . . . and hurl the sum of all my living out upon three hundred pages — then death could take my life, for I had lived it ere he took it: I had slain hunger, beaten death!"

But on his Western trip Wolfe had begun thinking about still a third book. As a man who kept late hours and roamed the streets at night, he had for years been fascinated by his discovery that "Americans are a night-time people," that a "chemistry of darkness" made life in America after dark very different from daytime life. He had long planned to make literary use of this difference, and, indeed, some of his best short stories, like "Only the Dead Know Brooklyn," had night settings. Originally he thought of writing "The Book of the Night" as a kind of grand prelude to "The Hills Beyond Pentland." But his friends were so fascinated by his descriptions of America after darkness fell that he began to think of writing "a great and original book" about the night, to be called "The Hound of Darkness." It would, he was confident, be in a great literary tradition, since "all American writing of the first rank has in it a quality of darkness and of night — I mention Poe, Hawthorne, Melville, Whitman (most decidedly), Mark Twain, and Sherwood Anderson."

When Wolfe returned to New York, he worked intermittently on all three of these projects, even while he was correcting the proofs of *From Death to Morning,* but increasingly "The Hound of Darkness" absorbed his energies. In this book he wanted to recapture all the diversity of life in America on a single night — sometimes he chose June 18, 1913, more often July 18, 1916, in order to include scenes related to the First World War.

His approach was cinematic. Wolfe belonged to the first gen-

eration of novelists to reach maturity after the development of
motion pictures, and he had been going to movies all his life. With
his father he had watched silent films in Asheville, and when he
was at Harvard he saw more, even though he sometimes professed
to be bored by their "banal sentimentality." When he moved to
New York, he made a habit of dropping in the newsreel theater on
Times Square, where he was fascinated by the juxtaposition of
film clips that showed what was happening in many parts of the
world at the same time. Often he went to regular movies with
John Terry, and he especially admired the acting of Leslie Howard,
Bette Davis, and Claudette Colbert. Wolfe had no understanding
of filmmaking or of film theory. When he saw Sergei Eisenstein's
Battleship Potemkin (1925), his only comment was: "Exciting picture — dull ending." But necessarily his thinking — like that of
such contemporaries as Joyce, Virginia Woolf, and John Dos
Passos — was influenced by the techniques of the cinema. Contrast editing, the intercutting of scenes from different narrative
lines, which began with such movies as D. W. Griffith's *The Birth
of a Nation,* made it possible for a filmmaker to tell more than one
story at a time, in a much more dynamic fashion than could the
narrator of a novel. Indeed, as some early film theorists claimed,
the cinema gave the viewer a "prodigious sense of simultaneity
and omnipresence." This was precisely the effect that Wolfe, restive under the constraints of a straightforward chronological narrative, hoped to achieve.

"The Hound of Darkness" would, then, begin with the omniscient eye of the camera-narrator zooming in ever more closely on
the earth, as it lay under "the still white radiance of the blazing
moon." Glimpsing first "the planetary distance of the continent"
of North America, it caught "the huge wink of the all-surrounding
seas." From the Eastern seaboard the camera panned ever farther
west, to the great central valley where the Mississippi and Mis-
souri rivers "burn like strings of steady silver in unchanging time,"
on to the "abrupt and basal ramparts of the Rocky mountains,"
which Wolfe had just visited, dipped through the High Sierra, on
to "the slopes of many vistaed California."

Initially all was silent save for a "vast, low and murmurous . . .
sigh" from the surrounding seas. But as the camera came in ever
closer there were the sounds of America at night, beginning with
the chucka-lucka, chucka-lucka of the great transcontinental train,

the Pacific Nine, "stroking the night with the pistoned velocity of its full speed," interrupting its beat only to hoot: "Ho-Idaho! Ho-Idaho-ho-ho-ho." Then followed the sound of the corn blades, very softly rustling in the wind: "Ah coarse and cool, ah coarse and cool, America."

"Who are you who keep silence in these watches of deep night?" then asks a listener, a boy. "Is it a lion in the mouth sulfurous, a fox in the eye humorous, a cat in the paw felonious, that prowls and breathes and stirs round night's great wall forever, and that will not let us sleep?"

To him the Hound of Darkness replies: "I am the beast that comes. . . . I'll show him rivers . . . — I'll give him plains for his hill-born heart . . . I'll give him his nation — part by part."

After this prologue followed scene after scene of unrelated episodes, linked only by the fact that they all occurred on the same night. One of the longest was "The House at Malbourne," which was obviously Elizabeth Lemmon's slightly disguised Virginia home, Wellbourne. Miss Lemmon appeared as "Margaret Latimer," and her visitor was Wolfe's first fictional characterization of Maxwell Perkins as "Foxhall Edwards," at this time still "a young man, a little past his thirtieth year, already a little deaf, holding his head a little to one side as he listens," with a face as innocent as a child's but also "as shrewd and subtle as a fox — strange mixture of gentleness and granite." In other scenes two drunken Mexicans emerged from the car they had wrecked near Santa Fe; the whores on Eagle Crescent in Asheville called softly to their clients; Mr. Saltonstall at his home on Louisburg Square read approvingly a denunciation of modern literature in the *Boston Evening Transcript*.

Some scenes for "The Hound of Darkness" Wolfe worked out in great detail, revising and rewriting them carefully; others he briefly sketched or simply named. He intended — if Perkins would let him — to use rougher language and to be more sexually explicit than in any of his previous writing. In one scene sailors passing through the tunnel under the Hudson River cried out: "Hey-y, Jack! . . . Let's start a fuckin' war against the Jews!" In a New Orleans scene a Negro boy shining shoes told a friend how "Mistah John says he slipped that ole French Tickler awn and when . . . he . . . shove it to huh . . . he say dat woman — hee-ee-ee! — he say dat woman — she mighty nigh went crazy."

In all he completed about half the planned scenes, in a manuscript that ran to about 100,000 words.

I

Though Wolfe was now back in New York and was in and out of the Scribners offices almost every day, he received no word of encouragement from Perkins about these three projected new books and no offer of a contract on any one of them. In part this silence was a reflection of company policy. A distinguished, conservative firm, Charles Scribner's Sons did not customarily offer a contract for a proposed book unless the author needed an advance against royalties. Since it was clear that Wolfe, with his accumulated earnings from *Of Time and the River,* was not in need, nobody at Scribners thought of giving him one.

Then, too, since Wolfe and Perkins were such close friends, no further formal arrangements between author and publisher seemed called for. Now that Wolfe was living on First Avenue, only two blocks away from the Perkins house, he was practically a member of his family. Initially, Louise Perkins was pleased to see Wolfe at all hours. She exchanged news and gossip with him and shared his love for outrageous puns: "What does the woman do who puts up apple sauce?" "Kansas." "What did the colored man say when he applied for a job?" "Arkansas (Ah can saw)." The Perkins daughters were less enthusiastic. They found Wolfe's size offputting, and they complained that his skin was very pale and unhealthy looking, his lower lip was often thrust out so far that it covered the upper one, and his hands were "really huge, very broad and heavy," and "felt so soft and clammy." But Perkins, who never paid much attention to the opinions of females anyway, was delighted that Wolfe visited almost every day.

Wolfe assumed that Perkins would guide the writing of his new book just as he had supervised the completion of *Look Homeward, Angel* and *Of Time and the River.* All his life he had turned to older figures — Mrs. Roberts, Horace Williams, George P. Baker, Aline Bernstein — for direction, and he now looked to Perkins for encouragement, love, and praise. Elizabeth Nowell called him "fanatically biased" toward Perkins, and in his lecture at Boulder he actually referred to his work with his editor as a "collaboration," as if he and Perkins were partners. Ready to get on with a new book, he asked the editor: "What are we to work on next . . . ? When do you want to publish next, and when do we begin to work again?"

He got no answers. As Wolfe complained later, Perkins showed "no anxiety whatever and . . . no immediate interest in his writing plans," and he manifested no enthusiasm for any of the three books that Wolfe projected. He actively disliked "The October Fair" manuscript. When Wolfe suggested pushing ahead to complete "The October Fair," Perkins told him "that it would be inadvisable to publish it without certain formidable deletions, or that perhaps we'd better wait a few years longer and see 'how everything works out.' " They stalled around until, as Wolfe said, "all the intensity and passion I had put into the book was lost, until I had gone stale on it, until I was no longer interested in it."

About "The Hills Beyond Pentland" Perkins had fewer reservations, though a great deal of it seemed to be a reworking of material already published in *Look Homeward, Angel.* In "The Hound of Darkness" project the editor took no interest. Now in his fifties, Perkins was visibly aging. His literary judgments, like his political opinions, were becoming increasingly conservative, and he saw no merit in Wolfe's attempt to write a cinematic novel. So far as he could tell, "The Hound of Darkness" had no structure and no plot. It was not in any conventional sense a novel, and it probably had no market. He maintained such a chilling silence about it that Wolfe abandoned the project. Only a fragment of it was published during his lifetime, under the title "A Prologue to America," in *Vogue,* which Wolfe derided as "the ladies' corset and hosiery encyclopedia."

II

By the middle of November 1935, Wolfe's interest began to shift from creation to criticism. *From Death to Morning,* published on November 14, got a chilly reception. Clayton Hoagland gave it an affectionate notice in the *New York Sun,* and a good many reviewers agreed with Herschell Brickell in the *New York Evening Post* that Wolfe was perhaps "the most important writer of fiction in this country." But nobody noted that the fourteen stories were thematically connected, each recounting a passing encounter between residents of two different worlds, who met, briefly shared an experience, and then parted to allow, as Wolfe expressed it, "each one [to] go alone to his appointed destination." Few reviewers paid attention to "The Web of Earth," which Wolfe and Perkins thought his best constructed and most carefully written story. Instead, they complained of Wolfe's gigantism and his verbal extravagance. In the *New Yorker* Clifton Fadiman lamented Wolfe's "incredibly tumescent language, piled on until the reader wearies under the load of it and gropes feebly for Mr. Hemingway, or anyone else who loves English wisely but not too well." "The total effect," Howard Mumford Jones agreed in the *Saturday Review*, "is to make one uneasy about Mr. Wolfe's future development as an artist." *From Death to Morning* sold only 5,392 copies during its first year in print.

"I will take a pounding on this book," Wolfe predicted, even before *From Death to Morning* was officially published, and he attributed the negative tone of the reviews to "the well-known 'reaction'" against his success in *Of Time and the River*. But believing that "as good writing as I have ever done is in this book," he decided to go on the offensive. In order to explain his purpose as an artist and his method as a writer, he turned back to the idea of publishing the talk he had given at Boulder.

Very proud of that lecture, both as a defense of his special approach to the writing of fiction and as an expression of his gratitude of Perkins, Wolfe on one level truly did want it published. At the same time, though, he obviously had unconscious reservations about it. Before he left on his Western trip he had asked Miss Nowell to edit his manuscript and find a magazine that would pay for it. After she drastically cut what he had given her and persuaded the *Atlantic Monthly* to accept it, Wolfe informed her that he had forgotten to give her the final half of his manuscript. Gallantly she cut that down to size and offered the *Atlantic* the two segments for the price agreed on for the first, but the editors found it too long to use. For some weeks Wolfe carried the edited manuscript around in his pocket — "like a baby kangaroo," Miss Nowell said. Once he left it in a bar where he and Perkins were having drinks. Another time it fell out of his pocket into the gutter at Broadway and 125th Street, where it remained, miraculously untouched, until an hour later when he missed it.

Eventually Henry Seidel Canby, the editor of the *Saturday Review of Literature,* accepted the revised lecture. It still did not have a title, but George Stevens, who had known Wolfe at Harvard and in Paris and who now worked for the *Saturday Review,* suggested calling it "The Story of a Novel." Under that title it appeared in three December issues of that weekly magazine.

Wolfe next wanted this defense of his approach to fiction to appear in a more permanent form, and he negotiated with Scribners for book publication of *The Story of a Novel.* In revising his manuscript for Scribners he mostly stayed with Miss Nowell's trimmed-down version of his lecture, so that this little book of 93 pages was the most colloquial and accessible that Wolfe ever wrote. But he also inserted a good many details about his method of writing, and he worked in, from passages deleted from the "Time and the River" manuscript, a hallucinatory dream sequence on Time and Guilt, which became the climax of the revised autobiography. The result was a deliberate heightening of effect, so that what started as a simple narrative became a contribution to confessional literature, resembling in tone and in structure Thomas De Quincey's *Confessions of an English Opium-Eater. The Story of a Novel* was published on April 21, 1936.

Wolfe's real purpose in publishing *The Story of a Novel* was to define his place in a literary landscape in which he felt increasingly isolated. He had few friends in the literary world. Despite Perkins's efforts, he and Hemingway did not take to each other. He kept up a distant acquaintance with F. Scott Fitzgerald out of respect for Perkins — "our common parent, Max," as Fitzgerald called him. It is not clear that Wolfe ever met John O'Hara, though he thought he was "a nasty writer" — as were Hemingway and Fitzgerald. He did not know Conrad Aiken or John Steinbeck; he had hearty contempt for Thornton Wilder; and he encountered William Carlos Williams only once.

Shortly after Wolfe came back from his Western trip he met John Dos Passos for the first time, at a dinner party given by the Perkinses. The two men got along amiably enough, and after dinner they took a walk and had coffee together. But they shared few interests, and Dos Passos felt that spending an evening with Wolfe was like "being with a gigantic baby." They never saw each other again.

Wolfe was also introduced to William Faulkner in the fall of 1935. Except for their general interest in Southern literature, the voluble, disheveled Wolfe and the dapper, courtly Faulkner had little in common. At this time Faulkner was much impressed by Wolfe's attempt to create a fictional world as distinctive as

Yoknapatawpha County but much broader in its expanse. Later, when asked to name the five most important contemporary American writers, he always put Wolfe at the head of his list, followed, usually, by himself, Dos Passos, Hemingway, and Erskine Caldwell, Willa Cather, or John Steinbeck. He defended his ranking on the grounds that Wolfe "tried to do the greatest of the impossible . . . to reduce all human experience to literature," even though he conceded that in the end Wolfe's effort "to put the whole history of the human heart on the head of the pin" was a "splendid magnificent bust." When Hemingway and other writers to whom he gave a lower rating complained, Faulkner regretted that he had ever offered such a list, and he began to backtrack. "To tell the truth," he said to one class at the University of Virginia, "I haven't read much of Wolfe." Another time he called Wolfe's books absurd: "it's like an elephant trying to do the hoochie-coochie."

Wolfe's enthusiasm for Faulkner was never more than lukewarm. He had read *Sanctuary, The Sound and the Fury,* and *As I Lay Dying* when they were published and concluded that Faulkner was a creator "of Pop-eye horrors, pederasts, [and] macabre distortions." After he met the Mississippi author he was willing to recognize Faulkner's "imaginative and inventive power," but he hoped that in the future he would write about more normal characters and situations, since he was obviously "a man with too extensive knowledge to deal merely with the horrible and the demented and the macabre types of life." Willingly he granted Faulkner a significant place in Southern literature, since "what he writes is not like the South, but . . . the South is *in* his books, and in the spirit that creates them." But not long afterwards, when a Faulkner enthusiast asked his opinion of the novels, Wolfe, to avoid controversy, said blandly that he had been too busy to read them. The two men met only once.

III

During the winter of 1935–1936 Wolfe felt not merely alone but under attack. The laudatory newspaper and magazine reviews of *Of Time and the River* were succeeded by sharply critical assessments in the literary quarterlies. In December, an informal and statistically meaningless poll reported in the *Saturday Review* accurately assessed Wolfe's standing: *Of Time and the River* received the most votes both for the best novel published in 1935 and for the worst novel of the year.

Some critics objected to Wolfe's treatment of Negroes, who, in fact, played a very small part in his fiction. Few of the named characters in either *Look Homeward, Angel* or *Of Time and the River* were black, and none played any significant role in either book. They were figures like Myrtis, a "little nigger servant girl," "the nigger Jacken, the fruit and vegetable man," and May (or Ella) Corpening, the Negro prostitute. In "The Face of the War," included in *From Death to Morning,* Wolfe gave a somewhat fuller account of a Negro regiment from Texas, halted at the point of embarkation at Newport News: "Cavorting with glee, their black faces split by enormous ivory grins," they gathered around their white officer, "like frantic children," patting his shoulders "with their great black paws."

Wolfe was not conscious of any prejudice, and he thought he was simply describing Negroes as they were. Indeed, had his books been published ten or fifteen years earlier, perhaps only the spokesmen for the National Association for the Advancement of Colored People would have criticized his characterizations. But because of the growing activism among blacks during the New Deal and the increasing general sensitivity toward human rights, a number of critics felt that Wolfe was contemptuous of Negroes and that the blacks who did appear in his books "hardly qualify as human beings." The charge baffled Wolfe. Equally incomprehensible to him was John Chamberlain's comment, in the *New York Times,* that "The Face of the War" presented none of the black soldiers as strongly marked individuals. Fuming, Wolfe admitted that he had not mentioned Booker T. Washington, Joe Louis, or W. E. B. Du Bois (about whom he was so ill informed that he called him "W. T. DuBose"), and he added that he had "also failed to say anything about Leonardo da Vinci, Michelangelo and the Queen of Sheba."

More troubling was the charge that he was anti-Semitic. Many readers objected to his treatment of Jewish characters in *Of Time and the River*. When Eugene Gant began teaching in New York City, he felt that he had plunged into a world overrun by Jews. His students had "Yiddish" faces, they were "beak-nosed," and they engaged in "Kike" laughter.

In the mid-1930s, such characterizations were bound to evoke protests. American Jews were better organized and more articulate than they had ever been before, and they were fearful that social or literary anti-Semitism could lead to the horrors taking place in Hitler's Germany. From Philadelphia, Simon Pearl wrote to Charles Scribner's Sons, objecting to Wolfe's "hymm of hate directed against an oppressed minority" and asking why a distinguished publishing house lent its name to "an anti-semitic treatise in the name of art and good literature." Others wrote to Wolfe himself. Harold Calo, a member of Wolfe's first class at New York University, reported that his friends were condemning Wolfe for "intolerance and anti-semitism." A Princeton correspondent found that Wolfe's novel "fairly reeks of the narrow-mindedness engendered in anti-Semitism." "Did you ever meet any Jew who was not swarthy, smelly, and horrible?" asked an anonymous writer, who suggested that Wolfe's novel should be retitled *Of Time and the Sewer*. "I take it you are a German. You should wear a brown shirt, and live in Germany. What a pal for Herr Hitler!"

Deeply hurt, Wolfe replied that the charge of anti-Semitism was "absolutely groundless." He asked Calo "to consider fairly whether you ever saw or heard me do anything [at New York University] that was unfair, intolerant, or unjust to any member of your faith," and he added the conventional cliché: "some of the best and most valued friends I have ever had here in New York have been Jews." Perkins also told Simon Pearl that Wolfe had "no anti-Semitic leanings" and that "he numbers Jews among his best friends." The editor pointed out that Wolfe was equally harsh in his descriptions of other American ethnic groups, particularly the Irish.

These were, at best, partial answers to an embarrassing question. Wolfe was, in fact, anti-Semitic. As a child he was brought up to deride and torment the few Jewish families in Asheville. At the same time he, like all the other members of his family, feared them. "In our small towns," he wrote, "we see our small tradesmen steadily driven to the wall, outwitted and outreached on every side by their Jewish competitor." In Cambridge and Boston he for the first time encountered a considerable number of Jews, and he disliked them. They were, he thought, materialistic, avaricious, money-grubbing — and, worst of all, successful. The chief tenet of the Jewish faith, he observed, was "keeping an eye on the main chance — a regulation the Jew observes with an iron pertinacity." A dramatic skit that he wrote at this time began: "Enter two Jews, arm in arm, gesticulating and exhorting each other loudly. Each bears a money bag in his free hand." They say to each other: "To de bank, to de bank, to de bank."

His move to New York reinforced his prejudices. He came to believe that Jews controlled the world of the theater, where Jewish producers catered to the demands of predominantly Jewish audiences for "the sensual, the thinly veiled, or the materialistic." Aline Bernstein was, of course, Jewish, and every quarrel with her reinforced his belief that Jews were treacherous, conniving, money-loving, and ostentatious.

But Wolfe usually tried to conceal his anti-Semitism. When he was growing up in the South he was taught that being a Jew was an unfortunate but ineradicable handicap and of course no gentleman would publicly refer to this deformity. What he said in his private letters or recorded in his pocket notebook was another matter — as were his virulently anti-Semitic outbursts when he was in his cups.

In his fiction, however, he intended to offer a portrait of America, and all his characters — except, perhaps, the immediate members of the Gant family — were not so much individuals as representative figures. Consequently he always took pains to identify the Jews in his stories by their ethnic or, as he thought of it, racial origins. In his own provincial way Wolfe thought that he was giving a balanced picture of Jewish life in America. Arrogance and aggressiveness, extravagance and sensuality were pairs of negative "racial" traits that he attributed to Jews in his fiction. But on the positive side he praised the "richness, color, and humor" of Jewish life, along with high intellectual achievement and love for rich foods, sumptuous clothing, and passionate sexual enjoyment, which made them "the most lavish and opulent race on earth." Since that balance was so much more flattering than his own personal assessment of Jews, he was both angered and baffled by critics who found his novels anti-Semitic.

Wolfe had anticipated the attacks of Marxist critics, who complained that his fiction lacked social significance. He was not particularly surprised when *Partisan Review* treated the novel as an account of Eugene Gant's repeatedly unsuccessful attempts to ingratiate himself with the rich rulers of the country and warned that if the author wanted "to find the strength that will give him certitude," he "must stay with the masses who gave birth to him and fed him and not seek to escape into a corrupt and alien atmosphere." More wounding was Edwin Berry Burgum's denunciation of *Of Time and the River* as an example of the worst in bourgeois novels. The New York University professor argued that Wolfe's idealistic or Nietzschean distortion of contemporary society was a preface to the rise of fascism.

Though Wolfe expected such criticism, he never fully understood it. He never read Marx, and since escaping the influence of Horace Williams he was uninterested in philosophy. "At twenty or twenty-one," he told a reporter, "I thought I was as sharp as hell, could absorb whole philosophies and economic doctrines one right after the other. But now," he admitted, "things go banging off about my head, and as far as these ideas have any value they have got to come through the slow process of growth." But he did not see how the Marxist critics could attack him as "a member of the bourgeois class in society and an upholder of the capitalistic system," since, he proudly and repeatedly announced, he came of working-class stock: "My father was a stone-cutter, his father before him was a farm laborer." With such roots, Wolfe was confident that he understood "our fellow workers" far better than those "great-hearted liberals" who were damning him as "a misbegotten Byronic son-of-a-bitch."

Wolfe exaggerated both the amount and the importance of Marxist criticism, but characteristically he tried to deflect these attacks by being charming and friendly to his critics. He assiduously courted Kyle Crichton of Scribners, who regularly wrote under the pseudonym "Robert Forsythe" in *New Masses,* and he allowed Crichton to persuade him to "keep writing the way he was and keep learning." Deliberately he cultivated the ebullient Marxist editor of the *Modern Monthly,* V. F. ("George") Calverton, who was a "notable contactman" for literary men of the Left. His plan paid off when Calverton reviewed *Of Time and the River* as the work of a "prose Walt Whitman," who "may become the greatest novelist in our literature."

But Wolfe found ingratiating himself with the literary Left both time-consuming and exasperating. Calverton, who was constantly trying to raise money for his magazine, planned a public dinner to celebrate the twelfth anniversary of the *Modern Monthly* in April

1936 and persuaded Wolfe to say that he would attend. Thinking that he had promised to speak at the dinner, Calverton printed advertisements listing him, along with Reinhold Niebuhr and George S. Counts, of Teachers College, as giving an address. Wolfe tried to get out of the engagement, but Calverton insisted and appealed to him "on the basis of cooperation with the radical movement." Reluctantly he did attend and made a pleasant after-dinner talk, praising the "very vital and valuable function" performed by the *Modern Monthly*. Afterwards, feeling that the price of this friendship was too high, he saw no more of Calverton.

IV

Feeling beset on the Left, Wolfe knew that he was also under attack from the Right, particularly from the Southern literary regionalists. Originally a small group of poets connected with Vanderbilt University who published a little magazine called *The Fugitive,* these writers by the 1930s were concerned with social and economic, as well as literary, issues. Their manifesto, *I'll Take My Stand: The South and the Agrarian Tradition,* appeared in 1930, just after the great stock market crash. In it, twelve Southerners — who included John Crowe Ransom, John Donald Wade, Donald Davidson, Allen Tate, Stark Young, and Robert Penn Warren — announced that they were defending "a Southern way of life against what may be called the American or prevailing way."

A curiously ambivalent relationship grew up between these Agrarians and Wolfe. Hoping for the emergence of a powerful and distinctive Southern literature, they had to recognize Wolfe as an important figure. In the early 1930s, after all, there were few other major Southern writers to whom they could point with pride: Ellen Glasgow insisted on shocking Virginians by saying unpleasant things about their ancestors; James Branch Cabell wrote naughty books; and William Faulkner seemed obsessed with gothic horrors. The Agrarians also sensed that Wolfe was in some ways a kindred spirit: he shared their recognition of the distinctiveness of Southern life, and he was as critical as they were of "progress" and of the New South ideology, which was intended to make the South resemble the North. Consequently they made an effort to link Wolfe, however loosely, to their movement. In 1935 when Robert Penn Warren joined Cleanth Brooks in starting the *South-*

ern Review at Louisiana State University, he promptly asked Wolfe to contribute a story to the first issue. Two years later, when Ransom was organizing a Vanderbilt Writers' Conference, he begged Wolfe to attend, assuring him that the conference would be twice as successful if he was present.

Wolfe had cautiously flirted with Southern literary regionalism as early as 1931, when Ellen Glasgow invited him to help organize and to attend a conference on "The Southern Writer and His Public" at the University of Virginia. He did not, in fact, go to that conference, and any plans he may have made for attending the one in Nashville were canceled when Ransom left Vanderbilt for Kenyon College. Warren's invitation to write for the *Southern Review* arrived while Wolfe was in Europe, and he never lived up to his promise to go through his box of manuscripts to find something suitable for that journal.

Nevertheless he thought of himself as a Southern writer and he was flattered by these attentions. Presently he struck up with several of the Agrarians the kind of easygoing instant friendship that Southerners so readily form with each other. He got to know Warren in Boulder and in San Francisco. Shortly after Wolfe returned from the West he met Stark Young, the Mississippi-born drama critic and novelist, and they exchanged mutually admiring letters. But he did not meet the others in the Agrarian group until December 1936, when he passed through Richmond during a meeting of the Modern Language Association, with a program that Caroline Gordon (Mrs. Allen Tate) characterized as "all Fugitives except Mark Van Doren." Striding through the lobby of the Hotel Jefferson, with his overcoat in one hand and a bottle of whiskey in the other, Wolfe spied Warren, went over and clapped him on the back, and said that they should get together for a talk. Warren invited him up to his room, where Ransom, the Tates, the Cleanth Brookses, and one or two others had already gathered.

They spent a long evening talking about the South. Wolfe had such a good time that, as he said later, "I did almost everything except become a Southern Agrarian. I suppose I don't understand enough about that." Some of the Agrarians were much less enthusiastic. Caroline Gordon reported that Wolfe was "drunk and dumb and extremely amiable." When the talk turned to Faulkner, Wolfe solemnly assured his fellow-Southerners that the whorehouse scene in *Sanctuary* was not authentic, because "he had intimate acquaintance with whore houses in many places."

Though Wolfe got along well with the Agrarians personally, he received some hard critical blows from them, for they never felt he was really a member of their movement. Some, like Stark Young, thought that Wolfe was "scarcely Southern," since he came from "a German family from Pennsylvania transplanted to N.C. on the wrong side of the tracks." Other Agrarians conceded that Wolfe was indeed Southern but believed that he knew only Appalachia, not the lowland South or the plantation South. Donald Davidson as early as 1930, in reviewing *Look Homeward, Angel,* accused Wolfe of entertaining "a certain hatred and loathing for the South, perhaps all the more because he recognizes it as part of himself."

More fundamental were the Agrarians' objections to the formlessness and the absence of restraint in Wolfe's prose. From the beginning there was a strong classical streak in Agrarian thought — as opposed to Wolfe's nineteenth-century romanticism — and many of them by the mid-1930s were on their way to becoming New Critics, who applied fine-honed intelligence to aesthetic issues. This basic difference was behind Warren's objection to *Of Time and the River* as a "chaos that steams and bubbles in rhetoric and apocalyptic apostrophe, sometimes grand and sometimes febrile and empty; . . . a maelstrom, perhaps artificially generated at times . . . [with] the flotsam and jetsam and dead wood spewed up, iridescent or soggy as the case may be."

Warren, after his friendly encounters with Wolfe in the West, never repeated that attack, but the inaugural issue of his *Southern Review* carried, instead of the requested story by Wolfe, a sharply critical review of *Of Time and the River* by John Donald Wade, who censured Wolfe for his failure to recognize "a disparity between Northern ways and Southern ways" and to admit that, deep down, he was "a Catawba, mama-and-papa-saying, Presbyterian Southerner." In a subsequent issue R. P. Blackmur, who was not an Agrarian but shared the New Critics' concern for form, dismissed *From Death to Morning* because of its "positive and overwhelming" weaknesses, which stemmed from "the heresy of expressive form: the belief, held to exaggeration, that life best expresses itself in art by duplicating its own confusion in the transferred form of the *spectator's* emotion." The first issue of the *Kenyon Review,* which Ransom edited after his departure from Vanderbilt, carried a remarkably hostile essay by John Peale Bishop arguing that "The meaning of a novel should be in its structure. But in Wolfe's novel . . . it is impossible to discover any structure at all." Caroline Gordon dismissed Wolfe for his "lack of artistic intelligence," and Allen Tate said scornfully that Wolfe "did harm to the art of the novel" and "moral damage to his readers."

Such criticism from fellow-Southerners deeply hurt Wolfe. Never understanding that the Agrarians were not really advocating a restoration of the Old South but were voicing their concern over the impersonality of modern urban life, he told Van Wyck Brooks that they "were bent on reviving . . . the old regime and all that was fraudulent in it." "They pretended," he went on, "that the old regime had favoured art and literature, dreaming of an aristocratic South that, as everybody knew, had actually despised the artist and the writer." In time he came to think of Agrarianism as "a form of high-toned fascism." But not until the publication of *The Web and the Rock* was Wolfe's anger at these "lily-handed intellectuals" who argued "the merits of a return to 'an agrarian way of life' " fully expressed. In that novel he denounced these "refined young gentlemen of the New Confederacy," who, as he thought, had failed to achieve recognition in the North and "retired haughtily into the South, to the academic security of a teaching appointment at one of the universities, from which they could issue in quarterly installments very small and very precious magazines which celebrated the advantages of an agrarian society."

V

Even without close literary friends Wolfe was remarkably happy during the first few months after he moved into his apartment on First Avenue. He had a comfortable place to live, and he had enough money. He had close ties to a group of Southerners living in New York City, many of them graduates of the University of North Carolina. They all shared a liking for Southern recipes, like string beans seasoned with bacon, a fondness for gossip, and a nostalgia for the Tar Heel State. At the center of the group was John Terry, who was still teaching at New York University. Whenever Terry came to Wolfe's apartment there were all-night sessions of Southern talk and Chapel Hill reminiscences.

Shortly before Christmas, Wolfe decided to have a Southern

party in his apartment for his friends. He intended to purchase all the food, but he was delighted when the women in the group volunteered to supply the Southern dishes he liked best: fried chicken, rice, string beans, cabbage, biscuits. Laughing and exuberant, he tried to help heat up the food that they brought, but he got in everybody's way. Finally dinner was served on his battered old writing table and on adjacent bridge tables, and they ate from his miscellaneous nicked dishes with the ill-sorted ten-cent-store knives and forks and spoons. In the happy glow of friendship Wolfe announced that there was no cooking in the world like Southern cooking and that Shakespeare must have had North Carolinians in mind when he spoke of "this happy breed." At the end of the evening, in a moment of exhilaration, he seized a large pencil, stood up to his full height, and wrote in large letters on the ceiling of his living room: "A Happy Christmas to all my good friends, Tom Wolfe."

Belinda Jelliffe was an important member of this group, and, now that Wolfe had ended his affair with Aline Bernstein, it seemed for a time that he might form a new permanent relationship with her. The wife of a distinguished psychiatrist, who was many years older and was entirely permissive, Mrs. Jelliffe was, as Wolfe said, "a whole-souled kind of person, who will go the whole hog, as we say in the South, for anything she believes in." She believed in Wolfe. The author of an autobiography, which he brought to Perkins's attention and which Scribners published, she understood the problems and the needs of a writer. Because she had grown up in the Southern Appalachians, she was familiar with Wolfe's background and was cheerfully indifferent to his wild swings in mood and to his obsessive suspiciousness. Perhaps drawing on her husband's psychiatric expertise, she recognized that Julia Wolfe played a dominant, sometimes overpowering, role in shaping her son's life, and she knew that, in order to convince himself that he was independent, he had to quarrel with even those he loved best. She made no demands on Wolfe — but she did not allow him to trample on her.

In December Julia Wolfe came up to New York, and she took an instant dislike to Mrs. Jelliffe, who, she said, "married an old man for his money." "Why don't she let Tom alone?" she asked. "Why can't he find a woman, unmarried." Indeed, she found Mrs. Jelliffe so much of a threat that, in a remarkable concession, she

allowed that even "the Jew woman" (Mrs. Bernstein) was pref-
erable. But she warned that "one or the other will be his down-
fall, wreck him some how." After Julia left, Wolfe's affair with
Mrs. Jelliffe cooled.

From that time he was simply promiscuous — not, indeed, that
he had confined his sexual interests to Mrs. Jelliffe earlier. Now he
took advantage of every opportunity, usually with a total absence
of affection toward or even interest in his partner. He was entirely
capable of going to a party, singling out an attractive young
woman, taking her into the bedroom for sex — and then, an hour
or so later, catching a glimpse of her across the room, he might ask
"Who's she?" A great many women found Wolfe attractive. Nearly
six and a half feet tall, now weighing two hundred and fifty pounds,
he was more of a man than most of their acquaintances. Though
his hair was thinning on the top and he was becoming a bit jowly,
there was still something irresistible about him. Women were
fascinated by his face, so expressive that one friend believed he
could see ideas crossing Wolfe's mind like trains passing across the
continent. Many were enchanted by his torrent of utterly
unselfconscious talk, mostly about himself. Others welcomed his
advances because he was famous. And most, after they came to
know him intimately, would have agreed with one of his passing
loves that he was "intolerable and wonderful and talked like an
angel and was a real son-of-a-bitch."

Women who took their brief affairs with Wolfe seriously — and
there were several, nearly all older than Wolfe — went on a roller-
coaster ride of emotions. "Amanda" wrote him after their first
time in bed: "Last night was so divinely perfect, every minute of
it that when I think of it little shivers of excitement and pleasure
and tenderness run through me." Several other "late evenings"
followed, and Amanda found Wolfe's lovemaking "so kind and
gentle . . . so strong and *direct* and so thrillingly relentless." Then
the affair began to unravel. She received a phone call from a
woman, seemingly drunk or deranged, who threatened her life if
she came to Wolfe's apartment again. Finding the whole situation
too complicated to handle, she suggested that Wolfe "retire from
the scene of the action." Deeply injured — because he always
liked to break off these affairs himself — Wolfe called her repeatedly, and they began quarreling "like shyster lawyers in a court-
room." Finally Amanda decided to move, divorce her husband,

and go back to her former lover. Feeling betrayed and insulted, Wolfe began to broadcast his version of their affair "at length and in blood curdling detail." According to Amanda, he announced to all their friends that she was an absolute fool, who bored him to death; that they had had "only labial" intercourse; and that, by falsely accusing him, she had done "a thing for which any whore would get her throat cut."

These aimless sexual adventures reflected Wolfe's growing sense of unhappiness and disorientation during the winter of 1935–1936. Feeling under critical attack from all sides, and unable to get Perkins interested in any of the new books he proposed, he was idle much of the time and began drinking far too much again. Alcohol always made him quarrelsome, and it sometimes seemed that he was trying to pick a fight with everybody he knew.

One of his first victims was Aline Bernstein, whom he now saw infrequently. Ever since Madeleine Boyd had brought her suit against him, Wolfe was obsessed with the notion that other persons from his past, to whom he had incurred obligations, would now emerge and demand repayment. For no reason at all he became especially suspicious of Aline, who had indeed over the years given him several thousand dollars. Shortly after he returned from Europe, he came up with a plan to settle accounts with her by a cash payment, but she would not accept his money. Now he pressed her to make a written acknowledgment that his gift of the great ledgers in which *Look Homeward, Angel* was drafted canceled his debts to her. Puzzled, Aline could not quite get the point. The ledgers, she accurately reported to Perkins, had been "a gift of love and affection," not a payment of a debt, and she had no intention of selling them. But if Wolfe wanted a written acknowledgment that he had given them to her, she was prepared to sign it. "Being Tom's friend, or his mistress or lover, whatever one chooses to call it," she sighed, "is certainly no dull business."

But that was not enough for Wolfe. Nor was he satisfied when Aline wrote that she had destroyed all receipts and accounts of any money that she had given him, and he nagged Perkins to secure a formal release. Finally, on April 9, he created a scene in her apartment, accusing her of being "in a class of Mrs. Boyd" because she too intended to rob him. "I am so hurt that nothing can be worse," she wrote Perkins the next day when she sent him the note that Wolfe demanded: "I acknowledge the repayment of any money that I gave to Thomas Wolfe in the past, by my possession of the manuscript of Look Homeward Angel."

Wolfe even managed to pick a fight with Elizabeth Nowell, whom, in his less disturbed moods, he recognized as "far and away the best agent I ever knew, absolutely honest and reliable." She had been working indefatigably in his behalf, and during 1935 she placed no fewer than thirteen of his stories and shorter pieces in magazines that ranged from *Scribner's Magazine* to *Esquire, Cosmopolitan,* and the *New Yorker.* Every one of these had required an immense amount of detailed editing, and Miss Nowell had developed exceptional skill in cutting out repetitious words, superfluous phrases, and unnecessary paragraphs in order to reduce these stories to a length that magazines could publish. She negotiated the prices for these periodical pieces and saw that the publishers made prompt payment. She spent many hours late at night searching through Wolfe's huge crate of manuscripts for sections that, with suitable framing and editing, could be made into publishable stories. Sometimes she sat up until dawn typing drafts and revisions from Wolfe's dictation. Above and beyond these professional services she gave him assistance in personal problems. From time to time one of the women with whom he was sleeping would tell him that she was pregnant, and he would grow "wild with worry and the injustice of it." When he confided his anxiety to Miss Nowell, she briskly instructed him on the subject of contraception — about which he was apparently wholly ignorant — and told him that any woman who did not wear a diaphragm had nothing to blame except "just her own dumb luck." Fascinated but still not quite sure of his facts, Wolfe told the next woman who announced that she was expecting that he could not be bothered with such matters and suggested, "Why don't you telephone Miss Nowell: she's my agent; she takes care of everything for me."

But by early 1936 even Miss Nowell had had enough. During the previous months she spent an extraordinary amount of time piecing together the several parcels of manuscript that went to make up "The Story of a Novel" and then whittling it down to a publishable length. She did not object to this labor, even though her earnings for a full week of work on the manuscript were only fifteen dollars — ten percent of the one hundred and fifty dollars that the *Saturday Review* paid Wolfe. Then Charles Scribner's Sons decided to publish *The Story of a Novel* as a book, and, since she was Wolfe's agent only for short stories and periodical articles, she would receive no commission on its earnings. Her sense of injustice boiled over, and she told Wolfe that she deserved a percentage of the royalties from the book too.

Angrily Wolfe told her that she was "a leech sucking unearned commissions," that she was "no damn good and a parasite . . . and a money-grubbing jew," and he turned her down.

Very upset, she wrote out a long account of all that she had done to make "The Story of a Novel" publishable, adding, accurately, that "the book would have remained one of those things you were going to do some day or that Perkins didn't have time to work on unless I'd salvaged it and cut it and sold it." "I dont care so much about the money even though I do think it's only fair," she concluded, "and if you still think I'm a blood-sucker after reading this . . . all right, I wont take the money."

Grudgingly, Wolfe gave in and assigned ten percent of his royalties on *The Story of a Novel* to her. The whole quarrel was over an insignificant sum: during the first two years after publication *The Story of a Novel* earned only $534.95 for the author, and he had risked losing his literary agent over a commission of $53.50.

More serious were the consequences of another quarrel in which Wolfe became embroiled during the winter of 1935–1936. This one had its origin back in February 1935, when Wolfe and Terry went out to have dinner with Mrs. Dooher, Kitty Hoagland's mother, who was at the time living in Bayside, Long Island. Wolfe was in high spirits because his book, after so many years of doubt and struggle, was about to be published. Indeed, he brought along his own copy, the first off the press, of *Of Time and the River,* in which he had begun to make marginal notes and corrections, and, in his exuberant mood, he promised to give it to Mrs. Dooher.

At this time he first met her son, Muredach (or, as it was sometimes anglicized, "Murdoch"), a stockily built young man of twenty-two, with remarkably luminous eyes. Young Dooher had a deep love for literature, especially for English poetry, and he hoped some day to become an editor of a literary journal. But times were hard, and he made his living by searching for rare and out-of-print books. At the same time he began building a valuable collection of literary autographs.

At dinner Dooher began talking about his work, and afterwards he brought out a few items from his collection — notably, a poem in A. E. Housman's own handwriting. Wolfe was much impressed by Dooher's stories about the value that dealers placed on modern literary manuscripts, for this seemed to open a door to opportunity. Still living on advances from Charles Scribner's Sons and about to pack up his papers, preparatory to his trip to Europe, he saw a chance to make some money. "For God's sake, Murdoch," he begged, "if you can get money for my manuscripts, please do."

The next week Dooher took a look at Wolfe's voluminous pile of papers. The two men discussed business arrangements, and Wolfe, who was used to paying a ten percent commission to his literary agents, had to be convinced that dealers in manuscripts usually receive twenty percent. Wolfe then discussed the whole idea with Perkins. The editor suggested that since Dooher was young and relatively inexperienced, it might be best to "try the market" by allowing him to market one short manuscript first. They picked out the typescript of "A Portrait of Bascom Hawke," which Dooher was confident he could easily sell. But as they talked further, all three came to realize that the Bascom Hawke piece could be more profitably sold as part of the "Time and the River" manuscript.

Since Wolfe was about to leave for Europe, nothing more was done at the time, but during his absence Dooher lined up several prospective buyers. After Wolfe got settled in his First Avenue apartment, Dooher approached him again. By this time Wolfe no longer really needed to sell his manuscripts, for *Of Time and the River* earned $17,474 in royalties during its first year after publication. He was, however, willing to have Dooher continue as his agent, partly because of his friendship with the young man's family, partly because there was always the possibility that he might come up with an exceptional offer for his papers.

A fiasco in January cooled Wolfe's interest. With Perkins's consent, he turned over to Dooher several manuscripts and typed drafts. The young man reported that he could sell them for six hundred and seventy-five dollars, a price that Perkins agreed was very good indeed. But the prospective purchaser, Barnet B. Ruder, a reputable rare book dealer in Manhattan, had to go to the hospital before the sale was completed, and when he got back on his feet, he decided that the price was too high. Crestfallen, Dooher returned the manuscripts to Wolfe.

His next attempt was more successful. Suggesting that Dooher test the market by presenting a single item, Wolfe allowed him to sell his annotated copy of *Of Time and the River* — the same copy that he had promised to give to Mrs. Dooher — and Ruder promptly bought it for one hundred and twenty-five dollars. Much encouraged, Dooher was now confident that he could readily find purchasers for all of Wolfe's manuscripts.

But by this time Wolfe was getting bored with the whole business. He thought Dooher was "importunate and demanding" when he asked to go through the boxes of papers in his apartment and considered him positively offensive when he proposed taking all the manuscripts out to Rutherford, New Jersey, to which Mrs. Dooher had returned. Mostly to get rid of Dooher, Wolfe sent him to Scribners and authorized him to pick up several further items — the handwritten notebooks in which he had jotted down his outline for *Look Homeward, Angel,* some term papers he had written at Harvard, and the typescript for *Of Time and the River.*

When Dooher took this material to Ruder's store, he discovered that what he had was not the typescript from which the printer had worked in setting *Of Time and the River* but a collection of materials, including some passages that had been deleted from the published book, and, even more exciting, unpublished drafts in Wolfe's own handwriting. Quite properly he reported his discovery to Wolfe, who became greatly agitated. Toward all his papers he had a proprietary attitude, but he was especially attached to anything unpublished, since this was, potentially, material for a future book.

He asked Dooher, then, to reclaim the manuscript and to bring it to his apartment on February 10, so that they could sort out the unpublished material. When Dooher arrived, Wolfe announced that he had a lunch engagement with Mrs. Jelliffe, which he was not willing to break, and he told the young man to take the manuscript over to the library at Scribners and begin the work of collating it with the book. After a long, liquid lunch, Wolfe went around to Scribners himself and found that Dooher, angry at having been dismissed like an errand-boy, had hardly begun the job. At just this moment Perkins came in to report that Frère-Reeves, of W. H. Heinemann, was in town and he insisted that Wolfe must join them for one drink. "I ought to have known better," Perkins later said ruefully, "because Tom was not a one-drink man."

When Wolfe finally did return to Scribners, around seven o'clock, he had decided to call off the sale of his manuscripts. Announcing "that this whole business had begun to take up too much of my time," he patronizingly asked Dooher, "What do I owe you for your trouble?"

By this time Dooher was furious. He thought of himself as a businessman, who had been conducting a business deal honestly and responsibly, and for his pains Wolfe had left him for seven hours to dawdle in the overheated Scribners library, only to return and fire him. Angrily he accused Wolfe of breaking his promises to him and to his family. He remarked — truthfully, but gratuitously — that he had never felt any friendship for Wolfe and called him "the meanest bastard that ever crossed the Mason-Dixon line."

"If you weren't a boy," Wolfe replied, "I'd slap you in the face." He order Dooher to leave the premises at once, he dismissed him as his agent, and he demanded the immediate return of all manuscripts still in his possession. As Dooher left, he said he would see Wolfe in court.

After this, as tempers cooled, the disagreement should have blown over, but it did not. Efforts to bring Wolfe and Dooher together failed. Wolfe hoped that Dooher's brother-in-law would mediate, but Hoagland laughed, shook his head, and said that Dooher was "a strange boy," who might well mean his threat to hold on to Wolfe's manuscripts until he was paid an agent's fee. Convinced that "the whole affair was a temporary explosion of Irish temperament and temper," John Terry said that he could see justice on both sides of the quarrel. "To see all sides," Wolfe fumed, is "a way people sometimes have of talking when what they mean is that they are broad enough to feather their own nest, and to see all sides on which their bread is buttered." Terry did go out to Rutherford with Wolfe in March, when they found Mrs. Dooher "extremely friendly and sympathetic" but wholly unable to make her son give in.

Once more Wolfe was back in court. When Dooher refused to return the manuscripts entrusted to him, Wolfe sued him, and Dooher brought a countersuit for breach of contract, claiming that Wolfe, by dismissing him, had deprived him of a twenty percent commission on sales that, he absurdly claimed, would certainly have reached ten thousand dollars. He really had no expectation of winning, but he felt aggrieved. He knew that, by employing an inexpensive local lawyer in New Jersey, he could for a very modest sum make Wolfe suffer.

The legal proceedings dragged on for the next two years and kept Wolfe in a state of excited irritability. He had only the loosest notion of what manuscripts he had turned over to Dooher, and he needed court orders both to compel Dooher to disclose what he had and to prevent him from selling these papers. He became almost frantic when one of his autobiographical notebooks, used in preparing *Look Homeward, Angel,* turned up for sale by a Los Angeles dealer; in these jottings he had used the real names of people in Asheville, and if these got out he could be subject to a dozen libel suits. Since his Manhattan lawyers — the same who had represented him in the Boyd case — were licensed to practice only in New York, they had to enlist a New Jersey firm, which, after a good deal of investigation and expense, suggested that Wolfe ought to settle out of court for five hundred dollars. Indignantly refusing to submit to what he called blackmail, Wolfe hired another New Jersey attorney, who promised to fight Dooher in court.

When the case finally did come to trial, in February 1938, the judge, as expected, ruled against Dooher, and Wolfe bragged that he had "won a complete and overwhelming victory." But the experience was emotionally draining and expensive. His legal costs ran to more than a thousand dollars. The personal costs were greater. Because of this suit he cut off relations with Clayton and Kitty Hoagland, who had been his most supportive friends. And, what was more painful, he no longer saw John Terry, who had failed to stand by him in this trial. "The plain truth is," Wolfe concluded sadly, "he is a very fat and sentimental man, who wants to avoid trouble and unfriendliness, if he can." At about this time he began drafting his slightly fictionalized caricature of Terry as "Jerry Alsop," the eunuch-like father-confessor of the college boys in *The Web and the Rock.*

VI

Far more costly in the long run were the quarrels with Perkins that began to erupt during this same winter of 1935–1936. In part they originated in proximity and idleness. Now that Wolfe was a neighbor, the Perkinses got to see him not just at his best but at his worst. With no book manuscript to talk about, he and Perkins frequently discussed general social and economic issues, on which Wolfe fancied he was much more radical than the editor. Since both men were drinking too much, their disagreements often turned into very angry quarrels, for Perkins was one of the most stubborn men in the world and Wolfe became highly excited during an argument. One night in late November, joining Max and Louise Perkins for dinner at Louis and Armand's restaurant, Wolfe got to ranting about "capitalistic injustice," and when Perkins did not appear to agree, he insultingly suggested that his editor ought to be named the "King Capitalist." "Listen, Tom," Louise felt obliged to write him after she got home, "if any one else were as mean to Max as you were tonight you would fight him! You know that he is your friend — really your friend — and that he is honorable. Isn't that enough?" Shamed, Wolfe apologized the next day, but the flare-ups continued.

Wolfe was at his worst during a dinner the Perkinses gave for Countess Eleanor Palffy, who had lost an eye in an accident and had just been released from the hospital. Affected and sophisticated, she was the kind of woman to whom Wolfe took an instant dislike and, having fortified himself beforehand with a number of drinks, he did everything he could to be outrageous. Thinking that the countess was a snob and therefore probably anti-Semitic, he told her that his father had been a rabbi, and he was baffled when, instead of being offended, she seemed genuinely interested in talking with him about Jewish culture. Once dinner was served Wolfe launched into a tirade about how he was as good as anybody, even a countess, and to prove his point jumped up from the table, tore off his coat to exhibit the label, a lion and a unicorn, "from the best tailor in London," he boasted. When the countess remained unimpressed, Wolfe announced that he did not give a damn whether she had only one eye or not. After taking the countess back to the hospital, Perkins, for the first time, shouted at Wolfe, who later told Mrs. Jelliffe ruefully that he could not understand how he could possibly have behaved so dreadfully.

Behind these eruptions there was something more than alcohol and idleness. Wolfe had a lifelong aversion to being dependent on anybody else, and he was uncomfortable because he owed so much to Perkins and to Charles Scribner's Sons. He rightly sensed that the people at Scribners did not think of him as fully adult or as competent to manage his own life. Indeed, over the years, he had given abundant evidence of his inability to cope; he called on Perkins to deal with everything from wiring emergency funds to his family in the South to getting rid of a girl who became sick in his apartment. Yet the more assistance he received, the more he resented having to ask for help.

He was especially unhappy because Scribners continued to manage his money for him. In fact, the system of having his royalty earnings in an account at Scribners, on which he could draw large or small sums in cash simply by dropping in at any time during the business day, was a great convenience to Wolfe, who was a nocturnal creature, rarely up and about before the New York banks closed. Yet, in his cups, he could lash himself into fury over his belief that Scribners was treating him like a child. One night at the James Thurbers', after a good many highballs, he burst into tears and sobbed, "I've never had a bank account. God damn it, I've never had a bank account." After brooding for a day or two, he decided to open one, and he shot off a telegram to Scribners: "Deliver one thousand and fifty dollars in cash to my apartment 865 1st Ave by eleven o'clock December 13, 1935." After failing to dissuade him, Perkins sent the money over, but that evening he discovered that Wolfe, euphoric after having taken such a decisive step, had stuffed the money into his pocket and fallen asleep again, not waking until the banks were shut. Perkins was afraid that he would lose the money or be robbed, but he did not need to fear. Julia's son took the wad of bills over to Mrs. Bernstein at the Hotel Gotham and had her put it in the safe until the next day. He then did open his account at the Chase National Bank, and three weeks later he deposited nearly twelve thousand dollars more from his Scribners royalties. Thereafter, since he rarely could get to the bank during business hours, he usually cashed small checks at the Hill Top Liquor Store, at the corner of First Avenue and 49th Street, where he was a familiar customer.

Wolfe's attempt to gain financial independence from Scribners was triggered by the news that he was being charged for the hundreds of changes and corrections that had been made in the proofs of *Of Time and the River*. Like most authors, he had a contract allowing him to make alterations up to ten percent of the cost of composing the whole book. But corrections in *Of Time and the River* came to nearly eighty percent of the total cost of setting type for the book, partly because Wolfe's manuscript was so disorganized and incomplete, partly because the second section of the novel ("The Young Faustus") had to be completely reset when Perkins split up the long segments on Uncle Bascom and on Professor Hatcher's playwriting class and interspersed sections of one with the other. Wolfe's bill came to $1,180.60.

Staggered, he confronted Perkins with this charge. The editor conceded that it did seem a little unfair, since he, as much as Wolfe, had been responsible for many of the changes. Still, he noted — in a gentle reminder that Wolfe had failed to read the proofs — that the number of alterations would undoubtedly have been much higher if the author had overseen the book himself.

Since Wolfe believed that Perkins was, in effect, Charles Scribner's Sons, he linked his financial problems with the company to Perkins's lack of interest in his new book, "The October Fair." Because he could not really believe that Perkins was afraid of a suit by Mrs. Bernstein, he tried to find some other explanation for his editor's behavior. Finally he hit on it: "Women." He had hitherto thought of Mrs. Perkins as a silly, flighty creature, but now he fancied that she had deep plans and powerful control over her husband. Without any evidence at all he attributed Perkins's opposition to "The October Fair" to his wife, who wanted one of her daughters to go on the stage and was counting "on Mrs. Bernstein, with her influence on the theatrical world, . . . to realize her theatrical ambitions."

An acrimonious dispute between Wolfe and Perkins in April 1936 indicated how strained their relationship had become. Wolfe wanted *The Story of a Novel* to sell for no more than seventy-five cents or a dollar, so that it could have wide circulation. When Perkins explained that Scribners' margin of profit on such an inexpensive book was too low, he agreed to a reduction of his royalties from fifteen percent of list price, which he had received on his fiction, to ten percent. But when *The Story of a Novel* appeared, he discovered that the price had been raised to a dollar and fifty cents — though his royalty rate remained at ten percent. Furious, he quarreled with Perkins. Admitting that Scribners had a "legal and contractual right" to change the price of the book and to adhere to the lower royalty rate, he protested that the company was capitalizing on his friendship, as it had done in loading him with the huge bill for author's alterations in *Of Time and the River*. "Don't you think that I . . . would be justified henceforth and hereafter, [in] considering my relations with you and Scribners were primarily of a business and commercial nature," he asked Perkins, "and if you make use of a business advantage in this way, don't you think I would be justified in making use of a business advantage too if one came my way? Or do you think it works only one way?" He ended with a warning: "You cannot command the loyalty and devotion of a man on the one hand and then take a business advantage on the other."

Perkins felt much put upon and misunderstood. He had never been enthusiastic about publishing *The Story of a Novel;* it was "a little trifle," the kind of short, inexpensive book that bookstores did not like to handle. To win over the Scribners sales department, he had to agree to increase the price, while keeping the royalty low, but he felt that he could not explain his tactics to Wolfe, "who would not have understood that, and would have been enraged by the idea." Perkins knew that reducing an author's rate of royalty is a very sensitive matter, touching his pride as much as his pocket, but he admitted very revealingly: "I wouldn't have thought of suggesting such a thing to most authors, but at that time Tom and I were so much at one, that I thought all would go well."

After an angry confrontation, both men backed down. Perkins ordered the author's royalty rate on *The Story of a Novel* raised. Wolfe refused the increase. Perkins prevailed, and the royalty rate was set at fifteen percent, so that during the next two years Wolfe received $185.10 more from the sale of this book than his contract had provided. Over this difference Scribners had risked losing one of its most prominent and successful authors. And over this sum Wolfe risked losing the editor whose friendship and support he now needed more than ever.

VII

Four days after Wolfe and Perkins quarreled over *The Story of a Novel,* Bernard DeVoto attacked it in the *Saturday Review of Literature.* Conceding that Wolfe's published lecture formed "one of the most appealing books of our time," DeVoto used his review to appraise Wolfe's whole career as a writer. When he read *Look Homeward, Angel* he had judged it "just the routine first-novel" of adolescence, but he was troubled that the story was encumbered with what he called "placental" material — "long, whirling dis-charges of words, unabsorbed in the novel, unrelated to the proper business of fiction, badly if not altogether unacceptably written, raw gobs of emotion, aimless and quite meaningless jabber, clap-trap, belches, grunts and Tarzan-like screams." To his dismay he had found an even larger proportion of such material in *Of Time and the River,* a book apparently intended to show that Eugene Gant was "clearly a borderline manic-depressive," suffering from "an infantile regression" that made him think all the other char-acters in the novel were "twenty feet tall, spoke with the voice of trumpets and the thunder, ate like Pantagruel, wept like Niobe, laughed like Falstaff and bellowed like the bulls of Bashan."

Surely "something was dreadfully wrong" with the author of these books, and now *The Story of a Novel* revealed to DeVoto what it was: Wolfe was an "astonishingly immature" writer who had "mastered neither the psychic material out of which a novel is made nor the technique of writing fiction." He lacked the "one indispensable part of the artist," critical intelligence. Wolfe himself appeared to believe the press releases of the Scribners publicity department touting him as a genius, but, DeVoto remarked ac-idly, "we could do with a lot less genius, if we got a little more artist." "However useful genius may be in the writing of novels," the review concluded, "it is not enough in itself."

The excitement produced by "Genius Is Not Enough" did not derive from DeVoto's attack on Wolfe's lack of form, his gigan-tism, and his rhetorical excesses. After all, many of the Agrarians had said the same things, though usually less bluntly. Nor did it stem from the unexpectedness of DeVoto's opinions, since a year earlier he had used what was ostensibly a review of James Boyd's *Roll River* to blast Wolfe for filling up *Of Time and the River* "with Mardi Gras grotesques who suffer from compulsion neuroses and walk on stilts and always speak as if firing by battery." Nor was it the viciousness of DeVoto's attack, for without any personal malice he made a practice of lambasting authors he did not like.

What did excite comment was his charge that Perkins had played a primary and indispensable role in shaping Wolfe's novels. Ac-cording to DeVoto, Wolfe had for years poured out words, as a volcano pours out lava, with no understanding of what was or-ganic and relevant to his story and what was detritus. This mate-rial had been hacked and shaped and compressed into something resembling a novel by "Mr. Perkins and the assembly-line at

Scribners'." In consequence it was hard "to trust the integrity of a work of art in which not the artist but the publisher has determined where the true ends and the false begins."

This was a charge that Perkins had always most feared. He knew that DeVoto's review would permanently damage Wolfe's reputation. And in later years he came to think that DeVoto's attack was ultimately responsible for Wolfe's decision to leave Scribners, because it "led him to believe he must prove that I was not necessary to him."

Surprisingly, Wolfe was not greatly upset by DeVoto's review. He made no public response, and even in his private letters he said only that "the De Voto thing didn't hurt me — it just made me mad." After all, his first three books had received a good deal of sharp criticism; when more was dumped on *The Story of a Novel* he was, if "not yet exactly resigned to it, . . . at least a little prepared for it and not google-eyed with astonishment when it happens." He did object that DeVoto had not really reviewed his book but had used the occasion "as a pivot, a threat, a stalking horse, or an excuse" to "express his dislike, his hostility, or his prejudice" against everything Wolfe had ever written. "I don't pretend that I didn't take the De Voto thing seriously," he explained to an admirer two months later, "but . . . it doesn't rankle, I have no vengeful feelings; in the end I may even get some good from it." Afterwards Wolfe always referred to DeVoto as "one of the little men."

At this time Wolfe did not, either in public or in private, refer to DeVoto's charge that he could not write a novel without Perkins's assistance. Later he mentioned this accusation to Perkins as "an untrue myth . . . venomously recorded by a man named De Voto," only to add: "How far from the truth these suppositions are, you know yourself better than anyone on earth." The fact that he had "utterly finished and completed" *Look Homeward, Angel,* down "to the final period, in utter isolation, without a word of criticism or advice from any one, before any publisher ever saw it," was evidence enough to refute DeVoto. From Wolfe's point of view, Perkins's great contribution, both to his first novel and to *Of Time and the River,* was not so much his generous, painstaking editorial assistance as his "aid of spiritual sustenance, of personal faith, of high purpose, of profound and sensitive understanding, of utter loyalty and staunch support, at a time when many people had no belief at all in me." It was this kind of help that he had intended to acknowledge in *The Story of a Novel,* and DeVoto had chosen to misinterpret his expression of gratitude as a confession of dependence.

VIII

Another reason why DeVoto's review left Wolfe relatively unruffled was that he was already under way on a new book. After a troubled winter, during which he felt he had been afflicted by "almost every kind of worry, threat and annoyance," he decided he needed to get away from New York for a few days. For Saint Patrick's Day he went to Boston, where an idea for another novel "came boiling to the surface all of a sudden." It was a possibility that he had toyed with since the publication of *Look Homeward, Angel:* a book about what happened to a man who wrote a book. This, it seemed, offered a solution to his problems. By getting to work on a new novel he could forget about the sycophants, the critics, and the lawyers who had been exhausting him, and by beginning a book that was not related to the Gant cycle he could perhaps overcome Perkins's reluctances and again work with his editor and friend. Buoyed by the thought, he started, and he telegraphed Perkins: "Wrote book beginning. Goes wonderfully. Full of hope."

When Wolfe got back to New York, he talked with Perkins about his idea. By telling what the reception of a book did to its author, he could write "a kind of tremendous fable," for this new book would be "the story of a good man abroad in the world — . . . the naturally innocent man . . . who sets out in life with his own vision of . . . what men and women are going to be like, what he is going to find, and then the story of what he really finds." It could be another *Candide* or *Don Quixote,* though, he noted, "of course it has got to be the book of an American, since I am an American." Parts of it were "going to be savage, parts fantastic, parts extravagant and grotesque, and some of it very coarse and very bawdy and . . . wonderfully comical and funny." All in all "it ought to be a wonderfully exciting and interesting book to read."

When Perkins heard Wolfe's plan, he snapped his fingers and exclaimed: "Do it, and do it now." It was just the thing Wolfe should write at this stage of his career. How much Perkins, who was becoming increasingly deaf, really understood of Wolfe's project is unclear, but no doubt he felt greatly relieved. After so many months of accomplishing nothing, his prize author was now ready to settle down to work — and on a book that had a real story line and on a subject that, so far as he could tell, was likely to bring on no lawsuits from Aline Bernstein or anybody else.

Elated, Wolfe settled down to write, and work made him happy. Shortly after Perkins gave him the go-ahead, Nancy Hale, a Scribners' novelist who lived near the Perkinses on 49th Street, heard Wolfe, at two or three o'clock in the morning, chanting as he strode toward his apartment: "I wrote ten thousand words today! I wrote ten thousand words today!" He could not, of course, keep up that pace, but several weeks later he was still turning out three thousand words a day. He had before him, he realized, "another long hard grind and a few thousand more hours of despair and agony, clutching at my hair and swearing I'll never write another word," but he felt confident about the outcome: "I know pretty directly and clearly in my mind where I am going."

After trying several other possibilities, he decided to call the new book "The Vision of Spangler's Paul," with a long subtitle:

> The Story of His Birth, His Life,
> His Going To and Fro in the Earth,
> His Walking Up and Down in It:
> His Vision also of the Lost, the
> Never-Found, the Ever-Here America.

"Spangler" he adopted from Spangler's Run, the stream that ran near his father's birthplace in Pennsylvania. The hero got his Christian name from the Apostle, and Wolfe thought of using a quotation from Acts on the title page: "And Paul said, I would to God that not only thou, but also all that hear me this day, were both almost, and altogether such as I am — except these bonds."

The body of the book would consist of what purported to be a manuscript completed by Paul Spangler, author of a controversial first novel, "Home to Our Mountains," before his mysterious disappearance or death. It would be prefaced by a long introduction by "A Friend," Edward Mason, an elderly lawyer (or in some drafts an architect) who was Spangler's friend.

Forced by the critics to reassess himself as a writer, Wolfe planned, by dividing this new book into two entirely separate parts, to overcome what had always been a major problem in his writing, the intermingling of his own thoughts and voice with the ideas and statements of his characters. In "Mason's" long introduction — it ran to ninety-two typed pages — he had ample opportunity to express his own feelings about the reception of his first book, to answer charges that he was an autobiographical novelist, and to explain the difficulties of beginning a second book. Presenting these ideas through an elderly narrator, instead of advancing them as his own complaints, allowed him to exhibit a sense of self-deprecating humor that had been sadly lacking in *Of Time and the River*. For instance, after listening to one of Spangler's tirades about his enemies and how they were out to ruin him, Mason observed coolly that "he was lashing himself up into a fit of violent and embittered recrimination — which had in it the seeds of all that was worst and weakest in him — distortion, prejudice, and self-pity," and he reminded him sharply: "Of all people I have known, you are perhaps least qualified to play the wounded faun." Paul Spangler, presented in Mason's flat, unemotional prose, became a far more credible figure than Eugene Gant had ever been.

After venting his own feelings in this introduction, Wolfe could make the second half of the new book more objective than anything that he had yet written. It would contain no authorial intrusions, no editorial comment, no lyrical dithyrambs. He knew that it was risky to try such a very different style of writing, but he deliberately was seeking to recapture "the enthusiastic eagerness, the desire to experiment and find out new ways, the fearlessness of conception and effort" with which he had begun as an author.

Since Spangler's last work was about what happened to a man who published a book, Wolfe needed to show in great detail the workings of a great New York publishing house, James Rodney and Company. Inevitably, the House of Rodney bore a close resemblance to Charles Scribner's Sons, the one publishing house that Wolfe knew well, and the principal characters were closely patterned after major figures at Scribners: Charles Scribner II; Whitney Darrow, the business manager; Wallace Meyer, the senior editor; and Maxwell Perkins. All were unquestionably portraits, for Wolfe kept the pledge he made himself to be more truly autobiographical in this book than anything he had previously written.

Then, in the late spring of 1936, "The Vision of Spangler's Paul" began to fade. Never willing to throw away anything that he had written, Wolfe began to see ways of inserting material that he had drafted earlier for "The Hills Beyond Pentland" and for "The Hound of Darkness" into this new book. After all, Paul Spangler's background, family, early life, and education had to be included, because they had prepared him to write "Home to Our Mountains." Back into Wolfe's outline, then, came more and more on the early history of Asheville, more on the Pentland clan, more adventures of his childhood that had been dropped from *Look Homeward, Angel*. Soon he even tacked on the story of his love affair with Aline Bernstein and the brawl at the Oktoberfest in Munich, episodes that he had planned to publish in "The October Fair." The new book was slowly becoming another, even more inclusive, autobiography of Thomas Wolfe.

About the same time Perkins discovered, apparently for the first time, that Wolfe was writing about Charles Scribner's Sons. In a vague way he had been prepared for this development, for he realized that virtually all of Wolfe's characters were drawn from life. "When Tom gets around to writing about all of us," he had warned his colleagues jovially, *"look out!"* But he did not realize that Wolfe was going to deal so extensively and so explicitly with the people at Scribners until he saw Wolfe's chapter on "Old Man Rivers," a very slightly fictionalized sketch of Robert Bridges, the former editor of *Scribner's Magazine* who appraised all manuscripts by measuring the length of their authors' listings in *Who's Who in America*. Since Bridges was dead, the piece seemed harmless enough and Perkins did not object to it, though he wrote Elizabeth Lemmon that this new book of Wolfe's "will be the end of me" and predicted "a worse struggle than *Of Time and the River* unless he changes publishers first." But Wolfe struck close to home when he produced "The Lion at Morning," a portrait of Charles Scribner II; it included an account of a breach-of-promise suit that a former Ziegfeld Follies girl, "a comely blonde of mature charms," brought against "Mr. Parsons," the head of the Religious Books Department at James Rodney and Sons.

Perkins had no objection to Wolfe's writing about him — and, indeed, it is hard to see how he could have found much to complain about in Wolfe's portrait of "Foxhall Edwards." But during his long, intimate friendship with Wolfe he had talked freely about personalities and minor scandals in the office. If Wolfe mentioned these, his source would become immediately and painfully apparent. Perkins's concern was probably unwarranted, and both Charles Scribner III and Wheelock told him not to worry. After all, during the past seven years Wolfe had been in and out of Scribners almost every day and had talked to everybody, from the company president to the stockroom boys. But Perkins was seriously upset.

Aware of Perkins's uneasiness, Wolfe decided to make a test of a chapter he completed in early June called "No More Rivers," the story of a sensitive editor who had thrown over his friends for a gold-digging chorus girl and had subsequently become a recluse. Hoping to publish it first as a short story, he asked Miss Nowell to "sound out" Perkins's reactions. As Perkins read it, he recognized that the central figure was based on the Scribners editor Wallace Meyer. Miss Nowell found Perkins sitting bolt upright at his desk, his cheeks flushed and his eyes blazing. At first he refused to talk about the story at all. Finally, over drinks at the Chatham Walk, he poured out his feelings to her. "Can't you see," he exclaimed, "if Tom writes those things up and publishes them, it'll ruin those people's lives, and it'll be *my fault!*" If these stories were published, he warned, "I'll hand in my resignation from Scribners and go live in the country. It's my duty — there's nothing else for me to do."

Though he gave Miss Nowell strict orders not to tell Wolfe what he said, she did so anyway, and he became equally upset. Perkins, he growled, was trying to make a martyr of himself. His threat to resign was attempted blackmail, because Perkins knew Scribners would never accept his resignation. Perkins was also being very unfair. Years ago when he learned that the characters in *Look Homeward, Angel* were based on real people — *"my own people in my native town"* — he had said it was "all right, fine," that the only thing that mattered was to have the best possible book. But now that Wolfe was writing about "his own fine friends at Scribners," Perkins seemed to regard them as "a special race." Wolfe "mustn't dare to say a word about them." "Well," Wolfe told Miss Nowell, "if that's going to be his attitude, it's just too bad. Because I'm going to write what I please, and as I please, and nobody is going to stop me!"

But the news that Perkins was ready to stop yet another of his projected books — thus adding "The Vision of Spangler's Paul" to "K-19," book publication of "No Door," a proposed early volume of short stories, "The October Fair," "The Hills Beyond Pentland," and "The Hound of Darkness" — threw Wolfe into a deep depression. Utterly exhausted after three months of intensive writing and thoroughly frustrated, he for the first time began seriously to consider leaving Scribners. In mid-June he drafted a letter that he thought of sending to Harpers, Viking, W. W. Norton, Little, Brown, and other publishers asking whether they would be interested in his new book. Admitting that his "physical resources, which have been generous, are at the present moment depleted; that the kind of vital concentration which has at times in the past attended the act of creation, is diffused," he expressed the new hope that his energy and power would return if he made "a new beginning in my creative life."

As Wolfe brooded over his problems, he began to drink again, very heavily. He started calling Miss Nowell at about 3 A.M. to announce dolefully, "Well, I've done it now." When she asked what he had done, he would reply, "Why, don't you know! I've left Scribners." Angrily she would tell him that he had done no such thing, that he was only drunk and ought to go home to bed. But a few nights later her phone would ring again, and the deep voice, more Southern in accent when he was under the influence of alcohol, would again announce: "I've done it now."

In fact, Wolfe did not send out his letter to other publishers. He drank and he brooded. He spent time watching the Olympic try-outs on Randall's Island. And he almost completely stopped working. Finally he hit on a way out of his difficulty — or at least a way to avoid having to make hard decisions. When Rowohlt Verlag wrote of the enthusiastic reception of the German translation of *Of Time and the River,* Wolfe learned that it had earned sizable royalties, which could not be shipped out of the country because of Hitler's restrictions on the currency. At about the same time the North German Lloyd Steamship Line, a company that was helping to promote the summer Olympics in Berlin, offered him half-fare passage for writing a few short travel articles. Cross and tired, Wolfe abruptly decided to take his seventh trip to Europe, and on July 23 sailed from New York on the *Europa.*

XII

Unmistakable and Most Grievous Severance

W OLFE FELT INSTANTLY AT HOME in Berlin. The city was
clean and orderly, for Hitler gave orders to make it a
showplace for visitors to the 1936 Olympics. Before
the Hotel am Zoo, where Wolfe stayed again, the streetcars,
"cream-yellow, spotless, shining as a perfect toy," slipped past
almost noiselessly, and "even the little cobblestones that paved the
tramways were spotless as if each of them had just been gone over
thoroughly with a whisk broom."

Wolfe's friends were expecting him. Rowohlt, happy to have
one of his major American authors in Germany, had Wolfe's royalty check waiting for him when he landed at Bremerhaven. Ledig
was overjoyed to see his old friend and on his first evening in
Berlin managed to obtain an invitation for him to attend a formal
reception for Charles A. Lindbergh, one of the few prominent
Americans considered friendly to the Nazi regime.

After Wolfe accepted he realized that he had not packed a dress
shirt, and he and Ledig rushed out on the Tauentzienstrasse to buy
one. At shop after shop obliging saleswomen measured his neck and
arms and reported that they had no shirt of such gigantic dimensions. Infuriated by these reminders of his ungainly size, Wolfe
barged down the street, cursing loudly and announcing — fortunately in English — that such incompetence was just what one
would expect to find in a country run by Nazis. At last the manager
of one elegant store, who mistook Wolfe for one of the famous

athletes participating in the Olympics, came up with a solution to the problem. He could dismember a regular large dress shirt, lengthen the sleeves, add a hidden extension to the collar, and insert a huge gusset in the back, which would not be seen when Wolfe had his coat on, and he promised the remade garment would be ready in time for the evening reception. Now as elated as he had formerly been unhappy, Wolfe chanted nonsense as he strode back toward his hotel, pausing amorously to embrace the trees along the sidewalk in an expression of his renewed ardor for Germany.

The Germans reciprocated his affection. In March Rowohlt Verlag had published Hans Schiebelhuth's sensitive translation of *Of Time and the River* in two volumes, under the title *Von Zeit und Strom,* and German reviewers praised it even more enthusiastically than *Look Homeward, Angel.* To be sure, there were some dissenters. Hermann Hesse, who had admired Wolfe's first novel, found this second book so lacking in artistic structure that he laid it aside without finishing it, and a Nazi critic in *Die Neue Literatur* declared that Wolfe was inferior to Theodore Dreiser, Upton Sinclair, and Sinclair Lewis. But the *Berliner Tageblatt* called Wolfe an epic poet; the *Kölnische Zeitung* said his "realistic-romantic epic" presented both a "photographically true environment" and "the dreamland of the soul"; and the *Magdeburgische Zeitung* ranked Wolfe above Whitman, Dostoievsky, Goethe, Dickens, Cervantes, and Homer because of the "original poetic breath of fire which issues . . . from the volcano of this spirit like a pure flame."

Again a celebrity, Wolfe was interviewed for the *Berliner Tageblatt,* whose reporter obviously had difficulty following his exceptionally incoherent remarks. Wolfe jumped from an announcement that if "there were no Germany, it would be necessary to invent one," to a momentary expression of interest in the Olympics, to a quite erroneous declaration that "two hundred years ago my forefathers emigrated from southern Germany to America." Fortunately, Ledig was present to provide the reporter with facts, for Wolfe's interest was completely focused on the artist who was drawing a sketch to accompany the interview. She was Thea Voelcker, whose fair skin, marvelous blue eyes, and lustrous yellow hair braided about her head made her look like one of the Valkyries. Wolfe had never seen such a beautiful woman.

The next morning Ledig brought him a copy of the *Berliner Tageblatt,* and he was devastated when he saw her drawing, which appeared alongside the interview. She made him look like a pig, he raged. Certainly he did not look like that. His mother had often said that he was the handsomest of her boys. Surely Thea had drawn a caricature, intended to humiliate him. Very probably she was connected with the Gestapo. Nothing Ledig said could console him, and he was not appeased by rumors — which were quite false — that she had a lurid past, including three or four divorces, and that from time to time she lapsed into periods of madness. For days afterwards Ledig caught Wolfe staring at his reflection in store windows, craning his neck and angrily comparing "his handsome, mighty head with the 'Schweingesicht' with which the artist had given the lie to his mother's opinion."

To everyone's surprise, he began a passionate pursuit of Thea. At a party Rowohlt gave for him, Wolfe caught a glimpse of Thea, whose six-foot height made her tower over the other women much as he himself stood out among the men. Abruptly breaking off his conversation, he worked his way across the room to her, talked with nobody else, and presently left in her company. From that night on Wolfe and Voelcker were inseparable.

The next few days were a round of dinners and parties, interrupted only by visits to the Olympic stadium, "the most beautiful and most perfect in its design that had ever been built." He had a standing invitation to use Ambassador Dodd's box, which was near that of Chancellor Hitler himself. Always patriotic — and never more so than when he was abroad — Wolfe supported the American contestants, including the great black athlete Jesse Owens. "Owens was black as tar," he said later, "but what the hell, it was our team and I thought he was wonderful. I was proud of him, so I yelled." On one occasion he cheered so enthusiastically for Owens that Hitler, who thought blacks belonged to an inferior race and ostentatiously turned his face away when Owens was in the lead, looked up angrily at the American ambassador's box to see who was making such a commotion.

But on this visit Wolfe's enchantment with Germany began to fade quickly. Indifferent as he had always been to public affairs, he could not help noticing the new spirit that was abroad in the Third Reich. Since his previous visit Hitler's bellicose intentions had become unmistakable. The German government began spending larger sums on armaments than any other country had ever done in peacetime. In March 1936, Germany had remilitarized the Rhineland, and in July Hitler had forced Austria to align its foreign policy with that of the Third Reich. Even the Olympic contests in Berlin were something more than sports spectacles; they were demonstrations of the "whole united power of Germany's enormous organizing and disciplining genius . . . collected in a single stroke as compact as the blow of a fist." Wolfe studied the unbroken wall of soldiers who lined Unter den Linden on the days that Hitler attended the Olympics. When Hitler approached in his shining car, "a little dark man with a comic-opera moustache, erect and standing, moveless and unsmiling, with his hand upraised, palm outward, not in Nazi-wise salute, but straight up, in a gesture of blessing such as the Buddha or Messiahs use," they sprang instantly to attention. Wolfe heard in "the solid smack of ten thousand leather boots as they came together" the "sound of war." "The great engines of war are ready," he concluded; they "are on the rails, are being constantly enlarged and magnified."

Internally, the Nazi regime had become more obviously oppressive in the year since Wolfe's last visit, more ruthless in crushing out dissent. In June all police forces in the country were placed under the control of Heinrich Himmler, the head of the SS (Schutzstaffel, security units), who was responsible only to Hitler himself. Persecution of Jews was now blatant and harsh. They had been deprived of their rights as citizens in September 1935, forbidden to intermarry with persons of "Aryan" blood, and excluded from most professions.

Just as he had done in 1935, Wolfe tried at first to discount the stories he heard of Nazi oppression, and he argued with Martha Dodd that injustice in Hitler's Germany ought to be compared to inequity in America. Before condemning Germans for repressing freedom of speech, Americans should remember that "in Germany you are free to speak and write that you do not like Jews and that you think Jews are bad, corrupt, and unpleasant people. In America you are not free to say this." He drew up a tally sheet on what he called "Fascism":

For	*Against*
Physical Clean-ness	Repression of Free Speech
Healthy People	A Cult of Insular Superiority
Effective Relief	With This A Need For Insular
A Concentration	Dominion
of National Energy	

But in 1936 the evidence of Nazi brutality was too strong for even Wolfe to dismiss. He sensed among all his acquaintances "an ever-present fear . . . a kind of creeping paralysis which twisted and blighted all human relations" in the Third Reich.

Wolfe was always more sensitive to social injustice when he was having personal difficulties, and his business arrangements in Germany were not proceeding smoothly. Despite extraordinary reviews, very few people in Germany were buying his books. In the first year after publication only 7,707 copies of *Von Zeit und Strom* were sold, and only 604 copies of *Schau Heimwärts, Engel!* In contrast Pearl Buck, Sinclair Lewis, and Thornton Wilder had a wide reading public, and some 300,000 copies of *Gone With the Wind* were sold in Germany. Wolfe began to question the sales reports given him by Rowohlt Verlag, especially since the company had persuaded him to accept a reduced rate of royalty on *Von Zeit und Strom* because it was such a long and expensive book. He took great offense at the German system of basing royalty payments on the price of a paperback edition of a book — even when, as in the case of *Von Zeit und Strom,* no paperback edition was actually published — and finally he felt obliged to hire a Berlin law firm to protect his interests.

Angry and disillusioned, he decided to leave Berlin and go with Thea Voelcker on a vacation in the Austrian Tyrol. They found a quiet inn in the village of Alpbach, in the shadow of the 2400-meter-high Galtenberg. During the day Wolfe added to his "Vision of Spangler's Paul" manuscript, and in the evenings he and Thea joined the local farmers at the bar, where he listened to the local harp and zither music. He enjoyed the folk dancing, though he would not join in and only tapped his feet. Over round after round of drinks, he talked, compulsively and endlessly, about America, about baseball, about his childhood, about his family.

Wolfe hated for these evenings to end, because he then had to go to his room and think — about himself, about Thea, and about his future. He claimed that he loved her and wanted to bring her to America as his wife, but he exhibited toward her the same extreme oscillations of emotion that he had shown to Aline Bernstein. He attacked her because she was so beautiful that she could not be good, and he berated her for her sins, real and imagined. Then, in an abrupt reversal of mood, he exhibited "wild repentance" and exclaimed: "I love you, Thea, you know it, I love you." But when she, asking and expecting nothing from him, expressed a desire not to marry him but to bear his child, he had a desperate sense of being trapped.

Much of the time, as Thea reported in her not quite idiomatic English, Wolfe was "in state of agony," and he crashed "from one violent state into the other." Sometimes he seemed to her a "possessed devel"; at others, he was a "tormented, trembling, vibrating creature, that helpless makes responsable the outer world for his pain"; then he would change again into a "destroying raging man, who with cold amusement — but always with the [i.e., his] own torment — ruined other persons." Often he talked to her about his editor. "Perkins forces me," he complained — only to add that he loved Perkins and wanted to be forced by him.

After about a week in Alpbach, Thea woke one morning to find Wolfe's place in the bed empty. Nobody knew where he was. Then a rumor spread that he had been seen on the Galtenberg, the most difficult mountain in the area. Early in the morning he had gone out alone and, despite his lack of experience or equipment, had managed to get to the top of the mountain, which, as he told Perkins later, "makes all your New England mountains look like toad-stools." "It damned near finished me," he reported, "but I did it."

By eleven o'clock he was back at the inn and he began to pack. He returned to Berlin alone, leaving Thea behind because, he explained to Ledig, while he was up on the mountain "he had the feeling of a female cow about her and just broke away."

A few days later he decided to leave Germany. On the train to Paris he shared a compartment with four other passengers, and as they traveled they all introduced themselves. Remembering that currency restrictions allowed them to take only the insignificant sum of ten marks (approximately thirty dollars) out of the Third Reich, Wolfe and a fellow-American decided to spend all they had in the dining car before they reached the border. Returning to the compartment in high spirits, they offered to carry any excess sums that the German travelers might have. A dreary, rather unpleasant German whom Wolfe mentally christened "Fuss-and-Fidget" entrusted ten marks to him. At the border police came aboard the train and arrested the man. Trembling "with a murderous and incomprehensible anger," Wolfe watched the police take the man away, as the other passengers whispered that he was a Jew, who was attempting illegally to leave the country with a great deal of money.

For the first time Wolfe understood, in personal terms, what the Nazi dictatorship was, and he began at once to plan a story based on his train ride. At first he thought of calling it, "I Have Them Yet," referring to the coins the Germans had entrusted to him. For a long time he kept these on his writing table, looking at them now and then, pursing his lips and shaking his head sorrowfully. But he settled on a better title, the phrase that Heinz Ledig so frequently used to introduce his comments on the way the Nazi regime operated: "I Have a Thing to Tell You."

"I've written a good piece over here," Wolfe reported to Miss Nowell when he reached Paris. "I'm afraid it may mean that I can't come back to the place where I am liked best and have the most friends, but I've decided to publish it." The story was, as he recognized, his farewell to Germany, "to that old German land with all the measure of its truth, its glory, beauty, magic and its ruin — to that dark land, to that old ancient earth that I had loved so long."

Except for this story, Wolfe did not write much while he was abroad, but, as he told Thea Voelcker after his return to New York, "my unconscious mind must have been busy at my book, because now that I am back, the whole plan, from first to last, has become clear to me, and I think I know exactly what I want to do." Giving up the scheme of dividing "The Vision of Spangler's Paul" into a largely autobiographical introduction and an objective narrative, he decided instead to produce a single enormous book that would recount the entire life history of Paul Spangler. The novel would begin with an account of Paul's divided heritage, from his Northern-born father, who was a mason and a builder, and his Southern mountain-born mother, who came from a family that was primitive and superstitious but also was hard-driving and prosperous. The book would trace Paul's search for his identity — in the mountain town, in the state, in the nation, and, at the end, on other continents. With this new structure Wolfe felt he could present "a real fable, [with] imaginary characters and everything." At the same time, by drawing so heavily on his own experience, it could be "far more autobiographical than I have ever been without seeming to be at all."

Rearranging what he had already written, he began to fill the gaps in his story. The work proceeded rapidly because he dictated most of his new material to his typist, sometimes pacing back and forth across the room, reenacting the scenes he was narrating, sometimes leaning against the windowsill near her desk. She produced a typed draft, either triple-spaced or single-spaced with very wide margins, which he later revised in pencil. Working very hard, he had almost no social life during the months after his return from Europe and he did very little drinking. Indeed, he was so busy that he neglected to get a haircut for two months. By December 4, according to his secretary's calculations, he had written 180,250 words.

Some of what he composed in the fall of 1936 offered, in effect, stage directions and a fully described cast of characters for the new book, beginning with those in the town where Paul Spangler grew up. Then he enumerated and characterized the people he met at the state university, an account in which "Big Ben Jolley" (later changed to Gerald Alsop), his hostile caricature of John Terry, figured prominently. The elaborate outline went on to characterize the Southerners in exile whom Paul Spangler encountered in New York.

But much of what he wrote during this period of enormous productivity was fully developed and carefully crafted narrative. He revised his German story, "I Have a Thing to Tell You," which he had begun in Paris, adding new detail and fleshing out characterizations. Most of his long account of Lloyd McHarg, his hardly disguised satirical portrait of Sinclair Lewis, was dictated during these months.

Wolfe showed none of this new writing (which was to make up a large portion of his posthumous novels, *The Web and the Rock* and *You Can't Go Home Again*) at the Scribners offices, for he had nearly reached the conclusion that he must change publishers. On the voyage home he told Marcia Davenport, another of Perkins's favorite authors, that he was leaving Scribners. But there was nothing like an open break until he learned from Miss Nowell that during his absence Perkins had reread his story, "No More Rivers," after she had cut the passages referring to Charles Scribner II and to Whitney Darrow and had changed the occupation of the central character, George Hauser, from editor to musician. Coolly Perkins commented: "I think the story could do no one any harm now, — except perhaps Thomas Wolfe."

On October 4, the first evening that he and Perkins spent alone together, Wolfe angrily burst out: "Maybe that story isn't the best one I've ever written, but it's not the worst one either." He thought Perkins disliked the story because it dealt with people at Charles Scribner's Sons, and writing about them was "a sin against the Holy Ghost." Perkins disclaimed any intention of censoring Wolfe — but he repeated his threat that, after publishing whatever Wolfe wrote about Scribners, he would immediately resign from the firm. From that point the argument spilled over into all the real and imaginary grievances that the two men held toward each other, and they parted in bitter anger.

The next day Wolfe sent a terse note to Irma Wyckoff, Perkins's devoted secretary: "From now on, will you please address and send any mail that may come for me to 865 First Avenue, New York City?" After that, he no longer dropped by Perkins's office almost every day, and, except in cases of real urgency, he communicated with Scribners only by mail or through Miss Nowell.

Wolfe's tense relations with his publisher worsened in November when Marjorie Dorman, his former Brooklyn landlady, sued him and Charles Scribner's Sons for libel. She and other members of her family sought damages totaling $125,000 because Wolfe's story "No Door," in *From Death to Morning,* portrayed her as "mad Maude Whittaker" and asserted that her father and her sisters shared her "hereditary trait of madness."

The suit surprised both Wolfe and Perkins. Miss Dorman had raised no objection to "No Door" when *Scribner's Magazine* published it in 1933; then it probably reached three hundred thousand readers, ten times the number that read *From Death to Morning.* At that time she asked Scribners to publish a book she proposed to write on "Thomas Wolfe in Verandah Place," carefully identifying herself as "the lady whom Tom calls Mad Maude Whittaker."

Wolfe blamed Charles Scribner's Sons for the libel suit. Without any evidence at all he concluded that Marjorie Dorman got the idea of suing him from the gossip columnist Walter Winchell, who announced in the *New York Daily Mirror* on September 21 that publication of Wolfe's next novel had been postponed until all the characters portrayed in it died; Winchell claimed that Wolfe's "last two slightly autobiographical tomes brought several libel suits." Wolfe was certain that Winchell's column could only stem from rumors, which were fairly widespread, that Perkins had discouraged publication of "The October Fair" because he feared a suit by Aline Bernstein. Therefore, from Wolfe's peculiar point of view, Perkins had, in effect, invited this new suit, which was for a sum larger than the author's lifetime earnings.

Scribners, of course, thought that Wolfe's writing was responsible for the suit, but the firm was unavoidably involved in the case. Wolfe was an important author, who had to be protected in order to defend the integrity of the firm. Besides, Perkins, conscious that "everything Tom wrote was more or less autobiographical," felt a personal responsibility; he said, "of course it was up to me to guard Tom from legal dangers in so far as possible." In addition to these professional considerations, the company was financially liable. The Dormans sued both the author and his publisher. If they won, damages could be assessed against both. Though Scribners could, in theory, require the author to pay the full amount, everybody knew that Wolfe did not have $125,000, and most of the money would have to come from the company. Consequently, Charles Scribner suggested that his firm and Wolfe employ the same attorney and share legal expenses, and he agreed to pay half of any damages awarded to the Dormans.

They retained Alfred A. Cook, of Cook, Nathan, Lehman & Greenman, an attorney strongly recommended to Charles Scribner by friends at the *New York Times*. Going with Scribner to Cook's hushed, book-lined office, Wolfe developed an instant distrust of the attorney, which was not dispelled when Cook, in response to his passionate declamation about the injustice of the Dormans' suit, replied: "This problem of yours . . . is not a matter that involves Justice. It is a matter of the Law." He became even more upset when Cook, "secure in wealth, in smugness, in respectability," asked whether he had ever lived in certain neighborhoods, whether he drank, and so on, remarking "that although he of course had never led 'that sort of life' he was — ahem, ahem — not narrow-minded and understood that there were those that did."

From that opening conversation it was evident that Cook would advise a settlement out of court, knowing, as an experienced lawyer, that the outcome of a libel case was always unpredictable. His aversion to going to trial, which would be held in Brooklyn before a Brooklyn jury, increased when Wolfe made a long, rambling deposition, full of loose, undocumented assertions about the peculiarities of the Dormans and of speculations about Marjorie Dorman's possible confinement to an insane asylum.

Scribners also pressed for a settlement. Charles Scribner did not want his firm involved in a case that might prove long, unsavory, and expensive. And Perkins felt very strongly that the suit must be ended quickly through compromise. He knew that Madeleine Boyd's suit, which had finally been settled in May 1936, and Muredach Dooher's suit, which was to continue until 1938, drove Wolfe "frantic and made it impossible for him to write." Continuing to treat Wolfe as a child from whom unpleasant reality had to be concealed, Perkins urged a settlement on the grounds of saving time and legal expenses and "did not give the chief reason which was that Tom would not be able to work properly while the suit was pending."

This apparent pusillanimity on the part of his lawyer, his publisher, and his editor forced Wolfe to conclude that his relationship with Charles Scribner's Sons must be fundamentally redefined or that he must, finally and after so many previous threatened departures, seek a new publisher. Shortly after the meeting with Cook, Wolfe asked Perkins for a letter formally acknowledging "that I have faithfully and honorably discharged all obligations to Charles Scribner's Sons, whether financial, personal or contractual, and that no further agreement or obligation of any sort exists between us." He needed an acknowledgment of "the unmistakable and grievous severance" of his relationship with his publisher, he said, because everybody assumed that he was under contract to Scribners, when in fact he was not. His present indefinite arrangement allowed Scribners "to exert . . . such control of a man's future . . . work as will bring . . . profit if that man succeeds, and absolves [the publisher] from any commitments of any kind should he fail."

Deeply disturbed, Perkins wrote the letter, but he simply could not understand the need for it. As he told Wolfe, "I never knew a soul with whom I felt I was in such fundamentally complete agreement as you." "You seem to think I have tried to control you," he continued in a second, and then a third, letter. "I only did that when you asked my help and then I did the best I could." If Wolfe was suggesting that he wanted a contract for his next book, of course he could have one. "You must surely know the faith this house has in you. There are, of course, limits in terms beyond which nobody can go in a contract, but we should expect to make one that would suit you if you told us what was required." Admitting that his New England heritage made it hard for him to "express certain kinds of feelings very comfortably," he wanted Wolfe to know that since 1929 "your work has been the foremost interest in my life."

After that, so far as Perkins or anybody else at Scribners knew, Wolfe seemed to lapse into silence for more than a month. In fact, though, he was drafting two letters reviewing his relationship with Scribners and summarizing his reasons for thinking that his connection with his publisher was now nearly at an end.

The shorter of these, which he called his "business letter," raised practical questions that he felt Perkins had left unanswered. Perkins's kind and flattering letter did not offer him a contract or suggest any financial terms, and, despite its general expressions of good will, it did not guarantee that Scribners would publish his next book.

In a much longer personal letter — it ran to about 12,000 words, or twenty eight typed pages — Wolfe reviewed the intellectual and literary differences that were increasingly separating him and Perkins. Not entirely coherent or reasonable, it was an eloquent statement of his disagreements with Scribners and an announcement of his future writing plans.

After an affectionate acknowledgment of all that Perkins had done for him in the past, Wolfe argued that he and his editor now were "in almost every respect of temperament, thinking, feeling and acting" at the "two opposite poles of life." "You in your essential self are the Conservative," he wrote, "and I, in my essential self, am the Revolutionary." By this he did not mean that Perkins was selfishly opposed to all change; instead, he was afflicted by "a kind of fatalism of the spirit . . . . a kind of unhoping hope, . . . a determined resignation, which believe that fundamentally life will never change." In designating himself as a "Revolutionary," Wolfe denied that he was "a Union Square or Greenwich Village communist," for he considered such self-styled radicals only "parasitic excrescences on the very society which they profess to abhor." But he did think of himself "a brother to the workers." Over the years he had developed an intense feeling "that this system that we have is evil, that it brings misery and injustice not only to the lives of the poor but to the wretched and sterile lives of the privileged classes who are supported by it." "Life can be made better," he declared, and to that end "I must henceforth direct every energy of my life and talent."

Wolfe thought that these differences in basic philosophy had increasingly affected his relationship with his editor. Perkins's social conservatism had limited his editorial vision. Professing great eagerness "to discover a manuscript of originality and power," he repeatedly rejected all innovative fiction. Though he claimed to be "waiting eagerly" to publish Wolfe's work, he had effectively discouraged him from completing the last three or four books that he had proposed.

That was the burthen of Wolfe's disagreement with Perkins. It was notable that he did not raise a number of other issues that he could have considered grievances. Wolfe did not protest because nobody at Scribners — not Perkins, not Wheelock, not anybody else — ever gave his manuscripts the close, line-by-line editing that they badly needed. Since Wolfe did not learn, either at the University of North Carolina or at Harvard University, to criticize his own work, he sorely needed an expert, trusted editor who could show him how to eliminate repetitious, redundant, inappropriate, and badly written phrases, sentences, and paragraphs. But Perkins, who had inordinate respect for the language his authors used, never did this.

Nor did he protest that Perkins had failed to recognize that Wolfe's most natural and effective literary form was the short novel. Although Perkins admired many of Wolfe's stories and considered "The Web of Earth" his most perfectly executed piece of work, he constantly urged Wolfe to produce grand, expansive books. Living out his secret fantasy of being a dwarf on the shoulder of a giant, directing his actions, he spurred Wolfe on in his attempts to write the Great American Novel. But if the editor's judgment in this matter was faulty, it was one in which the author himself concurred. Wolfe could not think of a writer of short novels as being a major author, and that was exactly what he intended to be.

What Wolfe did object to was the indifference or coolness that Perkins had exhibited toward the several projects he had proposed since the publication of *Of Time and the River*. Wolfe had now reached the point where he was afraid to show Perkins his extensive manuscript of "The Vision of Spangler's Paul," fearing that his inspiration and enthusiasm would be killed by Perkins's "cold caution, by indifference, by the growing apprehensiveness and dogmatism of your own conservatism."

The time had come, then, to make a declaration of literary independence. Confident now that "where I have been most wrong, most unsure in these past seven years" — i.e., since the publication of *Look Homeward, Angel* — "has been where I have yielded to this benevolent pressure" from Perkins, he announced that henceforth "I am going to write as I please." There would in the future be no censorship, overt or silent, of his ideas or his language. From now on he would use all the resources of the English language, "every word, if need be, in the vocabulary of the foulest-mouthed taxi driver, the most prurient-tongued prostitute that ever screamed an obscene epithet." In the future, he pledged, "no one is going to cut me unless I want them to." And he made a ringing affirmation:

> . . . I have at last discovered my own America, I believe I have found my language, I think I know my way. And I shall wreak out my vision of this life, this way, this world and this America, to the top of my bent, to the height of my ability, but with an unswerving devotion, integrity and purity of purpose that shall not be menaced, altered or weakened by any one. . . . No matter what happens I am going to write this book.

It was now up to Scribners to decide whether the firm wanted this new, independent Thomas Wolfe as an author on its list. Perkins had to stand resolutely by Wolfe and "make an end of all this devil's business." "If that can not be done any longer upon the terms that I have stated here," he said candidly, "then I must either stand alone or turn to other quarters for support, if I can find it. You yourself must now say plainly what the decision is to be."

Wolfe concluded his long letter with renewed expressions of affection for Perkins: "I know you are my friend. I value your friendship more than anything else in the world." Just because Perkins had given him "the greatest spiritual support and comfort I've ever known," even the contemplation of a severance with Scribners had caused Wolfe "the greatest distress and anguish of the mind for months." If the parting actually occurred, "it will seem to me like death."

After putting his powerful grievances and his dwindling hopes on paper, Wolfe did not mail these letters. Instead, he kept them on his table as he continued to work very hard, adding to his manuscript right up until Christmas. In an attempt to separate his personal friendship from his publishing relationship, he went to the Perkinses' for Christmas dinner. "They are," he told his mother, "a nice family."

I

Wolfe had said farewell to Germany. He had drafted, but not yet mailed, his farewell to Maxwell Perkins, his truest friend. He began to think it was now time also to say goodbye to the literary and publishing world of New York, which had caused him so much pain.

Increasingly he considered returning to the South, where so many other authors of his generation made their homes. Ellen Glasgow and James Branch Cabell flourished in Richmond, William Faulkner did most of his serious writing in Oxford, Mississippi, and Sherwood Anderson now spent most of his time in Marion, Virginia. The Louisiana novelist Hamilton Basso, who had published an appreciative portrait of Wolfe in the *New Republic,* had a house in Pisgah, North Carolina, and James Boyd lived comfortably on his 2500-acre estate at Southern Pines, North Carolina.

For some time Wolfe had been receiving indications that he would be warmly welcomed in the South. An invitation from his former classmate, William Polk, to address the annual meeting of the North Carolina Literary and Historical Association at Raleigh demonstrated that his native state was now proud, rather than ashamed, of its most famous author. Even in Asheville the furor roused by *Look Homeward, Angel* had abated, and Wolfe thought he could now end his self-imposed exile from his home town — an "exile" about which his New York friends tended to smile a little but one that was, he insisted, "the truth."

Not yet ready to attempt a frontal assault on Asheville, he began his Southern campaign with a long encircling movement. First he went to Richmond, where he encountered several of the Agrarians at the meeting of the Modern Language Association. Then he took the train for New Orleans, which he had not visited since he was

a child. He said he wanted nothing but quiet and rest, but he took
the precaution of asking Basso, who knew everybody in New
Orleans, for letters of introduction and recommendations of hotels, restaurants, and brothels.

Characteristically, he forgot to bring Basso's letter along, and
he reached New Orleans, unannounced and unexpected, on the
day of the Sugar Bowl game, when all the hotels were booked
solid. But by January 2 his presence in New Orleans was discovered, and the next day the *Times-Picayune* carried Wolfe's photograph with a story inaccurately titled, "Author Returns to Scenes
That Inspired His Pen." Soon the Hotel Roosevelt, where he finally found a room, was inundated by telephone calls, invitations,
and visitors. John T. McClure, a poet and former editor of the
Double Dealer, to which Faulkner and Anderson had contributed,
took him bar-hopping. Pat O'Donnell, whose novel, *Green Margins,* was a Literary Guild selection, clung onto him day after day.
A tiresome couple named Eldred, who felt they had a claim on
Wolfe because he had gone to school with Mrs. Eldred's brother,
seized him for endless rounds of drinks. Most persistent of all was
William B. Wisdom, a young New Orleans businessman, who
had already begun collecting Wolfe's writings and tried to get him
to discuss literature.

Among them they made Wolfe's week in New Orleans a round
of lunches, cocktails, dinners, parties, and balls, and they got
glimpses of the whole range of Wolfe's behavior: The celebrated
novelist, after a night of hard drinking with newspaper reporters,
standing on the grassy levee of the Mississippi River, announcing
oracularly: "Ah, this . . . fellows . . . this . . . this is America."
The royalty-conscious author, inscribing a Modern Library edition of *Look Homeward, Angel* to one of the newsmen: "I get five
percent on this one — and it costs a dollar — but fifteen percent
on the regular Scribner's edition — which costs two-fifty — But
you did show me the Mississippi levee at eight o'clock in the
morning — which was worth more to me than any river I ever
wrote about." The enchanted tourist, falling on his knees in the
so-called Mystery Room of Antoine's Restaurant, to sniff the ce-
dar sawdust that covered the floor. The literary naif, responding to
Wisdom's reference to conscious literary anachronisms in Chaucer:
"Do you really read that stuff? I think that's great." The gour-
mand, devouring at Antoine's the huge baked Alaska dessert with

"Thomas Wolfe" spelled out in white, soft meringue, and announcing: "I feel just like a cannibal eating this or worse, for I have the feeling that I am eating a part of me." The social rebel, standing in the sedate bar of the venerable Boston Club of New Orleans, loudly singing "Deutschland, Deutschland, Uber Alles." The middle-aged lecher, who decided that he wanted to meet some "pretty young unmarried girls, about eighteen," showed up at the elite Carnival Ball, insisted on occupying one of the "call-out seats" reserved for ladies participating in the Maskers' dance, and had to be asked to leave. The alcoholic author, passing out sometime after 3 A.M. and awaking in the empty bathtub of his hotel room, with all his clothes on but with the knee of his best trousers torn, telephoning a woman friend "to bring a bevy of girls and herself" to rub his head and back.

It was all very exciting and ego-boosting, but even during Wolfe's carnival week in New Orleans reality kept pressing in. Though he had given strict orders that his whereabouts during this vacation should not be divulged, his attorney in the Dooher case extracted from Perkins his probable New Orleans whereabouts. Furious, Wolfe dashed off a telegram to Perkins: "How dare you give anyone my address?" and drafted — but did not actually send — a letter accusing the editor of trying to "get out from under" at a time when Wolfe was menaced by "slander, blackmail, theft, and parasitic infamy." Spurning advice to settle the Dooher suit, Wolfe told his attorney not to consult with Scribners about these problems, since they had "now unmistakably indicated a desire for the complete severance of their publishing relations with me," or with Perkins, who was indeed "the greatest editor of this generation" but was also "a timid man . . . not a man for danger — I expect no help from him."

All this time Wolfe had been carrying around in his luggage the two letters he had written to Perkins before he left New York, and from time to time during his trip he had reread them, adding postscripts. Now he decided that it was time to "put the story of my relation to . . . Scribners upon the record." He did not mail the "business" letter, in which he discussed contracts and financial arrangements. Possibly as Miss Nowell judged, he did not really want a contract with Scribners for his next book; more probably he thought it unbecoming for an author of his stature to have to suggest advances, royalties, and other business arrangements to his publisher. But on January 10 he finally sent his long personal letter to Perkins, detailing all his grievances.

Emotionally drained after making this decision, Wolfe left New Orleans the next day, and the ineffable Eldreds persuaded him that he could get a real rest at their villa in Ocean Springs, on the Gulf Coast of Mississippi. One day with this garrulous, hard-drinking couple was all that he could take. "Youve been awfully nice to me and I appreciate all you've done for me," he told them, "but I've got to get away from here." He fled to the seclusion of a hotel in Biloxi, five miles away, where he made revisions in "I Have a Thing to Tell You." "I think he's not exactly right in his head," Eldred reported later; "you know how all these authors, these geniuses are, they work too hard and they get funny ideas."

Next Wolfe went, as he had promised, to visit some old friends in Atlanta. As usual, there were dinners, where Wolfe ate and talked too much. As usual, there were manuscripts of aspiring authors thrust on him, and promptly he sent them along to Miss Nowell. Newspaper reporters in Atlanta found Wolfe tired but tactful. No, he would not compare Atlanta and New Orleans, but everybody in both cities had been "most kind and hospitable, and I appreciate deeply all that has been done for me." No, he had not had a chance to meet Margaret Mitchell or to read *Gone With the Wind,* though he understood that she had written "a fine piece of work."★ "It's mighty good to be home," he told the reporters. "In the South, I mean."

From Atlanta he half-intended to go on to Asheville, but he was not sure he could face the emotional tumult of his loquacious family and he still was not certain that his hometown had forgiven him for *Look Homeward, Angel.* A confused telephone call from his excitable brother Fred confirmed his doubts, and he abruptly informed Fred that "his nerves would not permit him to visit Asheville and be pawed over at this time."

Instead, for the first time since his graduation from the University of North Carolina, Wolfe returned to Chapel Hill. The university was much larger than it had been in 1920, and he thought all the new dormitories made the campus look "like the outskirts of West Philadelphia." But he soon felt at home again, for

★Wolfe really thought *Gone With the Wind* was "an immortal piece of bilge."

much of the university had not changed at all and, most important, he found "the people are pretty much the way they always were."

He had promised Professor Phillips Russell, of the journalism school, to say a few words to his class in creative writing, and more than a hundred students crowded into the room to hear him. As always, Wolfe was late, and when he finally stumbled down the stairs, his face flushed and sweaty, he began in a stammering fashion: "I-I-I th-thought I was c-c-coming to sit in on a class-ss. . . . Wh-when I was here t-there weren't any more than th-th-this in school." Touched by the obvious stage fright of the distinguished visitor, the students listened supportively as he went on about how good it was to be back, how much larger and better the university was now than in the old days, how he had almost forgotten the beauty of the Southern landscape: "The color of our Carolina clay. I never remembered it was so red before."

George Stoney, an exceptionally perceptive listener, noted that Wolfe had three quite distinct ways of talking — all of which he used that day. The first was the halting, stuttering voice with which he began his talk, as he did most conversations, especially with strangers and at literary teas. Then, if he became comfortable, his second voice, "heavy, swift, full of the gurgle of rich laughter, the enthusiasm for life; manly and full of confidence, almost a swagger," replaced that awkward beginning. Finally, as he really got under way, his "literary voice" took over, and great torrents of words, sometimes lyrical, sometimes dramatic, poured out — on this occasion, an almost verbatim repetition of his published work, particularly of *The Story of a Novel*.

In Chapel Hill Wolfe stayed with his old fraternity brother, Corydon "Shorty" Spruill, now dean of the college, with whom he had maintained an intermittent correspondence over the years, and he spent most of his time visiting with friends. Relieved after mailing his letter to Perkins, he was relaxed and high-spirited. What the playwright Paul Green remembered most about his visit was the way Wolfe "talked, talked, talked."

Of all his friends at the University of North Carolina, Wolfe was most comfortable with Albert and Gladys Coates. Albert, the founder of the prestigious Institute of Government at the university, had attended Harvard Law School while Wolfe was in Cambridge, and Wolfe had met Gladys in New York. When they gave a breakfast party for him, featuring waffles and eggs — and, remembering stories about Wolfe's appetite, Mrs. Coates prepared more than twice as many as usual — it began about ten in the morning and lasted for six hours, until the other guests had to leave for a faculty tea. Knowing that Albert Coates was a professor in the law school, Wolfe recounted his troubles with New York lawyers in spirited detail. He vowed that he would depict them in his next book and thus make them repay him for all the money they had cost him.

That night, about nine o'clock, the Coateses were surprised to find Wolfe again at their door. He was being well treated at the Spruills, he explained, but they were teetotalers. "Gladys," he said, "can you give me a drink? I have been giving the Old Well a workout." After some liquid reinforcement, he asked what people in Chapel Hill did for night life, and the most exciting prospect the Coateses could offer was the local movie house, where a film about Wild Bill Hickok was showing. By the time they arrived, the theater was jammed, and they had to take the only remaining seats, very near the front row. Wolfe began making wisecracks about the movie, acting out his remarks, and soon the crowd — quite aware that the hulking giant whose head actually cast a shadow on the screen was Thomas Wolfe — was more interested in his comments than in the movie itself.

All in all, Wolfe's trip was a great success, and by the time he left, toward the end of January, he was ready to believe that the South could offer him the home and the place for work that he needed. He talked of returning, not to Asheville itself, but to the hills of Yancey County, where his grandfather Westall had been born. Here he thought he could find a house, live with his aging mother, and write his books.

II

The boost Wolfe's Southern trip gave to his spirits was short-lived. Back in New York, he still had to settle two urgent problems: his future relationship with Perkins and Scribners, and the libel suit brought by the Dormans. The two were interrelated.

Wolfe's long letter deeply hurt Perkins. It did not turn him against Wolfe or make him bitter, but it saddened and depressed him. "That particular letter," Wheelock remarked later, "very nearly killed Max." He did not put it in the general Scribners files but kept it in his own desk, pulling it out from time to time to restudy it and to read between the lines. Once Wheelock, entering the office unexpectedly, found him nearly in tears, studying the document, and without a word he slipped it almost furtively back into his drawer.

In the three letters he wrote in response, Perkins admitted that parts of Wolfe's long indictment made him angry, but otherwise he gave the author little evidence of the depth of his feeling. Instead, he patiently addressed Wolfe's complaints, one by one. He maintained that no philosophical differences separated him from Wolfe, though he granted that they were of different temperaments. If Wolfe fancied himself as Luther, Perkins would rather be Erasmus; if Wolfe called for revolution, Perkins preferred to wait "for natural forces to disclose their direction." But all this, he protested, was "getting to be too much of a philosophy of history or something." The important fact was that he and Wolfe "like and admire the same things and despise many of the same things, and the same people too, and think the same things important and unimportant."

Perkins denied the charge that he took vicarious pleasure in Wolfe's sufferings, at the hands of lawyers, newspaper reporters, and critics. "I do try to turn your mind from them and to arouse your humor," he admitted, but that was only "because to spend dreadful hours brooding over them, and in denunciation and abuse on account of them, seems . . . only to aggravate them."

Nor did he agree that he had weakly yielded to threats of libel. As for Mrs. Bernstein's protests against publication of "The October Fair," Perkins asserted stoutly, "I conceded nothing to her." If he suggested an out-of-court settlement in Dooher's case, it was only because "it was . . . very plain that this suit was such a worry that it was impeding you in your work."

On the more important issue of editorial control or censorship, Perkins took a different tack. He had objected to Wolfe's "radical, or Marxian, beliefs" in the manuscript of *Of Time and the River* because they were anachronistic in a book recounting Eugene Gant's adventures in the early 1920s. No changes in Wolfe's manuscripts had ever been forced on the author, Perkins pointed out, adding, "You're not very forceable, Tom, nor I very forceful." In all the discussions of his manuscript, "you were never overruled. Do you think you are clay to be moulded! I never saw anyone less malleable."

Self-effacing and still hoping for a reconciliation, Perkins refrained from telling his rebellious author some home truths. He did not mention that, after nearly every other possible publisher had turned down "O Lost," he had brought about the publication of Wolfe's first novel. He did not remind Wolfe that his cutting and shaping of that manuscript had transformed it from an imperfectly executed American *Ulysses* into a first-rate novel about a boy's growing up. He did not say that Wolfe had been unable to complete a second novel until Perkins helped him work out the organization of *Of Time and the River*. He did not hint that others at Scribners criticized him for spending so much time on that manuscript or mention that even Wheelock complained that he was wasting too much of his energy on a second-rate talent. And, most important, he did not say — as a lesser man might have said — that without Maxwell Perkins there would have been no Thomas Wolfe.

Instead, Perkins told Wolfe that his was "a fine letter, a fine writer's statement of his beliefs," which contained "brave and sincere beliefs uttered with sincerity and nobility."

So far as the future was concerned, he promised to play a less active role. If Wolfe wanted to write about people at Charles Scribner's Sons, Perkins accepted the fact "that you have the same right to make use of them as of anyone else in the same way." He agreed that it was always best for an author to cut and shape his own work, and he pledged that "unless you want help it will certainly not be thrust upon you." Should subsequent books prove excessively long, that problem "could be dealt with by publishing in sections." Anyway, Perkins noted, Wolfe was now such an important figure in American letters that he was "in a position to publish with less regard to any conventions of bookmaking, say a certain number of pages almost, whether or not it had what in a novel is regarded as an ending, or anything else that is commonly expected in a novel." In all these matters, Perkins felt, the writer "should always be the final judge," and he pledged that, "apart from physical or legal limitations not within the possibility of change by us, we will publish anything as you write it."

It was a noble response to Wolfe's indictment, high-toned and affectionate. But just as Wolfe's letter did not finally break off his connection with Scribners, Perkins's replies did not offer many concrete proposals for continuing that relationship. Notably absent from all Perkins's letters was any offer of a contract, any proposal of terms, any suggestions of an advance.

One reason for Perkins's inconclusiveness was the Dormans' libel suit, which was still pending. In all probability he was neither free nor willing to talk with Wolfe about specific terms for his next book until he agreed to an out-of-court settlement.

During the whole month of February, Wolfe resisted pressure from Perkins, Charles Scribner, and Cook, their lawyer, to settle. He feared that this suit would endanger his whole career. "As everyone knows," Perkins commented later, "he used real people in his books, and if libel suits were to be brought frequently, what could he do?" "To have to buy the privilege of doing one's work and earning one's living by the payment of hush money to anyone who cho[o]ses to use the law as the means of annoying and coercing you, is a heavy price to pay," Wolfe argued, "and furthermore a very dangerous and risky one, since . . . a dog once baited with a hunk of meat will [not] be permanently appeased, but finding getting easy will come yelping at the heels again."

Distrusting Cook, he was happy to run into Melville Cane, the lawyer and poet who had read "O Lost" in manuscript, and he poured out the story of the Dormans' suit to him. Finding that he was "in a highly agitated state and at times incoherent," Cane arranged to meet with him and Perkins at Scribners on March 2, when, after having a calmer report on the Dorman affair, he also advised Wolfe to settle out of court. Under such pressures, Wolfe finally capitulated and allowed negotiations with the Dormans' lawyers to begin. After some haggling, the Dormans at the end of March finally agreed to drop their suit for a cash settlement of $2850.

Wolfe and Charles Scribner's Sons each paid half of this settlement, and they also equally shared the legal expenses, which totaled $2640. The firm counted this settlement as a victory. For a total of $2745 it had avoided a court case that might have resulted in damages of $125,000. Wolfe, on the other hand, viewed it as a disaster. After his share was paid directly from his royalty account at Scribners, he was left owing the company over a thousand dollars. Wolfe was outraged. He had been given no warning that the total cost of the settlement would be so great. Scribners had betrayed him and had given away what little remained of the royalties from *Of Time and the River*. "Dammit," he swore, "they've taken me to the cleaners, and without telling me a damned word!"

In fact, Wolfe exaggerated his financial plight. He now had a comfortable cash balance of between five and six thousand dollars in his bank account. But he estimated that he needed about twenty-five hundred dollars a year to live on — in addition to income tax, agents' commissions, lawyers' fees, and gifts to members of his family. Since his books now brought in only about sixteen hundred dollars a year, he realized that he must have more income and that he must earn it speedily.

III

Before agreeing to settle with the Dormans, Wolfe insisted on having a letter from Charles Scribner III, giving formal assurance "that we have no option or moral claim on any of your future books." Perversely he chose to take that letter as proof that Charles Scribner's Sons did not wish to be his publisher. Now, he told Miss Nowell, he was on his own and he was broke.

He could not publish a new novel, for he had nothing that approached a finished book. During the winter he had come to feel that "The Vision of Spangler's Paul" failed to capture the sense of bewildered innocence that he sought, the feeling that would make it an American *Don Quixote* or *Candide*. Recasting his hero as a very ordinary, but confused and comic, man, Wolfe began to reshuffle the material that he had written and started outlining a book with the tentative title of "The Life and Times of Joseph Doaks." For the next twelve months Joe Doaks remained his protagonist, appearing briefly in several stories, but Wolfe recognized that his novel about an average man was far in the future.

For the present the only way he could make money was by selling short stories. Turning to his agent, he said that it was "up to you, Miss Nowell, to help me write these stories and see me through."

During the first six months of 1937, she worked very closely with him. After the Dorman settlement he could no longer afford to employ a typist to take dictation, and he returned to drafting stories in longhand on sheets of cheap yellow typing paper. Almost every evening Miss Nowell came to his apartment, gathered up what he had written during the day, and used his typewriter to make a legible copy. Then she worked with him to reduce his stories to a length that magazines would publish. It seemed to her later that she "sat up with him practically all night, night after night, while he talked about these stories, when he wrote the greater part of them."

Wolfe began to learn from her line-by-line editing. The revisions that she suggested were not much different from those she had offered on his earlier stories, but he had not paid much attention then. Considering himself primarily a novelist, working under Perkins's guidance, he had often accepted her cuts, though with a good deal of grumbling, as necessary for magazine publication, but in his books he usually went back to his more extensive original text. Up to this point he had never been "sure that he could write a saleable story deliberately," and when a magazine accepted one of his shorter pieces he thought it was "just kind of blind luck." But now that he no longer showed Perkins his work, he relied more on Miss Nowell, and he came to see that the changes she proposed were not just expedients but improvements. Ever since the publication of *From Death to Morning* he had been working toward a leaner, less lyrical style, and her detailed criticism helped him to write with more restraint. Up through 1935, she recalled later, she was able to cut his manuscripts by about fifty percent without much loss, but now she found that she could not reduce them by more than one-third.

Some of the stories that he worked on during the first half of 1937 came from his big crate of manuscripts drafted earlier. The *New Yorker* accepted his sketch of his London charwoman with royalist sentiments, and, after much fretting over the possibility of a libel suit, it also took "Mr. Malone," his satirical sketch based on Ernest Boyd, the pretentious Irish-American critic who was the former husband of Madeleine Boyd. A fragment on a Japanese sculptor received a new introduction and ending and appeared in *Harper's Bazaar*. The *American Mercury* took an episode based on his love affair with Aline Bernstein, intended for "The October Fair," and published it under the title "April, Late April."

More impressive were his newer stories. After his return from the South he drafted "The Lost Boy," a moving, very slightly fictionalized memoir of his brother Grover, who died in 1904 while the family was in St. Louis. With Miss Nowell he went through the manuscript closely, eliminating repetition, excessive descriptions, and brooding philosophical reflections. Then she suggested further deletions to get down to the length of a magazine story. "I've cut the hell out of it," she reported. "A lot of the places will probably make your heart bleed." Together they reduced an eighty-two-page draft to a forty-page final manuscript that was accepted by *Redbook,* which paid fifteen hundred dollars — by far the most money Wolfe had ever received for a story.

"The Child by Tiger," Wolfe's most carefully crafted short story, which he wrote during 1936–1937, demonstrated how much he learned from working with Miss Nowell. This was a fictional account of an episode well known in Asheville, when a black man, Will Harris, went berserk in 1906 and shot five citizens before a posse killed him. Wolfe had mentioned the incident in his outline for "O Lost," and he also thought of including the story of "the coon who is hunted by the posse," in *Of Time and the River.* But he did not actually begin writing about it until the fall of 1936, when a casual conversation with Kenneth Littauer, the fiction editor of *Collier's* magazine, who had been in Asheville in 1906, reminded him of Will Harris again, and he drafted an account of "Nigger Dick" intended for inclusion in "The Vision of Spangler's Paul." Now, in the spring of 1937, he worked very closely with Miss Nowell in revising that draft, delicately and consciously balancing symbols of good and evil, of light and dark, and he dictated the final section to her as she sat at his typewriter.

Evidence that Wolfe was becoming a more conscious literary craftsman, "The Child by Tiger" also demonstrated his widening social sympathies. Originally he had intended the story to illustrate the "basic savagery" of the black race. But over the years, as he became more sensitive to injustice and discrimination, he came to see in Dick Prosser — as he now called the man who was at once a most obedient and devout servant and a cold-blooded, sharpshooting murderer — the potential for violence that lay in the hearts of all men. Wolfe's portrait of Prosser, the one full-scale Afro-American in his writing, was neither patronizing nor prejudiced. Like all men, Prosser embodied the perpetually conflicting forces of good and evil; he was at the same time "a friend, a brother," and "a mortal enemy, an unknown demon." The murderous madness of this black man was neither more nor less comprehensible than the savage blood lust of the white mob that tracked him down and gloated over his mutilated corpse.

Because the story dealt with delicate racial issues, Miss Nowell had difficulty in placing it. Littauer was fascinated by it but thought it too daring for his *Collier's* readers. *Redbook* also turned it down. Then, surprisingly, the *Saturday Evening Post* mustered its courage and accepted it, saying "that they expect to lose some of their old readers as a result but they will gain a lot of younger and more intelligent ones." Paying two thousand dollars for the story, the *Post* editors planned to feature it on the cover of the magazine. Once the *Post* began "to make all kinds of hullabaloo" about it, Miss Nowell predicted, "the other big magazines will be considerably impressed and more apt to buy things [from Wolfe] — length, or no length."

Because Wolfe was working so hard, and under such great emotional stress, his health began to suffer during the first half of 1937. In February he fell ill with what he diagnosed as the flu. Instead of going to bed, he tried to keep on writing, and for several days he walked around with a fever, until Louise Perkins finally persuaded him to see a doctor. The physician found him exhausted and warned, as Wolfe reported later, "if I don't slow down I'm going to crash." He may have made X rays that revealed a suspicious dark area in his chest, for afterwards, pacing up and down in his apartment, Wolfe blurted out to Miss Nowell, "There's something the matter with my lung."

Always afraid of illness — and particularly frightened by tuberculosis, the dread disease of the "lungers" in Asheville, for which there was no known cure — Wolfe began to have melancholy thoughts about death. As he reworked "I Have a Thing to Tell You," which Miss Nowell had finally placed in the *New Republic,* he added to his farewell to Germany a passage that he had begun to work on in 1935 in Copenhagen, when he also feared he might be deathly ill. With little relevance to a story about Hitler's Germany, this eloquent conclusion obviously reflected Wolfe's present concern for his health:

Something has spoken to me in the night, burning the tapers of the waning year; something has spoken in the night; and told me I shall die, I know not where. Losing the earth we know for greater knowing, losing the life we have for greater life, and leaving friends we loved for greater loving, men find a land more kind than home, more large than earth.

Over the next several months he continued to brood about death. Once he besought a friend who had seen a man die to tell him all about it. "Did he give any sign of — of — anything?" he asked, answering himself: "I suppose not. I suppose no one ever really has." A little later he surprised his brother by inquiring: "Fred, do you think I'm going to die?"

In this depressed state of mind, Wolfe decided that he ought to make a new will, replacing the 1930 document that had divided his estate equally between his mother and Aline Bernstein. Again he called on Melville Cane for assistance in drawing up what was really a very simple document. He left one thousand dollars to his mother in cash and set up a ten-thousand-dollar trust fund for her, from which she was to receive monthly payments for the rest of her life. The rest of his estate was to be divided in equal shares among his surviving brothers and sisters and their children.

Wolfe probably calculated that his estate would not total much more than the eleven thousand dollars bequeathed to his mother. When he told Julia about the new will, he said that he was "a little bit in the position of the man who said: 'If we have some ham, we would have some ham and eggs if we had some eggs.' " That he did not leave all that he had to her outright reflected, in part, his fear of her incurable tendency to invest in speculative real estate. He also knew that, at just this time, the Wachovia Bank and Trust Company of Asheville was suing her for nonpayment of loans that dated back to 1927. If the bank was successful, it could foreclose on all her property, including the Old Kentucky Home. By now Wolfe had enough experience with lawyers and courts to realize that anything his mother received from his estate might simply go to pay off the claims of the bank.

The designation of Maxwell Perkins as executor and trustee suggested how mixed Wolfe's emotions were at this time, but his choice was not so puzzling as it might initially seem. Though he had condemned Perkins for moral cowardice and for editorial censorship, he never questioned the editor's probity. By selecting Perkins as his executor, he was attempting to define what he hoped would be their future relationship. He earnestly wished Perkins to continue to be his great and good friend, his moral and intellectual adviser, and his substitute father — but not his editor or publisher.

Both men had great difficulty in maintaining this distinction, and consequently their relations were rocky during the spring and early summer of 1937. Though Wolfe now rarely went to the Scribners offices, he continued to visit the Perkinses at home and to meet Max for drinks or dinner. No matter how hard they tried to talk about neutral topics, the conversation always came around to Wolfe and Scribners. Perkins could not let the subject alone. Down deep he really did not believe Wolfe would ever really leave the firm. Wolfe could not stop discussing it because he knew he really was going to break from Scribners but was unwilling to do so without Perkins's consent and blessing. Again and again they went over the same old litany of grievances and excuses, until finally Perkins exclaimed in exasperation: "All right then, if you *must* leave Scribners, go ahead and *leave,* but for heaven's sake, *don't talk about it any more!"*

About this time Wolfe drafted another of his letters "To All Publishers (other than Scribners)," announcing that he was looking for a new editor. As he wrote, he found himself explaining that his connection with Scribners had been "characterized from beginning to end on both sides by feelings of the deepest affection and respect." Moreover, at Scribners he had "enjoyed the friendship of an editor of extraordinary character and ability, who . . . stood by me and gave me without stint not only the benefits of his great technical and editorial skill but also the even more priceless support of his faith and belief." Understandably he put the draft letter away, unsent.

Only when Wolfe was drunk did his anger toward Perkins surface. In April, Noble Cathcart, the publisher of the *Saturday Review of Literature,* gave a dinner party at Cherio's restaurant for Mr. and Mrs. Jonathan Daniels, who were visiting from North Carolina, and invited the Perkinses and Wolfe. A cousin of Mrs. Cathcart, named Julia McWilliams, was also a guest. At first things went along pleasantly enough, though Wolfe, who arrived late, had been drinking and was darkly reflecting on the Dorman suit. Then Julia McWilliams, in the shock of recognition, turned to him and blurted out: "Oh, now I know who you are. I read an article

about you in the *Saturday Review*. It was by Bernard De Voto."
Intervening quickly to change the subject, Daniels tactlessly observed that only *Scribner's Magazine* seemed regularly to publish
Wolfe's short stories and asked Perkins what was wrong with that
financially faltering magazine anyway. Wolfe took the remark to
mean that *Scribner's Magazine* showed bad judgment in publishing
his work. His face grew white, as it often did when he was drunk,
and he began insulting everybody at the table.

As Perkins quietly motioned the others in the party to leave,
Wolfe turned his now nearly murderous rage on the editor. When
Perkins tried to quiet him, he shouted, "Let me alone, you god-
damned old woman!" and began swinging his arms, preparing to
hit him. Perkins insisted that if he wanted to fight, he had to step
outside. But as they emerged from the restaurant, a tall, black-
haired, handsome woman, whom neither of them had ever seen
before, ran up to Wolfe, threw her arms around him, and said,
"This is what I came to New York to see." Nobody else heard
what followed, but within three or four minutes the woman was
cursing Wolfe in vile language. This unexpected intervention di-
verted his attention from Perkins, and the fracas ended without an
actual exchange of blows.

Even after such an episode they made up again. Within a few
days of the threatened fistfight, Wolfe told Hamilton Basso, who
had heard rumors of the incident: "Max Perkins and I are all right.
I think we always were, for that matter. Periodically I go out and
indulge in a sixty-round, knock down and drag out battle with
myself but I think Max understands that." Perkins did understand,
but the strain of keeping up such a tumultuous friendship began to
tell on both men. By the end of April, Wolfe was so emotionally
exhausted as well as physically tired that he decided that the time
had finally come to go home.

IV

He did not, however, return to Asheville directly. Still uncertain
how he would be received, he drifted south in stages, at each stop
mustering courage to proceed farther. First he went to York
Springs, Pennsylvania, and visited the cemetery where his father's
family was buried. Then he moved down the Shenandoah Valley,
stopping at Roanoke, Virginia, to buy a copy of *Gone With the*

Wind, which had just won a Pulitzer Prize. Pausing in Bristol, Tennessee, he then approached Asheville from the rear, stopping off in the little town of Burnsville, thirty-eight miles to the northeast, in Yancey County, his mother's home territory. There, on a Saturday night, he stepped out of the drugstore into a gunfight, in which three local men were involved, and he avoided injury by prudently ducking behind a car.

At Burnsville he also visited his great uncle, John Westall, then ninety-five years old, who recounted his adventures in the 29th North Carolina Infantry during the Civil War and told in great detail about the fighting at Chickamauga in 1863. Over the next months Wolfe blended Westall's recollections and other family lore with a completely fictional love story into "Chickamauga," which was told entirely in the voice of the old veteran. Its language did not represent John Westall's careful, usually correct English but reflected Wolfe's deliberate attempt to recapture the speech of mountain folk while avoiding too much dialect and too many colloquialisms. The clear structure of the story and restrained use of language again demonstrated how much Wolfe had learned from working with Miss Nowell, and he rightly believed that "Chickamauga" was "one of the best stories I ever wrote." But in 1937, long before the Civil War Centennial, editors considered it neither history nor fiction, and most of the major magazines turned it down before it was accepted by the *Yale Review.*

Finally, on May 3, 1937, Wolfe arrived in Asheville, for the first time since 1929. All his apprehensions about coming home proved unjustified. No sooner was he settled in the Old Kentucky Home than Julia's telephone began ringing, and presently as many as five or six people at a time were waiting in the parlor to greet the prodigal. The almost complete collapse of Asheville during the Great Depression had blurred the sense of injury caused by *Look Homeward, Angel.* Many of the residents portrayed in the novel were now dead; some now took a kind of perverse pride that they were the originals from which characters in a famous novel had been drawn. Wolfe softened any lingering animosities by telling members of the Asheville Business Club: "If anything I have written has displeased anyone in my home town, I am genuinely and sincerely sorry for it."

"I feel perfectly at home," he told a newspaperman, with a certain note of surprise in his voice. He found Pack Square, where

W. O. Wolfe had his shop, much as it had been when he was a boy, and when he walked along his former paper route with the reporter he discovered something familiar at every turn. Asheville in 1937 seemed little changed from Asheville in 1917 or, for that matter, in 1907. Brooding over the unexpected continuity, Wolfe lifted his eyes to the rim of hills that surrounded the city and said to the somewhat puzzled reporter, "You can't change the mountains."

Pleased and relieved at his welcome, Wolfe began to plan spending the summer in or near Asheville. Fred drove him, Mabel, and Julia around the Smoky Mountain National Park, which had been created after he left North Carolina, and they looked at several possible places where he could work in quiet. Finally somebody brought to his notice a cabin at Oteen, about five miles east of Asheville, owned by Max Whitson, a former classmate and a cartoonist, that seemed ideal. For only thirty dollars a month he could rent a big living room, comfortably if informally furnished, a large bedroom, a kitchen, and a bath, all surrounded by fifteen acres of woods that would ensure quiet and privacy. Whitson's cabin was also close enough to Asheville that, with a twenty- or thirty-minute bus ride, Wolfe could easily come in to see his mother. "She will be seventy-eight her next birthday," he explained to a friend, "and I felt that since I have seen so little of the family during the past seven or eight years, it might be a good idea to be near them this summer."

Before going back to New York to pack his belongings, Wolfe had one duty to perform. Scott Fitzgerald was under treatment for alcoholism at nearby Tryon. Though Wolfe never really liked Fitzgerald, he now felt sorry for him. Shortly after Zelda had been committed to a mental institution, a reporter from the *New York Evening Post* insinuated himself into Fitzgerald's confidence and extracted a long, self-pitying story about his troubles. Indignant at this kind of "rotten, vicious, treacherous, cheap, sensational" journalism, Wolfe went over to Tryon to show his sympathy.

It was a sad meeting, for Fitzgerald was on the wagon and was obviously depressed. As Wolfe got ready to leave, Fitzgerald suddenly asked how old he was.

"Why, Scott," he replied, "I'll soon be thirty-seven."

"My God, Tom, I'm forty," Fitzgerald said, and he warned: "Look, bud, we're at the dangerous age. You know in this country we burn ourselves out at the work we are doing, and this is particularly true of writers."

They parted amicably, but afterwards both men reflected on how very different they were as writers. Admiring Wolfe's vigor and profuseness, Fitzgerald deplored his lack of artistic control, and in July, after he had sufficiently recovered to leave for Hollywood, he urged Wolfe to restrain himself, "to cultivate an alter ego, a more conscious artist." The greatest writers, like Flaubert, he argued, wrote novels of selected incidents; their artistry was defined by what they left unsaid. Lesser writers, like Zola, tried to include everything in their fiction. "So Mme Bovary becomes eternal while Zola already rocks with age." Admitting that Wolfe's talent was "unmatchable in this or any other country" while his own was "of narrow scope," Fitzgerald clearly thought he was the American Flaubert while Wolfe was an American Zola.

Wolfe welcomed the chance to respond to this bouquet "smelling sweetly of roses but cunningly concealing several large-sized brickbats." Since Fitzgerald's criticism was unsolicited and since Wolfe, now about to leave Scribners, no longer had to consider Perkins's feelings, he felt he could be blunt, and, as he told Hamilton Basso, he let Fitzgerald "have it with both barrels." As far as he could tell, Fitzgerald's letter really said only "that you think I'd be a good writer if I were an altogether different writer from the writer that I am." Why should anybody assume that a novelist who was not like Flaubert had to be like Zola? Would it not be better to compare *Madame Bovary* with *Don Quixote, The Pickwick Papers,* or *Tristram Shandy* — all indubitably great books, not because their authors presented "selected incidents" but because they were novels "that *boil* and *pour.*" "Don't forget," Wolfe reminded Fitzgerald, "that a greater writer is not only a leaver-outer but also a putter-inner, and that Shakespeare and Cervantes and Dostoievsky were great putter-inners . . . and will be remembered for what they put in — remembered . . . as long as Monsieur Flaubert will be remembered for what he left out."

Of course, he continued, "I want to be a better artist. I want to be a more selective artist. I want to be a more restrained artist. . . . But Flaubert me no Flauberts, Bovary me no Bovarys, Zola me no Zolas, and exuberance me no exuberances." Fitzgerald knew too much about writing to accept the myth that Wolfe simply poured out words, all keyed to the same high emotional pitch. "You have had to work and sweat blood yourself," Wolfe reminded him, "and you know what it is like to try to write a living word or create a living thing. So don't talk this foolish stuff to me about exuberance or being a conscious artist or not bringing things into emotional relief." "Leave this stuff for those who huckster in it," he warned. "Don't De Voto me. If you do I'll call your bluff."

Wolfe's exchange with Fitzgerald was one of the few entirely satisfactory occurrences during his summer at Oteen. When the news spread that he was living out at Whitson's cabin, it seemed that everybody in Asheville and the surrounding counties wanted to come out and "look at the elephant." Day after day his writing was interrupted by "people driving up to demand if I've seen anything of a stray cocker spaniel, gentlemen appearing through the woods with a four-pound steak and saying their name is McCracken and I met them on the train four weeks ago and they always bring their own provisions with them, and the local Police Court judge and the leading hot-dog merchant, and friends of my shooting scrape in Yancey County with bevies of wild females." Of course, he could have discouraged these intruders, but, as he told Fred, he did not want to "become an utter hermit." In fact, even as he lamented the interruptions to his work, he welcomed the guests. His secretary noticed that whenever he heard a car in the long driveway up to the cabin he dashed out to welcome the visitors. Their stay at the cabin was certainly not shortened by the fact that he always had a jug of whiskey stashed behind his couch.

Wolfe saw a great deal of his family during the summer. Julia and Mabel often came out to see him, and Fred came up from time to time from Spartanburg, South Carolina. He welcomed the opportunity to become reacquainted with Effie's children when the family drove up from Anderson, South Carolina, and he was proud that he could take them all out to dinner at the Gross Brothers Restaurant, just around the corner from the Old Kentucky Home, where the total bill came to eight or nine dollars. The younger children, like Edward Gambrell, wandered about his cabin, where they were much impressed with his "drink box" — a container of soft drinks on ice, like those found in filling stations. Of his nephews, Wolfe particularly enjoyed Dietz Wolfe, Frank's son, mostly because, preoccupied with the usual problems of adolescence, he was not deferential and did not ask inane questions about how it felt to be a great American author. Once, when they were having a meal together in the cabin, Wolfe jumped up from his chair, poked him in the ribs, and roared: "Dietz — did it ever occur to you that you were eating supper in Uncle Tom's Cabin?"

Wolfe was much less happy that Frank was also in Asheville. Julia's oldest son had a constriction of the esophagus that made it impossible to swallow solid food, and he feared that he had cancer. Feeling obliged to visit him, Wolfe could not suppress his detestation for this brother who had tormented him as a child, and he brutally asked why he didn't drink enough to kill himself. "You drink, don't do anything else but drink; you never have tried to make anything out of yourself. . . . Why don't you die?" Yet he also insisted that his ailing brother must be taken to a clinic for a complete set of X rays, and he was genuinely relieved when the doctors announced there was no cancer. With his usual reversal of moods, Wolfe then turned to Dietz and urged him not to be too hard on his father.

Wolfe saw something of Mr. and Mrs. Roberts during the summer, but their relationship was now distant. Mrs. Roberts had forgiven him for the pain that *Look Homeward, Angel* caused her, and she was happy that he had attained fame and success. But he was no longer her schoolboy protégé, whom she could encourage and advise. She did not now feel sufficiently close to rebuke Wolfe for drinking too much, even though she grew very angry to see him "butcher his genius with liquor."

He found more pleasure in meeting the younger college-educated people in Asheville, among whom he was a kind of hero, and as a distinguished literary figure he had entree to social circles into which his family had never been admitted. One of the happiest evenings of the summer was a little dinner party that Lillian ("Tot") Weaver gave for him and half a dozen other friends. Feeling relaxed and very much at home among friends who loved him and admired his writing, Wolfe read selections from Palgrave's *Golden Treasury* to the group. The slight hesitation or impediment in his speech disappeared as he got under way, and in his strong baritone voice, he read poems by Keats and Herrick. Then he turned to Milton's "Lycidas," and when he came to "Look homeward, angel, now, and melt with ruth," his listeners experienced a little shiver of recognition.

Despite all the interruptions, Wolfe did manage to get some work done during the first part of the summer. He decided to concentrate on a single, long episode, which would be both a short story and a section of his novel, based on the fire that he had witnessed in Aline Bernstein's Park Avenue apartment in 1930. The idea was not a new one; he had made notes for such a story as early as 1930 and had drafted part of it in 1933. He brought to Oteen a full, typed second draft, but he realized that it required major reshaping and revision. He wanted "The Party at Jack's" to be more than a fictional recreation of the Bernstein ménage, a portrait of wealthy, pretentious urban Americans so bored that they needed the diversion of Alexander Calder's inane puppet circus. This story of how their whole life was changed by the fire in the deep underground tunnels that burrowed through Manhattan was to be a kind of parable for the collapse of ostentatious capitalism at the outset of the Great Depression. Because the story had more than thirty identifiable characters, Wolfe found writing it "a terrifically complicated and difficult job." The design of the story was elaborate and, he felt, "somewhat Proustian," since "its life depends upon the most thorough and comprehensive investigation of character." From his recent work with Miss Nowell, he knew he had to include also a great deal of action.

Day after day he worked over the typescript, revising some passages, adding others, but more often writing a new, fuller version on the yellow second sheets that he favored. Miss Nowell's recent success in selling his short stories gave him money enough to hire a typist, and after briefly trying one young woman who, it proved, could neither spell nor type, he was fortunate enough to find Virginia Hulme, a local college girl, who came out every day to collect the pages that he brushed off on the floor, arranged them as best she could, and typed up a final draft. By the end of the summer, though the story was not quite complete, Wolfe was justifiably proud of "The Party at Jack's." "It was a very difficult piece of work," he reported to Miss Nowell, "but I think it is now a single thing, as much a single thing as anything I've ever written."

But the longer Wolfe remained at Oteen, the harder he found it was to reserve time for writing. There were too many invitations that he could not resist. He had to go to the steak supper that James S. Howell, who had roomed with him for a time at Chapel Hill, arranged for him and other boyhood friends at a cabin in the

Reems Creek section. He felt obliged to speak at the Veterans Hospital at Oteen, and he could not decline a request to address a University of North Carolina alumni rally. There was no way he could escape a fund-raising lunch of prominent business, civic, and political leaders at the George Vanderbilt Hotel to promote an Asheville auditorium and convention hall.

A good many of his social obligations he found emotionally as well as physically taxing. As a gesture of peace to his mother's family, who had been particularly outraged by *Look Homeward, Angel,* he accepted a dinner invitation from his cousin Jack Westall. Since he had no car, he was obliged to hitch a ride into Asheville with Virginia Hulme at the end of her working day. When he got into the car, that spunky young woman told him that he ought to wear a coat if he was going to a dinner party. Obediently Wolfe got out of the car, which rocked from side to side when relieved of his weight, and went into the cabin and found a coat. After he got back in, she suggested that he really ought to wash his hands, which were very dirty, and again he went in, washed, and returned. Then she noticed that his fingernails were long and grimy and told him, as she would a little boy, that he must clean them. "Great God!" he exclaimed. "You're enough to drive a man crazy!" But he did go and clean his nails. These efforts at neatness, combined with his nervousness over sitting down to dinner with his wealthy, critical cousins, were apparently too much for him. When they reached Asheville, he insisted on getting out at his mother's house, instead of going over to the Westalls' mansion. Virginia Hulme learned the next day that he never did get to the party, though he later wrote a very sweet note of apology to his neglected hostess.

Even more taxing was the summons he received to appear as a witness in a murder trial in Burnsville. The three men involved in the shooting fracas that Wolfe had observed resumed their battle a week later, and one of them was killed. Wolfe was called as a witness to the earlier disturbance, and James Howell, an attorney, told him he had to obey the subpoena or go to jail. Reluctantly Wolfe did give his evidence. In his summation, the defense lawyer urged the jury to take no account of his testimony, since he was "the author of an obscene and infamous book," *Look Homeward, Angel,* a man who "had held up his family, kin-folk, and town to public odium."

Renewal of these old charges was too much for Wolfe, who was already unhappy because his summer was dribbling away, with so little accomplished. That evening, back in Asheville, he got roaringly drunk, and two Asheville policemen had to detain him overnight in the city jail.

Finding that his cabin at Oteen did not give him the privacy he needed, Wolfe moved into the Battery Park Hotel, in the center of Asheville, only a few blocks from the Old Kentucky Home, but he gave his secretary strict instructions not to tell anyone, even his mother, his whereabouts. He tried to do more work on "The Party at Jack's," but by this time he was deeply depressed and was drinking heavily. His whole summer, as he told his mother later, had been "a calamity."

Early in September Wolfe left Asheville — as he had left Germany, as he had left Scribners — forever. After he returned to New York, a student who heard him at Chapel Hill asked whether he had really meant it when he said he would like to go back to North Carolina to live. A little bitterly, Wolfe replied: "I did then. But going back taught me this one thing. A man can't go back home again. . . . I could never go back there to live, back there or any other place for long. I have to move. My home is in my work, now."

XIII

A New World Is Before Me Now

EFORE HE LEFT ASHEVILLE, Wolfe finally began looking for
a new publisher. After drinking a good deal to bolster his
courage, he placed long-distance calls to Harcourt, Brace &
Company, Harper & Brothers, Doubleday, Doran & Company,
and Alfred A. Knopf, Inc., in New York and to Houghton Mifflin
Company and Little, Brown & Company in Boston. In no case
did he properly introduce himself or explain what was on his
mind. Instead he simply blurted out: "My name is Wolfe. Would
you be interested in publishing me?"

The recipients of his calls were puzzled, since the story of his
problems with Scribners had not been widely circulated. At Harpers he reached Leo Hartman, editor of *Harper's Magazine,* which
had never accepted any of Wolfe's stories. After initially thinking
that the call was a hoax, Hartman decided that the deep-voiced,
seemingly half-intoxicated man on the phone wanted him to publish a short story and replied loftily: "Send me something. I'll be
glad to look it over." Wolfe concluded that Harper & Brothers
was not interested in becoming his publisher.

At Knopf, Mrs. Blanche Knopf expressed a lively interest, and
she repeatedly telephoned Elizabeth Nowell, urging her to have
Wolfe "march right over with his manuscript." But Wolfe regretted calling Knopf almost as soon as he put down the telephone.
Perhaps he remembered that the Knopfs were great friends of

Aline Bernstein, and he may have heard that they were about to publish her autobiographical novel, *The Journey Down*. He concluded that the firm was an exhibitionist Jewish house and told Miss Nowell that he would have nothing more to do with it.

When Alfred Harcourt learned of Wolfe's call, he immediately consulted Charles Scribner and Maxwell Perkins, for Harcourt, Brace and Scribners had long-standing friendly relations. Both assured Harcourt that they would bear no hard feelings if he signed Wolfe up. Perkins said he "didn't think there was any other possibility," since Wolfe was too important a writer for any publisher to pass up. But Harcourt did not pursue the matter.

In fact, the people at Scribners were deeply hurt by Wolfe's actions. Though he had talked about leaving for nearly two years, they had not believed that he ever would do it. Perkins, in particular, grieved and worried. Nearly every day he called Miss Nowell's office to make inquiries about Wolfe, and he repeatedly insisted on having drinks with her, when he interminably reviewed the events that had led up to Wolfe's departure. "He has . . . turned his back on me, and Scribners," he wrote to Fred Wolfe — knowing that Fred would promptly pass the message along to his brother — and he professed a total inability to understand his decision. "He goes about town denouncing us for having got him into a libel suit," Perkins told Mrs. Bernstein, adding wryly: "There was one, you know, which resulted from a story he wrote, but he has some strange idea that we fomented it, even in the face of the very considerable expense to us."

But Wolfe was not denouncing anybody. Indeed, he was not talking much, for he was mostly worrying about his future. He was less than candid in saying that his funds were "almost exhausted" and that he was "right up against the wall"; at the end of September his balance in the Chase National Bank was $5,544.17. But now that he had severed his ties with Scribners and no other publisher had offered him a contract, he had no assured income.

At this point his most promising publishing connection seemed to be with Houghton Mifflin. Robert N. Linscott of that firm, whom Wolfe had met several years earlier over breakfast at the Algonquin Hotel, wrote on October 8 to express strong interest in becoming his publisher. Wolfe, he said, more than any other contemporary novelist, carried on "the tradition of indigenous American literature reflected in our own list since the days of Thoreau."

Linscott was confident that at Houghton Mifflin Wolfe would "find the understanding and enthusiasm essential for a lasting publishing alliance."

Deeply gratified, Wolfe wanted to talk at length with Linscott about "all the questions and difficulties involved" in becoming his publisher. "It is," he warned, "a question that involves the work of years, several million words of manuscripts, the material of at least three big books and a lot of stories, and the kind of use I am going to make of that material." He also suggested that the editor ought to have a full and frank discussion with Perkins, "the fine man who for eight or nine years has known more about me and my work than anyone else."

Coming down to New York, Linscott did visit Perkins, who told him "that Tom was half angel and half devil and that I was sure to run into trouble if I were lucky enough to get him." Then he spent the next day or two with Wolfe, whom he found "considerate and completely charming." Wolfe in turn liked Linscott, a ruggedly handsome man who faintly resembled Abraham Lincoln, and they were soon on first-name terms. Wolfe went over his grounds for leaving Scribners in such detail that Linscott believed he was really trying to clarify his own thoughts; privately the editor thought that much of the story "made little sense." Wolfe told Linscott that he was going to continue his huge autobiographical novel recounting the adventures of Joe Doaks — but he also suggested that he might interrupt that saga to write two or three other books, including "a sort of glorified and fictionalized travelogue of America" in the form of "a novel about an itinerant filling station attendant, who travels all over the country from job to job."

Impressed, Linscott talked about offering an advance against future royalties of ten thousand dollars, payable at the rate of five hundred dollars a month, which was what Wolfe said he needed to live on, but he had to explain that as a member of a conservative family-owned firm he had only limited freedom to offer contracts. Houghton Mifflin had a fixed rule that an advance could be given an author only after the company had seen at least a considerable portion of his manuscript.

But Wolfe had no manuscript to show Houghton Mifflin. In order to economize and to protect his privacy after the break with Scribners, he had given up his apartment on First Avenue, and he kept moving from one inexpensive hotel to another, not even giving his mother his address. All mail and telephone messages had to reach him through Miss Nowell's office. His furniture, books, and most of his papers were in the Mammoth Storage Warehouse in Brooklyn. Other batches of his manuscripts were still at Scribners.

Linscott tried to solve this difficulty by offering space for his papers in the New York offices of Houghton Mifflin. Wolfe himself went out to the Brooklyn warehouse with Paul Brooks, who worked for Houghton Mifflin, and they managed to haul back in a taxi the crate of papers. As for the manuscripts in Perkins's office, he took the coward's course of sending Miss Nowell to retrieve them. When his papers were finally assembled, Wolfe felt grandly pleased at having found a new publisher, and the people from Houghton Mifflin were, as Miss Nowell recalled, "dancing round with joy in the street."

Just before Wolfe left, however, Linscott handed him a letter formally acknowledging receipt of "1 packing case and 9 packages of Manuscripts," which, he noted, would be held at the Houghton Mifflin office "entirely at your risk." Offputting as Wolfe found this disclaimer of responsibility, he was even more upset by the fact that the letter was formally addressed "Dear Wolfe" and signed "R. N. Linscott." Angrily he drafted a reply: "You can not talk to a man over the dinner table and a drink about your belief and interest and enthusiasm for his work, and how your organization supports and upholds such people in failure or success, and then talk about who is to take the risk, or whose responsibility is whose when he brings his property into your office and entrusts it to your care."

He did not, however, mail the letter. After all, Houghton Mifflin was the only firm that had expressed a vigorous interest in becoming his publisher. Anyway, he was gradually becoming "accustomed to the idea that publishers were not divine institutions of generosity and light." Filing his letter, he went quietly to Houghton Mifflin the next day and removed his manuscripts.

But now he had to find a place where he could spread his papers out and work on them in safety and privacy. By chance he ran into Edgar Lee Masters, the author of *Spoon River Anthology,* who recommended the Chelsea Hotel, where he was living, and Wolfe recalled that much earlier Perkins had also spoken well of this old hotel on 23rd Street, which had for years been a residence for artists and writers. It was not very expensive, it was centrally located, and, most important of all, it had very large rooms with high ceilings, so that he would not feel cramped. The last week in October Wolfe rented a room at the east end of the Chelsea and, finding the hotel to his liking, soon moved to a suite at the west end. Here, for $138.68 a month, he had two very large rooms — "each of them . . . as big as a skating rink," he boasted — a small anteroom or foyer, and an enormous bathroom, which he called the "Throne Room," because the toilet was mounted on a pedestal. He made one of the large rooms his bedroom, deposited his crate of papers in the middle of the second, and set up his typist in the small room.

As he looked over his manuscript, he became less and less enthusiastic about showing it to Houghton Mifflin. He wrote Linscott that some of this "material for an enormous book" was in nearly final shape. But reexamining his manuscript "with a fresh eye after having been away from most of it for three or four years," he had to admit that much of his book was "not even yet in rough draft form." In fact, Miss Nowell remembered, his manuscript was in no shape for any publisher to read; "it was just a great mass of material he'd written."

To satisfy Linscott, Wolfe pulled out "The October Fair," the fictional account of his affair with Mrs. Bernstein, and tried to put it into final form. He reviewed his typed drafts, penciled in transitions between sections, and occasionally created new chapters from different segments of his other manuscripts. Attempting to explain to his new publisher, and perhaps to himself, what he was doing, he drafted a little preface that reviewed the "strange and troubled" history of "The October Fair." "Its chronology is vexed," he noted, for the book had been conceived in 1930, most of it had been written between 1931 and 1933, but other sections had been added between 1933 and 1937. In consequence, he admitted, "the whole thing is a maelstrom, the man [i.e., the protagonist in the love story] is like a hound set loose upon a dozen scents."

As Wolfe revised, his doubts about Houghton Mifflin began to grow. Though both Linscott and Brooks kept encouraging him with notes, Linscott did not come back to New York and continue his conversations with Wolfe as he had promised. He explained that an abscessed tooth kept him in Boston. Wolfe became suspicious. "Goddammit," he exploded to Miss Nowell. "Do you think he *really* has an abscessed tooth, or are they giving me the runaround? They say it's years since they 'moved toward a publishing alliance' with greater anticipation . . . but dammit all, . . . I can't see that we're moving toward anything at all!"

Wolfe was correct in suspecting that Houghton Mifflin was having second thoughts. Some in the office were troubled by a letter from Aline Bernstein, threatening to sue Houghton Mifflin if Wolfe's new novel depicted her in any way. Others, remembering how long and hard Perkins had to struggle with Wolfe over his first two novels, were not sure that Houghton Mifflin could take on such a responsibility. Someone came up with the idea of hiring Elizabeth Nowell as a special editorial consultant, whose duties would be to manage Thomas Wolfe. As Wolfe's agent, Miss Nowell felt she had to report this proposal to him, and he became very angry with Houghton Mifflin. "Here I had been dealing with them for weeks," he said, "only to discover that they were scared of me. I knew then that I was in the wrong church and the wrong pew."

I

At this point, early in November, Edward C. Aswell, assistant editor at Harper & Brothers, heard for the first time that Wolfe had left Scribners. The source of his information, improbably enough, was Wolfe's old enemy, Bernard DeVoto. He made an appointment to meet Wolfe at the Brevoort Hotel on November 11, and the two men immediately hit it off. Aswell, who had read everything that Wolfe had published, considered him the greatest living American writer. Neither then nor later did he doubt that Wolfe was a genius, "the greatest man I have had the good fortune to know, the most singularly honest intellectually, and the most lovable."

Wolfe took an immediate liking to Aswell, with whom he discovered that he had much in common. Both were Southerners, for Aswell came from Tennessee. Always a believer in omens, Wolfe felt it was significant that Aswell, too, had been born in October 1900, only six days after Wolfe. Both had attended Harvard, though in different years. While Wolfe had gone directly from high school to college to graduate school, Aswell had worked for a shoe company, first in Nashville and later in Chicago, for five years after high school and did not enter Harvard until 1922. At the university they had some of the same teachers, though Aswell, as an undergraduate who took his degree with distinction in history and literature, had closer ties to Harvard, for he had been chairman of the editorial board of the *Harvard Crimson* and class orator. After serving as assistant editor of the *Forum* and then of *Atlantic Monthly*, Aswell had joined Harper & Brothers in 1935.

After dinner the two men went to Wolfe's rooms at the Chelsea to continue their conversation. Taking off his coat and tie, unbuttoning his collar, and rolling up his sleeves, Wolfe paced back and forth as he told Aswell the whole story of his complicated relationship with Scribners and of his continuing affection for Perkins. As he recounted his luckless attempts to find a new publisher, Aswell realized that this man was deeply depressed, feeling that no one really wanted him and that he was now back where he had been at the beginning of his career as a writer.

Moved, he told Wolfe how much reading *Look Homeward, Angel* and *Of Time and the River* had meant to him and expressed confidence that Wolfe's future novels would be even more successful. To give substance to his encouraging words, he promised that Harpers would offer an advance of ten thousand dollars — even fifteen thousand dollars, if he insisted — on his next book, sight unseen. It was a daring — almost a foolish — thing for a junior editor, at a commercial house known to be more penny-pinching than most, to do, but Aswell thought that such a dramatic gesture was required to restore Wolfe's faith in himself.

Wolfe was deeply touched. The amount of Aswell's offer was impressive — "so large," he confessed, "that I was rather overwhelmed by it." Even more reassuring was the fact that Harpers, unlike Houghton Mifflin, would not make the advance contingent upon the receipt of an acceptable manuscript. He promised to think the offer over.

The next day Aswell hastened to inform his superiors, Cass Canfield, the president of Harper & Brothers, and Eugene Saxton, the editor-in-chief, of his unauthorized proposal. To his enormous relief, they approved, and both wanted to meet with Wolfe. A few days later Saxton invited Wolfe to join him, along with Canfield, Aswell, and another Harpers editor, for dinner at his place on

Gramercy Park. Afterward, when they sat with drinks before the fireplace in the living room, Wolfe told them the story of his life as a writer and the tale of his troubles with Scribners. Mostly the others listened with fascinated attention, but from time to time the third editor, who could not hold his liquor, staggered across the room and whispered loudly to Aswell: "He is the most Goddamned honest man I ever heard talk." The party did not break up until five in the morning.

Much impressed by the editors, Wolfe left convinced that the Harpers people "actually seem to be intensely and deeply interested in me as a man and as a writer, which, in a publishing connection, I think is a pretty important thing."

Still, he delayed for a full month before making a final decision. For one thing, James Poling, the managing editor of Doubleday, offered to match the contract terms offered by any other firm. Wolfe did not consider Doubleday seriously, for he thought it was a "Big-Production Factory," but he always found it hard to say no to anybody. Anyway, after such a long period when it seemed that no one wanted his books, it was flattering to be wooed by several publishers. Besides, he felt he had some commitment to Houghton Mifflin. Every time Wolfe worked himself up to the point of accepting the Harpers offer he drew back, explaining to Miss Nowell: "Goddammit . . . I *like* Bob Linscott. He looks like Abe Lincoln, and he's a wonderful man and I'm his friend."

Behind Wolfe's delaying tactics was the recognition that he was about to make his break with Scribners irreparable. Facing "one of the most grievous and painful decisions of my life," he began to drink heavily, and, as usual, alcohol made him suspicious and belligerent. At least once during these weeks of indecision he made a drunken call to Elizabeth Nowell, accusing her of gossiping about his plan to change publishers. On another night, while he was strolling through the lobby of the Chelsea Hotel, the switchboard operator, with whom he had been on easy, joking terms, called him "Toots," and her familiarity so offended his drunken ego that he protested to the manager. When the hotel manager offered to fire the offending young woman, Wolfe angrily denounced him for persecuting the help.

His most conspicuous flare-up was with Sherwood Anderson, whom he had visited in Virginia, on the way back from Asheville, and had liked very much. Now in New York, the Andersons asked Wolfe and a few other friends for dinner on December 1. Inevitably he arrived very late, and it was obvious that he had been drinking. There was a good deal of conversation about various liberal and radical causes in which the Andersons were much involved, and after a time guests began talking about the conservatism of the South. Mrs. Anderson, who was a native of Pennsylvania, observed that Southerners were intolerant of liberal views but did not challenge them directly; instead, they attacked liberals on other, extraneous grounds. For instance, she remarked, she had heard in the South that Wolfe was half-Jewish. Extremely upset, Wolfe jumped up from the table, announced that his father's Pennsylvania family was as good as Mrs. Anderson's and declared that he was going to take the next train to North Carolina, where his mother could refute this slander. After a time Anderson succeeded in calming him down, and by the end of the evening he appeared to have forgotten all about the matter.

But he did not. He continued to brood over Mrs. Anderson's remark, which undoubtedly stemmed from a rumor, which had bothered him since at least 1933, that Eleanor Jane Heikes, his father's mother, had been Jewish. Wolfe's halfhearted efforts to trace his genealogy had proved inconclusive, but he had convinced himself that the story was untrue. To revive it now, he concluded darkly, would affect "a lot of obscure decent people . . . pretty tragically in so many of the fundamental relations of life and their marital relations, [and] their social and business relations." Even more serious were the consequences that it could have for his own career, for up to this point he had been considered "a pretty American sort of writer, . . . indigenous to this country." In Wolfe's mind, Jews — whatever he might say in praise of their opulence, taste, and intellectual distinction — were clearly not truly American. This conclusion he claimed he had arrived at "honestly without a word or thought of prejudice toward any people, any race, or any creed."

More than two weeks after the dinner party Wolfe accidentally spotted Anderson, who was having lunch at the Brevoort Hotel, called him out into the lobby, and, as he reported to Miss Nowell later, "told old Sherwood off." After acknowledging that *Winesburg, Ohio* had been important to his generation of American writers, Wolfe charged that Anderson had failed them. His recent books about people "sitting around and talking, naked, on parlor sofas" — Wolfe was probably referring to Anderson's *Many Marriages* — proved that he "was done as a writer." Then, having told off the "Squire of Marion" — as both Hemingway and Faulkner had felt compelled to do earlier — Wolfe with drunken solemnity announced that Anderson "had done the best writing that had been done in this country in this century," shook his hand, and left.

Back at the Chelsea, Wolfe was dismayed to find a letter from Anderson, indirectly apologizing for "the queer row" that had erupted at the dinner and inviting him to a cocktail party and dinner. Before Wolfe could reply, he received a second note from Anderson, withdrawing the invitation: "As you have expressed such a hearty desire to chuck our acquaintance — why not."

Sobering up, Wolfe drafted a long reply — which he may not have mailed — apologizing for saying "some things which were out of order" about Anderson as a writer. His outburst against Anderson, he explained, was "just accidental." "I wasn't thinking about it or you so much when it happened, as about something else," he wrote. But if Anderson felt that his outburst had put an end to their friendship, Wolfe would have to accept his decision. "If this is the way it stands," he agreed, "it's got to stand this way — only I don't feel 'Why not?' "

The day after this quarrel with Anderson Wolfe chose Harpers as his publisher, and over the next few days he and Aswell worked out the details of an agreement. The publisher offered him a contract for his new novel, tentatively titled "The Life and Adventures of the Bondsman Doaks," with an advance of ten thousand dollars — a very substantial sum in the 1930s — charged against the fifteen percent royalties he would earn on the sales of the book.

Before accepting the contract, Wolfe followed Miss Nowell's advice and took it to the Authors League for review. He was a little concerned that the advance was for ten thousand dollars, not fifteen thousand, as he had understood Aswell to promise, but the lawyers at the Authors League convinced him that if he succeeded in getting more he might lose the company's good will. More troubling were provisions concerning subsidiary rights and motion picture rights, which he wanted Miss Nowell to continue to handle. "No one," he promised her, "is going to take one little penny of the ill-gotten gains which have enabled you thus far to wallow in luxury at my expense — no sir, by gum, not if I can help it."

The caution Wolfe exhibited toward the Harpers contract was an indication of what his relationship to his new editor would be. He liked Aswell and thought he was "a very fine fellow," who was "quiet, but very deep and true." In choosing him over Linscott he was affected by Aswell's belief "that I am the best writer there is." But he realized that he was "playing a personal hunch" in choosing an editor so young and relatively inexperienced, and he knew from the beginning that Aswell could never be the substitute father that Perkins had been, fulfilling "the wonderful image of our youth — that we will find someone external to our life and superior to our need, who knows the answer."

Consequently, as the Christmas season began, Wolfe felt as much sadness as he did joy. "I am worrying for the dead this Christmas," he wrote, "and for a lot of things that can't be helped." Improbably enough he sent a Christmas card to Charles Scribner III, assuring him: "I think you are not only the finest publishers, but among the finest people I have ever known."

Still, Wolfe knew that it was time to make a new beginning, and he accepted the Aswells' invitation to spend Christmas with them in Chappaqua. Late in the afternoon of Christmas Eve he showed up at Miss Nowell's office, drunk but not bellicose, to offer her a Christmas present of many boxes of Marlboro cigarettes, since he was constantly cadging cigarettes from her when they worked together. Then he insisted on taking Miss Nowell out for a Christmas drink, and by the time she managed to get him into a taxi to Grand Central Station, he had missed most of the trains.

Meanwhile at Chappaqua Aswell met every train, looking for his guest. Finally, at one o'clock on Christmas morning, Wolfe emerged as the final passenger on the last local. In one hand he had his overnight bag, and in the other was what Aswell at first took for a dead animal. It proved to be "the largest and ugliest stuffed toy dog anybody had ever seen." Gift-wrapped when Wolfe bought it, it had been used to wipe up the bars he had visited; the wrappings had come off, the box had disintegrated, and the tail was attached by only a few threads. "Sorry to be late, Ed," Wolfe greeted him. "I hadn't meant to do this, but I got something here for your boy for Christmas."

Aswell managed to get him to the house and to bed, where he

passed out and threw up in his sleep. The next morning when Aswell brought his little boy, Duncan, in to greet the guest, Wolfe pulled the bedclothes up to his chin in order to conceal the damage.

But after that things got better. Mary Lou Aswell had reread the description of Christmas dinner in *Look Homeward, Angel* and had prepared all Wolfe's favorite dishes. One of the other guests had brought the cranberry sauce, "with those whole cranberries all mushed up in it," and Wolfe told her that if she could also make lemon meringue pie he would marry her. At the end of the meal, when everybody was relaxed and happy, Mrs. Aswell asked Wolfe in a whisper if she could tell her friends the news. When he agreed, champagne was brought out, and she announced that Wolfe had chosen Harpers as his new publisher. "I tried to say something," Wolfe wrote a few days later, "and Ed tried to say something and neither could very well, and everyone had tears in their eyes, and I think they meant it, too." All told, he thought it was "a swell Christmas," "the best one I have had since I was a kid."

Back in New York, Wolfe nevertheless delayed as long as possible before signing his contract with Harpers. But Aswell reminded him that if he signed and received the first twenty-five hundred dollars of his advance before the end of the year he could save a considerable amount of income tax. On December 31, Aswell brought the check to the Chelsea, and Wolfe finally put his name on the contract. "I am committed utterly, in every way," he recognized, and he had "a strangely empty and hollow feeling, . . . the sense of absolute loneliness and new beginning." It was not "the hollowness of death, but a living kind of hollowness," he believed, for he was confident of the future: "A new world is before me now."

II

Then Wolfe settled down to work on his new book. He had not been idle since his return to New York in September, but his distracting personal and publishing problems made much of his effort fairly aimless. In addition, during these months his writing was taking a new direction. "I cannot say whether the direction is for better or for worse," he explained to Melville Cane. "I can only say that it was inevitable, and that I shall never again write the kind of book I wrote before." No longer did he wish his writing to be "largely concerned with the affairs and preoccupations of youth and of the world in terms of its impingements on my own personality." Instead, he wanted to write about "the life around me and . . . the broader social implications it has." But he was not certain how to deal with his new perception of reality or how to adapt it to his literary purposes.

During the fall of 1937 he had begun to talk with the left-leaning writers and intellectuals in Sherwood Anderson's circle. Up to this time he had thought of American Communists as members of a small, fashionable cult, who had to be placated from time to time because of the control they exercised over book reviewing and literary criticism, but the few people he knew in the party he neither liked nor respected. Now, through Anderson, he met genuine, dedicated party members, like the tough-minded, articulate Ella Winter, widow of Lincoln Steffens and veteran of a dozen Communist campaigns.

From their first meeting — at the dinner where he had such a row with the Andersons — Wolfe was impressed by Winter's intelligence and perceptiveness. When he told her about his recent visit to Asheville and of "his horror at going back to his home and what he found there," she promptly countered: "But don't you know you can't go home again?" Her words crystallized for Wolfe the still unarticulated lesson of his summer at home. "Can I have that?" he asked her eagerly. "I mean for a title? I'm writing a piece . . . and I'd like to call it that. It says exactly what I mean."

Over the next few days Wolfe brooded over her casual remark, which, the more he reflected on it, seemed to apply not merely to his return to Asheville but to so many of his other adult experiences. Unwittingly, he had for years been engaged in a "process of discovery" that, indeed, you can't go home again. A man could not go "back home to one's family, back home to one's childhood, back home to the father one has lost, back home to romantic love, to a young man's dreams of glory and of fame, back home . . . to lyricism, singing just for singing's sake, back home to aestheticism, to one's youthful ideas of the 'artist' and the all-sufficiency of 'art and beauty and love,' . . . back home to the escapes of Time and Memory." Winter's brief phrase, he concluded, expressed "a pretty tremendous fact and revelation."

Much impressed by Winter, Wolfe asked her to introduce him to some other Communists and — still rankling over the dinner with the Andersons — also to "some Jews." When she suggested Mike Gold, author of the proletarian novel *Jews Without Money*, he leapt at the chance, and the two men got along very well. Presently Wolfe contributed a story to *New Masses*, which Gold edited, a fictionalized version of how the National Cash Register Company had dictated the style of life and had dominated the thoughts of his brother-in-law, Ralph Wheaton, only to fire him when his sales fell off.

The news of Wolfe's association with these leftists spread, and, in this period when Moscow ordered its disciples to join in a Popular Front of all opponents of fascism, others sought to enlist him in radical causes. Almost daily he began to receive requests to sign left-wing petitions or to engage in radical demonstrations. He was asked "to . . . serve on committees of protest about the condition of the sharecroppers in the South — about the imprisonment of Tom Mooney — about the violation of civil liberties in various places — about the Scottsboro boys — about the Moscow trials — for or against the Stalinites or Trotskyites." Clifford Odets, who had long admired Wolfe's writing, begged him to endorse his new play, *Clash by Night*. George Seldes asked him to go with a group to Washington to picket against American neutrality in the Spanish Civil War. For the League of American Writers, Donald Odgen Stewart invited Wolfe to participate in a poll of writers, asking: "Are you for or are you against Franco and Fascism?" Freda Kirchwey, editor of the *Nation*, urged him to contribute to a symposium on "How To Keep Out of War."

Rival leftist factions tried to gain his endorsement. In the Communist party itself there was talk of recruiting him, but Henry Hart, who had known and disliked him since his early days at Scribners and thought him "a political ignoramus," blocked that move. Other Marxists were turned off by Wolfe's ignorance of the fine points of doctrinal squabbling that divided radicals. When S. L. Solon tried to get him to take sides on the purge trials then going on in Moscow, Wolfe replied: "Sure, S-Stalin has wiped them out. Why not? Those guys were probably out to get the Georgian bastard if they could. He just got there first, t-that's all."

Wolfe's indifference to Communist ideology did not mean that he was indifferent to the serious problems that beset the United States in the late 1930s. His awakening to social injustice had, he admitted, come late. At the onset of the Great Depression, when he was writing his second novel, he had, of course, been uncomfortably aware of the poor and the unemployed, but he had been brought up to think that laziness or inefficiency was responsible for their plight. Only gradually did the idea came to him, "soaking in like cold gray weather, soaking in like cold gray rain, soaking in with my own life and breath and work and blood and pulse," that it was not the jobless who were to blame for their situation but the economic and social system that had rejected them.

At about the same time, on his last two trips to Germany, he had become aware that Nazi totalitarianism was "a system of abominable works," a source of "unutterable pollutions." He had tried to warn against totalitarianism in his story "I Have a Thing to Tell You," but now it was increasingly evident to him that many Americans were attracted by the order and prosperity that fascism apparently guaranteed. In his darker moods he came to think that fascism, "in all its essential aspects," had already come to dominate "a considerable portion of American life," and the future seemed even more gloomy:

> When it happens if it happens, as it happens — it may not happen in any of the ways you feared, the ways you had heard about; nor speak any of the words you fear that it may speak; or say any of the things you thought it would say —
> It will just speak to you the same old words — "Fellow Americans" — "freedom: — "our great people" —
> And there will be no drums beat, and no grim compulsive beat —
> It will just come in quietly into the yards of a silent plant —
> And say "let the wheels turn" —
> When it happens, if it happens, as it happens.

Even if fascism did not infiltrate American society, Wolfe feared that it might conquer it. After the German Anschluss with Austria and the rape of Czechoslovakia, Hitler's intention of worldwide domination seemed obvious. The Führer had "furnished the world with a blueprint of his intentions in advance" and had been checking "his announced objectives off one by one with the precision of a riveting machine." Clearly, fascism was "a creature that thrives but is not appeased by compromise," and Wolfe thought it was "increasingly apparent that the only effective way to meet armed aggression may be armed resistance."

In that resistance he was willing to enlist the support of Communists, both at home and abroad. He did not think that Communism posed a real threat to the United States, but he did believe there was "a grave Fascist danger." If forced to choose, he concluded, "I should choose Communism: I cannot agree with people who say that both are equally bad, and identical." But he was not willing to accept Communist ideas uncritically. At a time when a great many other American intellectuals and writers were following the Communist party line, Wolfe did not forget that Communist regimes were like fascist governments in practicing "Suppression of Free Speech, Free Thought, Free Press" and in the "Oppression and Punishment of Minorities." He believed that freedom of thought and freedom of speech were not "just rhetorical myths" but were "among the most valuable realities that men have gained."

Wolfe defined his own political position as "definitely socialistic veering to the left." He was, he insisted, a social democrat, "a man who believes in socialism but not in communized socialism, and in democracy, but not in individualized democracy." Denying that democracy and capitalism were interdependent, he argued that "if democracy is to survive at all, it can do so only through the radical modification of capitalistic society as it now exists." In practical terms these views meant that Wolfe generally supported the policies of Franklin D. Roosevelt and hoped, perhaps naively, that the New Deal would bring about drastic changes.

But Wolfe's fundamental concern was less with political and economic conditions than with the spirit of America. To him the United States had originally been a chosen land, the country that promised "high and glorious fulfil[l]ment" to all its citizens. But this promise had been broken. A "dark wound" had been inflicted on the United States through "betrayal — vicious, cowardly betrayal — self-betrayal of ourselves." No longer was the country a single society. Now it was peopled by "a mongrel and disordered mob — a jargon of a thousand tongues, the mouthpiece of a million vicious and sensational rumors — but with no *faith,* no *freedom,* no *belief* — a slave-like swarm without the dignities of slavery." Long before most American intellectuals were involved in the ecology movement, Wolfe connected the disorders of the American spirit with the violation of the natural environment. From Sixth Avenue in New York, that "dreary street, tormented by its thousand dreary architectures, tormented by the jangle of its rusty signs, tormented by the rusty rackets of its elevated [railroad], tormented by . . . its little shops, hot-dog stands, grease-and-food emporiums [and] shooting galleries," to "the cesspool that is Jersey City," on to the small towns of America, cluttered with rubbish and filth, the whole country had become a "huge, sprawling, utterly confused, . . . mongrel dump-heap."

The chief duty of an American writer, Wolfe was convinced, was to remind his readers of the promise of American life, of the greatness that could still lie ahead for a nation begun "with an ideal of a free man's life, . . . fulfilling its whole purpose in an atmosphere of free and spacious enlightenment." But in order truly to love his country a writer had to understand its faults. "We've got to *loathe* America as we loathe ourselves," he concluded. "With loathing, horror, shame, and anguish of the soul unspeakable — as well as with love — we've got to face the total horror of our self-betrayal, the way America has betrayed herself."

III

Wolfe planned again to make Asheville the setting for a book that would reflect his growing social concerns. The action would concern events he had learned a great deal about during the previous summer: the failure of the First National Bank of Asheville, the conviction of its president for fraud, the suicide of the city mayor, and the end of the boom times of the 1920s. It seemed to him that what happened in Asheville in this period was "pretty important and significant in the light it throws on what happened to the whole country," and he asked both Mrs. Roberts and his cousin Jack Westall to help him gain access to newspapers and other records of the period.

Aware of the anger that *Look Homeward, Angel* had aroused in his home town, he assured his friends: "I have no intention of doing a job on Asheville." His new book was going to be "not about a town, nor about any certain group of people, but . . . about America and what happened here between 1927 and 1937." Its theme would be Ella Winter's phrase, "You Can't Go Home Again."

That same theme would apply to his fictional portrayal of his own relatives. On his visit home he learned to put some distance between himself and the problems of his family. He was sorry to hear that Ralph Wheaton, Mabel's husband, had contracted syphilis, but he refused to get excited about the problem and advised his sister not to worry about the scandal that she thought was brewing. He declined to get involved in another dispute among his brothers and sisters over the distribution of his father's estate, saying simply: "I did not get more than my share in 1922, neither did I ever consider that I got less." While sympathetic to his mother, who was being sued by the Wachovia Bank of Asheville, he recognized that she had brought on her own troubles by her real estate speculation and only hoped she would come out of the courts with enough to live on. In general his letters to his mother after the summer of 1937 were impersonal to the point of coolness. It was significant that in his new book the mother figure, "Aunt Maw" Joyner, shared little of the vitality of Julia Wolfe (or, for that matter, of Eliza Gant) but was a querulous, superstitious old woman.

In beginning a new book, Wolfe always jotted down outlines, which served both to fix in his own mind the scope and purpose of the novel and to indicate where passages and stories he had already written might fit in. The initial plan for "The Life and Adventures of the Bondsman Doaks" called for the novel to cover the period from September 1929 to September 1937. Though there was to be a certain amount of preliminary material, Wolfe intended to avoid retelling the story of his childhood and adolescence, which had been so fully presented in *Look Homeward, Angel,* and to omit most of his account of his love affair with Mrs. Bernstein, the tone of which he now found too personal for a novel of social commentary. The story proper would begin with a scene in Grand Central Station in New York, where the train to Libya Hill (as he now called Asheville) was boarded by residents of "Old Catawba" returning home. They included the president of the local bank, the mayor, the corrupt political boss, and, of course, the hero. This plan would allow Wolfe to begin with another of his magnificent train sequences — and he drew out of his box of papers the opening chapter of his rejected manuscript "K-19." There would, of course, be flashbacks — "time sweeps," as he called them — but the action would center on the failure of the bank, the consequent social and economic devastation of the community, and on the hero's discovery that he could not return to the past, that he could not go home again.

Though the hero of the novel had to be an interesting figure, Wolfe insisted that "his significance lies not in his personal uniqueness and differences, but in his personal identity to the life of every man." This new novel was intended to be "a book of discovery, hence union, with life; not a book of personal revolt, hence separation from life." It was important, therefore, that the hero should not be a self-centered aesthete like Eugene Gant in *Look Homeward, Angel* and *Of Time and the River,* and he promised that there would be "no trace of Eugene Gant-i-ness in the character of the protagonist." Instead of being a very tall man, he would be of about middle height, barrel-chested, with unusually long arms and fingers like paws. His heavy brows, his low forehead, and his head "thrust forward and turned upward with a kind of packed attentiveness" inevitably caused him to be nicknamed "Monk." He was, in fact, a resurrection of the almost identical figure of David "Jocko" Hawke, whom Wolfe had once intended to be the central figure of his second novel.

Wolfe spent a good deal of time thinking about the proper name for this hero. While "Joe Doaks" conveyed the sense of ordinariness that he desired, it had "too much a connotation of newspaper cartooning, slap-stick, [and] the fellow in the bleachers." Besides "Joe Doaks" gave no intimation of the role that his hero was to play in the new book. His life would weave together the stories of the many, diverse Americans that he encountered on his road to self-discovery. To stress this theme, he experimented with subtitles for the novel like "The Weft That the Weaver Hath Woven" and "The Web That the Weaver Has (Hath) Wrought." In the end he dropped the name "Joe Doaks" and announced firmly: "Let his name be Webber."

As Wolfe worked on the book during the early months of 1938, it changed in scope. As late as the middle of February he still planned to deal mostly with the Depression years, but in preparing a prospectus to show Aswell he began to sort through his piles of manuscript, some quite old, some very recent. He could not bear to discard any of it and began looking for a way to work it all into his new novel. And in a way the segments seemed to fit. All along Wolfe must have been troubled about developing the theme "You Can't Go Home Again" in a novel that began when the hero was twenty-nine years old; such a book would not describe the home to which Webber could not return. And since he intended to show how Webber's career was at every point shaped by the necessity of choosing between opposites — between the mountain-bred family of his mother and the Northern-born family of his father; between the South and the North; between the country and the city; between the American scene and the expatriate world — he obviously needed to begin the story with George Webber's birth.

Consequently, he made the inevitable decision. In a series of outlines he pushed the beginning of his story farther and farther back, to include Webber's early years in New York, his college experiences, his childhood and infancy, his ancestors and genealogy. In short, he was going to write another thinly fictionalized autobiography. By March, after he had worked his way through to this decision, he felt a great sense of satisfaction at having devised "a whole universe of the imagination into which I could pour *all* of the materials I had gathered."

IV

Most of the time while Wolfe was working on the new book he followed a regular routine. He continued to get up late in the morning, and he usually started writing without having any breakfast, though occasionally he sent down to the hotel lobby for coffee. He worked until about five or six o'clock, when he would break for a drink. After a large dinner — his one real meal of the day — he usually went back to his rooms and continued what he was writing. As he explained to Mrs. Roberts, "I can't stop thinking about it: it goes rumbling and roaring around in my head, or what serves me for a head. The result is that there is usually no sleep until long after midnight."

Even before he signed with Harpers he felt able to employ a secretary, Joan Lanier, who came in to type the manuscript that he had drafted in pencil on cheap yellow second sheets. She managed very well with the ribald genealogy that he contrived for his hero, which he called the Doaksology, but after Doaks became Webber and Wolfe began dictating stories about the Joyners, the earthy maternal ancestors of his hero, she felt he was going too far. Getting up from her desk and putting on her hat, she told Wolfe, "I can't listen to such language," and left.

Gwen Jassinoff succeeded her in January. This intelligent and attractive young woman, a recent graduate of the University of Wisconsin, quickly adapted to Wolfe's routine of work. Usually arriving at the Chelsea before Wolfe was out of bed, she would tidy up the little office and straighten up the living room, the floor of which was often littered with the pages he had written the night before and had shoved off the desk. By the time Wolfe got up, she was busy transcribing this material. While she worked at the type-writer, Wolfe would write at his big round table in the living room or, if his muscles were cramped, he would stand at the unused icebox in a corner of the bathroom.

Initially Miss Jassinoff simply typed for Wolfe, but when he learned that she could take dictation at the typewriter, he more often spoke, rather than wrote, his story. Pacing back and forth from the living room to her office, pausing from time to time to lean on the large bureau next to the window by her typewriter, he dictated rapidly, hardly pausing for breath, and he acted out the parts of the several characters in the story. Fascinated that he could compose so rapidly, without notes and without interruption, she asked how he was able to do it. "I write it in my mind first," he replied. Miss Jassinoff's first version of Wolfe's dictation was nec-essarily rough, and she would retype it to eliminate typographical errors. After Wolfe corrected this draft, often making extensive changes, she would type a finished version — unless he decided that still more changes were needed, which required further re-typing.

Of course there were inevitably some interruptions in his rou-tine of work. Even before signing on with his new publisher, Wolfe was obliged to resume relations with Perkins. In late De-cember his attorney notified him that his case against Muredach Dooher was coming up for trial. Because Perkins had been present during the discussions with Dooher, Wolfe had to enlist his aid and to secure his presence in court. "Honestly, Max, I hate like hell to bother you," he wrote his former editor, "but I do think this is one of those cases where people ought to stand together if they can, not only for personal or friendly reasons, but just be-cause it's taking a stand in favor of the human race."

"Of course I shall do anything possible to help in the Dooher matter," Perkins replied promptly. He was, however, human enough to get a little wry amusement out of the situation. "Tom said this was an occasion when he thought 'people ought to stand together,' " he wrote Hamilton Basso, "and a little later on that it would be 'for the sake of humanity.' And as I never really had a chance to strike a blow for humanity before, I thought I ought to do it, if only for the sake of Tom."

On February 8, Wolfe and Perkins, together with Barnet Ruder, the rare book dealer, and Mrs. Jelliffe, who also knew something of the arrangements with Dooher, trooped over to Jersey City for the trial. It was one of the rare occasions when Perkins, who was sensitive about his increasing deafness, wore his hearing aid in public, so as not to misunderstand any of the questions. On the stand Wolfe was remarkably composed and cogent, while Dooher seemed angry and immature, admitting that he had destroyed some pages of Wolfe's manuscripts because they contained filthy and pornographic material. As expected, the judge ruled in Wolfe's favor, and for the first time in three years he had no suit or legal threat hanging over him. On the ferry back to Manhattan he was so relieved that he was amusing and even witty on the subject of lawyers and justice. Then suddenly he broke out: "What do you suppose was on those two pages he destroyed? I must have used some absolutely new words! . . . I fear I'll never sink low enough to achieve such heights of obscenity again! What a loss to the field of belles lettres." This was the last time Wolfe and Perkins saw each other.

Shortly afterward, Wolfe had another final meeting, of a less pleasant kind. In February Aline Bernstein published her second book, *The Journey Down,* a novel about her love affair with Wolfe. The unnamed hero of her story was easily recognizable: he was gigantic physically, had grandiose ideas about himself as a writer, composed indescribably magnificent prose, and made love to the heroine by telling her that she came from the dung hill of the theater, that her breasts were like melons, and that she smelled like a Jew. Because of the danger of libel, reviewers did not openly identify him as Wolfe, but Bernard DeVoto, in the *Saturday Review of Literature,* gave hints that were obvious to readers who had followed his earlier attacks on Wolfe.

Wolfe was infuriated. Though he planned to publish his own fictional account of his affair with Aline, he was deeply upset by *The Journey Down.* Late one night, after brooding and drinking, he stormed up to the Bernsteins' apartment in the Gotham Hotel. He "started the most awful row about the Jews," Aline told a friend shortly afterward; "he denounced them at the top of his voice, said they should be wiped off the face of the earth." After attacking her Jewish friends by name, he called for three cheers for Adolf Hitler. At the end of her patience, Aline "launched out and punched him in the nose." Taken by surprise, he fell flat on his back on the floor, and she called for the porter to put him out. "It was the most sickening experience of my life," she wrote; "horrible, but it succeeded in finally freeing me from the spell. . . . I have always protected him so far as I could, and always allowed for his behavior because of a certain greatness I have felt about him; but this was too much."

Apart from these encounters, Wolfe's life during the early months of 1938 was relatively uneventful. Though he was now a well-known literary figure in New York, he rarely went out to parties and received few visitors. He saw more of Edgar Lee Masters than of anyone else. Masters, who was more than twice Wolfe's age, was as taciturn as Wolfe was loquacious. Masters was clearly near the end of a distinguished career, while Wolfe thought his best years were before him. But they got along beautifully. Masters admired Wolfe's "abounding vitality, his frankness and friendliness, his American spirit, the enthusiasm of his youthful heart." For his part, Wolfe recognized Masters's *Spoon River Anthology* as "one of the great books of his generation and one of the great books of the nation's literature."

From time to time Wolfe also met younger writers, who often sought to impress him. One of his greatest trials was James Agee, to whom the Aswells introduced him, on the assumption that their Appalachian background and Harvard experience would give them much to talk about. Wolfe knew nothing about Agee, who up to this point had published only a few undergraduate short stories and a book of poems, *Permit Me Voyage,* but Agee had read everything Wolfe had written. He felt that *Look Homeward, Angel* was such a definitive portrayal of small-town life in the South that there was nothing left for him to write about, and he complained that Wolfe "had stolen my whole childhood." Trying to impress Wolfe, Agee talked on and on, and Wolfe, who was also a natural monologist, resented being lectured to. At the end of one very long evening, when he finally got Agee to go home, Wolfe told Miss Nowell that he thought the young man was "crazy," because he "was always talking about things in spirals and on planes and things."

Much less demanding were the occasional visits from his relatives, to whom he could show the sights of New York. In January David Gambrell, Effie's son, came to Manhattan, and Wolfe took him on a tour of the city, up Fifth Avenue, through Grand Central Station, and down Broadway. David slept on a folding bed in Wolfe's room at the Chelsea, and he met all his uncle's friends at the hotel.

In April Virginia and Fredricka Gambrell, Effie's daughters, also visited New York. One evening he took them to the International Casino, which featured nearly nude women dancers. The nieces were "thrilled by this fabulous place," but their uncle kept making them promise not to tell Effie where they had been, because he was sure she would disapprove. Another evening, after dinner at Luchow's, an acquaintance suggested that he ought to take them to the Cotton Club in Harlem, and they were delighted at the idea. But Wolfe looked dubious and said that their mother, being from South Carolina, would not like them to go to a Negro nightclub. Instead, he decided that they must ride on the subway before leaving the city. With one girl on each arm, he walked them to the kiosk as they all sang "Rosalie." After the subway ride and a drink at Jack Dempsey's, they came back to the Chelsea, where Masters joined them for a nightcap.

Wolfe's reluctance about going into Harlem applied only to his nieces, not to himself. Escorted by Barnet Ruder, he went on what he called "our night club orgy," and the two men displayed "our skilled technique in the rhumba." "I had never been to a swell night club before," he wrote Ruder afterward. "Now when I see the name of Barnet B. Ruder on a letterhead — do I think of books? No, gentlemen, I think lasciviously of night clubs, and the dusky corybants of Harlem."

But such excursions were rare, and when Wolfe had company in the evening it was usually Miss Nowell or Aswell. As always, Miss Nowell was all business, and they smoked countless packages of cigarettes while they worked together to create short stories out of Wolfe's long manuscripts. Aswell was more relaxed, and Wolfe often talked with him for hours not merely about the book that he was writing but about future books that he might write. Once, while recovering from a very bad cold, which he

thought was turning into pneumonia, Wolfe said that he was going to do a book about doctors. Another of his favorite topics was
lawyers, with whom he had had so much unhappy experience
during the past three years.

One evening, stimulated by the news that a federal judge had
struck down the ban on the importation of Joyce's *Ulysses,* hitherto excluded as obscene, Wolfe asked Aswell whether "a book
pretty much limited to his sexual experiences could be published."
Up to this point, he explained, "he had never put much sex in his
books because he didn't want to touch the subject at all unless he
could do it as honestly as he tried to write about everything else."
But now the courts would permit him to be explicit, and he spent
four or five hours telling his editor what would be in such a book.
Like so many of Wolfe's other planned books, it was never written.

V

After working very hard throughout the spring of 1938, Wolfe
began to think about ways to escape from the heat of New York
City in the summer. He was invited to stay with friends but
hesitated to intrude his "large and not too tidy person" into anyone else's household. For a time he hoped to find a cool, comfortable old house, or even a barn with a floor, in upstate New
York. But an unexpected invitation settled his summer plans. The
department of English at Purdue University asked him to speak at
a literary banquet and offered a fee of three hundred dollars. Wolfe
remembered the great success he had had on a similar occasion
two years earlier at Boulder, and he accepted. "I am afraid my
delivery . . . is very bad," he told Ruder, "but for three hundred
dollars . . . I could put on a spirited exhibition of some sort, and
produce any variety of strange sounds, some of which, I trust,
may be mistaken for eloquence." Then, too, he thought the trip to
Purdue could serve "as a kind of springboard to a holiday" in the
West.

Even more important, he could "shoot the works" in this talk
at Purdue by making a public announcement of his growing concern for social issues. By drawing on his own experience he could
"state the relation of the author to the world and to the life around
him" and show that "the writer is a man who belongs to life, to

the world, who has work to do, a function to perform, a place in society just as much as an engineer, a lawyer, a doctor, or a business man."

He began dictating the lecture to Miss Jassinoff in early May, and he continued at top speed for about five days. He started with "a very plain and simple account of things" relating to his own evolution as a writer, but as he worked he increasingly saw the possibility of "transforming the material for the simple Purdue statement into the terms of poetic and imaginative fact — into the truth of fiction." Presently he came to see that his talk would serve as the concluding section of his massive novel, "a kind of epilogue that takes the form of personal address — to be called, 'You Can't Go Home Again' or 'A Farewell to the Fox.'" Ostensibly addressed by Wolfe's hero George Webber to his editor, Foxhall Edwards, this conclusion would be "a kind of impassioned summing up of the whole book."

As the time approached for his trip, Wolfe asked Aswell to store his manuscripts at Harpers during his absence. Before turning his papers over to the editor, he decided to separate the chapters and sections that belonged to his new novel from the other papers piled in his crate. For about ten days he and Miss Jassinoff sorted and arranged his numerous manuscripts, and on two weekends George Stoney, a young North Carolinian who had recently come to New York, helped him organize and label his materials. Finally Wolfe drew up an elaborate list, thirteen pages long, that would serve as an outline of the new book, which he now called "The Web and the Rock." It would cover the years from 1793 to 1937, in four large parts, each consisting of numerous "books." The outline listed the chapters of each book — both those that were completed and those that were only partly drafted.

Now that the parts were arranged in a rough order, Wolfe had for the first time "a sense of wholeness" about the novel and felt "a tremendous amount of comfort and satisfaction" in what he had done. He was convinced that he had "contrived a kind of legend or tremendous fiction," one even more ambitious than *Of Time and the River* had been. This new book, he explained, "will deal with a much greater sweep of time — over one hundred years, in fact. It will deal with a much greater variety of scenes, of characters, of events . . . , and it will present a narrative that is much more continuous and closely-woven." As a result, it "made a much more exacting demand upon my powers of invention and creation" than his earlier books had done.

Consequently he hesitated about allowing Aswell to read his manuscript during his absence. There was obviously a "tremendous labor of writing and revision" yet to be done. The entire manuscript, he believed, was in about the condition that *Of Time and the River* had been in December 1933, and, like the earlier book, it required at least another year of work. Showing such an incomplete and unfinished book to his editor was "like presenting someone with the bones of some great prehistoric animal he has never seen before," and he thought that Aswell might be bewildered by it. At the same time he realized that "it might be a good idea if the editor did get a general idea of the whole thing now." "He wanted very much to read it," Wolfe told Miss Nowell. "I had misgivings but he swore that I could trust him to understand the unfinished state of things and to *feel* what I am about." "I hope to God he does, and that it is all right for him to read it now," he concluded darkly. "It would be a crime if I were interrupted or discouraged now!"

But he was not willing to turn the manuscript over to Aswell until the very last minute. On the afternoon of May 17 he was still arranging and revising his papers. "He had two or three days' growth of beard, his hair was wildly dishevelled, he was in his shirt sleeves with the sleeves rolled up, no collar, and the neckband open, seated at a table in the middle of his big room," Aswell recalled. "Before him was a pile of manuscript which he was running through rapidly to see that all the pages were in order and that nothing had been omitted. Now and then he would come on some page or an entire chapter which he decided didn't belong in the book, and he would yank it out and throw it on the floor." Miss Jassinoff bustled about, gathering up these rejects and arranging them in neat piles.

Norman Kleinberg, one of the bartenders at the Chelsea, was waiting in the room, for Wolfe had asked him to pack his clothes for the trip. Since everything Wolfe owned was dirty and had been sent out to the cleaners, Kleinberg had nothing to do until seven o'clock, when the tailor came in, and then he began filling Wolfe's huge portmanteau, using his own judgment about what shirts, ties, and socks were to be included, since Wolfe did not care what he wore.

By 8:30 Wolfe had once more gone through his whole cache of papers. Finally he entrusted the manuscript of "The Web and the Rock," wrapped in two enormous bundles, to Aswell and relegated everything else to his crate, which would go into storage at Harpers. Late as it was, Wolfe still had not checked out of the hotel, and he had made no arrangements for packing his books and his few personal possessions. Grandly he turned these problems over to Kleinberg and began getting ready to catch his train. When Aswell left shortly before nine, he fully expected to hear the next morning that Wolfe had missed it, but by some miraculous burst of speed he got to the station before the train pulled out.

VI

"Not only very tired, but very happy also," Wolfe took the *Southwestern Limited* to Indianapolis. He was too keyed up to sleep, and as the train plowed into the Middle West at seventy-two miles an hour he did not miss "a house, a barn, a horse, a hog, a cow, or a plowed field." To the rhythm of the clicking train wheels he drafted a chant about the land: "the earth receding in an unending screen with infinite repetitiveness — field, furrow, silo, barn and house — field, furrow, silo, barn and [house] . . . — then streets spoking past again, and trees in leaf and box like houses — and the fat, flat, fertile earth again."

On May 19 he gave his lecture on "Writing and Living" at Purdue. Most of the talk explored his changing artistic and social views. In his early days at Chapel Hill and Harvard he had thought of the writer simply as an artist, but the Great Depression and the Nazi menace made him see that he had a responsibility to society. Any possibility that he might continue in the detached world of the aesthete had then been destroyed by "the huge conspiracy of the parasite — the whore, the harpy, the thief, the lawyer, the ambitious and the fashionable fool, the blackmailer" — that had sapped his energies for the past three years. But "from the desolation of these new discoveries" he felt he "had derived, by a strange paradox, a new sense of life, a newer and . . . a better hope," and a faith that "the common heart of man" could never be corrupted, never be defeated.

Wolfe ended his lecture with a peroration that must have reminded some of his Middle Western listeners of the poems of Carl Sandburg:

> The people! Yes, the people!
> The people that cannot ever be defeated or betrayed —
> The betrayed and the defeated people, the corrupted and the mis-
>   guided people, the duped and superstitious people, and the inert
>   and the submissive people —
> But in the end, always the people! just the people! —
> The rock bottom of the invincible and the everlasting people!

Though the audience of about three hundred people applauded warmly, Wolfe's lecture on "Writing and Living" was not the triumph that "The Story of a Novel" had been at Boulder. The acoustics were bad, and Wolfe's deep, throaty voice carried poorly over the amplifying system. The audiences for the two lectures were different. At Purdue there was no gathering of major creative writers but an assembly composed largely of university faculty members and their wives. And Wolfe, too, was different. No longer the youthful, handsome giant he had been in 1935, he was now very heavy and partially bald, and he wore spectacles. He was clearly an established, middle-aged writer, not a brilliant new-comer to the literary scene.

Yet neither Wolfe nor his hosts were unhappy about the talk. His sponsors were pleased to have a visiting lion at Purdue, and, once the talk was over, Wolfe was glad to be there. At a party afterward he took off his coat, leaned back in an easy chair, with a Scotch and soda in his hand, and talked for hours with faculty members. Genuinely interested in the people he met, he was soon calling them by their first names and insisting that they call him "Tom."

After two days in Lafayette he was ready to move on to Chi-cago, and he urged his new Purdue friends to come with him. "I've just made three hundred dollars," he told them, "and y-y-you've got to help me spend it." Finally seven of them piled into the car and they set off for the big city. Along the way they sang songs, and Wolfe joined in whether he knew the words or not and he even gave one solo, his father's favorite, "I Wonder Who's Kissing Her Now." He latched on to the "Heigh-ho" song from the recent motion picture *Snow White and the Seven Dwarfs* and kept singing it, as one member of the group recalled, long "after some of its original charm had worn off."

During the weekend in Chicago Wolfe and his companions drove all over the city, visiting "the *stupendous* University," exploring "the magnificent Lake Front and the not so magnificent slums," and spending a long time at the Brookfield Zoo, where he looked in vain for a baboon with a rump as colorful as one that he had seen as a boy. "It was like rainbow," he remembered. But he was charmed by the polar bears, "who wave their paws at you coyly," and he fed them several boxes of Crackerjack.

As his friends went home, Wolfe boarded the *Zephyr* for Denver. Full of excitement about his first ride on a streamlined train, he reserved a berth for the overnight trip, even though he knew he would get little use of it since he was too tall to fit into the bunk. "By God," he said, "I m-m-might as well go the whole hog."

In Denver he looked up the Ferrils, the Davisons, and other friends from his earlier visit. Originally planning to stay for only a day, he remained a week. "I'm afraid I talked and ate and drank them all into a state of exhaustion," he reported to Miss Nowell; "we have just eliminated sleep as a dispensable luxury." Then he pushed on to Cheyenne, where he was struck by "the white hot brightness of the air, the glare of heat and of aerial buoyancy." After that came Idaho, which he described as "the abomination of desolation," with "little pitiful blistered towns huddled down in the most abject loneliness underneath the huge light and scale and weather and the astounding brightness and dimensions of everything."

Arriving at Portland, Oregon, on June 7, Wolfe settled in at the University Club and was taken in hand by Stewart Holbrook, a leading historian of the Northwest, who shepherded him about the city and introduced him to other writers and journalists. At Gill's Bookstore he was upset to hear the rumor that salesmen from Charles Scribner's Sons, and indeed Maxwell Perkins himself, had been circulating derogatory reports about his character, his manner of living, and his literary future. The story, so far as Perkins himself was concerned, was untrue, but since feeling at Scribners toward Wolfe at this time was decidedly hostile, it was not altogether surprising that salesmen echoed this sense of betrayal. Outraged, Wolfe grew even more upset when Miss Nowell wrote him that Perkins had attempted to pump her about Wolfe's plans, "trying to find out in his 'fox' way if there was going to be anything about Scribner's in your book."

"Please — *please* don't tell him . . . anything about me, if you can avoid it," Wolfe promptly replied. "For six years he was my friend — I thought the best one I ever had — and then, a little over two years ago he turned against me — everything I have done since was bad, . . . it's . . . as if he were praying for my failure." "I don't think he *consciously* wants me to fail or come to grief," he conceded, "but it's almost as if *unconsciously* . . . he wants me to come to grief, as a kind of sop to his pride and his unyielding conviction that he is right in everything — the tragic flaw in his character."

In Portland Wolfe met Edward M. Miller, the Sunday editor of the *Oregonian,* and Ray Conway, of the Oregon Automobile Association, who were about to make a long trip by car to publicize the accessibility and inexpensiveness of the national parks in the West. Driving a white Ford, which bore the name of the Oregon Automobile Association on its side, they planned to drive to eleven national parks in a two-week period in order to demonstrate that ordinary travelers on a limited budget could enjoy these wonders of the West. On the spur of the moment, Miller invited Wolfe to join them.

Conway was rather less enthusiastic about adding this stranger to the party, for he had heard reports that Wolfe was a demanding sort of person, that he often drank too much, and that he kept late hours and did not get up early. But he relented after Wolfe pledged not to drink on the trip and to keep regular hours.

It was, as Miller said later, "not a particularly sensible trip" that they were planning, but the fact that it was "a little nutty" may have made it the more appealing to Wolfe, who decided that it offered him "the chance of a lifetime." A little troubled that this trip would extend his vacation by two weeks, he concluded that he would always regret it if he passed up this opportunity, since "when I get through I shall really have seen America (except Texas)."

On June 20 the three men set out from Portland, heading south to the Crater Lake National Park in Oregon and the Yosemite and Sequoia National Parks in California. Then, after driving across the Mojave desert, they inspected the Grand Canyon, went through Bryce Canyon and Zion National Parks, continued up through Utah and Idaho to the Grand Tetons and Jackson Hole and on to Yellowstone. From there they headed north to the

Glacier National Park, where they turned west, visiting the Grand Coulee, the site of the great dam and hydroelectric plant then under construction.

For the most part it was a journey without much incident. Usually Wolfe rode in the back seat of the car, where the constant jostling and bumping caused him to wear through two pairs of trousers. He got along easily with Miller but found it a little harder to like Conway, who was constantly concerned with the functioning of the car, the number of miles they covered each day, and the costs of the journey. Later when he learned of Conway's "great love and knowledge of mountains" and discovered that he had helped rescue many climbers who had suffered accidents, he came to have greater respect for this quiet, unemotional man. Throughout the tiring journey Wolfe was generally in good spirits, aware of "the gigantic unconscious humor of the situation," since he perceived that they were " 'making every national park' without seeing any of them."

He bought for the journey a bound notebook, in which he daily recorded his impressions of what he had seen. Mostly he jotted down disconnected phrases to remind himself of the scenery. Approaching Sequoia, he noted: "the bay-gold big barks — then cupreous masses — then forested peaks." The Grand Canyon, which for some reason he insisted on calling "the Big Gagoochy," he described as "a fathomless darkness peered at from the very edge of hell with abysmal starlight — almost unseen." The Mormon country in Utah displeased him. He found all the towns were "of architecture graceless, all denuded, with the curious sterility and coldness and frustration the religion has." Not even Salt Lake City impressed him, for he disliked its "harsh ugly temple, the temple sacrosanct, by us unvisited, unvisitable, so ugly, grim, grotesque, and blah."

Proud of his jottings, which he thought ran to 30,000 words — in fact, they were fewer than 12,000 — Wolfe thought that his journal preserved "a pretty clear record of the whole thing." When the trip was over he planned to have it typed up, "revising as much as I can but not taking too much time, and putting it down from the beginning like a spool unwinding at great speed." But as he looked back over his notes he conceded: "Perhaps it's not ready to use yet or won't be for a year or two."

By the time the three men reached Olympia, they were all tired, but they remained on amiable terms. They said goodbye, giving each other "new addresses, final instructions — [with] the casual-like wordiness of men with some sadness in their heart avoiding farewells." Miller and Conway headed back to Portland, and Wolfe took a bus to Seattle.

There he found waiting for him a telegram from Aswell: "Your new book is magnificent in scope and design, with some of the best writing you have ever done. I am . . . confident that when you finish you will have written your greatest novel so far." Much cheered by "this wonderful assurance," Wolfe pledged: "I'm going back and try to live up to it until its finished as I want it."

VII

Though still keyed up from his trip, Wolfe realized that he had very little rest during what was supposed to be a vacation, and he planned to go to some quiet place on Puget Sound "to loaf and rest for a few days." He had already made a quick visit to the Seattle area and had been struck by the quiet beauty of Port Townsend, across the sound on the Olympic Peninsula. "What a place to write a novel!" he exclaimed. If he could only go there to relax, he was sure that he would quickly regain his energy, because, as he told Miss Nowell: "This is a country fit for Gods — you've never seen anything like it for scale and magnificence and abundance. . . . You feel there's no limit, no end to anything. The East seems small and starved and meagre by comparison."

But as usual Wolfe's plan to rusticate himself never materialized. He had first to visit his relatives in the Seattle area. Seeing them revived his much earlier plan to end his saga of the Gants (now the Webbers) with an account of the diaspora of the family across the country, a final volume to be called "Pacific End." His literary acquaintances in Seattle made even more demands on his time. Holbrook had introduced him to James F. Stevens, a public relations officer of the West Coast Lumbermen's Association, best known for his version of the Paul Bunyan tales, and Stevens and his wife, Theresa, brought him into their circle of friends, which included many members of the English department at the University of Washington.

One party followed another, and Wolfe, though exhausted, insisted on going to them all, on talking more than anybody else, and on staying longer than any of the other guests. On July 3, Mrs. Stevens thought that he looked so flushed and feverish that he ought to take a sedative and get some rest, but the next day Wolfe insisted on watching the Fourth of July parade with them. But by evening it was clear that he was not well. At a party when a prominent local Communist asked him why he did not write like Mike Gold, Wolfe uncharacteristically snapped back, in a loud voice, "Why in hell doesn't Mike Gold write like me?"

The next day he decided to take the ferry to Victoria and Vancouver, British Columbia, apparently thinking that it would be ironical to spend the day after Independence Day under the British flag. Crossing the sound in a stiff gale on the deck of the Canadian Pacific Railroad coastal liner *Princess Kathleen*, he encountered what he later called a "poor shivering wretch," and they took turns drinking from his pint bottle of whiskey. By the time the ship arrived in Vancouver, Wolfe was chilled through and was feeling miserable. Instead of calling a doctor, he holed up in his hotel room, hoping to fight off what he thought was a cold, contracted from the man on the ship. On the second day he decided to return to Seattle by train, but, unwilling to lose this chance of seeing yet one more American city, he first hired a taxi driver to give him a short tour of Vancouver, which seemed "very slow and quaint after U.S." On the train ride he was very sick and feverish.

The next day, though he was still feeling dreadful, he forced himself to go to a party that Professor and Mrs. Sophus Winther of the University of Washington were giving in his honor. Arriving late, flushed in the face and wracked with a terrible cough, he nevertheless drew on his reserves of strength to give his usual party performance, reminiscing for hours about his days at Chapel Hill and Cambridge and talking about Maxwell Perkins.

But the following morning he had to give in. "Jim," he said, calling Stevens from his hotel room, "I've got to yell 'calf rope.' I'm afraid I'm pretty sick." Stevens promptly arranged for him to see Dr. Edward C. Ruge, his family physician, and in a brief examination the doctor found that Wolfe had a temperature of 102.4 degrees, a continuous, severe cough, rapid heartbeat with elevated blood pressure, and congestion in his right lung. His diagnosis was pneumonia. Always terrified by illness, Wolfe pleaded with Stevens: "I don't want to die out here, Jim. Don't let me be kept here to die."

Stevens and Ruge thought the best plan was to admit Wolfe to Firlawns, Ruge's private sanatorium at Kenmore, just north of Seattle, where there were no X-ray machines or other frightening hospital equipment. It was, by most accounts, a pleasant, relaxed place, though the locked steel-mesh doors in the corridors and the restraints across the windows were grim reminders that the inmates were mostly Ruge's mental patients. Still able to see a little humor in the situation, Wolfe told an early visitor: "They haven't yet made up their minds whether I'm Jesus Christ or Napoleon."

During the month that Wolfe remained under Dr. Ruge's care at Firlawns the course of his illness was erratic. With diathermy, cough-suppressing medication, and complete rest — which were almost the only measures a physician could take to battle pneumonia in the days before the introduction of antibiotics and before the widespread use of sulfa drugs — his temperature and his blood pressure dropped. On July 15, Dr. Ruge brought in a lung expert as consultant, Dr. Philip Schoenwald, who gave Wolfe a careful examination and declared that he was making good progress. Immensely relieved, Wolfe wired to Aswell, who, like all of Wolfe's friends in the East, was deeply worried about his illness: "Doctors say I'm out of danger now."

But Dr. Ruge found Wolfe's case a troubling one. Though some of his symptoms disappeared, he still had a wracking cough and the congestion in his right lung remained severe. The doctor attributed the slow recovery to Wolfe's "worn-out condition before the infection," for, he said, he "had absolutely no strength to fall back upon." He also blamed Wolfe's insistence that he had to get back on his feet and resume writing his book, which his publisher and, indeed, the world were waiting for. In a tactless effort to keep him from trying to work, Ruge reminded him that only a small number of people in the United States knew or cared about his book. Asking what difference it would make to humanity if he got well or not, he reminded Wolfe "that even such great men as Genghis Khan and Napoleon died." Speechless with fury, Wolfe would not talk to the doctor for two days. Later he told Ruge that if he ever did get back to work he was going to write him up in a novel.

Ruge also felt under attack from Wolfe's friends. The Stevenses, with the best intentions in the world, kept barging into Firlawns to visit, and each time they came Wolfe's temperature went up. The Winthers, who thought that Firlawns was a run-down asylum for mental patients and wanted to move Wolfe to a regular hospital, caused so much disruption that Ruge barred them from the premises. Aswell kept trying to interfere, long-distance, from New York, urging that other physicians be brought in to examine Wolfe, but professional courtesy prevented them from poaching on Dr. Ruge's case.

Feeling beset on all sides, Ruge decided that someone from Wolfe's family ought to come to Seattle — "just in case," as he told the Stevenses. Since Julia was too old to make the extended train trip and Mabel was nursing her sick husband, Fred was the only available family member, and he took a vacation from his job in Spartanburg, South Carolina, in order to be at his brother's bedside.

"O God, I'm finished," Wolfe protested when he learned that Fred was coming. "He'll kill me!" Much as he loved his brother, he knew that Fred's high-strung hysteria would only reinforce his own darkest fears. When Fred arrived, he nearly drove everybody crazy. He was, Mrs. Stevens thought, as "whole-hearted, well meaning, and as devoted as a Great Dane puppy" — and about as useful. He conceived an immediate and intense distrust of "this dam[n] man Ruge," who struck him as "sinister and mys[t]erious," and he constantly badgered the doctor with suggestions, complaints, and requests. Angry at having his authority questioned, Ruge ordered Fred out of his office. Urged on by Aswell, Fred wanted to dismiss Ruge from the case, but Wolfe in his feeble condition was even more reluctant than ever to make a hard decision. After all, he told Fred, if "the ship and he (Tom) had weathered the storm . . . he didn't want to leave the skipper in port."

By early August, though, it was clear that Wolfe was not recovering. His cough had virtually disappeared, but he continued to run a fever and he began to suffer from excruciatingly painful headaches. Under much pressure from Fred and from Aswell, Ruge took his patient to Providence Hospital in Seattle, where, on August 6, for the first time since he fell ill, X rays were made of his lungs. They showed "a large area of consolidation in the right upper lobe, involving one third to one half of the right lung." The official diagnosis was still "pneumonia with delayed resolution," but doctors for the first time began mentioning tuberculosis as a possibility. The suggestion terrified Wolfe. "When you intimate it or mention it to him," Fred warned his mother and sister, "it agitates him no end. He is terribly afraid of the word T.B. and it hurts him like the dickens to hear it."

The ominous diagnosis impelled Wolfe to insist that Fred bring him some paper and pencil to his room in Providence Hospital, where, propped up in bed, he drafted a letter to Maxwell Perkins. Gone now were the suspicions he had recently voiced about his former editor, and Wolfe wrote with the affection and trust that had so long characterized their friendship:

> I'm sneaking this against orders, but "I've got a hunch" — and I wanted to write these words to you.
>
> I've made a long voyage and been to a strange country, and I've seen the dark man very close; and I don't think I was too much afraid of him, but so much of mortality still clings to me — I wanted most desperately to live and still do, and I thought about you all a 1000 times, and wanted to see you all again, and there was the impossible anguish and regret of all the work I had not done, of all the work I had to do — and I know now I'm just a grain of dust, and I feel as if a great window has been opened on life I did not know about before — and if I come through this, I hope to God I am a better man, and in some strange way I can't explain I know I am a deeper and wiser one. If I get on my feet and out of here, it will be months before I head back, but if I get on my feet I'll come back.

It was the last letter he ever wrote.

The suggestion that he might have tuberculosis finally led Wolfe to dismiss Dr. Ruge and to put himself under the care of Dr. Charles E. Watt, the principal lung specialist at the Providence Hospital, who up to this point had been able to take only a peripheral interest in the case because Wolfe was the patient of another physician.

During the rest of August he remained in Providence Hospital. His friends and relatives in Seattle did what they could to make him comfortable. From New York Aswell repeatedly urged him to concentrate on getting well and not to worry about finishing his book. "Do please try to take it all as easy as you can," Miss Nowell begged. "Don't stew, don't worry." Sending him some recent light novels, Perkins advised him not to be impatient, since a long rest would improve his general health and the hospital experience would be future material for him as a writer.

About the middle of the month Fred, who hated the people and the climate of Washington and felt "like a *caged animal*" in Seattle, had to go back to his job, and Mabel came out to relieve him. When Wolfe first saw her he was disturbed, asking anxiously, "Have you come out to tell me that I'm very sick and am going to die?" But his sister reassured him. Like all the Wolfe family, she distrusted doctors and was confident that anyone who had as good an appetite as Tom's could not be seriously ill.

She got a great deal of help from a young Southern nurse, Annie Laurie Crawford, who was working toward an advanced degree at the University of Washington. Though Miss Crawford had not previously met the Wolfes, she had worked in an Asheville hospital and she knew the Westalls. When Wolfe learned that she was in Seattle, he begged her to visit him at Providence Hospital, because she was, he said, "one of us," somebody he could talk to. Presently she began coming every day, and he eagerly looked forward to her visits. She brought him an amaryllis; unlike most of the other flowers he received, which were sent promptly to the children's ward, he kept it by his bed, asking a nurse to move it from one side to the other so that he would wake up and see it. When he was feeling very low, she simply sat with him and held his hand. More often she listened.

"Let me talk at you," he would begin, and he told her all about his writing plans and of his hope that his next book would truly be worthy of all the praise that he had already received. Recognizing that when he was released from the hospital, he would have to stay for a while in Seattle to regain his strength, he told Miss Crawford that he was going to have a flat at the Spring Apartment Hotel, which he had inspected before he fell ill. There Mabel would cook for him and help care for him until he was able to get about. Then he planned to go to Palo Alto, where his friend Dr. Russel V. Lee would see that he fully recovered. In describing his plans to Miss Crawford, Wolfe usually began, "When I get well" — but sometimes he said, "If I get well."

But by early September it was clear that his dreams would not come true. Though his cough was gone and his fever had diminished, his headaches continued to be intolerably severe, and no medication relieved them. The only way he was able to get to sleep at night was by having Mabel or Miss Crawford rub his head with witch hazel — he disliked the smell of rubbing alcohol — until he was virtually drenched. On September 4, Dr. Watt's examination found Wolfe disoriented and confused. Examination of his eyes suggested the possibility of a metastic lesion in the brain, but the evidence was inconclusive. "The exact interpretation of all this is difficult to state," Dr. Watt was obliged to conclude. "Certainly this is no ordinary pneumonia."

He urged Mabel to take her brother to the Johns Hopkins Hospital in Baltimore, to be examined by Dr. Walter Dandy, the best brain surgeon in the United States. A certain desperation in Dr. Watt's tone indicated that he and the other physicians in the Pacific Northwest had done all that they could for Wolfe and that they feared that they would be blamed if the novelist died while under their care.

Until the transcontinental train trip could be arranged, Watt thought there was no harm in letting Wolfe move to the apartment his sister had rented. With the help of a cousin, she managed to get him out of the hospital and up to the seventh-floor apartment, where, exhausted, he collapsed across the big double bed that had been set up in the living room. But after a time he seemed stronger, began to watch from the window the boats moving back and forth across the sound, and told her: "You picked well this time, Mabel. . . . You picked a nice place; this is a fine hotel." He ate a big dinner, enjoying all the Southern dishes — like green beans cooked with bacon — that she had prepared for him, and she began to feel that maybe he was not so sick after all. Perhaps all he had needed was just to get out of the hospital.

But that evening Dr. George W. Swift, the brain specialist whom Aswell all along had wanted to put in charge of Wolfe's case, gave him a careful examination. Finding Wolfe lying in bed with a profuse perspiration, he listened to his chest, tested his reflexes, and examined his eyes. He diagnosed brain abscess, which might or might not be tubercular in origin, and urged Mabel to get her brother to Baltimore as quickly as possible.

The next day Wolfe, accompanied by Mabel and Annie Laurie

Crawford, boarded the *Olympian* for the five-day trip East. The doctors had given Miss Crawford morphine to relieve Wolfe's headaches during the journey, and they suggested that if he became much worse during the trip he might be taken to the Mayo Clinic. On the first night of the journey, he was delirious. While Mabel and Miss Crawford were trying to get a little rest, he climbed over the luggage with which they had tried to block the door and wandered down seven cars of the train in his pajamas, trying, as he explained to the porter who brought him back to his compartment, to send a telegram. After that he was mostly quiet, though often in pain, but he resisted taking morphine, which he said made him feel worse.

At Chicago Julia Wolfe joined them, bringing peaches and grapes from her own yard in Asheville. Since some of the time on the train Wolfe had seemed to think that he was heading for Palo Alto, Mabel decided to test his alertness by asking if he recognized the old lady. Looking up from the wheelchair in which he was being moved from one train to another, he smiled and said, "Mrs. Julia E. Wolfe of the Old Kentucky Home."

By the time the party reached Baltimore, Wolfe was disoriented and confused. As he was carried in a stretcher from the train to the waiting ambulance, he asked his sister, "Where are you taking me now, Mabel?" The news that he was going to the Johns Hopkins Hospital undoubtedly brought to his mind memories of the many times his father had been in that hospital — and of the inability of the physicians there to cure his cancer. "Well, Mabel," he said, "your ideas about Johns Hopkins may be all right, . . . but I have ideas of my own." But when asked what they were, he was too feeble to continue, and he said only, "I need a rest, Mabel. I'm awfully tired."

Admitted to the hospital on September 10, Wolfe was immediately given a preliminary examination. The doctor described him as "a very large middle aged man who is acutely ill. He does not seem well oriented, his speech is vague, wandering and incomplete. He seems distracted and quite ill." The only remarkable physical characteristic was that his skin was "loose and slightly wrinkled," because he had lost fifty pounds during the two months of his illness. The examining physicians concluded that he was most likely suffering from acute pulmonary tuberculosis, with a cerebral tubercle or possibly tuberculous meningitis, but they added that cancer or cerebral abscess were other, less probable diagnoses.

After studying the X rays and reviewing the notes of his associates, Dr. Dandy then made his own thorough examination of the patient. It was obvious that he was very ill. Much of the time he seemed entirely rational, but the crushing pain in his head sometimes caused him to stop in the middle of a sentence. "It was as though a shade had been drawn on a scene we had been watching," Mabel remembered. "He sat there for a moment, not looking around wildly or frightened, just blank." Then, when the pain abated, he would resume his sentence just where he had left off.

To give immediate relief Dr. Dandy proposed to open a small hole in his skull — a trephine — in order to release the fluid that he was sure was accumulating there. He found it difficult to explain this procedure to Julia, with her incurable optimism that there could not be much wrong with her son, and to Mabel, who was by this point hysterical, and doubtless he was relieved that Aswell, who had come down from New York, took charge and asked him to go ahead. When Dr. Dandy told Wolfe that he intended to "bore a little hole in your head, right back here," the patient seemed to accept the procedure and even asked: "Well, Doctor, you aren't going to bore all the way through my head, are you?" When the emergency operation was performed, fluid spurted from Wolfe's skull "with terrific pressure," shooting three feet into the air.

But this operation gave only temporary relief, and Dr. Dandy knew that the only possibility of saving Wolfe's life was through an exploratory operation on his cranium. If on opening his skull he discovered a removable abscess or tumor, there was a possibility that he might live, but if he found cancer or multiple tuberculosis, the case was hopeless. The chances were ninety-five percent against Wolfe, but Dr. Dandy thought the operation ought to be attempted. Reluctantly Julia and Mabel agreed. So did Fred, who arrived in Baltimore on the morning of the operation and went in to reassure his brother. "Tom," he said, "you're going to be all right. You are going to be fine, boy." "I hope so, Fred," Wolfe replied. "I hope so."

By the time of the operation on September 12, Perkins and Miss Nowell had both come down from New York, and they joined

Aswell. Mrs. Bernstein wanted to come but was told that her presence would be too upsetting to the family. After a two-hour operation, Dr. Dandy emerged to give the family and friends the news. He had discovered on the right lobe of Wolfe's brain "myriads of tubercles." An old tubercular lesion in his lung had been opened up during his illness, and the disease had spread to his brain. "Obviously," as the medical report of the operation read, "nothing could be done."

After the incision was closed, Wolfe was wheeled back to his room. He did not regain consciousness.* For the next three days his condition remained about the same, and at 5:30 in the morning of September 15 he died, just eighteen days short of his thirty-eighth birthday. He was buried in Riverside Cemetery in Asheville.

---

* Members of the Wolfe family later insisted that Wolfe regained consciousness after the operation and spoke some final words to them. Another report has him calling for Aline Bernstein. Wolfe's medical records show that he responded, with increasing difficulty and slowness, when his name was called, that he muttered irrationally several times, once calling out for "Scotch!" and that he seemed to recognize and speak briefly to both his brother and his sister on September 13. But Dr. Dandy told Aswell that he never truly regained consciousness.

Afterword: The Posthumous Novels of Thomas Wolfe

WOLFE'S DEATH IN SEPTEMBER 1938 left unresolved the fate of the huge manuscript on which he had worked for so many years. Since he had almost no other property and only a small income from the books he had already published, that manuscript constituted the major portion of his estate. In April 1937, well before his break with Charles Scribner's Sons, he had drawn up a will naming Maxwell E. Perkins the executor of his estate. Because Wolfe had left Scribners for Harper & Brothers and had chosen Edward C. Aswell as his new editor, Perkins found the role of executor unwelcome and embarrassing. He thought of declining to serve, but his sense of duty to his dead friend was too strong. As he wrote to his mother, "there did not seem to be any decent way of not doing it."

Under Perkins's general supervision, Aswell assumed the responsibility of preparing Wolfe's manuscript for publication. Out of the large bundle of papers Wolfe had left with him he shaped two long novels, *The Web and the Rock* (1939) and *You Can't Go Home Again* (1940). These were followed by *The Hills Beyond* (1941), which consisted of Wolfe's unfinished novel about the Joyner family and of ten short stories and essays, most of which had been previously published.

Just how familiar Aswell was with Wolfe's manuscript before the author's death is unclear. Certainly he "probably saw him more frequently than anyone" during the last six months of his life in New York, and the two men talked for hours about Wolfe's work in progress. Then, too, Wolfe had entrusted his manuscript to the editor before leaving on his Western trip and, with some reluctance, had allowed him to examine it. Aswell did read some of it, and he wired Wolfe in Seattle that it was "magnificent in scope and design." In all probability, however, he sampled the manuscript and did not go through the whole mass of papers that Wolfe had deposited with him.

After Wolfe's death, however, he had to deal with the manuscript as a whole, and he discovered, as he later told Richard S. Kennedy, that it was "a mess." It was so confusing that he labeled the jottings he made as he tried to read through it: "Notes I made to help bring order out of chaos."

The papers Wolfe left with Aswell did not form, in any proper sense, a novel at all. Perhaps the best way to characterize them is as a series of loosely interconnected long short stories or short novels. The material was in varying stages of completion: some of it was in handwritten first drafts; parts of it were typed versions of what Wolfe had dictated to his secretaries; some sections had been revised and retyped; considerable parts of it had already been published in various magazines. The manuscript included sections deleted from "O Lost" before it became *Look Homeward, Angel,* passages from the abandoned and unpublished novel "K-19," and segments cut from *Of Time and the River.* Other portions had been written much more recently.

Aswell tried to follow the long outline that Wolfe had drawn up for "The Web and the Rock," but he found it was not very helpful. Some of the chapters Wolfe listed had never been written; others existed only in fragmentary form; many more were present in several versions, differing sometimes slightly, sometimes very significantly. Parts of the manuscript were written in the first person, but other sections were told in the third person by an omniscient narrator. The protagonist was variously named Eugene Gant, David Hawke, Paul (or George) Spangler, Joe Doaks, and George Webber. Sometimes he seemed to come from a normal, if noisy, household; at other times he was the product of a broken marriage and lived with his ancient, superstitious Aunt Maw. In some parts of the manuscript the hero had brothers and sisters; in others he was an only child. Later he fell in love with a woman much older than himself who was named Alice, Irene, Esther, or Rebecca and who was married to a Mr. Jacobs, Jack, or Feitlebaum.

In attempting to put Wolfe's manuscript into some comprehensible shape, Aswell asked for the assistance of Perkins, who had a very clear memory of what Wolfe had written before 1936 though he knew little of his recent work. He also called on Gwen Jassinoff, who had been Wolfe's secretary during his final months in New York and had helped arrange his papers before he went to Purdue. And, most important, he got help from Elizabeth Nowell, whose knowledge of Wolfe's manuscripts was comprehensive since she, as his agent, had gone through much of this material with him, looking for publishable short stories. At Aswell's request, she carefully annotated Wolfe's outline for the new book, identifying as many of the chapters as she could, listing where some of the material had been previously published, and indicating whether Wolfe had thought the sections were in rough or almost final form.

There were both moral and legal constraints on what Aswell could do with Wolfe's manuscript. From their long conversations he knew how bitterly Wolfe resented the cutting and shaping of his earlier manuscripts that had taken place at Scribners, and he was aware that editorial interference with the integrity of the author's work had been a principal cause for Wolfe's break with Perkins. Before Wolfe left for the West, he had told Aswell that he expected to proceed with his work "without any great assistance," and he specified: "I do not believe that I am in need of just the same kind of editorial help at this moment as Mr. Perkins so generously and unselfishly gave me in 1933, 1934." Aswell had agreed with him, admitting that "any outside suggestions that might be made to you at this stage could very well prove premature and ill-founded." Though Wolfe's death obviously ended this understanding, his editor at first felt morally bound to do only the minimal amount of tampering with his friend's prose. Had he been inclined to do more, he had also to remember Wolfe's contract with Harper & Brothers, which stipulated that the publisher could make "no changes, additions, or alterations in the title or text" without the written consent of the author. With Wolfe's death that veto power devolved on Perkins, who reminded Aswell that the contract gave Harpers "no right whatever for detailed editing" of the manuscript.

At the same time both Aswell and Perkins knew that the contract provided that Wolfe's new novel could not exceed 750,000 words in length. By a rough count, his manuscript contained perhaps double that number. Or, to put the matter another way, what he had written was as long as ten novels of normal size and three times as long as the admittedly overlong *Of Time and the River*. As practical men, Aswell and Perkins knew that there was no reading public for a novel written on such a vast scale. To resolve this problem, Perkins came up with his own interpretation of the contract: If it did not give the publisher the right to make changes in Wolfe's prose, it did allow a "very considerable margin for omissions." In other words, Aswell could cut but not revise.

Presently Aswell proposed to deal with the problem of excessive length by dividing the manuscript into two separate novels. After consulting with Melville Cane, the lawyer who had drawn up Wolfe's will, Perkins gave the plan his blessing. Perhaps he remembered that he had faced an almost identical problem in dealing with Wolfe's excessively long manuscript of "Time and the River" and that he had found the same solution. After convincing Wolfe that he had written two separate cycles or stories, Perkins had persuaded him to ready the first half for the printer and to postpone publication of the second half.

Concentrating on the first half of Wolfe's manuscript, Aswell spent eight months getting it ready for publication. It formed, he thought, a reasonably coherent whole, since it recounted the early life of George Webber, his education at Pine Rock (as Chapel Hill became in this fictional version of Wolfe's own life), his move to New York and his efforts to begin a literary career, his turbulent love affair with Mrs. Esther Jack, and, finally, his flight abroad, where he was injured in a beer hall brawl in Munich. Aswell decided to call the new book "The Web and the Rock," a title that Wolfe had intended for the entire work.

Aswell also made an early decision to drop Wolfe's introductory chapters dealing with the Joyner family, the maternal ancestors of Wolfe's hero, George Webber. He felt justified in cutting out this material because Wolfe never got around to writing the parallel chapters he intended to include on Webber's paternal ancestors. He was also influenced by Miss Nowell's opinion that "lots of Joyner stuff" was readily "cuttable if Perkins allowed," since Wolfe's "book proper" began only with the second or third of his major sections. Perkins did agree — perhaps because he himself in editing "O Lost" had cut most of the introductory material on the early Gants and Pentlands in order to make *Look Homeward, Angel* begin with Eugene Gant. Aswell deferred publication of the Joyner chapters to another book, *The Hills Beyond.*

But as Aswell worked over the manuscript, he began to realize that he could not literally follow the moral and legal restrictions against altering Wolfe's prose. The more familiar he grew with the material, the more certain he became that many changes, both great and small, had to be made. For one thing, the names of the characters had to be standardized; Eugene, David, Paul, and Joe all became George. Since most of the book was written in the third person, the first-person sections — usually material written much earlier — had to be changed. Because George Webber was an only child, Aswell had to deal with the references that cropped up to his brother and his brother-in-law — who were really the siblings of Eugene Gant, Paul Spangler, or Joe Doaks, not George Webber.

More troublesome was the possibility that Wolfe's manuscript might be libelous, for both Fred Wolfe and John Terry advised him that many of Wolfe's characters were thinly disguised but readily recognizable caricatures of living persons. In one case Wolfe used the actual name of a man in describing a red-haired and red-bearded Asheville citizen who was in the habit of "talking — prowling . . . and yelling and cursing at people and with a sadistic lust for striking at the feet of young [paper] route boys in drunken glee." To prevent suits Aswell changed the names and slightly altered the descriptions of many minor characters. In some instances the changes had to be more extensive. In one chapter Wolfe told of a brutal one-eyed baker who forced his son, accused of stealing small sums of money from his employer, to enlist in the navy and threatened that he would shoot him if he ever showed his face again in Asheville. Aswell changed the man's name from Profitt to Lampley, made him a butcher rather than a baker, gave him "two good eyes in place of his blind eye," and altered a few other unessential but recognizable details.

Yet more serious was the legal danger posed by Wolfe's sketch of his Aunt "Pink" Westall, whom he detested, considering her, as did his brother Fred, a woman who came from "a cheap — vulgar, sneering — crowd of Mountaineers" and who used the wealth of their uncle and "the veneer of hypocritical Nigger-Baptistreligion" to look down on the Wolfes. Even in the manuscript of "O Lost" Wolfe had tried to get revenge by exposing his aunt's brutality to the orphan girls whom she took into her home, ostensibly out of charity but really in order to exploit them as slaveys. After Perkins persuaded him that the chapter was "highly dangerous," it was dropped from *Look Homeward, Angel,* but, characteristically, it now turned up again in the manuscript of "The Web and the Rock." Aswell did not discover the libel until very late, after the book had been set up in type, and, deciding that it was too risky to publish it, he deleted the entire chapter.

More questionable, though understandable, were Aswell's procedures for establishing a single text for chapters that Wolfe had drafted in several varying forms. For instance, there were two versions of Chapter 2, "Three O'Clock," which described George Webber at the age of twelve, introduced his querulous Aunt Maw, with whom he lived, told how some poor-white boys bullied and attacked George and how his best friend, the part-Cherokee Nebraska Crane, saved him, and ended with an account of several small black boys from the market area who used to bicycle in formation past George's front yard at exactly three o'clock each afternoon, insisting on calling him "Paul." The two drafts differed in length, and each contained details missing from the other.

Aswell constructed a final version by blending the two typescripts. Throughout he changed — as Wolfe himself had sporadically done on the carbon of one draft — the name of the boy from Spangler to Webber and deleted references to the boy's mother (Paul Spangler's mother had been alive, but George Webber's mother was dead). To prevent possible libel suits he altered the names of most of the boys who bullied young Webber. He eliminated some repetitious passages and drastically abridged Wolfe's tribute to the beauties and simplicity of North Carolina, which were contrasted to the exotic decadence of South Carolina. The editor also removed several of Wolfe's long rhapsodic passages, such as his invocation of the world of George Webber's Northern-born father:

> Ever the good green East again, the smell of paint and smoke in April, the smoke of morning, breakfast, afternoon, the talk of porches and the smell of gardens, and feel of home! Ever the good green East again — and thought of the great West unvisited, the

soaring range, the great Divide, the painted brilliance of the desert, and the ragged hackles of the Rocky Mountains, but ever the good green East again, and the green sweet flanks, the nearness, and the mountain hollows, evening, and the slant of late light on late green flanks, far voices in a hollow, a screen-door shut, and laughter, a sweet cool tinkle — and the thought of home! Ever the good green East again . . . [etc., etc.].

Aswell's editing of Wolfe's story of the love affair between George Webber and Esther Jack, which in the end formed about half of *The Web and the Rock,* was more controversial. This segment, which Wolfe called "The October Fair," had been written over a period of many years. From time to time he had revised parts of it, attempting "to tone it down, make it less personal, less over-written," but he was never satisfied with it. "He'd been too close to it when he first wrote it," as he told Miss Nowell, and he explained "that it would now be rewritten as 'emotion recollected in tranquillity,' " in order to make it not just his own story for one "typical of *all* young men in [a] first love affair." In the manuscript Wolfe left with Aswell there were many segments of the story, but they lacked clear organization, chronology, or point of view.

Aswell constructed a pastiche out of several drafts, rearranging the episodes in the love story, making the chronology more comprehensible, toning down George Webber's sexually explicit speeches, and eliminating his most virulently anti-Semitic remarks. Though there are legitimate questions about his shaping of this material, there can be no doubt that much editorial intervention was needed in order to make it comprehensible.

Much less defensible were Aswell's additions to Wolfe's manuscript. On finding that Wolfe had written "The Web and the Rock" — as he wrote all his novels — not as a sequential narrative but as a series of almost independent sections or "books," he tried to tie the story together by adding brief transitional passages, published in italics, between sections of the novel. These he wrote himself, often echoing passages from Wolfe's manuscript, but neither in the published novel nor in any Harpers publicity concerning it was any hint given that these were the work of the editor, not the author.

A final unfortunate decision led to the inclusion of what purported to be an introductory statement by Wolfe, announcing:

"This novel . . . marks not only a turning away from the books I have written in the past, but a genuine spiritual and artistic change. It is the most objective novel that I have written. I have invented characters who are compacted from the whole amalgam and consonance of seeing, feeling, thinking, living, and knowing many people." This statement was drawn from a long letter that Wolfe had begun to Aswell on February 14, 1938, in which he sketched the principal characters and indicated the basic themes of "The Web and the Rock." Dissatisfied with what he had written, Wolfe never finished the letter and never mailed it; Perkins discovered it among his papers after his death and showed it to Aswell. The editor then prepared a much abridged version of this letter to introduce Wolfe's first posthumous novel and, at Perkins's suggestion, he called it an "Author's Note." He affixed Wolfe's name to it and added the spurious date of May 1938.

Shaped by the editor, not by the author, this "Author's Note" misrepresented *The Web and the Rock*. Wolfe certainly intended to rework his manuscript so as to make it less lyrical and more objective, but he did not live to do so. Consequently *The Web and the Rock* was largely an echo, both in style and in substance, of his earlier novels. Nearly all reviewers thought this introductory note — which, of course, they thought Wolfe himself had written — was seriously misleading, since the new novel was "the same old Wolfe after all," "a thin, watered-down repetition" of his earlier fiction. Some found that *The Web and the Rock* confirmed their view of Wolfe as "a perennial adolescent, emotionally and intellectually."

I

Though few reviewers were enthusiastic, sales of the novel were healthy, and Aswell was encouraged to push ahead with editing the last half of Wolfe's manuscript the following year. This second section of "The Web and the Rock" manuscript he called *You Can't Go Home Again*, which, he reminded Mabel, "was Tom's own title, as you know."

Though the manuscripts from which this new book was formed were a jumble, they had greater consistency of style and theme than those used in *The Web and the Rock*. Most of this material was written during the last two years of Wolfe's life, when he was trying to restrain his lyrical impulse and to emphasize his concern for social issues. These pages included what were, in effect, a series of separate short novels. One dealt with George Webber's return to Libya Hill (as Asheville was called) when he witnessed the end of the boom times. A second, longer novelette, on which Wolfe had worked with great care during the summer of 1937, was "The Party at Jack's," which satirized the superficiality of wealthy New Yorkers in the 1920s and hinted that the imminent depression was about to put an end to their frivolous way of life. A third gave a very detailed account of George Webber's encounter in England with the celebrated visiting American novelist Lloyd McHarg (Sinclair Lewis). A fourth was the full version of "I Have a Thing to Tell You," Wolfe's story of his slow awakening to the barbarities of Hitler's Germany. And, finally, there was extensive material — some of which Perkins did not permit Aswell to publish — on the House of Rodney, Wolfe's fictional version of Charles Scribner's Sons.

In order to make a unified book out of this disparate material, Aswell edited with even less restraint than he had shown in the *The Web and the Rock*. He cut large segments of Wolfe's manuscript that did not seem to fit. Perhaps one-third of "The Party at Jack's" was dropped (and the name of the section was changed to "The World That Jack Built"), as was about half of the story of Lloyd McHarg.

To forestall suits for libel or invasion of privacy, Aswell systematically changed the names and descriptions of numerous characters. He also, in effect, invented a character. When Wolfe first drafted his story on the boom times in Asheville, his hero, John Hawke, had a brother, Lee (who, in fact, was clearly patterned on Fred Wolfe), and when he wrote his short story "The Company," his protagonist, then called Joe Doaks, witnessed the financial problems of his brother Jim (who was really Ralph Wheaton, Wolfe's brother-in-law). At some later point, Wolfe combined Lee and Jim into one character. But George Webber was an only child and, in order to use this material, Aswell decided to convert this brother into a childhood friend, Randy Shepperton, who had appeared briefly in *The Web and the Rock*.

For *You Can't Go Home Again* Aswell freely constructed chapters from Wolfe's fragments and drafts. So far as can be determined — and it is always possible that in the vast collection of

Wolfe's papers in the Houghton Library something can be over-
looked — Wolfe left no full draft for what became Chapter 5,
"The Hidden Terror." It recounted George Webber's return train
trip from New York to Libya Hill, during which he met Nebraska
Crane, now a professional baseball player, Jarvis Riggs, Mayor
Kennedy, and Parson Flack, the principal promoters of the Libya
Hill boom that was about to collapse, and the sinister Judge
Rumford Bland, the blind, syphilitic usurer, who asked George
searchingly, "Do you think you can go home again?" Instead,
Wolfe's papers included at least ten drafts of portions of this chapter (many with carbon copies on which Wolfe had made revisions). Some had been intended for "K-19" and *Of Time and the
River,* others had been written more recently. Of the forty two
printed pages of this chapter, about twenty-eight can be fairly
closely approximated in Wolfe's numerous drafts — though not
in the order in which they appear in the book. Aswell created the
others by patching together phrases and sentences of Wolfe's.

In editing *You Can't Go Home Again,* Aswell simply ignored
Perkins's injunction about changing Wolfe's language. In order to
provide a clear copy for the typesetter, he had most of the material
retyped, and it is, consequently, not always easy to determine just
what changes he did make. But a comparison of Wolfe's typescript, which was dictated to a secretary, describing his first meeting with Lloyd McHarg with the version published in *You Can't
Go Home Again* suggests the kinds of revision for which Aswell
was responsible.

Wolfe's Typescript	*You Can't Go Home Again*
To say that I was shocked at his appearance would be eloquent understatement. I was appalled. It was terrifying. I recognized him instantly. I had seen his pictures many times, but I now realized how mercifully inadequate, how beautifully unrevealing are the uses of photography. He was, I thought, the most fantastically ugly man I'd ever seen, and to this ugliness was added akind of personal ruin and devasta-	There was something almost terrifying in his appearance. George recognized him instantly. He had seen McHarg's pictures many times, but he now realized how beautifully unrevealing are the uses of photography. He was fantastically ugly, and to this ugliness was added a devastation of which George had never seen the equal.

Wolfe's Typescript

tion, of which I'd never seen the equal.

The first and most violent impression, perhaps, was his astonishing redness. Everything about him was red — a kind of fiery red that had an actual physical combustibility. At that moment, if smoke had begun to issue from his nostrils and he had burst out in flames all over, I don't think I should have been surprised. His hair was red, his large protuberant eyes were red, his eyebrows were red, his face was so red that it seemed to throw off heat. His eyelids were red, and, last of all, his bony, freckled, red-haired, knuckly hands — I realized now, why every one who knew him called him Knuckles —were also red. Moreover, it was a most alarming redness I've ever seen:

His face, for example, did not have that fleshy and high-colored floridity that one so often sees in the faces of men who have drunk long and earnestly. It was far past that. The man was thin, thin to the point of emaciation. I thought he looked shockingly ill and wasted. His face, moreover, which was naturally a kind of wry, puckish sort of face — as a matter of fact, as one got to know it better, a pugnacious but very attractive kind of face, full of truculence, homely as hell but also with a kind of impish humor, a homely, Yankee, freckled kind of modesty that was

You Can't Go Home Again

The first and most violent impression was his astonishing redness. Everything about him was red— hair, large protuberant ears, eyebrows, eyelids, even his bony, freckled, knuckly hands. (As George noticed the hands he understood why everyone who knew him called him "Knuckles.") Moreover, it was a most alarming redness. His face was so red that it seemed to throw off heat, and if at that moment smoke had begun to issue from his nostrils and he had burst out in flames all over, George would hardly have been surprised.

His face did not have the fleshy and high-colored floridity that is often seen in men who have drunk too long and too earnestly. It was not like that at all. McHarg was thin to the point of emaciation. He was very tall, six feet two or three, and his excessive thinness and angularity made him seem even taller. George thought he looked ill and wasted. His face, which was naturally a wry, puckish sort of face — as one got to know it better, a pugnacious but very attractive kind of face, full of truculence, but also with an impish humor and homely, Yankee, freckled kind of modesty

Wolfe's Typescript	*You Can't Go Home Again*
wonderfully engaging — this face seemed to have been all dried out, blistered by those fierce, red, fiery flames that had burned in it. In his photographs of course one did not see this, but this face, which was by nature wry and puckish, had been further dried and puckered up as if it were under the permanent control of a half green, red hot persimmon. It was furthermore all so scaled, carbuncled, scabbed, broken out in lumps and patches, that it suggested the corrugations of a washing board.	that were wonderfully engaging — this face now looked as puckered up as if it were permanently about to swallow a half-green persimmon, and it also seemed to be all dried out and blistered by the fiery flames that burned in it.

Aswell's numerous alterations did not basically change Wolfe's meaning, but they altered the rhythm of his sentences and blurred the focus of his portrait. In much of *You Can't Go Home Again,* the voice is that of the editor, not the author.

For *You Can't Go Home Again* Aswell once more wrote passages to connect the different segments or "books," but he was now less restrained than he had been in *The Web and the Rock* and did not attempt to construct them from Wolfe's own words. Indeed, he boasted to his wife that he "was *creating* the book," " 'creating' passages (he read some of them to [her]) to supply, he said, essential transitions." In one, relating how George Webber's experiences in Germany had led to his "effort of self-appraisal," Aswell wrote that Webber now had "the definite sense of new direction toward which he had long been groping, that the dark ancestral cave, the womb from which mankind emerged into the light, forever pulls one back — but that you can't go home again." Knowing how hostile Wolfe had always been toward Freudian imagery, Miss Nowell questioned this passage, and Aswell was obliged to admit that it expressed his own thought, and "was not quoted from anything Tom wrote nor even from anything he said."

Feeling that *You Can't Go Home Again* had no proper ending, the editor decided to transfer the concluding paragraphs of "I Have a Thing to Tell You" to the final page of George Webber's farewell letter to his editor, Foxhall Edwards. The published book therefore ended with a passage suggesting that Wolfe had a premonition of his death: "Something has spoken to me in the night, burning the tapers of the waning year; something has spoken in the night, and told me I shall die, I know not where." Later Aswell explained that he transposed this passage "so that the book would have a proper closing." "As you know," he told Miss Nowell, "the manuscripts had no form at all when Tom turned them over to me because he wasn't anywhere near finished with them. After his death I had to do the best I could to give them form and order according to the internal evidence."

II

Though most reviewers found *You Can't Go Home Again* a stronger novel than *The Web and the Rock,* a few expressed reservations about Aswell's handling of Wolfe's manuscripts. In particular Hamilton Basso, to whom Wolfe had shown some of his stories in draft, protested, in a long review in the *New Republic,* that Harpers was less than candid in stating that both *The Web and the Rock* and *You Can't Go Home Again* had been "finished and turned over to his publishers in May, 1938." Basso also felt that it was not honest to call this book a "new enterprise" on Wolfe's part, since he knew that some sections of *You Can't Go Home Again* had been written as early as 1934 and that much of the book had been drafted in 1935 and 1937.

Perhaps in response to such criticisms, Aswell included "A Note on Thomas Wolfe" in the last volume that he extracted from Wolfe's papers, *The Hills Beyond*. Giving a fascinating glimpse of Wolfe as a writer, the "Note" revealed for the first time that Aswell was the author of some passages in Wolfe's posthumous books. There were, he explained, large gaps between the sections of Wolfe's final novels. Claiming that "Tom had told me what was to go in most of these blanks," he admitted: "I wrote a few paragraphs as best I could to serve this purpose, drawing upon Tom's own words whenever they were available, and these passages were printed in italics and set on pages by themselves in order to distinguish them from Tom's own text."

But much of Aswell's "Note" was thoroughly misleading. Describing the "mountain of manuscript" that was turned over to him, he asserted that it had not all been intended for use in Wolfe's novel. Wolfe, he said, "wanted me to become familiar with every detail of it so that between us we could decide what really did belong in 'the book.' " In fact, as Aswell knew very well, Wolfe's elaborate outline indicated that all of his manuscripts were part of one gigantic novel — to be published perhaps in more than one volume — that he called "The Web and the Rock."

Though he admitted to initial bewilderment over Wolfe's pile of papers, Aswell declared that further study convinced him that Wolfe had "the whole conception of his work clear in his mind." Consequently the chapters of his posthumous novels, even when written at different times, all "fitted together like the pieces of a jigsaw puzzle." This claim was untrue. Moreover it was belied by Aswell's admission that much "extraneous matter," including "the unfinished fragments and great chunks of stuff that did not belong in the books," had to be deleted before the novels could be published.

Aswell's "Note" went on to defend Wolfe as a writer, claiming that critics exaggerated his repetitiousness and verbosity. If he piled adjective on adjective, it was in order to convey a precise meaning and to give a special rhythm to his sentences. Consequently, while "whole chunks and reams" of his manuscript could be deleted, "small cutting was often impossible because it would have ruined his style." Aswell failed to mention that he had made numerous such small changes in *The Web and the Rock* and that he had used his editorial blue pencil much more extensively in *You Can't Go Home Again.*

He also tried to refute the charge that Wolfe was an autobiographical novelist. Correctly he brought forward Nebraska Crane, the baseball player, and other figures as instances of fictional characters that Wolfe had created without an identifiable prototype. But he added to that list "Randy Shepperton, George Webber's Mercutio, who stood by him after his book came out when everybody else turned against him," as "another imaginative projection." He failed to note that Randy Shepperton was a projection created by Edward C. Aswell, not Thomas Wolfe.

Finally, he presented *The Hills Beyond* as "a work of almost pure imagination," Wolfe's most objective writing, in his lean and bare style. Acknowledging that one part of it had been published, as "The Bell Remembered," in 1936, Aswell argued that this fragment of a novel showed the direction that Wolfe's subsequent writing would have taken, because this was "the very last work he did." No doubt Aswell thought that this was the case, but, as Miss Nowell pointed out to him, Wolfe began the Joyner manuscript in the fall of 1935. Though Wolfe added some material after his visit to Asheville, she had read through the first six chapters of the unfinished novel in early 1937.

III

It is not possible to know why Aswell edited Wolfe's posthumous books as he did. An authoritarian personality, used to giving orders and having them unquestioningly obeyed, he was not introspective, and he felt no need to explain his actions to others. Certainly he expressed no doubts and voiced no guilt about his work as Wolfe's editor. He carefully preserved all his memoranda and letters about Wolfe's manuscripts, kept the typescripts and galley proofs that showed the changes he made, and made sure that all this material was safely deposited in the Houghton Library at Harvard University.

It is fair to speculate that his actions as Wolfe's posthumous editor were initially shaped by financial and professional considerations. As a very junior editor at Harper & Brothers, he had been responsible for offering Wolfe a contract for his next book, sight unseen, with a very large advance of ten thousand dollars. With Wolfe's death, recovery of that advance became problematical; Harpers could have sued Wolfe's estate, but the total assets of that estate were much less than this debt. Consequently, unless Aswell could shape a book, or books, from Wolfe's manuscript, Harpers would suffer a considerable financial loss. More important, as Aswell's wife noted, "Ed's reputation was compromised if [one or] more Great American Novels didn't emerge from Tom's literary remains because Ed had confidently assured his firm that they were there."

But there was more to it than that. When Aswell became Wolfe's editor he believed, as his wife said later, "that theirs was to be the Great Collaboration — Tom's genius combined with Ed's power of organization." Wolfe's death "almost literally diminished him." But gradually he convinced himself that "he was Tom's remaining *half.*" He thought he had a special understanding of the writer. He enormously admired, even adored, Wolfe, but he eventually came to the conclusion that there was an incurable immaturity about his writing. "Tom never grew up," he told a young friend. The more he worked with the manuscripts, the more convinced he became that Wolfe would never have been able to shape them into a novel without editorial assistance. Now that Wolfe was dead, it was his duty to do for his last books what Perkins had done for the early ones. He spoke to his wife of "his *obligation* to finish Tom's work."

How Aswell's editorial labors should be judged is another matter, and the subject has aroused a good deal of scholarly and even popular discussion. Few questions were raised before Aswell's death. Basso's careful review of *You Can't Go Home Again* did suggest doubts about the editing of Wolfe's posthumous novels or, at least, about the candor of the publisher's statements announcing those books. Miss Nowell also had some reservations about Aswell's work, but she could say very little since she was editing *The Letters of Thomas Wolfe,* a project that required the permission of the Estate of Thomas Wolfe, of which Aswell himself became administrator after Perkins's death in 1947.

The publication of Richard S. Kennedy's *The Window of Memory* in 1962 opened a new era in Wolfe scholarship. By a careful examination of all of Wolfe's papers, Kennedy was able to trace the evolution of the texts of his novels, from original handwritten jottings in his notebooks, to first drafts, through variant typescripts, to galley proofs and the final printed pages. For the first time it was possible to determine just what editorial changes Aswell made in Wolfe's last books. Kennedy concluded that Aswell "did more to bring Wolfe's book into order than Maxwell Perkins had done with *Of Time and the River.*" He thought that in organizing and rearranging the manuscripts for *The Web and the Rock* Aswell "did a piece of creative editing." But in working on *You Can't Go Home Again* he not merely cut and rearranged Wolfe's materials; he "tampered with Wolfe's style as he had not done before." In extenuation of Aswell's actions Kennedy noted that the material Wolfe had drafted for *You Can't Go Home Again* was "a crude product," consisting mostly of manuscripts written during the two years before his death and then "laid aside to season." "Editorial doctoring was badly needed," he concluded, since much of the manuscript had to be revised or reassembled. By "sensibly reordering" the sections, Aswell "placed the material . . . in the best possible sequence."

Kennedy's book, which has remained the most careful and thoughtful study of Wolfe's literary career, greatly influenced the views of other critics, who had not worked with Wolfe's manuscripts. After reading it, Louis D. Rubin, Jr., who had published a perceptive study, *Thomas Wolfe: The Weather of His Youth,* in 1955, concluded that *The Web and the Rock* and *You Can't Go Home Again* were "given their status as novels primarily by Edward Aswell." Arguing that the novels Aswell edited should be relegated "to the status of anthologies, to be given no more credence than the late 17th and early 18th century editions of Shakespeare," Rubin called for "a complete re-editing of all of Wolfe's writing from [*Of*] *Time and the River* onward." C. Hugh Holman, one of the most thoughtful critics of Wolfe's writing, agreed, noting that in assembling the posthumous novels Aswell "exercised great freedom in excision, rearrangement, and even rewriting on occasion."

Since these critical judgments were widely shared and generally known, it was puzzling when John Halberstadt in an article in the *Yale Review* in 1980 announced, as a newly discovered truth, that Aswell had tampered with Wolfe's texts. Most of Halberstadt's essay was unexceptionable, if naive, and it went over the same ground that Kennedy had covered. But his conclusions were more extreme: "Aswell's editing not only violated the spirit (if not the letter) of Wolfe's contract with Harper and Brothers, but also fundamentally changed the character of Wolfe's work." In published letters and newspaper interviews Halberstadt went on to charge that "the three posthumous novels of Thomas Wolfe, *The Web and the Rock, You Can't Go Home Again,* and *The Hills Beyond,* were not really written by Wolfe in the usual sense but were predominantly the work of an editor named Edward Aswell."

Halberstadt's publications caused a considerable literary brouhaha, especially among those who had not followed the previous critical and biographical studies that described Aswell's overly active role as editor. "In years past, I have often taught *The Web and the Rock* in American literature courses," one distinguished professor announced; "after reading Halberstadt, I would not dream of doing so again. It would be teaching an unacknowledged and profoundly misleading hybrid." Because Halberstadt published material from Wolfe's papers without the permission of the Estate of Thomas Wolfe or of the Houghton Library, where they are housed, he was denied further access to those papers and was not permited to use the library for a period.

Though a few scholars came to Halberstadt's defense, most considered his charges overstated. After a careful reexamination of the evidence, Kennedy branded "the recently publicized declaration that Aswell 'was the dominant contributor to the books that bore Wolfe's name' " as "simply untrue," and he repeated his judgment that Aswell's editing was "acceptable, even commendable, for a commercial publication." More recently Leslie Field prepared a book-length analysis, "Thomas Wolfe's Posthumous Publications," that thoroughly examined all the outlines that Wolfe drew up for his last books and traced the evolution from original draft to published book of a sample chapter from each of the novels. His view is similar to Kennedy's: "Wolfe wrote, revised, and rewrote as he adhered to his overall plan; Aswell edited."

My own conclusion falls between these two extreme positions. I find it absurd to speak of Aswell as the "author" of Wolfe's posthumous novels. I myself have read every draft, and every carbon copy, of all of Wolfe's manuscripts — not merely those in the two parcels he entrusted to Aswell but all the others that were in his great wooden packing case, which Perkins, as his executor, controlled — and I have compared these, on a line-by-line basis, both with the typescripts from which the printer worked in composing *The Web and the Rock* and *You Can't Go Home Again* and with the published books. Except for the introductory passages linking the "books" in these novels and for very occasional transitional sentences or paragraphs, Thomas Wolfe wrote these novels. They are not spurious or forged, and they are not the work of Edward C. Aswell. The structure of the novels is also Wolfe's; assisted by Miss Nowell, the editor followed Wolfe's outline for the books. Finally, the theme of the novels is Wolfe's, not Aswell's. Taken together, these two books tell the story of "one man's discovery of life and of the world," and, as Wolfe promised in the statement of purpose that he left for Aswell, they show how George Webber painfully learned, "through error and through trial, and through fantasy and illusion, through falsehood and his own damn foolishness, through being mistaken and wrong and an idiot and egotistical and aspiring and hopeful and believing and confused," that you can't go home again.

But I believe that it is equally misleading to speak of Aswell's work on Wolfe's posthumous novels as simply that of an editor. From standardizing the names and the tenses of Wolfe's manuscript, Aswell moved on to modifying the rhythm of his prose, to altering his characterizations, and to cutting and shaping his chapters. Greatly exceeding the professional responsibility of an editor, Aswell took impermissible liberties with Wolfe's manuscript, and his interference seriously eroded the integrity of Wolfe's text. Far from deserving commendation, Aswell's editorial interference was, both from the standpoint of literature and of ethics, unacceptable.

IV

Notably missing from these discussions is a consideration of what procedures Aswell or any other editor might have followed in dealing with Wolfe's unpublished papers. It is easiest to begin by eliminating choices that were not possible.

In some ways it might seem that the best solution was to publish "October Fair" — Wolfe's long, impassioned account of his love affair with Esther Jack — as a continuation of *Of Time and the River*. It was originally conceived as part of that novel. Publishing it as a sequel, or second volume, of *Of Time and the River* would greatly have strengthened that defective book, for it would have allowed much clearer development of Wolfe's portrayal of Eugene Gant as an American Candide, the innocent who painfully learns, in experience after experience, that things are not what they seem. But this plan could have been followed only in 1935 or 1936. After that Wolfe so frequently revised and reshaped the Esther Jack material that it was no longer a sequel to *Of Time and the River*. For instance, his short novel "The Party at Jack's" dealt with social issues irrelevant to the theme of the earlier book. This plan, then, was not available to Aswell.

Another impracticable option would have been to publish Wolfe's manuscripts just as he left them. In considering this possibility it is important to remember that Wolfe did not have anything that could be considered the manuscript or the typescript of a book. What he had was a pile of undigested and mostly unrelated fragments, chapters, sections, and, in a few instances, short novels. They had no common theme or story line. If published in full, these papers would have filled five or six large volumes. Certainly neither Harpers nor any other commercial publisher could afford to publish such a potpourri. Nor would there have been an audience for such a collection. Many years later when the University of North Carolina Press published in two hefty volumes *The Notebooks of Thomas Wolfe,* which contained, in addition to the entries in his pocket notebooks, large chunks of Wolfe's hitherto unpublished fragments, the number of readers was small.

Still another possibility would have been the publication of several small volumes, each containing a segment of Wolfe's manuscript that was self-contained and in most nearly finished shape. In some ways such little books would have been good for Wolfe's critical reputation. They would have demonstrated that, whatever Wolfe's limitations in crafting a long novel, he displayed a splendid sense of artistry in the short novel of 15,000 to 40,000 words. A few of Wolfe's contemporaries, like Perkins, recognized that "The Web of Earth," his short novel published in 1935, was the truest, most carefully planned story that he ever wrote. Years later C. Hugh Holman edited five of *The Short Novels of Thomas Wolfe,* which reminded readers that this was the form in which Wolfe worked best. Still, it is certain that publication of Wolfe's material as short novels would not have been acceptable to Harper & Brothers, or any other commercial publisher, in the late 1930s and 1940s. And, what is equally important, this form of piecemeal publication would not have satisfied Wolfe. As James Thurber remarked, Wolfe felt that short books did not represent real writing but "some kind of doodling in words." "If you said you were a writer," Thurber remembered, "he wanted to know where the books were, the great big long books."

The only remaining option was to arrange and edit Wolfe's manuscript, following as closely as feasible the outline that he left, the long letters describing the nature and purposes of his future books, and, in general, the spirit in which he wrote. These necessarily flexible guidelines are the ones that Aswell tried to follow. It is certain that another editor, with a different temperament and with a different literary sensibility, would have made different decisions. Yet it is not clear that another editor could have made better, or even considerably different, novels out of Wolfe's manuscripts.

What is certain is that there is no way to know what these last books would have been had Wolfe lived to complete them. Some critics have argued that these posthumous books show that Wolfe was not advancing as an artist, since he was retracing familiar ground, without the passion or the lyrical intensity that gave a special quality to his first books. Others, who find in these last books evidence of greater maturity and control, believe that they show Wolfe was just reaching his full stature as a writer. The controversy is not one that can ever be settled, partly because the posthumous books are the products of Aswell's editing as well as of Wolfe's creativity. Before Wolfe could complete his book, "death bent to touch his chosen son with mercy, love and pity, and put the seal of honor on him when he died." The quotation is from *The Web and the Rock,* and it was written by Edward C. Aswell.

Acknowledgments

It is a pleasure to acknowledge the assistance I have received from many sources during the six years that I have been working on this book. Without this aid the biography could not have been completed.

First I want to thank Mr. Paul Gitlin, Administrator, C.T.A., of the Estate of Thomas Wolfe, who has given me unrestricted access to all of Thomas Wolfe's papers and has allowed me to quote liberally from them. Since my book has been written with the permission and the encouragement of the Estate of Thomas Wolfe, it is in one sense an authorized biography. But it is not an official biography. The Estate imposed no conditions on my work, and it reserved no right to review or censor my findings.

To librarians all over the United States I am indebted for generous access to their collections and for answers to my frequent and tiresome letters of inquiry. My heaviest obligation is to the Houghton Library, at Harvard University, where I worked almost daily for three years. Mr. Rodney Dennis, Mr. Thomas Noonan, and Ms. Susan Halpert of that library have been unfailingly helpful. I also owe much to Ms. Marte Shaw, who was formerly on the Houghton staff. At the Widener Library of Harvard University Mr. Nathaniel Bunker has been indefatigable in locating dissertations and out-of-print items needed for my research.

To the North Carolina Collection at the University of North Carolina at Chapel Hill my obligation is also very great, and Dr. H. G. Jones, Ms. Frances Weaver, Ms. Alice Cotten, and Mr. Jerry Cotten have unstintingly given me help on my repeated visits.

Miss Jan Brackin, Mr. Edward Epstein, Miss Betty Lawrence, and Mr. John Tom all worked to put the Wolfe material in the Pack Memorial Library in Asheville at my disposal.

At the Princeton University Library Mr. Alexander Wainwright and Ms. Jean F. Preston expedited my research in the Archive of Charles Scribner's Sons. Through the kindness of Miss Katherine E. Desai, Mr. Ted Greider, and Mr. Bayrd Still I was able to use the significant Wolfe materials in the libraries of New York University.

Ms. Joan St. Clair Crane and Mr. Michael Plunkett made available manuscripts in the Alderman Library of the University of Virginia. Though I was not able to visit the Humanities Research Center at the University of Texas, Miss Ellen S. Dunlop helped me locate Wolfe manuscripts in that collection, and Miss Linda Eichorn and Mr. Everett Larsen made the faithful transcriptions from which I have worked.

I am also grateful for help provided by: Mr. Terry Abraham of Washington State University Library; Miss Dolores Altemus of the Morris Library at the University of Delaware; Miss Margaret E. Berg of the University of Michigan Library; Mr. Robert Buckeye of the Abernethy Library at Middlebury College; Miss Delina Stephens Buie of the University of Louisville Library; Mr. Robert Byrd of the William R. Perkins Library at Duke University; Mr. Bernard R. Crystal of the Columbia University Library; Miss Katherine Emerson of the Library of the University of Massachusetts in Amherst; Mr. David E. Estes of the Robert W. Woodruff Library at Emory University; Mr. David Farmer of the McFarlin Library at the University of Tulsa; Miss Ellen Garrison of the Sherrod Library at East Tennessee State University; Miss Diana Haskell of the Newberry Library; Miss Nancy Johnson of the American Academy and Institute of Arts and Letters; Mr. David E. Schoonover of the Beinecke Library at Yale University; Miss Sandra Taylor of the Lilly Library at Indiana University; Mr. Robert A. Tibbetts of the Ohio State University Library; and Mr. Brooke Whiting of the Library of the University of California at Los Angeles.

Mr. Gordon N. Ray and Mr. Stephen L. Schlesinger provided copies of Wolfe documents in the files of the John Simon Guggenheim Foundation, and Miss Robin Kuzen discovered important Wolfe materials in the Office of the Pulitzer Prizes at Columbia University. Dr. Ernest Hartmann, Mr. Paul Roazen, and Dr. Richard F. Sterba helped me attempt to verify the claim the Wolfe was psychoanalyzed in Vienna. Mr. Robert Saudek of the Museum of Broadcasting and Miss Catherine Heinz of the Broadcast Pioneers Library assisted in an unsuccessful effort to discover a recording of a radio broadcast that Wolfe was supposed to have made, and Mr. David G. Flanders and Miss Brenda Kerstetter, of the Freedom of Information–Privacy Branch of the Federal Bureau of Investigation, found after a search that no F.B.I. file was kept on Wolfe.

I owe a special debt to Dr. Curtis Prout and Dr. Gustave Dammin, of Brigham and Women's Hospital in Boston, who gave an expert reading and interpretation of the voluminous medical records of Wolfe's final illness in the Johns Hopkins Hospital.

Private collectors have generously made their holdings available to me. To Mr. and Mrs. William Hatchett my debt is very large, for they opened to me their treasure-trove, the Braden-Hatchett Thomas Wolfe Collection, not used by any previous biographer. Not merely did they allow me to work through their extensive holdings when I was in Memphis; afterwards they have regularly kept me informed of further additions to that important collection. My old friend and former student, Theodore V. Theobald, generously shipped to me most of his extensive collection of articles, essays, and other materials about Wolfe; he saved me weeks of work in the library. Mrs. Carole Klein shared with me not only important documents but also her deep understanding of the Wolfe-Bernstein relationship. Miss Elizabeth Evans lent me notes and allowed me to hear the important interview that she taped with Miss Annie Laurie Crawford. Mr. Aldo P. Magi has repeatedly made available the rareties of his extensive Wolfe collection and has never been too busy to answer my frequent inquiries. Mr. Alexander Wainwright very kindly allowed me to examine his small, but absolutely priceless, collection. Mrs. Pamela Rankin-Smith, Mrs. Simeon Braguin, and Mrs. Samuel J. Cole shared with me valuable Wolfe material in their possession.

One of the delightful advantages of writing about a twentieth-century American figure like Thomas Wolfe is that it is still possible to talk to, or to correspond with, people who knew him. The number is dwindling, and some of those whom I interviewed have since died. Unfortunately I began this project too late to meet Thomas Wolfe's brothers and sisters, but I have had the pleasure of talking or corresponding with Wolfe's surviving nieces and nephews: Dr. R. Dietz Wolfe, Mrs. H. Whitman Wilder, Mr. David W. Gambrell, and Mr. Edward C. Gambrell. All have been unstintingly cooperative.

On Wolfe's early years in Asheville and his college days at Chapel Hill, I have been privileged to talk with, to listen to, or to hear from, Mr. William H. Andrews; Mr. William H. Bobbitt; Mr. Albert Coates; Mrs. Gladys Coates; Mr. Benjamin Cone; Ms. Katherine Robinson Everett; Mr. Paul Green; Mrs. Elizabeth Green; Mr. Phillip Hettleman; Ms. Elizabeth McKie; Mr. Nathan Mobley; Mr. Moses Rountree; Mr. R. Hobart Souther; Mr. Corydon Spruill; Mr. Vance E. Swift; Miss Annie Westall; Miss Marie Westall; and Mr. Ralph D. Williams.

A number of people gave me their recollections of Wolfe as an aspiring playwright and New York University instructor: Ms. Laurie R. Abramson; Mr. George P. Baker; Miss Annabelle J. Barrera; Mrs. Marguerite Cohn; Mrs. Mina Kirstein Curtiss; Mr. Joe Gangemi; Mr. Boris Gamzue; Mr. Julius Kabat; Mr. Donald W. Keyes; Mr. Joseph Roberto; Mr. Guy Savino; Mrs. Edith Hertz Smith; Mr. George Stevens; Mrs. Mary Alice Thoma; and Mrs. Ann Tromka.

Others who knew Wolfe during the final decade of his life and have shared their memories with me, either in interviews or in letters, include: Mrs. Mary Lou Aswell; Mr. Jerome Bahr; Mrs. Hamilton Basso; Mr. Cleanth Brooks; Mrs. Bernard DeVoto; Mr. Robert Disraeli; Mr. Muredach J. Dooher; Mrs. Thelma Ezzell; Mr. Henry Hart; Mrs. Hjalmar Hertz; Mr. Clayton Hoagland; Mrs. Kathleen Hoagland; Dr. Francis Hulme; Mrs. Edwin K. Large, Jr.; Mr. Paul Magriel; Mrs. Osmer F. Muench; Ms. Margaret Painter; Mr. Louis Shaeffer; and Mr. George Stoney.

The recollections of Wolfe's secretaries and typists, who retain clear memories of his work habits, have proved especially valuable: Mrs. Peter Campbell; Mrs. Eleanor Breese; Ms. Joyce Maupin; and Mrs. George Gaillard.

Mr. Donald Klopfer, Mr. Heinz M. Ledig-Rowohlt, and Mrs. Alfred Stern shared their vivid memories of Wolfe's German adventures with me.

I have learned much about Wolfe's Western journeys from Mr. Peter Davison, Mr. Thomas Hornsby Ferril, Mr. Robert Liddell Lowe; Dr. Henry A. Murray, and Mr. Robert Penn Warren.

Wolfe scholars have freely shared their time and learning with me. I owe more than I can say to Mr. Wilson Angley; Mr. Scott Berg, Mrs. Andrea P. Brown, Miss Myra Champion, Miss Lucy Connif, Mrs. Mary Aswell Doll, Mr. Leslie A. Field, Mr. John Hagan, Mrs. Lou Harshaw, Mr. John L. Idol, Jr., Mr. John Phillipson, Mr. Louis D. Rubin, Jr., Mr. Duane Schneider, Ms. Clara Stites, and Dr. Preston Lea Wilds.

Many other scholars have helped me locate sources or have assisted me with special problems concerning Wolfe: Mrs. Ann Berthoff; Mr. Carl Bode; Mr. Robert Dallek; Mr. William Dusinberre; Mr. Frank B. Freidel; Mr. Arnold Gates; Mr. Earl Harbert; Mr. Thomas L. Johnson; Mr. Robert Kenzer; Mr. Charles Maier; Mr. Herbert Mitgang; Mr. Richard Poirier, Mrs. Susan Sheehan; Mrs. Wilma Dykeman Stokely; and Mr. J. Harvey Young.

I owe the title of this book to a suggestion from Mr. Daniel Bell.

For special favors and assistance I am grateful to Mr. Arthur S. Link and Mr. David Brion Davis. Among many others who have helped I want to thank Mr. and Mrs. Kenneth R. Andrews; Mrs. Pearl K. Bell; Mr. Stanley Coben; Mr. and Mrs. Roy Jacobsen; Mrs. Phyllis Krasilovsky; Mrs. Jane Langton; Dr. Robert Levin; Mr. and Mrs. Robert Preyer; Mr. Leonard Rapport; Col. M. David Samples; Dr. Howard Shevrin; Mr. Bennett H. Wall; Mr. C. Vann Woodward; Mr. Stephen Whitfield; Mr. Alden Whitman; Mrs. Nancy Wilner; and Mr. Harry Woolf.

Mr. Marc Dolan, Mr. Benjamin Edwards, Mr. David Leviatin, Miss Susan Moeller, Mr. Jeffrey Rayport, Mr. Christopher Schroeder, and Mr. Thomas A. Underwood are among the students who provided invaluable research assistance. I am also deeply indebted to Miss Elizabeth Horton and Mrs. Ruth DiPietro for research help and for excellent typing.

I am heavily indebted to several people at Little, Brown and Company. Mr. Roger Donald, my editor, has steadily maintained his interest in, and his faith in, this biography during the long years while it was in preparation. Miss Cynthia Reed provided indispensable guidance through the thicket of problems involved in securing rights and permissions. Mr. Michael Mattil, who oversaw the preparation of the final revision of the manuscript, proved that it is possible for an editor to be at once an excellent critic and a strong friend.

Much of my research on Wolfe and most of the writing of this book has been done on leaves of absence from my regular teaching duties, and I am grateful to the President and Fellows of Harvard College, to Dean Henry Rosovsky, Dean A. Michael Spence, and Dean Phyllis Keller for making these leaves possible. I am also deeply indebted to the John Simon Guggenheim Foundation for its support.

I wish that there were some way adequately to thank colleagues and friends who took time from their own important work to read and criticize this manuscript. Professor Daniel Aaron, of Harvard University, has gone over it line by line, giving me the benefit of his sensitivity to language and his unparalleled knowledge of American literary history. For much help in placing Wolfe in the Anglo-American literary tradition I am deeply indebted to Professor Marcus Cunliffe, of George Washington University. With the insight and skill that have made her such a superb editor at the Harvard University Press, Dr. Aida D. Donald has worked over my manuscript, page by page, and it is the better for her suggested revisions. Mr. Paul Gitlin's close reading helped me to catch a number of factual errors and important legal distinctions. Professor Richard S. Kennedy, of Temple University, drawing on his unequaled knowledge of Wolfe's manuscripts, has given me invaluable detailed criticism. Professor Kenneth S. Lynn, of the Johns Hopkins University, took time from his own work on Ernest Hemingway to share with me his mastery of twentieth-century American literature and to offer his brilliant psychological insights about Wolfe. The book is better because of the reading that Professor Richard Marius, of Harvard University, gave it, for he is both a native of Wolfe's Appalachian region and a distinguished biographer. To Mr. Arthur J. Rosenthal, Director of the Harvard University Press, I am grateful for a perceptive and critical reading of my early chapters. Finally, Professor Richard Walser, of North Carolina State University, whose rich store of knowledge is based on a lifetime study of Wolfe, gave the manuscript a detailed scrutiny, and his suggestions enabled me to correct dozens of factual slips. To all these readers I am deeply grateful. Their criticism and advice has made this a better book, but I alone am responsible for all errors of fact and opinion that remain.

8 March 1986   David Herbert Donald

Sources, Abbreviations, and Notes

I
A Note on Sources and Usage

SINCE THIS BOOK is so fully annotated, no formal bibliography seems necessary, but I want to mention some of the major sources on which it rests.

Anyone who writes about Thomas Wolfe has to deal with the fact that nearly all of his work was, in greater or lesser degree, autobiographical. Wolfe himself made two serious attempts to tell the story of his life as a creative artist. The first of these, *The Story of a Novel* (New York: Charles Scribner's Sons, 1936), emerged from the lecture he delivered at the Colorado Writers' Conference in Boulder. The second, a lecture delivered at Purdue University in 1938, was published after his death as *Thomas Wolfe's Purdue Speech: "Writing and Living,"* edited by William Braswell and Leslie A. Field (Lafayette, Ind.; Purdue University Studies, 1964). Recently these two small books have been combined in *The Autobiography of an American Novelist: Thomas Wolfe,* edited by Leslie Field (Cambridge: Harvard University Press, 1983).

Wolfe's fiction is also largely autobiographical. The life of Eugene Gant, as presented in *Look Homeward, Angel* (New York: Charles Scribner's Sons, 1929) and *Of Time and The River* (New York: Charles Scribner's Sons, 1935), is remarkably like the history of Thomas Wolfe. Though George Webber, in *The Web and the Rock* (New York: Harper & Brothers, 1939) and *You Can't Go Home Again* (New York: Harper & Brothers, 1940), bears no physical resemblance to Thomas Wolfe, his career and his ideas largely replicate those of the author. Most of Wolfe's stories in *From Death to Morning* (New York: Charles Scribner's Sons, 1935) are about Wolfe or members of his family, and "Gulliver" (pp. 134–149), which recounts the problems of "a man who was too tall — who lived forever in a dimension that he did not fit," hardly pretends to be fiction. Many of the pieces in *The Hills Beyond* (New York: Harper & Brothers, 1941) are also auto-biographical.

The problem is to tell what parts of Wolfe's fiction can be taken as fact. In general, I have been wary of drawing on Wolfe's novels for biographical information, because they so frequently exaggerate or misrepresent happenings in his own life. (Such distortion is, I hasten to add, entirely proper for a novelist, however much trouble it may cause his biographer.) On the whole I have found Wolfe's manuscript drafts of his fiction more revealing and more accurate than the edited published novels and stories. But before crediting his fiction, either in published or in manuscript form, I have tried to find independent corroborative evidence.

Fortunately, that evidence is abundant, for Wolfe, even at an early age, refused to throw away anything: letters he received, drafts or copies of letters he sent, canceled checks, bills, form letters, Christmas cards, and all the variant versions of his novels and stories. By far the largest body of Wolfe's papers is the William B. Wisdom Collection in the Houghton Library of Harvard University, which includes hundreds of letters to and from Wolfe, together with his pocket notebooks or diaries, the ledgers in which he drafted much of his fiction, manuscript and typed versions of most of his work, and galley proofs of many of his books. It is huge. When I began this biography I asked Mr. Rodney Dennis, Curator of Manuscripts at the Houghton Library, to give me an estimate of the size of the Wisdom Collection, and he replied, "Between three and six million pages." After turning every page in the collection, I judge that was a somewhat exaggerated figure, but this is certainly one of the largest collections of papers of any American author. In addition to manuscripts, the Wisdom Collection contains books and magazines from Wolfe's own library

(many of which he annotated), recordings of interviews with
Mabel Wolfe Wheaton and Fred Wolfe, newspaper clippings, and
photographs. An elaborate guide to this material, which runs to
218 typed pages, was prepared by Patrick Miehe in 1973.

In citing this collection I have used Miehe's numbering system
when referring to compositions by Wolfe. Since letters to and
from Wolfe are filed by author or recipient, I have not included
Miehe's numbers when citing correspondence.

Attached to the Wisdom Collection in the Houghton Library
are the very important Manuscripts of Elizabeth Nowell, Wolfe's
friend, editor, and biographer. The recently acquired Manuscripts
of Mrs. Marjorie Fairbanks, a friend of Wolfe's who collected
materials for an unpublished biography, are also in the Houghton
Library.

Rivaling the Wisdom Collection in size and importance is the
Thomas Wolfe Collection in the North Carolina Collection of the
University of North Carolina at Chapel Hill. This collection is
particularly strong on Wolfe's early years and on his family; it
includes his numerous letters to his mother. Also in the North
Carolina Collection are the Fred Wolfe Manuscripts and the very
helpful Manuscripts of John Skally Terry, an early biographer
who wrote very little but showed excellent instincts about collecting material.

The Braden-Hatchett Thomas Wolfe Collection, in private
hands in Memphis, Tennessee, is another large and important
group of papers, which supplements the materials at Harvard and
the University of North Carolina. It is especially strong on Wolfe
family materials. Recently its owners have built up a collection of
practically every known article or essay written about Wolfe. For
a guide to this invaluable body of material, see "The Braden-
Hatchett Thomas Wolfe Collection: Master Catalogue" (1981,
with numerous supplements).

Though the Thomas Wolfe Collection of the Pack Memorial
Library in Asheville contains relatively few manuscripts, it is very
rich in photographs and newspaper clippings, and the library is, in
general, strong on Asheville and its history.

The Fales Library of New York University has an important
collection of manuscripts relating to Wolfe's career as a teacher.
Some of these were published in *Thomas Wolfe at Washington Square,*
edited by Thomas Clark Pollock and Oscar Cargill (New York:

New York University Press, 1954), but many others have been used for the first time in this biography.

The Thomas C. Wolfe Collection (#6348), in the Clifton Waller Barrett Collection of Manuscripts in the University of Virginia Library at Charlottesville, is small, but every item in it is of great value. The same can be said of the private collection of Thomas Wolfe manuscripts of Mr. Alexander Wainwright in Princeton, New Jersey. Also important and useful are the Wolfe manuscripts in the Research Library at the Harry Ransom Humanities Research Center of the University of Texas at Austin.

An invaluable source is the Archive of Charles Scribner's Sons in the Firestone Library at Princeton University. In addition to containing letters from Wolfe to Maxwell E. Perkins and others at Scribners, it also preserves copies of many letters about Wolfe and information on contracts and sales not found elsewhere.

The Estate of Thomas Wolfe preserves a large body of materials concerning contracts and publication of Wolfe's books, together with important correspondence between Maxwell E. Perkins and Edward C. Aswell, significant family correspondence, and Aswell's drafts of stories that Wolfe told him. These papers are in the custody of Mr. Paul Gitlin, Administrator, C.T.A., of the Estate of Thomas Wolfe, in his New York office.

The earliest full-scale bibliography was George R. Preston, Jr., *Thomas Wolfe: A Bibliography* (New York: Charles S. Boesen, 1943). Though now largely superseded, it remains valuable for its precise descriptions of the first editions of Wolfe's books. Elmer D. Johnson, *Of Time and Thomas Wolfe: A Bibliography with a Character Index of His Works* (New York: Scarecrow Press, 1959), is now mainly valuable for the 29-page index of characters who appear in Wolfe's fiction, since Johnson has published a greatly expanded bibliography, *Thomas Wolfe: A Checklist* (Kent, Ohio: Kent State University Press, 1970). Unfortunately it is not free of errors and omits some important items. See Theodore V. Theobald, "Additions to Wolfe Bibliography," *The Thomas Wolfe Review* 5 (Spring 1981): 42–50. For an admirable critical listing, see John S. Phillipson, *Thomas Wolfe: A Reference Guide* (Boston: G. K. Hall & Co., 1977).

I have found all of these guides valuable in locating articles published about Wolfe. My search for this material was expedited when the Theodore V. Theobald Collection of Thomas Wolfe material was loaned to me for several months; it has since been deposited in the library of St. Mary's College, Raleigh, North Carolina. For rare or unique items I have also drawn frequently on the important Thomas Wolfe Collection of Aldo P. Magi.

Most of Thomas Wolfe's pocket notebooks, together with much other Wolfe material, have now been published in Richard S. Kennedy and Paschal Reeves, eds., *The Notebooks of Thomas Wolfe* (2 vols.; Chapel Hill: University of North Carolina Press, 1970). I have relied heavily on these admirably edited volumes, though I have also checked the original diaries, in the Houghton Library, for omitted materials, such as details on Wolfe's sexual exploits.

The largest published collection of Wolfe's correspondence is Elizabeth Nowell, *The Letters of Thomas Wolfe* (New York: Charles Scribner's Sons, 1956). The quality and accuracy of Miss Nowell's editing is high, though she was obliged to omit parts of many letters that referred to persons who were still alive. I have used the original letters, mostly in the Wisdom Collection. Next in importance are *The Letters of Thomas Wolfe to His Mother,* carefully edited by C. Hugh Holman and Sue Fields Ross (Chapel Hill: University of North Carolina Press, 1968). This volume largely supersedes *Thomas Wolfe's Letters to His Mother, Julia Elizabeth Wolfe,* edited by John Skally Terry (New York: Charles Scribner's Sons, 1951), which still remains useful, however, because of Terry's introduction.

Wolfe's correspondence with Aline Bernstein has been published in Suzanne Stutman, ed., *My Other Loneliness: Letters of Thomas Wolfe and Aline Bernstein* (Chapel Hill: University of North Carolina Press, 1983), and Stutman, ed., *Holding On For Heaven: The Cables and Postcards of Thomas Wolfe and Aline Bernstein* (The Thomas Wolfe Society, 1980). Both these collections are useful, but I have usually cited the original letters, in the Wisdom Collection.

Smaller but important collections of Wolfe's letters are Oscar Cargill and Thomas Clark Pollock, ed., *The Correspondence of Thomas Wolfe and Homer Andrew Watt* (New York: New York University Press, 1954), and Richard Kennedy, ed., *Between Love and Loyalty: The Letters of Thomas Wolfe and Elizabeth Nowell* (Chapel Hill: University of North Carolina Press, 1983).

The two previous full-length biographies of Wolfe are Elizabeth Nowell, *Thomas Wolfe: A Biography* (Garden City, N.Y.:

Doubleday & Co., 1960), and Andrew Turnbull, *Thomas Wolfe* (New York: Charles Scribner's Sons, 1967). I have learned much from both. Miss Nowell's book, rich with her own personal associations with Wolfe, was necessarily incomplete, because so many of the people deeply involved in Wolfe's life were still alive when she was writing and because Edward C. Aswell, then administrator of the Estate of Thomas Wolfe, imposed many constraints on her. Turnbull's biography is much more complete and objective on Wolfe's personal life, but Turnbull's primary interest, as he stated in the letters of inquiry that he sent out, was in Wolfe as a man, not in Wolfe as a writer.

Among several shorter biographical studies, Elizabeth Evans's *Thomas Wolfe* (New York: Frederick Ungar Publishing Co., 1984), and Bruce R. McElderry, *Thomas Wolfe* (New York: Twayne Publishers, 1964), are outstanding.

Richard Walser, *Thomas Wolfe Undergraduate* (Durham, N.C.: Duke University Press, 1977), admirably covers four critical years in Wolfe's life.

Anyone who hopes to understand Wolfe must learn a great deal about his lover, Aline Bernstein. Carole Klein's *Aline* (New York: Harper & Row, 1979), is a full, sympathetic biography. Readers will also learn much from Mrs. Bernstein's autobiographical fiction, *Three Blue Suits* (New York: Equinox Cooperative Press, 1933), and *The Journey Down* (New York: Alfred A. Knopf, 1938).

A. Scott Berg's *Max Perkins: Editor of Genius* (New York: E. P. Dutton, 1978) is a comprehensive biography of another central figure in Wolfe's life, warmly appreciative of its subject. Also important for understanding the Wolfe-Perkins relationship is *Editor to Author: The Letters of Maxwell E. Perkins,* edited by John Hall Wheelock (New York: Charles Scribner's Sons, 1950).

Of the many critical studies of Wolfe, Louis D. Rubin, Jr., *Thomas Wolfe: The Weather of His Youth* (Baton Rouge: Louisiana State University Press, 1955), was a pioneering, perceptive study. Paschal Reeves, *Thomas Wolfe's Albatross: Race and Nationality in America* (Athens: University of Georgia Press, 1968), is thoughtful and fair-minded. C. H. Holman's *The Loneliness at the Core: Studies in Thomas Wolfe* (Baton Rouge: Louisiana State University Press, 1975) is especially insightful. *Thomas Wolfe's Characters: Portraits from Life,* by Floyd C. Watkins (Norman: University of Oklahoma Press, 1957), is helpful on the autobiographical element in

Wolfe's fiction. Some of the essays in *Thomas Wolfe and the Glass of Time,* edited by Paschal Reeves (Athens: University of Georgia Press, 1971), are excellent. For a sampling of other critical literature, see Richard Walser, ed., *The Enigma of Thomas Wolfe: Biographical and Critical Selections* (Cambridge: Harvard University Press, 1953), and Leslie A. Field, ed., *Thomas Wolfe: Three Decades of Criticism* (New York: New York University Press, 1968).

In my notes I have cited many of the unpublished doctoral dissertations written about Wolfe. Much of this critical literature has not proved very useful, because only in a few instances have the authors had access to Wolfe's papers, which show how his books evolved.

A notable study is Richard S. Kennedy, *The Window of Memory: The Literary Career of Thomas Wolfe* (Chapel Hill: University of North Carolina Press, 1962). Granted access to the whole body of Wolfe's manuscripts, Kennedy labored among them indefatigably to discover how Wolfe's books were composed, edited, and published. His book remains the most authoritative study of Wolfe's literary career, and, even though I differ from its conclusions at some points, I have found it invaluable.

Paschal Reeves, ed., *Thomas Wolfe: The Critical Reception* (New York: David Lewis, 1974), contains a large sampling of contemporary reviews of Wolfe's books. Aldo P. Magi and Richard Walser, eds., *Thomas Wolfe Interviewed, 1929–1938* (Baton Rouge: Louisiana State University Press, 1985), shows how Wolfe appeared to newspaper reporters.

The Thomas Wolfe Review (until 1981 *The Thomas Wolfe Newsletter*), a biennial publication, contains numerous biographical and critical essays.

In general, I have taken as few liberties as possible with the materials quoted and cited in this book. I have spelled out a few abbreviations that might be unintelligible to a reader and have throughout transformed "&" into "and." All omissions within quotations are, of course, designated by the usual ellipses (. . .). But in quoting phrases or parts of sentences, I have not supplied introductory or concluding ellipses and have silently capitalized the first words of sentences.

In my notes I have given sources for quotations. With a few exceptions these notes do not distinguish between drafts and final versions of letters, nor between originals and carbon copies of manuscripts. Often it is not possible to determine whether Wolfe actually mailed a letter or merely blew off steam by writing it. Consequently my notes usually do not state whether a letter was sent. In these notes I have explained and developed a few points too obscure to interest a general reader, but I have not used the notes to correct errors that I have found in other books and articles. Nor have I tried to be compendious in my citations, listing all the material that I have read and studied on any particular topic.

This book, then, is not intended to serve as a survey and appraisal of the literature on Thomas Wolfe. It is, instead, a biography of Wolfe, drawn so far as possible from the original sources.

II
Abbreviations Used in the End Notes

AB	Aline Bernstein, Thomas Wolfe's lover.
Alexander Wainwright Coll.	Private collection of Thomas Wolfe manuscripts owned by Mr. Alexander Wainwright, of Princeton, New Jersey.
AOAAN	Leslie Field, ed., *The Autobiography of an American Novelist*. Cambridge: Harvard University Press, 1983.
Barrett Coll.	Thomas C. Wolfe Collection (#6348), in the Clifton Waller Barrett Collection of Manuscripts, University of Virginia Library, Charlottesville.
Berg	A. Scott Berg, *Max Perkins: Editor of Genius*. New York: E. P. Dutton, 1978.
BHW	Benjamin Harrison Wolfe, Thomas Wolfe's brother.
BLAL	Richard Kennedy, ed., *Between Love and Loyalty; The Letters of Thomas Wolfe and Elizabeth Nowell*. Chapel Hill: University of North Carolina Press, 1983.
Braden-Hatchett Thomas Wolfe Coll.	The Braden-Hatchett Thomas Wolfe Collection of papers concerning Thomas Wolfe and his family, in the personal possession of Mr. William Hatchett and Ms. Eve Braden Hatchett, Memphis, Tennessee.

Charles Scribner's Sons Archive	Archive of Charles Scribner's Sons, Princeton University Library, Princeton, New Jersey.
ECA	Edward C. Aswell, Thomas Wolfe's last editor.
EN	Elizabeth Nowell, Thomas Wolfe's literary agent.
Fairbanks MSS.	Marjorie C. Fairbanks Manuscripts, Houghton Library, Harvard University, Cambridge, Massachusetts.
FDTM	Thomas Wolfe, *From Death to Morning*. New York: Charles Scribner's Sons, 1935.
Fred Wolfe MSS.	Fred Wolfe Manuscripts, North Carolina Collection, University of North Carolina, Chapel Hill.
FW	Fred Wolfe, Thomas Wolfe's brother.
Gitlin MSS.	Papers belonging to the Estate of Thomas Wolfe, in the office of Mr. Paul Gitlin, Administrator, C.T.A., of the Estate, New York, New York.
HB	Thomas Wolfe, *The Hills Beyond*. New York: Harper & Brothers, 1941.
JEW	Julia E. Wolfe, Thomas Wolfe's mother.
Journey Down	Aline Bernstein, *The Journey Down*. New York: Alfred A. Knopf, 1938.
JST	John Skally Terry, Thomas Wolfe's first authorized biographer.
Kennedy	Richard S. Kennedy, *The Window of Memory: The Literary Career of Thomas Wolfe*. Chapel Hill: University of North Carolina Press, 1962.
Klein	Carole Klein, *Aline*. New York: Harper & Row, 1979.
LHA	Thomas Wolfe, *Look Homeward, Angel: A Story of the Buried Life*. New York: Charles Scribner's Sons, 1929.
LTHM	C. Hugh Holman and Sue Fields Ross, eds., *The Letters of Thomas Wolfe to His Mother*. Chapel Hill: University of North Carolina Press, 1968.
Letters	Elizabeth Nowell, ed., *The Letters of Thomas Wolfe*. New York: Charles Scribner's Sons, 1956.
MEP	Maxwell Evarts Perkins, Thomas Wolfe's first editor.
MOL	Suzanne Stutman, ed., *My Other Loneliness: Letters of Thomas Wolfe and Aline Bernstein*. Chapel Hill: University of North Carolina Press, 1983.
MWW	Mabel Wolfe Wheaton, Thomas Wolfe's sister.
Nowell	Elizabeth Nowell, *Thomas Wolfe: A Biography*. Garden City, N.Y.: Doubleday & Co., 1960.

Nowell MSS.	Manuscripts of Elizabeth Nowell, Houghton Library, Harvard University
OTATR	Thomas Wolfe, *Of Time and the River: A Legend of a Man's Hunger in His Youth.* New York: Charles Scribner's Sons, 1935.
Pack Mem. Lib.	Thomas Wolfe Collection, Pack Memorial Library, Asheville, North Carolina.
PN	Richard S. Kennedy and Paschal Reeves, eds., *The Notebooks of Thomas Wolfe.* Chapel Hill: University of North Carolina Press, 1970. 2 vols.
Pollock and Cargill	Thomas Clark Pollock and Oscar Cargill, *Thomas Wolfe at Washington Square.* New York: New York University Press, 1954.
SOAN	Thomas Wolfe, *The Story of a Novel.* New York: Charles Scribner's Sons, 1936.
TW	Thomas Wolfe
TW, AO	Thomas Wolfe, Autobiographical Outline, Wisdom, Nos. 190–191. Two notebooks, begun in July 1926, in which Wolfe jotted down phrases and sentences to remind him of events in his early life.
TWAHF	Mabel Wolfe Wheaton and LeGette Blythe, *Thomas Wolfe and His Family.* Garden City, N.Y.: Doubleday & Co., 1961.
TWATR	Thomas Wolfe, *The Web and the Rock.* New York: Harper & Brothers, 1939.
Terry MSS.	Manuscripts of John Skally Terry, North Carolina Collection, University of North Carolina, Chapel Hill.
Turnbull	Andrew Turnbull, *Thomas Wolfe: A Biography.* New York: Charles Scribner's Sons, 1970.
Walser, Enigma	Richard Walser, ed., *The Enigma of Thomas Wolfe: Biographical and Critical Selections.* Cambridge: Harvard University Press, 1953.
Walser, Undergraduate	Richard Walser, *Thomas Wolfe Undergraduate.* Durham, N.C.: Duke University Press, 1977.
Wisdom	The William B. Wisdom Collection of Thomas Wolfe Manuscripts, Houghton Library, Harvard University.
WJ	Thomas Wolfe, *A Western Journal: A Daily Log of the Great Parks Trip, June 20–July 2, 1938,* ed. by Agnes Lynch Starrett. Pittsburgh: University of Pittsburgh Press, 1951.

Wolfe Coll., UNC Thomas Wolfe Collection, North Carolina Collection, University of North Carolina, Chapel Hill.

Wolfe-Watt Corresp. Oscar Cargill and Thomas Clark Pollock, eds., *The Correspondence of Thomas Wolfe and Homer Andrew Watt.* New York: New York University Press, 1954.

WOW William Oliver Wolfe, Thomas Wolfe's father.

YCGHA Thomas Wolfe, *You Can't Go Home Again.* New York: Harper & Brothers, 1940.

III

Notes

FOR THE SAKE of smoother reading, I have dispensed with numbered footnotes. Instead, I have keyed my notes to the page and line of the text. In the following pages each note is preceded by two numbers, separated by a slash. The first refers to the page, the second to the line. Thus a note preceded by 315/22 gives the source of facts or quotations on line 22 of page 315.

Chapter I: *A Secret Life*

3/5 LHA, prefatory note, "To The Reader."

3/17 For a detailed investigation of this matter, see Floyd C. Watkins, *Thomas Wolfe's Characters* (Norman: University of Oklahoma Press, 1957).

4/19 LHA, pp. 68. 16.

5/10 Thomas Wolfe received his first name from his grandfather, Thomas Casey Westall. His middle name was that of an old friend of his mother's, Thomas Clayton Bowman, a lecturer on spiritualism.

5/18 Elizabeth Evans, interview with Annie Laurie Crawford, 1975, cassettes lent to me through the courtesy of Professor Evans.

5/30 *TW Newsletter,* vol. 3, no. 2 (Fall 1979): 30.

5/37 JST, notes on an interview with JEW, Terry MSS. See also Hayden Norwood, *The Marble Man's Wife: Thomas Wolfe's Mother* (New York: Charles Scribner's Sons, 1947), p. 199.

6/8 JEW, "Eliza Gant Talks," transcription by Ruth Davis of several recordings that JST made of interviews with JEW, Terry MSS. In the remaining pages of this chapter, all quotations, unless otherwise identified, are from these interviews. I have found these recordings much more accurate and revealing than the conversations that Hayden Norwood reported in *The Marble Man's Wife,* and they offer a much more candid picture of the

Wolfe household than the somewhat saccharine reminiscences in Mabel Wolfe Wheaton and LeGette Blythe, *Thomas Wolfe and His Family* (Garden City, N.Y.: Doubleday & Co., 1961).

6/14 On the Westfall family, see two articles by Richard Walser, "Thomas Westall and His Son William," *TW Review,* vol. 8, no. 1 (Spring 1984): 8–18, and "Major Thomas Casey Westall," ibid., vol. 8, no. 2 (Fall 1984): 1–10. For much further information about the Westalls I am indebted to Professor Walser and Mr. William Hatchett.

7/13 WOW to Julia E. Westall, Oct. 18, Oct. 25, and Nov. 15, 1884, Braden-Hatchett Thomas Wolfe Coll.; WOW to Julia E. Westall, Oct. 23, 1884, Fred Wolfe MSS.

7/24 Hilda Bottomley to Editor, Harper and Brothers, Sept. 16, 1938, Wisdom.

7/37 JEW to FW, April 4, 1939, Fred Wolfe MSS.

8/2 Norwood, *Marble Man's Wife,* p. 131.

8/9 On W. O. Wolfe's family, see Richard Walser, *Thomas Wolfe's Pennsylvania* (Athens, Ohio: Croissant & Co., 1978), especially pp. 1–5. W. O. Wolfe's mother was Eleanor Jane Heikes, daughter of Emanuel Heikes and Sarah Wierman. I am indebted to Professor Walser for further information on the Wolfe genealogy.

8/21 For a full account of these troubles, see Richard Walser, *The Wolfe Family in Raleigh* (Raleigh: Wolfe's Head Press, 1976), pp. 1–18.

8/32 Norwood, *Marble Man's Wife,* p. 144; TW, draft of "The Web of Earth," Wisdom, No. 321.

9/15 JEW to TW, Aug. 7, 1926, Wisdom.

10/24 TW, Autobiographical Outline, Wisdom, Nos. 190–191. In these two notebooks, begun in July 1926, Wolfe jotted down, in more or less chronological order, phrases and sentences to remind him of events in his early life. Though not always accurate, these outlines are much more factually reliable than his much expanded fictional account in *Look Homeward, Angel,* and wherever possible I have relied on them, rather than on the novel, for biographical information.

10/27 Norwood, *Marble Man's Wife,* p. 185.

12/4 Hilda Bottomley to MEP, May 20, 1943, Charles Scribner's Sons Archive.

12/20 ECA, "Thomas Wolfe," talk given before the Harvard Club, Oct. 13, 1953, courtesy of Dr. Mary A. Doll.

13/1 LHA, p. 84.

13/6 Walser, *Thomas Wolfe's Pennsylvania,* p. 7.

13/35 TW to Margaret Roberts, July 8 [?], 1927, Wisdom. Cf. TW, MS. draft of a passage intended for "Of Time and the River," Wisdom, No. 414.

14/15 TW, untitled MS. on FW, Wisdom, No. 1316. For a typical letter showing these mood swings, see TW to FW, Sept. 15, 1920, Terry MSS. On this pattern of emotional reversal I have greatly profited by conferences with Professor Henry A. Murray.

14/31 TW, AO.

14/37 *Letters,* p. 123.

14/40 The following paragraphs are not intended as a clinical diagnosis — the basic purpose of which would be therapy — but as a summary of my understanding of some patterns in Wolfe's behavior, a summary that draws on the psychoanalytic literature on secondary narcissism. My ideas have been much influenced by Heinz Kohut's *The Analysis of the Self* (1971). Howard Shevrin's unpublished paper, "Narcissism, Individual Development & Psychopathology," a copy of which he graciously supplied me, was also very helpful. For the American Psychiatric Association's 1978 list of diagnostic criteria for narcissistic personality disorders, nearly every one of which applies to Wolfe, see Normund Wong, "Borderline and Narcissistic Disorders: A Selective Overview," *Menninger Clinic Bulletin* 44 (1980): 118. I have also found useful suggestions in Joseph D. Lichtenberg, "Is There a Line of Development of Narcissism?" *International Review of Psycho-Analysis* 5 (1978): 435–447; Saul Tuttman, "Otto Kernberg's Concepts About Narcissism," *American Journal of Psycho-Analysis* 40–41 (1980–1981): 307–316; Ben Bursten, "Some Narcissistic Personality Types," *International Journal of Psycho-Analysis* 54 (1973): 287–300; and Arthur Mandelbaum, "Family Characteristics of Patients with Borderline and Narcissistic Disorders," *Menninger Clinic Bulletin* 44 (1980): 201–211.

See also William U. Snyder, *Thomas Wolfe: Ulysses and Narcissus* (Athens: Ohio University Press, 1981).

Most psychiatrists trace the origins of narcissistic personality disorders to conditions in the very early months of an infant's life. The records on Wolfe's earliest years are very sparse. His fictional portrait of this period of his life is one of happiness and abundance. But that view reflects not so much his feelings as a small child as the excessively high opinion he came to have of his father after W. O. Wolfe's death.

15/12 TW, AO.

15/22 ECA, "Love As Art, and Vice Versa: An Erotic Experience, As Told to Me by Thomas Wolfe," Gitlin MSS.

15/26 TW, AO.

15/33 Bursten, "Some Narcissistic Personality Types," p. 293. Cf. Kohut, *The Analysis of the Self*, pp. 48–49.

16/16 Elizabeth Bernard Hester to JST, May 7, 1944, Terry MSS.

16/34 TW, AO.

17/11 JST, notes of interview with JEW, Terry MSS.

17/29 TW's entries in Benjamin Harrison Wolfe's Composition Book, Grade 6, Wolfe Coll., UNC.

17/36 TW, The Tar Heel Composition Book, 3rd grade, Wisdom, No. 1255.

18/5 Mary Louise Wolf, "Thomas Wolfe Remembered," *TW Newsletter,* vol. 3, no. 1 (Spring 1979): 34–37; William B. Wisdom, "Table Talk of Thomas Wolfe," Wisdom.

18/24 MWW, "Remembering Papa," Wolfe Coll., UNC. See John Boone Trotti, "Thomas Wolfe: The Presbyterian Connection," *Journal of Presbyterian History* 59 (Winter 1981): 517–542.

18/31 TW, untitled MS., Wisdom No. 416.

18/35 Kennedy, p. 29.

18/38 For a sampling of TW's quotations from the Bible, see Hans Helmcke, *Die Familie im Romanwerk von Thomas Wolfe* (Heidelberg: Carl Winter, Universitätsverlag, 1967), pp. 294–295.

19/3 On the other hand, he often experienced a sense of deep shame. See Francis J. Broucek, "Shame and Its Relationship to Early Narcissistic Developments," *International Journal of Psycho-Analysis* 63 (1982): 369–378.

19/11 *Asheville Citizen,* Sept. 19, 1938.

19/26 TW, draft for "The Ordeal of the Bondsman Doaks," Wisdom, No. 780.

19/33 TW, AO.

20/10 LHA, p. 136. On Wolfe's attitude toward blacks, see Paschal Reeves, *Thomas Wolfe's Albatross: Race and Nationality in America* (Athens: University of Georgia Press, 1968), chap. 2.

20/28 " 'Who's Who — and Why?' A Weekly Record of the Copies sold in Asheville, North Carolina, by Each Individual Boy Who Represents The Saturday Evening Post," 1909, Wolfe Coll., Pack Mem. Lib.; TW to Effie Wolfe Gambrell, May 16, 1909, Wisdom.

21/8 TW, typescript of "O Lost," Wisdom, [passage omitted from LHA, p. 197].

21/22 Max Israel, Wolfe's boyhood playmate, was not Jewish.

21/32 TW, AO; TW, typescript of "O Lost," Wisdom [passage omitted from LHA, p. 96].

21/39 Laurel Shackelford and Bill Weinberg, eds., *Our Appalachia* (New York: Hill and Wang, 1977), pp. 177–179; Elizabeth Evans, interview with Annie Laurie Crawford, 1975.

22/8 J. Y. Jordan, Jr., to JST, Nov. 27, 1941, Terry MSS.

22/14 Turnbull, pp. 11–12.

22/21 TW, AO. In this outline Wolfe called the family the Gants.

22/33 J. M. Roberts to EN, Sept. 18, 1951, Nowell MSS. Other versions of the story have Mrs. Roberts saying, "We want this boy."

23/10 TWAHF, p. 134.

23/17 LHA, p. 213.

24/2 TW, AO. See TW, "A Treatise on the Subject of 'Horty,' " undated composition in the back of an examination book, Wolfe Coll, UNC. He did do well in spelling and won a prize in an interscholastic high-school spelling contest. *Asheville Gazette-News,* April 12, 1913.

24/12 TW, AO.

24/22 Mrs. Roberts's comments on an assignment dated February 1913, in TW, Notebook for English Composition, North State Fitting School, 1912, Wolfe Coll., UNC.

24/35 Turnbull, pp. 16–17.

24/40 William J. Cocke, *Johnny Park Talks of Thomas Wolfe* (Asheville, 1973), p. 11.

25/11 TW, exercise book for English, North State Fitting School, 1914, Wolfe Coll., UNC; TW to John Bryan, Dec. 18, 1933, Wisdom.

25/29 Margaret Roberts to TW, Mar. 13, 1921, Wolfe Coll., UNC.

25/37 TW to Frank Wells, Aug. 29, 1921, Wolfe Coll., UNC; TW to Frank Wells, Sept. 5, 1921, Wisdom.

26/3 *Letters,* p. 123.

26/12 Frank Wolfe to JST, June 6, 1947, Terry MSS.; TW, AO.

26/16 TW, AO.

26/38 TW, AO.

27/11 TW, AO.

27/33 Frank Wolfe to MWW, Feb. 10, 1931, Braden-Hatchett Thomas Wolfe Coll.

28/4 TW, draft of "Of Time and the River," Wisdom, No. 359.

28/8 JEW to TW, Mar. 15, 1931, Wisdom.

28/25 TWAHF, p. 37.

29/17 TW, AO.; TW to Margaret Roberts, July 8 [?], 1927, Wisdom. There has been some controversy over the economic standing of the Wolfe family. Using Thomas Wolfe's assertion in *Look Homeward, Angel,* that the Gants (i.e., the Wolfes) were worth $100,000 in 1912, William F. Kennedy, in "Economic Ideas in Contemporary Literature — The Novels of Thomas Wolfe," *Southern Economic Journal* 20 (July 1953): 35–50, calculated that they were in the upper one or two percent of the Asheville community in terms of wealth and income. But Wolfe had little idea of his parents' worth, and he tended to exaggerate in what was, after all, supposed to be a work of fiction. Richard S. Kennedy's conclusion (Kennedy, pp. 37–38) is more persuasive: "The Wolfe family moved in one generation from the working class, through the lower middle class, to the middle class." The income that Julia Wolfe received from the Old Kentucky Home, and the investments she made with that income, were critical in that shift.

29/28 *Asheville Citizen,* April 15 and June 1, 1916; TW, speech on preparedness, 1916, Wisdom, No. 1261.

30/13 TW, "Shakespeare: The Man," which also contains the judges' comments, Wisdom, No. 1257.

30/18 *Asheville Citizen,* June 2, 1916; Duncan Emrich, interview with Mabel Wolfe Wheaton, Feb. 23, 1947, recordings in Wisdom.

30/23 Acting on their advice, Wolfe as late as August 1916 was looking into preparatory schools in Raleigh, where Mabel and Ralph Wheaton lived. TW to Ralph Wheaton, Aug. 18, 1916, Wolfe Coll., UNC.

30/33 TW to Margaret Roberts, July [8?], 1927, Wisdom.

30/38 TW, typescript of "O Lost," Wisdom [passage omitted from LHA, p. 387].

31/11 TWAHF, pp. 137–138; MWW to Ralph Wheaton, Tuesday [1916] and Aug. 28, 1916, Braden-Hatchett Thomas Wolfe Coll.; *Letters,* pp. 2–3.

Chapter II: *The Magical Campus*

32/3 *Letters,* p. 192.

32/5 TW, AO. In the remaining pages of this chapter, all quotations, unless otherwise identified, are from these two autobiographical notebooks that Wolfe compiled in 1926.

32/8 On the university in Wolfe's time, see Louis R. Wilson, *The University of*

North Carolina, 1900–1930: The Making of a Modern University (Chapel Hill: University of North Carolina Press, 1957). William S. Powell, *The First State University: A Pictorial History of the University of North Carolina* (Chapel Hill: University of North Carolina Press, 1979), is admirably detailed.

33/6 For many details in this chapter I have relied heavily on Richard Walser's admirable and accurate monograph, *Thomas Wolfe Undergraduate* (Durham, N.C.: Duke University Press, 1977).

33/20 Walser, *Undergraduate,* gives full details on the places Wolfe roomed and on his roommates.

33/25 *Letters,* p. 3.

33/27 The University of North Carolina used a numerical grading system, in which a "1" equaled an "A," a "2" equaled a "B," and so on.

33/36 TW, typescript of "O Lost" [passage omitted from LHA, p. 396].

34/3 Vance E. Swift, in H. G. Jones, ed., *Thomas Wolfe of North Carolina* (Chapel Hill: North Caroliniana Society, 1982), p. 77.

34/33 Kennedy, p. 41; Turnbull, p. 27.

35/16 *Letters,* pp. 3–4; Walser, *Undergraduate,* p. 12.

36/6 TWAHF, pp. 164–165.

36/19 TW, undated recollections of college days, Wisdom, No. 1172; Don Bishop, "Thomas Wolfe Biography Is Promised Soon," *Asheville Citizen,* May 1, 1950; Swift, in Jones, *Thomas Wolfe of North Carolina,* pp. 77–78.

37/10 Cf. Wolfe's unflattering fictional account of Terry as Gerald Alsop in TWATR, chs. 11–12.

37/26 In LHA, pp. 412–416, Wolfe said that his fictional counterpart, Eugene Gant, was infested with pubic crabs, but I have followed the fuller account he wrote in an unpublished manuscript, "The Wonderful Books," Wisdom, No. 298. It fills in and explains the cryptic entries in his Autobiographical Outline: "Mamie Smith — all the passion and the fire — the second visit — Christmas home — The hotel and the red-haired woman — Discovery." The doctor's comment is from TW, typescript of "O Lost" [passage omitted from p. 346].

37/30 William Hatchett, interview with FW, May 6, 1977, videotape, Braden-Hatchett Thomas Wolfe Coll.

38/34 WOW to BHW, July 9, 1917, Braden-Hatchett Thomas Wolfe Coll.

38/37 WOW to BHW, July 13, 1917, Wolfe Coll., UNC.

39/7 *Letters* p. 66.

39/13 Turnbull, p. 327.

39/38 *Letters,* pp. 4–5.

40/13 LeGette Blythe, "The Thomas Wolfe I Knew," *Saturday Review of Literature* 28 (Aug. 25, 1945): 19.

40/18 LTHM, p. 4.

40/39 TW, typescript of "O Lost" [passage omitted from LHA, p. 399].

41/8 On Greenlaw, see Kennedy, pp. 42–45, and Walser, *Undergraduate,* ch. 4.

41/36 TW, essay for English 3–4, Wolfe Coll., UNC.

42/4 LTHM, p. 5.

42/8 TW to Mr. and Mrs. J. M. Roberts, Nov. 1917, Wisdom.

42/17 TW, autobiographical notes on his college days, Wisdom, No. 1172.

42/25 TW, typescript of "O Lost" [passage omitted from LHA, p. 486].

43/19 AOAAN, p. 104.

43/26 *Tar Heel*, Mar. 23, 1918.

43/27 *Asheville Citizen*, April 5, 1918.

43/32 WOW to TW, April 17, 1918, Braden-Hatchett Thomas Wolfe Coll.

43/38 WOW to TW, May 13, 1918, Wolfe Coll., UNC.

44/8 Eaton, "Student Days with Thomas Wolfe," *Georgia Review* 17 (Summer 1963): 150.

44/12 Jonathan Daniels, *Thomas Wolfe: October Recollections* (Columbia, S.C.: Bostick & Thornley, 1961), p. 11; Vance E. Swift to H. G. Jones, Dec. 1980, North Carolina Coll.; interview with Ralph Williams, April 11, 1981.

44/14 *Letters*, p. 7.

44/29 Cf. Wolfe's account of this visit in the typescript of "O Lost" [passage omitted from LHA, p. 483] with Walser, *The Wolfe Family in Raleigh* (Raleigh: Wolfe's Head Press, 1976), p. 25, and Elizabeth Lay Green's recollections in Jones, *Thomas Wolfe of North Carolina*, p. 56.

44/33 JEW to TW, Nov. 1917, and WOW to TW, Nov. 21, 1917, Wolfe Coll., UNC.

44/35 WOW to TW, April 4, 1918, Wolfe Coll., UNC.

45/4 WOW to TW, April 23, 1918, Fred Wolfe MSS.; WOW to BHW, May 1, 1918, Wolfe Coll., UNC.

46/3 LTHM, p. 4.

46/17 LTHM, p. 5.

48/3 JEW to TW, Nov. 1917, Wolfe Coll., UNC.

48/5 Tracy Wilder, interview with JEW, c. 1939, typescript dated Oct. 29, 1950, Wolfe Coll., UNC.

48/32 TW, fragment on BHW, Wisdom, No. 187; TW to MEP, incomplete, undated, Wisdom.

48/34 Elaine Westall Gould to TW, 1929, Wisdom.

48/37 TW to Esther Owens, Aug. 25, 1935, Barrett Coll. This was Wolfe's first draft of the dedication; the published dedication is shorter.

49/29 Phillip Hettleman, "Thomas Wolfe and the *Tar Heel*," in Jones, *Thomas Wolfe of North Carolina*, pp. 31–34.

49/38 Ernest Seeman to JST, Aug. 31, 1951, Terry MSS.

50/8 Hubert C. Heffner in *American Literature* 50 (Mar. 1978): 127–128; Corydon P. Spruill, in Jones, *Thomas Wolfe of North Carolina*, p. 82.

50/18 Vance E. Swift, ibid., p. 79.

50/22 John Y. Jordan, in *TW Newsletter*, vol. 4, no. 1 (Spring 1980): 43; George B. Lay, in Walser, *The Wolfe Family in Raleigh*, pp. 25–26.

50/37 Hettleman, in Jones, *Thomas Wolfe of North Carolina*, p. 33.

51/17 For slightly varying account of this episode, see LeGette Blythe, "Tom Wolfe's School Days," *State and Columbia* [S.C.] *Record*, Oct. 19, 1961; Benjamin Cone, in Jones, *Thomas Wolfe of North Carolina*, pp. 70–71; Turnbull, p. 31.

51/29 Walser, *Undergraduate*, p. 75.

51/34 Hilton West, Anecdotes about Thomas Wolfe, Feb. 26, 1947, Terry MSS.

51/39 Green, in Jones, *Thomas Wolfe of North Carolina,* p. 52.

52/4 *Tar Heel,* May 2, 1919; WOW to Frank Wolfe, June 13, 1919, Braden-Hatchett Thomas Wolfe Coll.

52/7 The University of North Carolina changed from the semester to the quarter system in 1918–1919.

53/4 Robert Watson Winston, *Horace Williams: Gadfly of Chapel Hill* (Chapel Hill: University of North Carolina Press, 1942), is admiring and anecdotal. For more balanced treatments see Walser, *Undergraduate,* ch. 8, and Mel Groth, "The Education of Thomas Wolfe: Roberts, Greenlaw, Williams, Baker," *St. Andrews Review* 2, no. 4 (Spring–Summer 1975): 261–273. There is an able assessment of Williams's strengths and weaknesses in Garland B. Porter to TW, Feb. 14, 1937, Wisdom.

53/6 *Letters,* p. 16.

54/28 On Williams's favoritism, see William H. Bobbitt, in Jones, *Thomas Wolfe of North Carolina,* p. 51; interview with Corydon P. Spruill, June 24, 1980; interview with Ralph Williams, April 11, 1981.

54/31 Horace Williams to TW, Dec. 20, 1920, Wolfe Coll., UNC.

54/33 Williams's statement in TW's application form, Harvard University Appointment Office, Mar. 24, 1922, copy, Nowell MSS.

55/15 TW, "Mass Movements in Labor," Wisdom, No. 1209; TW, *The Crisis in Industry* (Chapel Hill: Published by the university, 1919).

56/1 TW to Horace Williams, incomplete drafts of two letters, Wisdom.

56/3 AOAAN, p. 103.

56/17 Two full-scale accounts of Koch and his work, on which I have relied heavily, even though both take a more favorable view than I have been able to do, are John Patrick Hagan, "Frederick Henry Koch and the American Folk Drama" (unpublished Ph.D. dissertation, Indiana University, 1969), and Mel Groth, "Thomas Wolfe and the Koch Idea" (unpublished Ph.D. dissertation, Indiana University, 1975). See also Mel Groth, "The Education of Thomas Wolfe, II: Frederick Henry Koch, 'The Little Man With The Urge,' " *St. Andrews Review* 3 (Fall–Winter 1975): 83–96.

56/32 TW, typescript of "O Lost" [passage omitted from LHA, p. 596].

56/37 Hagan, "Frederick Henry Koch and the American Folk Drama," pp. 241–242.

57/10 Frederich H. Koch, ed., *Carolina Folk-Plays: First, Second, and Third Series* (New York: Henry Holt and Co., 1941), p. xi.

57/21 W. D. Macmillan III to JST, Oct. 28, 1926, Terry MSS.

57/27 LeGette Blythe, "About Tom Wolfe," *The Miscellany* [of Davidson College] 2 (Dec. 1966): 44.

57/32 Groth, "The Education of Thomas Wolfe," p. 83.

57/39 TW, "The Man Who Lives with His Idea," *Carolina Play-Book* 16 (Mar.–June 1943): 18.

58/6 Ibid., p. 19.

58/10 TW, "Letter to Proff Koch," *Carolina Play-Book* 16 (Mar.–June 1943): 24.

58/16 TW, "A Previously Unpublished Statement," *Carolina Quarterly* 11 (Spring 1960): 9.

58/19 For the text of the clipping, see Walser, *Undergraduate,* pp. 89–90.

58/36 Koch, *Carolina Folk-Plays,* p. xi.

59/6 Ibid.

59/13 Henderson, "The Puzzle Tom Wolfe Left for Posterity: The Riddle of Self," *Raleigh News and Observer,* Mar. 30, 1941.

59/16 *Tar Heel,* Mar. 28, 1919.

59/18 For the text of the play, see Frederick H. Koch, ed., *Carolina Folk Plays: Second Series* (New York: Henry Holt and Co., 1924), pp. 33–44.

59/26 TW, typescript of "O Lost" [passage omitted from LHA, p. 497].

59/28 *Letters,* p. 68.

59/31 "The Carolina Playmakers," *Review of Reviews* 60 (Sept. 1919): 302–303.

59/35 TW, "The Convict's Theory," Wisdom, No. 15. This play was published as "Deferred Payment" in *University of North Carolina Magazine* 49 (April 1919): 139–153.

60/3 TW, "The Strikers," Wisdom, No. 10.

60/13 TW, "The Third Night: A Play of the Carolina Mountains," *Carolina Play-Book* 12 (Sept. 1938): 70–75.

60/34 *Tar Heel,* Jan 10, 1920.

61/3 Ibid., Feb. 28, 1920.

61/14 Walser, *Undergraduate,* p. 112.

61/28 *Tar Baby,* vol. 1, no. 9 (April 10, 1920).

61/40 Nat Mobley, in Jones, *Thomas Wolfe of North Carolina,* p. 69. The full yearbook entry is reproduced in Walser, *Undergraduate,* facing p. 135.

62/4 *Letters,* p. 8.

62/15 This dramatic fragment is published in Walser, *Undergraduate,* pp. 135–141.

62/31 AOAAN, pp. 108–109.

62/40 TW, application for admission to the Graduate School of Arts and Science, Harvard University, Aug. 10, 1920, Harvard Archives.

63/5 Horace Williams to TW, Feb. 26, 1922, Wolfe Coll., UNC.

63/11 JEW, "Eliza Gant Talks," transcription by Ruth Davis of several recordings that JST made with JEW, Terry MSS.

63/21 TW to FW, Sept. 15, 1920, copy, Terry MSS.

63/25 JEW, "Eliza Gant Talks."

63/29 LTHM, p. 7.

64/4 JEW, "Eliza Gant Talks"; Hayden Norwood, *The Marble Man's Wife* (New York: Charles Scribner's Sons, 1947), pp. 178–179.

Chapter III: *By God, I Have Genius*

65/3 TW, AO.

66/2 LTHM, pp. 10–11; TW, MS. on the Farnsworth Room, Wisdom, No. 573.

66/13 The best biography of Baker is Wisner Payne Kinne, *George Pierce Baker and the American Theatre* (Cambridge: Harvard University Press, 1954).

66/37 Christina H. Baker to Marjorie C. Fairbanks, Nov. 17, 1948, Fairbanks MSS.

67/2 LTHM, p. 11.

68/8 *Letters*, p. 10. This play was probably "The Family," Wisdom, No. 16.

68/17 *Letters*, p. 11.

68/27 For the text of this play, together with informed comment, see TW, *The Mountains . . .* , ed. by Pat M. Ryan (Chapel Hill: University of North Carolina Press, 1970).

68/40 TW, "The Beginning of a Native American Drama Since 1890," Wisdom, No. 1285.

69/12 TW, *The Mountains*, pp. 55, 53.

69/21 Ibid., p. 54.

69/27 LTHM, p. 17.

69/30 TW to "Dear Old George," Feb. 10, 1921, Wisdom.

69/37 JEW to TW, Feb. 6, 1921, Wisdom.

70/8 TW, response to criticisms of the reading of "The Mountains," c. January 1921, Wolfe Coll., UNC.

70/12 TW to G. P. Baker, c. Fall 1922, Wisdom.

70/30 AOAAN, pp. 111–112.

70/32 *Letters*, p. 9.

71/9 Kennedy, p. 66.

71/16 TW, AO.

71/33 OTATR, p. 167.

72/11 Lowes, *The Road to Xanadu: A Study in the Ways of the Imagination* (New York: Vintage Books, 1959), pp. 4, 52, 394.

72/16 Ibid., p. 477.

72/25 *Letters*, p. 30.

72/30 TW, "The Supernatural in the Poetry and Philosophy of Coleridge," Wisdom, No. 1295.

72/40 *Letters*, p. 24.

73/5 Ibid., pp. 44–45. In *Of Time and the River*, Eugene Gant, Wolfe's fictional counterpart, read at least twenty thousand volumes in ten years. If Wolfe intended to assert this claim for himself, it was, as Van Wyck Brooks observed (*From a Writer's Notebook* [New York: E. P. Dutton & Co., 1958], p. 11), impossible and untrue. But there is no question that Wolfe did, as he claimed in his autobiographical outline, perform "enormous feats of reading" while at Harvard.

73/12 TW, AO.

73/24 TW to Mr. and Mrs. J. M. Roberts, c. February 1921, Wisdom.

73/33 Mrs. Henry A. Westall to TW, Oct. 13, 1920, Wolfe Coll., UNC.

74/11 TW to FW, June 1921, Wisdom. Wolfe never wrote this play, but in 1932 he published a thinly fictionalized account of his uncle's family, "A Portrait of Bascom Hawke," which was later incorporated into *Of Time and the River*. By that time Laura Westall was dead, but her husband found Wolfe's "calumnious treatment of his family" so "profane and obscene" that it ought to be suppressed by the postal authorities. He also applied to Wolfe for a loan, which he claimed was due to him because Wolfe had exploited "his family from information, obtained by his visits to Medford." Henry A. Westall to TW, Aug. 18, 1935, Braden-Hatchett Thomas Wolfe Coll.; Westall to MWW, Dec. 30, 1937, ibid.

74/26 LTHM, p. 8.

74/33 WOW to TW, Dec. 18, 1920, Fred Wolfe MSS.

74/39 JEW to TW, Dec. 18, 1920, Fred Wolfe MSS.; JEW to TW, Nov. 28, 1920, Wisdom.

75/12 JEW to TW, Mar. 6, 1921, Wisdom; Glen A. Alexander to JEW, June 12 and July 16, 1921, Wisdom, No. 123.

75/15 JEW, Memorandum, Mar. 4, 1921, Wisdom.

75/22 LTHM, p. 24.

75/34 William Hatchett, interview with Fred Wolfe, Aug. 5, 1977, Braden-Hatchett Thomas Wolfe Coll.

76/16 TW, undated fragments on Eugene Gant's first year in Boston, Wisdom, No. 392; TW, fragment on Boston, Wisdom, No. 580, Cf. M. A. Braswell to Albert Coates, Mar. 30, 1977, copy provided through the courtesy of Professor Coates.

76/33 LTHM, pp. 18–21. Cf. Louis D. Rubin, Jr., *Thomas Wolfe: The Weather of His Youth* (Baton Rouge: Louisiana State University Press, 1955), pp. 81–84, on Wolfe's changing attitudes toward the South.

77/10 TW, fragment from a draft of "Mannerhouse," Wisdom, No. 142.

77/29 TW, "Cambridge, The City and the Voyages" ledger, Wisdom, No. 233

77/35 TWATR, p. 449.

78/1 Letter from Louis Sheaffer, April 11, 1980.

78/11 TW, "Starwick — Boston — Reading *Ulysses*," Wisdom, Nos. 368 and 576; TW, "The Pension in Munich," Wisdom, No. 912.

78/17 TW To Sinclair Lewis, c. November 1930, Terry MSS.

78/25 TW to Sherwood Anderson, July 8, 1935, Anderson MSS., Newberry Lib.

78/39 AOAAN, p. 113; TW, undated fragment from the 1920s, Wisdom, No. 1317.

79/3 TW to G. P. Baker, c. June 1922, Wolfe Coll., UNC. On the reactions of Southern writers to Mencken, see Fred Hobson, *Serpent in Eden: H. L. Mencken and the South* (Chapel Hill: University of North Carolina Press, 1974), pp. 33–79.

79/24 TW, undated fragments on the South, Wisdom, No. 1207.

79/34 TW, undated entry in "The Good Child's River" ledger, Wisdom, No. 258.

80/12 TW to G. P. Baker, c. June 1922, Wolfe Coll., UNC. Cf. PN, I: 7–8.

80/22 TW, incomplete plays, Wisdom, Nos. 18–19; TW, scenes from incomplete plays, including "The House of Belmont," Wolfe Coll., UNC.

80/32 TW to Mr. and Mrs. J. M. Roberts, c. February 1921, Wisdom; *Letters*, p. 29.

80/37 *Letters*, pp. 13–14.

81/5 JEW to TW, Feb. 24, 1921, Wisdom.

81/15 JEW to TW, July 3, 1921, Braden-Hatchett Thomas Wolfe Coll.

81/22 TW to Mrs. J. M. Roberts, July 22, 1921, Wisdom.

81/40 TW,"The Hungry Dutchman," Wisdom, No. 558.

82/12 *Letters*, p. 12.

82/20 LTHM, p. 13; undated letter to me from Professor George P. Baker, the son of Wolfe's teacher.

82/30 TW to G. P. Baker, Aug. 28, 1921, Wolfe Coll., UNC; Gladys Taylor, statement on TW, Wisdom, No. 1346.

83/7 TW to JEW, c. Sept. 1921, Wisdom; LTHM, p. 29.

83/18 TW, prayer in notebook on English history, Wisdom, No. 1267.

83/36 *New York Post*, Sept. 21, 1938. Cf. George Stevens, *Speak for Yourself, John: The Life of John Mason Brown* (New York: Viking Press, 1974), p. 38.

84/13 TW, pocket notebook, Oct. 21–22, 1921, Wolfe Coll., UNC.

84/16 *Letters*, p. 427.

84/26 *Letters*, pp. 20–21.

84/34 TW, AO; *Letters*, pp. 427–428.

85/4 Wisdom, No. 1294.

85/11 Wisdom, No. 1299.

85/26 *Letters*, pp. 35–37, where this letter is incorrectly dated September or October 1922, instead of 1921. Some dialogue for this proposed play appears in Walser, *Undergraduate*, pp. 135–141.

85/38 LTHM, p. 30.

85/40 TW, "The Mountains," Wisdom, No. 42. The full text of this three-act play is most readily available in TW, *The Mountains . . .* , ed. by Pat M. Ryan, pp. 85–177.

86/19 *Letters*, p. 31.

86/27 TW, registration form with Harvard University Appointments Office, Mar. 24, 1922, copy, Nowell MSS. It has been said that Wolfe was actually offered the job at Northwestern at this time, but as late as June the English department there stated that it would be pleased to consider his application. Unsigned letter to TW, June 5, 1922, Wolfe Coll., UNC.

87/4 Program, "The 47 Varieties," May 26, 1922, Harvard Theatre Coll.; Kennedy, p. 75; TW, AO.

87/17 JEW to TW, April 3, 1923, Wisdom.

87/22 TW to G. P. Baker, c. June 1922, Nowell MSS.

87/28 OTATR, p. 246.

88/4 TW to G. P. Baker, c. June 1922, Nowell MSS.

88/7 LTHM, pp. 39–40.

88/10 LTHM, p. 43.

88/32 Interview with Mrs. Marie Westall Hall, June 18, 1982.

88/36 Turnbull, p. 65.

89/12 On these changes see *Asheville Handbook, 1929,* compiled by the Asheville Chamber of Commerce, pp. 17–18, 22; Mitzi Schaden Tessier, *Asheville: A Pictorial History* (Norfolk, Va.: Donning Co., 1982), pp. 118–141.

89/21 *Letters*, p. 33.

89/40 TW, "Niggertown," Wisdom, No. 67.

90/27 FW to TW, Jan. 26, 1938, Braden-Hatchett Thomas Wolfe Coll.; *Letters,*
pp. 704–705.

90/38 *Letters,* p. 33.

91/11 TW, AO.

91/14 TW, typescript for *Of Time and the River,* Wisdom, No. 372 [passage
omitted from published book, p. 169].

91/21 Barry, "Play #2," MS., Harvard Theatre Coll. I am indebted to Marc J.
Dolan's "The Art of His Technique: George Pierce Baker and His Students" (unpublished senior honors thesis, Harvard University, 1983), pp.
132–136, for this suggestion.

91/27 Bruce W. McCullough to Oscar Cargill, c. July 18, 1954, MS., Fales
Lib., N.Y.U.

92/2 Barber, "Tom Wolfe Writes a Play," *Harper's Magazine* 216 (May 1958):
72.

92/31 In *Of Time and the River,* which was published after Raisbeck's death,
Wolfe's alter ego, Eugene Gant, was shocked to discover in Paris that
"Starwick," Raisbeck's fictional counterpart, was homosexual. But
Wolfe's autobiographical outlines show that he clearly knew of Raisbeck's
sexual preferences much earlier. When Raisbeck died in mysterious
circumstances — perhaps murdered by a homosexual pickup to whom he
had given a ride in his car — Wolfe was fearful that his name might be
mentioned in the resulting scandal. About this time when a friend tried to
talk to him about Raisbeck's homosexuality he grew very excited and
told her: "I dont know anything about that. . . . I do know it exists but
I just dont know anything about it — I never ran into any." Marjorie C.
Fairbanks, fragment of an unpublished biography of TW, Fairbanks MSS.

93/16 Some of these fragmentary plays are in Wisdom, Nos. 43–48; others are
in the Wolfe Coll., UNC.

93/36 Wisdom, No. 52. One of the Bateson fragments is published in Hans
Helmcke, *Die Familie im Romanwerk von Thomas Wolfe* (Heidelberg: Carl
Winter, Universitätsverlag, 1967), pp. 296–300.

94/2 Turnbull, p. 68.

94/9 I am indebted to Professor George P. Baker for a letter sharing his memories of the Baker family's attitude toward Wolfe.

94/14 *Letters,* p. 31.

94/19 TW to G. P. Baker, c. June 1922, Wolfe Coll., UNC.

94/20 G. P. Baker to TW, Aug. 9, 1922, Fred Wolfe MSS.

95/16 TW to G. P. Baker, undated but 1922–1923, Wisdom; *Letters,* p. 47.

95/30 LTHM, p. 39.

95/36 Paschal Reeves, *Thomas Wolfe's Albatross: Race and Nationality in America*
(Athens: University of Georgia Press, 1968), p. 10.

95/40 TW to JEW, c. Nov. 1922, Wisdom.

96/4 LTHM, p. 35.

96/10 LTHM, p. 37.

96/12 For the (rechristened) text of "Niggertown" see Richard S. Kennedy,
ed., *Welcome To Our City: A Play in Ten Scenes* (Baton Rouge: Louisiana
State University Press, 1983). In dealing with this play, as well as with

Wolfe's other plays, I have relied heavily on Claude William La Salle, II, "Thomas Wolfe: The Dramatic Apprenticeship" (unpublished Ph.D. dissertation, University of Pennsylvania, 1964); Mary Charmian Green, "Thomas Wolfe: The Evolution of a Dramatic Novelist, 1918–1929" (unpublished Ph.D. dissertation, University of North Carolina at Chapel Hill, 1973); Ladell Payne, "Thomas Wolfe and the Theatre," in Paschal Reeves, ed., *Thomas Wolfe and the Glass of Time* (Athens: University of Georgia Press, 1971), pp. 123–135; and especially Marc J. Dolan, "The Art of His Technique: George Pierce Baker and His Students," cited above.

97/14 *Welcome To Our City,* pp. 30, 33, 112.

97/40 *Letters,* pp. 40–41.

 98/5 *Letters,* pp. 39–40.

98/12 *Letters,* p. 41.

98/14 There is nothing to indicate that the change was made because of the alleged sensitivity of Cambridge or New York audiences to racial slurs. Neither had objected to Edward Sheldon's play "The Nigger."

98/19 LTHM, p. 38.

98/25 Elizabeth Munroe's letter to G. P. Baker, April 18, 1923, quoted in EN to Mrs. Charles E. Bolster, Nov. 3, 1951, Nowell MSS.

98/29 TW to William T. Polk, April 1923, Wolfe Coll., UNC.

99/17 Barber, "Tom Wolfe Writes a Play," pp. 73–74.

99/25 Marjorie C. Fairbanks, Notebook 15, Fairbanks MSS.

99/30 Turnbull, p.72.

99/36 Albert Coates to EN, April 20, 1950, Nowell MSS.

99/38 TW to G. P. Baker, c. April 1923, Wolfe Coll., UNC.

100/4 For an excellent analysis of the problems of presenting the play in the Agassiz Theater, by a man who has himself directed, produced, and acted on that stage, see Dolan, "The Art of His Technique," pp. 104–109.

100/34 PN, I: 15.

100/38 Letter from Elizabeth McKie, June 28, 1980.

100/40 Both critiques are in the Wolfe Coll., UNC.

101/12 Elizabeth McKie to TW, May 11, 1923, ibid., Florence Milner to TW, May 16, 1923, ibid.

101/22 Elaine Westall Gould to TW, May 16, 1923, ibid.

101/33 For lists of the plays that were submitted, see G. P. Baker to Richard Herndon, June 5, 6, and 25, 1923, G. P. Baker MSS., Harvard Theatre Coll.; Herndon to Baker, June 8, 1923, ibid.

101/37 JEW to TW, June 17, 1923, Wisdom.

 102/2 TW to MWW, c. May 1923, Wisdom, No. 121; *Letters,* p. 42.

102/12 G. P. Baker to O. M. Sayler, Oct. 3, 1923, Wisdom.

102/26 LTHM, pp. 42–43, 46.

Chapter IV: *I Shall Conquer the World*

103/22 Kennedy, p. 81

104/1 For this longer version, see Phyllis L. Huffman, "An Edition of 'Welcome To Our City,' A Play by Thomas Wolfe" (unpublished Ph.D. dissertation, University of North Carolina at Greensboro, 1979).

104/3 Wisner P. Kinne, *George Pierce Baker and the American Theatre* (Cambridge: Harvard University Press, 1954), p. 229.

104/13 TW to G. P. Baker, [Oct. 20, 1921?], Nowell MSS.

104/21 TW, scenario for "The House at Belmont," Wolfe Coll., UNC.

104/28 TW, "The Heirs," Wisdom, No. 122.

104/38 *Letters*, p. 51.

105/5 JEW to TW, June 17, 1923, Wisdom.

105/11 *Letters*, p. 49.

105/19 G. P. Baker to JEW, Sept. 4, 1923, Fred Wolfe MSS.

105/20 *Letters*, p. 54.

105/25 LTHM, p. 48.

105/32 JEW to TW, June 17, 1923, Wisdom.

105/37 LTHM, p. 53.

106/7 TW, autobiographical notes, Wisdom, No. 1169. The Guild did not return his script and give him reasons for the rejection until December.

106/26 FW to JST, Dec. 11, 1950, Terry MSS.; William Hatchett, interview with FW, Aug. 5, 1977, Braden-Hatchett Thomas Wolfe Coll.

106/33 TW, autobiographical notes, Wisdom, No. 1169.

106/36 B. Lacy Meredith to JST, June 13, 1942. Terry MSS.

107/7 On the early history of the Theatre Guild, together with lists of its productions, see Walter Prichard Eaton, *The Theatre Guild: The First Ten Years* (New York: Brentano's, 1929); Roy S. Waldau, *Vintage Years of the Theatre Guild, 1929–1939* (Cleveland: The Press of Case Western Reserve University, 1972); and Norman Nadel, *A Pictorial History of the Theatre Guild* (New York: Crown Publishers, 1969).

107/21 LTHM, p. 46.

107/29 Miss Helburn strongly disliked Wolfe. *A Wayward Quest: The Autobiography of Theresa Helburn* (Boston: Little, Brown and Co., 1960), p. 331.

108/8 LTHM, pp. 50–51. Langner said later, "I doubted whether he would ever possess the discipline to observe the hard rules which the theatre imposes upon its writers." Lawrence Langner, *The Magic Curtain* (New York: E. P. Dutton & Co., 1951), p. 159.

108/29 *Letters*, pp. 59, 65; LTHM, p. 55; TW, untitled dramatic fragment on Baker, Wisdom, No. 151.

108/36 JEW to TW, Jan. 8, 1924, Wisdom.

109/14 *Letters*, p. 57.

109/27 On Washington Square College, see the essay by James B. Munn, in Theodore Francis Jones, ed., *New York University, 1832–1932* (New York: New York University Press, 1933), pp. 379–390, and the annual volumes of *New York University: Reports of Officers* (Washington Square, New York).

110/10 TW to Walter Bonamine, Sept. 30, 1927, MS., Fales Lib., NYU.

110/23 For unusually full accounts of Wolfe's teaching at Washington Square College, see Oscar Cargill, "Thomas Wolfe at Washington Square," in Pollock and Cargill, pp. 1–84, and Richard S. Kennedy, "Thomas Wolfe at New York University," *TW Review* 5 (Fall 1981): 1–10.

110/39 Wolfe-Watt Corresp., pp. 21–22.

110/40 Interview with Boris Gamzue, June 4, 1982.

111/6 Pollock and Cargill, p. 60.

111/13 Wolfe-Watt Corresp., p. 14.

111/21 On TW's appointments and salary at NYU see Thomas Clark Pollock to EN, Sept. 12, 1950, Nowell MSS. I have also been informed on this point by a letter from Professor Bayard Still, May 13, 1980.

111/25 Wolfe-Watt Corresp., p. 42.

111/37 Letters, p. 59.

112/17 LTHM, pp. 58, 61.

112/24 Wolfe-Watt Corresp., p. 42.

112/31 TW's class rolls, NYU, Wisdom, Nos. 1311 and 1314.

113/2 TW's passport, Sept. 25, 1924, Wolfe Coll., UNC. Wolfe was still growing. His next passport, dated March 17, 1930, gave his height at six feet, five inches.

113/6 Harold Rosenblatt, interview with Abraham Slotiniver, 1950, Terry MSS.; Pollock and Cargill, p. 88.

113/16 Earl Hamner, "Thomas Wolfe: A Biography in Sound," *Carolina Quarterly* 9 (Fall 1956): 7–8; Pollock and Cargill, pp. 88–89.

113/20 Helen Rosen to TW, April 19, 1926, Wisdom. Later Ms. Rosen concluded that her criticisms of Wolfe were "totally unfounded." Rosen to TW, May 19, 1926, ibid.

113/25 Harold Rosenblatt, interview with Abraham Slotiniver, 1950, Terry MSS.

113/34 OTATR, p. 419.

114/2 Letters, p. 61.

114/16 LTHM, p. 59; Letters, p. 61.

114/34 OTATR, p. 444.

114/37 TW to Walter Bonamine, Sept. 30, 1927, MS., Fales Lib., NYU.

115/16 TW's semifictional account is in OTATR, pp. 444–447, 455–468. It is confirmed and amplified in Kyle Crichton, *Total Recoil* (Garden City, N.Y.: Doubleday & Co., 1960), p. 74; interview with Mrs. Edith Hertz Smith, March 1982; and George Wald to Mrs. A. Arthur Smith, Nov. 10, 1968, a copy of which was generously made available to me by Mrs. Smith.

115/28 TW to Abe Smith, Jan. 16, 1931, Wisdom.

116/4 OTATR, pp. 457–468.

116/6 Interview with Mrs. Edith Hertz Smith, March 1982.

116/9 OTATR, p. 404.

116/13 TW, "The Train and the City," *Scribner's Magazine* 93 (May 1933): 285.

116/19 Charles F. Bopes, "Wolfe Reminiscences," Aug. 31, 1953, MS., Fales Lib., NYU.

116/21 Letters, p. 60.

116/31 LTHM, p. 48; OTATR, pp. 416–417.

117/5 LTHM, pp. 66–67.

117/29 Henry T. Volkening, "Tom Wolfe: Penance No More," *Virginia Quarterly Review* 15 (Spring 1939): 196–198.

117/32 Kwak Hyo-suk, "A Case of East Meeting West," *Korea Newsreview* 9 (Mar. 29, 1980): 22–23.

117/37 TW to Vardis Fisher, July 17, 1935, Wisdom.

117/40 James B. Munn to Oscar Cargill, Oct. 5, 1949, MS., Fales Lib., NYU.

118/35 TW to James B. Munn, June 7, 1929, Wisdom; Munn to Cargill, Oct. 5, 1949, MS., Fales Lib., NYU.

119/4 TW to William Polk, Spring 1924, Wolfe Coll., UNC.

119/18 LTHM, p. 61.

119/30 Letters, p. 63.

120/3 Letters, p. 62.

120/16 Letters, p. 69; LTHM, p. 70.

120/20 Letters, p. 67.

120/26 LTHM, pp. 69–70.

121/6 LTHM, pp. 67–68. TW's detailed fictional account of this visit (an account that was, in fact, a composite of several visits made over a number of years) is in OTATR, pp. 501–595. He gave further details in his draft of OTATR, Wisdom, No. 435.

121/12 TW to Olin Dows, 1925, Wisdom; TW to James B. Munn, June 7, 1929, Wisdom.

121/21 LTHM, p. 70.

121/33 LTHM, pp. 77, 79.

121/36 TW, fragmentary diary, Oct. 26, 1924, Wisdom, No. 157.

122/9 Letters, pp. 71–72.

122/16 Letters, pp. 72–73; PN, I: 44.

122/35 LTHM, pp. 83–85; interview with George Stevens, July 1981.

122/37 On TW's residences in Paris, see Brian N. Morton, *Americans in Paris: An Anecdotal Street Guide* (Ann Arbor: Olivia & Hill Press, 1984), p. 19.

123/8 The authoritative text is TW, *Mannerhouse: A Play in a Prologue and Four Acts,* ed. by Louis D. Rubin, Jr., and John L. Idol, Jr. (Baton Rouge: Louisiana State University Press, 1985). This completely supersedes TW, *Mannerhouse: A Play in a Prologue and Three Acts* (New York: Harper & Brothers, 1946), a version that was mangled and badly edited by ECA.

123/18 OTATR, pp. 544–549.

124/3 TW, *Mannerhouse,* ed. by Rubin and Idol, p. 114.

124/12 Letters, p. 104.

124/19 AOAAN, p. 26.

124/25 OTATR, p. 683.

125/11 On the Raisbeck-Fairbanks-Harding relationships I have been greatly assisted by Mrs. Fairbanks's unfinished and unpublished biography of TW, Fairbanks MSS.; by Leonie Sterner to TW, c. 1935, Wisdom; and the packet of letters from Raisbeck to Mrs. Fairbanks in the Fairbanks MSS. See also Richard Walser, "Boston's Elinor in Paris," *TW Review* 6 (Fall 1982), pp. 35–38.

125/32 OTATR, p. 683.

126/17 TW, MS. on Francis Starwick's character, Wisdom, No. 470.

126/24 Letters, pp. 85–86.

126/28 TW, final typescript of OTATR, Wisdom, No. 658.

126/30 Letters, p. 78.

126/39 Helen B. Harding to TW, Feb. 1, 1925[?], Wisdom.

127/16 TW to Helen B. Harding, undated, Wisdom; TW, final typescript for OTATR, Wisdom, No. 658; OTATR, p. 757.

127/24 TW to Helen B. Harding, undated, Wisdom. OTATR, pp. 770–784; TW to Raisbeck, 1925, Wisdom.

128/3 TW, drafts of numerous letters to Helen B. Harding, undated, Wisdom. There is no way to determine how many of these letters were actually mailed. "I did not keep any of Tom's letters, not knowing that some day they might be valuable. I was really only someone to be talked at in those days and never took any of it seriously. Nor did he mean a thing to me." Helen B. Harding to Marjorie C. Fairbanks, Mar. 1, 1948, Fairbanks MSS.

128/5 Nowell, p. 94.

128/21 FW to TW, Jan. 15, 1925, Wisdom; TW to Helen B. Harding, undated, Wisdom; LTHM, p. 87.

128/24 LTHM, p. 99.

128/32 OTATR, p. 858.

128/35 Unless otherwise identified, all quotations in the remainder of this section are from TW, "Passage to England," Wisdom, No. 185.

129/9 Letters, p. 95.

129/36 Letters, p. 96.

130/3 Mrs. J. M. Roberts to TW, June 7, 1925, Wisdom.

130/5 Asheville Citizen, July 19, 1925.

130/13 PN, I: 47.

131/12 Wolfe-Watt Corresp., pp. 14–15.

132/1 TWATR, pp. 309–313. Cf. AB's account of this first meeting in Journey Down, pp. 3–40.

132/7 Nowell, p. 100.

132/12 TWATR, p. 314.

132/14 Carole Klein's Aline (New York: Harper & Row, 1979) is a full, sympathetic biography.

132/35 TWATR, p. 374. Both TWATR and Journey Down avoid stating whether they had sex on that first night, but TW's autobiographical notes, Wisdom, No. 1169, are explicit.

133/5 Letters, pp. 101–102.

133/12 J. M. Roberts, Jr., in Life, Oct. 8, 1956, p. 22.

133/20 LTHM, pp. 100–101.

133/37 TWATR, pp. 318–319.

134/18 TWATR, p. 342.

134/24 In TWATR Wolfe makes "Esther" late for the meeting. But Aline's letter of Sept. 20, 1926, states: "I waited for you on the library steps for 20 minutes." MOL, p. 72.

134/37 TWATR, pp. 356–357.

136/14 TW to MEP, Jan. 19, 1931, Charles Scribner's Sons Archive.

136/19 LTHM, p. 100; JEW to TW, May 1, 1926, Wisdom.

136/39 Journey Down, p. 75.

137/7 Journey Down, p. 71.

137/9 TWATR, p. 443.

137/17 For comment on this passage, see EN to ECA, May 25, 1949, Nowell MSS.

137/32 TW, undated fragment, Wisdom, No. 243.

138/2 TW, undated fragment, Wisdom, No. 244.

138/9 TWATR, p. 370.

138/12 Mina Curtiss, "Wolfe Among the Monstres Sacres," *Nation* 206 (April 1, 1968): 446–448.

138/21 TW, autobiographical notes, Wisdom, No. 1169.

138/25 AB to TW, June 4, 1926, Wisdom.

138/27 TW to AB, June 5, 1926, Wisdom.

138/40 TW to AB, Dec. 1925, Wisdom; *Letters*, pp. 103, 109.

139/9 Lemon to TW, Nov. 6, 1925, Wisdom.

139/14 *Letters*, pp. 103–104.

139/24 AB to EN, undated, Nowell MSS.

139/30 Kennedy, p. 113.

139/36 AOAAN, p. 116.

140/6 For examples, see PN, I: 54–59.

Chapter V: *I Must Spin Out My Entrails*

141/5 TW to James Daly, [1926], Wisdom.

141/17 AB to TW, Nov. 22, 1926, Wisdom.

142/8 TW, AO.

142/20 TW, "My Record as a Writer," Wisdom.

142/33 AB, *Journey Down*, pp. 41–68; AB to EN, n.d., Nowell MSS.

143/14 ECA to EN, April 23, 1938, Nowell MSS.

143/30 TW's undated critique of AB's *Journey Down*, Wisdom, No. 1193.

144/18 *Letters*, pp. 112–113; TW to AB, Aug. 26 [1926], Wisdom.

144/27 TW, AO.

144/30 *Letters*, p. 113.

145/4 *Letters*, p. 472. Wolfe included novels by Hardy, James, and Howells in lists for student book reports at NYU. Kennedy, p. 89.

145/40 PN, I: 61.

146/6 *Letters*, p. 113.

146/18 *Letters*, p. 111; TW, "Things For Which I Have Cared, Being Young," Wisdom, No. 189.

146/22 TW, AO.

146/35 On the autobiographical element in Wolfe see Henry A. Murray, Introduction to Herman Melville's *Pierre* (New York: Farrar Straus, 1949), pp. xxxi–xxxii; C. Hugh Holman, *The Loneliness at the Core* (Baton Rouge: Louisiana State University Press, 1975), ch. II; and Richard N. Coe, *When the Grass Was Taller: Autobiography and the Experience of Childhood* (New Haven: Yale University Press, 1984).

147/23 *Letters*, p. 110.

147/40 Anthony C. Hilfer, *The Revolt from the Village, 1915–1930* (Chapel Hill: University of North Carolina Press, 1969), p. 150.

148/8 TW to Margaret Roberts, Sept. 16, 1924, Wisdom; *Letters,* p. 107.

148/12 LTHM, p. 119, *Letters,* p. 123.

148/23 TW to AB, Nov. 8, 1926, Wisdom.

149/19 TW, "O Lost," Ledger IX, pp. 192–200, Wisdom.

149/24 TW, "My Record as a Writer," Wisdom.

149/30 LTHM, p. 119.

150/7 Kennedy, pp. 129–130, 116; Larry Rubin, "Thomas Wolfe and the Lost Paradise," *Modern Fiction Studies* 11 (1965): 250–258.

150/24 LHA, p. 2; Kennedy, p. 118; TW, MS. fragment, Wisdom, No. 162. See also W. P. Albrecht, "The Title of *Look Homeward, Angel; A Story of the Buried Life,*" *Modern Language Quarterly* 2 (1950): 50–57.

150/32 TW to AB, [Sept. 1926] and Sept. 25 [1926], Wisdom.

151/11 *Letters,* p. 115.

151/20 TW to AB, Sept. 27 [1926], Barrett Coll.; TW to AB, [Sept. 1926], Wisdom.

151/27 TW to AB, Oct. 4 [1926], Wisdom.

152/8 TW to AB, Nov. 1 [1926], Wisdom; William J. Cocke, *Johnny Park Talks of Thomas Wolfe* (Asheville, 1973), pp. 17–18; W. J. Cocke to his mother, Nov. 20, 1926, Cocke MSS., Duke University Library.

152/16 LTHM, p. 108.

153/10 TW to AB, Oct. 21 and 26, 1926, Wisdom.

153/18 TW to AB, Nov. 8, 1926, Wisdom.

153/30 Quotations in this and the following paragraphs are from the following letters: TW to AB, Sept. 11, 1926; Wisdom; AB to TW, Sept. 2, 1926, Wisdom; TW to AB, Dec. 1 [1926], Barrett Coll.; AB to TW, [Sept. 1926] and Oct. 2 [1926], Wisdom; TW to AB, [Nov. 24, 1926], Wisdom.

154/21 TW to AB, Dec. 1 [1926], Barrett Coll.; TW to AB, Oct. 4, 1926, Wisdom.

154/33 TW to AB, Sept. 11 and 22, Oct. 2, and Nov. 15, 1926, Wisdom.

155/5 TW to AB, Aug. 22, Sept. 11, and Oct. 2, 1926, Wisdom.

155/24 TW to AB, June 5, Aug. 26, Oct. 21 and 25, 1926, Wisdom.

155/40 TW to AB, Sept. 11, 1926, Wisdom; AB to TW, Sept. 9 and 13, Oct. 12, 1926, Wisdom; TW to AB, Dec. 1 [1926], Barrett Coll.

156/5 TW to AB, Nov. 10, 1926, Wisdom.

156/18 TW to AB, Nov. 14, 1926, Wisdom.

157/4 PN, I: 74; TW to AB, Nov. 13, 1926, Wisdom; TW to AB, Dec. 1 [1926], Barrett Coll.

157/26 PN, I: 83, 85; TW to AB, [Dec. 10, 1926], Wisdom.

158/3 TW to AB, Nov. 9, Dec. 10 and 12, 1926, Wisdom.

158/10 TW to AB, Dec. 10 and 24, 1926, Wisdom.

158/30 TW to AB, Oct. 15 and 16, Nov. 14, Dec. 5 and 9, 1926, Wisdom.

158/34 PN, I: 96.

159/12 TW, autobiographical notes, Wisdom, No. 1169.

160/3 PN, I: 97–98.

160/14 *Letters,* p. 120.

160/25 TW to Olin Dows, [1927], Wisdom.

160/31 LTHM, p. 117.

161/13 PN, I: 96; TW to Olin Dows, [1927], Wisdom; Pollock and Cargill, p. 79; William Y. Tindall to Oscar Cargill, Jan. 3, 1950, Fales Lib., NYU; Tindall to Louis Cohn, Dec. 7, 1944, Alexander Wainwright Collection, Princeton.

161/22 TW to Homer A. Watt, Mar. 7, 1927, Wisdom.

161/27 PN, I: 111, 98.

161/31 *Letters*, p. 586.

161/35 SOAN, pp. 8–9.

162/7 LHA, pp. 271–272.

162/22 LHA, pp. 330–338.

162/25 TW, "O Lost," Ledger XIII, pp. 172–184 and 368, Wisdom. James R. Blackwelder, "The Dimensions of Literature in *Look Homeward, Angel*" (unpublished Ph.D. dissertation, Emory University, 1968), lists and identifies poetic fragments in the novel. For Wolfe's use of poetry see Louis D. Rubin, Jr., *Thomas Wolfe: The Weather of His Youth* (Baton Rouge: Louisiana State University Press, 1955), pp. 8–12; Nathan L. Rothman, "Thomas Wolfe and James Joyce: A Study in Literary Influence," in Walser, *Engima*, pp. 263–289; Floyd D. Watkins, "Thomas Wolfe's High Sinfulness of Poetry," *Modern Fiction Studies* 2 (1956): 197–206. Less persuasive is Mark D. Hawthorne, "Thomas Wolfe's Use of the Poetic Fragment," *Modern Fiction Studies* 11 (1965): 29–34.

163/39 TW, "Starwick — Boston — Reading Ulysses," Wisdom, No. 368.

164/11 PN, I: 100.

164/29 PN, I: 111; *Letters*, p. 121; Bruce W. McCullough to Oscar Cargill, [July 18, 1954], Fales Lib. NYU.

165/15 Nowell, p. 108; AB, *Journey Down*, pp. 130–165.

165/30 PN, I: 119.

166/6 PN, I: 112.

166/25 *Letters*, pp. 124–125; LTHM, pp. 116, 120.

167/8 TW, Autobiographical Notebook, II (Wisdom), contains only a few words on Clara Paul (who became Laura James in the novel): "Clara — Moonlight and the holding of a hand — How her firm little breasts seem to spring forward, filled with life [—] the festered wrist — Her tender care — Parting — the train — the letter." It contains nothing on the Italian woman.

167/15 TW, draft on "Eugene's" writing plans, Wisdom, No. 614.

167/25 AB to TW, [June 29, 1927], Wisdom.

167/33 LTHM, p. 120; *Letters*, p. 124.

168/29 *Letters*, pp. 126–127; PN, I: 120.

169/12 PN, I: 121–127.

169/21 PN, I: 129–130.

169/37 LTHM, p. 124; Klein, pp. 201–202.

170/36 Klein, pp. 205–208.

171/9 William Y. Tindall to Oscar Cargill, Jan. 3, 1950, Fales Lib. NYU.

171/36 TW, "O Lost," Ledger I, pp. 305–306, Wisdom.

172/7 LTHM, p. 128; *Letters*, p. 132.

Chapter VI: *Like Some Blind Thing Upon the Floor of the Sea*

173/8 *Letters*, p. 120.

174/6 TW to AB, Munich, [Sept. 1928], Wisdom; T. R. Smith to TW, April 30, 1928, Wisdom; John Tebbel, *A History of Book Publishing in the United States* (New York: R.R. Bowker Company, 1978), 3: 135–145.

174/28 Madeleine Boyd, *Thomas Wolfe: The Discovery of a Genius,* ed. Aldo P. Magi (The Thomas Wolfe Society, 1981); Madeleine Boyd, "And a Genius Came into My Life," UNC; TW to George Wallace, June 25, 1928, Wisdom.

175/17 Mrs. Donald S. Friede, "Reader's Report" on "O Lost," Alexander Wainwright Collection; Princeton; Pascal Covici to EN, Nov. 7, 1949, Nowell MSS.

175/28 William M. Sloane, "Literary Prospecting," *Saturday Review of Literature* 19 (Dec. 3, 1938): 4–5.

176/5 Melville Cane, "Thomas Wolfe: A Memoir," *American Scholar* 41 (Autumn 1972): 637–639; *Letters*, p. 137.

176/12 I owe this figure to Professor Richard Walser. See the excellent discussion of characterization in *Look Homeward, Angel* in Mary Charmian Green, "Thomas Wolfe: The Evolution of a Dramatic Novelist, 1918–1929" (unpublished Ph.D. dissertation, University of North Carolina, 1973), ch. VII.

177/8 LHA, p. 79.

177/27 LHA, p. 456.

178/6 *Letters,* pp. 129–131.

178/15 Helen White Childers, "American Novels about Adolescence, 1917–1953" (unpublished Ph. D. dissertation, George Peabody College for Teachers, 1958); W. Tasker Witham, *The Adolescent in the American Novel, 1920–1960* (New York: Frederick Ungar Publishing Co., 1964).

178/25 TW, "The Ordeal of the Bondsman Doaks," Wisdom, No. 780.

178/38 Ibid.

179/25 PN, I: 288; TW to AB, [Oct. 1928], Wisdom.

179/39 TW, "The River People," Wisdom, No. 233. I am indebted to Mr. Gore Vidal for pointing out that Wolfe's literary isolation was not unique. Indeed, Mr. Vidal observes, American novelists are not really sequential, except, of course, in time, because they tend to discover models among European writers who are their contemporaries, rather than among their American predecessors. Thus the fiction of Henry James owes less to Hawthorne than to Flaubert.

180/5 *Letters*, p. 135; TW to AB, [Oct. 1928], Wisdom.

180/16 TW to AB, June 7, 1928, Wisdom; LTHM, p. 132; Pollock and Cargill, p. 106.

180/38 *Letters*, p. 133; L. Ruth Middlebrook, "Reminiscences of Tom Wolfe," *American Mercury,* 63 (November 1946): 546; William Y. Tindall to Oscar Cargill, Jan. 3, 1950, Fales Library, NYU.

181/13 Helen Resor to TW, July 6, 1928, Wisdom.

181/19 William Y. Tindall to EN, Oct. 26, 1949, Nowell MSS.

181/30 TW to MEP, Jan. 19, 1931, Charles Scribner's Sons Archive; Nowell, p. 117; AB to TW, [May 1928], [July 6, 1928], and [Oct. 27, 1928], Wisdom.

182/6 AB to TW, [June 1928], [July 1928], and Aug. 6, 1928, Wisdom.

182/14 Margaret Roberts to TW, July 3, 1928, Wisdom.

182/32 PN, I: 191.

183/12 TW to AB, [Aug. 1928], Wisdom.

183/24 TW to AB, [July? 1928], Wisdom; PN, I: 142.

184/5 PN, I: 237, 251, 259.

184/16 *Letters,* p. 135.

184/19 TW to AB, before July 5, 1928, Wisdom.

184/23 Emil Hilb to EN, Sept. 2, 1961, Alexander Wainwright Collection, Princeton.

185/4 PN, I: 136–138. For further discussion of "The River People" see Kennedy, ch. XI.

185/17 *Letters,* p. 135; PN, I: 150; TW, "The River People," esp. ch. II, Wisdom, No. 233.

185/35 TW to AB, Aug. 27 and Sept. 7, 1928, Wisdom.

186/5 PN, I: 163, 190, 194.

186/18 TW to AB, [October] and Oct. 25 [?], 1928, Wisdom.

186/29 TW to AB, undated fragment [June 1928], and Aug. 11–12, 1928, Wisdom.

187/4 TW to AB, June 7, [August], and Aug. 11 12, 1928, Wisdom.

187/12 AB to TW, [Sept. 1928], Wisdom.

187/26 TW to AB, Aug. 11–12, Oct. 27, and June 7, 1928, Wisdom.

187/34 TW to AB, [Aug. 4–8], Oct. 9, 1928, Wisdom.

187/37 AB to Nancy C. Wylie, [May 26, 1945], Pack Mem. Lib.

188/2 TW to MEP, Jan. 19, 1931, Charles Scribner's Sons Archive.

188/22 TW to AB, [July 28, 1928], Wisdom.

188/33 TW to AB, Aug. 1, 1928, Wisdom.

188/40 TW to AB, Aug. 11–12, 1928, Wisdom.

189/14 TW to MEP, Jan. 19, 1931, Charles Scribner's Sons Archive; AB to TW, [July 6, 1928], Wisdom; TW, MS. draft of "The Quarrel," Wisdom, No. 815.

190/2 TW to AB, July 26, [August], and July 28, 1928, Wisdom; AB to TW, [Aug. 20, 1928], Wisdom.

190/10 TW to AB, [July 28], July 19, 1928, Wisdom.

190/25 TW to AB, [Aug. 14, 1928], Wisdom.

191/4 TW to AB, [Aug. 1928], Wisdom.

191/12 TW to AB, [before Sept. 7, 1928], Wisdom.

191/32 PN, I: 272, 194; *Letters,* p. 143.

192/20 *Letters,* pp. 144–145; TW to Margaret Roberts, Jan. 12, 1929, Wisdom; PN, I: 199–200, 271–272.

193/4 Irving H. Page to William Hatchett, Mar. 31, 1981, Braden-Hatchett Thomas Wolfe Coll.; Eugene F. DuBois to EN, Sept. 23, 1950, Nowell MSS.; *Letters,* pp. 146–147.

193/10 TW to Margaret Roberts, Jan. 12, 1929, Wisdom.

193/33 PN, I: 200–203; TW to AB, Oct. 9, 1928, Wisdom.

194/14 PN, I: 204, 150; TW to AB, Nov. 8, 1928, Wisdom; PN, I: 261.

194/33 Madeleine Boyd to TW, Oct. 15, 1928, Wisdom; AB to TW, Oct. 16, 17, 19, 1928, Wisdom; TW to AB, Oct. 29 and 30, Nov. 17, 1928, Wisdom.

195/3 MEP to TW, Oct. 22, 1928; *Letters,* pp. 158–159.

195/29 TW to AB, [Oct. 1928], Wisdom.

195/40 TW to AB, Oct. 10 and Nov. 30, 1928, Wisdom.

196/8 TW to AB, Nov. 28, 1928, Wisdom.

196/21 TW to AB, Nov. 10 and 28, 1928, Wisdom.

Chapter VII: *A Miracle of Good Luck*

197/18 MEP, "Thomas Wolfe," *Harvard Library Bulletin* 1 (Autumn 1947): 271.

198/17 The best biographical treatments are A. Scott Berg, *Max Perkins: Editor of Genius* (New York: E. P. Dutton, 1978), and Malcolm Cowley, "Unshaken Friend," *New Yorker,* 20 (April 1, 1944): 32–36, 39–41, and (April 8, 1944): 30–40.

199/8 *Letters,* pp. 168–170.

199/36 John Hall Wheelock in "Thomas Wolfe: Biography in Sound," Earl Hamner, ed., *Carolina Quarterly* 9 (Fall 1956): 8–9; MEP, "Thomas Wolfe," p. 270; MEP's recollections, enclosed in MEP to JST, Oct. 22, 1948, Wisdom. Wolfe believed that Meyer had been the first to read his manuscript for Scribners. TW to Henry Volkening, July 9, 1929, Wisdom.

200/18 PN, I: 301–302; *Letters,* p. 170.

200/28 Contract between Chales Scribner's Sons and Thomas Wolfe, Jan. 9, 1929, Gitlin MSS.

200/38 *Letters,* p. 162.

201/13 Pollock and Cargill, pp. 59–60.

201/15 Mary Lindsay Thornton, ed., " 'Dear Mabel': Letters of Thomas Wolfe to His Sister, Mabel Wolfe Wheaton," *South Atlantic Quarterly* 60 (Autumn 1961): 473.

201/22 *Letters,* pp. 173, 175, 199–200; Guy J. Forgue, ed., *Letters of H. L. Mencken* (New York: Alfred A. Knopf, 1961), p. 312.

201/34 *Letters,* p. 175; Berg, p. 133.

202/19 MEP to William B. Wisdom, April 6, 1943, Charles Scribner's Sons Archive; MEP's recollections, enclosed in MEP to JST, Oct. 25, 1948, Wisdom. In his recollections Perkins mistakenly remembered that Gant's return had preceded the passage describing the wanderings of Eugene and his friend through Altamont on the way home from school.

202/21 Berg, p. 139.

202/27 For a detailed account of the editing of "O Lost," see Francis E. Skipp, "Thomas Wolfe and His Scribner's Editors" (unpublished Ph. D. dissertation, Duke University, 1962), ch. II.

203/14 MEP's recollections, in MEP to JST, Oct. 25, 1948, Wisdom; MEP to William B. Wisdom, April 6, 1943, Wisdom.

203/35 *Letters,* pp. 586, 129.

204/18 PN, I: 310; Kennedy, p. 178.

204/27 Berg, p. 134.

204/32 *Letters,* p. 200.

205/9 *Letters,* p. 213. Ominous for their future relations was a sentence I have omitted: "Later, they must discover that such answers have to come out of their own hearts. . . ."

205/22 PN, I: 322–325.

205/28 MEP, "Thomas Wolfe," p. 271.

205/39 For further examples of how Wolfe changed the names of people and places see Myra Champion, "Notes and Map of Asheville," Wisdom, No. 1341.

206/9 SOAN, p. 21; MEP, "Thomas Wolfe," p. 272.

207/6 TW to Henry Volkening, July 4, 1929, Wisdom; Pollock and Cargill, p. 94; L. Ruth Middlebrook, "Reminiscences of Tom Wolfe," *American Mercury* 63 (Nov. 1946): 544–545; Middlebrook, "Further Memories of Tom Wolfe," ibid. 64 (April 1947): 418.

207/16 Pollock and Cargill, pp. 101, 93.

207/32 PN, I: 317; TW, "Cambridge, The City and Voyages" Ledger, Wisdom, No. 233.

208/8 PN, I: 313.

208/15 PN, I: 402; II: 431.

208/29 PN, II: 424.

209/23 MEP's memorandum to JST, Oct. 29, 1945, Wisdom; PN, II: 416.

210/6 *Letters,* pp. 183–184; pages torn from Cambridge-Boston Ledgers, Wisdom, No. 807.

210/19 Wheelock to TW, July 17, 1929, Charles Scribner's Sons Archive; *Letters,* p. 189.

210/33 *Letters,* pp. 195–196.

211/16 PN, I: 358, 325; *Letters,* pp. 176–177.

211/20 *Letters,* p. 199.

211/33 Floyd C. Watkins's *Thomas Wolfe's Characters* (Norman: University of Oklahoma Press, 1957) shows that the people in Wolfe's books were "Portraits from Life," but because a number of these people were still alive in 1957 Watkins could not always specifically identify them in print. On the autobiographical problem in general see C. Hugh Holman, "Thomas Wolfe and the Stigma of Autobiography," *Virginia Quarterly Review* 40 (Autumn 1964): 614–635; and B. R. McElderry, Jr., "The Autobiographical Problem in Thomas Wolfe's Earlier Novels," *Arizona Quarterly* 4 (Winter 1948): 315–324.

212/26 PN, I: 365–368.

213/2 PN, I: 365–366.

213/9 *Letters,* p. 203; PN, I: 367.

213/25 *Letters,* p. 203; Duncan Emerich, recorded interview with MWW, Feb. 23, 1947, Wisdom. Cf. TWAHF, p. 215.

214/3 LTHM, p. 152.

214/15 TW to AB, Oct. 3, 1929, Wisdom.

214/25 Horace Sutton, "Look Homeward, Asheville," *Saturday Review of Literature* 37 (Nov. 6, 1954): 48; TW to Madeleine Boyd, Jan. 5, 1929 [i.e., 1930], copy in Madeleine Boyd to MEP, Jan. 8, 1936, Charles Scribner's Sons Archive.

215/19 Paschal Reeves, ed., *Thomas Wolfe: The Critical Reception* (New York: David Lewis, 1974), pp. 1–6.

215/26 George W. McCoy, *Asheville and Thomas Wolfe* (pamphlet reprinted from *North Carolina Historical Review* 20 [April 1953]: 200–217); Betty Lynch Williams, *Asheville and Thomas Wolfe: A Study in Changing Attitudes* (pamphlet reprinted from *Appalachian Heritage* 3 [1975]); Floyd C. Watkins, "Thomas Wolfe and Asheville Again and Again and Again," *Southern Literary Journal* 10 (Fall 1977): 31–55.

216/5 Duncan Emerich, recorded interview with MWW, Feb. 23, 1947, Wisdom; Lucile J. Babcox to Scribner & Sons, [1929], Charles Scribner's Sons Archive; Mary Johnston Avery, "Asheville People Smart Under Lash," *Charlotte Observer,* Mar. 30, 1930; Jack Westall, "Asheville's Reactions to Look Homeward, Angel," Dec. 2, 1947, Westall Family MSS., Duke University; Oliver Wolfe to TW, [1929], Wolfe Coll., UNC.

216/21 *Asheville Times,* Oct. 27, 1929,; "A Friend" to Superintendent, Asheville Public Library, undated, Pack Mem. Lib.

216/29 SOAN, pp. 18–19; *Letters,* p. 209.

217/10 Margaret Roberts to TW, May 11, 1936, Wisdom; J. M. Roberts to EN, Sept. 18, 1951, Nowell MSS.

217/32 Oliver Wolfe to TW, [1929], Wolfe Coll., UNC.; Roy Wilder, interview with JEW, Brooklyn, c. 1939, ibid.; JEW, "Eliza Gant Talks," transcription by Ruth Davis of recordings that JST made of interview with JEW, Terry MSS.; Duncan Emerich, recorded interview with MWW, Feb. 23, 1947, Wisdom.

217/36 JEW, "Eliza Gant Talks"; Effie Gambrell to TW, Aug. 25, 1930, Wisdom.

217/39 Frank Wolfe to FW, May 6, 1931, Braden-Hatchett Thomas Wolfe Coll.

218/4 FW to TW, Mar. 31, 1930, Wisdom. Cf. FW to ECA, Mar. 28, 1955, Fred Wolfe MSS.

218/20 TWAHF, pp. 215–233; Duncan Emerich, recorded interview with MWW, Feb. 23, 1947, Wisdom; MWW to George McCoy, Jan. 9, 1953, McCoy-Love Family Papers, Duke University; MWW to TW, [1930], Wisdom.

218/25 TW, "The Vision of Spangler's Paul," Wisdom, No. 768.

218/40 TW to MWW, Nov. 30, 1929, Wisdom; Vardis Fisher, "My Experiences with Thomas Wolfe," *Tomorrow* 10 (April 1951): 28; Volkening, "Tom Wolfe: Penance No More," p. 206.

219/15 *Letters,* p. 215.

219/28 TW to Mrs. J. M. Roberts, Feb. 2, 1930, Wisdom; TW to Albert Coates, Nov. 19, 1929, Wisdom.

219/38 *Letters,* pp. 207–208; LTHM, p. 157.

220/19 Reeves, *Thomas Wolfe: The Critical Reception,* pp. 6–11.

220/27 Volkening, "Tom Wolfe: Penance No More," p. 206; *Letters,* p. 221.

220/39 Reeves, *Thomas Wolfe: The Critical Reception,* pp. 16–17, 20; *Scribner's Magazine* 86 (Dec. 1929): 24, 28.

221/11 James Earl Bassett, "The Critical Reception of *Look Homeward, Angel,*" *TW Review* 6 (Spring 1952): 45–47. Not all North Carolina reviews were unfavorable. Richard Walser, "The Angel in North Carolina," ibid. 3 (Fall 1979): 19–25.

221/20 Christopher P. Baker and Alan P. Clarke, eds., "An Unpublished Thomas Wolfe Letter," *Mississippi Quarterly* 25 (Fall 1971): 467–479.

221/37 *Letters,* p. 203; Edman to T. Walsh, Nov. 19, 1929, Wisdom; Bynner to TW, Feb. 6, 1930, Wisdom; Roger Burlingame, *Of Making Many Books* (New York: Charles Scribner's Sons, 1946), p. 16.

222/9 Schorer to TW, Oct. 22, 1929; Wisdom; Flaccus to TW, [1929], Wisdom; Derleth to TW, Sept. 8, 1930, Wisdom.

222/13 Irma Wyckoff to EN, Sept. 27, 1951, Nowell MSS.

222/20 Joseph Blotner, *Faulkner: A Biography* (New York: Random House, 1974), I: 633; Carlos Baker, *Ernest Hemingway: A Life Story* (New York: Charles Scribner's Sons, 1969), p. 205.

223/7 PN, I: 375–376; Earl Wilson, in *New York Post,* Sept. 16, 1938; Jessie Schroeder to TW, Nov. 1, 1929, Wisdom.

223/18 W. Y. Tindall, notes for two lectures on TW, enclosed in Tindall to Louis Cohn, Dec. 7, 1944, Alexander Wainwright Coll.

224/5 Ann Preston Bridgers, "Thomas Wolfe: Legends of a Man's Hunger in His Youth," *Saturday Review of Literature* 11 (April 6, 1935): 599.

224/14 Tindall to Oscar Cargill, Jan. 3, 1950; MS., Fales Lib. NYU. TW's records of his sexual exploits have been removed from his pocket notebooks in the Wisdom Collection and are kept in the vault of the Houghton Library.

224/40 Mina Curtiss to EN, Oct. 4, 1949, Wisdom; Mina Curtiss, "Giants and Pygmies," from her unpublished autobiography.

225/16 Alexander Calder, *Calder: An Autobiography with Pictures* (New York: Pantheon, 1966), pp. 106–107; Jean Lipman and Nancy Foote, eds., *Calder's Circus* (New York: E. P. Dutton & Co., 1972).

226/7 For a full, amusing account of the party and the circus, see Klein, pp. 248–253.

226/20 Mina Curtiss, "Giants and Pygmies."

227/2 Factual accounts of the fire appeared in the *New York Times,* Jan. 4–5, 1930.

227/13 PN, I: 388–389.

227/19 TW to Mrs. J. M. Roberts, Feb. 2, 1930, Wisdom.

227/22 PN, II: 425–426.

228/2 LTHM, pp. 162–163.

228/19 John Hall Wheelock to EN, July 1 and 29, 1952, Nowell MSS.

229/4 *Letters,* p. 644.

229/10 The exact figures are not easy to determine. According to a memorandum signed by Perkins, Wolfe's book had earned $3,484.50 by April 11,

1930 (MEP to Mr. Brown, Jan. 5, 1931, Archive of Charles Scribner's Sons). That meant that 9,958 copies had been sold. But John Hall Wheelock prepared a memorandum for John S. Terry indicating much smaller sales, because it showed that Wolfe received only $2,263.75 from Scribners in 1930 (Wolfe Coll., UNC). In still a third reckoning, Irma Wyckoff, Perkins's secretary, reported that by April 11, 1930, *Look Homeward, Angel* had sold 11,399 copies (Wyckoff to EN, Sept. 27, 1951, Nowell MSS). If correct, this report meant that, after deducting the $500 advance Wolfe had received in 1929 and after further deducting Mrs. Boyd's ten-percent fee as agent, Wolfe's royalty check came to $3,172.16. But still a fourth account of royalties on *Look Homeward, Angel* (an unsigned, undated memorandum in the Archive of Charles Scribner's Sons), shows that by April 11, 1930, the author's royalties totaled $3,984.50 — presumably before the advance and Mrs. Boyd's fee were deducted. If this reckoning is accurate, his first royalty check was for $3,136.05. Whatever the exact figures, not all of this royalty money was immediately available to Wolfe. Scribners issued semiannual statements, in February and in August, but payment was not due to the author until four months after each statement.

229/25 TW, sheets torn from "October Fair" ledgers, Mar. 2, 1930, Wisdom, No. 244.

229/36 All these letters of recommendation are in the files of the John Simon Guggenheim Memorial Foundation.

230/2 Carbon of a letter, presumably from Charles Scribner II, to TW, Dec. 18, 1929, Charles Scribner's Sons Archive.

230/14 Pollock and Cargill, pp. 146–151.

230/36 PN, I: 399; II: 417, 423, 436.

231/6 PN, I: 391; TW, Pocket Notebook 13, Wisdom.

231/24 PN, I: 399–400.

231/34 PN, I: 398: AB's *Three Blue Suits* (New York: Equinox Cooperative Press, 1933), pp. 49–72.

232/4 PN, II: 433, 429.

232/18 In this generous calculation of his assets TW must have included royalties from LHA, the advance from Scribners on his next novel, and his Guggenheim award.

232/25 PN, II: 442.

Chapter VIII: *Penance More*

233/10 Fletcher to Frank D. Fackenthal, Mar. 10, 1930, Archives of the Pulitzer Prizes, Columbia University.

233/14 Whitney Darrow to TW, June 3, 1930, Wisdom.

233/18 TW, draft of the David Hawke story, Wisdom, No. 649.

233/21 TW to Esther Owens, April 17, 1936, Barrett Coll.

234/3 Fletcher to Fackenthal, Jan. 16, 1930, Archives of the Pulitzer Prizes.

234/14 TW to George M. Babbitt, May and December, 1930, Wisdom; Harry Mandelbaum to TW, April 14 and 24, June 9, 1931, Wisdom.

234/22 PN, II: 454.

234/24 Enclosure in TW to MEP, Sept. 27, 1930, Wisdom.

235/3 AB's note added to Jean Roscoe (secretary to Dr. Babbitt) to AB, Oct. 1930, Terry MSS.; AB to TW, May 23, June 2 and 15, 1930, Wisdom.

235/12 TW to Theodore Bernstein, May 1930, Wisdom.

235/25 Letters, p. 233.

235/36 Letters, p. 249.

236/7 TW, "Woman's Letter," Wisdom, No. 819. On TW and *Finnegans Wake*, see Walter Voigt, *Die Bildersprache Thomas Wolfes* (München: Max Hueber, 1960), pp. 233–234.

236/10 Letters, p. 286.

236/25 Emily Davies Thayer to TW, May 22, July 31, 1930, and undated, Wisdom; PN, II: 455.

236/38 PN, II: 455, 460.

237/34 ECA, "Love as Art, and Vice Versa: An Erotic Experience, as Told to Me by Thomas Wolfe," Gitlin MSS.

238/5 PN, II: 460.

238/13 PN, II: 465.

238/21 Letters, p. 282.

238/35 Letters, p. 235.

239/6 Letters, p. 245.

239/20 Letters, p. 234.

239/26 Letters, p. 241.

239/38 Letters, p. 282; Kennedy, p. 192.

240/7 Letters, p. 234; TW to Henry Volkening, June 10, 1930, Wisdom.

240/24 Letters, pp. 255, 273; TW to A. S. Frère-Reeves, Aug, 2, 1930, Wisdom.

240/32 Letters, p. 237.

241/3 Andrew Turnbull, ed., *The Letters of F. Scott Fitzgerald* (New York: Charles Scribner's Sons, 1963), pp. 224, 251.

241/24 Letters, pp. 237–238, 263.

242/6 Letters, p. 240, PN, II: 511; Turnbull, p. 159.

242/19 AB to TW, July 3, Aug. 12, and undated, 1930, Wisdom. Most of these communications are included in Suzanne Stutman, ed., *Holding on for Heaven: The Cables and Postcards of Thomas Wolfe and Aline Bernstein* (The Thomas Wolfe Society, 1985).

242/29 PN, II: 485–486.

242/37 Letters, p. 264.

243/14 *The Times*, July 22, 1930; *Everyman*, June 12, 1930; *Referee*, July 6, 1930; *Times Literary Supplement*, July 24, 1930.

243/27 *Spectator*, Aug. 2, 1930; *Observer*, Aug. 17, 1930; *London Evening News*, Aug. 6, 1930.

243/39 TW to A. S. Frère-Reeves, July 26, 1930, Wisdom; *Letters*, pp. 257–258.

244/9 TW to A. S. Frère-Reeves, Sept. 2, 1930, Wisdom; TW to Richard Aldington, Sept. 28, 1930, MS., UCLA; *Letters*, p. 261.

244/25 Letters, pp. 261–262; TW to FW, Sept. 26, 1930, Wolfe Coll., UNC.

244/34 PN, II: 514, 525.

245/9 *Letters,* p. 274.

245/27 TW, "October Fair" Ledger, begun June 6, 1930, Wisdom; PN, II: 494.

245/35 *Letters,* p. 236; MEP to TW, Dec. 23, 1930, Wisdom.

246/14 PN, II: 518, 509.

246/27 *Letters,* p. 287.

247/19 LTHM, p. 165; *Letters,* p. 272; PN, II: 530.

247/33 LTHM, p. 165.

248/16 TW to FW, Sept. 26, 1930, Wolfe Coll., UNC.

248/22 *Letters,* p. 276.

249/8 Lewis to TW, Oct. 23, 1930, Wisdom; clipping from *New York Herald-Tribune,* in MEP to TW, Folder 8, Wisdom; Harry E. Maule and Melville H. Cane, eds., *Man From Main Street* (New York: Random House, 1953), pp. 7, 17.

249/18 *Letters,* pp. 271, 388; TW to JST, incomplete letter, 1930, Wisdom.

249/27 TW, "The Earth: England," Wisdom, No. 1013; Garland B. Porter to EN, July 7, 1957, Nowell MSS. Cf. Mark Schorer, *Sinclair Lewis: An American Life* (New York: McGraw-Hill, 1961), p. 559.

249/40 TW, final typescript for YCGHA, pp. 785–788, Wisdom, No. 1026.

250/8 Allen Austin, "An Interview with Sinclair Lewis" *University of Kansas City Review* 24 (March 1958): 208; *Horizon* 22 (March 1979): 48–49.

250/18 AB to TW, Oct. 14, 1930, and undated, Wisdom.

251/11 TW to MEP, Jan. 19, 1931, Charles Scribner's Sons Archive.

251/20 TW to FW, Nov. 25, 1930, Wisdom; PN, II: 528.

251/28 *Letters,* p. 269; TW to MEP, Jan. 19, 1931, Charles Scribner's Sons Archive.

251/38 MEP to TW, Jan. 31, 1931, Wisdom.

252/13 Berg, pp. 123–125.

252/22 *Letters,* p. 289.

252/32 *Letters,* p. 294; TW to MEP, Feb. 24, 1931, Charles Scribner's Sons Archive.

253/6 *Letters,* p. 248; TW to JST, Jan. 21, 1931, Wisdom.

253/25 TW, statement to Alfred A. Cook, Dec. 7, 1936, Wisdom, No. 1323; interview with Margaret Painter, May 6, 1980; *Scribner's Magazine* 94 (July 1933): 10.

254/4 *Letters,* pp. 323–324; PN, II: 795; Marion L. Starkey, "Thomas Wolfe of North Carolina," *Boston Evening Transcript,* Sept. 26, 1931.

254/15 *Letters,* p. 328; PN, II: 569; interview with Mrs. Edith H. Smith, Feb. 22, 1982.

254/26 Donald Wayne to Myra Champion, Oct. 20, 1952, Wolfe Coll., Pack Mem. Lib.

254/31 *Letters,* p. 296.

255/7 Interview with Margaret Painter, May 6, 1980.

255/14 Tindall to Oscar Cargill, Jan. 3, 1950, MS., Fales Lib., NYU.

255/22 *New York Evening Post,* April 4, 1931. Cf. Kwak Hyo-suk, "A Case of East Meeting West," *Korea Newsreview* 9 (Mar. 29, 1980): 22–23.

255/33 LTHM, p. 170.

256/5 Interview with Mrs. Hjalmar Hertz, Dec. 20, 1982.

256/16 YCGHA, pp. 349–350.

256/27 Claire Turner Zyve to TW, undated, Wisdom; *Letters,* pp. 297–298.

257/3 AB to TW, Mar. 24, 1931, Wisdom.

257/18 TW to AB, March 1931, Wisdom.

257/24 AB to TW, April 1931, Wisdom.

257/33 AB to TW, May 30, 1931, and undated, Wisdom; TW, Pocket Notebook, No. 19, Wisdom.

258/5 Interview with Mrs. Hjalmar Hertz, Dec. 20, 1982.

258/21 *Letters,* p. 299; PN, II: 556–557.

259/4 *Letters,* p. 310; FDTM, p. 5; interview with Margaret Painter, May 6, 1980; TW, notes on Marjorie Dorman, 1936, Wisdom, No. 1213; LTHM, p. 174.

259/26 FDTM, pp. 183–184.

260/6 MEP to TW, Aug. 27, 1931, Charles Scribner's Sons Archive; *Letters,* pp. 305–309.

260/11 PN, II: 562.

260/35 Sinclair Lewis to MEP, Jan. 12, 1932, Charles Scribner's Sons Archive; Ernst Rowohlt Publishing House to TW, Dec. 28, 1931, ibid.; MEP to Paul Weiss, Sept. 30, 1940, ibid.; TW to Sinclair Lewis, Jan. 1932, Wisdom; TW to A. S. Frère-Reeves, April 15, 1932, Wisdom.

261/13 FW to TW, April 30, May 4, June 2, 1931, Wolfe Coll., UNC; TW to FW, May 1, 1931, ibid.; TW to FW, May 27, 1931, Braden-Hatchett Thomas Wolfe Coll.; FW to TW, Aug. 23, 1931, Wisdom.

261/27 SOAN, pp. 59–60; PN, II: 568.

261/36 *Letters,* p. 302; LTHM, p. 173.

262/19 *Letters,* p. 316.

262/39 *Scribner's Magazine* 91 (April 1932), 193–198, 239–256.

263/5 Matthew J. Bruccoli, ed., *Selected Letters of John O'Hara* (New York: Random House, 1978), p. 75.

263/35 *Letters,* p. 336.

264/11 LTHM, p. 178; TW to MWW, Nov. 4, 1931, Wolfe Coll., UNC; FW to Richard K. Brunner, Feb. 25, 1959, Fred Wolfe MSS.

264/28 JEW to TW, May 5 and Oct. 4, 1931, Wisdom; JEW to MWW, April 26, 1931, Braden-Hatchett Thomas Wolfe Coll. As early as April 1931 Wolfe suggested that Aline ought to talk about their relationship with his mother, who was coming up for a short visit. Julia did not see her at that time, though afterwards she did briefly meet her at Mabel's apartment in Washington. TW to AB, April 9, 1931, Wisdom.

264/36 Interview with Mrs. Hjalmar Hertz, Dec. 20, 1982.

265/3 Unless otherwise identified, all quotations in the following paragraphs are from JEW, "Eliza Gant Talks," transcription by Ruth Davis of several recordings that JST made of interviews with JEW, Terry MSS.

266/2 AB to TW, Jan. 1932, Wisdom.

266/15 AB to TW, Jan. 14, 1932, Wisdom.

266/35 *Letters,* p. 341.

267/7 *Letters,* p. 339.

267/21 Kyle Crichton, *Total Recoil* (Garden City, N.Y.: Doubleday & Co., 1960), p. 34.

267/33 TW, fragments intended for inclusion in SOAN, Wisdom, No. 686.

268/19 *Publishers Weekly,* July 30, 1932, p. 352; *Letters,* p. 353.

268/32 *Letters,* p. 336; TW to George McCoy, Mar. 22, 1932, Wisdom.

268/35 *Letters,* p. 337.

269/7 PN, II: 575, 579.

269/16 MEP to Julian Meade, May 4, 1932, Charles Scribner's Sons Archive. A copy of this rare dummy book, "K-19," is in the Pack Memorial Library in Asheville. In 1983 it was reprinted in a limited edition by the Thomas Wolfe Society, as *K-19: Salvaged Pieces,* ed. by John L. Idol, Jr.

269/38 "The Man on the Wheel," pp. 70, 215–216, Wisdom, No. 312.

270/5 *Letters,* p. 333.

271/11 *Letters,* pp. 343, 345.

Chapter IX: *A Miserable, Monstrous Mis-begotten Life*

272/9 *Letters,* p. 363.

272/17 Nowell, p. 213; *Letters,* p. 344.

273/6 *Letters,* p. 352, 353.

273/18 PN, II: 606; *Letters,* p. 355.

273/24 *Scribner's Magazine* 93 (May 1933): 285–294.

273/34 Marjorie K. Rawlings to MEP, June 7, 1933, Charles Scribner's Sons Archive.

273/36 *Scribner's Magazine* 93 (June 1933): 333–338, 378–388.

274/10 *Scribner's Magazine* 94 (July 1933): 7–12, 46–56.

274/25 *Letters,* p. 370.

275/13 *Scribner's Magazine,* 94 (July 1933): 7, 56. I have arranged these passages in verse form in order to stress their poetic quality.

275/32 Robert Raynolds, *Thomas Wolfe: Memoir of a Friendship* (Austin: University of Texas Press, 1965), p. 37.

276/2 *Letters,* p. 359.

276/18 E.g., *Letters,* p. 386; LTHM, pp. 207, 213.

276/24 AOAAN, p. 59.

277/4 MEP to MWW, Feb. 11, 1933, Wolfe Coll., UNC.

277/28 Incomplete, unpublished review, Wisdom, No. 1191.

277/32 Carlos Baker, ed., *Ernest Hemingway: Selected Letters, 1917–1961* (New York: Charles Scribner's Sons, 1981), p. 347; MEP to TW, Dec. 23, 1932, Charles Scribner's Sons Archive.

278/9 MEP to JST, Nov. 21, 1945, Wisdom; *Book-of-the-Month Club News,* July 1960; Frank A. Dickson, in *Anderson (S.C.) Independent,* Aug. 21, 1948, copy in Braden-Hatchett Thomas Wolfe Coll.

278/12 May Cameron, *Press Time* (1936), pp. 247–248. This "interview" was mostly written or extensively revised by Wolfe. Aldo P. Magi and Richard Walser, eds., *Thomas Wolfe Interviewed, 1929–1938* (Baton Rouge: Louisiana State University Press, 1985), pp. 58–64.

278/21 *Green Hills of Africa* (New York: Charles Scribner's Sons, 1935), p. 71; Baker, ed., *Ernest Hemingway: Selected Letters*, pp. 726, 681.

278/34 *Letters*, p. 358.

279/2 The manuscript is in Wisdom, No. 267.

279/19 *Letters*, p. 323; AOAAN, p. 51.

280/15 *Letters*, p. 321.

280/24 PN, II: 611.

280/31 On the consequences of the shift from first- to third-person narrative, see C. Hugh Holman, *The Loneliness at the Core: Studies in Thomas Wolfe* (Baton Rouge: Louisiana State University Press, 1975), pp. 82–83. But for a thoughtful dissenting opinion, see Richard S. Kennedy, in Paschal Reeves, ed., *Thomas Wolfe and the Glass of Time* (Athens: University of Georgia Press, 1971), pp. 33–39.

281/8 *Letters*, p. 362.

281/20 MEP, "Thomas Wolfe: A Writer for the People of His Time and To-morrow," *Wings* 13:5; *Letters*, p. 398. Wolfe made a confused explanation to the head of the Guggenheim Foundation: "The chief reason for this [shift from first- to third-person] being that in most of these magazine pieces the 'I' is not the central character but the narrator of events." TW to Henry Allen Moe, Feb. 8, 1934, Guggenheim Foundation.

281/29 *Letters*, p. 358.

282/7 PN, II: 612–613.

282/20 PN, II: 611–613.

282/25 MEP to Charles Scribner III, April 18, 1933, Charles Scribner's Sons Archive.

282/34 The two unsigned contracts, dated May 2 and May 3, 1933, are in the Charles Scribner's Sons Archive.

283/2 Signed, undated contract for "Time and the River," Wisdom, No. 1323.

283/10 MEP to Collector of Internal Revenue, June 18, 1934, Charles Scribner's Sons, Archive.

283/21 For Perkins's attempt to explain a bank account, see MEP to TW, May 11, 1934, Charles Scribner's Sons Archive. For TW's withdrawals, see "Advance on Time and the River," account of TW with Charles Scribner's Sons, Wisdom, No. 1323.

283/32 MEP to Charles Scribner III, April 18, 1933, Charles Scribner's Sons Archive.

284/13 PN, II: 613–614, 643.

284/40 For accounts of Wolfe's habits of writing, see memoirs by several of his typists: Georgia Watts, "Typist to Thomas Wolfe," *London Magazine,* June 1969, pp. 57–61; Alladine Bell, "T. Wolfe of 10 [sic] Montague Terrace," *Antioch Review* 20 (Fall 1960): 377–390; Eleanor Buckles's unpublished "Wolfe Re-visited"; and Joyce Maupin's unpublished memoir.

285/11 *Letters*, p. 382; TW, draft of chapter intended for OTATR, Wisdom, No 438.

285/20 TW, draft of "Fox and Foxman: November 1933," Wisdom, No. 1130.

285/28 Charles Norman, *Poets & People* (Indianapolis: Bobbs-Merrill Co., 1972), pp. 134–135.

285/40 TW, memorandum dated Jan. 20, 1934, Wisdom, No. 1173.

286/9 Klein, pp. 282–283.

286/25 AOAAN, pp. 67–68; TW, miscellaneous MS. fragments, Wisdom, No. 300.

287/3 TW to Henry Carlton, Aug. 25, 1933, Wisdom; *Letters,* pp. 365, 374.

287/20 Kyle Crichton, *Total Recoil* (Garden City, N.Y.: Doubleday & Co., 1960), pp. 20–21.

288/2 Raynolds, *Thomas Wolfe,* pp. 41, 95.

288/18 Clayton and Kathleen Hoagland, *Thomas Wolfe, Our Friend, 1933–1938* (Athens, Ohio: Croissant & Co., 1979); Earl Hamner, ed., "Thomas Wolfe: Biography in Sound," *Carolina Quarterly* 9 (Fall 1956): 11–12; interview with Mr. and Mrs. Clayton Hoagland, June 29, 1983.

288/28 Mary Lindsay Thornton, ed., " 'Dear Mabel': Letters of Thomas Wolfe to His Sister, Mabel Wolfe Wheaton," *South Atlantic Quarterly* 60 (Aug. 1961): 479.

288/37 *Letters,* pp. 365, 385–386; LTHM, p. 215.

289/24 For descriptions of Wolfe's apartment see Eleanor Buckles's unpublished memoir, "Wolfe Re-visited"; Sanderson Vanderbilt, in *New York Herald-Tribune,* Feb. 18, 1935; Belinda Jelliffe, "Recollections," Nowell MSS.

290/7 For a full account of Miss Nowell and her relationship with Wolfe see Richard S. Kennedy, ed., *Beyond Love and Loyalty: The Letters of Thomas Wolfe and Elizabeth Nowell* (Chapel Hill: University of North Carolina Press, 1983). Cf. EN, "Wolfe and Perkins as I Knew Them," Wisdom, No. 1344.

290/23 BLAL, p. xxi; EN, "Dates in Wolfe's Life," Nowell MSS.

290/40 EN, "Dates in Wolfe's Life," Nowell MSS.

291/16 TW, typescript of "Boom Town," Wisdom, No. 342.

291/31 Maxim Lieber in *Times Literary Supplement,* June 16, 1961, p. 373.

291/34 *American Mercury* 32 (May 1934): 21–39. For an account of the publication of this story that stresses the role played by the editor of *American Mercury,* see Charles Angoff, *The Tone of the Twenties and Other Essays* (New York: A. B. Barnes and Co., 1966), pp. 84–92.

292/9 BLAL, pp. 6, 8, 15.

292/15 John Hall Wheelock to Gertrude Michalove, July 27, 1933, Charles Scribner's Sons Archive.

292/25 MEP to A. S. Frère-Reeves, Sept. 23, 1933, Charles Scribner's Sons Archive.

292/28 AOAAN, p. 62.

292/35 Nowell, p. 222; MEP to JST, Dec. 19, 1945, Wisdom.

293/14 MEP to Mr. Merrick, Dec. 7, 1940, copy, Fred Wolfe MSS.

293/19 PN, II: 621.

293/34 *Letters,* p. 398–399.

293/38 MEP to TW, Dec. 16, 1933, Wisdom.

294/19 AOAAN, p. 73. The decision to divide the novel was made before January 18, 1934, because on that date Perkins wrote A. S. Frère-Reeves that Wolfe's manuscript "comes at present to 344,000 words." (Charles

Scribner's Sons Archive). This was about half the length of the complete manuscript of "Time and the River."

294/30 AOAAN, p. 72–73; Whitney Darrow to MEP, July 17, 1934, Charles Scribner's Sons Archive.

295/3 MEP to JST, Oct. 29, 1945, Wisdom.

295/17 Mrs. Osborne wrote to Wolfe in both 1933 and 1935 (Wisdom). He drafted a long and unconvincing letter to her on July 18, 1935 (*Letters*, pp. 481–482), but her death made it unnecessary for him to send it.

295/30 Aline Bernstein, *Three Blue Suits: Mr. Froelich, Herbert Wilson, Eugene* (New York: Equinox Cooperative Press, 1933). See Henry Hart, *A Relevant Memoir: The Story of the Equinox Cooperative Press* (New York: Three Mountains Press, 1977), pp. 44–51.

295/39 *Letters*, pp. 391–397.

296/19 TW to Edward Goodnow, July 10, 1935, Wisdom. Cf. *Letters*, p. 430.

296/31 MEP to Thomas Beer, Mar. 13, 1935; MEP to MWW, Mar. 8, 1935, Charles Scribner's Sons Archive; PN, II: 613.

297/2 TW, typescript of OTATR, p. 909, Wisdom, No. 658.

297/19 PN, II: 612–613, 638.

297/23 The best general account of the editing of the manuscript is Francis Edward Skipp, "Thomas Wolfe and His Scribner's Editors" (unpublished Ph.D. dissertation, Duke University, 1962), ch. IV.

298/25 JST, "'En Route to a Legend," *Saturday Review of Literature* 31 (Nov. 27, 1948). 8, MEP to JST, Oct. 29, 1945, Wisdom; MEP, "Thomas Wolfe," *Harvard Library Bulletin* 1 (Autumn 1947): 272.

298/36 *Letters*, p. 404; TW to FW, Jan. 20, 1934, Wolfe Coll., UNC.; MEP to FW, Mar. 6, 1934, Fred Wolfe Coll., UNC.

299/2 TW to Mr. and Mrs. Beverley Smith, July 3, 1934, Wisdom.

299/13 AOAAN, p. 70.

299/30 MEP, "Thomas Wolfe," *Harvard Library Bulletin* 1: (Autumn 1947) 272.

300/6 The typewritten draft of this section is in Wisdom, No. 581; AOAAN, p. 78.

300/16 MEP, "Scribner's and Tom Wolfe," *Carolina Magazine* 68 (Oct. 1938): 15–16.

300/24 Berg, p. 237.

301/5 TW to Helen Trafford Brown, April 11, 1934, Barrett Coll.

301/16 MEP to A. S. Frère-Reeves, May 12, 1934, Charles Scribner's Sons Archive.

301/21 TW to Norman H. Pearson, Mar. 7, 1938, Wisdom.

302/5 MEP, "Scribner's and Tom Wolfe," *Carolina Magazine* 68 (Oct. 1938): 16; MEP to Peter Jack Munro, Sept. 29, 1938, Charles Scribner's Sons Archive; MEP, "Thomas Wolfe," *Harvard Library Bulletin* 1 (Autumn 1947): 272–273; *Letters*, p. 416; John Hall Wheelock, ed., *Editor to Author: The Letters of Maxwell E. Perkins* (New York: Charles Scribner's Sons, 1950), p. 91.

302/31 Turnbull, p. 201; *Letters*, p. 416.

303/4 Berg, p. 245.

303/19 MEP to Paul Weiss, Sept. 30, 1940, Charles Scribner's Sons Archive. See the excellent discussion in Richard S. Kennedy, "What the Galley Proofs of Wolfe's *Of Time and the River* Tell Us," *TW Review* 9 (Fall 1985): 1–8.

303/30 Joyce Maupin, unpublished memoir.

304/17 *Letters*, p. 420; Wheelock, ed., *Editor to Author*, pp. 98, 180–181.

304/28 The original of this memorandum is in Wisdom, No. 1345, along with a letter from EN to William H. Bond, Sept. 4, 1949. See also EN to ECA, April 19, 1949, and Irma Wyckoff to EN, Aug. 27, 1949, Nowell MSS.

305/16 Cf. TW, typescript for OTATR, pp. 467–469, Wisdom, No. 656, and OTATR, p. 254. For further discussion, see Francis E. Skipp, "Thomas Wolfe, Max Perkins, and Politics," *Modern Fiction Studies* 23 (Winter 1967–1968), 503–511.

306/6 The two sets of galley proofs for these different versions of *Of Time and the River* are in the Wisdom Collection. The recently discovered first forty galleys are in the Wolfe Collection, University of North Carolina.

306/20 Nowell, "Dates in Wolfe's Life," Nowell MSS.; Berg, pp. 247–248.

306/33 *Letters*, p. 429; TW to Belinda Jelliffe, Jan. 4, 1935, Pack Mem. Lib.; Van Doren, "The Art of American Fiction," *The Nation*, April 25, 1934, p. 473. In public Wolfe was silent. But he planned to include in his "Preface" for *Of Time and the River* — a preface that was never published — a rebuke to those "people none of whom knew anything about my life but who found my failure to publish a [second] book . . . a matter so remarkable that it called for mockery and contempt." TW, handwritten draft of Preface, Wisdom, No. 351.

307/3 *Letters*, p. 425.

307/9 *Letters*, p. 429. Wolfe had dictated correspondence to his typist earlier, especially after his arm was injured.

307/23 Belinda Jelliffe, "Recollections," Nowell MSS.; TW, "Notes," Wisdom, No. 1318.

307/39 MEP to TW, Jan. 21, 1935, Wisdom; *Letters*, p. 446.

308/15 TW to A. S. Frère-Reeves, Sept. 13, 1934, Wisdom; *Letters*, p. 415; TW, variant drafts of dedication to OTATR, Wisdom, No. 353.

308/30 MEP to TW, Jan. 21 and Feb. 8, 1935, Wisdom; Berg, p. 251.

308/36 TW, "Preface," Wisdom, No. 1318.

309/8 MEP to TW, Jan. 21, 1935, Wisdom; MEP to A. S. Frère-Reeves, Feb. 6, 1935, Charles Scribner's Sons Archive; *Letters*, p. 429.

309/13 LTHM, p. 242.

310/4 *New York Herald-Tribune*, Feb. 18, 1935. Cf. Magi and Walser, *Thomas Wolfe Interviewed*, pp. 21–26.

310/17 JST, Recollections, Terry MSS.; Belinda Jelliffe, "Recollections," Nowell MSS.

311/9 Belinda Jelliffe, "Recollections," Nowell MSS.; JST to JEW, April 23, 1935, Wolfe Coll., UNC.

Chapter X: *The Famous American Novelist*

312/9 *Letters*, p. 433; TW, "Log of Trip," Mar. 4–7, 1935, Wisdom, No. 1174.

312/24 TW to John S. Terry, Mar. 28, 1935, Terry Coll, UNC.; *Letters*, p. 438.

313/9 PN, II: 675.

313/27 PN, II: 676, 684; Sylvia Beach, *Shakespeare and Company* (New York: Harcourt, Brace, 1959), p. 208; Noel Riley Fitch, *Sylvia Beach and the Lost Generation* (New York: W. W. Norton & Co., 1983), p. 352.

313/32 MEP to TW, Mar. 14, 1935, Wisdom.

314/2 PN, II: 674, 676, 679.

314/11 TW to JST, Mar. 28, 1935, Terry Coll., UNC.

314/17 *Letters*, p. 437.

314/22 PN, II: 712; *Letters*, p. 444.

314/32 For extensive samplings of reviews see Paschal Reeves, ed., *Thomas Wolfe: The Critical Reception* (New York: David Lewis, 1974), pp. 33–76, and *Book Review Digest*, 1935, pp. 1090–1091.

315/5 Reeves, p. 39; *Saturday Review of Literature* 11 (Mar. 9, 1935): 529–530.

315/25 Reeves, pp. 39, 44, 48; *Forum* 93 (April 1935): 218; *Modern Monthly* 9 (June 1935): 249–250; *Current History* 42 (April 1935): iii.

315/41 Reeves, p. 35; *New Yorker* 11 (Mar. 9, 1935): 79–82; *New Republic* 82 (Mar. 20, 1935): 163–164.

316/10 *Saturday Review of Literature* 11 (Mar. 9, 1935): 529–530; *Nation* 140 (Mar. 27, 1935): 366; *New Yorker* 11 (Mar. 9. 1935): 79–82; *New Republic* 82 (Mar. 20, 1935): 164.

316/24 *New Yorker* 11 (Mar. 9, 1935): 79–82; *New York Times*, Mar. 12, 1935; *New Outlook* 165 (April 1935): 10.

316/32 *New York Times*, Mar. 12, 1935.

316/36 PN, II: 718.

317/8 *Letters*, pp. 447–450.

317/14 MEP to EN, Oct. 23, 1934, Charles Scribner's Sons Archive.

317/30 *Letters*, p. 445; TW to John Hall Wheelock, April 9, 1935, Charles Scribner's Sons Archive.

317/37 John Hall Wheelock to TW, Mar. 27, 1935, Wisdom.

318/1 MEP to TW, April 30, 1935, Wisdom.

318/23 PN, II: 698; *Letters*, p. 458.

318/35 *Letters*, p. 444.

319/10 PN, II: 691, 698, 702.

319/24 PN, II: 720–721, 727, 729.

319/31 PN, II: 741, 735.

319/35 The first German edition of *Schau Heimwärts, Engel!* bears the date 1932, but it was not actually published until March 1933. William W. Pusey III, "The German Vogue of Thomas Wolfe," *Germanic Review* 23 (April 1948): 132.

320/1 Hermann Hesse, *My Beliefs* (New York: Farrar Straus, 1974), pp. 346–349.

320/11 The Wisdom Collection contains clippings of most major German reviews. See, in addition, a three-page typed translation of excerpts from these reviews in that collection.

320/19 Martha Dodd to TW, Monday [1935], Wisdom.

320/30 H. M. Ledig-Rowohlt, "Thomas Wolfe in Berlin," *American Scholar* 22 (Spring 1953): 186.

321/2 PN, II: 748; TW to Clayton Hoagland, May 27, 1935, Wisdom; *Letters,* pp. 466–467.

321/16 B. J. Engelmann, "Notes by Engelmann," Fairbanks MSS.

321/33 For some reason this story seems not to have appeared in 1935, but TW's "Begegnung mit Rowohlt" was published in the *Berlin Kurier,* Mar. 19, 1950, a copy of which is in the Fairbanks MSS.

322/9 Pusey, pp. 139–140; Ledig-Rowohlt, pp. 190–191.

322/33 Anne M. Springer, *The American Novel in Germany* (Hamburg: Cram, de Gruyter & Co., 1960), pp. 90–91; C. Hugh Holman, "Thomas Wolfe's Berlin," *Saturday Review* 50 (Mar. 11, 1967): 66, 69, 90; *Letters,* p. 460.

323/7 Ledig-Rowohlt, p. 192.

323/17 TW to unidentified correspondent, Copenhagen, undated, copy, Harry Ramsom Humanities Research Center, University of Texas, Austin; letter from Martha Dodd Stern, Oct. 27, 1983.

323/28 Martha Dodd Stern to EN, April 1950, Nowell MSS.; Martha Dodd, *Through Embassy Eyes* (New York: Harcourt, Brace and Co., 1939), pp. 89–95.

324/37 *Letters,* p. 460; TW to FW, May 27, 1935, Wolfe Coll., UNC; TW to MEP, May 23, 1935, Wisdom.

325/2 Interview with Donald Klopfer, Nov. 17, 1983.

325/15 Ledig-Rowohlt, p. 190; letter from Martha Dodd Stern, Jan. 26, 1984.

325/28 PN, II: 748; TW to JST, June 23, 1935, Wisdom. See also EN to ECA, May 25, 1949, Nowell MSS., and EN to Ernst Ledig-Rowohlt, Feb. 22, 1954, Nowell MSS.

325/36 PN, II: 757.

326/5 C. H. Clemmensen, in Copenhagen *Daily News,* June 18, 1938, translated by Mrs. Ruth Shaw, Braden-Hatchett Thomas Wolfe Coll.

326/9 TW to JST, June 23, 1935, Wisdom.

326/14 Wheelock to TW, July 4, 1935, Wisdom.

326/34 *New York Times,* July 5, 1935; *New York Herald-Tribune,* July 5, 1935; *Time* 26 (July 15, 1935): 45.

326/38 MEP to JST, Nov. 1, 1945, Wisdom.

327/34 AB to MEP, Mar. 31, 1935, Charles Scribner's Sons Archive; Klein, p. 299; Berg, p. 273.

328/24 MEP to JST, Nov. 1, 1945, Wisdom; Belinda Jelliffe, Recollections, Nowell MSS. In constructing this account of Wolfe's first day back in New York I have drawn on the unpublished monograph on Belinda Jelliffe by Richard Walser and Aldo P. Magi, who have had access to the correspondence of Mrs. Jelliffe.

328/32 PN, II: 805; TW to MEP, Aug. 12, 1938, Wisdom.

329/16 Helen E. Marston to TW, April 7, 1936, Wisdom; Eleanor Beckman Martin to TW, April 2, 1935, Wisdom; Eva Needle to TW, Mar. 20, 1935, Wisdom; Esther R. Hauser to TW, May 7, 1935, Wisdom; Helen H. Tait to TW, Aug. 28, 1935, Wisdom; G. Ashton to Charles Scribner's Sons, April 29, 1935, Charles Scribner's Sons Archive; Jane Doe to TW, [1935], Wisdom. (For reasons of privacy the name has been changed.)

329/26 Sherwood Anderson to TW, [1935], Wisdom.

330/2 Harry Weinberger to MEP, Mar. 13, 1935, Charles Scribner's Sons Archive; Bill of Complaint by the Plaintiff in the case of Madeleine Boyd vs. Thomas Wolfe, before the Supreme Court of the State of New York, County of New York, May 29, 1935, Wisdom, No. 1324.

330/23 TW to MEP, May 26, 1935, Wisdom.

331/2 MEP to Cornelius Mitchell, Jan. 9, 1936, Charles Scribner's Sons Archive; Mitchell to TW, July 31, 1935, Wisdom; TW to Mitchell, Aug. 13, 1935, Wisdom.

331/10 AB to TW, July 11, 1935, Charles Scribner's Sons Archive.

331/38 EN to Dr. Else K. LaRue [Mar. 1954], Nowell MSS.; Dr. E. K. LaRue to TW, July 15, 1935, Wisdom; Klein, pp. 300–301.

332/8 Klein, p. 302.

332/16 Letters, p. 594.

332/20 Klein, p. 302.

332/27 The Sixth Annual Writers' Conference in the Rocky Mountains, July 22–August 9, 1935 (Boulder, 1935), in Charles Scribner's Sons Archive.

333/14 TW to JEW, Sept. 23, 1934, Wisdom.

333/30 PN, II: 759–760.

333/41 TW to Edward Davison, July 8, 1935, Wisdom.

334/15 TW to E.A. Cross, July 18, 1935, #330 in Catalogue No. 44 of Robert F. Batchelder, Ambler, Pa.

334/30 Dorothy Heiderstadt, "Studying under Thomas Wolfe," Mark Twain Quarterly 8 (Winter 1950): 7.

334/34 Letters, p. 518.

335/11 Heiderstadt, pp. 7–8; Lou Myrtis Vining, "Thomas Wolfe — In Memoriam," Writers' Digest 19 (July 1939): 47–50.

335/23 On the internal dynamics of the conference, see the valuable newspaper clippings in the Braden-Hatchett Thomas Wolfe Collection, which also contains a Supplement to the University of Colorado Extension News 3 (May 1935), announcing Wolfe's appointment.

335/34 Warren, "A Note on the Hamlet of Thomas Wolfe," American Review 5 (May 1935): 191–208; interview with Robert Penn Warren, April 27, 1983.

336/26 Kennedy, p. 294; Letters, p. 535; "Notes by E. D. [Edward Davison]," c. August 1951, Nowell MSS.

336/31 The Silver & Gold, Aug. 8, 1935, clipping in Braden-Hatchett Thomas Wolfe Coll.

337/2 St. Louis Star-Times, Sept. 20, 1935; Letters, p. 488.

337/26 Desmond Powell, "Of Thomas Wolfe," Arizona Quarterly 1 (Spring 1945): 28–36.

337/35 Mabel Dodge Luhan to TW, May 16, 1935, Wisdom.

338/20 For an amusing account of this visit, see Turnbull, pp. 221-223. See also Letters, p. 486; TW to Alfred Dashiell, [Aug. 26, 1935], quoted in Dashiell to EN, Nov. 20, 1952, Nowell MSS.; EN to Dashiell, Nov. 22, 1952, Nowell MSS.

338/25 Mabel Dodge Luhan to TW, Aug. 25, 1935, Wisdom.

338/41 Interview with Henry A. Murray, April 2, 1982.

339/11 *Letters,* p. 488.

339/18 George Oppenheimer, *The View from the Sixties* (New York: David McKay Co., 1966), pp. 41–43; Sam Marx, *Thomas Wolfe and Hollywood* (Athens, Ohio: Croissant & Co. 1980).

339/32 AOAAN, p. 99; Daniel Fuchs to EN, Jan. 27, 1954, Nowell MSS.

339/41 Russel V. Lee to Myra Champion, Sept. 7, 1956, Wolfe Coll., Pack Mem. Lib.

340/7 Interview with Robert Penn Warren, April 27, 1983.

340/28 *St. Louis Star-Times,* Sept. 20, 1935.

340/35 *Letters,* pp. 478, 492–493.

341/5 Belinda Jelliffe, "Recollections," Nowell MSS.

341/12 JST to JEW, Oct. 9, 1935, Wolfe Coll., UNC.

341/29 Jelliffe, "Recollections." Nowell MSS.; AB to TW, [fall 1935], Wisdom; Dorothy Jackson to TW, Sunday [1935], Wisdom.

341/39 Jelliffe, "Recollections," Nowell MSS., Mrs Jelliffe remembered the sum that Wolfe owed her as $8.67, but a memorandum, by John Hall Wheelock, of charges against Wolfe's royalty account at Scribners gives the correct figure. Nowell MSS.

342/3 *Letters,* p. 536.

342/25 *Letters,* p. 523; Cornelius Mitchell to TW, May 18, 1935, Wisdom; LTHM, p. 263; Final Agreement in the case of Madeleine Boyd vs. Thomas Wolfe, New York Supreme Court, New York County, June 23, 1936, copy, Nowell MSS.; MEP to Paul Weiss, Sept. 30, 1940, Charles Scribner's Sons Archive.

342/29 LTHM, p. 264.

342/35 Contract between Charles Scribner's Sons and TW, Dec. 26, 1934, Wisdom. Wolfe was to receive a fifteen-percent royalty on the list price of all volumes sold.

343/8 *Letters,* pp. 462, 478.

343/20 *Letters,* p. 485.

343/26 MEP to TW, Aug. 20 and Aug. 30, 1935, Wisdom.

343/39 *Letters,* p. 487.

344/8 John Hall Wheelock, ed., *Editor to Author: The Letters of Maxwell E. Perkins* (New York: Charles Scribner's Sons, 1950), p. 106.

344/12 It is not clear whether Wolfe or Perkins made the decision to include only the first section of "No Door" in *From Death to Morning,* probably for the reason that most of the later sections had already been published, in a slightly different form, in *Of Time and the River.* In "The Web of Earth" the Hawke family was changed to the Gant family, and two pieces on early North Carolina history, "Polyphemus" and "Old Catawba," which had been published separately, were reunited in "The Men of Old Catawba." Kennedy, pp. 282–285.

344/26 Marjorie K. Rawlings to MEP, Oct. 15, 1935, Charles Scribner's Sons Archive; MEP to Marjorie K. Rawlings, Oct. 18, 1935, ibid.; AOAAN, p. 45.

344/39 *Letters,* p. 491.

345/17 Charles Angoff, "Thomas Wolfe and the Opulent Manner," *Southwest Review* 48 (1963): 81–84.

Chapter XI: *Almost Every Kind of Worry*

346/16 *Letters,* pp. 473, 478.

346/21 *Letters,* p. 478.

347/14 Cf. Kennedy, pp. 300–301.

347/31 *Letters,* p. 489; TW, "A Note on the Quality of Night and Darkness in American Writing," Wisdom, No. 1214.

348/25 For TW's occasional comments on movies, see TW to Gladys Taylor, summer 1920, Wisdom; JST, undated memoir concerning movies and plays TW attended in New York, Terry MSS.; PN, I: 101. In discussing the relationship between the movies and fiction I have relied heavily on Stephen Kern, *The Culture of Time and Space, 1880–1918* (Cambridge: Harvard University Press, 1983), esp. pp. 20–30, 70–77; Claude-Edmonde Magny, *The Age of the American Novel: The Film Aesthetic of Fiction Between the Two Wars* (New York: Frederick Ungar Publishing Co., 1972); Keith Cohen, *Film and Fiction: The Dynamics of Exchange* (New Haven: Yale University Press, 1979); Seymour Chatman, *Story and Discourse: Narrative Structure in Fiction and Film* (Ithaca: Cornell University Press, 1978); and Donald M. Lowe, *History of Bourgeois Perception* (Chicago: University of Chicago Press, 1982).

348/36 Unless otherwise identified, all quotations in the following paragraphs are from TW's typescript, "The Hound of Darkness," Wisdom, No. 1113.

349/10 TW, "Hound of Darkness" ledger, Wisdom, No. 737.

349/40 Ibid.

350/28 Louise Perkins to TW, [1935], Wisdom; Nancy Perkins, "Tom Wolfe as I Remember Him," [April 16, 1943], Terry MSS.

350/37 EN to Vardis Fisher, Dec. 10, 1935, Fisher MSS., Yale University; AOAAN, p. 71. This passage was omitted from SOAN, p. 76.

351/3 *Letters,* p. 490.

351/14 *Letters,* pp. 594, 602.

351/28 *Letters,* p. 702. In 1986 the Thomas Wolfe Society published a limited edition of *The Hound of Darkness,* edited by John L. Idol, Jr.

352/13 *New York Sun,* Nov. 14, 1935; *New York Evening Post,* Nov. 15, 1935; *New Yorker,* Nov. 16, 1935, p. 107; *Saturday Review of Literature,* 13 (Nov. 30, 1935): 13. For other reviews see Paschal Reeves, ed., *Thomas Wolfe: The Critical Reception* (New York: David Lewis, 1974), pp. 79–84.

352/19 *Letters,* p. 494.

352/38 Nowell, pp. 301–302.

353/3 Interview with George Stevens, July 1, 1981.

353/18 Kennedy, pp. 292–293.

353/24 Fitzgerald to TW, April 2, 1934, Wisdom, published in Andrew Turnbull, ed., *The Letters of F. Scott Fitzgerald* (New York: Charles Scribner's Sons, 1963), p. 508.

353/26 TW, undated notes on writers, Wisdom, No. 1211.

353/36 Dos Passos to Myra Champion, Nov. 22, 1951, Pack Mem. Lib.

354/16 On Faulkner's opinions of Wolfe, the best guide is Richard Walser, "On Faulkner's Putting Wolfe First," *South Atlantic Quarterly* 78 (Spring 1979): 172–181. See also Lavon Rascoe, "An Interview with William Faulkner," *Western Review,* 15 (Summer 1951): 304; Frederick Gwynn and Joseph Blotner, eds., *Faulkner in the University* (Charlottesville: University of Virginia Press, 1959), p. 144; Joseph Blotner, *William Faulkner: A Biography* (New York: Random House, 1984), p. 483; Harvey Breit, "A Walk with Faulkner," *New York Times Book Review,* Jan. 30, 1955, p. 4; James B. Meriwether and Michael Millgate, eds., *Lion in the Garden: Interviews with William Faulkner, 1926–1962* (New York: Random House, 1968), pp. 81, 107, 268; Joseph Blotner, ed., *Selected Letters of William Faulkner* (New York: Random House, 1977), pp. 185, 251; Malcolm Cowley, *The Faulkner-Cowley File* (New York: Penguin Books, 1978), pp. 14, 111–112.

354/32 *Letters,* pp. 448, 495; May Cameron, *Press Time,* p. 248; William Wisdom, "Table Talk of Thomas Wolfe," Wisdom, No. 1347.

355/3 *Saturday Review of Literature,* 13 (Dec. 7, 1935): 26.

355/16 FDTM, p. 90. See Paschal Reeves, *Thomas Wolfe's Albatross: Race and Nationality in America* (Athens: University of Georgia Press, 1968), ch. 2.

355/34 Reeves, *Wolfe's Albatross,* p. 23; TW to Kimball Flaccus, Dec. 5, 1935, Pack Mem. Lib.

355/40 OTATR, pp. 419–420, 440, 447, 458, 465, 468. See Howard H. Ribalow, "Of Jews and Thomas Wolfe," *Chicago Jewish Forum* 13 (1954): 89–99; Leon Spitz, "Was Wolfe an Anti-Semite?" *American Hebrew* 158 (Nov. 19, 1948): 5; and Reeves, *Wolfe's Albatross,* ch. 3.

356/18 Pearl to Charles Scribner's Sons, April 17, 1935, Charles Scribner's Sons Archive; Calo to TW, [1935], Wisdom; Hebert Shapiro to TW, Nov. 15, 1936, Fan Mail File, Wisdom; Anon. to TW, Jan. 16, 1937, Wisdom.

356/29 TW to Calo, July 10, 1935, Wisdom; MEP to Simon Pearl, April 20, 1935, Charles Scribner's Sons Archive.

357/5 For examples of TW's early anti-Semitic utterances, see PN, I: 21–23.

357/19 For instance, after a long, amiable association with "Captain" Louis Cohn, founder of the House of Books in Manhattan, Wolfe began to suspect that Cohn was making a profit by selling copies of his novels that he had autographed for him personally. Drunk, he visited the Cohns and berated them in a scurrilous anti-Semitic diatribe. Interview with Mrs. Marguerite Cohn, Jan 21, 1982.

357/35 Reeves, *Wolfe's Albatross,* pp. 83–84.

358/4 *Partisan Review* 2 (April–May 1935): 89. This was followed shortly by Joseph Freeman's attack, "Mask, Image, and Truth," ibid., 2 (July–Aug. 1935): 3–17.

358/8 Walser, *Enigma,* p. 310. Later Burgum offered a much more positive appraisal in "Thomas Wolfe's Discovery of America," *Virginia Quarterly Review* 22 (1946): 421–437.

358/24 May Cameron, *Press Time,* p. 252; TW, undated manuscript fragments, Wisdom, Nos. 301 and 1316.

358/31 Joseph North, ed., *New Masses: An Anthology of the Rebel Thirties* (New York: International Publishers, 1969), pp. 211–214.

358/36 *Modern Monthly* 9 (June 1935): 249–250. On Calverton see Daniel Aaron, *Writers on the Left* (New York: Harcourt, Brace & World, 1961), pp. 322–333.

359/10 Calverton to TW, April 8, 1936, Wisdom; Joyce Maupin, unpublished recollections of TW; TW, typescript for address to Modern Monthly dinner [1936], Wisdom, No. 1195; EN to Richard Kennedy, July 4, 1950, Nowell MSS.

359/22 I have found the following studies of the Fugitives and the Agrarians particularly helpful: John L. Stewart, *The Burden of Time: The Fugitives and the Agrarians* (Princeton: Princeton University Press, 1965); Thomas Daniel Young, *Gentleman in a Dustcoat: A Biography of John Crowe Ransom* (Baton Rouge: Louisiana State University Press, 1976); Louis D. Rubin, Jr., *The Wary Fugitives: Four Poets and the South* (Baton Rouge: Louisiana State University Press, 1978); and Virginia J. Rock, "They Took Their Stand: The Emergence of the Southern Agrarians," *Prospects* 1 (1975): 205–295.

359/24 On TW and the Agrarians I have relied heavily on Floyd C. Watkins, "Thomas Wolfe and the Nashville Agrarians," *Georgia Review* 7 (Winter 1953): 410–423; John Daniel Walther, "The Springs of Conflict: Reaction and Resolution in the Fiction of Thomas Wolfe" (unpublished Ph.D. dissertation, Vanderbilt University, 1971), pp. 148–188; and, especially, Thomas A. Underwood's excellent paper, "Thomas Wolfe and the Vanderbilt Agrarians: Catharsis and Control in the Southern Literary Renaissance," prepared for my seminar at Harvard in 1984.

360/33 Sally Wood, ed., *The Southern Mandarins: Letters of Caroline Gordon to Sally Wood, 1924–1937* (Baton Rouge: Louisiana State University Press, 1984), pp. 204–205; interview with Robert Penn Warren, April 27, 1983; Cleanth Brooks to Thomas A. Underwood, April 21, 1984; PN, II: 861.

360/37 *Letters,* p. 615.

361/2 Wood, *Southern Mandarins,* p. 205.

361/13 John Pilkington, ed., *Stark Young: A Life in the Arts* (Baton Rouge: Louisiana State University Press, 1975), 2:1216; Cleanth Brooks to Thomas A. Underwood, April 21, 1984; *Nashville Tennessean,* Feb. 16, 1930.

361/25 Quoted in Walser, *Enigma,* p. 128.

361/33 Wade, "Prodigal," *Southern Review* 1 (July 1935): 198.

361/39 Ibid. 1 (Spring 1936): 898–899.

362/3 Bishop, "The Sorrows of Thomas Wolfe," *Kenyon Review* 1 (Winter 1939): 9. Bishop had made up his mind about OTATR before he read it. Thomas Daniel Young and John J. Hindle, eds., *The Republic of Letters in America* (Lexington: University Press of Kentucky, 1981), p. 145.

362/6 Caroline Gordon, "Rooted in Adolescence," *New York Times Book Re-*

view, Mar. 7, 1948, pp. 10–12; Watkins, "Thomas Wolfe and the Nashville Agrarians," p. 412.

362/16 Van Wyck Brooks, *Days of the Phoenix* (New York: E. P. Dutton & Co., 1957), pp. 124–125; PN, II: 836.

362/25 TWATR, pp. 242–243.

363/16 JST, untitled reminiscences, Terry MSS.

363/23 TW to Ralph Lum, Feb. 1, 1938, Wisdom.

364/4 JEW to FW, Jan. 22, 1936, Fred Wolfe MSS.

364/24 Turnbull, pp. 231–232.

365/7 All these letters (written in 1935–1936) are in the Wisdom Collection. ("Amanda" is a fictitious name, for reasons of privacy.)

366/2 AB to MEP, Jan. 21, Mar. 18, and April 10, 1936, Gitlin MSS.

366/5 TW to Vardis Fisher, July 17, 1935, Wisdom.

366/9 For a list see Aldo P. Magi, "Thomas Wolfe: A Publishing Chronology," *TW Review* 7 (Fall 1983): 17; EN, "Dates in Wolfe's Life," Nowell MSS.

366/32 EN to MWW, Sept. 25, 1952, Nowell MSS.; EN, "Dates in Wolfe's Life," ibid. Wolfe used condoms when having intercourse with prostitutes, but his purpose was to prevent disease, not pregnancy.

367/16 BLAL, pp. 33–38.

367/23 In addition to sources specifically cited below, my account of Wolfe's quarrel with Dooher is based on my interview with Muredach J. Dooher, Mar. 28, 1984; on TW's " Statement" [answers to interrogatories posed by his attorney, William Morrison], June 26, 1936, Nowell MSS.; on MEP to Claude Simpson, Jr., Aug. 13, 1940, Charles Scribner's Sons Archive; and on the voluminous correspondence between Wolfe and his lawyers in Wisdom, Nos. 238–239 and 450–451. Mr. Jerald E. Podair has generously supplied me a copy of the file of the New Jersey Superior Court (formerly the Chancery Court) in the case of Wolfe vs. Dooher (Docket 115, page 304).

367/34 Both Terry and Wolfe commented on Dooher's eyes. JST to TW, May 23, 1935, Wisdom; and TW to Ralph Lum, Jan. 28, 1938, Wisdom.

369/17 TW to [Charles Scribner's Sons], Jan. 13 and 21, 1936, Wisdom; and Jan. 17, 1936, Barrett Coll.

369/40 MEP to JST, Jan. 3, 1946, Wisdom.

370/34 TW to Ralph Lum, Dec. 29, 1937, and Feb. 1, 1938, Wisdom; MEP to Cornelius Mitchell, Mar. 16, 1936, Charles Scribner's Sons Archive; TW to FW, July 16, 1936, Braden-Hatchett Thomas Wolfe Coll.

371/23 *New York Times,* Feb. 9, 1938, p. 21; TW to W. N. Cox, Feb. 9, 1938, copy, Pack Mem. Lib.

371/31 TW to Ralph Lum, Dec. 29, 1937, Wisdom.

372/17 Berg, p. 287; Louis Perkins to TW, [1935], Wisdom.

372/36 MEP to JST, Nov. 13, 1945, Wisdom.

373/17 Helen Howard Gude to Oscar Cargill, Dec. 31, 1952, Fales Lib., NYU. In fact, Wolfe had had a bank account — which was usually overdrawn — when he was attending Harvard.

373/30 Draft of telegram, TW, "Hound of Darkness Ledger," Wisdom, No. 737; MEP to John Hall Wheelock, Dec. 14, 1935, Charles Scribner's Sons Archive.

374/5 Statement from Charles Scribner's Sons to TW, Sept. 25, 1935, Wisdom.

374/11 *Letters,* pp. 505–506; John Hall Wheelock, ed., *Editor to Author* (New York: Charles Scribner's Sons, 1950), pp. 111–112.

374/24 For Wolfe's deterioriating relations with Mrs. Perkins, see PN, II: 959; Berg, p. 291; EN, "Dates in Wolfe's Life," Nowell MSS; and Anne W. Armstrong to JST, Nov. 12, 1943, Terry MSS.

375/8 *Letters,* pp. 505–507.

375/21 MEP to JST, Oct. 29, 1945, Wisdom.

375/33 Unless otherwise identified, all quotations in the following paragraphs are from Bernard DeVoto, "Genius Is Not Enough," *Saturday Review of Literature* 13 (April 25, 1936): 3–4, 14–15.

376/32 *Saturday Review of Literature* 11 (April 27, 1935): 1, 5.

376/34 DeVoto never met Wolfe. Interview with Mrs. Bernard DeVoto, Oct. 19, 1981. Though DeVoto denied that he was carrying on a feud with Wolfe (Wallace Stegner, ed., *The Letters of Bernard DeVoto* [Garden City: Doubleday & Co., 1975], pp. 250–254), he continued to attack Wolfe's novels — e.g., in the *Saturday Review of Literature* on October 24, 1936 (p. 5), August 21, 1937 (pp. 8, 14), and August 26, 1939 (p. 4), and in the *Atlantic Monthly,* January 1940 (pp. 69–71).

377/9 MEP to JST, Nov. 13, 1945, Wisdom.

377/25 *Letters,* pp. 528, 511; TW to Kent Roberts Greenfield, June 23, 1935, Wisdom; ECA to FW, Jan. 3. 1940, Fred Wolfe MSS.

378/3 *Letters,* pp. 556, 576–577.

378/10 *Letters,* p. 502.

378/20 *Letters,* pp. 534, 496.

378/34 *Letters,* p. 526.

378/36 *Letters,* p. 534.

379/12 Nowell, p. 300.

379/18 TW to LeGette Blythe, May 18, 1936, Wisdom.

379/31 *Letters,* p. 527; Kennedy, pp. 305–306.

380/18 TW, "An Introduction By A Friend," pp. 37, 40, Wisdom, No. 990.

380/28 *Letters,* p. 518.

381/21 Nowell, p. 321.

381/31 Turnbull, p. 233.

382/24 Nowell, p. 322; MEP to JST, Nov. 9, 1945 and Dec. 18, 1945, Wisdom.

382/39 Nowell, p. 322.

383/15 *Letters,* p. 538.

383/24 Nowell, p. 323.

Chapter XII: *Unmistakable and Grievous Severance*

384/8 SOAN, p. 237.

385/9 H. M. Ledig-Rowohlt, "Thomas Wolfe in Berlin," *American Scholar* 22 (Spring 1953): 193–194; interview with H. M. Ledig-Rowohlt, Mar. 31, 1984.

385/25 William W. Pusey III, "The German Vogue of Thomas Wolfe," *Germanic Review* 23 (April 1948): 146; Lawrence Marsden Price, *The Recep-*

tion of United States Literature in Germany (Chapel Hill: University of North Carolina Press, 1966), p. 151; *Berliner Tageblatt,* April 19, 1936; *Kölnische Zeitung,* April 26, 1936; *Magdeburgische Zeitung,* April 19, 1936.

385/33 "Wir sprachen Thomas Wolfe," *Berliner Tageblatt,* Aug. 5, 1936.

386/11 Ledig-Rowohlt, "Thomas Wolfe in Berlin," pp. 195–196; Ledig-Rowohlt to Marjorie C. Fairbanks, Aug. 12, 1952, Fairbanks MSS.

386/32 YCGHA, p. 626, Turnbull, p. 234; Martha Dodd, *Through Embassy Eyes* (New York: Harcourt, Brace & Co., 1939) p. 212.

387/15 PN, II: 840; YCGHA, pp. 627–628; *Letters,* p. 552.

388/4 PN, II: 829, 831; YCGHA, p. 631.

388/21 Royalty statement of Rowohlt Verlag to Thomas Wolfe, Jan. 30, 1937, Wisdom, No. 1324; PN, II: 834–835, 839–840.

388/32 Janice Warnke, "Thomas Wolfe Entertains Alpbach," MS., Fales Lib., NYU.

389/15 Thea Voelcker to TW, Nov. 14, 1936, Wisdom; Thea Voelcker to MEP, Sept. 25, 1938, Charles Scribner's Sons Archive.

389/24 EN to Alfred Dashiell, Dec. 19, 1956, Dashiell MSS., Princeton; *Letters,* p. 540.

389/28 H. M. Ledig-Rowohlt to Marjorie C. Fairbanks, Aug. 12, 1952, Fairbanks MSS.

390/14 PN, II: 835. "I Have a Thing to Tell You" appeared in three installments in the *New Republic* of March 10, 17, and 24, 1937.

390/21 *Letters,* p. 541; *New Republic* 90 (Mar. 24, 1937): 207.

390/27 *Letters,* p. 545.

390/41 TW to Olin Dows, Nov. 28, 1936, Wisdom.

391/12 PN, II: 841.

391/34 Marcia Davenport, *Too Strong for Fantasy* (New York: Avon Books, 1979), pp. 224–226.

391/41 MEP to EN, Aug. 26, 1936, Charles Scribner's Sons Archive.

392/11 Nowell, pp. 338–339.

392/17 *Letters,* p. 543.

392/20 On the Dorman suit, see, in addition to the sources specifically cited in the following notes, TW's rejoinder in the case of Marjorie Dorman *et al.,* Wisdom, No. 1323; TW's "Statement" to his lawyers, Dec. 7, 1936, Wisdom, No. 1323; MEP to JST, Nov. 1945, Wisdom; and TW to Emil Goldmark, Mar. 10, 1937, Wisdom.

392/24 Marjorie Dorman to Charles Scribner's Sons, May 11, 1935, Charles Scribner's Sons Archive.

393/12 MEP to JST, Nov. 1945, Wisdom.

393/18 For advice on these legal matters, I am indebted to Mr. James A. Sharaf, Office of the General Counsel, Harvard University.

393/35 For TW's very slightly fictionalized account of this interview, see "Justice Is Blind," in Walser, *Enigma,* p. 97; *Letters,* p. 589.

394/15 MEP to Claude Simpson, Aug. 13, 1940, Charles Scribner's Sons Archive.

394/32 *Letters,* p. 559.

395/7 John Hall Wheelock, ed., *Editor to Author: The Letters of Maxwell E. Perkins* (New York: Charles Scribner's Sons, 1950), pp. 115–117.

395/18 *Letters,* pp. 598–603.

395/24 All quotations in the following paragraphs are from *Letters,* pp. 575–596.

398/7 LTHM, p. 269.

398/32 *Letters,* p. 587.

398/34 In the following pages I have relied heavily on Elizabeth Evans's excellent essay, "Thomas Wolfe's 1937 Visits South: You Can Go Home Again," *TW Review* 8 (Fall 1984): 36–48.

399/8 My account of Wolfe's stay in New Orleans is based principally on William Wisdom, "The Table Talk of Thomas Wolfe," Wisdom, Nos. 1347–1348, and on William H. Fitzpatrick's letter to Andrew Turnbull, Feb. 18, 1963, copy, Theobald Collection.

400/14 Thomas Sancton, "Time and the River," *New Orleans Item,* Oct. 26, 1950; *Letters,* p. 571.

400/30 *Letters,* p. 574.

401/14 Wisdom, "The Table Talk of Thomas Wolfe."

401/26 *Atlanta Sunday American,* Jan. 17, 1937; *Atlanta Constitution,* Jan 17, 1937; Garland B. Porter to EN, July 7, 1957, Nowell MSS.

401/33 FW to JEW, Jan. 18, 1937, Fred Wolfe MSS., UNC.

402/3 TW to Bill Dowd, Feb. 1, 1937, Wisdom.

402/28 George Stoney, "Eugene Returns to Pulpit Hill," *The Carolina Magazine* 48 (Oct. 1938): 11–14.

402/35 H. G. Jones, ed., *Thomas Wolfe of North Carolina,* p. 53.

402/23 Interview with Albert and Gladys Coates, June 21, 1980; Albert Coates, *Tom Wolfe As I Remember Him,* offprint from University of North Carolina *Alumni Review,* Nov. 1975.

404/1 Berg, p. 321.

404/10 For Perkins's three letters, see Wheelock, *Editor to Author* (pp. 119–126), which, however, omits the reference to Mrs. Bernstein.

406/14 MEP to Claude Simpson, Aug. 13, 1940, Charles Scribner's Sons Archive.

406/20 TW to Charles Scribner, Jan. 21, 1938, Wisdom.

406/27 Cane, "Thomas Wolfe: A Memoir," *American Scholar* 41 (Autumn 1972): 640–641. For the correct dates of these encounters see TW's bill from Ernst, Cane & Berner, April 19, 1937, Wisdom.

406/31 Receipt signed by Marjorie Dorman *et al.,* Mar. 29, 1937, Wisdom, No. 1324.

406/34 Wheelock to EN, May 10, 1951, Nowell MSS.

407/4 JST to Mabel and Ralph Wheaton, June 4, 1949, Fred Wolfe MSS., UNC.

407/16 Charles Scribner to TW, Feb. 18, 1937, Wisdom.

407/35 For the nature and extent of Miss Nowell's assistance to Wolfe, see EN to MEP, April 1, 1947, MS., office of Paul Gitlin; Richard S. Kennedy's essay, "Thomas Wolfe and Elizabeth Nowell: A Unique Relationship"; Benjamin Appel, "Elizabeth Nowell and Thomas Wolfe," *Carleton Miscellany* 8 (Winter 1967): 70–79; and Elizabeth Evans, "Elizabeth Nowell: Thomas Wolfe's Agent and Friend," *TW Newsletter* 4 (Spring 1980): 32–38.

408/26 EN, "Dates in Wolfe's Life," Nowell MSS.

408/33 On the editing of "Mr. Malone," see BLAL, pp. 58–59, and Katherine S. White in *New York Times Book Review,* Feb. 5, 1961, p. 44.

409/11 The edited typescript of "The Lost Boy" is in Wisdom, No. 1031.

409/17 For a comparison of the actual persons and events in the Harris affair with Wolfe's fictional recreation, see Floyd C. Watkins, *Thomas Wolfe's Characters* (Norman: University of Oklahoma Press, 1957), pp. 102–109.

409/31 On the evolution of "The Child by Tiger," see Kennedy, pp. 315–319; PN, II: 518, 851–852; and EN to MEP, April 1, 1947, Gitlin MSS.

410/16 BLAL, pp. 56, 72, 74.

410/27 LTHM, p. 270; TW to Esther Owens, Feb. 17, 1937, Barrett Coll.; Richard J. Calhoun and Robert W. Hill, " 'Tom, Are you Listening'— An Interview with Fred Wolfe," *South Carolina Review* 6 (April 1974): 41; Nowell, p. 378.

411/4 *New Republic* 90 (Mar. 24, 1937): 207.

411/10 Turnbull, p. 267; Calhoun and Hill, " 'Tom Are You Listening,' " p. 41.

411/19 Last Will and Testament of Thomas Wolfe, April 17, 1937, office of Paul Gitlin.

411/24 LTHM, pp. 278–279.

412/19 Nowell, p. 375.

412/30 *Letters,* p. 611.

413/21 MEP to JST, Nov. 13, 1945, Wisdom; Jonathan Daniels, *Thomas Wolfe: October Recollections* (Columbia, S.C.: Bostick & Thornley, 1961), pp. 18–19; Harrison Smith to EN, June 25, 1958, Nowell MSS.

413/27 *Letters,* p. 616.

414/24 John S. Phillipson, "Thomas Wolfe's 'Chickamauga': The Fact and the Fiction," *TW Review* 6 (Fall 1982): 9–22. On dialect, see TW to Helen McAfee, fourth page of an incomplete, undated letter [1938], Wisdom, No. 213; *Letters,* p. 625.

414/26 On Wolfe's Asheville visits, see George W. McCoy, *Asheville and Thomas Wolfe* (reprint from *North Carolina Historical Review,* April 1953); Betty Lynch Williams, *Asheville and Thomas Wolfe: A Study in Changing Attitudes* (1975), pp. 29–32; and Evans, "Thomas Wolfe's 1937 Visits South."

414/38 TW, draft of remarks before the American Business Club of Asheville, [May 1937], Wisdom, No. 1198.

415/8 *Asheville Times,* May 4, 1937.

415/25 TW to LeGette Blythe, May 20, 1937, Wisdom; TW to Esther Owens, May 25, 1937, Barrett Coll.; TW to Mrs. Robert F. Armstrong, May 20, 1937, Wisdom.

416/2 TWAHF, pp. 241–243; FW to JST, Jan. 13, 1952, Terry MSS.; Fred Wolfe, interview with William Hatchett, Aug. 5, 1977, Braden-Hatchett Thomas Wolfe Coll. On the rather pointless controversy over whether either man was drinking on this occasion, see Hamilton Basso in *New York Times Book Review,* Jan. 22, 1961, p. 6, and Fred Wolfe's reply, ibid., Mar. 5, 1961, p. 42.

416/15 Fitzgerald to TW, [July 19], 1937, Wisdom, published in Andrew Turnbull, ed. *The Letters of F. Scott Fitzgerald* (New York: Charles Scribner's Sons, 1963), p. 552.

417/7 *Letters,* p. 641–646.

417/27 *Letters,* p. 645, 623; interview with Virginia Chapman Gaillard, June 19, 1982.

418/5 Interview with Edward Gambrell, June 1982; letters from Dr. R. Dietz Wolfe, Aug. 7 and Oct. 28, 1980.

418/13 JEW, "Eliza Gant Talks," transcription by Ruth Davis of recordings that JST made of interviews with JEW, Terry MSS.

418/26 Turnbull, p. 280.

418/40 Interview with Francis Hulme, June 19, 1982.

419/21 *Letters,* pp. 647, 631.

419/35 BLAL, p. 75.

420/29 Interview with Virginia Chapman Gaillard, June 19, 1982.

420/40 *Letters,* p. 19.

421/5 Asheville police envelope, for repository of arrested person's possessions, dated Aug. 18, 1937, Wisdom, No. 1323.

421/13 *Greensboro Daily News,* Aug ?, 1964; LTHM, p. 288.

421/22 Stoney, "Eugene Returns to Pulpit Hill," p. 12.

Chapter XIII: *A New World Is Before Me Now*

422/18 ECA, "Thomas Wolfe Did not Kill Maxwell Perkins," *Saturday Review of Literature* 34 (Oct. 6, 1951): 44. Elizabeth Nowell claimed that Wolfe's decision to seek a new publisher was precipitated by reading a further attack by Bernard DeVoto, "English '37: The Novelist and the Reader," published in *Saturday Review of Literature* on August 21, 1937. (Nowell, p. 392). She admits, however, there is no record of how or when Wolfe saw this essay, and nothing in his letters indicates that he was in any way affected by it.

423/4 [Blanche Knopf] to ECA, Mar. 16, 1949, Alfred A. Knopf MSS., Harry Ransom Humanities Research Center, University of Texas, Austin, copy provided through the courtesy of Susan Sheehan; Bernard Smith to TW, Sept. 20, 1937, Wisdom; EN's note on TW to Robert N. Linscott, Oct. 16, 1937, in her typescript of Thomas Wolfe Letters, Houghton. Some years later Alfred Knopf censured Wolfe for deserting Scribners, declared that his firm "refused under any circumstances" to publish him, and felt "it would have reflected great credit on my colleagues had they all sent Wolfe back on his knees to Scribner's." Alfred A. Knopf to Struthers Burt, June 11, 1951, Knopf MSS.

423/11 Berg, p. 333.

423/26 MEP to FW, Nov. 1, 1937, Charles Scribner's Sons Archive; MEP to AB, Oct. 14, 1937, Gitlin MSS.

423/30 *Letters,* pp. 662–663.

424/3 Linscott to TW, Oct. 8, 1937, Wisdom.

424/12 TW to Linscott, Oct. 16, 1937, Barrett Coll.

424/29 Statement by Linscott, Nov. 8, 1949, Nowell MSS.

425/16 EN, "Dates in Wolfe's Life," Nowell MSS.

425/29 Linscott to TW, Oct. 22, 1937, Wisdom; *Letters,* p. 661.

425/35 EN, "Dates in Wolfe's Life," Nowell MSS.

426/11 TW to Mrs. C. S. Bates, Nov. 30, 1937, Wisdom.

426/22 *Letters,* p. 683; EN, "Dates in Wolfe's Life," Nowell MSS.

426/36 Kennedy, pp. 381–382; TW, "To The Reader," Wisdom, No. 790.

427/6 Nowell, p. 399.

427/20 ECA, "Thomas Wolfe Did Not Kill Maxwell Perkins," p. 45.

427/31 Harvard College, Class of 1926, *The Quindecennial Report* (Cambridge, 1941), p. 12.

428/28 ECA, "Thomas Wolfe Did Not Kill Maxwell Perkins," pp. 44–46; EN, "Dates in Wolfe's Life," Nowell MSS.

428/34 *Letters,* p. 686.

429/8 Turnbull, pp. 285–286.

429/12 *Letters,* p. 686.

429/17 PN, II: 878.

429/24 Linscott to TW, Dec. 1, 1937; EN to Linscott, Oct. 30, 1949, Nowell MSS.

429/37 *Letters,* p. 688; BLAL, p. 89; Turnbull, p. 290.

430/16 Mrs. Sherwood Anderson to William A. Jackson, Jan. 11, 1949, copy, Nowell MSS.; Anderson's diary quoted in Amy Nyholm to EN, Feb. 10, 1950, ibid.

430/33 *Letters,* p. 689.

431/7 Howard Mumford Jones, ed., *Letters of Sherwood Anderson* (Boston: Little, Brown & Co., 1953), pp 401–402; *Letters,* pp. 686–687, 690; TW to Hamilton Basso, undated draft [1938], Wisdom.

431/13 Anderson to TW, Dec. 17 and Dec. 18, 1937, Wisdom, published in Jones, ed., *Letters of Sherwood Anderson,* pp. 393–394.

431/22 *Letters,* pp. 688–690.

432/2 TW to Linscott, Dec. 20, 1937, Barrett Coll.; EN to ECA, Oct. 9, 1951, Nowell MSS.: TW to EN, Dec. 29, 1937, Wisdom.

432/13 *Letters,* pp. 656, 695; LTHM, pp. 283–284.

432/19 *Letters,* pp. 688, 692, 697.

432/28 EN to Mina Curtiss, Oct. 12, 1949, Nowell MSS.

433/3 EN, "Dates in Wolfe's Life," Nowell MSS.; Earl Hamner, ed., "Thomas Wolfe: A Biography in Sound," *Carolina Quarterly* 9 (Fall 1956): 14–15.

433/17 Turnbull, p. 287; *Letters,* p. 696.

433/29 *Letters,* p. 698.

434/6 TW to Melville Cane, Jan. 22, 1938, Wisdom; TW to Margaret Roberts, Feb. 14, 1938, Wisdom.

434/25 Ella Winter to EN, May 4, 1949, Nowell MSS.

434/38 *Letters,* pp. 711–712, 686.

435/8 Ella Winter to EN, May 1947, Nowell MSS.; Ella Winter, *And Not To Yield* (New York: Harcourt Brace & World, 1963), p. 176: TW, "The Company," *New Masses,* Jan. 11, 1938, pp. 33–38.

435/26 *Letters,* p. 738; Kennedy, p. 366.

435/30 Interview with Henry Hart, June 18, 1984. See Harvey Klehr, *The Hey-*

day of American Communism: The Depression Decade (New York: Basic Books, 1984), ch. 18.

435/36 Solon, "The Ordeal of Thomas Wolfe," *Modern Quarterly* 11 (Winter 1939): 50–51.

436/9 AOAAN, pp. 135–136.

436/18 AOAAN, p. 143; TW, handwritten draft for "The Company," Wisdom, No. 931.

436/29 TW, fragmentary diary entry, [June 17, 1938], Wolfe MSS., Harry Ransom Humanities Research Center, University of Texas, Austin.

436/39 Quotations in this and the following paragraphs are from TW, undated [1937–1938] manuscript fragments on politics, and an untitled manuscript on fascism, Wisdom, Nos. 1210, 1214.

438/36 Letters, pp. 708, 730, 739, 762.

439/9 Letters, p. 733.

439/24 PN, II: 929–937.

440/16 PN, II: 941–943. Cf. *Letters*, p. 745; PN, II: 424–425.

440/31 Letters, pp. 712, 714–715, 719; PN, II: 954.

441/17 TW to Margaret Roberts, Mar. 7, 1938, Wisdom; *Letters*, p. 739 (italics added).

441/28 Letters, p. 730.

441/37 For an expurgated version of the passage to which she objected, see HB, p. 225.

442/26 Interview with Mrs. Peter Campbell, June 4, 1984; Mrs. Campbell to William Braswell, May 16, 1962, copy provided through the courtesy of Leslie Field.

442/37 Letters, p. 694.

443/5 MEP to TW, Dec. 29, 1937, Wisdom; MEP to Hamilton Basso, Jan. 3, 1938, Charles Scribner's Sons Archive.

443/24 Belinda Jelliffe, "Recollections," Nowell MSS.; *New York Times*, Feb. 9, 1938; MEP to Claude Simpson, Aug. 13, 1940, Charles Scribner's Sons Archive.

443/36 DeVoto, in *Saturday Review of Literature* 17 (Feb. 26, 1938): 19.

444/12 AB to Bella Spewack, [Feb. 1938], copy provided by Carole Klein. Cf. Mina Curtiss, "Wolfe among the Monstres Sacres," *Nation* 206 (April 1, 1968): 446–448.

444/25 Masters to MWW, Nov. 26, 1938, Wolfe Coll, UNC. One of Wolfe's last manuscripts, scribbled on both sides of his hotel bill at Empress Hotel, Victoria, B.C., July 5, 1938, dealt with Masters (Wisdom). ECA read the name Wolfe gave him as "Bastard," but I think it is clearly "Bustard."

445/2 Laurence Bergreen, *James Agee: A Life* (New York: E. P. Dutton, 1984), p. 74; EN, "Dates in Wolfe's Life," Nowell MSS.

445/9 Interview with David Gambrell, June, 1982; TW to FW, Jan. 22, 1938, Braden-Hatchett Thomas Wolfe Coll.

445/24 Interview with Mrs. H. Whitman Wilder, Feb. 25, 1982; LTHM, pp. 286–287.

445/32 TW to Ruder, May 12, 1938, Barrett Coll.

446/15 ECA to EN, Oct. 2, 1951, Nowell MSS.; ECA, "Love As Art and Vice Versa," Gitlin MSS.

446/20 TW to Arthur Mann, April 23, 1938, in Charles Hamilton Auction *Catalogue*, No. 39 (Jan. 29, 1970), p. 65.

446/32 TW to Ruder, May 12, 1938, Barrett Coll.

447/3 TW, notes for a lecture [1938], Alexander Wainwright Coll.; *Letters*, p. 750.

447/16 *Letters*, p. 751.

447/30 Mrs. Peter Campbell to William Braswell, May 16, 1962, copy provided through the courtesy of Leslie Field; *Letters*, p. 751; interview with Mrs. Peter Campbell, June 4, 1984; George Stoney, Recollections of TW, delivered at the Thomas Wolfe Society, New York, May 20, 1983. This outline, which is in Wisdom No. 1336, was published with elaborate annotation in Kennedy, pp. 415–437. The allegation of Patrick Miehe that Aswell, and not Wolfe, drew up this outline ("The Outline of Thomas Wolfe's Last Book," *Harvard Library Bulletin* 21 [Oct. 1973]: 400–401) is refuted by EN's letter to TW, May 27, 1938, BLAL, p. 112. See also Richard S. Kennedy, "Thomas Wolfe's Last Manuscript," *Harvard Library Bulletin* 23 (April 1975): 203–211.

448/19 *Letters*, pp. 764–766, 759; TW to Margaret Roberts, Mar. 7, 1938, Wisdom; LTHM, p. 290.

449/11 ECA, "Publicity Release on Wolfe," June 8, 1939, Nowell MSS.

449/21 *Letters*, p. 765; TW, fragmentary journal, May 18, 1938, Wolfe MSS., Harry Ransom Humanities Research Center, University of Texas, Austin.

450/9 AOAAN, pp. 132, 142–145. I have put the peroration in verse form to emphasize the similarity to Sandburg's poetry.

450/39 William Braswell, "Thomas Wolfe Lectures and Takes a Holiday," *College English* 1 (Oct. 1939): 11–13.

451/8 Braswell, pp. 15–21; *Letters*, p. 766.

451/25 *Letters*, pp. 767–768; TW, fragmentary journal, Wolfe MSS., Harry Ransom Humanities Research Center, University of Texas, Austin.

452/10 V. L. O. Chittick, "Tom Wolfe's Farthest West," *Southwest Review* 48 (1963): 93; BLAL, pp. 118–120.

452/20 The following paragraphs on Miller, Conway, and the trip through the national parks is based on Chittick, pp. 94–98; JST to Josephine D. Terry, Aug. 6, 1940, Terry MSS.; Conway to Miller, April 21, 1958, Nowell MSS.; Miller to EN, July 3, 1950, and Jan. 18, 1958, ibid.; Brian F. Berger, *Thomas Wolfe: The Final Journey* (West Linn, Ore.: Willamette River Press, 1984); and "The Final Journey" (1968), a cassette containing the recorded reminiscences of Conway and Miller, in the Braden-Hatchett Thomas Wolfe Collection.

452/33 *Letters*, p. 769.

453/17 Except where otherwise identified, all quotations in the following paragraphs are from WJ.

453/39 *Letters*, pp. 774–775.

454/12 *Letters*, pp. 774, 776.

454/24 *Letters*, pp. 774–775; James Stevens's recollections on the cassette "The Final Journey" (1968).

455/9 Chittick, pp. 98–99.

455/24 LTHM, p. 296.

455/28 The following paragraphs on the early weeks of Wolfe's illness draw heavily on Chittick's very full account (pp. 99–101), on James F. Stevens to EN, Jan. 30, 1958, Nowell MSS., and on Dr. Edward C. Ruge to FW, July 18, 1938, Wolfe Coll., UNC.

456/24 *Letters*, p. 776.

456/40 Ruge to FW, July 13, 1938, Wolfe Coll., UNC; JST to Josephine Terry, Aug. 8, 1940, Terry MSS.

457/10 Chittick, pp. 103–105; ECA to EN, April 23, 1958, Nowell MSS.; ECA to Henry M. Hart, July 14, Aug. 24 and 26, 1938, Wisdom.

457/33 JST to Josephine D. Terry, Aug. 8, 1940, Terry MSS.; Chittick, p. 104; FW to MWW, Aug. 15, 1938, Wisdom.

458/4 Charles E. Watt to Russel V. Lee, Sept. 5, 1938, Thomas Wolfe Medical Records at the Johns Hopkins Hospital, in Fairbanks MSS.

458/7 FW to MWW, Aug. 12, 1938, Wisdom.

458/28 TW to MEP, Aug. 12, 1938, Wisdom. On the circumstances in which Wolfe's final letter was written, see FW to JEW, May 23, 1939, Braden-Hatchett Thomas Wolfe Coll.

459/13 Mabel Wolfe Wheaton gave at least three versions of her brother's final weeks: a series of recordings made by the Library of Congress, Feb. 23, 1947 (copies in Wisdom); tape-recordings rather inaccurately transcribed in Lou Harshaw, *Asheville: Places of Discovery* (Lakemont, Ga.: Copple House Books, 1980), pp. 117–147; and *Thomas Wolfe and His Family* (Garden City, NY: Doubleday & Co., 1961), which she wrote with the collaboration of LeGette Blythe. What is most remarkable is that the three versions, made at very different times and in different circumstances, are virtually identical. Since Mrs. Wheaton's book is most easily available to readers, quotations in the following pages are from that source.

459/39 On Miss Crawford and her role, see Annie Laurie Crawford to EN, Feb. 1, 1958, Nowell MSS.; Elizabeth Evans, "Wolfe's Final Days: The Correspondence of Elizabeth Nowell and Annie Laurie Crawford," *TW Newsletter* 4 (Fall 1980): 1–14; and Elizabeth Evans's interviews with Miss Crawford, 1975, copies of which Professor Evans graciously lent me.

460/12 Watt to Russel V. Lee, Sept. 5, 1938, Wolfe Medical Records.

460/15 J. DeWitt Fox, "Walter Dandy — Super-Surgeon," *Henry Ford Hospital Medical Journal* 25 (1977): 149–170; William Lloyd Fox, *Dandy of John Hopkins* (Baltimore: Williams and Wilkins, 1984).

460/32 TWAHF, p. 287.

460/39 George W. Swift to FW, Nov. 4, 1938, Fred Wolfe MSS.

461/19 TWAHF, p. 293; Stewart Johnson, "Mrs. Julia Wolfe," *New Yorker* 34 (April 12, 1958): 41.

461/30 TWAHF, p. 295–296.

462/2 Reports on preliminary examinations by Drs. George Berkheimer and William Gray Watson, Sept. 10, 1938, Wolfe Medical Records.

462/12 TWAHF, p. 298.

462/26 Dr. Watson's postoperative notes, Sept. 10, 1938, Wolfe Medical Records; TWAHF, p. 301.

463/8 Postoperative notes of Drs. Dandy and Watson, Sept. 12, 1938, Wolfe Medical Records. Dr. Dandy's operative notes, Sept. 10 and 12, 1938, were enclosed in William M. Shelley to Michael L. Furcolow, Mar. 11, 1970, a copy of which Dr. R. Dietz Wolfe had kindly supplied me. There has been some controversy about the nature of Wolfe's final illness and the cause of his death, largely because most of his medical records were removed from the Johns Hopkins Hospital at the instigation of Mrs. Marjorie Fairbanks, who hoped to prepare a biography of Wolfe. The unwillingness of the Wolfe family to allow an autopsy also contributed to the uncertainty. In consequence the theory was suggested that Wolfe did not have tubercular meningitis but instead contracted desert fever (coccidiodomycosis) on his drive across the Mojave Desert. See James Meehan, "How Did Thomas Wolfe Die?" *The State*, Sept. 1973, pp. 18–20, 30; and Meehan, "Seeds of Destruction: The Death of Thomas Wolfe, *South Atlantic Quarterly* 73 (Spring 1974): 173–183. But Wolfe's medical records at the Johns Hopkins Hospital were preserved in Mrs. Fairbanks's papers, recently given to the Houghton Library, and I was fortunate enough to discover them. Dr. Gustave J. Dammin and Dr. Curtis Prout, both of the Harvard Medical School, have generously taken the time to examine these records and other medical evidence about Wolfe's final illness. Pointing out that coccidiodomycosis produces some characteristic changes in the blood, sputum, and tissues that were not evident in Wolfe's case, both agree that Wolfe died of pulmonary tuberculosis with basilar meningitis. Dr. Frank C. Wilson, of the University of North Carolina Medical School, has made an independent study of the evidence and arrived at the same conclusion as Drs. Dammin and Prout. Dr. Wilson reported his findings to the May 1986 meeting of the Thomas Wolfe Society in New York City.

Afterword: The Posthumous Novels of Thomas Wolfe

464/13 Berg, pp. 359–360.

464/21 In addition Aswell worked with Miss Nowell to prepare an abridged version of Wolfe's notes on his tour of the Western national parks ("A Western Journey," *Virginia Quarterly Review* 15 [Summer 1939]: 335–357), and he oversaw publication of a nearly complete edition of those notes (*A Western Journal: A Daily Log of the Great Parks Trip, June 20–July 2, 1938*, Agnes Lynch Starrett, ed. [Pittsburgh: University of Pittsburgh Press, 1951]).

465/3 HB, p. 353.

465/12 Kennedy, p. 401.

NOTES 557

466/2 For an excellent statement of these problems, see Kennedy, p. 388.

466/17 EN's notes on TW's Outline for the Web and the Rock, Wisdom, No. 1336.

466/31 *Letters*, pp. 758–759; ECA to TW, May 9, 1938, Wisdom.

467/12 John Halberstadt, "The Making of Thomas Wolfe's Posthumous Novels," *Yale Review* 70 (Autumn 1980): 83–86; Leslie Field, "Thomas Wolfe's Posthumous Publications," p. 326. I am indebted to Professor Field for making a copy of this manuscript available to me.

467/22 MEP to FW, Mar. 2, 1938, Wolfe Coll., UNC.

468/1 EN's notes on TW's Outline for the Web and the Rock, Wisdom, No. 1336.

468/26 FW to ECA, Mar. 24, April 9, and Sept. 24, 1939, Wisdom; JST, Memorandum to ECA, June 30, 1940, Terry MSS.

468/35 ECA to FW, April 14, 1938, Wisdom. See also the corrected typescript and galley proofs of *The Web and the Rock* in Wisdom.

469/10 ECA to FW, April 14, 1939, and FW to ECA, April 16, 1939, Wisdom.

469/22 Both of these drafts are in Wisdom, Nos. 832–837.

470/7 Cf. TW's draft, Wisdom, No. 833, and TWATR, p. 30.

470/18 EN's notes on TW's outline of The Web and the Rock, Wisdom, No. 1336.

470/27 Cf. Kennedy, p. 390. For a case study of how one chapter (ch. 37) of TWATR, "The Quarrel," was constructed from TW's several variant drafts, see Field, ch. 4.

471/15 Cf. *Letters*, pp. 710–714, and "Author's Note," TWATR, p. vi.

471/27 Paschal Reeves, ed., *Thomas Wolfe: The Critical Reception* (New York: David Lewis, 1974), pp. 123, 130–131.

471/33 ECA to MWW, Mar. 8, 1939, Wolfe Coll., UNC.

472/37 Halberstadt, p. 88; Richard S. Kennedy, "The 'Wolfegate' Affair," *Harvard Magazine* 84 (Sept.–Oct. 1981): 53.

473/17 Cf. Wolfe's typescripts in Wisdom, Nos. 964–973, and YCGHA, pp. 45–89.

473/26 Wolfe's typescript, "The Earth: England (October–April, 1930–1931)," is in Wisdom, No. 1013; the published passage is in YCGHA, pp. 545–546. For another example of Aswell's editing, see Kennedy, pp. 404–405.

475/27 Mary Lou Aswell to Andrew Turnbull, Jan. 21, 1963, copy provided by Mary A. Doll.

475/36 YCGHA, p. 706; ECA to EN, Dec. 7, 1951, Nowell MSS.

476/11 YCGHA, p. 743; ECA to EN, Oct. 8, 1951, Nowell MSS.

476/23 Reeves, pp. 147–150.

476/26 All quotations in the following paragraphs are from Aswell's "Note," HB, p. 351–386.

478/7 EN to ECA, [1949], Nowell MSS.

478/11 Cf. the unflattering fictional portrayal of Aswell as the "Weasel" in William Styron's *Sophie's Choice*.

479/9 Mary Lou Aswell to Andrew Turnbull, Jan. 21, 1962, copy supplied by Mary A. Doll; Mary Lou Aswell to Pearl K. Bell, Mar. 18, 1981, copy provided by Mrs. Bell; Thomas Hardesty in *Harvard Magazine* 84 (Mar.–April 1982): 16–18.

479/20 Wolfe's will had designated Nathan Mobley, a University of North Carolina classmate who was a lawyer in New York City, as Perkins's successor, but Mobley declined to serve. H. G. Jones, ed., *Thomas Wolfe of North Carolina* (Chapel Hill: North Caroliniana Society, 1982), pp. 69–70.

479/22 *The Window of Memory: The Literary Career of Thomas Wolfe* (Chapel Hill: University of North Carolina Press, 1962).

480/2 Kennedy, pp. 389–391, 403–405.

480/14 Rubin, quoted in *New York Review of Books*, July 16, 1981, p. 51; Rubin, "Creating the Great American Novelist," *New Leader* 46 (Jan. 7, 1963): 26.

480/18 Holman, *The Loneliness at the Core: Studies in Thomas Wolfe* (Baton Rouge: Louisiana State University Press, 1975), pp. 88–89.

480/22 Halberstadt, "The Making of Thomas Wolfe's Posthumous Novels," *Yale Review* 70 (Autumn 1980): 79–94.

480/33 Halberstadt, "Who Wrote Thomas Wolfe's Last Novels?" *New York Review of Books*, Mar. 19, 1981, pp. 51–52; " 'Crying Wolfe': An Exchange," ibid., July 15, 1951, pp. 50–51. Eliot Fremont-Smith, "Wolfegate: Of Time, the River, and Fraud," *Village Voice*, Feb. 25–Mar. 3, 1981, pp. 36–37; Edwin McDowell, "Paper on Thomas Wolfe Stirs Debate on Scholarship vs. Privacy," *New York Times*, April 6, 1981, p. C-11.

481/1 Quoted in *New York Review of Books*, Mar. 19, 1981, p. 51.

481/5 Halberstadt gave as one reason for rushing into print without these necessary and customary authorizations his fear that I might "scoop" his work by publishing "a quick article." He also claimed that he believed he could not get permission from the Estate of Thomas Wolfe because the administrator of that estate had signed with me "an exclusive three-year contract, such that no one else in the field can publish anything." *New York Review of Books*, Mar. 19, 1981, p. 52. Since Halberstadt was working in the Houghton Library reading room with me day after day for months on end, he could readily have determined the falsity truth of these assertions by simply asking me. In fact, my contract specifies that the Estate of Thomas Wolfe will not authorize other *biographies* of Wolfe while my own book is in progress, and it makes no reference at all to literary or critical studies like Halberstadt's. The incorrectness of Halberstadt's assertions is evident in the publication of numerous studies of Wolfe — many of which contain a large component of biography — after my contract was signed — e.g., Leslie Field, ed., *The Autobiography of an American Novelist: Thomas Wolfe* (Cambridge: Harvard University Press, 1983); H. G. Jones, ed., *Thomas Wolfe of North Carolina* (Chapel Hill: North Caroliniana Society, 1982); Richard S. Kennedy, ed., *Beyond Love and Loyalty: The Letters of Thomas Wolfe and Elizabeth Nowell* (Chapel Hill: University of North Carolina Press, 1983); Kennedy, ed., *Thomas Wolfe: A Harvard Perspective* (Athens, Ohio: Croissant & Co., 1983); and Suzanne Stutman, ed., *My Other Loneliness: Letters of Thomas*

Wolfe and Aline Bernstein (Chapel Hill: University of North Carolina Press, 1983).

481/12 Kennedy, "The 'Wolfegate' Affair," *Harvard Magazine* 84 (Sept. -Oct., 1981): 48–57, 62.

481/19 Field, "Thomas Wolfe's Posthumous Publications," p. 197.

483/11 Richard S. Kennedy and Paschal Reeves, eds., *The Notebooks of Thomas Wolfe* (Chapel Hill: University of North Carolina Press, 1970).

483/22 New York: Charles Scribner's Sons, 1961.

483/32 Malcolm Cowley, ed., *Writers at Work* (New York: Viking Press, 1958), pp. 94–95.

From the Thomas Wolfe Collection of the Pack Memorial Library at Asheville, permission granted by the Pack Memorial Library.

From unpublished Thomas Wolfe manuscripts in the Harry Ransom Humanities Research Center at the University of Texas in Austin, permission granted by the librarian.

From the Thomas Wolfe Collection of Alexander Wainwright, permission granted by Mr. Wainwright.

From unpublished letters in the Alfred Dashiell Papers and the Archive of Charles Scribner's Sons, permission granted by Princeton University Library.

From *Selected Letters: Sherwood Anderson*, Charles E. Modin, ed. (University of Tennessee Press, 1984) and *Letters of Sherwood Anderson*, Howard Mumford Jones, ed. (Little, Brown, 1953), permission granted by Harold Ober Associates; from the Sherwood Anderson Papers, permission granted by the Newberry Library.

From the unpublished letters and manuscripts of Edward Aswell, permission granted by Mary Aswell Doll.

From the unpublished letters of Aline Bernstein, permission granted by Missy Cusick.

From the unpublished autobiography and letters of Mina Kerstein Curtiss, permission granted by Lincoln Kerstein.

From the unpublished letters of Sinclair Lewis, permission granted by Ernst, Cane, Berner & Gitlin.

From the unpublished letters of Edgar Lee Masters, permission granted by Mrs. E. L. Masters.

From the unpublished letters of Elizabeth Nowell, permission granted by Clara Stites.

From the unpublished letters of Maxwell E. Perkins, permission granted by Mrs. John Frothingham and Mrs. Louise King.

From unpublished letters in the Archive of Charles Scribner's Sons, permission granted by Charles Scribner's Sons.

From the unpublished letters of Martha Dodd, permission given by Martha Dodd Stern.

Index